anthropology

CONTEMPORARY PERSPECTIVES | **FOURTH EDITION**

DAVID E. K. HUNTER • PHILLIP WHITTEN

Anthropology

CONTEMPORARY PERSPECTIVES

Anthropology

CONTEMPORARY PERSPECTIVES

FOURTH EDITION

EDITED BY

David E. K. Hunter

YALE UNIVERSITY

AND

Phillip Whitten

BENTLEY COLLEGE

Little, Brown and Company

BOSTON   TORONTO

Library of Congress Cataloging in Publication Data
Main entry under title:

Anthropology : contemporary perspectives.

    1. Anthropology — Addresses, essays, lectures.
I. Hunter, David E.   II. Whitten, Phillip.
GN29.A59   1985   306   84-21768
ISBN 0-316-38267-1

Library of Congress Catalog Card Number 84-21768

ISBN 0-316-38267-1

9 8 7 6 5 4 3 2

SEM

Published simultaneously in Canada
by Little, Brown & Company (Canada) Limited

Printed in the United States of America

Cover photo: Douglas Mazonowicz/Art Resource, NY. Thunderbird
motif and symbols. Rock painting, California, Seriagraph transcript.

This book is dedicated with love and appreciation to
KATHY
whose friendship, intelligence, and laughter
have enriched my life beyond measure.
P.W.

Preface

· ·

Anthropology is an exciting discipline. And why not? It encompasses all of the human experience: from the evolutionary processes that have molded us; to the civilizations, both ancient and modern, that we have forged; to the ways we communicate with each other; to the kaleidoscopic variety of human culture.

Anthropology is also a fast-changing discipline—enlivened by new discoveries, theories, problems, and debates on issues of fundamental importance to the understanding of human nature, society, and behavior.

• In the area of human evolution, for example, important fossil finds have been unearthed in the badlands of East Africa and elsewhere with startling regularity since the mid-1970s. Each discovery has broadened our understanding of our evolutionary history while simultaneously raising new and intriguing problems. In fact, these finds have so altered our ideas about the evolution of our own species that in each edition of this anthology we have been compelled to rework the entire section on human evolution.

• The publication of Edward O. Wilson's blockbuster book, *Sociobiology*, in 1975, raised anew (and at a more sophisticated level than before) the question of the extent to which human behavior is governed by our genetic inheritance. Are we, indeed, captives of our own genes—or, to put it more scientifically, is there a human biogram? Are certain behaviors biologically, rather than culturally, determined? These are some of the questions anthropologists have tackled with gusto. And from the research and writing—not to mention the storm of controversy—they have engendered, no doubt will come a deeper understanding of just what kind of creature *Homo sapiens* is.

• Sex roles is another topic of intense and heated debate these days. And it is a debate to which anthropology can contribute a great deal. Are the sex roles we have grown up with "natural," that is, biologically ordained? Or are they cultural conventions, created in the past to solve challenges posed by the environment and hence subject to modification as the physical and social environment changes? If the latter, what are the benefits and costs—both to the individual and to society as a whole—of radically altering a society's traditional sex roles? In the mid-1980s, this controversy was rekindled and brought to a boiling point by the publication of Derek Freeman's *Margaret Mead and Samoa: The Making and Unmaking of An Anthropological Myth* (1983). In his book Freeman attacks both Margaret Mead's scientific integrity and her research on Samoan society as reported in her classic book, *Coming of Age in Samoa* (1928). Because anthropology, far more than any other social science, takes a cross-cultural perspective, it can bring a great deal of research and knowledge to bear on the question of the diversity in human sex roles and other related questions.

These are just a few of the many important and exciting issues with which anthropologists are grappling today. In this, the fourth edition of *Anthropology: Contemporary Perspectives*, we have attempted to convey the excitement and relevance of contemporary anthropology to beginning students. The needs and interests of these students were foremost in our minds when we selected the articles for this anthology. The selections had to strike a balance between academic quality and level of difficulty. They had to be intrinsically interesting to students, both in subject matter and in writing style. And they had to relate to the introductory course in anthropology as it is taught in most North American colleges and universities. The resulting collection thus reflects both the important ongoing work of modern anthropology and the ways introductory anthropology is taught, while providing interesting, enjoyable reading for the college undergraduate.

The articles come from a broad range of sources, including major books and such journals and semipopular magazines as *American Anthropologist, Discovery, Harvard, Horizon, Human Nature, Human Organization, Mosaic, Natural History, Science, Science Digest, Scientific American, Smithsonian, Society,* and *The Sciences.* Some articles were written specifically for this volume. Most of the articles are recent (approximately 80 percent date from the 1970s and '80s, and almost one-third were first published in the last four years), and many reflect new discoveries and changes in the discipline of anthropology. But we also have included a number of the "classic" articles as well. The authors include such prominent anthropologists as Joan Ablon, Laura Bohannan, Napoleon A. Chagnon, Morton H. Fried, Ernestine Friedl, Edward T. Hall and Mildred Reed Hall, Michael Harner, Marvin Harris, Lowell D. Holmes, William W. Howells, Jane B. Lancaster, Richard Borshay Lee, Richard E. Leakey, David Maybury-Lewis, Horace Miner, Martin K. Nickels, William L. Rathje, Marshall D. Sahlins, Lauriston Sharp, Ralph S. Solecki, Melford E. Spiro, S. L. Washburn, and Peter M. Worsley, as well as leading individuals in other social and behavioral sciences and professional science writers.

This fourth edition of *Anthropology: Contemporary Perspectives* is actually a major revision of the book, both in subject matter and in organization. Almost one-third of the articles are new to this edition, and they explore such subjects as human evolution; the earliest primates; sociobiology; human diversity ("race"); the use of high technology in archaeology; the "garbage project"; the nature of human language; language and the coding of reality; doing fieldwork in middle-class America; politics and social control; personality and sex roles; the debate over Margaret Mead's research in Samoa; and the impact of modernization and industrialization on small, marginal societies throughout the world. Articles that were retained from the first three editions of the book were those judged most successful in a poll of instructors who have adopted the book and by students in introductory anthropology classes during the 1983-84 school year.

We have reorganized the fourth edition of *Anthropology: Contemporary Perspectives* to increase its compatibility with the leading textbooks in both introductory anthropology and cultural anthropology, and to allow it to be used as the *only* book in either of these courses.

• There are five main sections of the book, with sections II through V corresponding to the major subdisciplines within anthropology.

• Within the five sections there are fourteen topics, corresponding to the subject matter common to virtually all texts and courses in introductory anthropology: human evolution, primatology and human behavior; human diversity; archaeology; language, thought, and communication; fieldwork; kinship and marriage; political and economic organization; personality and sex roles; belief and ritual; and so on.

• In addition, we have significantly expanded both the section and topic introductions, explaining important basic concepts and providing students with a carefully detailed framework that will enhance their understanding and appreciation of the selections that follow.

• Also, we have added an extensive Glossary containing definitions of more than five hundred important terms used in the book.

• Finally, we have retained the popular facsimile format of the book in the fourth edition, keeping original photographs and artwork wherever possible.

In revising the book we were helped enormously by three of Phillip Whitten's students during the 1983-84 school year. Suzanne Laydon led a team including Charles Tate and Scott Maxwell that did an elaborate computer analysis of more than a thousand student evaluations of the articles in the third edition, which was invaluable in revising the book.

We are also deeply indebted to the following instructors who provided indepth critiques of the third edition and of our plans for its revision: Dean E. Arnold, Wheaton College; Monica Barnes, Community College of Allegheny County; Mary Jane Berman, Hartwick College; Barry Bogin, University of Michigan–Dearborn; Peter J. Brown, Emory University; Maribeth Hamby, University of Nevada–Reno; Gary Heidinger, Roane State Community College; Joseph Hickey, Emporia State University; Thomas Kiefer, Harvard University; Herb Kuehne, Briar Cliff College; Laurence D. Loeb, University of Utah; Debra L. Martin, Hampshire College; Elaine Mayer, Salve Regina College; Daniel E. Moerman, University of Michigan–Dearborn; Lisa O'Steen, University of Georgia; Deborah Padgett, Florida Southern College; Robert E. Polley, Edinboro University of Pennsylvania; Bruce E. Raemsch, Hartwick College; Rosalind Ribnick, Humboldt State University; Paul W. Sciulli, Ohio State University; Leslie E. Sponsel, University of Hawaii–Honolulu; N. J. Vasantkumar, Susquehanna University; Malcolm C. Webb, University of New Orleans; Brian Wilson, St. Norbert College; John S. Wozniak, St. Mary's College; and Ina Jane Wundram, Georgia State University.

We would also like to thank the college division staff at Little, Brown, with whom we worked so effectively: our editor, Brad Gray, who offered valuable suggestions in revising the book and was always helpful; his cheerful and highly competent administrative assistant, Anne Bingham; and Kathryn Daniel, the book editor, who has worked on the production of this book since its first edition. We also appreciate enormously the fine work done by our administrative assistant, Iris Stein.

Finally, we owe a debt of gratitude to the original authors whose articles we selected. Without their work, and their permission and that of their publishers to reprint it, this book literally would not have been possible.

Contents

IV

Language and Communication 97

V

Cultural Anthropology 126

Anthropology

....

CONTEMPORARY PERSPECTIVES

Peoples and Sites Discussed in This Book

(Article numbers are in parentheses.)

Driftwood Creek (12)

Putu (12)

Old Crow (12)

Bering Land Bridge (12)

• Girl's Hill (12)

The Eskimo (Inuit) (15, 30, 36)

Purgatory Hill (2)

The Naskapi (30)

Anzick (12)

The Shoshoni (10, 30)

Calico Hills (12)

The "Nacirema" (22)

Santa Rosa Island (12)

• The Paiute (30)

Cahokia (14)

The Iroquois (36)

Del Mar (12)

The Hopi (16)

• Folsom (12)

The Garbage Project (11)

The Aztecs (33)

Teotihuacan (33)

Tenochtitlán (33)

Tikal (33)

Valley of Mexico (13)

Tlapcoya (12)

The Yanomamö (19, 35, 44)

The Machiguenga (30, 31)

The Mehinacu (30)

Huaca Prieta (13)

Pikimachay Cave (12)

Fell's Cave (12)

Neander Valley (4)

Cro-Magnon (4)

La Chapelle-aux-saints (14)

La Ferrassie (4)

• Jebel Irhoud

The Tiv (

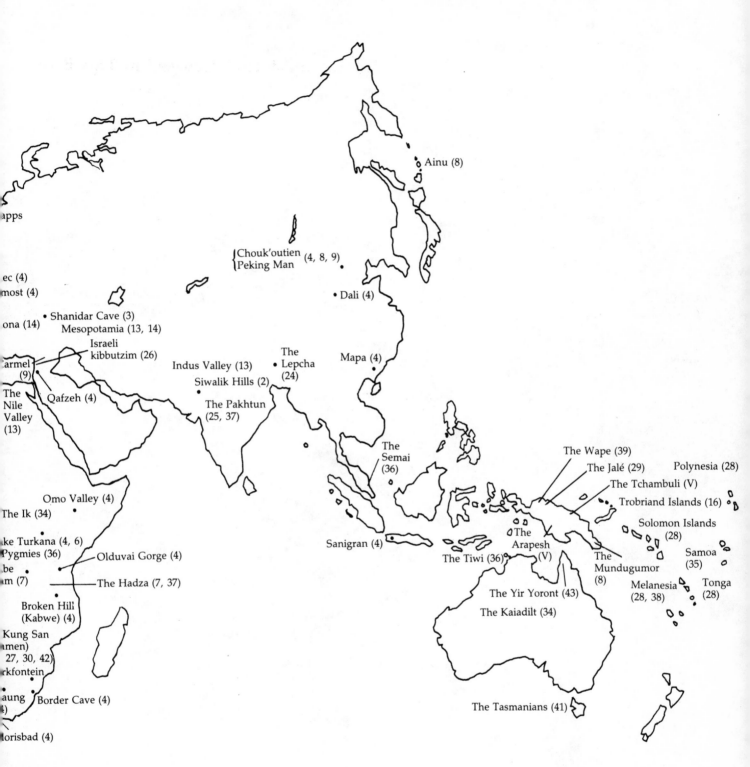

apps

ec (4)
most (4)

ona (14)

• Shanidar Cave (3)
  Mesopotamia (13, 14)

Israeli
kibbutzim (26)

Carmel
(9)

The
Nile
Valley
(13)

Qafzeh (4)

Indus Valley (13)
  • Siwalik Hills (2)

The Pakhtun
(25, 37)

The
• Lepcha
(24)

Chouk'outien
Peking Man } (4, 8, 9)

• Dali (4)

Mapa (4)

Ainu (8)

Omo Valley (4)
The Ik (34)

ke Turkana (4, 6)
Pygmies (36)
be
m (7)   The Hadza (7, 37)

Olduvai Gorge (4)

Broken Hill
(Kabwe) (4)

Kung San
men)
27, 30, 42)
kfontein

aung   Border Cave (4)

orisbad (4)

The Semai
(36)

Sanigran (4)

The Tiwi (36)

The Yir Yoront (43)

The Kaiadilt (34)

The Tasmanians (41)

The
Arapesh
(V)

The Wape (39)
  The Jalé (29)
    The Tchambuli (V)
Trobriand Islands (16)

The
Mundugumor
(8)

Melanesia
(28, 38)

Polynesia (28)

Solomon Islands
(28)

Samoa
(35)

Tonga
(28)

I
Introduction to Anthropology

This collection of articles will introduce you to some of the many facets of anthropology. In each section we provide a general framework and some historical comments to help you understand the significance of the readings within the general discipline of anthropology. The introductory notes are especially extensive in sections II (Physical Anthropology) and III (Archaeology), because these topics are more likely than others to lie outside of the realm of the daily world of discourse of most students.

We introduce you to anthropology in Topic One, The Study of Anthropology. Here, we sketch both the historical roots and the modern subdisciplines of anthropology in order to provide you with an overall framework on which to organize your reading of the articles collected in this reader.

TOPIC ONE

The Study of Anthropology

· ·

What is anthropology? For one thing, it is an academic discipline whose history, subdisciplines, and major theories we trace in the article that opens this anthology. But we believe deeply that anthropology is more than just an "academic" discipline, for its scope embraces all of humankind—past and present. Whether or not you go on to concentrate your studies in an anthropology major, we believe that taking an introductory course in anthropology will enrich your life and broaden your perspectives. It will expose you to foreign peoples, strange places, unexpected customs, new

viewpoints, and—again and again—the universals at the heart of the human condition everywhere.

We leave it to you to discover these universals, to find yourself in the enormous diversities of peoples and cultures, life-styles and world views represented in the articles reprinted here.

In the article title "What Is Anthropology?" the editors of this volume provide you with a guide to sampling the fruit of a tree whose roots are deep and whose boughs spread wide.

What Is Anthropology?

BY DAVID E. K. HUNTER AND PHILLIP WHITTEN

Anthropology is a way—or rather a collection of many different ways—of studying human beings and their closest primate relatives. The term *anthropology* comes from two Greek words: *anthropos*, meaning "man" (in the sense of human being), and *logos*, meaning "to reason" (or study).

THE BRANCHES OF ANTHROPOLOGY

If one thinks of the overall discipline of anthropology as a tree, then it is a tree consisting of four major branches and many smaller branches and twigs. The four major branches are physical anthropology, archaeology, linguistics, and cultural anthropology.

1. *Physical anthropology* is the study of human biology—but not just biology alone. Whether studying the fossil remains of our ancestors, the distribution of diverse genes among the world's contemporary populations, the mechanisms of genetic inheritance, the differing shapes and colors characterizing people in various regions, or even the behavior patterns of humans and their primate relatives, physical anthropologists are concerned with the manner in which all these things are related to the natural and social environments in which the subjects are living. So physical anthropology really is the study of the biological processes of humans and their primate relatives in their natural and social contexts or environments.

2. *Archaeology* is the retrieval and study of human remains. This includes not only their bodily remains (which certainly can tell us a great deal about how they lived and died), but also the remains of the things they built, produced, and made use of. In other words archaeologists attempt to find and study all the traces that human groups have left behind—of themselves and of all their activities—and they seek to understand the ways these remains are related to each other and the environments in which they occur.

3. *Linguistics* is the study and analysis of human communication systems, but most especially of language. Some linguists attempt to reconstruct the earlier language forms from which our present languages have evolved. Others study modern languages in order to learn how they encode the range of human experiences, what grammatical forms they feature, or what separates language from the communication systems of other species. Some linguists are concerned with what language usage can reveal about the different social groups within a society. Others are interested in what can be learned about the nature of the human mind from the study of language. So linguistics is *not* what many people take it to be—the mere learning of a lot of different languages—rather it embodies the use of research into languages in order to better understand the nature of human beings as a species.

4. *Cultural anthropology* is the study of culture and cultures. Culture consists of the shared patterns of behavior and associated meanings that people learn and participate in within the groups to which they belong. Every group, down to each individual family, has its own culture, and each culture is unique. Of course some cultures are quite similar to each other (say, the family cultures of a specific community); others are very different (nomadic Arab culture and Eskimo culture, for example). Some anthropologists study the nature of culture in general as an element of human existence; others are more interested in studying a specific culture (perhaps the culture of a Norwegian fishing village or a *barrio* in Mexico City). Culture, by providing "designs for living," enables humans to be extremely flexible and resourceful in solving problems posed by the natural environment, and our species is unique in that it inhabits virtually every niche that nature has wrought on our planet. The better we understand culture, the closer we shall come to understanding what it means to be a human being.

At this point it might be helpful to return to the image of the "tree of anthropology" with which we opened this essay. Until now we have concentrated on a description of its branches—its four main branches and even a number of its smaller branches and twigs. Some readers might even be tempted to ask whether, in all this diversity of interests encompassed by anthropology, there is in fact any trunk to the tree. Is there a central core that holds the whole thing together?

That is a reasonable question, and at times even anthropologists have had cause to ask it. In fact there is a trunk to be found. It is worth looking for because it is in the trunk of the tree that we find what makes anthropology different from all the other social sciences and also what makes it a worthwhile discipline to study and practice. We shall lead you to an appreciation of the trunk somewhat indirectly, however, by first describing some of the major roots of anthropology. We do this because we think that an understanding of the origins and development of the discipline will make its current practice more comprehensible and enticing.

THE ROOTS OF THE TREE

The origins of anthropology—as indeed of so much of our civilization—can be traced back to ancient Greece and the civilization of the Middle East. Historians claim as their father a Greek named Herodotus (484?–425? B.C.), and so might anthropologists as well. He traveled widely and recorded the life-styles of some fifty different peoples. He also formulated the idea that all peoples are *ethnocentric*—that is, they consider their own way of life superior to all others, and they judge other life-styles (for the most part negatively) in terms of the norms and values of their own.

With the fall of Rome in the fifth century A.D., much of the knowledge and thought of the classical civilizations were lost to Europeans for almost a thousand years. Medieval scholars were not so much interested in human beings or even in the nature of the world around them as they were in discovering as much as could be learned about God. Of course, they attempted to learn about God by studying the universe that God had created, and they did make many important discoveries about the world. But their concern to find "divine order" and "divine principles" underlying the manifest world blinded them to many of its most interesting features. It really was not until the Renaissance emerged in the fifteenth century, bringing with it a rediscovery of the treasures of classical learning, that European scholars began to investigate the natural environment as well as human societies with a view to understanding them on their own terms.

Already in medieval times, however, Europeans had been exposed to the existence—on distant shores accessible only to the hardiest of travelers—of many "strange and exotic" peoples. Throughout the Renaissance and Enlightenment periods, as Europe extended its economic interests ever farther abroad, exploration and colonization enabled scholars to visit these faraway places and make records (often fantastically misinformed and distorted) of the peoples they discovered and observed. By the eighteenth century, the vast riches to be made through control of the populations and resources of Africa, Asia, and the Americas induced governments and private enterprises to take more seriously the value of careful study of these so-called primitive peoples. After all, the better one understood them, the more efficiently one could set about exploiting them.

The Church too was quick to grasp the opportunity to extend its influence through missionary activities. Naturally, in order for their activities to be successful, these missionaries required information about the languages and customs of the people they would seek to convert to Christianity.

For many reasons, then, Europeans came to be interested in acquiring information about foreign peoples. Travelers, missionaries, sea captains, colonial administrators, adventurers, traders, and soldiers of fortune ranged across the world recording their impressions of the peoples they encountered. They brought these accounts back with them to European "armchair scholars," who attempted to study them by comparing them to each other—and to European society—in a more or less systematic manner. Inevitably, these efforts tended to "prove" the superiority of European society over all the "primitive" societies thus studied. These eighteenth- and nineteenth-century researches developed into what has come to be called the *comparative method* of social science research. Through the application of this method, a great many schemes of social and cultural evolution were put forward, all of which placed the institutions of European society securely at the top of the evolutionary pyramid.

Until the middle of the eighteenth century, there was no separate discipline that one might call social science. To the extent that society was studied, it was done within the all-purpose framework of history. But by around 1750, the study of society had become sufficiently specialized to deserve the label "social science"—a separate discipline having split off from historical studies and embarked on its own development. For about one hundred years, the study of human nature and society evolved along the lines we have already described, embodying loosely all the different approaches to the building of a science of humankind.

A century later Darwinian evolutionism arrived. The impact of Darwinism on human thought was profound, and its effects on social science were no less dramatic. The two outstanding changes in the study of human nature and society that resulted were (1) the application of evolutionary theory to virtually all aspects of the study of humankind, and (2) the split of such studies into increasingly specialized, separate disciplines.

The Emergence of Evolutionary Thought

The Christian doctrine that Creation had been a single event (pinpointed at 9:00 A.M. on September 23 in 4004 B.C. by Archbishop James Ussher in the early 1600s, who deduced that time from a careful study of Genesis) became more and more troublesome. Already in the sixteenth century Vasco Núñez de Balboa discovered that America was not an extension of Asia but, rather, a separate continent—and the origin of the "Indians" became a source of heated argument. This debate rapidly expanded into controversy about the degree of relatedness—and inherent levels of ability—of all the diverse peoples around the world.

To the *polygenists* the differences between human groups were so vast that they could not accept even a common origin for all people. Rebelling against a narrow acceptance of Genesis, they insisted that scientific inquiry must prevail over the Bible (a courageous position at the time). They argued that God must have created human beings a number of times in different places and that all people were not then descendants of Adam and Eve. Their numbers included many of the period's leading skeptics and intellectuals, such as Voltaire and David Hume. It is hardly surprising that these thinkers, attaching as they did such great significance to human physical variation, should have been racial determinists and indeed racists, ascribing to their own "stock" superior mental abilities. Voltaire, for instance, discussing the state of civilization among Africans, argued:

> If their understanding is not of a different nature from ours, it is at least greatly inferior. They are not capable of any great application or association of ideas, and seemed [sic] formed neither for the advantages nor the abuses of philosophy (quoted in Harris 1968:87).

Monogenicism defended the Scriptures' assertion of a single origin for all humans. Isolated groups, such as the "Indians," were accounted for by the claim that they had come from Atlantis (a mythical continent that was believed to have stretched from Spain to Africa before sinking beneath the waters of the Atlantic Ocean) or that they were the descendants of one of the lost tribes of Israel. Monogenists accounted for "racial" differences in terms of populations adapting to the problems posed by different environments—an idea that would become central to Darwin's principle of natural selection. But they also tended to believe, along with the French biologist Jean Baptiste de Lamarck (1744–1829), that physical characteristics acquired by an individual in the course of his or her lifelong development could be

passed on biologically from one generation to the next (an idea rejected by Darwin and the mainstream of subsequent evolutionary thought).

Because monogenists tended to defend the validity of the Biblical version of human origins, they also accepted the very recent dates that Biblical scholars had established for human creation. Thus although they, like the polygenists, divided the human species into "races," they deduced that these "races" must be of very recent origin and that, although people exhibited differences in response to environmental pressures, these differences were of minimal importance with regard to basic human abilities. For instance, Johann Friedrich Blumenbach (1752–1840), a German physician who developed an interest in comparative human anatomy, published a study in 1775 in which he identified five "races": Caucasian, Mongolian, Ethiopian (including all sub-Saharan blacks), Malayan, and American. For this effort he is frequently called the "father" of physical anthropology. However, Blumenbach was far from convinced that these categories were anything more than artificial constructions of convenience in the service of science: "When the matter is thoroughly considered, you see that all [human groups] do so run into one another, and that one variety of mankind does so sensibly pass into the other, that you cannot mark out the limits between them." And he adds, with a tone of wryly modern wisdom, "Very arbitrary indeed both in number and definition have been the varieties of mankind accepted by eminent men" (cited in Montagu 1964:41).

(The debate between monogenists and polygenists raged on through the nineteenth century and continues to this day. Although most human biologists since Darwin have aligned themselves in the monogenist camp, the writings of Carleton S. Coon (1904–1981), a contemporary anthropologist, were firmly polygenist. He argued in *The Origin of Races* (1963)—a controversial work—that the human species evolved five different times into the five "races" that he believed constitute the population of the world today.)

Let us return, however, to our account of the emergence of the theory of evolution. By the late eighteenth and early nineteenth centuries, discoveries (especially in biology and geology) were gradually forcing scholars to reassess their acceptance of a date for the creation of the earth derived from scriptural study. More and more geological strata in the earth's crust were coming to light, and it became clear that the thickness of some strata, and the nature of the mineral contents of many, demanded a very long developmental process. In order to account for this process, these scientists faced the need to push back the date of Creation, as we will see shortly. In addition, the fossilized record of extinct life forms accumulated, obliging scientists to produce plausible explanations for the existence and subsequent disappearance of such creatures as the woolly mammoth and the saber-toothed tiger.

In 1833, Sir Charles Lyell (1797–1875) published the third and last volume of his *Principles of Geology,* a work that had a tremendous influence on Darwin. Lyell attacked such schools of thought as *diluvialism,* whose followers claimed that Noah's flood accounted for what was known of the earth's geological structure and history, and *catastrophism,* whose adherents proposed that localized catastrophes (of which the Biblical flood was merely the most recent) accounted for all the layers and cracks in the earth's crust. He argued that the processes shaping the earth are the same today as they always were—uniform and continuous in character—a position that has come to be called *uniformitarianism.* However, Lyell was unable to free himself entirely from a doctrinaire Christian framework. Although he could envision gradual transformations in the inanimate world of geology, when he discussed living creatures, he continued to believe in the divine creation of each (unchanging) species, and he accounted for the extinction of species in terms of small, localized natural catastrophes.

Some biologists did comprehend the implications of comparative anatomy and the fossil record. For instance, Lamarck advanced his "developmental hypothesis," in which he arranged all known animals into a sequence based on their increasing organic complexity. He clearly implied that human beings were the highest product of a process of organic transformation and had been created through the same processes that had created all other species. However, Lamarck's imagination was also bound by theological constraints, and he did not carry his research through to its logical conclusion. Rather than limiting himself to natural forces as the shapers of organic transformation, Lamarck assumed an underlying, divinely ordered patterning.

Before scholars could fully appreciate the antiquity of the earth and the processes that gave rise to all species—including the human species—they had to free themselves from the constraints of nineteenth-century Christian theology. A revolution of perspective was necessary, a change of viewpoint so convincing that it would overcome people's emotional and intellectual commitment to Christian dogma. The logic of the new position would have to be simple and straightforward and would have to rest on a unified, universally applicable principle.

As we shall see shortly, students of human *society* had been grappling with these issues for almost a century. Herbert Spencer (1820–1903) developed the theory of evolution as applied to societies and based it (in the now immortal phrase) on the "survival of the

fittest." His writings and those of Thomas Malthus (1766–1834), the political economist who pessimistically forecast a "struggle for survival" among humankind for dwindling resources, profoundly influenced two naturalists working independently on the problem of the origins of species: Both Alfred Russel Wallace (1823–1913) and Charles Robert Darwin (1809–1882) arrived at the solution at the same time. They hit on the single, unifying (and natural) principle that would account for both the origin and the extinction of species—*natural selection.* In 1858, they presented joint papers on this topic, and the next year Darwin published *On the Origin of Species,* a book that captured scholars' imaginations and became the first influential work that popularized the concept of evolution as applied to the world of living organisms.

What is natural selection? It can be put simply and straightforwardly: *Natural selection is the process through which certain environmentally adaptive features are perpetuated at the expense of less adaptive features.*

Two very important points must be stressed with regard to natural selection: (1) *It is features—not individuals—that are favored,* and (2) *no features are inherently "superior."* Natural selection is entirely dependent on the environment. Change the environment, and the favored adaptive features change as well.

Evolutionism in Social Thought

As we have mentioned, since medieval times, Europeans had been exposed, through the reports of adventurous travelers, to the existence of many "strange" peoples living in "exotic" places on distant shores. Thus, European scholars accumulated a body of information (much of it quite unreliable) about foreign societies, and quite a few set about trying to compare societies in more or less systematic ways. By the late eighteenth century and throughout the nineteenth century, the *comparative method* of social science resulted in the elaboration of theories of social and intellectual progress that developed into full-blown evolutionary theories, frequently referred to as *classical* or *unilineal evolutionism.* The Marquis de Condorcet (1743–1794), for instance, identified ten stages of social evolution marked by the successive acquisition of technological and scientific knowledge: From the limited knowledge needed for hunting and gathering, humanity passes through the development of pastoralism, agriculture, writing, and the differentiation of the sciences, then through a temporary period of darkness and the decline of knowledge in the Middle Ages, leading to the invention of the printing press in 1453, the skeptical rationalism of René Descartes' philosophy, then to the founding of the French Republic of Condorcet's day, and eventually, through the application of scientific knowledge, to a world of peace and equality among the nations and the sexes. His *Outline of the Intellectual Progress of Mankind* (1795) is viewed by many as the outstanding work of social science produced in eighteenth-century Europe, even though its ethnocentric bias is blatant (Harris, 1968:35).

Auguste Comte (1798–1857), who is sometimes called one of the "fathers" of social science, followed Condorcet's approach to social evolution. For him, too, the progress of the human intellect moved social evolution forward. However, he identified only three stages of evolution, characterized respectively by "theological thought," in which people perceive the universe as animated by a will much like their own (evolving from animism through polytheism to monotheism); "metaphysical thought," in which abstract laws of nature are discovered; and finally "positive thought," represented by the scientific method (of which his own writings were the embodiment in the social sciences). By the way, it is interesting to note that Comte also believed that each person passes through these three stages in the course of his or her individual development.

The writings of Herbert Spencer on social evolution were preeminent during much of the middle and late nineteenth century. As mentioned earlier, it was he who first introduced the term *evolution* into the scientific literature. And in his classic *First Principles*, published in 1862,[1] he provides a definition of the term that has not significantly been improved upon to this day. *Evolution*, Spencer points out, *is not merely change*. It is "change from an indefinite, incoherent homogeneity to a definite, coherent heterogeneity; through continuous differentiations and integrations." In other words, to Spencer *evolution is the progress of life forms and social forms from the simple to the complex*.

Spencer's work is often neglected by contemporary anthropologists, who tend to trace their historical roots to two other major nineteenth-century evolutionists, Sir Edward Burnett Tylor (1832–1917) and Lewis Henry Morgan (1818–1881). Morgan's work in many ways is derived from that of Spencer. Like Spencer, he viewed social evolution as the result of societies adapting to the stresses of their environments. In his classic study, *Ancient Society* (1877), Morgan identified seven stages of social evolution:

I. Lower Status of Savagery
   Marked by simple food gathering

II. Middle Status of Savagery
   Marked by knowledge of fishing and the invention of fire

III. Upper Status of Savagery
   Marked by the invention of the bow and arrow

IV. Lower Status of Barbarism
   Marked by the invention of pottery

V. Middle Status of Barbarism
   Marked by the domestication of plants and animals, irrigation, and stone and brick architecture

VI. Upper Status of Barbarism
   Marked by the invention of iron working

VII. Civilization
   Marked by the invention of the phonetic alphabet

Sir Edward Tylor lacked the concern with social systems of Spencer and Morgan. He was more concerned with *culture* than with society, defining culture all-inclusively as "that complex whole which includes knowledge, belief, art, morals, law, custom, and any other capabilities and habits acquired by man as a member of society" (1958:1; orig. 1871). Tylor attempted to demonstrate that culture had evolved from simple to complex and that it is possible to reconstruct the simple beginnings of culture by the study of its "survivals" in contemporary "primitive" cultures.

In spite of the fact that their individual evolutionary schemes differed from one another in important ways, these classical evolutionists shared one overriding conviction: Society had evolved from simple to complex through identifiable stages. Although it could not be claimed that every single society had passed through each of the stages they described, nevertheless they believed they had found sequences of developmental stages through which a "preponderant number" of societies had passed (Carneiro 1973:91) and that these sequences represented progress. At the turn of the century, this position came under furious assault by Franz Boas and his students and vanished from the American intellectual scene. It reemerged in the 1940s to become one of the major conceptual tools that prehistorians and archaeologists use to reconstruct the human past.

The Emergence of Specialized Disciplines

As we noted earlier, until the mid-eighteenth century, the social sciences had no separate identities—the study of history embodied them all. And it wasn't until the rise of evolutionary theory in the nineteenth century that the social sciences began to differentiate themselves, began to split off from each other through a specialization of interests and research methodologies.

Perhaps the major splitting of the social sciences in the mid-nineteenth century was the emergence of the separate disciplines of sociology and anthropology, which to this day have maintained their distinct and individual identities. Sociologists tended to follow the

---

1. The word *evolution* does not appear in Darwin's *On the Origin of Species* until the 1872 edition!

positivist approach of Auguste Comte described earlier and shared with Comte a preoccupying interest in European society. Anthropologists, on the other hand, remained interested in a far broader range of data: archaeological finds, the study of "races" and the distribution of diverse human physical traits, human evolution, the comparative study of cultures and cultural evolution—all more or less unified by evolutionary theory. And whereas sociologists focused on European society, anthropologists, in their worldwide search for data, tended to concentrate on the "primitive" or preindustrial societies (Voget 1975:114–116.) It is in this context that the four main branches—physical anthropology, archaeology, linguistics, and cultural anthropology—emerged as separate, but still interrelated, subdisciplines.

THE TRUNK OF THE TREE

As you have seen, the roots of anthropology go very deep and they spread wide across the world. Its branches, large and small, are numerous and diverse. Where then is its trunk? What holds anthropology together?

In order to work—to plan, execute, and evaluate their research—all scientists must be trained in the sets of beliefs and practices that characterize their disciplines in a fundamental way. This set of beliefs and practices—in essence the core and underpinning of a scientific discipline—is sometimes termed the *paradigm* of that science. Although no scientist will ever fully utilize all the elements of a paradigm in his or her research, nevertheless such research is planned, undertaken, and evaluated by other scientists in terms of the ways in which it contributes to and reflects the paradigm as a whole.

Anthropology has such a paradigm—which is the trunk of the tree. It consists of five themes that have developed gradually as anthropology has emerged as a distinct discipline. These are the *comparative*, the *holistic*, the *systems and process*, the *case study*, and the *"insider-outsider"* themes. Before we explain and elaborate on each of these, we wish to emphasize one important point: Not all anthropologists conduct their day-to-day work in terms of all five themes, but all anthropologists do appreciate their importance and understand their own and others' work within the context these themes provide.

The Comparative Theme

As we mentioned above, a major aspect of the split between anthropology and sociology in the nineteenth century was that whereas sociology focused on Western society, anthropology continued the tradition of comparing and contrasting peoples and cultures throughout the world. These comparisons are made in two ways: (1) by *synchronics*, which is the comparison of anthropological data across a wide geographical area (including many peoples and cultures) at one point in time (usually the present or recent past); and (2) by *diachronics*, which involves comparison of such data through a very extended period of time but limited to one geographical region (and only a few peoples and cultures), thus revealing patterns of evolution (be it biological, social, or cultural).

The Holistic Theme

Another feature of the sociology-anthropology split was that sociologists came to concentrate their attention on society and social systems, whereas anthropologists continued to attempt to tie together all aspects of human biology and behavior—that is, biology, society, culture, and even psychology. The concern with the *whole* picture of the human condition is termed *holism*, and it is a fundamental aspect of anthropology. That is one reason anthropologists find themselves at odds with so many contemporary scholars and popularizers who wish to account for human behavior by reducing it to one simple underlying determinant, such as "race," territoriality, sexual dimorphism, or the structure of the human brain.

The Systems and Process Theme

Herbert Spencer introduced the concept of the *social system* in the early nineteenth century. In the last few decades anthropologists have rediscovered the fact that it is not very productive to describe and analyze societies and cultures in terms of static lists of their traits. Rather societies and cultures are understood as open systems, each possessing many subsystems and all such systems containing their own patterned processes. For example, archaeologists are no longer satisfied merely to catalog the material remains that they retrieve from prehistoric societies. Rather, they attempt to understand what such remains can tell us about the ways these societies adapted to and utilized the elements of their natural environment, how they organized themselves into social groups, the ways such groups interacted among themselves and with each other, and so forth. Physical anthropologists have essentially abandoned the static concept of "race" as useless and have turned instead to investigating the ways in which genes express themselves changeably in different environments. This concern with systems, processes, and dynamics has greatly enriched the discipline of anthropology.

The Case Study Theme

You will recall that anthropology developed on the fringes of European society and continued with a preoccupation with distant and remote peoples and places. Those hardy souls who ventured forth to study such out-of-the-way societies found themselves cut off, for long periods of time, from contacts with their homes. They lost track of current events in European affairs and consequently immersed themselves in the detailed study and description of the daily happenings among the people they were studying. It was a challenge to keep their objectivity while at the same time working to gain people's trust and even their affection. This form of social research is called *participant observation*. It is characteristic of much of the research undertaken by anthropologists, who seem on the whole to be much less comfortable with grand abstractions than with the concrete world of stones and bones, phonemes and morphemes, rituals, economic transactions, and pottery sherds. For every grand (and grandiose!) theory of society or human behavior that is so lightly bandied about in the popular media, one is sure to hear a quiet but insistent anthropological gadfly asking, "But what about the case of the Tasaday?" or "But how does that fit with what we know about forest-dwelling baboons?" Sadly, the wider public remains for the most part uninformed of the objections anthropologists have raised to the widely proliferated, pseudoscientific writings claiming "proof" for such things as prehistoric extraterrestrial visitors.

The "Insider-Outsider" Theme

Because anthropologists, more than other social scientists, have concentrated so much of their research on studying remote peoples with life-styles, mores, values, subsistence systems, and languages very different from our own, it has fallen on anthropologists to grapple with the problem of translating the *perspective of the people being studied* (the "insider's" view) into the *perspective of Western social science* (the "outsider's" view). Neither view is inherently correct, of course, and both complement and supplement each other. But it is easy to get them mixed up both during the process of learning about the people one is studying, and again after having completed one's research when trying to make it meaningful to colleagues, students, and even the public at large. After all, anthropologists are just as vulnerable as anybody else to succumbing to the insidious distortions of ethnocentric thought. Guarding against this is an important element of anthropological research. Because anthropologists are sensitized to the many and subtle ways people look down upon one another, the study of anthropology can be a valuable contribution to an individual's maturation and education.

THE TREE OF ANTHROPOLOGY

In this brief introductory essay, we have presented you with the branches, roots, and trunk of the "tree of anthropology." The articles that follow are many of its fruits. Naturally, we have selected this offering to make the study of anthropology enticing. We think the articles are clear and informative, and not a few of them are warmed by a sense of humor. We have been careful, however, to allow as many as possible of the voices of our discipline to be heard in these pages. The differences of opinion, the disputes and controversies that currently enliven the lives of anthropologists, are offered to you for your own consideration.

We hope that you will pause a while at the tree of anthropology, that you will taste of its fruit and rest in its shade. We hope that some of you will be moved to climb up into its branches, to see the world from the unique vantage points they offer. But most of all, we hope that those of you who choose to wander on through the other niches of the garden of academia will have found your stay here refreshing, that you will have acquired a new set of perspectives, perhaps a new understanding or awareness. If that is the case, then this awareness will enrich all of your future travels.

References

Carneiro, Robert
    1973 "The Four Faces of Evolution," in John J. Honigmann (ed.), *Handbook of Social and Cultural Anthropology*, Chicago: Rand McNally, pp. 89–110.
Coon, Carleton S.
    1963 *The Origin of Races*, New York: Alfred A. Knopf.
Harris, Marvin
    1968 *The Rise of Anthropological Theory: A History of Culture*, New York: Thomas Y. Crowell.
Montagu, Ashley
    1964 *Man's Most Dangerous Myth: The Fallacy of Race* (4th ed., rev.), New York: Meridian Books.
Tylor, Sir Edward Burnett
    1958 (orig. 1871) *The Origins of Culture*, Part I of *Primitive Culture*, New York: Harper Torchbooks.
Voget, Fred W.
    1975 *A History of Ethnology*, New York: Holt, Rinehart and Winston.

II
Physical Anthropology

○ ○

Physical anthropology has broadened a great deal over the last three decades, and it now includes many subjects that overlap with other disciplines. In a loose way, we may define physical anthropology as the study of primate biology in its natural and social environments—with a special emphasis on the study of our own species. Yet it is useful to break apart this large and rather loosely connected branch of anthropology into two major subbranches: *paleontology*, the study of our extinct ancestors (through their fossilized remains); and *neontology*, the comparative study of living primate groups.

Many scholars trace the origins of modern physical anthropology to the work of Johann Blumenbach (1752–1840), who systematically undertook to collect and study human skulls from many populations around the world. He devised ways of making very precise measurements on these skulls and used these measurements to produce an encyclopedic work on what he called the "races" of the world.

One of Blumenbach's central ideas was that the "races" developed as biological responses to environmental stresses. This notion was elaborated upon in the nineteenth century by numerous scholars, such as Anders Retzius (1796–1860), who in 1842 devised a formula for computing long-headedness and narrow-headedness:

$$\frac{\text{head breadth}}{\text{head length}} \times 100 = \text{cephalic index}$$

A low cephalic index indicates a narrow head; a high index a broad head. Fourteen years later, Retzius published a survey of cranial indexes based on the measurement of skulls from private collections, in which he distinguished a vast number of "races" determined by virtue of their cephalic indexes.

Others followed the lead of Blumenbach and Retzius, and a wide number of techniques were developed through which the human body could be systematically measured. Such measuring is called *anthropometry* and remains to the present day an important aspect of physical anthropology. Anthropometry contributes to our understanding of fossil remains by providing scholars with precise methods for studying them. It also provides concrete data on variations in body shape among human populations, replacing what previously had been rather impressionistic descriptions. Thus body measuring became one of the major tools for determining "racial" classifications. However, by the end of the century, it was being attacked by scholars who pointed out that anthropometric traits of all ranges could be found represented among individuals within each of the so-called "races."

After the publication of Darwin's *On the Origin of Species* in 1859, natural selection became the core concept of physical anthropology, and evolution its primary concern. Thomas Huxley (1825–1895), a naturalist who enthusiastically took up Darwin's theories, added great impetus to the study of human evolution by showing that the human species was not qualitatively distinct from other primates but, rather, only the most complex in an evolutionary continuum from the primitive lower primates through monkeys, the great apes, and finally humankind.

The study of the fossil evidence for human evolution was slow in developing. By 1822, reports had come from Germany about findings of the fossilized remains of many extinct animals in limestone caves. These reports impelled William Buckland (1784–1856), reader of geology at Oxford University, to investigate the limestone Paviland Cave on the Welsh coast. There Buckland found the same kinds of extinct animals as had been reported in Germany—as well as flint tools and a human skeleton. This skeleton came to be called the Red Lady of Paviland, because it had become stained with red ochre. (Subsequently it was determined that the skeleton was that of a male.) As a Christian minister, Buckland was hard pressed to explain this human presence among extinct creatures. He resorted to the contorted conclusion that the animal remains had probably been swept into the cave by flooding and that the human skeleton had been buried there long after Noah's flood by local inhabitants.

Similar mental gymnastics kept scholars from acknowledging what, in fact, their eyes were seeing: ancient human remains among extinct animals, attesting to a vastly longer human existence than Christian doctrine permitted. Only after the Darwinian revolution could people permit themselves to make accurate interpretations of these fossil materials. In 1860, for example, Edouard Lartet (1801–1873), while investigating a cave near the village of Aurignac in southern France, found human remains associated with the charred bones of such extinct animals as the woolly mammoth, the woolly rhinoceros, the cave bear, and the bison. The evidence he reported finally convinced many people, including the prominent geologist Charles Lyell, of the antiquity of humankind. It is hardly coincidental that these events happened the year after the publication of Darwin's *On the Origin of Species*.

Eight years later, in 1868, Louis Lartet followed his father's lead and excavated an ancient rock shelter that had been exposed in the course of the construction of a railway in the Dordogne region of France. He found five human skeletons: three adult males, one adult female, and one unborn baby. These people were associated with the same kinds of extinct animals and cultural artifacts as those found by his father at Aurignac. They came to be viewed as representatives of the so-called Cro-Magnon population (fully modern humans) that produced the impressive Aurignacian Upper Paleolithic culture.

In 1857, fragments of a human skeleton were found in a limestone cave near Düsseldorf in Germany. The skull cap, however, displayed what at the time seemed to be shockingly ape-like features. It was extraordinarily thick, had massive ridges over the eyes, and had little in the way of a forehead. This specimen, which came to be called Neanderthal man (sometimes spelled Neandertal, in keeping with current German spelling), raised for scholars the possibility of finding fossil populations of primitive people who were ancestral to the Cro-Magnon types and, thus, to modern human beings. In 1889, Eugene Dubois (1859–1940) traveled to Southeast Asia with the deliberate intention of finding such fossilized evidence of human evolution. There, during 1891 and 1892, in a site on the bank of the Solo River on the island of Java, he found some molars, a skull cap, and a femur (thighbone) of so primitive a nature that he thought them at first to be the remains of an ancient chimpanzee. By 1892, he revised this assessment and decided that he had, indeed, found an evolutionary ancestor of the human species, a creature he eventually called *Pithecanthropus erectus* (erect apeman). Naturally, as with all such finds, a great debate about its evolutionary status ensued; but today we agree with Dubois that his Solo River find is indeed a human ancestor, one of many that have since been found and are now grouped together under the term *Homo erectus* (erect man).

Although physical anthropology emerged as a fully developed discipline only after the theory of evolution had established itself in the minds of Europe's leading thinkers, already in the 1700s, scholars were engaged in the serious study of human population biology—as in the researches of Blumenbach and Retzius. However, as we indicated in "The Tree of Anthropology" (Hunter and Whitten) with which we opened this reader, eighteenth-century research on human biology was marred by the polarizing effects of the Great Debate of the day: the bitter feud between the *polygenists* and the *monogenists*. The former saw the biological and behavioral differences between the world's populations as being so substantial in nature that they could not accept a common origin for all the world's peoples. They argued (contrary to the teachings of the Scriptures) that God must have created people a number of different times in a number of different places. Monogenists, on the other hand, argued for a single origin for all peoples. Whereas polygenists perceived "racial" characteristics as permanent and immutable, monogenists insisted that they were changeable and came about as a result of the influence of the natural environment upon local groups.

Blumenbach himself was a member of the monogenist camp and recognized that the five "races" he posited were as much a matter of classificatory convenience as they were a reflection of the real world. Nevertheless, this debate proved rather fruitless until a means could be found to resolve it. That means proved to be the revolutionary theory proposed jointly by Alfred Russel Wallace (1823–1913) and Charles Robert Darwin (1809–1882) in 1858, and popularized by the publication in the following year of Darwin's masterpiece, *On the Origin of Species*.

If there is any one concept that united the discipline of physical anthropology, it is the theory of evolution. Its assumptions, axioms, hypotheses, and premises are the foundation upon which virtually all work in this area rests. It is important that you grasp how all-pervasive evolutionary thought is—how it has been assimilated into virtually all the social and biological sciences. Many of the readings in this and other sections of this book make explicit and implicit reference to evolutionary theory. We shall let them speak for themselves; but first we wish to clarify one aspect of the theory that is widely misunderstood and yet is also its central principle—the principle of natural selection.

Simply, *natural selection* can be defined as *the process through which certain environmentally adaptive features are perpetuated in organisms at the expense of less adaptive features*. That really is it. But its simplicity is deceptive, and the concept frequently (perhaps generally) is misunderstood. Here we shall address two widely held misconceptions about natural selection:

1. There is no such thing as an evolutionary "favored" individual. *Features* are favored, not individual organisms.

2. There is no such thing as an inherently "superior" feature (let alone an individual organism). What is meant by the term *superior* is the degree to which a feature is adapted to its environment. Change the environment, and a "superior" feature may well become an "inferior" feature.

Natural selection, then, is relative—relative to the environment. And because the environment is always changing, natural selection is an ever-changing process. No group, individual organism, or specific feature will ever reside permanently on top of the evolutionary ladder. Here, as elsewhere, the one constant is change.

In the context of this general introduction, we now present the articles of this section. They are grouped into three topics: Human Evolution, Primatology and Human Behavior, and Human Diversity. We discuss each of these separately.

Human Evolution

· ·

When the editors of this reader were college under-graduates (in the early 1960s) taking their first anthropology courses, the academic world still was in uproar over the fossil skull and teeth found by Mary and Louis Leakey in 1959 at Olduvai Gorge in northern Tanzania (East Africa). These fossilized remains, named *Zinjanthropus boisei* by the Leakeys, were dated at 1.75 million years old—almost a million years older than similar fossils that had been found in southern Africa. The possibility that the australopithecines—the direct ancestors of human beings (at least that is what they were thought to be then)—could be over a million years old was absolutely shocking.

The following two and a half decades have seen the unearthing of previously undreamed of riches in fossil finds. And most of these finds have not been limited to specimens of Neanderthals and *Homo erectus*, our two most direct and recent ancestors. Rather, the bulk of the finds have been of much older hominids and even of *their* remote ancestors—the earliest primates. In "Our Forebears' Forebears," Phillip Whitten and Martin K. Nickels survey what the latest discoveries have taught us about the evolution of the early primates. They discuss how plate tectonics (continental drift) and changing climatological conditions helped shape primate evolution, and they explore the major controversies surrounding our early ancestors.

As more fossils, and more ancient fossils, have been unearthed, you should not imagine that scholars have reacted calmly. Almost every significant new find has produced a flurry of heated debate over (1) its taxonomic status (that is, its place in the evolutionary hierarchy) and (2) its significance (that is, the degree to which it confirmed or invalidated previous views of human evolution). At first, it was merely a matter of pushing back the emergence of human ancestors earlier and earlier: The australopithecines became "older" throughout the 1960s, 1970s and early 1980s—first one, then two, then three, and now more than five million years old. But then, as more and more

fossils were found, the questions became more profound and subtle. For instance, what was the relationship between the emergence of erect bipedalism (walking on two legs) and the evolution of the large, complex human brain? Did large brains favor the invention of tools or, the other way around, did the invention of tools promote the enlarging of the brain?

One of the most recent debates and, in many ways, the most interesting one concerns hominid finds from East Africa. There Mary Leakey and her son Richard Leakey, working respectively at Laetoli (thirty miles south of Olduvai George) and at Lake Turkana (in Kenya), have found remarkable hominid specimens. They identify these specimens, some of which are as old as 3.35 to 3.75 million years, as belonging to our own genus *Homo*. Their main antagonist is Donald Johanson, whose fieldwork has been mainly in the Afar Triangle (in Ethiopia), west of the lower end of the Red Sea. Johanson's finds are the same age or slightly older than the Leakeys', and one of them, a skeleton he calls Lucy, is remarkably complete (over 40 percent of her bones were found). Johanson gives his finds the taxonomic label *Australopithecus afarensis*. He claims that the Leakey finds older than 2 million years are members of that *same* species, and that this species is the earliest example of a true hominid ancestor to human beings.

One of the most puzzling problems confronting students of human evolution was the fact that the interpretations of early hominid fossil remains did not fit in with the studies comparing human and ape amino acid molecules. Scientists studying amino acid molecules had, for over a decade, shown that systematic comparisons of these molecules from related species could be used to compute how far back in the evolutionary past their ancestors had split apart. Using these methods, Allan Wilson and Vincent Sarich of Berkeley arrived at a date of 5 to 6 million years ago for the split between pongids (apes and their ancestors) and hominids (humans and their ancestors). On the other hand, fossil studies, which counted *Ramapithecus* as the first true hominid, set the date of that split some 9 million years earlier. There seemed to be no way out of this dilemma other than to favor one view or the other (and most anthropologists favored the latter). Some authors even went so far as to suggest that the amino acid time clock might be accurate for the whole animal kingdom—but not for human beings. Two developments contributed to a solution to this puzzle: (1) the reinterpretation of ramapithecine remains and (2) the discovery of Lucy.

David Pilbeam of Harvard has been one of the world's foremost students of ramapithecines, the small creatures who inhabited Africa and Asia 8 to 15 million years ago and whose jaws seemed to show true hominid features. In the 1980s, after more complete remains of *Ramapithecus* were discovered (before then only ramapithecine jaws had been found), Pilbeam realized that *Ramapithecus* was not in the human family line at all, but most likely was ancestral to the orangutan. *Sivapithecus*, a form related to *Ramapithecus*, has now been proposed by some physical anthropologists as the first true hominid. Another possibility is that a *later* fossil population would be found, one that might qualify as the earliest hominid. This would make possible a meeting of the minds between those who studied fossils and those who studied amino acid time clocks. The first fully hominid fossils might indeed be only 5 or 6 million years old.

But was there such a fossil population? Richard Leakey thinks he and his associates have found one—a creature he has named *Homo habilis* ("handy man"). *Homo habilis*, which dates back over 2 million years, produced stone tools and had a brain one-third to one-half as large as our own. This population clearly was ancestral to *Homo erectus*, the immediate ancestors of *Homo sapiens*. But what was the origin of *H. habilis*?

Leakey believes that *H. habilis* evolved directly from a much earlier pongid ancestor, possibly the cat-sized pongid *Aegyptopithecus* (Egyptian ape), whose remains, found near Cairo, date back some 28 million years. Therefore Leakey views the other main fossil populations that are similar to, and precede or are contemporary with, *H. habilis* to be parallel side-branches of hominids—that is, evolutionary deadends.

This is where Johanson's discovery of Lucy becomes important. When discovered, she was the earliest, most complete, fully erect and bipedal hominid remain

ever found. Johanson coined the term *Australopithecus afarensis* for the population of fossils to which Lucy belongs. In 1984, David Pilbeam announced the discovery of some *A. afarensis* fossils dating back over five million years, the earliest hominid remains yet uncovered. Though it walked on two legs, *A. afarensis* had a smaller brain than *H. habilis*, and Johanson believes that *A. afarensis* is the ancestor of the "handy man," the link between *H. habilis* and the pongid line. In this view, *H. habilis* joins *A. afarensis* and *A. africanus* (found in southern Africa) as one single, continuous evolutionary line. (In this view the more rugged, "robust" line of australopithecines remains an evolutionary *cul-de-sac*.)

At least one very important issue is at stake in the Leakey-Johanson debate. If Leakey's view is right, it would appear that bipedalism and large brains evolved more or less together and that they were associated with the manufacture and use of tools. If Johanson's view is right, then our ancestors first evolved an upright posture and tool use, and only afterwards did the brain become enlarged.

In "The Emergence of Homo Sapiens," Boyce Rensberger takes up the tale at a later but equally important time. He accepts the Johanson interpretation of early hominid origins and focuses on the evolution of *H. sapiens*, our direct ancestor, from *H. erectus*. Here, too, there is debate, especially over the position of the large-headed, heavy-browed, stoop-shouldered Neanderthals. The "replacement hypothesis" portrays Neanderthals as evolutionary deadends, whereas the "unilinear hypothesis" views them as an early form of our own species who evolved into modern Europeans.

Rensberger lays out the arguments and data offered by both sides of this debate—and in the end suggests that it is too early to take sides. Regardless of which side ultimately is right, however, Ralph Solecki argues that it is important to recognize the cultural sophistication of Neanderthals. In "Neanderthal Is Not an Epithet but a Worthy Ancestor," Solecki shows you the "human" side of Neanderthals: their caring for the aged, their sentimentality, perhaps even their religiosity. Although social and cultural evolution in the last 100,000 years has been vast, it appears that, by the time of the Neanderthals, the basic features of human society (and possibly even human personality) were already well developed.

2

Our Forebears' Forebears

BY PHILLIP WHITTEN AND MARTIN K. NICKELS

FOUR TO FIVE MILLION YEARS AGO, the earliest humanlike creatures first strode upright across the
rolling savannas of East Africa, gazed over the vast
plain, and began competing with much stronger, faster,
and deadlier carnivores for a place in the sun. But long
before our remote forebears built the first fire and huddled around it to ward off the night (about one and a half
million years ago), eons before their predecessors fash-
ioned the first crude stone tools (almost four million
years ago), or even began to walk on two legs, primates
had inhabited the Earth for well over fifty million years,
evolving the set of physical characteristics—grasping
hands, binocular vision, short snouts, and large cortexes
—that they would later pass on to *Homo sapiens*. And
while Africa was undoubtedly the birthplace of our own
immediate ancestors and the genus *Homo* itself, the earliest primates appear to have arisen not in Africa or Asia,
but on the North American continent.

Despite the variety within the order of primates, the
nearly two hundred living species are bound by a common ancestral lifestyle that has shaped their distinctive
features. The distant relatives of today's prosimians (lemurs, tarsiers, lorises, and galagos or bush-babies), monkeys (both Old World and New World forms), apes (chimpanzees, gorillas, orangutans, gibbons, and siamangs),
and humans all shared a life history that began in and
amongst the trees. Some spent all of their lives in the
branches, while others most likely concentrated their
activities close enough to the trees so that they could flee
into them during times of danger and sleep in them at
night, safe from ground-stalking predators. But all primates developed dexterous fingers and toes with nails
(rather than claws) ideal for grasping and clinging to
branches as well as for capturing small insects and lizards;
and all of them developed eyes that faced forward with
overlapping fields of vision that enabled them to judge
accurately the distance to the next perch or the next meal.
As vision became more important for their survival and
their eyes moved from the sides of the head to the front,
the primates' olfactory apparatus diminished both in importance and size. Finally, the selective pressures of arboreal life caused the primate brain to change. The visual
cortex became enlarged and elaborated as it processed

more information. At the same time, complex cortical
motor control areas developed to coordinate rapid movements through trees.

The first primate (or proto-primate), however, was not
a very impressive fellow. From the rather meager fossil
record of only a few teeth, we can tell that it was a rodentlike animal (before there were true rodents). It probably
spent much of its time either hunting for insects or avoiding being unceremoniously squashed by the dinosaurs
that ruled as unchallenged lords for more than 160 million years, dominating both land and sea until they disappeared about 65 million years ago.

Oddly enough, the fossilized remains of this early form
have been found only in North America, a continent with
no indigenous primate species today. Its remains, along
with those of fearsome dinosaurs like *Triceratops,* were
discovered in 1964 by scientists from the University of
Minnesota, in Montana's Bug Creek area, among the
chalky rubble of Purgatory Hill (hence the primate's
name, *Purgatorius*). As if to confirm the American origins of the first primate, other bones appeared nearby.
Last year, in Wyoming, Robert T. Bakker, of Johns Hopkins University, discovered the fossil foot bones of a fif-
ty-two-million-year old lemurlike animal called *Cantius*.
These fossils are the oldest evidence of a grasping big toe,
a characteristic that some scientists consider more important than teeth for tracing primate evolution.

It is tempting to conclude from these discoveries that
the origin of all primates may have been on this continent,
but the fossil evidence is both skimpy and controversial.
And even though the oldest bones we now have come
from North America, it is always possible that still older
and more conclusive evidence may be found elsewhere.
Furthermore it is difficult to argue, with only a handful
of North American teeth and foot bones, that primates
first arose on this continent. After all, except for South
American monkey fossils, most fossil evidence relating
to the evolutionary rise of the higher primates (humans
included) comes from Africa, Asia, and Europe.

Still the question nags: What of the bones found in
North America? They date from the dawning of the Paleocene epoch (the earliest division of the Cenozoic era),
when North America and Eurasia were one continuous

continent called Laurasia; when South America and Africa may still have been linked by a land bridge; and when North and South America were not yet connected. Flowers, deciduous trees, and grasses were beginning to spread out, creating forest, bush, and savanna habitats that covered the northwestern United States and Europe with lush tropical rain forests.

ONE OF THE CREATURES that lived during this green era some sixty-five million years ago was *Plesiadapis,* a squirrel-sized animal very much like a rodent, whose remains have been found in both North America (Colorado) and Europe (France). *Plesiadapis* itself is not thought to be a direct ancestor of later primates—it had claws instead of nails, relied more on smell than sight, and had teeth specially adapted to eating fruits, seeds, and vegetables. But this rodentlike creature had already adapted to climbing and living in trees, the distinctive ecological niche occupied by almost every primate form. In fact, *Plesiadapis* so resembles the prosimians that came later that it is sometimes classified as one even today.

The indisputable evolutionary attributes of the primates did not appear until the next Cenozoic epoch, the Eocene. Like their Paleocene predecessors, the fossilized remains of Eocene primates come almost exclusively from the Eurasian-North American landmass. Unlike their predecessors, they had more manipulative digits, protected by flat nails instead of claws, and a body structure that allowed them to cling, hop, and leap, as some modern prosimians do. Fossil evidence of this period, which is the most complete for any of the early primate eras, also attests to the great diversity and adaptive success of these animals. Probably both nocturnal and diurnal, lemurlike and tarsierlike forms abounded. But despite their adaptive success, even these primates died out.

New mammalian groups, especially the rodents, began to invade the prosimians' econiches, and climatic changes forced many prosimians either into more restricted zones or into extinction. Prosimian supremacy among the primates eventually gave way to the superior arboreal adaptations of the anthropoids, the suborder that includes monkeys, apes, and humans. The earliest known anthropoids had larger and more complex brains than the prosimians, quite possibly color vision, more mobile and dexterous digits, and perhaps even more complex social adaptations. And by this time primate evolution had shifted toward the Asian half of the Eurasian-North American landmass. In 1980, when a team of Burmese and American scientists discovered fossilized fragments of the earliest known anthropoid primates—*Amphipithecus* and *Pondaungia*—in the hills of northern Burma, they noted that both creatures were about the size of a modern gibbon, and that their jaws were strikingly similar to those of present-day humans. Most astounding of all was their age: the fossils were dated to forty million years ago, more than ten million years before the earliest anthropoid remains found in Africa.

These earliest known anthropoid primates, though, also turned out to be virtually the last on the North American-Eurasian landmass, for the cooling climate that began at the end of the Eocene continued into the next epoch, the Oligocene. The northern and middle latitudes cooled so much that the forests that had flourished during the Paleocene and the Eocene turned into grasslands. And the primates, which had adapted to forest life, soon began to vanish. In fact, only two primates from this epoch have been found in North America, reflecting the disappearance of the climate that was once so congenial to them. The next primate to occupy this continent would be *Homo sapiens,* who migrated here from eastern Asia less than fifty thousand years ago.

In the Americas, primate evolution shifted during the Oligocene to South America, where the climate was milder. The oldest known specimen comes from Bolivia and has features of both monkeys and prosimians. However, the actual origin of primates in South America is still uncertain and highly controversial. Since there was no isthmus connecting North and South America at this time, the possibility of an African origin cannot be ruled out.

In the Old World, the stage for primate evolution moved to North Africa, to a fossil-rich area known as the Fayum depression, near present-day Cairo. These primates may have traveled from Asia to Africa beginning about thirty-five million years ago. Though the Fayum today is a desolate, wind-swept desert, then it was lush and tropical. Among the tall trees growing along its river banks lived at least six different kinds of primates: two genera of monkeys and four of apes, but apparently no prosimians. The virtually simultaneous appearance of monkeys and apes in the Fayum deposits and their similarities—small size, teeth designed for fruit eating, and four-legged posture—strongly indicate that they evolved either from some common anthropoid ancestor or from separate prosimian ancestors, but not one from the other.

About twenty-eight million years ago, some sixty million years after that unimpressive rodentlike animal appeared in North America, the first ape emerged from the basic stock of the Old World anthropoids. This cat-sized creature, known as the Egyptian ape, *Aegyptopithecus,* was discovered by Elwyn Simons, of Duke University, in 1960. Like the prosimians, it had a long snout, suggesting that its sense of smell was still relatively important. But its eyes faced directly forward and its brain, though smaller than that of comparably sized modern monkeys, was distinctly anthropoid. Presumably a social animal like most anthropoids, it lived mainly in the arboreal canopy high above the Fayum delta. But unlike some modern apes, it did not swing through the trees hand over hand, but rather ran among the branches on all four legs as monkeys do. This creature is especially important for understanding later events: Simons thinks it was ancestral to the apes that came to dominate the primate world in the next epoch and, in turn, almost certainly gave rise to modern apes and humans.

APE AND PLANET evolved together during the next epoch, the Miocene. India, which until that time had been an island in the Indian Ocean, drifted north and collided with southern Eurasia, forming the Himalayan Mountains. The Arabian Peninsula joined Africa and Eurasia together, and the Mediterranean Sea apparently evaporated, sometime between six and twelve million years ago, allowing animals (including primates) to pass between North Africa and southern Europe across the Arabian peninsula. Another land bridge connected Alaska with Siberia during the middle part of the Miocene. And around five million years ago, Central America arose from a bed of lava between North and South America. The Earth became drier as well.

While the forests of southern Europe and Asia dried into open grasslands, inadequate for apes, the African forests of the early Miocene richly supported the ape way of life. And so the Miocene in Africa was the heyday of the apes, the time when they reached their evolutionary peak. Simons estimates that there were about twenty times more kinds of apes than monkeys during this period. It was also in Africa some eighteen to twenty million years ago that a small tree-dwelling ape, known as *Proconsul,* stepped onto the evolutionary path that ultimately led to the development of the human species. First discovered half a century ago, *Proconsul*'s status as a human ancestor has been debated ever since. Based on analyses of a remarkably complete skeleton that Alan Walker, of the Johns Hopkins University School of Medicine, and Martin Pickford, of the National Museums of Kenya, reconstructed, Walker argues that *Proconsul* was almost certainly the direct ancestor of the dryopithecines, the most common apes of the Miocene.

Proconsul dates to the mid-Miocene in Africa, and soon thereafter migrated to Asia and Europe, where a new genus, *Dryopithecus,* evolved. Though *Dryopithecus* was very successful, surviving some ten million years, it began to disappear as its forest habitat gave way to expanding grasslands. By ten million years ago, the combination of receding forests and competition, especially from monkeys, proved too much for most of the Miocene apes, and they vanished from the Earth. Some species of this ape may have evolved into the still surviving orangutan, gorilla, and chimpanzee, but even these modern apes live in steadily shrinking forest habitats and are likely to become extinct in the wild by the end of this century.

The last and possibly most important ape form in the Miocene epoch was *Ramapithecus* (and its close cousin, *Sivapithecus*), which lived eight to fourteen million years ago, when the great forests were shrinking and the savannas expanding. Ever since the first ramapithecine jawbone was unearthed from the Siwalik Hills of northwest India, in the first decade of this century, anthropologists have argued over the status of this enigmatic primate with its mixture of apelike and humanlike features. Remains have since been found in Africa, Pakistan, Hungary, and Greece, as well as India, confusing rather than resolving the mystery of this ape. Was *Ramapithecus* the first ancestral hominid, a cousin of our true ancestor, or just an evolutionary dead end?

Some have argued that its thickly enameled molar teeth indicate that *Ramapithecus,* like *Homo sapiens,* ate mostly hard-covered fruits, nuts, and seeds, rather than the softer forest fruits and vegetation that most monkeys and apes feasted on. Others have held that *Ramapithecus* may have stood upright and walked on two legs, a prelude to human posture. But most of these early conclusions have been revised or abandoned in recent years. The number of alleged ancestral humanlike features have been either steadily reduced or seen in other, related forms, such as *Gigantopithecus* and *Sivapithecus.* And with the recent discovery of some fossilized limb bones, it now appears that *Ramapithecus* was more quadrupedal than previously thought, and quite likely more arboreal than terrestrial, even though it may well have been able to move on the ground on occasion, perhaps much as the modern chimpanzee and gorilla do today but without their more specialized "knuckle-walking" gait.

In the past ten years, many scholars have moved further and further from according hominid status to *Ramapithecus.* But the debate continues. Recently, there have been two significant developments. In 1981, Richard F. Kay, an anatomist at Duke University Medical Center, published an analysis of ramapithecine molars, in which he argues that this gentle creature was, indeed, probably our own great-great-grandfather, many times removed. On the other hand, last January, David Pilbeam, an anthropologist at Harvard University, reported on an eight-million-year-old skull from Pakistan, which he considers evidence that neither *Ramapithecus* nor *Sivapithecus* belong in the hominid lineage. Pilbeam even suggests that these forms more properly belong in the ancestral closet of the orangutan.

Regardless of whether *Ramapithecus* was the first hominid or a proto-orangutan, there is about a four-million-year gap in the fossil record after its disappearance and before the arrival of *Australopithecus* (southern ape) on the plains of eastern and southern Africa four million years ago. Late last year, Hidemi Ishida, of Osaka University, in Japan, and Richard E. Leakey, director of the National Museums of Kenya, announced the discovery in Kenya of a hominoid fossil that they argue may provide some of the missing pieces. Leakey describes the humanlike jawbone with five teeth as "a critical specimen—definitely a hominoid, and clearly neither a dryopithecine nor an australopithecine." He is cautious about fixing a firm date for the fossil pending the results of potassium-argon analyses, but he feels confident that it does date from about eight million years, judging from the fossilized fauna found in association with it. If Ishida and Leakey are correct, the fossil may provide the first evidence of the evolutionary divergence of humans and apes. However, the odds are small that it represents the last common ancestor of hominids and apes.

For the next form, the hominid *Australopithecus,* there is abundant fossil evidence. Larger-brained than *Ramapithecus* and fully erect, this creature walked as efficiently on two legs as we do. The adults stood less than five feet tall and weighed only 50 to 130 pounds. But they probably found safety in numbers. Walking the savannas in small bands, they likely gathered nuts, fruits, and berries, and perhaps even hunted and scavenged for meat. Despite their numbers, *Australopithecus* often fell prey to the larger and more powerful hunters of the African plain, particularly lions and leopards.

Within one million years after *Australopithecus* appeared, between two and three million years ago, hominid forms abounded on the vast African grasslands. One of them had a slightly larger brain and more modern-looking teeth than its australopithecine contemporaries.

Like them, it was a small, erect, bipedal creature that probably lived in nomadic bands. But its proficiency in shaping and using stone tools distinguished it from the others and suggested its name, *Homo habilis*—handy man. An evolutionary odyssey that seems to have begun ninety million years ago with an unpretentious ratlike creature thus eventually produced the first member of our own genus, *Homo*. And the story of human life on Earth began to unfold.

3

Neanderthal Is Not an Epithet but a Worthy Ancestor

BY RALPH S. SOLECKI

The top of a skull was perched on the edge of the yawning excavation in the huge cavern. At first it was difficult to realize that we had before us an extreme rarity in human paleontology.

Except for its heavy brow ridge, the skullcap looked like a gigantic egg, soiled and broken. When fully exposed on the narrow excavation shelf, it was an awesome sight—obviously the head of a person who had suffered a sudden, violent end. The bashed-in skull, the displaced lower jaw and the unnatural twist of the head were mute evidence of a horrible death.

As we exposed the skeleton which lay under a heavy burden of stones, we had confirmation that this individual had been killed on the spot by a rockfall. His bones were broken, sheared and crushed on the underlying stones. A large number of rocks must have fallen on him within a split second, throwing his body backward, full-length down the slight slope while at the same time a block of stone severed his head and neck from his trunk.

Among his remains there were small concentrations of mammal bones, which might have been rodent nests. But it is equally possible these bones were dropped there as part of a funeral feast for the dead.

This was "Nandy," as we called him, a member of the species *Homo neanderthalensis* who had died about 48,000 years before. In the scientific literature he is referred to as Shanidar I, because his were the first adult human remains that we identified as Neanderthal from a cave near the village of Shanidar high in the mountains of Kurdistan in northern Iraq.

Large, airy, and conveniently near a water supply, Shanidar Cave is still a seasonal home for modern Kurdish tribesmen, as it has been for various groups of men for thousands upon thousands of years. I had led our expedition to Shanidar Cave in a search for cultural artifacts from the Old Stone Age in this part of Kurdistan, Iraq. Human remains, much less Neanderthal remains, were not the goal, yet altogether in four expeditions from 1951 to 1960 we uncovered nine Neanderthal skeletons.

Laboratory studies of these remains continue to this day and the results are bringing the Neanderthals closer to us in spirit and mind than we would ever have thought likely.

The Neanderthals have been a nettling problem ever since the first find was made more than 100 years ago. This was the famous faceless skull and other skeletal parts found during quarrying operations around a cave in the Neander Valley not far from Düsseldorf in Germany. Primarily through the writings of one man, Marcellin Boule, who was a greatly respected Frenchman in the field of human paleontology, the owner of the Neander skull was soon cast in the role of a brutish figure, slow, dull and bereft of sentiment.

Although we now know much more about Neanderthal man—there have been at least 155 individuals uncovered in 68 sites in Europe, the Near East and elsewhere—he still seems to hang in space on the tree of human evolution. Some anthropologists feel that he had reached a "dead-end" branch on this tree. In any case, his time span on Earth (about 80,000 years) was more than double that of modern man who replaced him, but roughly one-tenth of the time span of *Homo erectus* who preceded him.

An abundance of Neanderthals

The classical hypothesis, now abandoned, was that Neanderthal man was an ancestral stage through which *Homo sapiens* passed. A second theory is that Neanderthal man was a species apart from *Homo sapiens*, contemporary but reproductively isolated, as donkeys are from horses. The third is that Neanderthal man was a subspecies of early *sapiens*, forming a geographic race. On the whole, the evidence appears to indicate that the Neanderthal did not gradually change into *sapiens*, but was replaced by invading

Reprinted from *Shanidar: The First Flower People*, by Ralph S. Solecki, by permission of Alfred A. Knopf. Inc. Copyright © 1971 by Ralph S. Solecki.

sapiens. The greatest difficulty for human paleontologists is that there is a real scarcity of skeletal finds to which they can point with confidence as *sapiens* of an age comparable to that of the Neanderthals.

There was, however, no scarcity of Neanderthals at Shanidar Cave. Prior to the discovery of Nandy, or Shanidar I, we had recovered the remains of an infant. It was later identified as Neanderthal by our Turkish colleague, Dr. Muzaffer Senyürek of the University of Ankara. When it was found, we had little reason to suspect that it was a Neanderthal child.

But not so with Nandy. "A Neanderthal if I ever saw one," is the comment in my field notes for the day of April 27, 1957, the day we found him. Although he was born into a savage and brutal environment, Nandy provides proof that his people were not lacking in compassion.

According to the findings of T. Dale Stewart, the Smithsonian Institution physical anthropologist who has studied all the remains of the Shanidar Neanderthals (except for the Shanidar child), Shanidar I lived for 40 years, a very old man for a Neanderthal—equivalent to a man of about 80 today. He was a prime example of rehabilitation. His right shoulder blade, collar bone and upper arm bone were undeveloped from birth. Stewart believes that his useless right arm was amputated early in life just above the elbow. Moreover, he must have been blind in his left eye since he had extensive bone scar tissue on the left side of his face. And as if this was not enough, the top right side of his head had received some damage which had healed before the time of his death.

In short, Shanidar I was at a distinct disadvantage in an environment where even men in the best condition had a hard time. That Nandy made himself useful around the hearth (two hearths were found close to him) is evidenced by his unusually worn front teeth. Presumably, in lieu of his right arm, he used his jaws for grasping. But he could barely forage and fend for himself, and we must assume that he was accepted and supported by his people up to the day he died. The stone heap we found over his skeleton and the nearby mammal food remains show that even in death he was an object of some esteem, if not respect, born of close association against a hostile environment.

The discovery of Shanidar I was for us a major, and unexpected, event. The discovery, about a month later on May 23, of Shanidar II was overwhelming.

The initial exposure was made by Phil Smith, then a Harvard University graduate student, who laid bare the great eye sockets and broken face of a new Neanderthal. My first impression was of the horror a rockfall could do to a man's face. The lower jaw was broken, the mouth agape. The eye sockets, crushed out of shape by the stones, stared hollowly from under a warped heavy brow ridge, behind which was the characteristic slanting brow of the Neanderthal.

From later reconstruction of the event, we determined that Shanidar II was killed by a relatively minor rockfall, followed closely by a major rockfall that missed the dead man. His demise did not go unnoticed by his companions. Sometime after the tumult, thunder and subsiding dust of the crashing rocks, they returned to see what had happened to their cave mate. It looks as though a small collection of stones was placed over the body and a large fire lit above it. In the hearth we found several stone points, and several split and broken mammal bones nearby that may have been the remains of a funeral feast. It appears that, when the ceremony was at an end, the hearth was covered over with soil while the fire was still burning.

As with the first two adults, Shanidar III was found in the course of cleaning and straightening the profile of an excavation. It was as if some Near Eastern genie was testing my alertness by tucking away the skeletons on the borders of the excavation proper.

Like the other two, Shanidar III had been accidentally caught under a rockfall and instantly killed. One of his ribs had a strange cut. X rays taken at Georgetown University Hospital revealed that he had been wounded by a rectangular-edged implement of wood and the wound had been in the process of healing for about a week when he died. Most likely, he had been disabled in a conflict with unfriendly neighbors and was recuperating when he was killed. Clearly, the dangers of the caveman's life were by no means shut out when he crossed the portal to his airy home.

On August 3, 1960, during our fourth and last season at Shanidar, we uncovered the fragile and rotted bones of Shanidar IV. While Stewart exposed these remains, I started to explore the stones and soil near the place where three years before we had found Shanidar III. Parts of his skeleton were missing and unaccounted for in our collection.

In my first trowelings, several animal bones turned up. One did not look like an animal bone; it looked human. Later I encountered a rib bone that Stewart authenticated as human, but it was not until I uncovered a human molar tooth that we confirmed the presence of Shanidar V. This was becoming too much.

Within four days we found several other bones of this fifth Neanderthal including the scattered fragments of the skull. It appeared that he too was killed by a rockfall, perhaps the same one that killed Nandy.

There was yet another discovery to be made. Stewart was clearing around the southern side of Shanidar IV when he encountered some crushed pieces of a humerus near the skull. "It doesn't make sense," said Stewart, "not in anatomical position." His immediate reaction was that he hated to think that there was yet another Neanderthal in the cave. Furthermore, there were already two humeri for Shanidar IV, the correct number, and now a third: Here was Shanidar VI.

In the space of only five days we had discovered three Neanderthal skeletal groups. Before us were the vast problems of preserving, recording and transporting the remains safely to the Iraq Museum in Baghdad. In the course of feverishly carrying out these activities, we discovered—in some loose material associated with Shanidar VI—more bones which later proved to be from yet another Neanderthal, Shanidar VII. These two, VI and VII, were females. We also retrieved some bones of a baby.

The skeleton remains of IV (a male), VI, VII and the baby (VIII) all appeared to lie in a niche bounded on two sides by large stone blocks. The nature of the soft soil and the position of the stone blocks leads me to believe that a crypt had been scooped out among the rocks and that the four individuals had been interred and covered over with earth. The child had been laid in first; the two females next, perhaps at a later time. The remains of these three were incomplete. Shanidar IV, the adult male, received the main attention of the burial. Probably, to make room for Shanidar IV, the bones of the others were disturbed.

As part of the archaeological routine, I had taken soil samples from around and within the area of Shanidar IV and Shanidar VI, as well as some samples from outside the area of the skeletal remains. These were sent for pollen analysis to Mme. Arlette Leroi-Gourhan, a paleobotanist in Paris.

Under the microscope, several of the prepared slides showed not only the usual kinds of pollen from trees and grasses, but also pollen from flowers. Mme. Leroi-Gourhan found clusters of flower pollen from at least eight species of flowers—mainly small, brightly colored varieties. They were probably woven into the branches of a pine-like shrub, evidence of which was also found in the soil. No accident of nature could have deposited such remains so deep in the cave. Shanidar IV had been buried with flowers.

Someone in the Last Ice Age must have ranged the mountainside in the mournful task of collecting flowers for the dead. Here were the first "Flower People," a discovery unprecedented in archaeology. It seems logical to us today that pretty things like flowers should be placed with the cherished dead, but to find flowers in a Neanderthal burial that took place about 60,000 years ago is another matter and makes all the more piquant our curiosity about these people.

Regarding their livelihood, we can certainly say the Neanderthals of Shanidar were hunters/foragers/gatherers. They most likely made a seasonal round of their wilderness domain, returning to shelter in Shanidar Cave.

The animals they hunted are represented in the cave by the bones of wild goat, sheep, cattle, pig and land tortoise. More rare are bear, deer, fox, marten and gerbil. It should be noted that the most common animals represented are the more docile type, the gregarious herbivorous mammals. It is likely that the Neanderthals caught them by running them over cliffs in herds or, conceivably, by running them into blind canyons where they could be slaughtered. There are several such canyons within easy striking distance of Shanidar Cave.

Communal life in a cultural backwater

The picture of the lone stalker cannot be ruled out in the case of the Neanderthal but, since these people lived in a communal setting, it would be more natural for them to have engaged in communal hunting. And the fact that their lame and disabled (Shanidar I and Shanidar III) had been cared for in the cave is excellent testimony for communal living and cooperation.

By projecting carbon 14 dates that we have received for certain portions of the cave, I estimate that its first occupation was at most about 100,000 years ago. For perhaps 2,000 generations, over a period of some 60,000 years, we think that groups of Neanderthals—probably numbering 25 members at a time—made their seasonal home in Shanidar Cave. Preliminary findings from the analysis of pollen samples show that, through the long history of their occupation of the cave, the climate vacillated from cool to warm.

Yet throughout the period, the Neanderthals changed little in their means of adapting to these climatic changes. Their tool kit remained much the same throughout: It included their flaked stone tools identified as a "typical Mousterian" industry of points, knives, scoopers and some perforators, all struck off from locally derived flint pebbles. Only a few fragments of bone tools were found. With this meager tool kit Neanderthal man was able to survive and prosper in his own way.

Shanidar seems to have been a kind of cultural backwater, a "refuge" area bypassed by the stream of history because of the remoteness of the area—a condition still reflected in the Kurdish tribal compartmentalizations of today.

Then, around 40,000-35,000 B.C., the Neanderthals were gone from Shanidar Cave, replaced by a wave of *Homo sapiens* whom we have called Baradostians. We have no skeletal remains of these people but ample evidence that they possessed a brand new stone tool kit. Using the same raw materials available to their predecessors, the Baradostians used the Upper Paleolithic technique of flint-knapping, striking off blades which were used as blanks for tools. They had more stone tool types, a variety of bone tools and they also possessed a woodworking technology such as the Neanderthals never had. Probably they used elaborate wood-carving stone tools to fashion traps and more advanced kinds of hunting apparatus and with this equipment they pursued much the same kind of game animals (mainly goats) as their extinct Neanderthal predecessors had.

By 35,000 B.C., the Neanderthals seem to have disappeared from the world altogether and we may well ask, what did Upper Paleolithic *Homo sapiens* have that the Neanderthals did not have? To my way of thinking, there were probably two things that weighed heavily in the balance. One was language. Jacquetta Hawkes, the English student of language and prehistory, feels that although the Neanderthal was a skilled toolmaker, his tool kit shows a conspicuous lack of invention and adaptability. He was probably handicapped because he did not develop a fully articulate and precise language. This was the new weapon which we think his Upper Paleolithic replacement possessed and used to make a tool kit so diversified that in the graver category he had more working edges than master cabinetmakers are accustomed to working with today. With his greater articulateness, he was able to describe and demonstrate the details of the manufacture of these stone tools to his people, including the children who were to carry on the group's activities.

The second critical cultural achievement of Upper Paleolithic man, in my opinion, is his ability to keep track of events for the future. Alexander Marshack, a research fellow at Harvard, has provided us with this recent and powerful insight into prehistoric man. Thousands of notational sequences have been found on engraved bones and stones dating as far back as at least 30 millennia. These markings have been puzzled over or guessed about by archaeologists since the time they were first discovered more than 100 years ago. Marshack has determined that they served Upper Paleolithic man as a kind of farmer's almanac tied in with a lunar notational count. Some are illustrated

with the natural history of the events, giving the possessor of the object a mnemonic device reminding him when to expect the change of seasons and the movements and dispersal of game.

An ancestor of sympathetic character

In short, this was of tremendous economic advantage to Upper Paleolithic man, and it gave him a control over his environment and destiny such as was evidently denied to his predecessor, the Neanderthal.

So, men with these remarkable abilities and all that flowed from them overtook and presumably eliminated the Neanderthals. We have long thought of the Neanderthals as ultimate examples of the Hobbesian dictum that the life of a primitive man is "nasty, brutish and short." They have been characterized as having a near-bestial appearance with an ape-like face in profile, a thick neck, stooped shoulders and a shuffling gait. But now it appears that they were actually very similar to *Homo sapiens* in skeletal structure. Stewart's study of the Shanidar Neanderthals led him to the conclusion that below the head there was not too much difference between these early men and modern man. Of course, one cannot deny the bulging prominent eyebrows and the heavy coarse-featured face of the Neanderthal in general, though Anthropologist Earnest Hooton once said: "You can, with equal facility, model on a Neanderthaloid skull the features of a chimpanzee or the lineaments of philosopher."

His own biological evolution is something man really does not have conscious control over. But his culture, his social and religious life, is something else. In the millions of years of evolution that began with the ape-like hominids of Africa it is among the Neanderthals that we have the first stirrings of social and religious sense and feelings: the obvious care with which the lame and crippled were treated, the burials —and the flowers. Flowers have never been found in prehistoric burials before, though this may simply be because no one has ever looked for them. And to be sure, only one of the burials in Shanidar Cave yielded such evidence. But the others buried there could have died during the wrong season for flowers, since death knows no season.

The Neanderthal has been ridiculed and rejected for a century but despite this he is still our ancestor. Of course we may still have the privilege of ridiculing him, but in the face of the growing evidence, especially in the light of the recent findings at Shanidar, we can not actually reject him. And what person will mind having as an ancestor one of such sympathetic character, one who laid his dead to rest with flowers?

4

The Emergence of *Homo sapiens*

BY BOYCE RENSBERGER

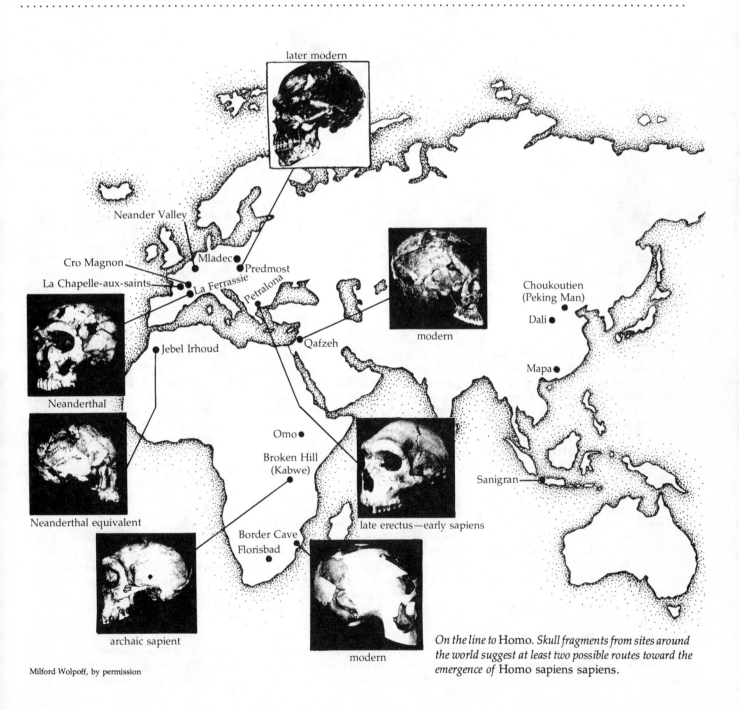

later modern

Neander Valley

Cro Magnon

La Chapelle-aux-saints

Mladec

Predmost

La Ferrassie

Petralona

Neanderthal

modern

Choukoutien
(Peking Man)

Dali

Jebel Irhoud

Qafzeh

Mapa

Neanderthal equivalent

Omo

Broken Hill
(Kabwe)

Sanigran

late erectus—early sapiens

archaic sapient

Border Cave
Florisbad

modern

On the line to Homo. *Skull fragments from sites around the world suggest at least two possible routes toward the emergence of* Homo sapiens sapiens.

Milford Wolpoff, by permission

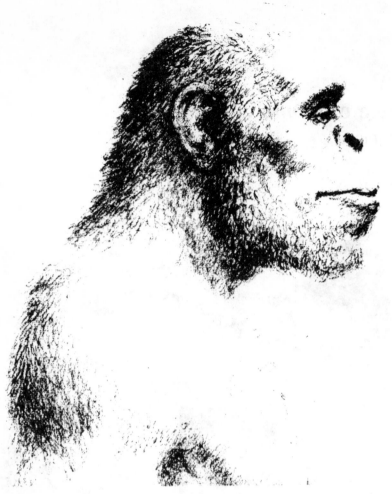

Australopithecus afarensis

According to one side of paleoanthropology's most enduring controversy, a confrontation that was to become humanity's most dramatic clash of two cultures took place in Europe's Upper Paleolithic period, some 35,000 years ago. On the one hand there were the Neanderthals, ostensibly beetle-browed hulks who trudged about Europe and the Middle East for more than 30 millennia, starting at least 70,000 years ago. Massively built people, they purportedly made up in brute strength what they lacked in wit and cunning.

At the same time, somewhere beyond Neanderthal's mostly European range—perhaps in Africa or Southwest Asia—a new breed of human being was on the rise, fully modern, anatomically and intellectually indistinguishable from ourselves. These people would soon produce magnificent cave paintings and sculpture. The most durable evidence of their culture is sophisticated weaponry indicative of a hunting prowess well beyond that of the Neanderthals.

In a geological moment, as some interpret the stratigraphy of excavations all over Europe, the Neanderthals disappeared. They were succeeded instantly by the moderns, sometimes called Cro-Magnon after the French site where several specimens were found. By 35,000 BP (before the present) the Neanderthals were gone. Fully modern people were the sole surviving form of human being on earth.

Where did the Cro-Magnons and their ilk come from? Did they exterminate the native Neanderthals? Did they simply outcompete them for food and other resources? Did they interbreed, producing genetic mixtures that survive as today's Europeans? Or was there no sharp division at all but rather a gentle evolutionary blurring as one form of creature developed naturally into another more suited to changing times?

The replacement hypothesis—the notion that a group from outside invaded the Neanderthals' range and superseded them through extermination, outcompeting or in-

terbreeding—is only the most popular guess as to what actually happened to the Neanderthal. As with so many other questions in paleoanthropology, the data that must be relied upon to answer this one have vexingly limited reliability. Many fossils are not securely dated, skeletons are often only fragmentary and it is frequently unclear whether a group of skeletons from the same site represents one or many populations. Honest but widely divergent opinions are common. The evidence supporting Neanderthal replacement, for example, can also be read to suggest a unilinear hypothesis: that fully modern human beings descended directly from the Neanderthals with relatively little contribution from outside of Europe or the Middle East.

Neanderthal's place

Since the original discovery of a Neanderthal skull in the Neander Valley of Germany in 1856—the first extinct form of human being ever found—scientific thinking about the emergence of fully modern humans has been in more or less continuous ferment. The evidence is, in some ways, more obscure than that for the earlier stages of human evolution. In recent years the effort to understand the final steps in human evolution—the steps that gave rise to our own kind, to people indistinguishable from us—has been overshadowed, at least in public perception. More attention, for example, has been drawn to the search for the earliest hominids, the first, still-apelike creatures considered to be on the direct evolutionary line to *Homo*, even though kinship to us might lie in hardly more than two-legged locomotion. (For a fuller discussion of human evolution up to the hominid divergence see the *Mosaic* special on human origins: Volume 10, Number 2.)

The earliest known creatures that are undisputedly hominids (members of the human family after it diverged from the pongid, or ape, family) date from 3.8 million years ago. They are of the species known as *Australopithecus afarensis*, a two-legged animal with a body of rather human proportions, but not much more than a meter tall and with a head only slightly different from an ape's. According to a newly emerging interpretation, *A. afarensis*, named in 1978, could have been the common ancestor of two lineages. One included the two previously known forms of *Australopithecus: A. africanus* and *A. robustus*. The other lineage was *Homo*. The oldest *Homo* known, usually called *Homo habilis*, is represented by the famous skull 1470 from Kenya, dated at about 1.8

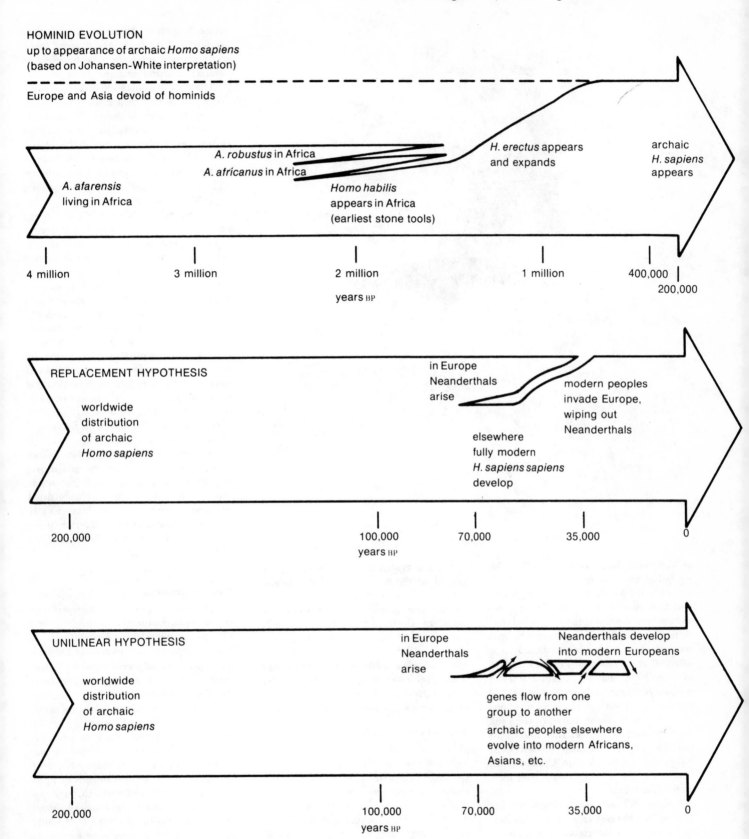

HOMINID EVOLUTION
up to appearance of archaic *Homo sapiens*
(based on Johansen-White interpretation)

Europe and Asia devoid of hominids

A. robustus in Africa

A. africanus in Africa

A. afarensis
living in Africa

Homo habilis
appears in Africa
(earliest stone tools)

H. erectus appears
and expands

archaic
H. sapiens
appears

4 million   3 million   2 million   1 million   400,000
200,000

years BP

REPLACEMENT HYPOTHESIS

worldwide
distribution
of archaic
Homo sapiens

in Europe
Neanderthals
arise

modern peoples
invade Europe,
wiping out
Neanderthals

elsewhere
fully modern
H. sapiens sapiens
develop

200,000   100,000   70,000   35,000   0

years BP

UNILINEAR HYPOTHESIS

worldwide
distribution
of archaic
Homo sapiens

in Europe
Neanderthals
arise

Neanderthals develop
into modern Europeans

genes flow from one
group to another
archaic peoples elsewhere
evolve into modern Africans,
Asians, etc.

200,000   100,000   70,000   35,000   0

years BP

The place of Neanderthals. Time line represents hominid evolution and two theories of Neanderthals' place in the line to modern Homo: *In the unilinear hypothesis, they are in the main stream; in the replacement hypothesis, they were bypassed.*

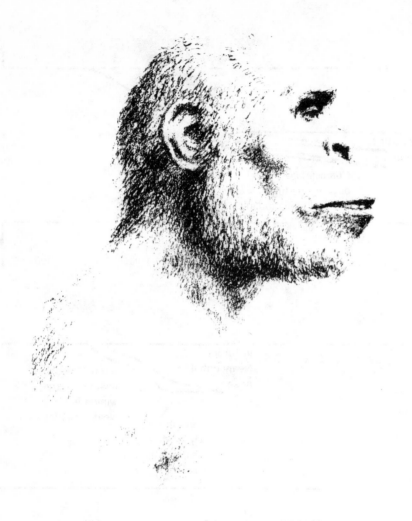

Australopithecus robustus

million years. Its brain was only half the size of that of people living today.

By about 1.5 million years ago, *H. habilis* had evolved into *H. erectus*. This appears to have been the first hominid to spread from Africa into Eurasia. Peking Man, who may have lived anywhere from 700,000 BP to 400,000 BP, is one well-known example. Not until the final 10 percent of the 3.8 million-year span—within the last 400,000 years—did the earliest examples of *Homo sapiens* emerge. These, however, were still not fully modern people. Their brains, for one thing, were only about 83 percent as big as ours on the average. Usually called "archaic sapiens," they ranged over most of the Old World.

Only in still more recent times—perhaps around 70,000 years ago—did they evolve, in Europe, into the classic Neanderthals, who are designated *Homo sapiens neanderthalensis*. The archaic sapiens also evolved into fully modern peoples, *Homo sapiens sapiens*.

There is evidence that the evolutionary growth of the brain—a trend that began early and slowly in hominid evolution—attained its present level something like 115,000 years ago—the last 3 percent of the 3.8 million years of the hominid career. Some say it was not until the last one percent. It remains one of the great challenges of anthropology to discover which of those figures is so: by what route—through, around or over Neanderthal—archaic sapiens became modern.

Another way

While the replacement hypothesis is perhaps the most widely held answer to the challenge, advocates of the unilinear hypothesis have not been overborne. They hold that the transition in Europe from Neanderthal to fully modern people may not have been as instantaneous as is often implied. Many thousands of years can disappear into a geological instant and, advocates note, the skeletons called Neanderthal show a high degree of variation that cannot be ignored.

Some Neanderthals are decidedly more modern looking than others; some specimens even appear transitional between classic Neanderthals and moderns.

After all, the differences between the Neanderthals and their modern successors are largely matters of degree. Brains are already at their maximum size. Nearly all the differences involve decreases in the robustness of bones. People become less heavily muscled and bones become correspondingly lighter and thinner. Skeletal buttressing diminishes. Once-massive brow ridges become smaller, and what is left of a snout continues to recede under the eyes and nose.

In the unilinear view there was no cultural clash, just a gradual evolution, largely confined to Europe in the case of the Neanderthals, though similar changes would have been taking place independently and perhaps, though not necessarily, coincidentally in Africa and Asia as well. Australia, like the New World, remained uninhabited until quite recently. People first reached Australia around 40,000 BP. They appear to have been fully modern. Entry into the New World is more controversial, with most estimates ranging from 12,000 to 30,000 BP. (See "Pre-Clovis Man: Sampling the Evidence," *Mosaic*, Volume 11, Number 5.)

For years the Neanderthal controversy rested at this point, with few new developments pointing either way. Adherents of neither side could point to reliably dated remains of fully modern people much older than about 35,000 years, and certainly not from anywhere outside of Europe and the Middle East.

Ancient moderns

Then a controversial new interpretation of ancient human bones—first found some 40 years ago in Border Cave in South Africa, 400 meters from the Swaziland border—suggested that modern people were living in southern Africa a startling 115,000 years ago. This was fully 45,000 years before the more primitive Neanderthals first appeared. As some view it, the replacement hypothesis received a major boost, and the unilinear hypothesis a major setback, at Border Cave.

Was Africa the real birthplace of *Homo sapiens sapiens*? Did descendants of those early Africans spread north through the Middle East to swamp the Neanderthals and become the ancestors of today's Europeans? Or did modern peoples evolve independently in Africa and Europe and, presumably, in Asia too? Those are among the questions that hang on the Border Cave dates. Unfortunately, the dates are far from secure;

again, vexingly, the evidence can be read several ways.

"There's no doubt that the Border Cave specimens are fully modern," says G. Philip Rightmire of the State University of New York at Binghamton. His detailed study of the single, adult partial skull found there (the other remains are an infant skull and an adult mandible) has established that fact. Using a statistical analysis of 11 measurements of the partial skull (including such things as the projection of the brow ridges and the distances between various bony landmarks), Rightmire has established that the Border Cave *Homo* falls within the range of variation exhibited by living peoples. Further, it comes closest to resembling today's so-called Hottentots, a South African ethnic group similar to the Bushmen (or San) but rather distinct from African Negroes. "The idea that fully modern humans appeared only 35,000 to 40,000 years ago is certainly subject to quite drastic change...."

"The problem is, though, that the dating isn't that solid. There's a good deal of assumption-making going on before one can arrive at the date of 115,000 years," Rightmire observes.

The scientist principally responsible for the date, Karl W. Butzer of the University of Chicago, is rather more confident. And he sees major implications not only in such an early emergence of modern humans but in that it may have taken place in Africa. Since most anthropologists are of European ancestry, he observes, it has been almost a foregone conclusion that Europe must be the homeland of modern human beings. "Border Cave completely explodes contemporary thinking about *Homo sapiens sapiens*," says Butzer.

Assumptions and inferences

Like many other fossils and artifacts from the crucial period in human evolution between 400,000 BP, when *Homo erectus* died out, and about 35,000 BP, when modern forms become well established, the Border Cave remains are not easily datable. They are too old for such reliable standbys as radiocarbon dating and not suitable for potassium/argon dating, which requires volcanic minerals. One new method, amino acid racemization, has yielded a date at Border Cave that supports the 115,000-year estimate. The technique, however, is controversial and not widely accepted. Another, molecular evolution, requires soft tissue. More sensitive methods of radiocarbon dating are in development and within a few years may be able to reach about 100,000

Australopithecus africanus

years or more. (For more on these subjects, see "Pre-Clovis Man; Sampling the Evidence," in *Mosaic*, Volume 11, Number 5; "Molecular Evolution; A Quantifiable Contribution," *Mosaic*, Volume 10, Number 2; "The Significance of Flightless Birds," *Mosaic*, Volume 11, Number 3; and "Extending Radiocarbon Dating," *Mosaic*, Volume 9, Number 6.)

The chain of assumptions and inferences necessary to reach any date at all for Border Cave is typical of the problems anthropologists face at many of the key sites that bear on this crucial stage of human evolution. Butzer's Border Cave date is based on a detailed analysis of sedimentary deposits in the cave. There are some 20 layers of dust, grit, rubble and the detritus of human occupation. Each layer has distinctive geological and chemical attributes. Some, for example, contain extensive amounts of rock particles that flaked off the cave roof because of frost weathering. These layers indicate a period of colder climate. Other layers show certain

mineral transformations that require protracted warm and humid periods.

The younger sediments in the cave, back to one laid down about 50,000 years ago, have been radiocarbon dated. Using intervals between the radiocarbon dates, Butzer has calculated rates of sediment accumulation and extrapolated the rates to older sediments. He has also correlated the cave's cold-phase sediments with climatological data from ocean cores. By these methods, Butzer calculates that the skeletal remains at issue came from sediments deposited 115,000 years ago during a period of cool and moderately wet climate. From the bones of animal species found at the same level, it has been deduced that the habitat was then a mosaic of woodland and savanna.

The assumptions necessary to calculate a finite date in Border Cave are enough to inspire skepticism among some anthropologists, although such methods are commonly relied upon after expression of certain caveats. At Border Cave, one additional caveat is of people with a high degree of intelligence and adaptability.

Archaic sapients

Locality aside, there is general agreement among paleoanthropologists that *Homo erectus* was the ancestor of all later forms of human beings. From about 1.5 million years ago until perhaps 400,000 years ago *Homo erectus* was the sole human species on the planet. Specimens are known from many parts of Africa, Europe, China and Indonesia.

The transition from *Homo erectus* to *Homo sapiens* could have taken place anywhere in this vast range. Fossil skulls with features that seem intermediate between *Homo erectus* and modern people—those usually termed archaic sapients—have been found in Europe, Asia and Africa.

The best known African specimen of archaic *Homo sapiens* was once called Rhodesian man. It is a remarkably complete skull that was found in 1921 near what was then Broken Hill in Northern Rhodesia and is today Kabwe, Zambia. It was once estimated to be 40,000 years old; newer evidence, putting it in line as a possible ancestor to the Border Cave people, suggests it is at least 125,000 years old and perhaps much older.

Butzer believes the case for a southern African origin of modern human beings is now strong. From there, the Chicago researcher suggests, this evolutionary trend toward more modern features gradually spread northward, reaching the Middle East by about 50,000 BP. This date is based on some fairly modern-looking human remains from Qafzeh, in Israel. The Qafzeh bones have proved difficult to date (various methods have yielded widely differing dates), but a reasonable compromise puts the bones at around 50,000 BP. From the Middle East, gateway from Africa to Eurasia, Butzer speculates, modern peoples spread out, to replace the Neanderthals and their ilk.

Strong dissent

While several American, British and South African anthropologists tend to agree with Rightmire and Butzer about the significance of the Border Cave, there are prominent dissenters. Among them is Richard G. Klein of the University of Chicago. He has specialized in interpreting the hunting skills of peoples living over the last 130,000 years, especially in southern Africa.

"Those Border Cave remains didn't come out of excavations. They came out of dumps," says Klein, recalling the guano diggers churning through the cave deposits. (They never did find any guano.) "To me that's not evi-

Homo habilis

that the critical adult skull did not come from a controlled excavation. It was found in a dump outside the cave, having been tossed there in 1940 by someone digging in the cave for guano.

An important link between the skull and the 115,000-year-old layer is that bits of sediment wedged into cracks in the bone match most closely the sediments of that layer. Even more important, in Butzer's view, was a 1941 excavation that *did* carefully document an infant skull in the same beds. And in 1974 a fully modern adult jaw was excavated from a layer estimated at 90,000 BP. It was well below the layer radiocarbon-dated to more than 50,000 years. "Dating of the key fossils to between 90,000 and 115,000 years is not proved beyond a reasonable doubt," Butzer concedes, "but

it's very probable. The probabilities of being mistaken are very small."

In Butzer's view, anatomically modern people probably originated in southern Africa some time before 115,000 BP. The area meets certain geographic criteria: that evolution is thought to take place chiefly on the periphery of a species' range and that in such locales environments are often different enough from those at the core of the range, so that different traits are favored by natural selection. Southern Africa, at one extreme of the hominid range, which included much of Africa and Eurasia, would seem an ideal site. It had the added advantage, Butzer suggests, of offering a wide variety of habitats within a small area. The range, from seacoast to plains to desert to mountains, should have favored the survival dence. I remain to be convinced that the bones are as old as they say. We've all too often been misled by this kind of thing."

Like many paleoanthropologists dealing with what they consider to be equivocal or isolated pieces of evidence, Klein prefers to set this one aside. It is better, he feels, to try to make sense of unarguable data. In Klein's view this approach leaves the title of oldest anatomically modern *Homo sapiens* with the Qafzeh people in Israel, if one accepts an age for them of around 50,000 years. (Various methods have given dates from 33,000 to 56,000 BP.)

Klein believes there was a replacement of Neanderthals by modern people, but that the Middle East probably makes a better candidate place of origin than does Africa. His analysis of European sites suggests that, while the replacement in any one place may have been rapid, it took some 5,000 years (from 40,000 to 35,000 BP) for the wave of replacement to sweep from the Middle East westward to the Atlantic.

Among advocates of the replacement hypothesis there is debate about whether the invaders slaughtered the natives or interbred. Most suspect both and argue about the ratio. Klein, however, takes an extreme position, rejecting flatly the notion of interbreeding: "I would think that the behavioral gulf between these two very different kinds of people would have been so great that there would have been no desire at all to mate."

Klein remains unconvinced, for example, that the Neanderthals, along with other archaic *Homo sapiens*, had crossed the mental threshhold that makes modern peoples distinctive. He disputes the contentions of other scientists that Neanderthals, who produced no art, buried their dead with grave goods. (See "On the Emergence of Language," *Mosaic*, Volume 10, Number 2.) More important, Klein argues that the Neanderthals were unable to make superior weapons. They were "rotten hunters," he declares.

Additionally, from his studies of South African sites where the bones of prey animals were preserved, Klein has deduced that people of the African Middle Stone Age, who were culturally comparable to the European Neanderthal of the period called the Middle Paleolithic, were able to bring down only the weakest and least dangerous animals. Using fossil teeth to determine the maturity of the prey species, Klein has proposed that Middle Stone Age hunters generally killed animals under a year old. Very few animals in their prime are represented in the preserved garbage of those times. The

Homo sapiens (archaic)

prey-age distribution is comparable to that of lions. The two exceptions are the eland and the bastard hartebeest. Unlike other bovids, both can be driven in herds. Klein suspects that Middle Stone Age hunters learned this and drove entire herds off cliffs.

Fully modern people from the Later Stone Age, comparable to Europe's Upper Paleolithic, Klein has found, were able to kill any animal they chose. Bones from such sites reflect an age distribution closer to that of living groupings and also include remains of more dangerous animals such as wild pigs.

The difference, Klein suspects, was in the weaponry. Armed with little more than rocks and clubs, neither the Middle Stone Age *Homo* nor the Neanderthal could get close enough to an animal in its prime and they dared not approach dangerous prey. They

lacked the ability to invent such superior weapons as the spear thrower or the bow and arrow that make it possible to kill from a distance. The remains of such weapons have been found in sites of modern peoples in Africa and Eurasia, but not in sites occupied by their evolutionary predecessors. Later sites also show abundant remains of fish and flying birds, species absent from earlier sites. Since fishing and fowling require specialized tools and skills, Klein suspects these findings help differentiate the mental abilities of archaic and modern *Homo sapiens* on any continent.

New skills

Once the transition from Neanderthal to modern occurred, whether by competition, breeding or succession, there appears to have

Homo erectus

been a great population explosion. It has been estimated that the density of post-Neanderthal humans was anywhere from 10 to 100 times that of Neanderthals. Erik Trinkhaus of Harvard has suggested that one reason may have been the Neanderthals' greater need for food energy. He estimates that, on the basis of the massiveness of Neanderthal skeletons and the necessary corresponding musculature, they may have needed twice as many calories to stay active as their more slender successors. This, however, would account for only part of the population difference. Klein argues that, since the basic resources available to both groups were the same, modern people could have been so numerous only if they were more effective exploiters of their environment.

"I don't know what it was," Klein says, "but the people who appeared 35,000 years

ago knew how to do an awful lot of things their predecessors didn't. Something quite extraordinary must have happened in the organization of the brain."

It could not have been an increase in brain size, for Neanderthal brains were already just as large as ours today. Much of the older literature, in fact, asserts that they were larger, though this is now thought to be the result of early Neanderthal samples that included mostly males. Even among people today male brains are, on the average, considerably larger than female brains with, obviously, no difference in intellectual power.

"I'm quite convinced," Klein says, "that in Europe it was a physical replacement of one kind by another. And I'm prepared to bet that that's what happened in Africa too and at about the same time."

The unilinear view

Milford H. Wolpoff would take that bet. Wolpoff, at the University of Michigan, is one of the leading advocates of the unilinear hypothesis—the view that there was no sudden, single replacement of one kind by another. Rather, he suggests, the Neanderthals by and large evolved into today's Europeans. The anatomically modern population represented at Qafzeh did not invade Europe but, instead, having derived from an archaic *Homo sapiens* there, gave rise to today's Middle Easterners and North Africans. The Border Cave people, whatever their age, then would be the ancestors of today's southern Africans. Other fossil remains from Asia, such as the Neanderthal-like people represented at Mapa and Dali in China, are in the line that led to modern Asians.

"Any theory of human evolution," Wolpoff notes, "has got to account for the differences among modern populations. A modern European skull looks different from a modern African skull. And both of them look different from a modern Chinese or a modern Australian."

Indeed, while all living peoples unquestionably belong to the subspecies *Homo sapians sapiens*, most members of each population—sometimes designated a race or ethnic group—share certain distinctive skeletal features. In fact, using the kind of statistical comparison of measurements that Rightmire applied to the Border Cave skulls, it is often possible to distinguish between rather closely related groups such as the Bushmen and the Hottentots.

"You look at what the distinctive features of modern Europeans are and then you look at the fossil populations to see where those features first appear, and you find them in the Neanderthals," Wolpoff says. One feature he likes to cite is the big nose. European anthropologists tend to euphemize the feature, including it in what they call the "midfacial prominence," but it is clear that people of other races find Europeans distinctive because, among other things, of their noses. Europeans have the most prominent noses of the living races. It begins jutting out at a fairly sharp angle just below the brow. In Africans and Asians, the nasal bone descends well below the browline before curving outward. The fleshy part of the nose may be broader in some groups but it rarely protrudes farther than or begins to protrude as high as the Europeans'.

Neanderthals had big noses. Only half jokingly, Wolpoff says their noses must have resembled that typified by Charles de Gaulle. In Neanderthals the feature is often considered an adaptation to a cold climate, because a larger nose is presumed better for warming inhaled air. Anatomically-modern fossil populations from outside Europe, such as the people of Qafzeh or of Border Cave, lack this feature.

Wolpoff cites a variety of other anatomical features that, in the same way, are characteristic of a modern race and that first appear in the archaic *Homo sapiens* fossils from the same area. These include various subtle contours of the skull bones: for example the more flattened face of Asian peoples and the slight bulge that bridges the brow ridges above the nasal root in the African skull.

"To me it makes the most sense to assume that those distinctive features were inherited from the people who were already living in the area and who already had the feature," Wolpoff says. For most other parts of the world, most anthropologists accept such parsimony, he declares, but not for Europe.

Neanderthal types

One of the chief reasons, in Wolpoff's unilinear view, that the Neanderthal controversy continues is too great a reliance on typological thinking. In other words, when people think of the Neanderthals, one particular skull—often beetle-browed—or a closely related group of skulls comes to mind. And when people think of more modern successors, they think of another set of distinctive skeletal traits, including less prominent, loftier brows. Between the two stereotypes there are great differences, and they lead to the view that the earlier could not have given rise to the later in so brief a time.

"People forget just how much variation there is in every population," Wolpoff observes, pulling, as he talks, various casts from cabinets in his laboratory and arranging them on a table. (He maintains what is considered to be the most complete collection of fossil hominid casts in the United States.) "Every feature that is considered to distinguish modern Europeans from Neanderthals can be found in [one or another] Neanderthal sample."

Modern features are rare among Neanderthals and certainly not typical, he concedes, but this is exactly what would be expected of evolution. Natural selection works by acting on traits that are already expressed. A trait may be represented at a very low frequency in a given population; if it becomes advantageous, after many generations it will come to predominate.

The Neanderthals, in Wolpoff's view, were far from homogeneous either at any one time or throughout the 35,000 or so

Homo sapiens neanderthalensis

years they existed. Modern traits—less massive bones or higher foreheads, for example—are present but rare in the earliest specimens. In the later Neanderthal populations, such traits become more common. There are even some skulls that appear to be a blend of Neanderthal and modern features, so much so that some authorities have guessed them to be hybrids. Unilinear advocates, on the other hand, see them as evidence of evolutionary transition.

Even *Homo erectus*, the immediate ancestor of *neanderthalensis* and other *Homo sapiens*, and often said to have been remarkably stable in its million-year career, actually changed with time. Brain size, for example, grew some 20 to 25 percent between the earliest and latest specimens.

And the transition from *H. erectus* to *H. sapiens* was gradual. There is no gen-

erally accepted way to define the boundary. There are specimens that look like hybrids of the two types and might have been taken for such if they were not dated to about 400,000 BP, when the transition was in progress. There are similarly gradual transitions elsewhere in human evolution. There are, for example, specimens that look intermediate between the archaic sapiens and classic Neanderthals. And there are, among the fossils called "anatomically modern," many examples that are considerably more archaic in appearance than are living people.

Again, because of the lack of reliable dates for many of the specimens, it is not always possible to arrange them in chronological order. But by using estimated dates and archaeological associations, it is possible to produce what amounts to a morphological continuum from *H. erectus* to *H. sapiens*

Homo sapiens sapiens (Cro Magnon)

sapiens into which *H. sapiens neaderthalensis* fits nicely.

Wolpoff holds that the Neanderthals were simply European representatives of a phase of human evolution through which people also evolved in Asia and Africa. This has sometimes been misunderstood as an assertion that archaic sapiens from Asia and Africa were Neanderthals. Rather simplified, Wolpoff's idea is this: Since the parent stock of all modern peoples was *Homo erectus*, and since modern people today despite minor differences all differ from *Homo erectus* in the same way, people everywhere had to evolve through intermediate stages that exhibit similar intermediate features.

These intermediate features, along with the results of natural selection in the unique European environment, in Europe produced a classic Neanderthal. In Africa, the same gradation is represented by specimens found in Ethiopia's Omo Valley, at Florisbad in

South Africa and at Jebel Irhoud in Morocco. They lack certain distinctive Neanderthal features; instead, they have uniquely African traits. Comparable Asian specimens would be the skulls from Mapa and Dali in China.

Mainstream Neanderthals

Wolpoff also asserts that the Neanderthals were not the dull-witted brutes that Klein envisions. In fact, he sees no reason to doubt that they were anything other than squarely on the intellectual continuum, almost if not already the equal of modern human beings.

One recent discovery in France lends new support to this view. Bernard Vandermeersch of the University of Paris has found a Neanderthal skeleton in clear and direct association with stone tools more sophisticated than the Mousterian tools that are typical of most Neanderthals. These advanced tools

are of a type known as Chatelperronian. The kit includes such Mousterian examples as scrapers and irregularly shaped flakes for cutting. But it also includes some of the long, regularly shaped blades, struck from a flint core, that are typical of the tool kit of more modern people.

Until now the finer, Chatelperronian tools have always been considered early examples of the work of modern people. Now it appears that Neanderthals were capable of just that transition to more advanced technologies. Additionally, the modern people of Qafzeh, considered by replacement advocates as possible sources of the invasion, made and used the cruder Mousterian tools. 'What is all comes down to,'' Wolpoff argues, ''is that if you look at all the European evidence, there is no great jump. You don't need invasions.''

But are there inconsistencies? Would the people of Border Cave, assuming they were fully modern 115,000 years ago, have bided their time in Africa while less advanced peoples occupied Eurasia? Wolpoff is reserving his opinion on the reliability of the Border Cave date. But, he argues, it makes little difference how old those people are. Citing Rightmire's conclusion that they most closely resemble modern Hottentots, Wolpoff suggests that they were simply the ancestors of today's southern Africans. The distinctively African features in the Border Cave skeletons do not appear in any European fossils. From this, Wolpoff concludes that the Border Cave people are unlikely to have contributed in any large part to modern European ancestry.

The unilinear hypothesis should not be understood to rule out mating between otherwise separated groups. Indeed, most authorities assume it must have been a common occurrence. It is the norm today in many traditional cultures for men and women to seek their mates from other bands or clans or villages. This practice, if extended indefinitely, means that genes are flowing more or less continuously over the entire inhabited range. One effect of this practice, well documented for living peoples, is that physical traits that are predominant in one area slowly diffuse to the surrounding areas. If a trait is advantageous in all environments, it will quickly spread. But if the environment of the surrounding area does not favor the trait, the introduced gene will remain at a low frequency. If bearers of this gene in the surrounding area chance to mate with someone from an area still more distant from the trait's center, the gene will be spread farther but still at a frequency related to its utility.

Shared traits

Many physical traits among modern peoples (skin color, height, head shape, etc.) are distributed in this way and will continue to exist in continua so long as there is outbreeding at the range margins. So long as the environment at the core of the area exhibiting the trait continues to favor that trait, it should remain common there. Like ripples on a pond, the trait should continue spreading so long as the force making the ripples remains active.

In this way, Wolpoff suggests, traits that are only locally advantageous will spread some distance away but will remain rare at that distance. On the other hand, traits that are advantageous in all environments, such as a larger brain, will spread throughout the inhabited region and reach high frequencies throughout.

The flow of universally advantageous genes, Wolpoff suggests, would be likely to spread them to neighboring peoples before the originating population progressed so far that it could use the advantage to invade or exterminate its neighbors.

Replacement advocates, of course, disagree. They envision early peoples as so widely dispersed that, from time to time, groups became cut off—perhaps isolated by a desert or a mountain range. These insular groups would not spread any of their newly evolved advantages until they had developed well beyond their contemporaries elsewhere and then breached the isolating constraints. Thus big-brained peoples, if isolated long enough, might eventually break out and replace their small-brained contemporaries.

There is no clear sign that the controversy over the emergence of anatomically modern peoples will be resolved soon. Undoubtedly more fossils will be found. But perhaps more important, existing discoveries must be reanalyzed with the aid of new techniques, new or extended dating methods and fresh eyes. One very serious handicap to any single investigator is the difficulty of access to most of the original fossils (which are housed in isolated collections around the world) or even to casts of the bones (which are either expensive or unavailable). Hominid fossils are often treated as the personal property of their discoverer and sometimes access is granted only to a favored few. A full description of the bones may be years or decades in coming, and until then convention dictates that no one else may analyze or interpret the material in detail.

Compared to the rich and active lives led by thousands or millions of members of now extinct hominid species in the many past environments of the planet, the bits of bone that have been found in the past century—in all only a few score—are a pitifully meager basis from which to develop a believable story of human evolution. Still the broad outline of a fairly coherent story has emerged. Indeed, the origin of human beings in apelike ancestors is among the best documented speciation events in paleontology. Only the details remain troublesome.

And as the details come closer to illuminating the differences and similarities among living peoples, we may rightly become more rigorous and, inevitably, more contentious in evaluating the evidence. Clues to many of the most important events or processes in human evolution may never amount to proof, at least in the eyes of other disciplines.

And yet it is nothing less than the heritage of our species that is at stake. We have, after all, come a long way from the view of the shocked lady who is alleged to have said, when Darwin's ideas of descent from the animals first burst forth, "Let us hope that it is not true, but if it is, let us pray it does not become generally known."

Like orphans searching for our parents, we want to know where we came from, how we got here, how we are really related to the rest of the living world. It can be argued, in fact, that providing this knowledge is paleoanthropology's highest use. In this light, even the smallest quibbles about how human evolution took place are matters of vital substance for us all.

Primatology and Human Behavior

· ·

Human beings are mammals, members of the order Primates. And they are very closely related to some living primates, most notably chimpanzees, gorillas, and orangutans. As primates, human beings have certain evolutionary traits in common with other primates (and other mammals as well); but our species is also distinctly different from all other animal species. At this moment, scholars are actively debating the degree to which it is possible to understand or explain human behavior in terms of the behavior patterns that seem to be innate in other species, particularly other primates.

Edward O. Wilson is, at this moment, a very controversial figure. In 1975, he published a book called *Sociobiology: The New Synthesis,* in which he gathered together all the information biologists had accumulated about genetically transmitted behavior among the world's animals. But he went one step further: he argued that, contrary to the cherished beliefs strongly held by many anthropologists, human behavior also has fundamentally, innate patterns. Three years later, in 1978, Wilson developed these views at length in his next book, *On Human Nature.*

Initially, Wilson's arguments stimulated heated debate which, at times, became ugly and personal. Several of his colleagues at Harvard organized the Sociobiology Study Group of Science, which became a forum for attacking Wilson and his followers. The study group argued that any attempt to account for human behavior genetically will inevitably cater to reactionary politicians seeking to protect the interests of groups with social, economic, and political power in society. In a letter to *The New York Review of Books,* they proclaimed that "Wilson joins the long parade of biological determinists whose work has served to buttress the institutions of their society by exonerating them from responsibility for social problems" (Dec. 11, 1975:60–61).

A careful reading of Wilson's books reveals, however, that he has made no direct, declarative statements tying human behavior to genes. Rather, he uses what to his critics is a maddening "suppositional" style; he

supposes there *might* be genes that would favor certain forms of social behavior, then proceeds to ponder how such genes might be expressed. His critics point out, with some justification, that many lay readers are apt to miss this reserve and read Wilson's speculations as definitive. (Indeed, subsequent works by others have done so, most egregiously in the area of the study of sex roles, where Wilson himself is apt to use language decidedly deterministic in flavor. See Topic Twelve for a fuller discussion of these materials.)

Both Wilson and his adversaries have recently toned down their public rhetoric. But the debate and its bitterness does show that science is not pursued in a vacuum. Its findings can be and often are appropriated for social, economic, and political purposes—regardless of scientists' intentions. Thus, in a society still organized to some degree along "racial" (and sexual) lines in its distribution of wealth and access to institutions of power, scientific theories and findings that even suggest the possibility that social institutions may, to whatever degree, be rooted in innate biological traits will be used to justify the status quo and undermine pressures for change. For example, if certain research suggests that intelligence is unevenly distributed among the "races" of our society, some pressure groups will use these findings to justify terminating programs like Head Start, which are designed to compensate for social inequalities. It was fear of such misuse of Wilson's work that fueled the bitterness of his critics' attacks.

All the articles in Topic Three address these issues. In the first, S. L. Washburn objects to comparisons made by Wilson between human social behavior and that of our primate relatives in "What We Can't Learn About People From Apes." Along the way, Washburn notes that in the twentieth century, "biological explanations are considered more scientific than social ones," a telling point that partly accounts for sociobiology's widespread appeal. But his most subtle and important point—and one that is least well understood by lay persons—is this: "It is impossible to infer that special genes account for human behavior simply because the behavior has a biological basis." You will find out why when you read this article.

In "Is It Our Culture, Not Our Genes, That Makes Us Killers?" Richard E. Leakey and Roger Lewin attack Konrad Lorenz's notion that innate aggression in human beings is so powerful that it will overwhelm all social structures designed to curb it. Rather, they argue, human life—though rooted in biology—is determined primarily by culture; that is, the behavior patterns and their meanings are learned, taught, and shared by members of social groups.

The final article in this topic takes a different tack to criticize Lorenz and others who argue for the innate primacy of human aggression. In "Sharing in Human Evolution," Jane B. Lancaster and Phillip Whitten argue that, to the extent that there is a human "biogram" (as Wilson would put it), the evidence from both fossil remains and cross-cultural comparisons with still-surviving hunting and food-gathering groups argues that human beings are characterized primarily by a predisposition toward cooperation and sharing, rather than toward violence and aggression. This article shows how looking for biological foundations for human behavior rooted in our evolutionary past need not reduce human beings to "naked apes."

What We Can't Learn About People From Apes

BY S. L. WASHBURN

The past decade has witnessed an upsurge of interest, both popular and scholarly, in animal behavior, marked by an explosion of books and articles that stress the similarities between human beings and other animals. In the 1960s, researchers like Desmond Morris and Konrad Lorenz promoted the idea that by studying the behavior of other animals we could achieve greater understanding of human behavior. In the 1970s, sociobiologists like Edward O. Wilson have attempted to create a new science out of this approach.

The idea that human beings can learn more about themselves by studying animals that exhibit similar traits is deceptively captivating. After all, the study of animal behavior is fun as well as science. Most people find it fascinating to learn how bees communicate and the reasons fish and birds migrate; note the current popularity of animal behavior courses at universities. And it is easy to be charmed by a lovable chimpanzee that has been taught to brush its teeth, wash dishes, and speak in sign language (as indeed some have) so that we see it as being almost human—or, put another way, as a less-evolved form of human being.

But, of course, chimpanzees are not human beings, however endearing they may be, and although we can learn a great deal about chimpanzees by studying them, I question whether we can directly apply what we learn to interpreting the varieties of human social behavior. Because of my early research on the social organization of baboons, my work is often cited to support theories about the animal origins of human behavior. Obviously, we studied animal behavior to find both possible similarities and possible differences. As time has passed it is the differences that seem more important, especially when considering social behavior. Human evolution produced a unique kind of creature. The point I would like to stress is that a meaningful study of the complexities of human behavior must begin with human beings, *not* with other animals.

Theories about human behavior should proceed from an understanding of the relationship between nature (or biology) and nurture (or learning). In developing new theories of human behavior, emphasis has too often been placed on one to the relative exclusion of the other. Proponents of nurture commanded the field throughout the 1950s and most of the 1960s, as evidenced by the focus on environmental factors in human behavior. Now the pendulum seems to have swung back to nature, which is to say biology, as a means of explaining fundamental behavior patterns.

Sociobiology is part of this trend. The sociobiologists would have us believe that human beings are governed by a set of genetic universals. Their aim, in E. O. Wilson's words, is to develop "general laws of the evolution and biology of social behavior," which may then be applied to human beings. In their view, genes are responsible for a disparate mix of everyday human activities—from cheating and spite to creativity and altruism. As one means of supporting their theoretical contentions, sociobiologists select animals whose behavior matches certain preconceived notions of human contact. Based on observations of these animals—such as monkeys or apes—they will then draw conclusions about the behavior of human beings.

As an example of the ludicrous extreme to which this sort of reasoning can be taken, I can cite a recent textbook in which the author uses the behavior of nonprimates to make significant statements about primates. At one point a picture of a musk ox in a defensive posture is used to illustrate the possibility of atavistic behavior in human beings. By way of demonstrating the absurdity of this method of proof, let me reverse the situation. Try to imagine the reaction of the editor of a zoological magazine if I sent him an article on the musk ox in which the animal's defensive stance was illustrated by the British square formations at the Battle of Waterloo. The editor would surely think me a bit daft. Yet this type of reasoning is considered acceptable when animal behavior is compared with human behavior.

The claim that genes are responsible for different types of behavior in animals and in people is the most controversial part of sociobiological theory. More to the point, this way of thinking, in its application to human behavior, repeats the errors of past generations of evolutionists, social Darwinists, eugenicists, and racists. It is useful to recall that the eugenicists argued that genes were responsible for an assortment of human social ills, including crime, alcoholism, and other forms of behavior they regarded as undesirable. Zoologists Peter B. and J. S. Medawar aptly described this form of geneticism as "the enthusiastic misapplication of not fully understood genetic principles in situations to which they do not apply."

S. L. Washburn

accounts provided by travelers, hunters, and local people. One might reasonably ask how professional scientists could uncritically accept questionable information gathered in such a random manner. Part of the answer lies in the 19th Century view of animals as simple creatures of nature, whose behavior was largely instinctive. Given such a view, the reports of untrained observers gained an undeserved credibility. Besides, apes, with their human-like appearance and apparent similarities in behavior, fit nicely into evolutionary theory. Faith in the theory of evolution was so great that misinformation substantiating it was readily accepted without verification. Clearly, a theory should be seen as a license for serious research, not as a substitute for it. Yet the nature of ape behavior and its relation to human behavior was debated for more than a century before reliable studies were available.

We have had more than a century of such misapplication of scientific theories, of people believing what they want to, often without any substantive data to support their claims. As a case in point, we might compare early studies of the behavior of the great apes with more recent investigations. Ape behavior received considerable attention in the late 19th Century as part of the general interest in human evolution. Literally hundreds of papers and monographs were written about these animals (R. M. and A. W. Yerkes compiled over 500 references in their 1929 work *The Great Apes*), many involving heated controversies over such aspects of ape behavior as promiscuity and monogamy.

However, none of these studies was based on scientific data collected through careful field studies. Instead, these early reports were essentially anecdotal, relying on

During that period the image of the gorilla shifted from the 19th Century vision of a fearsome beast, who in romantic literature was seen confronting the brave hunter, to the more recent view of the peaceful gorilla and its cousin, the friendly chimpanzee. Neither perception is wholly accurate, but they are both examples of people in different times believing what they wanted to about these animals. It is only in the past 15 years, thanks to zoologist George Schaller's study of the gorilla and Jane Goodall's continuing investigations of the chimpanzee, that more reliable information has emerged. The evidence today is that chimpanzees, far from being docile, playful creatures, are by nature aggressive animals that jealously guard their territory even to the point of violence. Observers record situations in which chimpanzees from one group have killed and eaten an infant from another group. Similarly, gorillas are known to fight and sometimes kill other gorillas.

The current view of the violent apes does not sit well with those who would like to believe that apes (and therefore human beings) are inherently peaceful. Accounts of gorilla violence by Dian Fossey and last year's Leakey Foundation lecture by B. Galkidas-Brindamour describing the battle scars she found on Indonesian orang-utans were discomforting to listeners. Their distress points up the obvious conflict between behavioral fact and popular desire.

Although the information we now have on ape behavior is vastly superior to what was available before the Second World War, we still depend on the spadework of a small group of researchers operating in a limited number of geographical areas. Much more field work will have to be done before we have an adequate understanding of the social behavior of gorillas, chimpanzees, and other members of the ape family. Even with the aid of comparative anatomy, the fossil record, and studies of captive primates, it will likely be some years before meaningful comparisons between human behavior and that of our nearest animal relatives can be made. It is certainly premature to attempt to do so now.

Let me provide an example to clarify the issues I have raised. Sociobiologists, with their fundamentalist belief in a biological basis for all sorts of human behavior, have resurrected the old theory that the lack of regular mating cycles, or estrus, among human females is a primary reason for the rise of the human family unit. According to this hypothesis the loss of female estrous behavior during the evolutionary process led to monogamy—which, of course, is the bedrock of marital relationships in most human societies. Explaining the origin of the human family and of the social group in nonhuman primates in terms of sexual attraction has an obvious appeal. It combines 19th Century romantic notions about sex with the 20th Century need for a scientific rationale; and in our culture, biological explanations are considered more scientific than social ones.

But biological interpretations tend to be simplistic. When the available data are examined, the sexual-attraction theory does not hold up, whether we are dealing with human beings or our ape and monkey cousins. The most recent investigations of nonhuman primate behavior reveal that male-female relationships run the gamut from near-promiscuity, to consort relations of varying duration, and even to lifelong pair bonds. Furthermore, whether mating cycles are monthly or yearly, the social systems of these primates continue to function. Thus we learn from the studies of Ronald

Nadler, a psychologist at the Yerkes Primate Research Center, that the gorilla, the most continuously social of the great apes, has the shortest mating cycle. At the other extreme, the orang-utan, the most solitary of the great apes, will mate at any time, whether the female is in heat or not. Gibbons are the least sexually active of the apes and yet they form lasting pair bonds.

If even ape behavior is so complicated that it resists being categorized by a few labels like monogamy and promiscuity, then there ought to be caution about casually applying them to human beings. Yet sociobiologists attempt to reduce the extraordinary variety of human male-female customs to monogamy. But the word monogamy is not a label for any clearly defined behavior that could have a genetic base. It may mean a continuing relationship, such as marriage or the currently fashionable "living together," or a temporary one, and it may be modified by all sorts of variations in economic and social conditions as well as by diverse sexual practices.

The point I would emphasize about terms like monogamy or polygamy, when used to describe human behavior, is that they refer to systems of marriage, not to mating. Mating can and does occur outside of marriage in every known society; marriage is a social and legal contract involving rights and obligations and encompassing far more than sexual behavior. (Animal behaviorists seeking to draw conclusions about human behavior often ignore this fundamental difference.) In their use of words like monogamy, sociobiologists show a gross misunderstanding of social science. Insofar as they overlook different cultural interpretations of these terms, they also make the arrogant assumption that our culture is synonymous with human nature.

To my way of thinking, students of animal behavior are much too free in their use of the behavior of nonhuman species to make points about human behavior. They may cite evidence of aggression in insects, birds, lions, and a range of other creatures and then generalize about human aggression—as Konrad Lorenz did in his book *On Aggression*. Animal behavior is quite diversified—even within one species, as we saw in our discussion of the apes—and virtually any thesis can be defended if its proponent can randomly select any animal whose behavior supports his contention.

In promoting the idea that genes account for human behavior, sociobiologists are able to minimize the difference between what is learned and what is genetically determined—in other words, our biologically inherited behavior. But learning is the crucial factor in the two basic abilities that distinguish human beings from all other primates: the ability to walk on two legs (bipedalism) and human speech.

We now know from the fossil record that our ancestors were standing erect and using only their legs for walking at least three million years ago. The evolution of this new means of locomotion was the behavioral event that led to the separation of man from his ape relatives. And yet the brain of early man was no larger than that of apes, and both shared a similar anatomical structure. Therefore it was the uniqueness of the human brain that gave man the ability to *learn* how to do things that his fellow primates were unable to do.

Of course there is a biological basis for walking, and through the process of natural selection a complex anatomical restructuring of the human body—involving changes in bone structure and a reorganization of muscles—occurred that made bipedal locomotion possible. But the important point is that human beings do not instinctively walk; they must learn to walk, just as they must learn to speak. Interestingly, we make much of the fact that learning to speak takes years but tend to overlook the long period of time it takes for a child to learn to run and walk properly.

Since human walking is unique and far better understood than the ways other animals move about, it is more productive to start with what we know about human beings before we shift to comparisons with other animals. Observing chimpanzees knuckle walking will provide no information about the internal anatomical changes that led to fundamental differences between chimpanzees and human beings.

Further, the fact that all human beings share essentially the same biological base, with some minor anatomical variations, does not mean that they will all behave similarly. For example, a common biological base makes swimming theoretically possible for all human beings and other primates as well. But apes cannot swim and most human beings never learn how. Granted human intelligence, many of us may learn to use our arms and legs in a variety of ways that permit us to swim. But the structure of our arms (primarily the result of man's early life in the trees) and of our legs (which evolved for walking on land) did not evolve specifically to enable us to swim. Nor are special genes required. Swimming is a learned behavior that uses parts of our bodies that evolved for other purposes.

We can see from this example that even when a certain behavior has a particular biological basis, it is not possible to infer that special genes are involved. Human hands can be trained to do many different things, but although the behavior of the hands may be varied, the basic biology of bones, joints, and muscles is the same. Also, human beings elaborate on everything they do. People do not just walk and run; they hop, skip, and dance. They may also swim in many different ways, and there is no evidence that these elaborations are based on biological variations.

As in the case of walking, there is a biological basis for speech. The human brain makes it possible for us to learn languages, but there is nothing to suggest that the brain determines the language to be learned. Any normal human being is able to learn the language of his group, and even others if necessary or desired. The basic biology sets limits and possibly accounts for some linguistic universals, but there is an immense freedom of learning. The constraints are primarily in the difficulties human beings from one language group may encounter in learning to make the sounds that are peculiar to the languages of another group.

Human speech is based on a phonetic code, on a system in which short, meaningless sounds are combined into meaningful units, or words. Like all codes, the system is based on a relatively small number of units that may be combined in an almost infinite number of ways. Therefore the human system of communication is open; we can and do create new words to meet our needs, and no limit has yet been approached. The phonetic code is unique to our species; there is nothing comparable in any other animal, whether primate or nonprimate. In spite of great efforts by researchers, apes cannot be taught to speak in the human sense of the word.

Speech is the main form of human communication, and anyone who wishes to understand speech as distinguished from animal sounds must start with the human phonetic code. And the only way we know that such a code exists is by studying human beings. Comparisons between human and animal communication must begin with human behavior. If we start with monkey communication we learn that monkeys make roughly two to three dozen sounds, and we could speculate that adding more sounds could lead to speech. But closer examination reveals that when monkeys communicate they use a combination of gestures and sounds; and the gestures are nearly always the more important of the two. When the sounds are separated from the gestures and treated as an independent means of communication, the monkey system of "talking" falls apart.

The varieties of human languages, the ease with which they are learned, and the speed with which they change all combine to distinguish the behavior of *Homo sapiens* from that of the other primates. There may be minor regional differences in nonhuman primate communication—in the same way that there are dialects in the sounds birds make—but there is nothing comparable to the incredible diversity of human language. For instance, in one relatively small region of Africa—what is now Tanzania—over 100 tribal groups speak many languages. In that same area, all baboons use the same system of communication.

Language then is probably the best illustration of a common biological base facilitating the learning of an extraordinary variety of behavior. Viewed in this manner, biology actually validates two basic assumptions of the social sciences: first, that human populations, not individuals, have the same human potentials, and second, that human social systems are not determined by the basic biology of the species. Consequently, language gives the nature versus nurture (or genetic versus learning) controversy over human behavior an entirely new dimension. No comparable mechanism, nor any alternative biological system, allows virtually unlimited communication as well as the development of new symbols when needed.

Furthermore, human social groups can adapt to different situations because of knowledge and organization, both of which depend on speech. And it is this language-based knowledge and organization that lead, in turn, to technical progress. We might, in fact, define social science as the science that studies the nature, complexity, and effectiveness of human conduct that is made possible by language. Granted such a definition, it becomes clear that human behavior cannot usefully be reduced to that of other animals—even our closest primate relatives.

It has now been fairly well established on the basis of fossil records that, granting basic human biology, learning was the dominant factor in determining behavior even 30,000 to 40,000 years ago. Or, putting it somewhat differently, human cognitive abilities, speech, and social systems—which is to say, human nature as we know it today—had fully evolved more than 30,000 years ago. But in applying evolutionary theory to human conduct, sociobiologists generally make little effort to understand the complexity of human behavior. Instead they use the theory of evolution to make questionable comparisons between human and animal behavior without the neces-sary research to validate their claims. Unsubstantiated opinions by researchers are too often presented as facts—or at least as worthy contributions to scholarship.

I would be the first to agree that the full understanding of the behavior patterns of any species must include biology. But the more that learning is involved, the less there will be of any simple relation between basic biology and behavior. The laws of genetics are not the laws of learning. As a result of intelligence and speech, human beings provide the extreme example of highly varied behavior that is learned and executed by the same fundamental biology. Biology determines the basic need for food, but not the innumerable ways in which this need may be met.

Out of the present controversy, which, on a positive level, has stimulated renewed interest in human and animal behavior, a new interdisciplinary biologically and socially based behavioral science may emerge. But in applying biological thinking we must take care not to ignore history, sociology, and comparative studies. For if we do, we will be condemned to repeat the scientific errors of the past.

For further information:

Bateson, P. P. G., and R. A. Hinde. *Growing Points in Ethology.* Cambridge University Press, 1976.

Dolhinow, P. J. *Primate Patterns.* Holt, Rinehart, and Winston, 1972.

Washburn, S. L., and Elizabeth R. McCown. *Human Evolution.* Benjamin/Cummings, 1978.

Wilson, E. O. *Sociobiology.* Harvard University Press, 1975.

6

Is It Our Culture, Not Our Genes, That Makes Us Killers?

BY RICHARD E. LEAKEY AND ROGER LEWIN

· ·

"The blood-bespattered, slaughter-gutted archives of human history from the earliest Egyptian and Sumerian records to the most recent atrocities of the Second World War accord with early universal cannibalism, with animal and human sacrificial practices or their substitutes in formalized religions, and with the world-wide scalping, head-hunting, body-mutilating and necrophilic practices of mankind in proclaiming this common bloodlust differentiator, this predaceous habit, this mark of Cain that separates man dietetically from his anthropoidal relatives and allies him rather with the deadliest of Carnivora." The message of these stirring words, written by Paleoanthropologist Raymond Dart, is clear: humans are unswervingly brutal, possessed of an innate drive to kill each other.

On the same subject, the Nobel Prize winner Konrad Lorenz, one of the founders of modern ethology, wrote with even more eloquence: "There is evidence that the first inventors of pebble tools—the African australopithecines—promptly used their weapons to kill not only game, but fellow members of their species as well. Peking Man, the Prometheus who learned to preserve fire, used it to roast his brothers: beside the first traces of the regular use of fire lie the . . . roasted bones of *Sinanthropus pekinensis* himself."

Lorenz sounded these dramatic phrases 14 years ago in his celebrated book *On Aggression,* the main burden of which is that the human species carries with it an inescapable legacy of territoriality and aggression, instincts which must be ventilated lest they spill over in ugly fashion. All these—archaeological evidence of cannibalism, the notion of territorial and aggressive instincts, of an evolutionary career as killer apes—were woven together to form one of the most dangerously persuasive myths of our time: mankind is incorrigibly belligerent; war and violence are in our genes.

This essentially pessimistic view of human nature was assimilated with unseemly haste into a popular conventional wisdom, an assimilation that was further enhanced by Desmond Morris (with *The Naked Ape*) and Robert Ardrey (with *African Genesis, The Territorial Imperative, Social Contract,* and more recently *The Hunting Hypothesis*). We emphatically reject this conventional wisdom for three reasons: first, on the very general premise that no theory of human nature can be so firmly proved as its proponents imply; second, that much of the evidence used to erect this aggression theory is simply not relevant to human behavior; and last, the clues that do impinge on the basic elements of human nature argue much more persuasively that we are a cooperative rather than an aggressive animal.

The rules for human behavior are simple, we believe, precisely because they offer such a wide scope for expression. By contrast, the proponents of innate aggression try to tie us down to narrow, well-defined paths of behavior: humans are aggressive, they propose, because there is a universal territorial instinct in biology; territories are established and maintained by displays of aggression; our ancestors acquired weapons, turning ritual displays into bloody combat, a development that was exacerbated through a lust for killing. And according to the Lorenzian school, aggression is such a crucial part of the territorial animal's survival kit that it is backed up by a steady rise in pressure for its expression. Aggression may be released by an appropriate cue, such as a threat by another animal, but in the protracted absence of such cues the pressure eventually reaches a critical point at which the behavior bursts out spontaneously. The difference between a piece of behavior that is elicited by a particular type of stimulus, and one that will be expressed whether or not cues occur is enormous, and that difference is central to understanding aggression in the human context.

There is no doubt that aggression and territoriality are part of modern life: vandalism is a distressingly familiar part of the urban scene, and there is war, an

As excerpted in *Smithsonian,* November 1977 from *Origins,* by Richard E. Leakey and Roger Lewin. Copyright © 1977 by Richard E. Leakey and Roger Lewin. Reprinted by permission of the publishers, E.P. Dutton. Photograph by Roger Lewin.

apparent display of territoriality and aggression on a grand scale. Are these unsavory aspects of modern living simply part of an inescapable legacy of our animal origins? Or are they phenomena which have entirely different causes?

To begin with, it is worth taking a broad view of territoriality and aggression in the animal world. Why are some animals territorial? Simply to protect resources, such as food, a nest or a similar reproductive area. Many birds defend one piece of real estate in which a male may attract and court a female, and then move off to another one, also to be defended, in which they build a nest and rear young. Intruders are soon met with territorial displays, the intention of which is quite clear. The clarity of the defender's response, and also of the intruder's prowess, is the secret of nature's success with these so-called aggressive encounters.

Such confrontations are strictly ritualized, so that on all but the rarest occasions the biologically fitter of the two wins without the infliction of physical damage on either one. This "aggression" is in fact an exercise in competitive display rather than physical violence. The biological common sense implicit in this simple behavioral device is reiterated again and again throughout the animal kingdom. For a species to transgress, there must be extremely unusual circumstances. We cannot deny that with the invention of tools, an impulse to employ them occasionally as weapons might have caused serious injury, there being no stereotyped behavior patterns to deflect their risk. And it is possible that our increasingly intelligent prehuman ancestors may have understood the implications of power over others through the delivery of one swift blow with a sharpened pebble tool. But is it likely?

The answer must be no. An animal that develops a proclivity for killing its fellows thrusts itself into an evolutionarily disadvantageous position. Because our ancestors almost always lived in small bands, in which individuals were closely related to one another, and had as neighbors similar bands which also contained blood relations, in most acts of murder the victim would more than likely have been kin to the murderer. As the evolutionary success is in the production and well-being of as many descendants as possible, an undifferentiated innate drive for killing individuals of one's own species would soon have wiped that species out. Humans, as we know, did not blunder up an evolutionary blind alley, a fate that innate, unrestrained aggressiveness would undoubtedly have produced.

To argue, as we do, that humans are innately nonaggressive toward one another is not to imply that we are of necessity innately good-natured toward our fellows. In the lower echelons of the animal kingdom the management of conflict is largely through genetically-

seated mock battles. But farther along the evolutionary path, carrying out the appropriate avoidance behavior comes to depend more and more on learning, and in social animals, the channel of learning is social education. The capacity for that behavior is rooted in the animal's genes, it is true, but its elaboration depends also on learning.

For instance, among the Micronesian Ifaluk of the western Pacific, real violence is now so thoroughly condemned that "ritual" management of conflict is taught in childhood. The children play boisterously, as any normal children do; however a child who feels that he or she is being treated unfairly will set off in pursuit of the offender—but at a pace that will not permit catching up. As other children stand around, showing looks of disapproval, the chase may end with the plaintiff throwing pieces of coconut at the accused—once again with sufficient care so as to miss the target! This is ritual conflict, culturally based, not genetic.

Animal conflict occurs both between animals of different species and between individuals of the same species, and under differing environmental conditions. Anyone who argues for inbuilt aggression in Homo sapiens must see aggression as a universal instinct in the animal kingdom. It is no such thing. Much of the research on territoriality and aggression concerns birds. Because they usually must build nests, in which they will then spend a good deal of time incubating eggs, and still longer rearing their young, it is a biological necessity for them to protect their territory. It is therefore not surprising that most birds possess a strong territorial drive. But simply because greylag geese and mockingbirds, for instance, enthusiastically defend their territory, we should not infer that all animals do so. And it is not surprising that hummingbirds show considerably more territorial aggression than lions, even though the king of beasts is a lethal hunter. Our closest animal relatives, the chimpanzees and gorillas, are notably nonterritorial. Both of these species are relatively mobile and so they can forage for food over a wide area.

The animal kingdom therefore offers a broad spectrum of territoriality, whose basic determining factor is the mode of reproduction and style of daily life. Indeed, an animal may find it necessary to assert ownership of land in one situation and not in another.

That territoriality is flexible should not be surprising. If food resources and space are scarce, then there may well be conspicuous territorial behavior. Some individuals will fail to secure sufficient food or a place in which to rear a brood. These individuals are, of course, the weakest, and this is what survival of the fittest through natural selection really means.

Territorial behavior is therefore triggered when it

is required and remains dormant when it is not. The Lorenzians, however, take a different view: aggression, they say, builds up inexorably, to be released either by appropriate cues or spontaneously in the absence of appropriate cues. A safety valve suggested by Lorenzians for human societies is competitive sport. But such a suggestion neglects the high correlation between highly competitive encounters and associated vandalism and physical violence—as players, referees and crowds know to their cost through Europe and the Americas. More significantly, research now shows a close match between warlike behavior in countries and a devotion to sport. Far from defusing aggression, highly organized, emotionally charged sporting events generate even more aggression and reflect the degree to which humans' deep propensity to group identity and cohesion can be manipulated.

We can say therefore that territoriality and aggression are not universal instincts as such. Rather they are pieces of behavior that are tuned to particular lifestyles and to changes in the availability of important resources in the environment.

When the practice of hunting and gathering was becoming firmly rooted in the fertile soil of prehuman society, our ancestors would of course not have operated sophisticated kinship networks. But we do know that chimpanzees know who are their brothers and sisters and who are not. And we know too that chimpanzees and baboons do migrate between their various troops. The biological benefits of reducing tension and conflict between groups through exogamy almost certainly would have been achieved early in hominid evolution. The notion of hostile neighboring hordes is an image born of the mistaken belief in a belligerence written ineradicably into the human genetic blueprint.

Food shortage, either on the hoof or rooted in the ground, must nevertheless have been a cause of potential conflict between bands. Indeed, severe famine may well have forced hominids into belligerent confrontation with one another in open competition for the scarce food. And the band that lost out may even have ended as the victors' supper. But there is neither evidence nor any reason to suggest that hominid flesh, either roasted or raw, appeared on our ancestors' diet, specifically as a source of food, in any but the most extreme circumstances. A much more likely consequence of conflict over food resources, so far as can be judged from what we know of both animals and present-day hunter-gathers, would have been the dispersal of bands and even the temporary scattering of individuals, a practice that ensures the best use of the limited food that is available.

Along with lions, humans are one of the few mammals who on occasion deliberately eat each other.

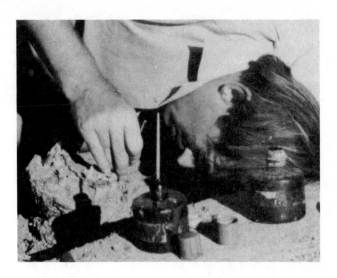

Author Leakey painstakingly recovers more evidence of Man's past at the Lake Turkana site in Kenya.

When a male lion wins control of a pride, he will often consume the young cubs and set about producing offspring of his own. Ruthless and wasteful though it may appear, the biological reason for the dominant male's behavior is evident: the offspring produced by the pride will have been sired by a very powerful animal, providing a brutal but efficient method of natural selection. Cannibalism in humans, however, takes place for different reasons.

Two kinds of human cannibalism

Broadly, there are two sorts of cannibalism and the distinction between them is crucial. First, there is the eating of members of one tribe of individuals by another—usually as the end result of raids; such is the conventional version of the practice, and it is known as exocannibalism. In the second form, known as endocannibalism, people eat members of their own tribe.

Human cannibalism takes place primarily as part of some kind of ritual. Even among the infamous tribes in the highlands of New Guinea, the context is one of extensive tribal ritual. Months of preparation—weaving symbolic adornments and the carving of elaborate wooden images—precede a raid, and it is abundantly clear that the entire exercise has a powerful unifying effect on the tribe. The habits of the New Guinea tribes are, in any event, extremely rare, and as against cannibalism manifested in this extreme form we may set the other extreme, in which people swallow a small morsel of a dead relative as a mark of love and respect.

Altogether, then, the notion that humans are inherently aggressive is simply not tenable. We cannot deny that 20th-century humans display a good deal of aggression, but we cannot point to our evolutionary past either to explain its origins or to excuse it. There are many reasons why a youth may "spontaneously" smash a window or attack an old lady, but an inborn drive inherited from our animal origins is probably not one of them. Human behavior is extraordinarily sensitive to the nature of the environment, and so it should not be particularly surprising that a person reared in unpleasant surroundings, perhaps subjected to material insecurity and emotional deprivation, should later behave in a way that people blessed with a more fortunate life might regard as unpleasant. Urban problems will not be solved by pointing to supposed defects in our genes while ignoring real effects in social justice.

The fallacy of thus adducing our animal origins should be evident for wars as well. Wars are planned and organized by leaders intent on increasing their power. In war men are more like sheep than wolves: they may be led to manufacture munitions at home, to release bombs from 10,000 feet up, or to fire long-range guns and rockets—all as part of one great cooperative effort. It is not insignificant that those soldiers who engage in hand-to-hand fighting are subjected to an intense process of desensitization before they can do it.

With the growth of agriculture and of materially based societies, warfare has increased steadily in ferocity, culminating in our current capability to destroy even the planet. We should not look to our genes for the seeds of war; those seeds were planted when, 10,000 years ago, our ancestors for the first time planted crops and began to be farmers. The transition from the nomadic hunting way of life to the sedentary one of farmers and industrialists made war possible and potentially profitable.

Possible, but not inevitable. For what has transformed the possible into reality is the same factor that has made human beings special in the biological kingdom: culture. Because of our seemingly limitless inventiveness and our vast capacity for learning, there is an endless potential for difference among human cultures, as indeed may be witnessed throughout the world. An important element of culture, however, consists in those central values that make up an ideology. It is social and political ideologies, and the tolerance or lack of it between them, that brings human nations to bloody conflict. Those who argue that war is in our genes not only are wrong, but in addition they commit the crime of diverting attention from the real cause of war.

One supreme biological irony underlies the entire issue of organized war in modern societies—the cooperative nature of human beings. Throughout our recent evolutionary history, particularly since the rise of a hunting way of life, there must have been extreme selective pressures in favor of our ability to cooperate as a group: organized food-gathering and hunts are successful only if each member of the band knows his task and joins in with the activity of his fellows. The degree of selective pressure toward cooperation, group awareness and identification was so strong, and the period over which it operated was so extended, that it can hardly have failed to have become embedded to some degree in our genetic makeup.

We are not suggesting that the human animal is a cooperative, group-oriented automaton. That would negate what is the prime evolutionary heritage of humans: their ability to acquire culture through education and learning. We are essentially cultural animals with the capacity to formulate many kinds of social structures; but a deep-seated urge toward cooperation, toward working as a group, provides a basic framework for those structures.

Unfortunately, it is our deeply rooted urge for group cooperation that makes large-scale wars not only possible, but unique in their destructiveness. Animals that are essentially self-centered and untutored in coordinated activity could neither hunt large prey nor make war. Equally, however, massive warfare would not be possible without the inventive intelligence that has produced the increasingly sophisticated hardware of human conflict. It is therefore as unhelpful to blame the scourge of war on our cooperativeness as it would be to blame it on our intelligence. To do either is to evade the real issue—those ideological values and behavioral habits on which nations are based, through which governments manipulate their people.

If we wish to, we can change our social structures without any fear of some primal urge welling to the surface and sucking us back into some atavistic pattern. We are, after all, the ultimate expression of a cultural animal; we have not totally broken free of our biological roots, but neither are we ruled by them.

7

Sharing in Human Evolution

BY JANE B. LANCASTER AND PHILLIP WHITTEN

"There is evidence," wrote famed ethologist Konrad Lorenz in 1963, "that the first inventors of pebble tools—the African australopithecines—promptly used their weapons to kill not only game, but fellow members of their species as well. Peking Man, the Prometheus who learned to preserve fire, used it to roast his brothers: beside the first traces of the regular use of fire lie the . . . roasted bones of *Sinanthropus pekinensis* himself."

Thus was promulgated the view of humans as clothes-wearing "killer apes." Despite the fact that this concept ignores a vast array of cultural anthropological data and relies on misinterpretations and erroneous extrapolations of ethological observations, it undoubtedly has caught on. Books by Lorenz (*On Aggression, Behind the Mirror*), Robert Ardrey (*African Genesis, The Territorial Imperative, The Social Contract*), Desmond Morris (*The Naked Ape, The Human Zoo*), Lionel Tiger and Robin Fox (*Men in Groups*), and others all have sold remarkably well—some even making the best-seller charts. According to this view, humans, unlike their primate relatives, are innately territorial and warlike. Indeed, it is argued, this unique propensity for killing and violence is the one most responsible for our evolutionary success.

Proponents of the killer-ape theory make what appears at first glance to be a strong case. One does not need to look far to find evidence of human violence and destruction. In fact, however, the theory is wrong on both counts: aggression is *not* the characteristic that distinguished our early ancestors from the apes; and humans are *not* the only primates who kill their fellows.

Jane Goodall and her colleagues in Tanzania's Gombe Stream Reserve have observed a community of chimpanzees that split in two in 1970. By 1972 the observers noted a cooling of relations between the two groups. In 1974 several males from the original group attacked a single male from the splinter group, beating him savagely for about twenty minutes until he died. Since that time, a series of brutal gang attacks—including one in which a rock was thrown at a prostrate victim—has completely wiped out the second chimp community (*Science News*, 1978).

If aggression is not the trait that distinguished our forebears from other primates, what is? The answer lies in a distinctively human characteristic—sharing—and the evolutionary mechanism that made it possible.

BIPEDALISM

Sometime between five and ten million years ago our ancestors began to spend much of their time on the ground, walking on two legs. Long before we had developed large brains, before we had language with which to communicate, and before we could manipulate the environment to our own ends, we were bipedal.

Bipedalism was one of the earliest evolutionary changes that distinguished the human way of life from that of the ape. Some experts claim that hominids (the family of primates that includes human beings and our earlier fossil ancestors) first stood in order to run, or to fight, or to free their hands for using tools. But these scenarios are unlikely. The first adventurers on two legs, like toddlers learning to walk, were probably very clumsy and inefficient. Such awkwardness would be of little value in combat or in flight. Similarly, tool using by itself cannot explain the significance of bipedalism, since tools can be used as easily while sitting down as standing up. More likely the adaptive value of bipedalism lay in the social behavior that it helped bring about—cooperation and sharing.

Walking on the hindlimbs while clutching food to be shared with others in the forelimbs would have been an advantage to a primate group utilizing a large home range. In this context, bipedalism could evolve slowly over hundreds of thousands of years—as it undoubtedly did. Thus, rather than being violent killer apes, our ancestors—and we—can more accurately be described as *sharing* apes.

Unfortunately, we know very little about the original differentiation and emergence of the human family. The period between five and ten million years ago is virtually an archaeological blank. The fossil record picks up about four and a half million years ago with scraps of hominid bone and teeth, and later with simple stone tools. By about three to one-and-a-half million years ago, a new way of life had been firmly established—a way of life fundamentally different from that of the apes and distinctly human in its broadest features. This original adaptive system of the hominids was very successful, lasting several million years—most of the history of the human line.

There are only a limited number of ways we can use to reconstruct this stage in human evolution. The archaeological record, though reasonably full, is limited to accidents

Reprinted by permission from the authors.

of preservation. However, we can expand our interpretation of the record by making judicious comparisons between the behavior of humans and of our closest living relatives, monkeys and apes. Other evidence can be gleaned from studies of the world's few remaining hunting-and-gathering societies.

THE BASIC PRIMATE PATTERN

There are few generalizations that can be made about all the higher primates. But some patterns seem to be so widespread among the Old World monkeys and apes that we can cautiously assume they must be very ancient and fundamental to the higher primate adaptation of life in social groups. The most significant of these patterns is the relationship between young animals and adults.

In all higher primate species, young animals spend years in physical and social dependence upon adults. This long dependence begins at birth, when the newborn first establishes a close one-to-one relationship with its mother. Unlike many other mammals, higher primates are not born into litters and hidden away in dens or nests. Instead, a single offspring is born, which for the first months of its life stays continuously in contact with its mother, clinging to her while she is moving, and resting in her arms to sleep. As Blurton-Jones (1972)

has pointed out, adaptations for continuous contact with mother involve many different anatomical, physiological and behavioral systems. These range from the anatomy of the hands and feet, distribution of body fat, composition of breast milk, sleep and sucking patterns, ease of satiation, tendency to vocalize, to the need for body contact for feeling secure.

Although this basic pattern holds true for all the higher primates (Old World monkeys, apes, and humans), there is a striking contrast in how this continuous contact relationship between mother and infant is maintained. Among all the Old World monkeys the responsibility of maintaining the relationship rests heavily with the infant. From the moment of birth, an infant monkey must be able to cling to its mother for long periods of time while she feeds, travels, grooms, or even leaps to safety. Infants unable to maintain body contact are likely to be eliminated through accident or predation from the gene pool. Monkeys need all four limbs for locomotion; clutching a weak or sick infant to the chest while trying to hobble on three legs is difficult and leaves the pair vulnerable to predators.

The same basic pattern is true for the great apes—though newborn apes are less developed than monkeys and are poor at clinging for the first few weeks of life. Mother apes help their poorly coordinated infants by walking on three legs and by restricting their movements and social interactions for several weeks after giving birth.

The close, continuous relationship between mother and infant gradually loosens as the infant is weaned and gains independence in locomotion. Once a young monkey or ape is weaned, it has sole responsibility for feeding and drinking. If it is too weak from illness or injury to do so, it will die before the concerned eyes of its mother. The mother will defend her youngster, groom it, sleep with it cradled in her arms, but feeding it solid foods is beyond her comprehension. Although isolated instances of food sharing among chimpanzees have been observed, basically the nonhuman primates are individual foragers.

In contrast with their early independence in feeding behavior, young monkeys and apes are dependent upon adults for protection for many years. Young primates remain at least until puberty in the safety of the group in which they were born; many never leave it. The prolonged period of juvenile development occurs in all the higher primates. During the years of development, the young primate has plenty of time to play, as well as to learn and practice the social and physical skills needed in adulthood.

CHIMPANZEE AND HUMAN BEHAVIOR

The general cleverness of chimpanzees has long been known. But it was not until the long-term field studies in Central Africa that particularly humanlike aspects of chimpanzee behavior were observed (Goodall, 1976; van Lawick-Goodall, 1971; Teleki, 1974, 1975). One of the most striking of these was the wide variety of tool use by chimpanzees in everyday life. These tools include the now-famous grass blades, vines or sticks used to "fish" for ants and termites in their nests; leaf sponges used to collect water, honey or wipe dirt off the body; twigs and sticks used to investigate and probe unfamiliar objects; rough hammer stones used to break open nuts; leafy twigs used as fly whisks; and finally sticks, stones and vegetation used as missiles in aggressive display. Chimpanzee tool use is similar to human in the sense that tools are an adaptive means to meet a wide variety of problems posed by the environment.

One of the marked differences between the use of tools by humans and chimpanzees is in the casualness and impermanence of the ape's tools. Although chimpanzees make their own tools in the sense that they strip a stick of leaves and side branches or chew up a mass of leaves for a sponge, they do not try to keep a particularly well-made tool for future use. Chimpanzees discard their tools because it is difficult for them to carry anything for long distances. When Goodall and her colleagues established a central feeding station at the Gombe Stream Reserve that provided bananas for the wild chimpanzees in the area, many came to load up a supply of bananas. They tried to carry bananas in every possible way: held in their mouths, hands and feet, tucked under armpits and chins, even slipped between flexed thighs and groins. Loaded up in this way, they retreated to climb nearby trees, dropping bananas every step of the way.

Another aspect of chimpanzee behavior that has excited students of human evolution is their sporadic attempts at the collective killing of small game. Sometimes these hunts involve several adult and subadult males who coordinate their movements to encircle the prey, some acting as diversions while others slip close enough to dash in for the capture. Prey (usually small gazelles) are killed and eaten immediately, the participants in the hunt dividing the prey simply by tearing it to pieces. Latecomers may get a mouthful by persistent attempts to pull off a piece or by begging.

The killing and eating of meat is clearly a special event in chimpanzee life. Witnesses of a kill show great interest and excitement and a clear desire for even a taste. The highly social, as opposed to nutritional, nature of chimpanzee cooperative killing and eating of prey has been noted by Geza Teleki (1975), who observed that a dozen or more chimpanzees may take a whole day to consume an animal weighing less than 10 kg (22 lbs). The small size of game killed by primates (baboons have also been reported to hunt small mammals on occasion) is very striking. The largest prey is under 10 kg—well under the body weight of an individual hunter. Shared foods are most often minuscule scraps, more social tokens than major sources of protein.

In spite of their tool use and hunting, the behavior of modern chimpanzees still fits squarely into the pattern described earlier for other primates. They are in no way quasi human. Like other monkeys and apes, they are basically individual foragers who live in long-term social groups. The infant is dependent on the mother for many years, but this relationship is based on a physical and psychological need for the mother's protection. Once weaned, young chimpanzees feed themselves. The basic diet is typical of many primates living in the tropics: vegetables, fruits and nuts, with some animal protein in the form of insects, small vertebrates and occasional small mammals. The important contrast between the feeding habits of human and nonhuman primates is not so much in what is eaten; rather it lies in whether each individual must forage for itself or whether there is a collective responsibility for gathering and sharing food between adults and young.

MODERN HUNTER-GATHERERS

In recent years the ways of life of hunter-gatherers have attracted renewed interest (Lee and Devore, 1968, 1976). Although only a few hunting-gathering groups remain in the modern world, they take on special significance when it is recalled that fully ninety-nine percent of human history was spent in the hunting-gathering stage. The peculiar demands of this life-style may well have left imprints on modern human biology and behavior.

There are certain ecological relationships and social behaviors found in all known tropical hunter-gatherers, which stand out in sharp relief when contrasted with the behavior of monkeys and apes. The first of these is a diet based on a balance of plant and animal foods. This balance is highly flexible and varies according to season, geographic location and long-term cycles in food availability. Our understanding of sex roles and the ecological basis of early human societies has shifted away from an emphasis on females as camp and infant tenders and males as food providers (Isaac, 1976; Tanner and Zihlman, 1976). In the process, our concept of "man, the hunter" has been modified to "humans, the hunter-gatherers."

Data from modern hunter-gatherers in the tropics indicate that meat is an important part of the diet, but always comprises well under fifty percent of the total. The basic day-to-day diet is provided by the collecting efforts of adult women, and consists mainly of vegetable foods and animal protein in the form of insects and nestling birds or eggs. Animal protein in large "packages"—that is, animals weighing over 20 kg—is provided by the efforts of adult males. Hunting, even in the tropics, is a risky occupation. It not only is potentially dangerous, but it is often unpredictable. Richard Lee (quoted in Hassan, 1975:35) found that among the San of the Kalahari, most hunters kill only one or two large animals a year. Among the Hazda of East Africa, as many as half the adult males fail to kill even one large animal a year, and some men kill only one or two in a lifetime. The question of whether or not a growing child eats or starves does not depend on the uncertain hunting success of a few adult males. As Isaac (1971:279) noted some time ago, the evolution of human behavior from a primate pattern involved not simply an increasing intensity of predation, but the unusual development of "a flexible system of joint dependence on plant and animal foods."

It is informative to look at the basic material possessions of a hunting-gathering woman who lives in the tropics. She must be able to carry all her possessions herself when she moves, because men are responsible for their own hunting equipment and for protecting the group. The most important items a woman possesses include a digging stick, a sling or net bag for carrying her infant, and a variety of bark and skin trays and containers for carrying and preparing food. This is all she needs to provide for her family. Significantly, none of these materials leaves a trace in the archaeological record.

The importance of carrying infants in a sling should be underscored because it is a major factor in human evolutionary history. Unlike Old World monkeys and apes, human infants are unable to cling to their mothers. In fact, they are dependent on their mothers to hold them for many months. Hunting-gathering women keep their infants with them continuously during their daily foraging. They use a sling, which suspends the infant from the mother's shoulder while leaving her hands and arms free. It appears that one of the costs our species paid for evolving larger brains was a prolonged period of infant helplessness. The invention of such a simple tool as a skin sling to carry an infant may have been a crucial turning point in human history because it permitted the survival of infants born with small, immature brains and the potential for major growth after birth.

The lives of hunter-gatherers differ sharply from those of other primates in the tropics by virtue of one very important behavior pattern: carrying and sharing. The carrying of infants, tools, or food to be shared allowed our ancestors to shift away from individual foraging to a pattern emphasizing the sharing of gathered and hunted foods within the social group. Among the Kalahari hunter-gatherers plant foods collected by women are shared among close family members. Meat—food which comes in much larger packages—is shared in a larger network.

The success of a system of sharing foods depends on one other behavioral innovation which sets humans off from other primates. This is the evolution of the home base, or camp. A home base need not be permanent. It can be nothing more than an agreed-upon location where members of the group can meet in order to share foods. Many monkeys and apes have favorite clumps of sleeping trees, where they often return for the night. A home base, however, is not just a location for sleeping. Rather it serves a much more important function as the site for the sharing of food among members of the social group. Like the shift from individual foraging to sharing, this represents a way novel among primates of utilizing a niche.

THE ARCHAEOLOGICAL RECORD

Glynn Isaac (1976), an archaeologist at the University of California at Berkeley, suggests that these behavioral elements—a flexible diet of plant and animal foods, food sharing, the carrying of food and equipment, and a home base—form a behavioral platform upon which the distinctly human way of life was established. The evidence for the early building of this behavioral platform comes from the fossil record, although not all elements of the pattern are equally clear. Accidents of preservation, and the bias against perishable plant foods and materials in favor of stone and bone, give a skewed view of the past.

Some of the earliest evidence of the shift in diet from foraging to hunting-gathering can be found at Olduvai Gorge and Koobi Fora in East Africa—sites dating from around three million to one-and-a-half million years ago. Here early stone tools are found in association with broken up mammal bones. These animals range in size from small

rodents to elephants, but it is clear that many are far larger than the 10 kg mentioned by Teleki as the largest prey taken today by nonhuman primates. The dismembering of a large mammal like an elephant or a hippopotamus suggests strongly that meat was not only killed cooperatively, but shared as well.

Evidence about the equipment of early hominids is very limited. Both at Olduvai and Koobi Fora, the two basic classes of stone tools—core tools and flakes—can be found. The rest of the probable technology and equipment of the early hominids—sharpened sticks for digging and stabbing, and slings and nets for carrying and gathering—will probably never be found in the archaeological record. At Olduvai a semi-circular stone windbreak has been discovered, perhaps the oldest structure built by our hominid ancestors. Concentrations of stone tools and broken bones here and at other sites attest to an essential element of the adaptive platform: a home base. The artifacts and bones tend to be located in particular ecological settings: patches about five to twenty meters in diameter, a size similar to the campsites of modern hunter-gatherers. They are usually located next to sandy streams, the kind which today provide strips of shade and are bounded by fruit trees. These bases were home for our remote ancestors. They were places where the hominids gathered together at night for warmth and protection against the great carnivores, and to share food.

The creatures living in these camps were fully bipedal, with brains somewhat larger than might be expected if they were apes. Although their molar teeth were massive by modern standards, there were no protruding canines like those used by other primates in aggression. The relatively small size of their crania clearly shows that the human adaptation of bipedalism, tool use, and home base long preceded the expansion of the brain and elaboration of culture so obvious later in the archaeological record. It is doubtful that these early hominids had language in any modern sense of the word. The small size of the brain argues against it, and their hunting and gathering activities and manufacture of simple tools did not demand language. Their life in small, face-to-face social groups suggests a communication system like that of modern chimpanzees.

SHARING AND SOCIAL ORGANIZATION

The elementary human adaptation, the one upon which all else is built, depends on a simple but unique change in ecological and social relations. This change was the shift from the individual foraging and feeding pattern of other primates to a system of sharing and cooperation, in which adults feed infants and juveniles. Associated with this assumption of responsibility to feed the young was a new economic interdependence between the sexes, one in which females gathered and males hunted. This ancient division of labor, permitting the flexible, joint dependence on plant and animal food, probably accounts for the early success of the first hominids. After all, they were small-sized, small-brained primates moving into a niche already crowded with highly successful group hunters such as lions, hyenas and wild dogs.

It is interesting to speculate on the effect of the economic division of labor on the social organization of early hominids. Comparative studies of Old World monkeys and apes indicate that attachment based on descent is one of the prime organizers of monkey and ape societies (Lancaster, 1975). This ancient principle is based on the attachment of an infant to its mother. In multigenerational primate societies, the early attachment is expanded to include other close relatives and descendents of the mother. It is reasonable to assume that the first social network through which hominids shared food was joined by female links. Much of the food was probably gathered by females. Male hunting must have added a new element to the equation. For the first time in primate evolution, males and females shared responsibility for feeding their offspring. Eventually this mutual economic interest probably led to the formation of a second set of emotional attachments, ones that linked specific males to specific females. It is unlikely that the early hominids had anything like the institution of marriage. But it is not unreasonable to speculate that couples formed special, more-or-less-enduring attachments that facilitated the feeding of offspring.

HUMANS: THE SHARING APES

What distinguishes our own species from our primate relatives is not any innate proclivity toward violence and aggression. Rather we can accurately be described as cultural animals whose outstanding characteristics are cooperation and sharing. What separated our family from the apes was a reorganization of the relationships between the sexes and between adults and young. This shift, which favored cooperative activities, permitted early hominids to exploit a niche new to primates. The ability to exploit this new niche rested on a few, rather simple behavioral patterns. These included bipedalism, the use of tools, the division of labor between male hunters and female gatherers, a home base, and most important—cooperation and sharing.

The archaeological record, the study of modern primates, and the behavior of present-day hunter-gatherers all attest to the significance of sharing in human evolution. It is the rock upon which all human culture is built; it is what makes us human.

REFERENCES

Blurton-Jones, N. 1972. Comparative aspects of mother-child contacts. In N. Blurton-Jones (ed.), *Ethological Studies of Child Behaviour*. London: Cambridge University Press.

Goodall, Jane. 1976. Continuities between chimpanzee and human behaviour. In Isaac and McGown (eds.), *Human Origins*. Menlo Park, CA: Staples Press, pp. 81–96.

Hassan, F.A. 1975. Determination of the size, density, and growth rate of hunting-gathering populations. In S. Polgar (ed.), *Population, Ecology, and Evolution*. The Hague: Mouton, pp. 27–52.

Isaac, Glynn. 1971. The diet of early man: aspects of archaeological evidence from lower and middle Pleistocene sites in Africa. *World Archaeology* 2:278–298.

Isaac, Glynn. 1975. The activities of early African hominids: A review of archaeological evidence from the time span two and a half to one million years ago. In Isaac and McGown (eds.), *op. cit.*, pp. 483–514.

Lancaster, Jane B. 1975. *Primate Behavior and the Emergence of Human Culture*. New York: Holt, Rinehart and Winston.

Van Lawick-Goodall, Jane. 1971. *In the Shadow of Man*. Boston: Houghton Mifflin.

Lee, Richard B. and I. DeVore (eds). 1968. *Man the Hunter*. Chicago: Aldine.

Lee, Richard B. and I. DeVore (eds). 1975. *Kalahari Hunter-Gatherers*. Cambridge, MA: Harvard University Press.

Science News. 1978. Chimp killings: Is it the 'man' in them? *Science News* 113:276.

Tanner, N. and A. Zihlman. 1976. Women in evolution. Part 1: Innovation and selection in human origins. *Signs* 1:385–602.

Teleki, Geza. 1975. Primate subsistence patterns: collector-predators and gatherer-hunters. *Journal of Human Evolution* 4:125–184.

TOPIC FOUR

Human Diversity

Since the beginnings of recorded history, the physical differences characterizing human populations have been of interest to both scholars and lay persons. Neontology, the study of the distribution of human biological traits, is a major area of interest of physical anthropologists.

In the eighteenth century, Johann Blumenbach, you will recall from the essay introducing this section, developed rigorous standards for measuring physical traits and used clusters of these measurements to identify "races." The concept of "race" quickly became incorporated into the scientific literature, and much of the research on human diversity has been undertaken using this concept. The term generally means a population that is distinguished from all other groups by virtue of manifesting an aggregate or cluster of innate biological traits. Indeed, the concept of "race" has won general (not just scientific) acceptance—so much so that, if you were to tell your neighbor that human "races" don't exist, you would be dismissed as a fool.

Yet anthropologist Ashley Montagu has demonstrated clearly the ambiguities of the term "race." He points out that experts on the subject cannot agree either on a definition of the term or on the number of so-called races into which the human species is divided. Further, use of the term tends to distort biological research, and with its static connotations, it is rather incompatible with evolutionary theory (a cornerstone of physical anthropology).

In 1969, Arthur Jensen, an educational psychologist at the University of California at Berkeley, published an article in the *Harvard Educational Review* purporting to show that black people are innately less intelligent than whites. Jensen's conclusions were based in large part on studies by the late British psychologist Sir Cyril Burt—studies that have since been shown to be fraudulent. Nevertheless, Jensen and others have persisted in their attempts to demonstrate a relationship between "race" and intelligence, with devastating social consequences.

In recent years, numerous scientific books and articles have been written in an attempt to answer such questions as: What is "race"? What is the connection between skin color and intelligence? In 1978, biologist Paul R. Ehrlich and psychologist S. Shirley Feldman published a book called *The Race Bomb,* the first book addressed to the educated layperson to tackle these subjects.

Like most scientists, Ehrlich and Feldman see human races as artificial groupings based on skin color and a few other characteristics arbitrarily chosen by the classifier. This reduces the whole question of racial intelligence to one of skin color and IQ, which is as trivial—and as valid—as considering the relationship between eye color (or height or shoe size) and mental ability. It is true, of course, that people vary greatly in numerous characteristics. Some are taller, run farther, swim faster, are darker skinned, or more intelligent than others. Part of these differences can no doubt be explained by the different genetic inheritances of the individuals. But the fact that one individual may be taller or darker-hued than another tells us absolutely nothing about his or her mental ability.

From an anthropological and biological point of view, there is no such thing as "race." Scientists who study human diversity focus not on the characteristics of artificial "races," but rather on the worldwide distribution of specific genes. *Why,* for example, do people from colder climates tend to have lighter colored skin than people from tropical climates? *Why* do people from certain regions of Africa, Asia and southern Europe have a greater likelihood than others to be born with sickle-cell anemia? By studying such questions, physical anthropologists attempt to show the adaptive function a specific gene plays in relationship to specific environmental stresses. In "Racial Odyssey," Boyce Rensberger explores the fascinating topic of human diversity and divulges what we have learned in recent years.

But races have a *social* reality, of course. And this reality can be very powerful indeed. It was the social reality of race that allowed Adolph Hitler to murder six million Jews; it is the social reality of race that permits discrimination against blacks, Orientals, Native Americans, and other groups in our society. In his classic article, "A Four Letter Word That Hurts," Morton A. Fried discusses some of the consequences of the social reality of race.

In the United States, a person is socially—and even legally—defined as "black," regardless of personal color-coding, if any known ancestor was black. Thus, former U.S. Senator Edward Brooke invariably is described as "black" despite his light skin color.

Other societies, however, define racial groups differently, as Ehrlich and Feldman point out. Brazil, for example, has a much more flexible system of classification, based on wealth as well as skin color. In Brazil, a "Negro" is any of the following: a poverty-stricken white, a poverty-stricken or poor mulatto, a poverty-stricken black, a poor black, or a black of average wealth. In contrast, a "White" is defined as: a wealthy white, a white of average wealth, a poor white, a wealthy mulatto, a mulatto of average wealth, or a wealthy black. (See the table below.)

Montagu proposes substituting the term "ethnic group" for "race"—an idea with which we agree. However, because the concept of "race" still captures the popular imagination, because people still treat "races" as significant social groupings, and because in our society at least the political economy is "racially" stratified—"races" therefore are socially real entities whose existence must be acknowledged, even if their biological validity is questionable. For this reason, we continue to use the term "race," but we enclose it in quotation marks.

The Social Reality of Race in Brazil

Skin Color	Economic Status			
	Poverty-stricken	Poor	Average Wealth	Wealthy
White	N	W	W	W
Mulatto	N	N	W	W
Black	N	N	N	W

In Brazil, both skin color and economic status are used to determine "race." The groups marked N in the table are considered Negroes, whereas the groups labeled W are considered whites.

8

Racial Odyssey

BY BOYCE RENSBERGER

. . . .

The human species comes in an artist's palette of colors: sandy yellows, reddish-tans, deep browns, light tans, creamy whites, pale pinks. It is a rare person who is not curious about the skin colors, hair textures, bodily structures and facial features associated with racial background. Why do some Africans have dark brown skin, while that of most Europeans is pale pink? Why do the eyes of most "white" people and "black" people look pretty much alike but differ so from the eyes of Orientals? Did one race evolve before the others? If so, is it more primitive or more advanced as a result? Can it be possible, as modern research suggests, that there is no such thing as a pure race? These are all honest, scientifically worthy questions. And they are central to current research on the evolution of our species on the planet Earth.

Broadly speaking, research on racial differences has led most scientists to three major conclusions. The first is that there are many more differences among people than skin color, hair texture and facial features. Dozens of other variations have been found, ranging from the shapes of bones to the consistency of ear wax to subtle variations in body chemistry.

The second conclusion is that the overwhelming evolutionary success of the human species is largely due to its great genetic variability. When migrating bands of our early ancestors reached a new environment, at least a few already had physical traits that gave them an edge in surviving there. If the coming centuries bring significant environmental changes, as many believe they will, our chances of surviving them will be immeasurably enhanced by our diversity as a species.

There is a third conclusion about race that is often misunderstood. Despite our wealth of variation and despite our con-stant, everyday references to race, no one has ever discovered a reliable way of distinguishing one race from another. While it is possible to classify a great many people on the basis of certain physical features, there are no known feature or groups of features that will do the job in all cases.

Skin color won't work. Yes, most Africans from south of the Sahara and their descendants around the world have skin that is darker than that of most Europeans. But there are millions of people in India, classified by some anthropologists as members of the Caucasoid, or "white," race who have darker skins than most Americans who call themselves black. And there are many Africans living in sub-Sahara Africa today whose skins are no darker than the skins of many Spaniards, Italians, Greeks or Lebanese.

What about stature as a racial trait? Because they are quite short, on the average, African Pygmies have been considered racially distinct from other dark-skinned Africans. If stature, then, is a racial criterion, would one include in the same race the tall African Watusi and the Scandinavians of similar stature?

The little web of skin that distinguishes Oriental eyes is said to be a particular feature of the Mongoloid race. How, then, can it be argued that the American Indian, who lacks this epicanthic fold, is Mongoloid?

Even more hopeless as racial markers are hair color, eye color, hair form, the shapes of noses and lips or any of the other traits put forth as typical of one race or another.

NO NORMS

Among the tall people of the world there are many black, many white and many in between. Among black people of the world there are many with kinky hair, many with straight or wavy hair, and many in between. Among the broad-nosed, full-lipped people of the world there are many with dark skins, many with light skins and many in between.

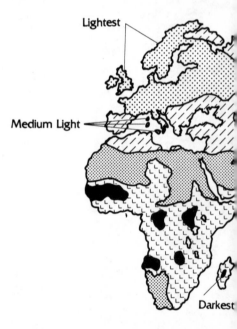

Lightest

Medium Light

Darkest

How did our modern perceptions of race arise? One of the first to attempt a scientific classification of peoples was Carl von Linne, better known as Linnaeus. In 1735, he published a classification that remains the standard today. As Linnaeus saw it there were four races, classifiable geographically and by skin color. The names Linnaeus gave them were *Homo sapiens Africanus nigrus* (black African human being), *H. sapiens Americanus rubescens* (red American human being), *H. sapiens*

 Reprinted from *Science Digest*, January/February 1981 by permission of the author.

Asiaticus fuscusens (brownish Asian human being), and *H. sapiens Europeaeus albescens* (white European human being). All, Linnaeus recognized, were members of a single human species.

A species includes all individuals that are biologically capable of interbreeding and producing fertile offspring. Most matings between species are fruitless, and even when they succeed, as when a horse and a donkey interbreed and produce a mule, the progeny are sterile. When a poodle mates with a collie, however, the offspring are fertile, showing that both dogs are members of the same species.

Even though Linnaeus's system of nomenclature survives, his classifications were discarded, especially after voyages of discovery revealed that there were many more kinds of people than could be pigeonholed into four categories. All over the world there are small populations that don't fit. Among the better known are:

● The so-called Bushmen of southern Africa, who look as much Mongoloid as Negroid.
● The Negritos of the South Pacific, who do look Negroid but are very far from Africa and have no known links to that continent.
● The Ainu of Japan, a hairy aboriginal people who look more Caucasoid than anything else.
● The Lapps of Scandinavia, who look as much like Eskimos as like Europeans.
● The aborigines of Australia, who often look Negroid but many of whom have straight or wavy hair and are often blond as children.
● The Polynesians, who seem to be a blend of many races, the proportions differing from island to island.

To accommodate such diversity, many different systems of classification have been proposed. Some set up two or three dozen races. None has ever satisfied all experts.

CLASSIFICATION SYSTEM

Perhaps the most sweeping effort to impose a classification upon all the peoples of the world was made by the American anthropologist Carleton Coon. He concluded there are five basic races, two of which have major subdivisions: Caucasoids; Mongoloids; full-size Australoids (Australian aborigines); dwarf Australoids (Negritos—Andaman Islanders and similar peoples); full-size Congoids (African Negroids); dwarf Congoids (African Pygmies); and Capoids (the so-called Bushmen and Hottentots).

In his 1965 classic, *The Living Races of Man,* Coon hypothesized that before A.D. 1500 there were five *pure* races—five centers of human population that were so isolated that there was almost no mixing.

Each of these races evolved independently, Coon believed, diverging from a pre-*Homo sapiens* stock that was essentially the same everywhere. He speculated that the common ancestor evolved into *Homo sapiens* in five separate regions at five different times, beginning about 35,000 years ago. The populations that have been *Homo sapiens* for the shortest periods of time, Coon said, are the world's "less civilized" races.

The five pure races remained distinct until A.D. 1500; then Europeans started sailing the world, leaving their genes—as sailors always have—in every port and planting distant colonies. At about the same time, thousands of Africans were captured and forcibly settled in many parts of the New World.

That meant the end of the five pure races. But Coon and other experts held that this did not necessarily rule out the idea of distinct races. In this view, there *are* such things as races; people just don't fit into them very well anymore.

The truth is that there is really no hard evidence to suggest that five or any particular number of races evolved independently. The preponderance of evidence today suggests that as traits typical of fully modern people arose in any one place, they spread quickly to all human populations. Advances in intelligence were almost certainly the fastest to spread. Most anthropologists and geneticists now believe that human beings have always been subject to migrating and mixing. In other words, there probably never were any such things as pure races.

Race mixing has not only been a fact of human history but is, in this day of unprecedented global mobility, taking place at a more rapid rate than ever. It is not farfetched to envision the day when, generations hence, the entire "complexion" of major population centers will be dif-

THE DISTRIBUTION OF HUMAN SKIN COLOR IN 1500
(North and South America not included)

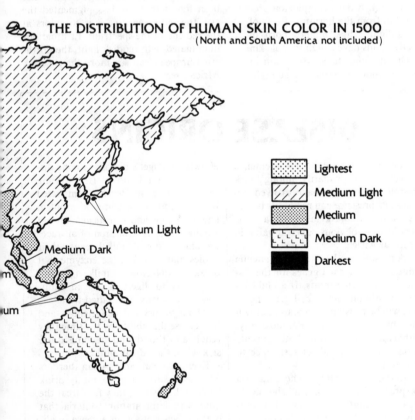

Lightest
Medium Light
Medium
Medium Dark
Darkest

The map above suggests the distribution of people in terms of skin color about 1500. In fact, edges between groups have always been blurred, speculative, and difficult to pin down, and since 1500 the picture has been changed drastically and often by massive, worldwide population shifts.

ferent. Meanwhile, we can see such changes taking place before our eyes, for they are a part of everyday reality.

HYBRID VIGOR

Oddly, those who assert scientific validity for their notions of pure and distinct races seem oblivious of a basic genetic principle that plant and animal breeders know well: too much inbreeding can lead to proliferation of inferior traits. Crossbreeding with different strains often produces superior combinations and "hybrid vigor."

The striking differences among people may very well be a result of constant genetic mixing. And as geneticists and ecologists know, in diversity lies strength and resilience.

To understand the origin and proliferation of human differences, one must first know how Darwinian evolution works.

Evolution is a two-step process. Step one is mutation: somehow a gene in the ovary or testes of an individual is altered, changing the molecular configuration that stores instructions for forming a new individual. The children who inherit that gene will be different in some way from their ancestors.

Step two is selection: for a racial difference, or any other evolutionary change to arise, it must survive and be passed through several generations. If the mutation confers some disadvantage, the individual dies, often during embryonic development. But if the change is beneficial in some way, the individual should have a better chance of thriving than relatives lacking the advantage.

NATURAL SELECTION

If a new trait is beneficial, it will bring reproductive success to its bearer. After several generations of multiplication, bearers of the new trait may begin to outnumber nonbearers. Darwin called this natural selection to distinguish it from the artificial selection exercised by animal breeders.

Skin color is the human racial trait most generally thought to confer an evolutionary advantage of this sort. It has long been obvious in the Old World that the farther south one goes, the darker the skin color. Southern Europeans are usually somewhat darker than northern Europeans. In North Africa, skin colors are darker still, and, as one travels south, coloration reaches its maximum at the Equator. The same progression holds in Asia, with the lightest skins to the north. Again, as one moves south, skin color darkens, reaching in southern India a "blackness" equal to that of equatorial Africans.

This north-south spectrum of skin color derives from varying intensities of the same dark brown pigment called melanin. Skin cells simply have more or less melanin granules to be seen against a background that is pinkish because of the underlying blood vessels. All races can increase their melanin concentration by exposure to the Sun.

What is it about northerly latitudes in the Northern Hemisphere that favors less pigmentation and about southerly latitudes that favors more? Exposure to intense sunlight is not the only reason why people living in southerly latitudes are dark. A person's susceptibility to rickets and skin cancer, his ability to withstand cold and to see in the dark may also be related to skin color.

The best-known explanation says the body can tolerate only a narrow range of intensities of sunlight. Too much causes sunburn and cancer, while too little deprives the body of vitamin D, which is synthesized in the skin under the influence of sunlight. A dark complexion protects the skin from the harmful effects of intense sunlight. Thus, albinos born in equatorial regions have a high rate of skin cancer. On the other hand, dark skin in northerly latitudes screens out sunlight needed for the synthesis of vitamin D. Thus, dark-skinned children living in northern latitudes had high rates of rickets—a bone-deforming disease caused by a lack of vitamin D—before their milk was routinely fortified. In the sunny tropics, dark skin admits enough light to produce the vitamin.

Recently, there has been some evidence that skin colors are linked to differences in the ability to avoid injury from the cold. Army researchers found that during the Korean War blacks were more susceptible to frostbite than were whites. Even among Norwegian soldiers in World War II, brunettes had a slightly higher incidence of frostbite than did blonds.

EYE PIGMENTATION

A third link between color and latitude involves the sensitivity of the eye to various wavelengths of light. It is known that dark-skinned people have more pigmentation in the iris of the eye and at the back of the eye where the image falls. It has been found that the less pigmented the eye, the more sensitive it is to colors at the red end of the spectrum. In situations illuminated with reddish light, the northern European can see more than a dark African sees.

DISEASE ORIGINS

The gene for sickle cell anemia, a disease found primarily among black people, appears to have evolved because its presence can render its bearer resistant to malaria. Such a trait would have obvious survival value in tropical Africa.

A person who has sickle cell anemia must have inherited genes for the disease from both parents. If a child inherits only one sickle cell gene, he or she will be resistant to malaria but will not have the anemia. Paradoxically, inheriting genes from both parents does not seem to affect resistance to malaria.

In the United States, where malaria is practically nonexistent, the sickle cell gene confers no survival advantage and is disappearing. Today only about 1 out of every 10 American blacks carries the gene.

Many other inherited diseases are found only in people from a particular area. Tay-Sachs disease, which often kills before the age of two, is almost entirely confined to Jews from parts of Eastern Europe and their descendants elsewhere. Paget's disease, a bone disorder, is found most often among those of English descent. Impacted wisdom teeth are a common problem among Asians and Europeans but not among Africans. Children of all races are able to digest milk because their bodies make lactase, the enzyme that breaks down lactose, or milk sugar. But the ability to digest lactose in adulthood is a racially distributed trait.

About 90 percent of Orientals and blacks lose this ability by the time they reach adulthood and become quite sick when they drink milk.

Even African and Asian herders who keep cattle or goats rarely drink fresh milk. Instead, they first treat the milk with fermentation bacteria that break down lactose, in a sense predigesting it. They can then ingest the milk in the form of yogurt or cheese without any problem.

About 90 percent of Europeans and their American descendants, on the other hand, continue to produce the enzyme throughout their lives and can drink milk with no ill effects.

It has been suggested that Europeans developed lighter eyes to adapt to the longer twilights of the North and their greater reliance on firelight to illuminate caves.

Although the skin cancer-vitamin D hypothesis enjoys wide acceptance, it may well be that resistance to cold, possession of good night vision and other yet unknown factors all played roles in the evolution of skin colors.

Most anthropologists agree that the original human skin color was dark brown, since it is fairly well established that human beings evolved in the tropics of Africa. This does not, however, mean that the first people were Negroids, whose descendants, as they moved north, evolved into light-skinned Caucasoids. It is more likely that the skin color of various populations changed several times from dark to light and back as people moved from one region to another.

Consider, for example, that long before modern people evolved, *Homo erectus* had spread throughout Africa, Europe and Asia. The immediate ancestor of *Homo sapiens, Homo erectus,* was living in Africa 1.5 million years ago and in Eurasia 750,000 years ago. The earliest known forms of *Homo sapiens* do not make their appearance until somewhere between 250,000 and 500,000 years ago. Although there is no evidence of the skin color of any hominid fossil, it is probable that the *Homo erectus* population in Africa had dark skin. As subgroups spread into northern latitudes, mutations that reduced pigmentation conferred survival advantages on them and lighter skins came to predominate. In other words, there were probably black *Homo erectus* peoples in Africa and white ones in Europe and Asia.

Did the black *Homo erectus* populations evolve into today's Negroids and the white ones in Europe into today's Caucasoids? By all the best evidence, nothing like this happened. More likely, wherever *Homo sapiens* arose it proved so superior to the *Homo erectus* populations that it eventually replaced them everywhere.

If the first *Homo sapiens* evolved in Africa, they were probably dark skinned; those who migrated northward into Eurasia lost their pigmentation. But it is just as possible that the first *Homo sapiens* appeared in northern climes, descendants of white-skinned *Homo erectus.* These could have migrated southward toward Africa, evolving darker skins. All modern races, incidentally, arose long after the brain had reached its present size in all parts of the world.

North-south variations in pigmentation are quite common among mammals and birds. The tropical races tend to be darker in fur and feather, the desert races tend to be brown, and those near the Arctic Circle are lighter colored.

There are exceptions among humans. The Indians of the Americas, from the Arctic to the southern regions of South America, do not conform to the north-south scheme of coloration. Though most think of Indians as being reddish-brown, most Indians tend to be relatively light skinned, much like their presumed Mongoloid ancestors in Asia. The ruddy complexion that lives in so many stereotypes of Indians is merely what years of heavy tanning can produce in almost any light-skinned person. Anthropologists explain the color consistency as a consequence of the relatively recent entry of people into the Americas—probably between 12,000 and 35,000 years ago. Perhaps they have not yet had time to change.

Only a few external physical differences other than color appear to have adaptive significance. The strongest cases can be made for nose shape and stature.

WHAT'S IN A NOSE

People native to colder or drier climates tend to have longer, more beak-shaped noses than those living in hot and humid regions. The nose's job is to warm and humidify air before it reaches sensitive lung tissues. The colder or drier the air is, the more surface area is needed inside the nose to get it to the right temperature or humidity. Whites tend to have longer and beakier noses than blacks or Orientals. Nevertheless, there is great variation within races. Africans in the highlands of East Africa have longer noses than Africans from the hot, humid lowlands, for example.

Stature differences are reflected in the tendency for most northern peoples to have shorter arms, legs and torsos and to be stockier than people from the tropics. Again, this is an adaptation to heat or cold. One way of reducing heat loss is to have less body surface, in relation to weight or volume, from which heat can escape. To avoid overheating, the most desirable body is long limbed and lean. As a result, most Africans tend to be lankier than northern Europeans. Arctic peoples are the shortest limbed of all.

Hair forms may also have a practical role to play, but the evidence is weak. It has been suggested that the more tightly curled hair of Africans insulates the top of the head better than does straight or wavy hair. Contrary to expectation, black hair serves better in this role than white hair. Sunlight is absorbed and converted to heat at the outer surface of the hair blanket; it radiates directly into the air.

White fur, common on Arctic animals that need to absorb solar heat, is actually transparent and transmits light into the hair blanket, allowing the heat to form within the insulating layer, where it is retained for warmth.

Aside from these examples, there is little evidence that any of the other visible differences among the world's peoples provide any advantage. Nobody knows, for example, why Orientals have epicanthic eye folds or flatter facial profiles. The thin lips of Caucasoids and most Mongoloids have no known advantages over the Negroid's full lips. Why should middle-aged and older Caucasoid men go bald so much more frequently than the men of other races? Why does the skin of Bushmen wrinkle so heavily in the middle and later years? Or why does the skin of Negroids resist wrinkling so well? Why do the Indian men in one part of South America have blue penises? Why do Hottentot women have such unusually large buttocks?

There are possible evolutionary explanations for why such apparently useless differences arise.

One is a phenomenon known as sexual selection. Environmentally adaptive traits arise, Darwin thought, through natural selection—the environment itself chooses who will thrive or decline. In sexual selection, which Darwin also suggested, the choice belongs to the prospective mate.

In simple terms, ugly individuals will be less likely to find mates and reproduce their genes than beautiful specimens will. Take the blue penis as an example. Women might find it unusually attractive or perhaps believe it to be endowed with special powers. If so, a man born with a blue penis will find many more opportunities to reproduce his genes than his ordinary brothers.

Sexual selection can also operate when males compete for females. The moose with the larger antlers or the lion with the more imposing mane will stand a better chance of discouraging less well-endowed males and gaining access to females. It is possible that such a process operated among Caucasoid males, causing them to become markedly hairy, especially around the face.

ATTRACTIVE TRAITS

Anthropologists consider it probable that traits such as the epicanthic fold or the many regional differences in facial features were selected this way.

Yet another method by which a trait can establish itself involves accidental selection. It results from what biologists call genetic drift.

Suppose that in a small nomadic band

a person is born with perfectly parallel fingerprints instead of the usual loops, whorls or arches. That person's children would inherit parallel fingerprints, but they would confer no survival advantages. But if our family decides to strike out on its own, it will become the founder of a new band consisting of its own descendants, all with parallel fingerprints.

Events such as this, geneticists and anthropologists believe, must have occurred many times in the past to produce the great variety within the human species. Among the apparently neutral traits that differ among populations are:

Ear Wax—There are two types of ear wax. One is dry and crumbly and the other is wet and sticky. Both types can be found in every major population, but the frequencies differ. Among northern Chinese, for example, 98 percent have dry ear wax. Among American whites, only 16 percent have dry ear wax. Among American blacks the figure is 7 percent.

Scent Glands—As any bloodhound knows, every person has his or her own distinctive scent. People vary in the mixture of odoriferous compounds exuded through the skin—most of it coming from specialized glands called apocrine glands. Among whites, these are concentrated in the armpits and near the genitals and anus. Among blacks, they may also be found on the chest and abdomen. Orientals have hardly any apocrine glands at all. In the words of the Oxford biologist John R. Baker, "The Europids and Negrids are smelly, the Mongolids scarcely or not at all." Smelliest of all are northern European, or so-called Nordic, whites. Body odor is rare in Japan. It was once thought to indicate a European in the ancestry and to be a disease requiring hospitalization.

Blood Groups—Some populations have a high percentage of members with a particular blood group. American Indians are overwhelmingly group O—100 percent in some regions. Group A is most common among Australian aborigines and the Indians in western Canada. Group B is frequent in northern India, other parts of Asia and western Africa.

Advocates of the pure-race theory once seized upon blood groups as possibly unique to the original pure races. The proportions of groups found today, they thought, would indicate the degree of mixing. It was subsequently found that chimpanzees, our closest living relatives, have the same blood groups as humans.

Taste—PTC (phenylthiocarbamide) is a synthetic compound that some people can taste and others cannot. The ability to taste it has no known survival value, but it is clearly an inherited trait. The proportion of persons who can taste PTC varies in different populations: 50 to 70 percent of Australian aborigines can taste it, as can 60 to 80 percent of all Europeans. Among East Asians, the percentage is 83 to 100 percent, and among Africans, 90 to 97 percent.

Urine—Another indicator of differences in body chemistry is the excretion of a compound known as BAIB (beta-amino-isobutyric acid) in urine. Europeans seldom excrete large quantities, but high levels of excretion are common among Asians and American Indians. It has been shown that the differences are not due to diet.

No major population has remained isolated long enough to prevent any unique genes from eventually mixing with those of neighboring groups. Indeed, a map showing the distribution of so-called racial traits would have no sharp boundaries, except for coastlines. The intensity of a trait such as skin color, which is controlled by six pairs of genes and can therefore exist in many shades, varies gradually from one population to another. With only a few exceptions, every known genetic possibility possessed by the species can be found to some degree in every sizable population.

EVER-CHANGING SPECIES

One can establish a system of racial classification simply by listing the features of populations at any given moment. Such a concept of race is, however, inappropriate to a highly mobile and ever-changing species such as *Homo sapiens*. In the short view, races may seem distinguishable, but in biology's long haul, races come and go. New ones arise and blend into neighboring groups to create new and racially stable populations. In time, genes from these groups flow into other neighbors, continuing the production of new permutations.

Some anthropologists contend that at the moment American blacks should be considered a race distinct from African blacks. They argue that American blacks are a hybrid of African blacks and European whites. Indeed, the degree of mixture can be calculated on the basis of a blood component known as the Duffy factor.

In West Africa, where most of the New World's slaves came from, the Duffy factor is virtually absent. It is present in 43 percent of American whites. From the number of American blacks who are now "Duffy positive" it can be calculated that whites contributed 21 percent of the genes in the American black population. The figure is higher for blacks in northern and western states and lower in the South. By the same token, there are whites who have black ancestors. The number is smaller because of the tendency to identify a person as black even if only a minor fraction of his ancestors were originally from Africa.

The unwieldiness of race designations is also evident in places such as Mexico where most of the people are, in effect, hybrids of Indians (Mongoloid by some classifications) and Spaniards (Caucasoid). Many South American populations are tri-hybrids—mixtures of Mongoloid, Caucasoid and Negroid. Brazil is a country where the mixture has been around long enough to constitute a racially stable population. Thus, in one sense, new races have been created in the United States, Mexico and Brazil. But in the long run, those races will again change.

Sherwood Washburn, a noted anthropologist, questions the usefulness of racial classification: "Since races are open systems which are intergrading, the number of races will depend on the purpose of the classification. I think we should require people who propose a classification of races to state in the first place why they wish to divide the human species."

The very notion of a pure race, then, makes no sense. But, as evolutionists know full well, a rich genetic diversity within the human species most assuredly *does*.

9

A Four Letter Word That Hurts

BY MORTON H. FRIED

Taking the great white race away from today's racists is like taking candy from a baby. There are sure to be shrieks and howls of outrage. But it will be very hard to take away this piece of candy, because, to drop the metaphor, nothing is harder to expunge than an idea. The white race is not a real, hard fact of nature; it is an idea.

In 1959 a young anthropologist named Philip Newman walked into the very remote village of Miruma in the upper Asaro Valley of New Guinea to make a field study of the Gururumba. It was late that first afternoon when it began to dawn upon his native hosts that he had made no move to leave. Finally a man of some rank plucked up his courage and said, "How long will you stay, red man?"

Most people are probably amused, but a few will be puzzled and chagrined to know that what passes in our own culture as a member of the great white race is considered red by some New Guineans. But when did anyone ever really see a *white* white man? Most so-called white men are turned by wind, rain, and certain kinds of lotion to various shades of brown, although they would probably prefer to be thought bronze. Even the stay-in who shuns the sun and despises cosmetics would rarely be able to be considered white in terms of the minimal standards set on television by our leading laundry detergents. His color would likely be a shade of the pink that is a basic tint for all Caucasoids. (That, like "Caucasian," is another foolish word in the service of this concept of race. The Caucasus region, as far as we know, played no significant role in human evolution and certainly was not the cradle of any significant human variety.)

Actually, even the generalization about pink as a basic skin tint has to be explained and qualified. In some people the tint of the skin is in substantial measure the result of chemical coloring matter in the epidermis; in others there is no such coloring matter, or very little, and tinting then depends on many factors, including the color of the blood in the tiny capillaries of the dermis. Statistically, there is a continuous grading of human skin color from light to dark. There are no sharp breaks, no breaks at all. Since nobody is really white and since color is a trait that varies without significant interruption, I think the most sensible statement that can be made on the subject is that there is no white race. To make this just as true and outrageous as I can, let me immediately add that there never *was* a white race.

While at it, I might as well go on to deny the existence of a red race, although noting that if there was such a thing as the white race it would be at least esthetically more correct to call it the red race. Also, there is not now and never has been either a black race or a yellow race.

To deny that there are differences between individuals and between populations is ridiculous. The New Guineans spotted Dr. Newman as an off-beat intruder as soon as they clapped eyes on him. Of course, they were noticing other things as well and some of those other things certainly helped to make the distinctions sharper. After all, Newman was relatively clean, he had clothes on, and, furthermore, he didn't carry himself at all like a Gururumba—that is to say like a human being. I was spotted as an alien the first time I showed up in the small city of Ch'uhsien, in Anhwei province, China, back in 1947. Even after more than a year in that place, there was no question about my standing out as a strange physical type. During the hot summer, peasants who had never seen anything like me before were particularly fascinated by my arms protruding from my short-sleeved shirt, and I almost had to stop patronizing the local bath house. I am not a hirsute fellow for someone of my type, but in Ch'uhsien I looked like a shaggy dog, and farmers deftly plucked my hairs and escaped with souvenirs. Another time, a charming young lady of three scrambled into my lap when I offered to tell her a story; she looked into my eyes just as I began and leaped off with a scream. It

Reprinted from *Saturday Review*, October 2, 1965, by permission of the author.

was some time before I saw her again, and in the interval I learned that in this area the worst, bloodthirsty, child-eating demons can be identified by their blue eyes.

Individual differences are obvious, even to a child. Unfortunately, race is not to be confused with such differences, though almost everybody sees them and some people act toward others on the basis of them. I say "unfortunately," because the confusion seems so deeply embedded as to make anyone despair of rooting it out.

Most laymen of my acquaintance, whether tolerant or bigoted, are frankly puzzled when they are told that race is an idea. It seems to them that it is something very real that they experience every day; one might as well deny the existence of different makes and models of automobiles. The answer to that analogy is easy; cars don't breed. Apart from what the kids conjure up by raiding automobile graveyards, and putting the parts together to get a monster, there are no real intergrades in a machinery of this kind. To get a car you manufacture parts and put them together. To get our kind of biological organism you start with two fully formed specimens, one of each sex, and if they are attracted to each other, they may replicate. Their replication can never be more than approximate as far as either of them, the parents, is concerned, because, as we so well know, each contributes only and exactly one-half of the genetic material to the offspring. We also know that some of the genetic material each transmits may not be apparent in his or her own makeup, so that it is fully possible for a child to be completely legitimate without resembling either side of the family, although he may remind a very old aunt of her grandfather.

The phenomenon of genetic inheritance is completely neutral with regard to race and racial formation. Given a high degree of isolation, different populations might develop to the point of being clearly distinguishable while they remained capable of producing fertile hybrids. There would, however, be few if any hybrids because of geographical isolation, and the result would be a neat and consistent system.

Much too neat and consistent for man. Never in the history of this globe has there been any species with so little *sitzfleisch*. Even during the middle of the Pleistocene, way down in the Lower Paleolithic, 300,000 or more years ago, our ancestors were continent-hoppers. That is the only reasonable interpretation of the fact that very similar remains of the middle Pleistocene fossil *Homo erectus* are found in Africa, Europe, and Asia. Since that time movement has accelerated and now there is no major region of this planet without its human population, even if it is a small, artificially maintained, nonreproductive population of scientists in Antarctica.

The mobility so characteristic of our genus, Homo, has unavoidable implications, for where man moves, man mates. (Antarctica, devoid of indigenous population, is perhaps the only exception.) This is not a recent phenomenon, but has been going on for one or two million years, or longer than the period since man became recognizable. We know of this mobility not only from evidence of the spread of our genus and species throughout the world, but also because the fossils of man collected from one locality and representing a single relatively synchronic population sometimes show extraordinary variation among themselves. Some years ago a population was found in Tabun Cave, near Mt. Carmel, in Israel. The physical anthropologists Ashley Montagu and C. Loring Brace describe it as "showing every possible combination of the features of Neanderthal with those of modern man." At Chouk'outien, a limestone quarry not too far from Peking, in a cave that was naturally open toward the close of the Pleistocene geological period, about 20,000 years ago, there lived a population of diverse physical types. While some physical anthropoligists minimize them, those who have actually pored over the remains describe differences as great as those separating modern Chinese from Eskimos on one hand and Melanesians on the other. All of this, of course, without any direct evidence of the skin color of the fossils concerned. We never have found fossilized human skin and therefore can speak of the skin colors of our ancestors of tens of thousands of years ago only through extrapolation, by assuming continuity, and by assuming the applicability of such zoological rules as Gloger's, which was developed to explain the distribution of differently pigmented birds and mammals.

The evidence that our Pleistocene ancestors got around goes beyond their own physical remains and includes exotic shells, stones, and other materials in strange places which these objects could have reached only by being passed from hand to hand or being carried great distances. If our ancestors moved about that much, they also spread their genes, to put it euphemistically. Incidentally, they could have accomplished this spreading of genes whether they reacted to alien populations peacefully or hostilely; wars, including those in our own time, have always been a major means of speeding up hybridization.

Even phrasing the matter this way, and allowing for a goodly amount of gene flow between existing racial populations through hundreds of thousands of years of evolution, the resulting image of race is incredibly wrong, a fantasy with hardly any connection to reality. What is wrong is our way of creating and relying upon archetypes. Just as we persist in thinking that there is a typical American town (rarely our own), a typical American middle-class housewife (never our wife), a typical American male ("not me!"), so we think of races in terms of typical, archetypical, individuals who probably do not exist. When it is pointed out that there are hundreds of thousands or millions of living people who fall between the classified races, the frequently heard rejoinder is that this is so now, but it is a sign of our decadent times. Those fond of arguing this way usually go on to assert that it was not so in the past, that the races were formerly discrete.

In a startlingly large number of views, including those shared by informed and tolerant people, there was a time when there was a pure white race, a pure black race, etc., etc., depending upon how many races they recognize. There is not a shred of scientifically respectable evidence to support such a view. Whatever evidence we have contradicts it. In addition to the evidence of Chouk'outien and Tabun mentioned above, there are many other fossils whose morphological characteristics, primitivity to one side, are not in keeping with those of the present inhabitants of the same region.

Part of the explanation of the layman's belief in pure ancestral races is to be found in the intellectually lazy trait of stereotyping which is applied not only to man's ancestry but to landscape and climate through time as well. Few parts of the world today look quite the way they did 15,000 years ago, much less 150,000 years ago. Yet I have found it commonplace among students that they visualize the world of ages ago as it appears today. The Sahara is always a great desert, the Rockies a great mountain chain, and England separated from France by the Channel. Sometimes I ask a class, after we have talked about the famous Java fossil *Pithecanthropus erectus*, how the devil do they suppose he ever got there, Java being an island? Usually the students are dumbfounded by the question, until they are relieved to discover that Java wasn't always cut off from the Asian mainland. Given their initial attitudes and lack of information, it is not surprising that so many people imagine a beautiful Nordic Cro-Magnon, archetypical White, ranging a great Wagnerian forest looking for bestial Neanderthalers to exterminate.

Once again, there is no evidence whatsoever to support the lurid nightmare of genocide that early *Homo sapiens* is supposed to have wreaked upon the bumbling and grotesque Neanderthals. None either for William Golding's literary view of the extirpation of primitive innocence and goodness. The interpretation that in my view does least damage to the evidence is that which recognizes the differences between contemporary forms of so-called Neanderthals and other fossil *Homo sapiens* of 25,000 to 100,000 years ago to have been very little more or no greater than those between two variant populations of our own century. Furthermore, the same evidence indicates that the Neanderthals did not vanish suddenly but probably were slowly submerged in the populations that surrounded them, so that their genetic materials form part of our own inheritance today.

Then, it may be asked, where did the story come from that tells of the struggle of these populations and the extinction of one? It is a relatively fresh tale, actually invented in the nineteenth century, for before that time there was no suspicion of such creatures as Neanderthals. The nineteenth century, however, discovered the fossils of what has been called "Darwin's first witness." After some debate, the fossil remains were accepted as some primitive precursor of man and then chopped off the family tree. The model for this imaginary genealogical pruning was easily come by in a century that had witnessed the hunting and killing of native populations like game beasts, as in Tasmania, in the Malay peninsula, and elsewhere. Such episodes and continuation of slavery and the slave trade made genocide as real a phenomenon as the demand for laissez-faire and the Acts of Combination. It was precisely in this crucible that modern racism was born and to which most of our twentieth-century mythology about race can be traced.

In the vocabulary of the layman the word "race" is a nonsense term, one without a fixed, reliable meaning, and, as Alice pointed out to Humpty Dumpty, the use of words with idiosyncratic meanings is not conducive to communication. Yet I am sure that many who read these words will think that it is the writer who is twisting meaning and destroying a useful, common-sense concept. Far from it. One of the most respected and highly regarded volumes to have yet been published in the field of physical anthropology is *Human Biology*, by four British scientists, Harrison, Weiner, Tanner, and Barnicot (Oxford University Press, 1964). These distinguished authors jointly eschewed the word "race" on the ground that it was poorly defined even in zoology, *i.e.*, when applied to animals other than man, and because of its history of misunderstanding, confusion, and worse, when applied to humans.

Similar views have been held for some time and are familiar in the professional literature. Ashley Montagu, for example, has been in the vanguard of the movement to drop the concept of human race on scientific grounds for twenty-five years. His most recent work on the subject is a collation of critical essays from many specialists, *The Concept of Race* (Free Press, 1964). Frank B. Livingstone, a physical anthropoligist at the University of Michigan, has spoken out "On the Non-existence of Human Races" (*Current Anthropology*, 3:3, 1962). In the subsequent debate, opinions divided rather along generational lines. The older scientists preferred to cling to the concept of race while freely complaining about its shortcomings. The younger scientists showed impatience with the concept and wished to drop it and get on with important work that the concept obstructed.

Quite specifically, there are many things wrong with the concept of race. As generally employed, it is sometimes based on biological characteristics but sometimes on cultural features, and when it is based on biological traits the traits in question usually have the most obscure genetic backgrounds. The use of cultural criteria is best exemplified in such untenable racial constructs as the "Anglo-Saxon race," or the "German race" or the "Jewish race." Under no scientifically uttered definition known to me can these aggregates be called races. The first is a linguistic designation pertaining to the Germanic dialects or languages spoken by the people who about 1,500 years ago invaded the British Isles from what is now Schleswig-Holstein and the adjacent portion of Denmark. The invaders were in no significant way physically distinct from their neighbors who spoke other languages, and in any case they mated and blended with the indigenous population they encountered. Even their language was substantially altered by diffusion so that today a reference to English as an Anglo-Saxon language is quaint and less than correct. As for the hyperbolic extension of the designation to some of the people who live in England and the United States, it is meaningless in racial terms—just as meaningless as extending the term to cover a nation of heterogeneous origin and flexible boundaries, such as Germany or France or Italy or any other country. As for the moribund concept of a "Jewish race," this is simply funny, considering the extraordinary diversity of the physical types that have embraced this religion, and the large number that have relinquished it and entered other faiths.

The use of cultural criteria to identify individuals with racial categories does not stop with nationality, language, or religion. Such traits as posture, facial expression, musical tastes, and even modes of dress have been used to sort people into spurious racial groups. But even when biological criteria have been used, they have rarely been employed in a scientifically defensible way. One of the first questions to arise, for example, is what kind of criteria shall be used to sort people into racial categories. Following immediately upon this is another query: how many criteria should be used? With regard to the first, science is still in conflict. The new physical anthropologists whose overriding concern is to unravel the many remaining mysteries in human evolution and to understand the role that heredity will play in continuing and future evolution are impatient with any but strictly genetic characters, preferably those that can be linked to relatively few gene loci. They prefer the rapidly mounting blood factors, not only the ABO, Rh, MNS, and other well-known series, but such things as Duffy, Henshaw, Hunter, Kell, and Kidd (limited distribution blood groups named for the first person found to have carried them). Such work has one consistent by-product: the resultant classifications tend to cross-cut and obliterate conventional racial lines so that such constructs as the white race disappear as useful taxonomic units.

Some scientists argue that a classification based on only one criterion is not a very useful instrument. On the other hand, the more criteria that are added, the more abstract the racial construct becomes as fewer individuals can be discovered with all the necessary characteristics and more individuals are found to be in between. The end result is that the typical person is completely atypical; if race makes sense, so does this.

That racial classification is really nonsense can be demonstrated with ease merely by comparing some of the most usual conceptions of white and Negro. What degree of black African ancestry establishes a person as a Negro? Is 51 per cent or 50.1 per cent or some other slight statistical preponderance necessary? The question is ridiculous; we have no means of discriminating quantities of inherited materials in percentage terms. In that case can we turn to ancestry and legislate that anyone with a Negro parent is a Negro? Simple, but totally ineffective and inapplicable: how was the racial identity of each parent established? It is precisely at this point that anthropologists raise the question of assigning specific individuals to racial categories. At best, a racial category is a statistical abstraction based upon certain frequencies of genetic characters observed in small samples of much larger populations. A frequency of genetic characters is something that can be displayed by a population, but it cannot be displayed by an individual, any more than one voter can represent the proportion of votes cast by his party.

The great fallacy of racial classification is revealed by reflecting on popular applications in real situations. Some of our outstanding "Negro" citizens have almost no phenotypic resemblance to the sterotyped "Negro." It requires their acts of self-identification to place them. Simultaneously, tens of thousands of persons of slightly darker skin color, broader nasal wings, more everted lips, less straight hair, etc., are considered as "white" without question, in the South as well as the North, and in all socioeconomic strata. Conversely, some of our best known and noisiest Southern politicians undoubtedly have some "Negro" genes in their makeup.

Why is it so hard to give up this miserable little four-letter word that of all four-letter words has done the most damage? This is a good question for a scientific linguist or a semanticist. After all, the word refers to nothing more than a transitory statistical abstraction. But the question can also be put to an anthropologist. His answer might be, and mine is, that the word "race" expresses a certain kind of unresolved social conflict that thrives on divisions and invidious distinctions. It can thrive in the total absence of genetic differences in a single homogeneous population of common ances-

try. That is the case, for example, with the relations between the Japanese and that portion of themselves they know as the Eta.

In a truly great society it may be that the kinds of fear and rivalry that generate racism will be overcome. This can be done without the kind of millenarian reform that would be necessary to banish all conflict, for only certain kinds of hostilities generate racism although any kind can be channeled into an already raging racial bigotry. Great areas of the earth's surface have been totally devoid of racism for long periods of time and such a situation may return again, although under altered circumstances. If and when it does, the word "race" may drop from our vocabulary and scholars will desperately scrutinize our remains and the remains of our civilization, trying to discover what we were so disturbed about.

III

Archaeology

∘ ∘

Archaeology is the systematic retrieval and study of the remains (both of people and their activities) that human beings (and their ancestors) have left behind on and below the surface of the earth. Like physical anthropology, archaeology gradually emerged as a separate discipline in the course of the nineteenth century. It split off from the generalized study of ancient history as scholars—mostly geologists, initially—began to focus on finding material remains of ancient precivilized populations in Europe.

Actually, it was a geological debate that helped lay the groundwork for the emergence of archaeology. The prevailing view among geologists until well into the nineteenth century was that the various strata that compose the earth's crust were the result of either Noah's flood (diluvialism) or a series of catastrophes of which the flood was the most recent (catastrophism). One of the first geologists to dispute these notions was William Smith (1769–1839). Dubbed "Strata" Smith by his detractors, he assembled a detailed table of all the known strata and their fossil contents and argued a uniformitarian position: that the eternally ongoing processes of erosion, weathering, accumulation, and the movement of the continents accounted for their large number. He was supported by James Hutton (1726–1797) in his influential work *Theory of the Earth*, published in 1795.

Combat was joined by the greatly respected William Buckland (the discoverer of the "Red Lady of Paviland," which we discussed in the introduction to Section II), who in 1823 published his work *Reliquiae Diluvianae, or Observations on the Organic Remains contained in Caves, Fissures and Diluvial Gravel, and on Other Geological Phenomena attesting to the Action of an Universal Deluge,* in which he vigorously attacked the uniformitarian views that so directly contradicted Church dogma. Only the appearance of Sir Charles Lyell's *Principles of Geology* (1830–1833) managed finally to turn the tide of scholarly sentiment in favor of the uniformitarian view of the earth's history.

Because of the nature of their work, it was for the most part amateur and professional geologists who most frequently encountered fossilized human remains, generally embedded in strata in the floors of limestone caverns. In the roughly six decades following the 1790s, an impressive array of evidence with regard to human antiquity was found in a number of such caves in Europe and England; but the finds were dismissed or their importance unrecognized. As early as 1797, for example, John Frere (1740–1807) found chipped flint tools twelve feet deep in his excavation at Hoxne (northeast of London). These stone tools were closely associated with the remains of extinct animal species. To Frere these finds suggested a very ancient human existence, even older than the commonly accepted 6,000-year antiquity of Creation. Nobody listened. Forty years later, in 1838, Boucher de Perthes (1788–1868), a customs collector at Abbeville in the northwest of France, disclosed news of some flint "axes" he had found in gravel pit caves on the banks of the Somme River. The world laughed at his assertion that these tools were manufactured by "antediluvial man," even though they had been found in the immediate vicinity of the bones of extinct cold-adapted animals. In 1846, he published *Antiquités Celtiques et Antediluviennes,* in which he formally argued his thesis—and was attacked as a heretic by the Church.

We have already discussed William Buckland's inability in 1822 to comprehend the significance of his own find, the so-called Red Lady of Paviland. The powerful grip of Christian theology on scholars' minds blinded the intellectual establishment of the period, keeping them from seeing and appreciating the overwhelming pattern that these and numerous other finds presented. As we have emphasized repeatedly, it was the emergence of Darwinism in 1859 that freed people's vision and enabled them to face and reinterpret these materials correctly. The evolutionary perspective, then, was of critical importance for the emergence of archaeology. Without it, there was no way to interpret accurately the significance of the ancient remains that were being turned up with increasing frequency.

The excavation of rock shelters revealing human cultural remains of great antiquity was only one of several kinds of archaeological research being undertaken in the nineteenth century. The excavation and description of large prehistoric monuments and burial mounds, begun in the wake of emergent nationalism in the seventeenth century and eighteenth centuries, continued. So did the retrieval and preservation of materials accidentally brought to light by road, dam, and building excavations as the industrial revolution changed the face of the earth. By the 1800s, vast quantities of stone and metal implements had been recovered and had found their way into both private and public collections. As the volume of such artifacts mounted, museum curators were faced with the problem of how to organize and display them meaningfully.

In 1836, Christian Jurgensen Thomsen (1788–1865), curator of the Danish National Museum, published a guide to its collections in which he classified all artifacts in terms of the material from which they were made. He argued that the three classes he thus identified represented stages in cultural evolution: a *Stone Age* followed by a *Bronze Age* and then an *Iron Age*. The idea was not new—it had been proposed by Lucretius in ancient Rome—but it was new for its time. However, the *Three-Age System* fit well with the contemporary writings of early nineteenth-century social evolutionists and was of such usefulness that it quickly spread to other countries.

The Three-Age System was clearly evolutionary (and hence radical) in nature. It contained a geological perspective in that it proposed clearly defined sequences of cultural stages modeled after geological strata. It was of tremendous value in providing a conceptual framework through which archaeologists could begin systematically to study the artifacts they retrieved from the earth, and also in that it tended to support those scholars arguing for a greatly expanded vision of human antiquity.

Combined with Darwinian evolutionism, the Three-Age System became an even more powerful conceptual tool. In 1865, Sir John Lubbock (1834–1913) published his tremendously influential book *Prehistoric Times*, in which he vastly extended the Stone Age and divided it in two. He thus proposed that human prehistory be viewed in terms of the following stages: the *Paleolithic* (Old Stone Age, marked by flint tools); the *Neolithic* (New Stone Age, marked by the appearance of pottery); the *Bronze Age*; and the *Iron Age*. Although this system has continued to be refined, it still forms the basis of our understanding of world prehistory, and we continue to make use of its terminology.

At about the time Lubbock was formulating his broad outline of the stages of cultural evolution, Edouard Lartet (whom we discussed earlier) and his English colleague Henry Christy were exploring the now famous rock shelters in the Dordogne region of France. In one cave, called La Madeleine, Christy and Lartet found not only an abundance of spectacular cave art and small engravings of extinct species, such as the woolly mammoth, but also a magnificent collection of tools, including intricately carved implements of antler bone and ivory. These became the "type complex" for the identification of the Magdalenian culture, easily the most advanced and spectacular culture of Upper Paleolithic times.

Using the art work they found in the ten or so caves they explored in this region, Lartet and Christy developed a system to classify the materials they uncovered. Their approach was based on the fact that renderings of different species of animals predominated during different periods. The succession of stages they worked out for the Dordogne region was the following: (1) the Age of the Bison; (2) the Age of the Woolly Mammoth and Rhinoceros; (3) the Age of the Reindeer; and (4) the Age of the Cave Bear.

Gabriel de Mortillet (1821–1898) took the work of Lartet and Christy a step further by developing a chronology of the same region based on the tool industries found at *type sites* (sites used to represent the characteristic features of a culture). The series he ultimately settled on in the 1870s had six stages: Thenaisian, Chellean, Mousterian, Solutrean, Magdalenian, and Robenhausian. Although these materials have been reinterpreted a great deal since that time, prehistoric archaeologists still use Mortillet's approach to naming archaeological cultures and even most of the names he proposed.

The archaeologist of the late nineteenth century who most attracted public attention was probably Heinrich Schliemann (1822–1890). After intensive study of the Homerian epics, Schliemann set out to find the ancient city of Troy. He accomplished this in 1871 at a place called Hissarlik, near the western tip of Anatolia (modern Turkey). He was a romantic figure, and his quest to find the sites of Homeric legend excited public fancy and brought forth private funds to support both his own and other archaeological research. Unfortunately he was not a very skilled excavator: While digging up the highly stratified site at Hissarlik he focused his attentions on what turned out to be the wrong layer—and virtually destroyed the real Troy in the process.

As the frontiers of knowledge about human origins expanded in Europe with the emergence of increasingly specialized subdisciplines, a parallel development was taking place in the Americas. Wild speculation about the origins of Native Americans gave way to increasingly systematic research by scholars and learned amateurs. In 1784, for example, Thomas Jefferson (1743–1826) excavated an Indian burial mound in Virginia. Although his digging techniques were crude, he approached his task in a very modern manner. Rather than setting out simply to collect *artifacts*, Jefferson cut into the mound to collect *information*. His cross-section of the mound revealed ancient burial practices similiar to those of known historic groups and refuted the popularly held notion that the mound builders had buried their dead in an upright position.

By the 1840s, John Lloyd Stephens and Frederick Catherwood had established new standards for care in the recording of details in their magnificent reports about, and drawings of, the ruins of the Mayan civilization in the Yucatan peninsula, published in works such as Stephens's *Incidents of Travel in Central America: Chiapas and Yucatan* (1842).

The mounds of the southeastern United States attracted a number of excavators, most notably E. G. Squier and E. H. Davis, who described their research in an important monograph published in 1848. By the middle of the century, sufficient work had been done to justify a long synthesis of American archaeology by Samuel Haven published in 1856.

Archaeology in the New World was always very tightly connected to cultural anthropology—much more so than in Europe. This stemmed from the fact that whereas Europeans engaged in archaeological research as an extension of their researches backward from known historical times to their distant prehistoric past, Americans were investigating "foreign" societies—whether they were digging in their own backyards or engaging in ethnographic research with their displaced (and decimated) Native American neighbors. To this day this difference persists: In Europe archaeology is usually thought of as a humanity (an adjunct to history), whereas in the United States archaeology is practiced as a subdiscipline of anthropology and is viewed as a social science.

Doing Archaeology

How do we learn about the past? What kinds of evidence remain behind after ancient societies have vanished? How do we go about retrieving these remains, analyzing them, interpreting them? These are the concerns of archaeology.

Archaeological remains are the material things left behind by people and retrieved from the earth by archaeologists. They may be collected from the surface of a site or dug up. In general, people leave three kinds of remains behind after they have passed from the scene (and even while they are inhabiting a site, for that matter): remains of the environment, remains of their behavior, and their own (skeletal) remains.

Archaeologists have developed specialized and sophisticated techniques to retrieve and interpret this evidence from the past. After a site has been inspected, it is excavated carefully and systematically, with well worked-out strategies depending both on the nature of the site and on the reasons for its excavation. Good modern excavation is based on a careful initial investigation and sampling of a site's remains and has built-in feedback systems that provide the flexibility to modify excavation plans in the light of discoveries made in the course of digging.

The remains that are uncovered are then preserved, repaired, cleaned, inspected, described in great detail, and finally categorized. The artifacts are then dated using any of a variety of techniques including such recent developments as radiocarbon dating, potassium-argon dating, and so on.

In the past decade, archaeology increasingly has adapted the resources, tools, and techniques of other sciences to learn more about the past—from satellite-mapping to computer-assisted analysis. In "New Tools Unearth the Past," Dina Ingber describes some of these new techniques that have allowed us intimate glimpses into the previously hidden lives of people long dead.

Although archaeology has been soaring into space and using the fruits of high technology, it remains ultimately a science firmly rooted in the earth, one that will use any technique, no matter how humble, to advance our knowledge of the past. In "The Garbage Project," William L. Rathje describes perhaps the most humble—and one of the most celebrated—archaeological research projects of recent decades. By analyzing what people discard, we can learn a lot about how they live. Rathje shows us how.

10

New Tools Unearth the Past

BY DINA INGBER

How do archeologists piece together a richly detailed history of a tribe that vanished thousands of years ago?

Can you guess which scientific tools make such discoveries possible?

Imagine putting together a story that tells you:

The site was first inhabited in 1250 B.C. by a small tribe, 40 to 50 men, women and children. The women wore bright beaded jewelry, and many of the men had their front teeth sanded down, perhaps as a symbol of bravery.

They came from somewhere farther north, searching for food and shelter. On their arrival, they felled several dozen trees near the creek, choosing only the hardest woods to carve into tent poles. There was an accident and one young brave died of ax wounds.

That spring, over 3,000 years ago, the men went out on a hunt, bringing down at least 70 young bison—enough to keep the tribe well fed and clothed. The carcasses were hauled to a cave in the nearby mountainside for butchering. Most of the meat was later roasted over open fire pits in the valley below, while the tougher parts were stone-boiled for soup. For this kind of cooking, stones were heated in a fire until red hot. Then the stones were placed in a pot of water to make the water boil.

The bones of the bison were kept in the cave. Some were whittled into spear shafts and other tools, but only two of the best tribal craftsmen were allowed to handle this job. The unusable bones were dumped into a garbage heap toward the back of the cave. Here, broken spearheads, shattered pottery and even human excrement were discarded.

HUNTING AND GATHERING

While the men hunted, the women gathered nuts and berries. Hackberries were the favorite. That first year was a prosperous one. Over 23 inches of rain fell. The area was lush and provided sustenance for over 100 species of animals and dozens of varieties of plants. The tribe could keep a few wild dogs as pets.

A wandering tradesman came to visit that year and brought seeds for a new kind of edible plant—seeds that the women used to start a crop. The visitor also brought trinkets: turquoise beads and strange bits of sharp-edged material called obsidian, which had been found near a faraway volcano. Together with bits of shell and animal teeth, these were brought to the women's work tent to make more necklaces.

In the year 1245 B.C., a great drought hit the area, followed by a hard winter. Crops shriveled. The creek dried out. Many of the tribespeople, including an 8-month-old-baby and a 70-year-old tribal elder, died from hunger or cold. The tribe resorted to cannibalism, eating the remains of their dead to keep alive.

The area began to change. The forests and lush fields were replaced by a parched and dusty landscape. The tribe was forced to move on in search of better hunting grounds.

There are no written records of these events, no pictures or legends passed down through the years. How can we know how many people lived lived there, when they settled, what they ate? The answers come from unusual sources: from pollen grains, animal dung and broken glass; from bits of bone, rock and trash.

Some conclusions seem fairly obvious. For example, a layer of cracked pebbles covering the hearth tells the archeologist that the food was cooked by the stone-boiling method. When stones are heated quickly and then immersed in water, they shatter, littering the hearth with tiny bits of rock when the pit is emptied.

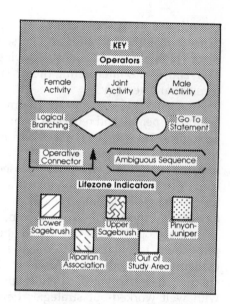

A computer was 85 percent correct when it calculated where artifacts of the Shoshoni Indians of central Nevada would be found. This flow chart begins (top left) in early summer. The tribe is living in its lower lifezone, at an altitude of 6,500 feet. It feeds itself by hunting, gathering and fishing. In late summer, supplies run short. The tribe eats berries and tule (cattails) until it moves to its winter village when the protein-rich pinyon nuts have ripened at 7,000 to 8,000-foot levels to provide additional food until spring. Working with weather conditions from the 1840s and other data, the computer predicted the movements of the tribe so well that 3,500 artifacts were found.

 Reprinted from *Science Digest*, November/December 1980, by permission of the author.

Sometimes the evidence is harder to analyze. And so today's archeologist is accompanied by geologists, ecologists, plant geneticists, chemists, physicists . . . even computer programmers. Bones are tested for radioactive messages, minerals are placed in atomic reactors, plant remains are studied under microscopes.

The astonishingly complete picture we have just presented is a composite made up of details discovered at several digs, but it is only a sampling of what science has made it possible for today's archeologists to uncover.

In *Clues to America's Past* Louis de la

Haba has told how, out of a jumbled pile of 40,000 bones and about 150 stone tools found at a site in Colorado, the archeologist Dennis Stanford reconstructed a detailed story of a bison hunt that took place 10,000 years ago—including the time of year, the number of animals and hunters involved, and even the location of trees and shrubs as they then stood.

To re-create the terrain, Stanford turned to the botanists and ecologists. "We found where the trees had stood by reconstructing habitats from animal remains such as snail shells," Stanford explained. "Certain snails live in leaf litter,

others in decaying logs, others under the roots of trees or in grass or in water. So we're identifying all the different snail shells we've found in this area and plotting them like a map. We can then superimpose the habitats of other animals—animals that liked to live around fallen trees or to burrow in dead leaf mulch. It gives us a picture of the ecology ten thousand years ago."

Stanford then brings in the zoologists and biologists. "The size of the herd we get from bone counts. And bones also give the sex of the animals. We can tell the age of the animals from teeth—their stage of eruption and the wear patterns."

POLLEN CLUES

Pollen—the microscopic grains produced by seed-bearing vegetation—has become a prime thread in the archeological tapestry. Pollen that falls into anaerobic (oxygenless) conditions such as peat bogs or lake bottoms is protected against bacterial attack and may be preserved for centuries. It gives botanists a picture of the vegetation that existed during that period. Sometimes pollen from plants that existed only at certain times can help archeologists date surrounding materials such as farm implements. And an overabundance of one kind of pollen may indicate that a certain crop was brought in as animal feed or fertilizer and tell us about agricultural techniques.

The remains of tiny creatures can tell amazing stories. Beetles are particularly important because many species live in precisely defined habitats: grasslands, forests, river banks, dead wood. The remains of a particular kind of beetle may show that an area was once woodland, an open plain, or even under water. In a Roman pit in England, beetles proved that the area was once a garbage dump containing animal dung, general domestic waste and the sweepings from a primitive leather-goods factory.

Even feces have their value. Both human and animal excrement can tell about the foods eaten and the environments exploited. So the study of coprolites—fossil dung—is now a science, with entire laboratories devoted to it.

Archeologists can discover how one culture related to other cultures—what they traded and how their crafts spread. A technique called Neutron Activation Analysis can give materials such as obsidian a kind of fingerprint. An obsidian sample is put into an atomic reactor and bombarded with neutrons to make it highly radioactive. Obsidian from one area contains trace elements that are different from those of obsidian from an-

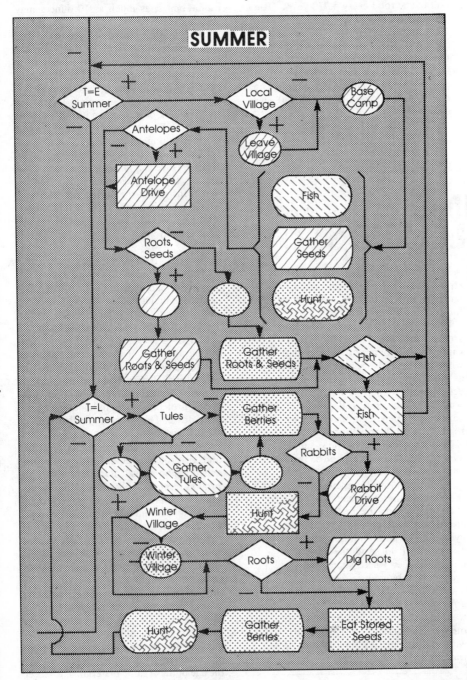

SUMMER

other area. Because of the trace elements, the wavelengths of the radiation are different. Thus, obsidian found in Hopewell Indian sites in Ohio was found to come not from Mexico as suspected but from Wyoming. The archeologist can then begin to draw maps of trade routes and cultural contacts.

How are archeological finds dated? Tree-ring dating, or dendrochronology, is one of the oldest techniques. It not only tells us about the age of the wood but about the weather during its lifetime.

Every year, trees grow a new layer, which varies in size with climatic changes. At the start of the growing season, the tree manufactures new cells just beneath the bark. As spring turns to summer, the cells produced are smaller and more densely packed, and by wintertime the growth has stopped completely. A cross section of each tree shows a series of concentric rings consisting of a row of pale springtime cells and a row of darker cells. This light-dark ring pattern is re-peated for each year of the tree's life. Thin rings usually mean a drought or cold spell that stunted growth, and thick rings mean a year of abundant water and sunshine. Starting at the outer layers where the rings can be matched with recorded climatic events, dendrochronologists have been able to work their way back thousands of years.

The workhorse of archeological dating has been the carbon-14 method. All living things contain radioactive carbon-14 isotopes, which are unstable and disintegrate. Beginning at death, an organism's C-14 level diminishes at a fixed rate: one half of the total every 5,730 years. Using a Geiger counter, a scientist can tally the C-14 impulses emitted by an ancient specimen, then compare the result with the count from a living sample. If the living material gives, say, 75 disintegrations per minute and the ancient sample 37.5, the scientist knows his find is 5,730 years old.

SAMPLES DESTROYED

Dr. Willard Libby, who developed the technique and won a Nobel Prize for his work, originally tested it on wood from Egyptian tombs, the linen wrapping of one of the Dead Sea Scrolls, and a baker's roll buried in the volcanic ash of Pompeii.

C-14 dating can be relied upon for determinations as far back as 40,000 years. But it has obvious drawbacks. Because the level of C-14 in any sample is low—one atom in every million million ordinary carbon atoms—large samples must be used. From charcoal and wood, almost an ounce is necessary for testing. And for some bones, as much as 10 ounces may be used.

These samples are destroyed in the dating process. It's no wonder that many archeologists are reluctant to submit their precious finds for testing. The Shroud of Turin, claimed by many to be Jesus' death garment, is a case in point. Destroy a large chunk of it to prove its authenticity or leave it be and have its true age remain forever in doubt?

The University of Rochester physicist Harry Gove has developed a new C-14 dating that may eliminate those problems. Instead of measuring the electrical signal emitted by the C-14 deterioration, Gove has found a way to measure the actual C-14 atoms.

100,000 YEARS

The advantages of Gove's technique are great. Samples don't have to be destroyed; a much smaller sample is needed; and accurate dating for perhaps as far back as 100,000 years can be achieved.

But C-14 is not the only key to measuring the age of finds. The question "When did it die?" is being answered in other ways. Jeffrey Bada, of the Scripps Institute of Oceanography, has been analyzing protein changes in bone that occur after death. This process is called Amino Acid Racemization.

"All living organisms contain proteins, and all proteins contain little molecules called amino acids," Bada said about his process recently. "There are about twenty kinds of amino acids and each of them can exist in a kind of left-handed or right-handed configuration."

Living organisms use only left-handed amino acids (L-isomers). But once an organism dies, the process of racemization starts. The amino acids begin to reverse themselves into right-handed (D-isomers) states in order to reach a balance of one right-handed for one left-handed. This change takes place at a steady and predictable rate and by analyzing the ratio of D-isomers to L-isomers Bada can tell the age of the organic material. The closer

FLYING ARCHEOLOGISTS

From the air, an archeologist can look down on a field of corn and detect signs of ancient buildings, burial grounds or irrigation systems.

A black-and-white aerial photograph of a field will tell him that some parts of the crop are growing taller and darker than others. This would indicate that long ago a ditch had been dug in the soil beneath those plants, perhaps to irrigate the field for some ancestral farmer. The digging had increased the depth of humus, and the plants growing over the ditch are darker and taller because they get more nourishment than those on either side.

Or, the shorter, lighter plants may show that the remains of some ancient buildings lie beneath. The structures block the plants' access to nourishment and stunt their growth.

Such crop patterns once helped the archeologist Leonard Wooley locate the exact site of ancient Syrian graves. The field he was studying was covered with sparse, shallow-rooted growth. But mixed in were clumps of sturdier weeds, each clump about six feet across. The soil had been broken in the past, allowing these plant roots to penetrate deeply. And, he theorized, it had been broken into the right shapes for graves. He was right.

Using the Digicol Color Monitor, archeologists can assign colors to the various shades of gray that black-and-white film records. Solid masses such as roads and walls then show up as yellow, while the soil shows up as blue. And by a technique called edge enhancement, they can make ancient roads show on high-altitude photos.

Infrared photography now supplements black-and-white photos. Infrared radiation is heat radiation. Objects have individual heat capacities, which show up as different densities of color.

Electronic and magnetic scanners also detect underground irregularities by sensing variations in the patterns of a magnetic field. And the variations indicate places where something has been built in by man.

Once the archeologist in search of a site was as limited as Stone Age man, waiting for some artifact to show him the way. Today he can probe the Earth with sophisticated technology and release its secrets.

the ratio between D and L is to one to one, the older the object is. Bada has used his technique to date fossil shark bone from the floor of the Pacific Ocean at a whopping eight million years of age.

The archeologist can not only discover the age of a piece of material but calculate when a man made it into a tool. Ancient potters used crystalline minerals such as feldspar and quartz to strengthen their clay. When these minerals are heated to 932 degrees Fahrenheit, they emit light, or thermoluminescence (TL). It comes from the release of extra electrons absorbed by the crystals over the years.

When an ancient potter fired his piece at high temperatures, the thermoluminescence was released. The material in the piece of pottery promptly began absorbing electrons again. By measuring this thermoluminescence accumulated since the firing, scientists can tell when the pottery was made.

Obsidian—a glass formed in the cooling of lava—was made into knives and weapons by those living in volcanic areas. This volcanic glass contains an unstable uranium isotope, and the isotope decays at a regular rate. As it does so, it leaves "fission tracks" on the obsidian and by counting them a scientist can tell when the obsidian was formed.

These fission tracks are even more useful in man-made glass. The obsidian might have been lying around accumulating fission tracks for hundreds of years before an Indian picked it up to make an arrowhead. But man-made glass has fission tracks that tell us when the glass was fired, in other words, when the goblet or bowl itself was created.

Recently, a technique called Obsidian Hydration Rim Dating has given us a way to determine when man actually made the sharp-edged obsidian into a useful object. When obsidian is fractured to make a tool, fresh surfaces are exposed and begin to absorb water. This hydrated rim gradually swells and develops a series of microfractures that refract light in a different way than the unaltered glass beneath does. This change in light refraction can be measured, and from it scientists can figure out how long the rim has been absorbing water. They cannot calculate the obsidian's absolute date, but they can tell whether it is older or younger than some other obsidian tool.

CROSS-CHECKING

Even the most absolute dates indicated by one method are rarely considered accurate unless supported by other tests. Dendrochronology is often used to verify C-14 dates. By cross-checking the two, it was discovered that for the period 1000 to 5000 B.C. radiocarbon dates are somewhat inaccurate. This may be due to changes in the Earth's atmosphere that changed the C-14 levels at that time. A chart, based on the cross-check with tree rings, allows scientists to correct the C-14 dates.

It has become difficult to keep track of all this information and sort it into a coherent pattern. That's why archeologists are turning to the computer—sometimes installing a terminal at the dig. Dr. David Hurst Thomas, of the American Museum of Natural History, fed data on the Western Shoshoni Indians into a computer: types of tools used, food eaten, climate. The computer then simulated the movements of these Indians over a 1,000-year period. It plotted a map of archeological sites, predicting where the Shoshoni would have lived. Dr. Thomas checked these sites and about 85 percent of the predictions turned out to be correct!

These incursions of science into archeology are relatively new, and it is impossible for one archeologist to be familiar with all the analytical techniques.

To help solve the problem, Dr. Stuart Fleming, director of the University of Pennsylvania Museum, hopes to form the first complete scientific-dating lab, using every sort of laboratory analysis needed in archeology. His dream is to have archeologists send all the artifacts from a single dig to his lab so they can be studied, compared and fitted together.

The result may tell us not only *what* the ancients did but *why* they did it. The new "motivational archeology" is trying to relate environmental to cultural changes and discover the reasons men behaved as they did. It may help us unravel some mysteries of ancient human behavior and let us trace man's creativity and development, as expressed in everything he did—from pottery to palaces, from coprolites to carvings.

11

The Garbage Project

BY WILLIAM L. RATHJE

. . . .

Each day the city of Tucson, Arizona, expends a tremendous effort to discard the 250 tons of material resources it generates at the household level, which will perhaps become the basis for studies by archeologists of the distant future. But these data need not be wasted by contemporary archeologists. The fact that household discard of commodities is observable as a process in our ongoing society provides archeologists with an interesting analysis potential.

Analyses of contemporary industrial societies using traditional archeological methods and measures can make behaviors today comparable to those of the past. This comparability provides a link to the work of other archeologists in the form of a cap to the long time sequences they have reconstructed and produces a unique perspective that relates past to present.

An archeological focus also provides a unique materialist perspective on our present society that contrasts to most sociology and psychology studies based on interviews. The kinds of observations archeologists record on human behavior—material culture interactions—are easily quantifiable on standard scales. In addition, the measurements and measurers themselves need not intrude on the activities they seek to record. (Interview–garbage comparisons, at both the census tract and household level, demonstrate that (a) there are significant differences between "front door" and "back door" data; and (b) these differences are patterned. For beer and cigarettes, garbage data recorded significantly more drinkers and smokers and higher rates of consumption than reported in interviews in the same neighborhoods.) This advantage of material–behavior studies has attracted the attention and even some emulation from sociologists.

Using an archeological perspective, researchers can analyze modern industrial societies in order to contribute to long-term and short-term views of the workings of complex social–material systems. This potential can be illustrated with a few comments about one aspect of the University of Arizona's Garbage Project—specifi-

cally, the analysis of resource discard from both a long- and short-term perspective (for more detailed studies see Rathje and Hughes 1975, Rathje and McCarthy 1977, Rathje and Harrison 1977, and Rathje in press).

The rationale for garbage research is clearly drawn from archeology. From this discipline has come an emphasis on the unique kinds of information that material culture contains about human activities and an appreciation for the significant part played in these activities by material commodities. Archeologists have developed methods to analyze old garbage in order to discover the relationships among resource management, urban demography, and social and economic stratification that once existed in ancient urban centers. Contemporary garbage can be used to obtain a new insight on the same relationships.

All archeologists study garbage; the Garbage Project's raw data are just a little fresher than most.

Each bag of household refuse is a neat time capsule of diverse, but directly related, behavior sets. Over 140 variable categories were selected to record garbage data in a way to meet as wide a range of problems as could be foreseen covering health, nutrition, personal and household sanitation, child and adult education and amusement, communication, and pet-related materials [see Figure 1]. Each item (usually clearly labeled food packaging) in sampled refuse is recorded by general category, specific type, input volume, cost, brand, material composition, and weight of any edible food discard (not including bones, skins, peels, rinds, or tops) [see Figure 2]. The project's sampling design was based on grouping Tucson's 66 urban census tracts into 7 clusters derived from 1970 federal census population and housing characteristics. From 1973 up to 1977, household samples have been consistently drawn from 13 census tracts selected to be representative of Tucson's 7 tract clusters. The total recorded garbage represents around 3000 3.5-day household refuse accumulations—more than 140,000 individual items. The raw data were collected by Tucson Sanitation Divi-

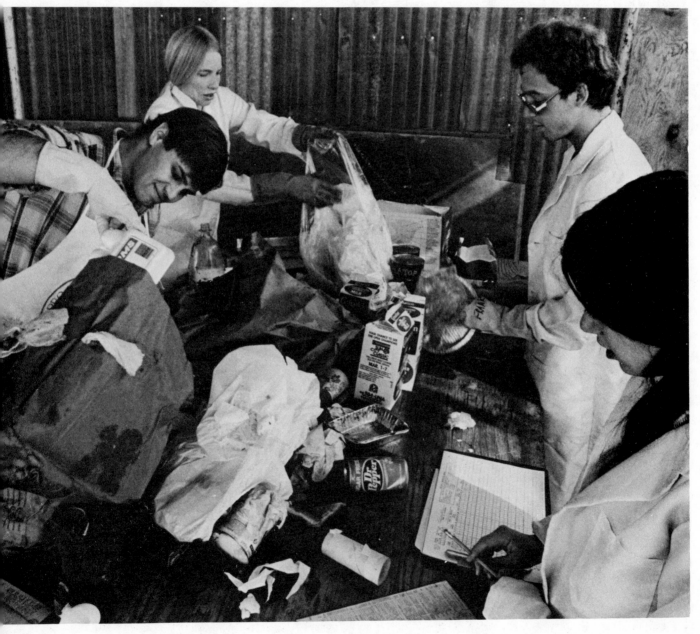

Lori Stiles

FIGURE 1   Garbage Item Code List

BEEF *	001
OTHER MEAT (not bacon)*	002
CHICKEN	003
OTHER POULTRY	004
FISH (fresh, frozen, canned, dried)*	005
CRUSTACEANS & MOLLUSKS (shrimp, clams, etc.)	006
T.V.P. TYPE FOODS *	007
UNKNOWN MEAT	008
CHEESE (including cottage cheese)	010
MILK *	011
ICE CREAM (also ice milk, sherbet)*	012
OTHER DAIRY (not butter)	013
EGGS (regular, powdered, liquid)*	014
BEANS (not green beans)*	015
NUTS	016
PEANUT BUTTER	017
FATS: Saturated *	018
Unsaturated *	019
Bacon, saltpork *	020
Meat trimming *	021
CORN (also corn meal and masa)*	022
FLOUR (also pancake mix)*	023
RICE *	024
OTHER GRAIN (barley, wheat germ, etc.)	025
NOODLES (pasta)	026
WHITE BREAD	027
DARK BREAD	028
TORTILLAS *	029
DRY CEREALS: Regular	030
High Sugar (first ingredient only)	031
COOKED CEREALS (instant or regular)	032
CRACKERS	033
CHIPS (also pretzels)	034
UNKNOWN PRODUCE *	040
FRESH VEGETABLES *	041
CANNED VEGETABLES (dehydrated also)*	042
FROZEN VEGETABLES *	043
POTATO PEEL *	044
FRESH FRUIT *	045
CANNED FRUIT (dehydrated also)*	046
FROZEN FRUIT *	047
FRUIT PEEL *	048
RELISH, PICKLES, OLIVES *	049
SYRUP, HONEY, JELLIES, MOLASSES	051
PASTRIES (cookies, cakes and mix, pies, etc.) *	052
SUGAR *	053
ARTIFICIAL SWEETENERS	054
CANDY *	055
SALT *	056
SPICES & FLAVORINGS (catsup, mustard, pepper, etc.)*	057
BAKING ADDITIVES (yeast, baking powder, etc.)*	058
POPSICLES	060
PUDDING	061
GELATIN	062
INSTANT BREAKFAST	063

DIPS (for chips)	064
NON-DAIRY CREAMERS & WHIPS	065
HEALTH FOODS *	066
SLOP *	069
REGULAR COFFEE (instant or ground)*	070
DECAF COFFEE	071
EXOTIC COFFEE *	072
TEA *	073
CHOCOLATE DRINK MIX OR TOPPING *	074
FRUIT OR VEG. JUICE (canned or bottled)	075
FRUIT JUICE CONCENTRATE	076
FRUIT DRINK, pdr. or lqud. (Tang, Koolaid, Hi-C)*	077
DIET SODA	078
REGULAR SODA	079
COCKTAIL MIX (carbonated)	080
COCKTAIL MIX (non-carb. liquid)	081
COCKTAIL MIX (powdered)	082
PREMIXED COCKTAILS (alcoholic)	083
SPIRITS (booze)	084
WINE (still & sparkling)	085
BEER *	086
BABY FOOD & JUICE *	087
BABY CEREAL (pablum)	088
BABY FORMULA (liquid)*	089
BABY FORMULA (powdered)*	090
PET FOOD (dry)	091
PET FOOD (canned or moist)	092
TV DINNERS (also pot pies)	094
TAKE OUT MEALS	095
SOUPS *	096
GRAVY & SPECIALTY SAUCES *	097
PREPARED MEALS (canned or packaged)*	098
VITAMIN PILLS & SUPPLEMENTS (commercial)*	100
PRESCRIBED DRUGS (prescribed vitamins)	101
ASPIRIN *	102
COMMERCIAL STIMULANTS & DEPRESSANTS *	103
COMMERCIAL REMEDIES *	104
ILLICIT DRUGS *	105
COMMERCIAL DRUG PARAPHERNALIA	106
ILLICIT DRUG PARAPHERNALIA	107
CONTRACEPTIVES: MALE	108
FEMALE	109
BABY SUPPLIES (diapers, etc.)*	111
INJURY ORIENTED (iodine, bandaids, etc.)	112
PERSONAL SANITATION *	113
COSMETICS *	114
CIGARETTES (pack)*	124
CIGARETTES (carton)*	125
CIGARS	126
PIPE, CHEWING TOBACCO, LOOSE TOBACCO	127
ROLLING PAPERS (also smoking items)	128

HOUSEHOLD & LAUNDRY CLEANERS *	131
HOUSEHOLD CLEANING TOOLS (not detergents)	132
HOUSEHOLD MAINT. ITEMS (paint, wood, etc.)	133
COOKING & SERVING AIDS	134
TISSUE CONTAINER	135
TOILET PAPER CONTAINER	136
NAPKIN CONTAINER	137
PAPER TOWEL CONTAINER	138
PLATIC WRAP CONTAINER	139
BAGS (paper or plastic)*	140
BAG CONTAINER	141
ALUMINUM FOIL SHEETS	142
ALUMINUM FOIL PACKAGE	143
WAX PAPER PACKAGE	144
MECHANICAL APPLIANCE (tools)	147
ELECTRICAL APPLIANCE & ITEMS	148
AUTO SUPPLIES	149
FURNITURE	150
CLOTHING: CHILD *	151
ADULT *	152
CLOTHING CARE ITEMS (shoe polish, thread)	153
DRY CLEANING (laundry also)	154
PET MAINTENANCE (litter)	155
PET TOYS	156
GATE RECEIPTS (tickets)	157
HOBBY RELATED ITEMS	158
PHOTO SUPPLIES	159
HOLIDAY VALUE (non-food)*	160
DECORATIONS (non holiday)	161
PLANT & YARD MAINT.	162
STATIONERY SUPPLIES	163
JEWELRY	164
CHILD SCHOOL RELATED PAPERS *	171
CHILD EDUC. BOOKS (non-fiction)	172
CHILD EDUC. GAMES (toys)	173
CHILD AMUSEMENT READING	174
CHILD AMUSEMENT TOYS (games)	175
ADULT BOOKS (non-fiction)	176
ADULT BOOKS (fiction)	177
ADULT AMUSEMENT GAMES	178
LOCAL NEWSPAPERS *	181
NEWSPAPERS (other city, national)*	182
ORGANIZATIONAL NEWSPAPERS OR MAGAZINES (also religion)*	183
GENERAL INTEREST MAGAZINES *	184
SPECIAL INTEREST MAGAZINE OR NEWSPAPER *	185
ENTERTAINMENT GUIDE (TV Guide, etc.)	186
MISCELLANEOUS ITEMS (specify on back of sheet)*	190

*Special Notes Used in Recording Procedures, see Appendix.

FIGURE 2 Sample Item Analysis

PAGE 1/1

CENSUS TRACT 16 17 18: A29

COLLECTION MO 19 20: 02 DAY 21 22: 08

NAME OF RECORDER: Hughes/Westfall

DATE OF ANALYSIS: 2 Feb 84

TRACT: A29 TOTAL PGS. 1/1

MATERIAL COMPOSITION CODES

CODE (LIST MOST PREVALENT MATERIAL FIRST)
A PAPER
B FERROUS (STEEL/TIN)
C ALUMINUM
D PLASTIC (CELLOPHANE)
E NON-RETURN GLASS
H RETURNABLE GLASS
J AEROSOL CANS
K WOOD
M CERAMICS
P LEATHER
Q RUBBER
R COPPER AND BRASS
S BIODEGRADABLE PLASTIC
T TEXTILES
V CORRUGATED CARDBOARD
X OTHER (SPECIFY ON BACK)

#	ITEM CODE 23 24 25	NO. OF ITEMS 26 27 28	FLUID OUNCES 29 30 31 32 33	SOLID OUNCES 34 35 36 37 38	COST 41 42 43 44	WASTE (GRAMS) 45 46 47 48	SPECIAL IND. 49	BRAND 50-57	TYPE 58-65	MATERIAL COMPOSITION CODE 66 67 68
1	041	1		16.0		70		MARSHBUR	CARROT	D
2	086	3	36.0		.95			COORS	LIGHT	C
3	079	2	24.0					SEVENUP	UNCOLA	C
4	028	1		16.0	.90	292		ARNOLD	WHEAT	D
5	051	1	64.0		1.60			SHAMROCK	WHOLE	A
6	051	1		32.0		54		WELCHS	JELLY	EB
7	041	1				60			LETTUCE	
8	010	1				260			CHEDDAR	
9	048	1						STAR	BANANA	A
10	081	2							DAILY	
11	044	1				98		ROYALOCC	VODKA	E
12	094	1	25.4	10.7					BUNS	
13	027	1			.50	105		CAMPBELL	TURKEYNO	B
14	098	1		16.0				WESTERN	MARGARIN	A
15	018	1						MARLBORO	FILTER	A
16	124	1		20.5	4.05	372		SAFEWAY	RIBSTEAK	D
17	001	1								
18	069	1						BAYER	ASPIRIN	D
19	102								PAPER	A
20	140	4								

sion foremen, who randomly selected households within the sample tracts. Data recording was done by more than 100 student volunteers—the real core of the project—who were forced to submit to immunizations and coerced into wearing lab coats, rubber gloves, and face masks.

To protect the anonymity of specific households, garbage samples were recorded only by census tract. No names, addresses, or other specific personal data were either examined, recorded, or saved. To place present types of resource discard into a meaningful frame of reference, long-term data are needed. Without these, modern data are often equivocal or misleading.

Because we have so little comparative data, we often think of ourselves today as ardent recyclers. Coors, Olympia, the beverage industry, the Iron and Steel Foundation, Alcoa, Reynolds, and everyone else seems to be recycling metal cans. Until the slump in the building industry, there were incessant newspaper drives. At Christmas we all receive an onslaught of Christmas cards printed on recycled paper. Our potential conceit is placed in some perspective by the fact that at present, generally, we are recycling less than we did in the recent past. For example, today only 19% of all wood fiber is recycled. This stands in marked contrast to the 35% that was recycled during World War II.

Analyses of even older data indicate exponential changes in rates of reuse, recycling, and resource discard. Bunny Fontana's classic study of bottles excavated from mid 1800s trash deposits in Magdelena, Mexico is an example (Fontana 1968). Fontana noted that after glass containers were first introduced, only broken bottles were found in trash, and in each case where bases were recorded, they were worn almost paper thin from long-term reuse. Even after bottles became more common and the infrequent discard of whole bottles began to appear, all bases, on both whole and broken bottles, continued to show signs of long-term reuse.

Garbage Project data from modern Tucson are a striking contrast. The average Tucson household discards 500 whole glass bottles each year. Around 50 of these bottles (10%) are made of returnable glass and could be reused, ideally up to 40 times if returned to distributors. The other 450 bottles could be turned in to local recycling plants and ground into cullet for making additional bottles. Nevertheless, almost all bottles seem to be discarded as soon as the original contents are emptied; none show any trace of reuse.

Another example of time depth in resource discard may be nearer and dearer to the hearts of archeologists. A report by James Deetz on his excavations at Plymouth Plantation in New England (Deetz 1973) shows a change in discarded ceramics. The Joseph Howland site was occupied for 50 years, between 1675 and 1725. Deetz's photograph of the ceramics from its trash pits shows eight puny piles of broken pieces spread out on a spatious lab table. The same table is smothered by a deep layer of ceramics from a century later. The majority of the later pottery seems only slightly damaged by cracking and chipping, and an almost complete eight-place table setting is discernible in the piles of porcelain. This entire load was produced by a single family in only 5 years, between 1830 and 1835.

Tucsonans today do not often discard serving items, they concentrate instead on high-turnover packaging materials. The average household each year discards 1800 plastic items, both wraps and containers; 850 steel cans; 500 recyclable all-aluminum cans; and more than 13,000 individual items of paper and cardboard (largely packaging). The EPA estimates that as a nation in 1966, the United States produced 55 billion pounds of food packaging; most of it was discarded after a single use and disposed of in dumps and landfills at a cost of over $400 million. The majority of this packaging was developed to decrease food discard due to spoilage, and for this purpose it has been effective. Although considerable variability between sociodemographic groups has been identified by the Garbage Project and although the only other large-scale food discard data for households were presented almost 50 years ago without any clear statement of methodology of collection, it seems fair to say that packaging (along with other technological changes) has cut household food discard from 20 to 25% of total input by volume during World War I to between 10 and 15% of input by volume today in Tucson.

However, this technological solution to waste has been bought by a trade-off of nonrenewable resources (iron ore, oil, bauxite for aluminum) or slowly renewable resources (forests) in exchange for such rapidly renewable resources as corn and beef and apples.

It is important to study the development of this trade-off and to quantify various aspects of it now because many ramifications of our material—behavior interactions go unrealized while our response alternatives become increasingly limited by the size and inelasticity of our resource demands.

This resource–discard trade-off is a good long-term problem for archeologists to develop because their data base can place resource trade-off behaviors in an extremely useful perspective for modern consumers as well as provide unique data to test general regularities in long-term man–material interactions. Long-term trade-offs to decrease edible food discard lead into a study of food waste at the household level over the short-term—specifically, over the last 3 years in Tucson, Arizona.

Edible food discard has long been a concern of the government (most notably the USDA), consumer educators and nutritionists, and household managers; but it is not easy to obtain data on its extent, much less useful information on its social and behavioral correlates.

The limitations of traditional interview–survey techniques present problems for gathering accurate data on household-level food discard behavior in the U.S. The concept of "food waste" is fraught with moral implications. Few Americans will admit that they unnecessarily discard edible food even to themselves, and mere participation in a study of waste behavior is sure to bias results (Adelson et al. 1961, 1963).

On the other hand, garbage provides quantifiable data on food discard unbiased by the kinds of problems facing interviewers. There are, of course, other biases—garbage disposals, pets, fireplaces, and compost piles; but all these factors work in one direction: to minimize food discard. Thus, garbage data represent minimum levels of food utilization and waste. As a data base developed in 1973 and 1974, the Garbage Project began to correlate edible food discard patterns with sociodemographic population segments. Although patterns emerged around group means, there was a great deal of variability that cut across these groups and the question was clearly, Are there more general and useful correlates of food discard behavior?

Data from the 1973 beef shortage provided an initial clue. As prices went up and beef became less available, household purchase behaviors changed rapidly and radically: Shoppers bought new cuts, they bought in new quantities (either trying to stock up or trying to cut down), and they bought more or less frequently than usual. As this variety came in the front door, an all-time high waste of beef—9% of the volume purchased (not including the weight of bone and fat)—spilled out the back.

As beef purchase behaviors stabilized however, in 1974 and 1975, the quantity wasted decreased drastically to 3% of input volume. These data led to an hypothesized "food discard equation." This simple formula states that the amount of regularity in purchase–consumption behaviors varies inversely with the percentage of food input that is discarded. This waste equation is only an hypothesis and must be tested rigorously with our current data; however, we have had success in predicting and retrodicting relative waste rates among different population segments over a 3-year time frame for a wide variety of food commodities. Nevertheless, the formula remains applicable only to Southwestern U.S. communities that purchase modern processed foods that are prepared and consumed at the household level.

From this formula we were able to anticipate food discard behavior in relation to the sugar shortage. As the variety of purchases increased along with sugar prices and scarcity in the spring of 1975, the quality of waste of pastries, kiddie cereals, candy bars, and even sugar in granular form was double its previous rate.

The formula is also useful in evaluating the waste associated with commonly utilized commodities that do not rapidly fluctuate in price under normal conditions. "White" bread is an example. Bread discard associated with standard 24-ounce and 16-ounce packages is less than 5% of total input. Bread packaged in less than 16-ounce wrappers is less than 5% of total input. Bread packages less than 16-ounce are usually a special variety of sizes. As expected, the waste associated with these less regularly utilized breads is high, almost 10% of total bread waste.

Food discard may be at a lower rate today than in 1918, but edible food in refuse adds up to as much as 8% of the total weight of household garbage, and a considerable quantity of nutrients end up in dumps and sanitary landfills. Extrapolations from Garbage Project data suggest, for example, that in 1974 the 360,000 plus residents of Tucson discarded more than 9500 tons of edible food, worth between 9 and 11 million dollars. But to make any kind of dent in this behavior, the basic correlates of food discard must be identified, and attempts by consumer educators and nutritionists to modify behavior must be evaluated. It is obvious that if the discard formula is correct, awareness of waste is not enough to decrease discard; purchase behavior must be modified. It is now important for the Garbage Project to refocus on the sociodemographics of households in order to identify their correlation with specific patterns in food purchases and the effect of these patterns on food discard. The general implication of this short-term study and its tentative food discard formula for the study of long-term resource discard is that it too may be understandable in relation to general patterns and regularities of the interaction between human behavior and material culture.

This kind of synergism between long-term and short-term analyses is what the Garbage Project seeks to develop in its continued short-term archeology of household refuse and in its long-term comparisons of these data with the remains from much older household middens.

REFERENCES

Adelson, S. F., E. Asp and I. Noble
1961   Household records of foods used and discarded. *Journal of the American Dietetic Association* 39 (No. 6): 578–584.

Adelson, S. F., I. Delaney, C. Miller and I. Noble
1963   Discard of edible food in households, *Journal of Home Economics* 55 (No. 8): 633–638.

Deetz, J. J. F.
1973   Ceramics from Plymouth, 1635–1835; The archaeological evidence. In *Ceramics in America*, edited by I. M. G. Quimby. Virginia: The University Press of Virginia. Pp. 15–40.

Fontana, B. L.
1968   Bottles and history: The case of Magdalena de Kino, Sonora, Mexico. *Historical Archaeology* 1968: 45–55.

Rathje, W. L.
n.d.   Archaeological ethnography. In *Ethnoarchaeology: From Tasmania to Tuscon*, edited by R. A. Gould. School of American Research and the University of New Mexico Press. (in press.)

Rathje, W. L. and G. G. Harrison
1977   Monitoring trends in food utilization: Application of an archaeological method. *Proceedings of the Federation of American Societies for Experimental Biology* 37 (No. 1): 49–54.

Rathje, W. L. and W. W. Hughes
1976   The Garbage Project as a nonreactive approach: Garbage in . . . garbage out? In *Perspectives on attitude assessment: Surveys and their alternatives*, edited by H. W. Sinaiko and L. A. Broedling, Champaign-Urbana. Pendleton. Pp. 151–167.

Rathje, W. L. and M. McCarthy
1977   Regularity and variability in contemporary garbage. In *Research strategies in historical archaeology*, edited by S. South. New York: Academic. Pp. 261–286.

Issues in Archaeology

• •

In this topic we approach the study of archaeology by focusing on some of the major questions that scholars are attempting to answer today. The first article looks at one of the livelier debates in American archaeology: the question of when the New World first was populated. No serious scholars doubt any longer that the Americans were populated by fully evolved modern human hunting and food-gathering bands—probably migrating in pursuit of big game on the Siberian plains. They crossed over the Bering Strait land bridge connecting Alaska and Siberia during the last glacial period, which marked the end of the Ice Age, and found themselves in a paradise rich in wild game and bountiful in plant life. They thrived, and their numbers grew rapidly as they expanded southward and eastward, seeking out the incredibly diverse environmental niches that met their needs and fit their fancies. Eventually they evolved a spectacular variety of lifestyles that included high civilizations in the jungles of Mesoamerica, vital communities of salmon fishers on the Northwest Coast, dazzling mound builders in the midwestern plains of North America, canal-building adobe dwellers high in the Andes Mountains of Peru, and countless bands of semi-nomadic hunters and food-gatherers from the Inuit (Eskimo) of Alaska to the Yahgan of Tierra del Fuego in Argentina. The question vexing archaeologists is: When did the first bands cross the Bering Strait from Siberia to Alaska?

In "The First Americans: Who Were They and When Did They Arrive?" Ben Patrusky is evenhanded in presenting the two main competing views. The older of the two, and still the one more widely held, is that this epic migration was relatively recent—about 12,000 years ago. Many sites have been found scattered across North America (and a few in South America, too) that date from around 11,000 B.P. (before the present) and that feature, in the collections of stone tools they exhibit, versions of the so-called Clovis Point (named after a site in New Mexico): a medium-sized, leaf-shaped projectile point with a hollow groove in the base. In the view of many scholars these points were brought to the New World by Siberian migrants. Moreover, the spread of this tool kit across the continent marks the rapid expansion of the migrating groups, who encountered a fresh, virtually limitless, and unbelievably rich environment. (And, in the course of but a few centuries, the Clovis people seem to have hunted into extinction many of the great mammals that lived there, from giant sloths to horses and elephants.)

But there are dissidents—an increasing number—who believe that human groups first crossed over from Siberia much earlier, 25,000 to 50,000 years ago. In the mountains of Peru, for instance, Richard MacNeish believes he has found pre-Clovis tools perhaps 25,000 years old. He and others point to tantalizing bits and pieces of evidence indicating the presence of humans in the New World thousands of years before the Clovis culture emerged. For example, an analysis of American Indian languages seems to point to at least two, and possibly three, distinct migrations; and further, in 1984 an urban settlement was discovered in southern Chile, on the southernmost tip of South America, dating back about 11,000 years. In this view, the Clovis tool horizon represents the diffusion of a new tool from one already established group to another. It may have been invented in the Americas, or it may have been brought in by a late-arriving Siberian "second wave" migration. Although pre-Clovis finds remain controversial, we believe that, eventually, this latter view of the population of the New World will prove true. But the data are here in Patrusky's article for you to evaluate and decide for yourself.

The invention of agriculture was the first salvo in a triple revolution that forever changed the lives of human beings on this planet. Where and when was agriculture first invented? Until the 1980s, we thought we could answer this question with confidence. But recent discoveries have challenged many of our notions about the origin of agriculture. People living in widely scattered parts of the world—from southern Europe to western Egypt to the Nile Valley to Kenya—may well have domesticated some plants and animals as early as 19,000 years ago, 8,000 years before domestication began in Mesopotamia. But these early experiences in domestication did not lead to the second and third great revolutions in human cultural evolution—the emergence of cities and the rise of civilization.

In "The Origin of Agriculture," Charles B. Heiser discusses the events leading to the beginnings of plant and animal domestication in the Far East, the Middle East, and the Americas, and the profound consequences that resulted from this radical change in human life-style.

What are some of the unintended consequences of agriculture that have become a part of human destiny? For one thing, agriculture permanently altered the natural environment. Many species of wild plants and animals failed to survive the pressures farmers exerted on the environment in order to create conditions that promoted favored species. Then, agriculture also damaged the land, depleting it of nutrients and (paradoxically) creating conditions that promoted the predominance of weeds. Irrigation, the most productive form of farming, caused people to crowd together and farm more limited lands while rats bred and thrived in the canals and ditches.

The concentration of farming populations into smaller land areas meant that groups of people could seize control of the land and thereby exert political control over large masses. Thus, in some regions, the *state* emerged as a new sociopolitical form. (However, the state also arose in some nonagricultural populations, as well.)

A popular misconception is that agriculture was in-vented to relieve people from the unending drudgery and insecurities embodied in the previous, hunting and food-gathering subsistence strategy. This is far from true. Recent research by Richard B. Lee, Marvin Harris, and others shows that agriculture requires more intensive and enduring labor than does hunting and food-gathering (see articles 27, 30, and 31). The enormous increase of agriculturally created food surpluses has never been used to reduce the amount of time or energy expended in work, but rather it has been utilized again and again to enable ever larger numbers of people to live crowded into increasingly complex social groupings.

Thus, the emergence of agriculture underlies another immensely significant, rather recent, human sociocultural invention: the city. "How Were Cities Invented?" asks John Pfeiffer—and in doing so he also totes up the pros and cons of urban life. Most of us take cities for granted, but archaeology reveals how profoundly city dwelling has changed human existence in the last seven to eight thousand years. Thus, it can't be denied that some of the most spectacular achievements in philosophy, mathematics, the natural sciences, technology, the arts, and literature were rooted in the urban way of life. In fact, most specialists refined their crafts and arts as city dwellers. But on the other side, cities also created the conditions of poverty by piling on top of each other landless, unskilled, and often unemployed workers and their families. Garbage and waste disposal poses health problems in cities, and epidemic diseases in cities become extremely difficult to control. So the city, a hallmark of our civilization, is a problematic development at best—and archaeology has much to tell us of its origins, development, and possibilities.

12

The First Americans:
Who Were They and When Did They Arrive?

BY BEN PATRUSKY

. . . .

No serious archaeologist argues about the origins of the first human inhabitants of the Western Hemisphere or about how they arrived. These paleo-Indians strode—or drifted—in, from what is now Siberia across the Bering Strait, over a land bridge that joined the Old World to the New during the last great ice age. They came as big-game hunters on the trail of moving herds of giant elephants and other megafauna of the Pleistocene epoch. They were first occupants of Beringia—a continent-sized landmass linking Asia and North America—which lured them as it lured their game. Then shifting needs and opportunities propelled them farther east and south.

Not much of this is in question. But one big question remains: When did they come; how early were early humans in the New World? Since the early days of the 20th century, New World archaeologists have been debating the issue—often heatedly. Timetables abound. Robert L. Humphrey of George Washington University has dubbed the ongoing controversy "The Hollywood Complex, or my early man site is earlier than your early man site."

The heat of the debate doesn't surprise Dennis Stanford, director of paleo-Indian archaeology at the Smithsonian Institution. "People digging at the roots of America's ancestry tend to be highly messianic," he explains. "They've invested time, money, thought and often reputation. Sure they want their labors and finds to prove significant. Sometimes they're not very careful about interpreting their results."

The debate about humankind's dawning in the New World is far from settled. But in recent years highly trained archaeologists have begun to accumulate impressive bits of evidence that suggest migrations at a time much farther back than might have been accepted only a few years ago. Some human occupancy as much as 20,000 or 25,000 years ago is beginning to look, if not feasible, at least arguable. Dates much older than that, however, while postulated, still strike more heat than light from among the disputants. At the present stage of knowledge and of dating technology, there is slim chance for the dispute over Western humankind's antiquity soon to be settled. But a critical look at the evidence and the inferences to be drawn from it can be highly suggestive.

Clovis and before

The pivotal point of the debate is on the order of 12,000 years ago—or 12,000 BP, for "before the present," in the parlance of the professionals. That represents the earliest totally accepted date for human appearance in the New World.

Evidence of human presence then is incontrovertible. It takes the form of a special kind of artifact: a man-made tool, a projectile point with a highly distinctive shape, a manufactured weapon for killing mammoths and other big game. The points are bifacially fluted; longitudinal flakes have been chipped from the base on both sides to form grooves. With fluting, the point could be attached to a wooden shaft for use as a spear or dart. These fluted points have been found at sites ranging from the Pacific coast to the Atlantic coast of North America and from Alaska to central Mexico. In the sites where carbon 14 dating is unequivocal, all the projectile points have been found to date within a very narrow window of time—11,500 to 11,000 BP.

Because the points were first found in abundance in a locale called Clovis in Blackwater Draw, New Mexico, the points have been designated Clovis points—and their manufacturers the Clovis Culture. The Clovis Culture is also often referred to by another name: the Llano Complex, for the Llano High Plains region of the Southwest. The designation embraces not just the fluted projectile points but the entire bone and stone "tool kit" associated with them.

But were the bearers of the Clovis Culture the first inhabitants of the New World? Or were there earlier bands of migrant-hunters whose groping cultural evolution ultimately gave rise to the technologically advanced Clovis? That question is at the heart of the peopling of America debate.

That the Clovis people were the very first Americans is a position promulgated by Paul S. Martin of the University of Arizona. He has introduced the "overkill theory" to support his arguments. Martin contends that the Clovis people, already skilled big-game hunters, swept into the Americas from Alaska in a single, rapid migration about 12,000 years ago. There they encountered a hunter's paradise: a land teeming with mastodons and mammoths, sloths, giant cats, horses, camels and bison. The archaeological record shows that many of these species became extinct coincidentally with the advent of Clovis. Clovis, according to Martin, cut a rapacious swath through the hemisphere, exterminating these Ice Age mammals.

Other New World archaeologists contest the overkill hypothesis. In their view dramatic changes in climate and vegetation, in the wake of a significant glacial retreat, were the agents of extinction. More to the point, a number of these investigators are convinced that humans trod the soil of the New World far in advance of Clovis's distinctive appearance. Says Richard S. MacNeish, director of the Robert S. Peabody Foundation for Archeology: "There can be little doubt that man was here well before 12,000 years ago, as we have about 30 sites with more than 2,000 recognizable artifacts and with more than 60 radiocarbon determinations before 10,000 B.C.E. (Before the Common Era)." How much earlier than 12,000 years ago? MacNeish suggests that humans "may have first crossed the Bering Strait land bridge into the Western Hemisphere between 40,000 and 100,000 years ago."

Reprinted from MOSAIC, National Science Foundation, September/October 1980. The original title was "Pre-Clovis Man: Sampling the Evidence."

The pre-Llano vista

One of the most prominent figures in the controversy over New World habitation is anthropologist and geoscientist Vance Haynes, also of the University of Arizona. To Haynes, a self-styled "archaeological conservative" who has been stalking Clovis for more than two decades, has been delegated the *ad hoc* role of both arbiter and devil's advocate in the assessing and validating of evidence presumptive of prehistoric migrations into the New World. Haynes's judgment: "There is no one place where the evidence (for pre-Llano cultures) is so compelling that if you looked at it in a court of law you would want to be tried on the basis of that evidence."

The evidence to date for a pre-Llano presence in the New World is not yet "airtight," admits the Smithsonian's Dennis Stanford. "But some of what we do have looks really good and very compelling and can't be lightly dismissed."

Some of the key pieces of evidence of the existence of a pre-Llano people include:

• **Pikimachay Cave in Highland Peru,** where MacNeish has uncovered artifacts he insists date back as much as 21,000 to 25,000 years. "My excavations of Pikimachay Cave have proved to me that pre-10,000 B.C.E. and pre-20,000 B.C.E. remains of man do exist," he says unequivocally.

MacNeish discovered the cave in 1967. It is a huge rock shelter, 85 meters long and 25 meters deep, situated halfway up a hill stepped by ancient terraces. Meticulous excavation has revealed sequential strata of habitation, "a series of floors on which man had clearly lived," declares MacNeish. A roof-fall that occurred about 9,000 years ago securely sealed off the lower, earlier deposits from any

possible intrusion or artifact contamination from strata lying above and representing a later chronology.

Beneath this rocky lid lie seven strata, showing evidence of a number of occupations by man back as far as 25,000 years. Using carbon-14 dating, University of California at Los Angeles scientists assigned BP time slots of 19,660 ± 3,000; 16,050 ± 1,200; 14,700 ± 1,400, and 14,150 ± 180 to the upper four strata, respectively, though the lowest has not been so dated. The antiquity of the earliest dated level, MacNeish reports, is confirmed by an independent analysis by Isotopes, Inc., which reported an age for that stratum of 20,200 ± 1,000.

All told, says MacNeish, almost 300 "indisputable" artifacts were unearthed in association with more than 800 bones of sloths and other extinct Ice Age mammals. Perhaps the best evidence was turned up at the upper level, dated at 14,150 BP, which was found to contain 133 artifacts, including stone projectile points and scrapers. Many of the recovered artifacts are very crude, says MacNeish, and a far cry from the sophistication of Clovis, suggesting that they were the tools of unspecialized hunters and gatherers.

• **Valsequillo Basin, Puebla, Mexico,** where in the early 1960s investigators stumbled upon a trove of extinct-animal bones as well as some crude stone artifacts along a dry river bed. Subsequent stratum-by-stratum excavation turned up an ever receding chronology of hunters slaughtering Ice Age animals. At about 30 meters down, at a level dated by carbon-14 at 22,000 years, archaeologist Cynthia Irwin Williams found evidence of a mastodon dismemberment by ancient butchers.

• **Tlapacoya, Valley of Mexico, near Valsequillo,** where Mexican investigators Jose Lorenzo and Lorena Mirambell found bones in association with a shallow depression containing charcoal that yielded a carbon-14 date of 24,000 BP (give or take 4,000 years) and presumed to be the remains of an ancient hearth. Moreover, the investigators uncovered some obsidian artifacts, including a curved blade found buried under a large tree trunk, that gave the same 24,000 BP date.

• **Del Mar in Southern California.** A group of 11 human skeletons has been found along the California coast and dated by Jeffrey Bada of the University of California at San Diego, using a technique called amino acid racemization. It is based on the assumption that amino acids in protein undergo a configurational change—from the so-called L or left-handed sort to the D or right-handed kind—as bone fossilizes, and that this switching goes on at a measurable, clocklike rate until the sample reaches half-and-half equilibrium. The oldest date determined on a skull found at Del Mar gave a racemization number of 48,000 BP. Two other samples—dated at 23,000 and 17,150 BP—have been confirmed by radiocarbon dating on bone collagen performed by the University of California at Los Angeles' Rainer Berger.

• **Santa Rosa, California,** an island 25 miles off the coast of Santa Barbara, where Berger and Phillip Orr, curator of the Santa Barbara Museum, discovered a red burn area about three meters in diameter in association with stone tools and the bones of dwarf mammoths. The supposition: that the burn area actually had served as a hearth where paleo-Indians cooked the horse-sized mammoths as far back as 40,000 years ago. Carbon-14 dates derived from bits of charcoal found in the firepit suggest the age. According to Berger, during the late Pleistocene (100,000–10,000 years ago) Santa Rosa and three other nearby islands may have formed a single landmass that was joined to the mainland via a narrow neck of land across which foraging dwarf mammoths and their human predators could readily wander.

• **Meadowcroft Rockshelter, Pennsylvania.** On a sandstone outcrop 65 kilometers southwest of Pittsburgh, James M. Adovasio of the University of Pittsburgh has unearthed an assemblage of unifacial tools associated with radiocarbon ages of 13,250, 14,850 and 15,120 years. One especially significant find was a bifacial projectile point—"like a fluted point except that it has no fluting"—that dates earlier than the Clovis point and may be ancestral to it. (A detailed discussion of

Peruvian cave. Excavations of Pikimachay Cave in Peru offer evidence that humans were in the Western Hemisphere before 20,000 B.C.E.

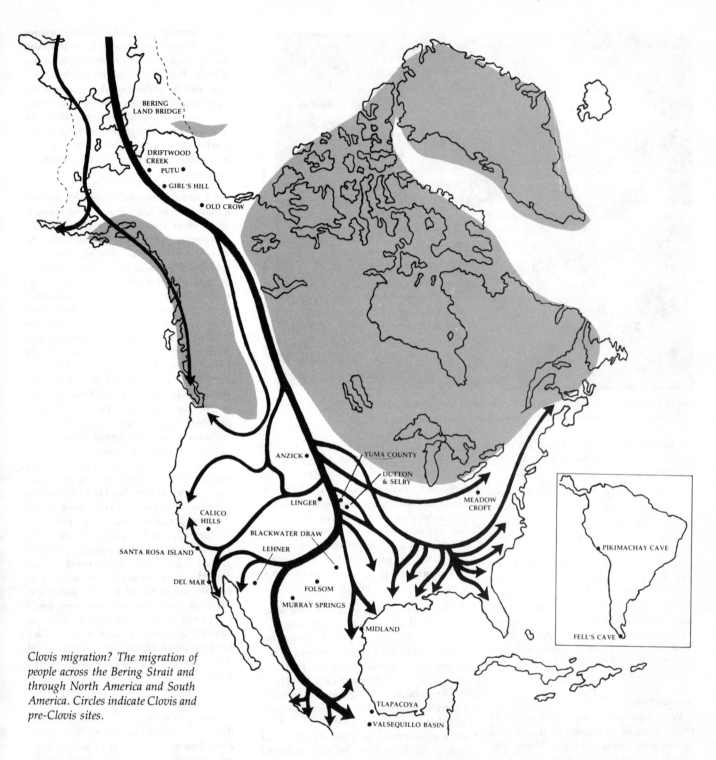

Clovis migration? The migration of people across the Bering Strait and through North America and South America. Circles indicate Clovis and pre-Clovis sites.

paleo-Indian sites in Pennsylvania and Virginia appeared in *Mosaic*, Volume 8, Number 2.)

• **The Selby and Dutton sites in eastern Colorado.** In 1975 pond-dredging crews on farms near Wray, Colorado, unearthed two Pleistocene fossil sites. Alerted to the discovery, a Smithsonian Institution archaeological team that happened to be working nearby raced to the scene. In

subsequent (and as yet far from complete) excavations, under the direction of Dennis Stanford, the team initially discovered fluted projectile points and other manifestations of Clovis. Digging deeper, they found evidence of the presence of earlier cultures that included what are called bone expediency tools. These are manufactured by producing a spiral fracture in bone and using the sharp edges for butchering or hide-working. Bone

flakes presumably the waste or debitage from tool production, and bone, apparently processed for the removal of marrow, were also found. The tools, made from the bones of Ice Age horse, bison, mammoth and camel, were found in "chronologically secure" layers extending back a possible 20,000 years. What makes the site especially exciting, according to Robert L. Humphrey, is that it "reveals the only evidence to date of an archaeological

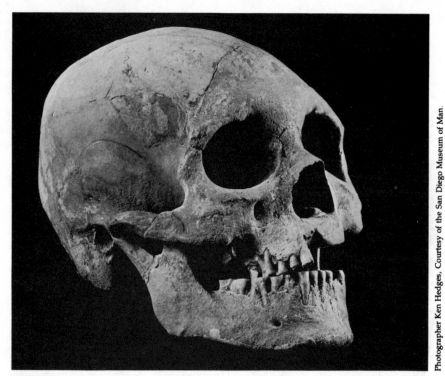

Photographer Ken Hedges, Courtesy of the San Diego Museum of Man.

Ancestral skull? This paleo-Indian skull was dated at nearly 50,000 years old through a still-controversial amino-acid dating process developed by Jeffrey L. Bada.

culture stratigraphically *in situ* below a level containing Clovis fluted points and other manifestations of the Llano Complex."

• **Old Crow Basin, Yukon Territory,** where in 1966 was discovered a caribou leg bone that had clearly been worked by human hands to produce a tool called a flesher—a back-scratcher-like implement used to scrape animal hides. William Irving of the University of Toronto and Richard Morlan of the National Museum of Man, in Ottawa, who now direct major archaeological research projects in the basin, established a carbon-14 date for the flesher of 27,000 BP. Since then, other worked-bone specimens have been found and dated as far back as 41,000 years.

Not foolproof

What says Clovis specialist Haynes to all this? "Tantalizing but not foolproof. . . .I am a skeptic. I remain a skeptic. I have yet to see *unequivocal* evidence of pre-Clovis. Each (site) has some kind of uncertainty connected with it." On his list of "uncertainties," Haynes includes:

• **Skepticism about radiocarbon dates.** Samples may become contaminated by groundwater, he says, and throw the true carbon-14 date off accordingly. Case in point: the Meadowcroft site. It is possible, he says, that rainwater could have brought in dissolved

carbon from nearby coal deposits, thus disturbing the precision of the radiocarbon date. Haynes isn't saying that is what happened. "It's just that we can't be sure it didn't happen." Haynes also expresses doubts about "one of the best pieces of evidence around for a pre-Clovis presence in the New World," the Old Crow flesher. "There's no way to say for sure that the bone was not pulled out of the ground and worked over at a much later date," he says.

• **Suspicion about amino acid racemization.** In a thorough review of this dating technique, David von Endt, a research chemist at the Smithsonian Institution, writing in a monograph on pre-Llano cultures published in 1979 by the Anthropological Society of Washington, D.C., concludes: "I view no projected amino acid date as reliable." Reason: The rate of turnover from *L*- to *D*-form amino acids depends on a mix of complicated factors that have yet to be fully reckoned into the racemization clock.

• **Uncertain primary or cultural context.** "The primary requirement," says Haynes, "is. . .an assemblage of artifacts that are clearly the work of man. Next, this evidence must lie *in situ* within undisturbed geological deposits. . . .Lastly, the minimum age of the site must be demonstrable by primary association with fossils of known age or

with material suitable for reliable isotopic dating. These requirements have now been met repeatedly for the late paleo-Indian period (Clovis) but they have not yet been met repeatedly for earlier periods." Example: the "questionable" primary context of the Santa Rosa firepit. Haynes wonders whether this so-called hearth may not actually be the product of a natural brush fire—not an uncommon phenomenon on this chaparral-dense island.

• **Artifact versus geofact, or when is a tool a tool?** Haynes talks about a "bandwagon effect, where some archaeologists see artifacts everywhere they look." In many cases, he says, the artifacts are nothing more than geofacts or ecofacts, pseudotools produced by agents other than human. "I think if we were to dig anywhere there are Pleistocene, coarse-grained sediments or bones," says Haynes, "(we) would find something that could be interpreted as artifact. In other words, there is a sort of 'background noise' in the buried record of things that can be taken as artifacts." Case in point: Calico Hills in the Mojave Desert, near Yermo, California, where in 1968 archaeologists spotted what they proposed to be crude, very ancient flint artifacts in a massive deposit of alluvial gravels of Pleistocene age. The investigators contend that some of the stone specimens show flaking marks that could have resulted only from human intervention. But Haynes, who has examined the site and specimens on six different occasions, reads the "evidence" another way. As he puts it: "Evidence for artifacts remains uncompelling. . .(and) a natural origin cannot be precluded. In fact, normal natural processes are adequate to explain the origin of all the phenomena observed. Even the best specimens could have been chipped and flaked naturally, especially in view of the fact that each 'artifact' has been selected from literally hundreds of thousands of individual pieces of chert." Similarly, two criteria seem to distinguish bone artifacts: evidence of a spiral fracture (a fundamental step in tool production or marrow processing) and of polishing (in-dicative of tool use). But other forces, agents other than man, can break or polish bone—e.g., trampling and gnawing by other animals.

• **Absence of stone artifacts.** Thus far Old Crow and the Selby/Dutton sites (at strata below Clovis) have yielded only bone artifacts. No stone tools are in evidence and, according to Haynes, "you can't produce flake scars by hitting bone against bone. Further, there's little to support the validity of an all-bone culture. If there were stone tools at Dutton or Old Crow, where are they?'' Haynes remains skeptical about the seven tiny stone ''impact flakes'' suggestive of human origin turned up by Stanford's team at Dutton and described as tailings produced as a result of impact from a chopping tool.

Counterarguments

Needless to say, Haynes's arguments breed counterarguments among those convinced of a significant pre-Llano presence. Old Crow archaeologist William Irving, for example, suggests that stone tools may not be all that essential to the support of human life. In fact, he contends, bones that could have performed all the necessary tasks of hunting, piercing, butchering, skinning and perforating have been recovered from deposits at Old Crow and elsewhere. Two years ago, Dennis Stanford gave a dramatic demonstration of bone's versatility. Using only bone tools, Stanford showed how it was possible to butcher and process the remains of an elephant, operating on one that had died of natural causes at a Boston zoo.

As for the artifact versus geofact issue, Stanford readily concedes that archaeologists may be led astray by wishful thinking— ''seeing what they want to see.'' But, he points out, with bone, for instance, there are criteria to help the investigator with a trained eye to distinguish between tool and pseudo-tool. For example: With tools, only the ends—the working parts—tend to become polished and worn. This discriminatory polishing doesn't often happen in nature, unless only the ends have been gnawed. But then there would generally be tooth marks to help make the distinction.

Also, bones that exhibit spiral fracture by other-than-human cause are often those broken after the bone had dried or as a result of the animal's falling or twisting its leg. In both cases these bones are not likely to exhibit impact depressions suggestive of human workmanship. Moreover, says Stanford, at the Selby and Dutton sites most of the bone-artifact specimens were broken the same way; they show single and multiple points of impact located in the same area of the bone. ''These suggest a pattern that cannot be attributed to the random breakage patterns expected if the bones were either broken or polished due to natural conditions,'' he says.

In an effort to eliminate all doubt about bone-artifact authenticity, Stanford has been overseeing a number of experimental studies aimed at producing hard, quantifiable data on bone fracturing, modification and use. From his elephant-butchering trials, for instance, he has developed information regarding tool-wear patterns. Another study

Clovis tools. These Clovis fluted points are from the Naco Mammoth site in Arizona, contemporary with the Clovis site.

has Gary Haynes, a doctoral student, feeding buffalo and horse bones to bears in the National Zoological Park in Washington, D.C., to see just how the animals break and gnaw bones. Haynes is also observing how the bones of wood bison, newly killed by wild wolves in Canada, are altered by the natural environment. In an applied offshoot, Stanford is consulting with veterinarians who are analyzing bone breaks in race horses. Are the breaks natural, or did someone break a horse's leg intentionally? The ability to discriminate has relevance for insurance companies as well as archaeologists. Stanford is hopeful that he will soon get permission to put elephant bones around a pond at the National Zoo's Conservation and Research Center near Front Royal, Virginia, to see if and how other free-to-roam animals treat the specimens.

Meanwhile, at Santa Rosa Island, museum curator Phillip Orr has built model pit barbecues to help determine whether the red-char area he and Rainer Berger discovered actually served the earliest immigrants as a hearth or whether, in fact, it was the result of a natural brush fire. His experiments produced the same kind of deep-soil burning (to a depth of about 80 centimeters) as seen in the purported pre-Llano firepit, but different from the burn pattern of a natural chaparral fire.

Whither Clovis

When Haynes, eminently known for his ''insistence on methodological exactitude,'' drops his devil's-advocate mask, he readily professes a belief in a human presence that

may far antedate Clovis, a presence he believes will become demonstrable and unquestionable in time. In fact, he now seems near-convinced about the validity of MacNeish's Pikimachay Cave finds—specifically those from the 14,150 BP level. The Valsequillo deposits, dating from 9,000 to 21,000 years ago, also enthrall him (although the picture there remains clouded by another kind of uncertainty: unsubstantiated charges that workmen may have deliberately planted some of the would-be artifacts).

But far from quashing the debate, the strong indications of a pre-Llano presence have introduced a major new wrinkle to the controversy, having to do with the origins of the Clovis Culture. Is it, as Martin, Vance Haynes and others contend, an import by a technologically advanced people who brought their Upper Paleolithic wisdom with them from Siberia? Or is it, as MacNeish, Stanford and other pre-Llano advocates maintain, a homegrown product—an evolutionary outgrowth of already-in-place, pre-Clovis cultures? Asked another way: Is the Clovis point, that superior paleo-Indian invention that allowed Llano hunters to take full advantage of the megafauna-rich Pleistocene environment of the New World, a candidate for the first truly American patent?

In Haynes's view, even if pre-Llano hunting cultures entered the Americas more than 30,000 years ago, they did not develop into technologically skilled artisans anywhere near the caliber of Clovis. As he sees it, Clovis represents an entirely independent migratory swarm, a late-glacial sweep distinct from earlier, ''inconclusive'' movements into the

New World. "It now appears," says Haynes, "that the *main* peopling of the New World took place during deglaciation, when something akin to a population explosion occurred between 11,000 and 11,500 years ago by mammoth hunters entering from Alaska and finding abundant and untapped resources."

Haynes offers up this scenario: During the peak of the most recent glacial epoch—anywhere from 14,000 to 20,000 years ago, he says—a large portion of the earth's ocean water was stored in Northern Hemisphere ice sheets, causing the sea level to drop by scores of meters. What emerged was the 1,600-kilometer-wide Bering land platform, which made Alaska as much a part of the Asian continent as the North American and which allowed for easy migration from Old World to New.

The bridge, however, was not a thoroughfare from the Old world to the *whole* of the New; two great icecaps—the Cordilleran on the west, and the Laurentide on the east—covered much of Canada and much of the United States. Joining as they did at the foot of the Canadian Rockies, the giant glaciers created an ice barrier, a wall to southerly migration.

The hunters remained mired in an Alaskan cul-de-sac until about 12,000 years ago, when a period of marked glacial retreat opened a north-south corridor between the two icecaps. The progenitors of Clovis, confined until then in central Alaska, swept south in pursuit of the mammoth and other quarry. Once through, they dispersed rapidly across all of North America and into Mexico. All Clovis dates bear this out; from east to west, north to south, the Clovis artifacts fall within that 11,000-11,500 BP slot. Nor did expansion—or technological innovation—cease. For the Clovis point gave rise to an even sleeker, more advanced projectile point, dubbed the Folsom point, after Folsom, New Mexico, where a specimen was first uncovered in association with the skeletons of extinct bison. Similar fishtail stone points have been found as far as the southernmost tip of South America—Fell's Cave in Tierra del Fuego—and dated at about 10,000 BP.

Pleistocene extinctions

The transition from the use of Clovis to Folsom points approximately 11,000 years ago coincides with the extinction of Pleistocene mammoths, horses, camels and several other varieties of megafauna—which prompted Haynes's colleague, Paul Martin, to formulate the "overkill theory," ascribing extinction to the Llano influx and insisting that they were the first inhabitants of the Americas.

Proponents of the idea of a substantial pre-Llano presence take issue with these speculations. For one, they assail the proposition that megafauna extermination stemmed directly from an invasion of Clovis. More to blame, they say, were drastic changes in climate. With deglaciation, the desert moved north, wiping out huge areas of grassland once used for foraging. They cite the work of Russell Graham of the Illinois State Museum who, having recently completed a comprehensive examination of Pleistocene fauna, concludes: "Man's pernicious effect on the modern environment is not necessarily indicative of his impact on ancient environments. . . . Undoubtedly man's predation had an effect on the megafauna, but climatic changes are the best explanation for Pleistocene extinction." Opponents of "overkill" also wonder how it is that one of the most heavily hunted of the species, a variety of bison, is still with us, while hundreds of other animal species that Clovis and Folsom did not hunt perished. Says Dennis Stanford: "Throughout life's entire history animals have gone extinct—in most cases without any help from man."

Pre-Llano proponents also have trouble accepting the presumption of Clovis's lightning-like sweep through the hemisphere. Says Stanford: "I find it impossible to accept this idea of rapid migration. Primitive cultures tend to be conservative, hunters who explore, retreat, explore, retreat. As they move from environment to environment, they must learn to adapt, and that doesn't happen overnight." MacNeish has similar reservations: "A group of primitive people traveling into completely unknown territory would have frequently taken the wrong direction, and the group would have always been saddled with household equipment and baggage, babies, pregnant women and hobbling elders."

MacNeish proposes yet another sort of paleo-Indian-advance theory—small-group filtering or, more colloquially, the "hurry-up-and-wait" process: A band of migrants might be especially adapted for subsistence in broad ecological zones, he says, "and within these zones they would be able to move rapidly, but movement from one zone to the other would require that they build up a whole new subsistence complex; that would take considerable time. The hypothesis that Clovis and Folsom moved through dozens of radically different environmental zones from the Bering Strait to Tierra del Fuego in a thousand years thus seems unreasonable."

As such, the pre-Llano advocates suggest that Clovis, with his advanced tool kit, developed from an indigenous population in the Americas before 11,500 years ago. "It wasn't the people that swept through America," says Stanford, "but the (technology) that diffused rapidly through already existent populations—much as the idea of tobacco use traveled from the United States through Europe to the Eskimos all in a matter of a few years."

The Siberian connection

But if paleo-Indians did indeed poke their way into the Americas long before the emergence of the Clovis Culture, who were these migrants and how did they get here, considering that a severe ice age was upon the land? Stanford: "Soviet archaeologists have found evidence that man inhabited Siberia certainly 35,000 years ago and perhaps as early as 70,000 years ago. The discovery of early occupations of Siberia greatly increases the time available for man to come across the Bering land bridge."

Moreover, he says, there is now reason to belive that the ice-free corridor from Alaska to North America was open for movement south for much longer periods than previously supposed. "In fact," says Stanford, "it may have been closed for only a short time during the whole (Ice Age) period. So it would have been possible for early hunters. . .to have entered North America long before 12,000 years ago and to have moved southward, continuing to exploit grassland environments." Further, he says, there is now even a slim possibility that an "alternative route" to the interior corridor may have been available—an ocean-side roadway that trailed down along the emerged Pacific coast.

Haynes has strong objections to this idea of a coastal route. "Even if there were such a route between the glacial ice and the ocean," he says, "it would have been an incredibly treacherous environment to negotiate. Under the prevailing circumstances it's hard to imagine people moving down the coast even in boats."

By the same token, Haynes has no problem in living with the notion of Clovis's rapid migration. As he explains: "The phenomenal dispersal of Clovis sites is more compatible with a distinct migration, related to a relatively rapid, natural event—the separation of the ice sheets to form a trans-Canadian passage—than with a sudden outgrowth from meager, indigenous cultures after 12,000 years of sluggish development for which a continuity has yet to be demonstrated."

Native technology

And how does Haynes respond to the contention that Clovis's technological know-how was born in the Americas, a product of progress in home-grown artisanship and not an import? "I do not see anything that is on a developmental sequence leading to Clovis," he says. "What you see is technology akin to Eurasia, to mammoth hunters of the Old World." He sees likenesses in the tool kits of Clovis and Old World hunters, including bifacial stone scrapers, burins (chisel-like implements), flakeknives, a bone technology of bevel-based, cylindrical points and foreshafts, shaft wrenches and the use of red ocher with burials. "The similarities are unmistakable," he says, "and to invoke independent development of all these traits in the New World from a population base for which there is only tenuous evidence does not seem reasonable as does an origin from the Siberian Paleolithic."

Conpicuously absent from the Old World tool kit, however, is the centerpiece of the Clovis Culture: the fluted projectile point. This absence is probably the key piece of evidence against those who propose an Old World origin and rapid dispersal for Clovis. Haynes, in response, explains that the development of fluted, bifacial projectile points could have taken place in Alaska or along the ice-free corridor between 14,000 and 12,000 years ago. But if so, goes the counterargument, why is there no good evidence of Clovis points in this initial New World dwelling place as is the case elsewhere in the hemisphere?

The fact is, a few fluted points *have* been found in the Far North in recent years. However, one Alaskan find, said to date from the post-Clovis period, about 9,000 years ago, is held up as evidence that Clovis developed out of an already-extant American paleo-Indian culture, and that this new technology traveled not from north to south but from south to north, representing a cultural backwash. But two other fluted points, from the Putu site in the Brooks Range, have been related to a charcoal date of 11,500 years ago. "If this date is valid," says Haynes, "it makes at least two Alaskan fluted points as old as the oldest fluted points from interior North America."

Ultimately, settlement of the controversy over the early peopling of America will likely come only with the discovery of new archaeological sites. If, for the sake of argument, a site with a Clovis point were to be found in Central America, bearing a date beyond 14,000 years ago, that would all but demolish the Clovis fast-migration theory. One the other hand, one in Alaska more than 14,000 years old would help support it. But when and where new sites will turn up remains unpredictable. "Most early man sites, probably 99 percent of them, tend to be destroyed by climate almost immediately or by subsequent geologic processes," says Stanford. "When we find one, we're usually dealing with a geological freak."

On balance then: The evidence, if not altogether conclusive, certainly strongly suggests that the New World was visited and settled by migrant hunting bands from the Old World in the shadowy recesses of time back far beyond 12,000 years ago. But it remains to be determined whether the Llano Complex developed from a local, as-yet-undiscovered, indigenous progenitor or whether it originated in the Old World and spread by way of rapid dispersal. At the moment, both positions seem equally defensible. Perhaps the wisest counsel for now is for New World archaeologists to wait and see—to postpone final judgment until new, clarifying evidence comes to light. In Haynes's words: "I think that if pre-Clovis man was really here, good evidence will be found. The important thing is not to rush into it.... What we are actually looking for is what really happened, not what we think happened."

13

The Origin of Agriculture

BY CHARLES B. HEISER, JR.

. . . .

In the sweat of thy face thou shalt eat bread.

Genesis 3:19

People have been on earth for some two million years. Except for a minute fraction of that time, they have been hunters of animals and gatherers of plants, strictly dependent upon nature for their food. They must, at many times during their long history as hunter-gatherers, have enjoyed full stomachs, when vegetable foods were abundant or ample game was available. Early humans certainly must have experimented with nearly all of the plant resources, thus becoming experts on which ones were good to eat. They became excellent hunters and fishermen. Contrary to earlier opinion, recent studies suggest that they didn't always have to search continually just to find enough to eat and, at times, must have had considerable leisure.

There undoubtedly were times and places, however, in which people did have to spend most of their waking hours searching for food, and hunger probably was common throughout much of the preagricultural period. Certainly there could never have been much of an opportunity for large populations to have built up, even among the successful hunter-gatherers. People probably lived in small groups, for with few exceptions a given area would provide enough food for only a few. Disease and malnutrition probably contributed to keeping populations small, and it is likely that there were also some sorts of intentional population control, such as infanticide.

Then, about 10,000 years ago, food-producing habits began to change, and in the course of time our ancestors became food producers rather than hunter-gatherers. At first they had to supplement the food they produced with food they obtained by hunting and gathering, but gradually they became less dependent on wild food sources as their domesticated plants and animals were increased in number and improved. The cultivation of plants and the keeping of animals probably required no less effort than did hunting and gathering, but in time they gave a more dependable source of food. Having a dependable food source made it possible for larger numbers of people to live together. More mouths to feed were no longer disastrous, but rather were advantageous, for with more bodies to till and reap, food could be produced more efficiently. Although some urban centers may have developed before agriculture, food production was probably the chief stimulus for the growth of villages and eventually of cities, and with the latter came civilization.

When food production became more efficient, there was time to develop the arts and sciences. Some hunter-gathers, as was already pointed out, must have had considerable leisure, but they never made any notable advances toward civilization. An important difference between hunter-gatherers and farmers is that the former are usually nomadic whereas the latter are sedentary. But even those preagricultural people, such as certain fisherman, who had fairly stationary living sites did not develop in civilizing ways comparable to those of farmers. Agriculture probably required a far greater discipline than did any form of food collecting. Seeds had to be planted at certain seasons, some protection had to be given to the growing plants and animals, harvests had to be reaped, stored, and divided. Thus, we might argue that it was neither leisure time nor a sendentary existence but the more rigorous demands associated with an agricultural way of life that led to great cultural changes. It has been suggested, for example, that writing may have come into existence because records were needed by agricultural administrators. Plants and animals were being changed to suit needs; living in a new relation with plants and animals was, in turn, changing the way of life.

In recent years archaeological work has greatly increased our knowledge of the beginnings of agriculture, and without doubt future archaeological work will add a great deal more information. In contrast to previous generations of archaeologists who were mostly concerned with spectacular finds—tombs, and temples, the contents of which would make showy museum exhibits—recent archaeologists have taken a greater interest in how people lived, what they ate, and how they managed their environment. A few charred seeds or broken bones may appear rather insignificant in a museum, but they can reveal a great deal about early human activities. As a result of recent work in archaeology, done in cooperation with scientists from many other fields, we are beginning to understand the ecology of prehistoric people in many different parts of the world.

Our knowledge of what humans ate and did thousands of years ago comes from the remains of plants and animals recovered from archaeological excavations. Unlike many tools, which were made of stone and are indestructible, foods are perishable and are preserved only where conditions are ideal. The best sites are in dry regions, often in caves, and from such sites we obtain remains to use in the reconstruction of our ancestors' diet. Other human artifacts, such as flint sickles and stone querns, or grinding wheels, may also provide clues about diet, but they leave us to speculate about what plants were being harvested and prepared, and whether these were wild or cultivated. Obviously, the record of what prehistoric people ate is very incomplete, and for many areas of the earth, significant remains have yet to be found.

Drawings of animals, particularly from the later prehistoric periods, have come down to us and sometimes (but not always, by any means) can be fairly readily identified, but it is animal bones, or even fragments of them, that provide the best clues about the animals that were closely connected with people. An expert zoologist can identify species from bones, but it is not always possible to say whether remains are from domestic or wild animals.

Plant remains comprise a variety of forms. Most are seeds or fruits, but other parts, such as flower bracts, stalks, and leaves are sometimes found. A few remarkably well-preserved seeds are recovered, looking as if they had been harvested only a year before, but most seeds are charred and broken. A skilled botanist can identify such plant remains, and it can often be determined if they are from domesticated or wild plants.

Another source of information about the ancient diet is coprolites—fossil feces. By suitable preparation they can be restored to an almost fresh condition (sometimes, it is said, including the odor). Whole seeds have been found in coprolites, but most of the food material is highly fragmented and requires lengthy, painstaking analysis for identification. Such analysis is highly significant because it tells us what was actually eaten, in what combinations, and whether it was cooked or raw.

Unfortunately, material collected at an archaeological dig is sometimes not accurately identified, as has been shown for some of the early archaeological reports from Peru. Fortunately, however, the material recovered from archaeological sites is usually preserved in museums, and future investigators can examine the material to verify or correct identifications.

With the development of radiocarbon methods of dating it became possible to date, fairly accurately, the beginnings of plant cultivation. Sometimes radiocarbon dates, for one reason or another, may be open to suspicion, but when different materials from the same site are analyzed and several dates agree, we have fair assurance that they are correct within a few hundred years.

The evidence that has accumulated over the past several years indicates that agriculture probably had its origins in the Near East*—although not necessarily, as earlier supposed, in the fertile river valleys of Mesopotamia (which were to be important centers of early civilization), but more likely in the semiarid mountainous areas nearby. Dates determined for flint sickles and grinding stones discovered in these areas indicate that before 8000 BC humans had likely become collectors of wild grain, and there is evidence that a thousand or so years later they were actually cultivating grains and keeping domesticated animals. Several sites are now known in the Near East (see Figure 1) that give evidence of early agriculture. One of the first sites to give such evidence was at Jarmo, in Iraq, where investigations were conducted under the direction of R. J. Braidwood. In deposits dated at 6750 BC, seeds of wheat and barley and bones of goats were found. Other evidence of cultivation, dating from approximately the same time, has been found at several other sites in the Near East. Since the plants in these sites apparently represent cultivated species, we must suppose that there was an earlier period of their incipient domestication, which may have lasted for a few hundred years or more. How long it takes a plant to become fully domesticated cannot be answered precisely and it probably varies considerably from species to species. In deposits accumulated after 6500 BC we find evidence of other plants being cultivated in the Near East and Greece, and bones of various domesticated animals become more abundant.

Other centers of agriculture developed in the Old World. Whether these developments were stimulated by knowledge of agriculture in the Near East or

---

*The *Near East* (see map, Figure 1) is the term used by archaeologists to refer to the countries of southwest Asia. The term *Middle East*, widely used in the news today, includes the Near East.

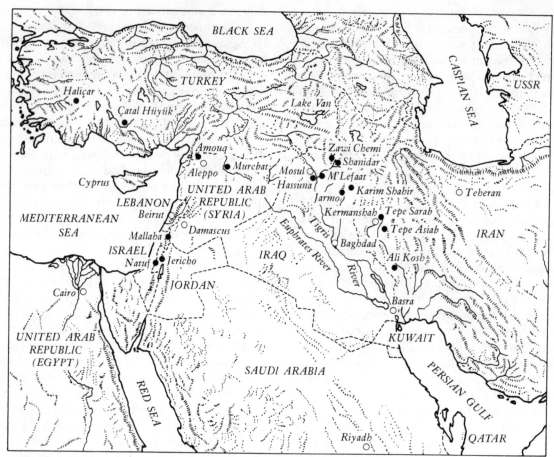

Figure 1   Selected archaeological sites that show evidence of early agriculture in the Near East (solid dots).

whether they were independent developments is not certain, but the fact that some of them were based on completely different plants from those of the Near East might support the latter view. For a long time southeastern Asia had been considered an ancient center for domesticated plants, but until recently there was no archaeological support for this view; this is not wholly unexpected, since the climate for the most part in that area of the world is hardly conducive to preservation of food remains. In 1969, however, a report was published of an assemblage of plants from Thailand, including possibly a pea and a bean, dated at 7000 BC. As it is not definitely clear whether the plants recovered represented wild or cultivated species, we cannot yet say that agriculture was practiced as early here as it was in the Near East. We do not yet know when rice, which was to become the basic food plant of southeastern Asia, was first brought under cultivation, but it was probably considerably later than the cereals of the Near East.

In the New World, agriculture began a few thousand years later than in the Near East and had its origins in Mexico and Peru. Through a series of ex-

cavations directed by R. S. MacNeish, we now have a remarkable sequence of plants giving evidence of the period of incipient domestication in Mexico. Some indication of the earliest cultivated plants is found in the mesquite-desert regions of southwestern Tamaulipas, with gourds, squashes, beans, and chili peppers being found at levels dated at between 7000 and 5500 BC.

Following investigations at Tamaulipas, MacNeish made deliberate efforts to search for evidence of the domestication of maize, which eventually became the most important plant in the Americas. A group of caves in the arid highlands near Tehuacan in south central Mexico showed promise, and a series of excavations was begun in 1961. The results give us the best picture yet of the transitional stages leading to full-scale agriculture. Humans were probably in the Tehuacan area by 10,000 BC and for several millennia they depended on wild food sources, both plant and animal. Gradually more and more plants were cultivated, some perhaps having been domesticated at this site, others introduced from other regions. The first suggestion of cultivated plants occurs in material dated at about 5000 BC, with maize, squash, chili pepper, avocado, and amaranth being found. These plants were definitely cultivated during the next period (4900–3500 BC), together with various fruits and beans toward the end of the period. During the next thousand years other plants were added, including cotton and two new kinds of beans. The dog, which is known from historic records to have been an important food item in Mexico, is first associated with humans in the archaeological record at this time. At about the beginning of the Christian era, the inhabitants of Tehuacan had also acquired the turkey. From remains of the same period there are reports of some other plants: guava, pineapple, and peanut. The presence of these plants would be of particular interest, for the peanut is definitely South American in origin and the pineapple and guava perhaps are also, which would suggest that the peoples of this area had contact with South America at this time. None of these plants has been found in any other archaeological sites in Mexico to date. A study of historical records of both peanuts and pineapple would suggest that they arrived in Mexico recently, perhaps after the coming of the Spanish.

Another early development of agriculture in the Americas occurred in Peru, perhaps even earlier than in Mexico. Two kinds of cultivated beans and a chili pepper, dated at around 6000 BC or earlier, have been recovered in a highland valley at Callejon de Huaylas in north central Peru. Previous to this discovery, archaeological plant material had been found in dry coastal sites, such as Huaca Prieta in northern Peru. Gourds, squashes, cotton, lima beans, and chili peppers are among the first plants cultivated on the coast; present evidence indicates that agriculture developed here about 2000 years later than in the highlands.

At present it is difficult to say whether agriculture in the Americas appeared first in Peru or Mexico. The fact that many of the same plants were cultivated in the two areas might suggest that agriculture spread from one of the areas to the other, but the chile peppers and the squashes of the two regions belong to different species, and it seems possible that the common bean was domesticated independently in Mexico and Peru. Thus, although the possibility remains that agriculture, or at least the idea of growing plants, diffused from one area to the other, it is just as likely that agriculture arose independently in Mexico and Peru. That there was diffusion between the two areas at a later time is clear because maize, which almost certainly had its origin in Mexico, appears in Peru by 2500–3000 BC and, as already mentioned, certain South American plants may have appeared in Mexico in pre-Columbian times.

From the foregoing account it can be seen that agriculture arose in widely separated parts of the earth, probably quite independently from place to place. But agriculture begin in the Old World more than a thousand years earlier than it did in the New—could the idea of agriculture have come to the New World from the Old? The New World was peopled by immigration across the Bering Strait long before agriculture was known, and if there were subsequent crossings at this place, it was by hunters rather than agriculturists. Thus, we would have to postulate a long ocean voyage at a very early date to account for agricultural knowledge being brought to the New World. Some anthropologists have postulated that there were such voyages in prehistoric times, but much later than the time at which agriculture was established in Mexico. Therefore, it seems highly unlikely that agriculture had but a single origin. It is, in fact, likely that it had several origins in both the Old and the New World, although some people still believe that it was invented only once.

An examination of the list of food plants from all the early sites in both the New and the Old World reveals that all of the plants were propagated by seed. A large number of present-day food plants, including such important ones as the white and the sweet potato, manioc, yams, bananas, and sugar cane are pro-

Figure 2 Selected New World archaeological sites that show evidence of early agriculture (solid dots).

pagated vegetatively—by stem cuttings, tubers, or roots—rather than from seed. Some people, notably the geographer Carl Sauer, have reasoned that cultivation of plants probably began with vegetative propagation, arguing that such cultivation is much simpler than seed planting. There is also some evidence from Old World mythology suggesting that vegetative cultivation is older than seed planting. The archaeological record, unfortunately, has not been able to provide us with clearcut answers, for many of the vegetatively cultivated plants are crops of the wet tropics, areas where the preservation of prehistoric food materials is rather unlikely. Moreover, even in dry areas, tubers and other fleshy plant parts are far less likely to be preserved than are relatively dry materials, such as seeds. While we cannot, perhaps, entirely rule out the possibility that agriculture based on vegetative propagation was earlier than seed-propagation agriculture, it seems fairly clear that it was seed planting that led to the most profound changes in our way of life. All the early high civilizations whose diets are known to us were based on seed-reproducing plants—wheat, maize, or rice—with or without accompanying animal husbandry.

Following the domestication of plants and animals, the next great advance in agriculture came with the control of water. Irrigation arose in the Near East around 5000 BC and in Mexico shortly after 1000 BC. With irrigation, considerably more food could be produced in many areas; as a result, a few people could produce enough food to feed a large population, permitting others to spend time in pursuit of the arts and crafts and of religion. Elaborate temples, many of them standing today, were constructed by early societies that had perfected methods of irrigating their crops and testify to the amount of human labor that was made available for other pursuits.

Another important development in Old World agriculture was the use of animals to prepare the fields for planting, which was never done in the New World in prehistoric times. Along with this difference there was a basic difference in planting techniques. In the Old World the cereals (wheat, for example) were planted by broadcasting handfuls of grain, whereas in the New World the grains of maize were planted individually.

With the domestication of plants and animals there should have been a dependable food supply and, so it might be thought, hunger should have disappeared from the earth. As any intelligent person is acutely aware, however, hunger is still very much with us today. Harmony with nature has yet to be established. With the advent of agriculture, humans began changing their environment drastically. Irrigation, which initially led to greater food production, eventually destroyed some of the most fertile areas. Without adequate drainage, irrigation leads to an accumulation of salts in the soil that few plants can tolerate. That this happened in prehistoric times in the Near East is evident from archaeological findings; for barley, which is more salt tolerant than wheat, replaced the latter plant in some regions after irrigation was developed. The use of animals to till the soil led to increased areas being planted, which in time must have been accompanied by increased soil erosion. Then, along with the plants and animals that people brought under their control came others that they did not want and could not control. Rusts, smuts, and weeds soon found cultivated plants and fields a fertile territory for their development, and insects, rodents, and birds moved in to appropriate the new foods for themselves. Competition for the more fertile agricultural land led to warfare on an escalating scale, for which the powers of some of the domesticated animals were used. Hunger has always accompanied war.

Deserts now occupy many of the areas where high civilizations once flourished. Natural climatic change may in part be reponsible for some of these deserts, but humankind most likely contributed through misuse of soil and water. Alteration of the environment, which began in a modest way 10,000 years ago, continues in the present on a scale never known before.

14

How Were Cities Invented?

BY JOHN PFEIFFER

The most striking mark of man's genius as a species, as the most adaptable of animals, has been his ability to live in cities. From the perspective of all we know about human evolution, nothing could be more unnatural. For over fifteen million years, from the period when members of the family of man first appeared on earth until relatively recent times, our ancestors were nomadic, small-group, wide-open-spaces creatures. They lived on the move among other moving animals in isolated little bands of a few families, roaming across wildernesses that extended like oceans to the horizon and beyond.

Considering that heritage, the wonder is not that man has trouble getting along in cities but that he can do it at all—that he can learn to live in the same place year round, enclosed in sharp-cornered and brightly-lit rectangular spaces, among noises, most of which are made by machines, within shouting distance of hundreds of other people, most of them strangers. Furthermore, such conditions arose so swiftly, practically overnight on the evolutionary time scale, that he has hardly had a chance to get used to them. The transition from a world without cities to our present situation took a mere five or six millenniums.

It is precisely because we are so close to our origins that what happened in prehistory bears directly on current problems. In fact, the expectation is that new studies of pre-cities and early cities will contribute as significantly to an understanding of today's urban complexes as studies of infancy and early childhood have to an understanding of adolescence. Cities are signs, symptoms if you will, of an accelerating and intensive phase of human evolution, a process that we are only beginning to investigate scientifically.

The first stages of the process may be traced back some fifteen thousand years to a rather less hectic era. Homo sapiens, that new breed of restless and intelligent primate, had reached a high point in his career as a hunter-gatherer subsisting predominantly on wild plants and animals. He had developed special tools, special tactics and strategies, for dealing with a wide variety of environments, from savannas and semideserts to tundras and tropical rain forests and mountain regions. Having learned to exploit practically every type of environment, he seemed at last to have found his natural place in the scheme of things—as a hunter living in balance with other species, and with all the world as his hunting ground.

But forces were already at work that would bring an end to this state of equilibrium and ultimately give rise to cities and the state of continuing instability that we are trying to cope with today. New theories, a harder look at the old theories, and an even harder look at our own tendencies to think small have radically changed our ideas about what happened and why.

We used to believe, in effect, that people abandoned hunting and gathering as soon as a reasonable alternative became available to them. It was hardly a safe or reliable way of life. Our ancestors faced sudden death and injury from predators and from prey that fought back, disease from exposure to the elements and from always being on the move, and hunger because the chances were excellent of coming back empty-handed from the hunt. Survival was a full-time struggle. Leisure came only after the invention of agriculture, which brought food surpluses, rising populations, and cities. Such was the accepted picture.

The fact of the matter, supported by studies of living hunter-gatherers as well as by the archaeological record, is that the traditional view is largely melodrama and science fiction. Our preagricultural ancestors were quite healthy, quite safe, and regularly obtained all the food they needed. And they did it with time to burn. As a rule, the job of collecting food, animal and vegetable, required no more than a three-hour day, or a twenty-one-hour week. During that time, collectors brought in enough food for the entire group, which included an appreciable proportion (perhaps 30 per cent or more) of dependents, old persons and children who did little or no work. Leisure is basically a phenomenon of hunting-gathering times, and people have been trying to recover it ever since.

Another assumption ripe for discarding is that civilization first arose in the valleys of the Tigris, Euphrates, and Nile rivers and spread from there to the rest of the world. Accumulating evidence fails to support this notion that civilization is an exclusive product of these regions. To be sure, agriculture and cities may have appeared first in the Near East, but there are powerful arguments for completely independent origins in at least two other widely separated regions, Mesoamerica and Southeast Asia.

In all cases, circumstances forced hunter-gatherers to evolve new ways of surviving. With the decline of the ancient life style, nomadism, problems began piling up. If only people had kept on moving about like sane and respectable primates, life would be a great deal simpler. Instead, they settled down in increasing numbers over wider areas, and society started changing with a vengeance. Although the causes of this settling down remain a mystery, the fact of independent origins calls for an explanation based on worldwide developments.

An important factor, emphasized recently by Lewis Binford of the University of New Mexico, may have been the melting of mile-high glaciers, which was well under way fifteen thousand years ago, and which released enough water to raise the world's oceans 250 to 500 feet, to flood previously exposed coastal plains, and to create shallow bays and estuaries and marshlands. Vast numbers of fish and wild fowl made use of the new environments, and the extra resources permitted people to obtain food without migrating seasonally. In other words, people expended less energy, and life became that much easier, in the beginning anyway.

Yet this sensible and seemingly innocent change was to get mankind into all sorts of difficulties. According to a recent theory, it triggered a chain of events that made cities possible if not inevitable. Apparently, keeping on the move had always served as a natural birth-control mechanism, in part, perhaps, by causing a relatively high incidence of miscarriages. But the population brakes were off as soon as people began settling down.

One clue to what may have happened is provided by contemporary studies of a number of primitive tribes, such as the Bushmen of Africa's Kalahari Desert. Women living in nomadic bands, bands that pick up and move half a dozen or more times a year, have an average of one baby every four years or so, as compared with one baby every two and a half years for Bushman women living in settled communities—an increase of five to eight babies per mother during a twenty-year reproductive period.

The archaeological record suggests that in some places at least, a comparable phenomenon accompanied the melting of glaciers during the last ice age. People settled down and multiplied in the Les Eyzies region of southern France, one of the richest and most-studied centers of prehistory. Great limestone cliffs dominate the countryside, and at the foot of the cliffs are natural shelters, caves and rocky overhangs where people built fires, made tools out of flint and bone and ivory, and planned the next day's hunt. On special occasions artists equipped with torches went deep into certain caves like Lascaux and covered the walls with magnificent images of the animals they hunted.

In some places the cliffs and the shelters extend for hundreds of yards; in other places there are good living sites close to one another on the opposite slopes of river valleys. People in the Les Eyzies region were living not in isolated bands but in full-fledged communities, and populations seem to have been on the rise. During the period from seven thousand to twelve thousand years ago, the total number of sites doubled, and an appreciable proportion of them probably represent year-round settlements located in small river valleys. An analysis of excavated animal remains reveals an increasing dietary reliance on migratory birds and fish (chiefly salmon).

People were also settling down at about the same time in the Near East —for example, not far from the Mediterranean shoreline of Israel and on the border between the coastal plain and the hills to the east. Ofer Bar-

Yosef, of the Institute of Archaeology of Hebrew University in Jerusalem, points out that since they were able to exploit both these areas, they did not have to wander widely in search of food. There were herds of deer and gazelle, wild boar, fish and wild fowl, wild cereals and other plants, and limestone caves and shelters like those in the Les Eyzies region. Somewhat later, however, a new land-use pattern emerged. Coastal villages continued to flourish, but in addition to them, new sites began appearing further inland— and in areas that were drier and less abundant.

Only under special pressure will men abandon a good thing, and in this case it was very likely the pressure of rising populations. The evidence suggests that the best coastal lands were supporting about all the hunter-gatherers they could support; and as living space decreased there was a "budding off," an overflow of surplus population into the second-best back country where game was scarcer. These people depended more and more on plants, particularly on wild cereals, as indicated by the larger numbers of flint sickle blades, mortars and pestles, and storage pits found at their sites (and also by an increased wear and pitting of teeth, presumably caused by chewing more coarse and gritty plant foods).

Another sign of the times was the appearance of stone buildings, often with impressively high and massive walls. The structures served a number of purposes. For one thing, they included storage bins where surplus grain could be kept in reserve for bad times, when there was a shortage of game and wild plants. They also imply danger abroad in the countryside, new kinds of violence, and a mounting need for defenses to protect stored goods from the raids of people who had not settled down.

Above all, the walls convey a feeling of increasing permanence, an increasing commitment to places. Although man was still mainly a hunter-gatherer living on wild species, some of the old options no longer existed for him. In the beginning, settling down may have involved a measure of choice, but now man was no longer quite so free to change locales when the land became less fruitful. Even in those days frontiers were vanishing. Man's problem was to develop new options, new ways of working the land more intensively so that it would provide the food that migration had always provided in more mobile times.

The all-important transition to agriculture came in small steps, establishing itself almost before anyone realized what was going on. Settlers in marginal lands took early measures to get more food out of less abundant environments—roughing up the soil a bit with scraping or digging sticks, sowing wheat and barley seeds, weeding, and generally doing their best to promote growth. To start with at least, it was simply a matter of supplementing regular diets of wild foods with some domesticated species, animals as well as plants, and people probably regarded themselves as hunter-gatherers working hard to maintain their way of life rather than as the revolutionaries they were. They were trying to preserve the old self-sufficiency, but it was a losing effort.

The wilderness way of life became more and more remote, more and more nearly irretrievable. Practically every advance in the technology of agriculture committed people to an increasing dependence on domesticated species and on the activities of other people living nearby. Kent Flannery of the University of Michigan emphasizes this point in a study of one part of Greater Mesopotamia, prehistoric Iran, during the period between twelve thousand and six thousand years ago. For the hunter-gatherer, an estimated one-third of the country's total land area was good territory, consisting of grassy plains and high mountain valleys where wild species were abundant; the rest of the land was desert and semidesert.

The coming of agriculture meant

that people used a smaller proportion of the countryside. Early farming took advantage of naturally distributed water; the best terrain for that, namely terrain with a high water table and marshy areas, amounted to about a tenth of the land area. But only a tenth of that tenth was suitable for the next major development, irrigation. Meanwhile, food yields were soaring spectacularly, and so was the population of Iran, which increased more than fiftyfold; in other words, fifty times the original population was being supported by food produced on one-hundredth of the land.

A detailed picture of the steps involved in this massing of people is coming from studies of one part of southwest Iran, an 880-square-mile region between the Zagros Mountains and the Iraqi border. The Susiana Plain is mostly flat, sandy semidesert, the only notable features being man-made mounds that loom on the horizon like islands, places where people built in successively high levels on the ruins of their ancestors. During the past decade or so, hundreds of mounds have been mapped and dated (mainly through pottery styles) by Robert Adams of the University of Chicago, Jean Perrot of the French Archaeological Mission in Iran, and Henry Wright and Gregory Johnson of the University of Michigan. Their work provides a general idea of when the mounds were occupied, how they varied in size at different periods—and how a city may be born.

Imagine a time-lapse motion picture of the early settling of the Susiana Plain, starting about 6500 B.C., each minute of film representing a century. At first the plain is empty, as it has been since the beginning of time. Then the pioneers arrive; half a dozen families move in and build a cluster of mud-brick homes near a river. Soon another cluster appears and another, until, after about five minutes (it is now 6000 B.C.), there are ten settlements, each covering an area of 1 to 3 hectares (1 hectare = 2.47 acres). Five

minutes more (5500 B.C.) and we see the start of irrigation, on a small scale, as people dig little ditches to carry water from rivers and tributaries to lands along the banks. Crop yields increase and so do populations, and there are now thirty settlements, all about the same size as the original ten.

This is but a prelude to the main event. Things become really complicated during the next fifteen minutes or so (5500 to 4000 B.C.). Irrigation systems, constructed and maintained by family groups of varying sizes, become more complex. The number of settlements shows a modest increase, from thirty to forty, but a more significant change takes place—the appearance of a hierarchy. Instead of settlements all about the same size, there are now levels of settlements and a kind of ranking: one town (7 hectares), ten large villages (3 to 4 hectares), and twenty-nine smaller villages of less than 3 hectares. During this period large residential and ceremonial structures appear at Susa, a town on the western edge of the Susiana Plain.

Strange happenings can be observed not long after the middle of this period (about 4600 B.C.). For reasons unknown, the number of settlements decreases rapidly. It is not known whether the population of the area decreased simultaneously. Time passes, and the number of settlements increases to about the same level as before, but great changes have occurred. Three cities have appeared with monumental public buildings, elaborate residential architecture, large workshops, major storage and market facilities, and certainly with administrators and bureaucrats. The settlement hierarchy is more complex, and settlements are no longer located to take advantage solely of good agricultural opportunities. Their location is also influenced by the cities and the services and opportunities available there. By the end of our hypothetical time-lapse film, by the early part of the third millennium B.C., the largest settlement of all is the city of Susa, which covers some thirty hectares and will cover up to a square kil-

Hillel Burger, Peabody Museum, Harvard University

Female figurine from Tepe Yahya, Iran. A variety of sites throughout the world have yielded astonishingly ancient objects created by men who farmed and built permanent dwellings such as this stone figurine found in Tepe Yahya, Iran—a settlement that was in contact with Susa before 4000 B.C.

ometer (100 hectares) of territory before it collapses in historical times.

All Mesopotamia underwent major transformations during this period. Another city was taking shape 150 miles northwest of Susa in the heartland of Sumer. Within a millennium the site of Uruk near the Euphrates River grew from village dimensions to a city enclosing within its defense walls more than thirty thousand people, four hundred hectares, and at the center a temple built on top of a huge brick platform. Archaeological surveys reveal that this period also saw a massive immigration into the region from places and for reasons as yet undetermined, resulting in a tenfold increase in settlements and in the formation of several new cities.

Similar surveys, requiring months

and thousands of miles of walking, are completed or under way in many parts of the world. Little more than a millennium after the establishment of Uruk and Susa, cities began making an independent appearance in northern China not far from the conflux of the Wei and Yellow rivers, in an area that also saw the beginnings of agriculture. Still later, and also independently as far as we can tell, intensive settlement and land use developed in the New World.

The valley of Oaxaca in Mexico, where Flannery and his associates are working currently, provides another example of a city in the process of being formed. Around 500 B.C., or perhaps a bit earlier, buildings were erected for the first time on the tops of hills. Some of the hills were small, no more than twenty-five or thirty feet high, and the buildings were correspondingly small; they overlooked a few terraces and a river and probably a hamlet or two. Larger structures appeared on higher hills overlooking many villages. About 400 B.C. the most elaborate settlement began to appear on the highest land, 1,500-foot Monte Albán, with a panoramic view of the valley's three arms; and within two centuries it had developed into an urban center including hundreds of terraces, an irrigation system, a great plaza, ceremonial buildings and residences, and an astronomical observatory.

At about the same time, the New World's largest city, Teotihuacán, was evolving some 225 miles to the northwest in the central highlands of Mexico. Starting as a scattering of villages and hamlets, it covered nearly eight square miles at its height (around A.D. 100 to 200) and probably contained some 125,000 people. Archaeologists are now reconstructing the life and times of this great urban center. William Sanders of Pennsylvania State University is concentrating on an analysis of settlement patterns in the area, while Rene Millon of the University of Rochester and his associates have prepared detailed section-by-section maps of the city as a step toward further extensive excavations. Set in a narrow valley among mountains and with its

own man-made mountains, the Pyramid of the Sun and the Pyramid of the Moon, the city flourished on a grand scale. It housed local dignitaries and priests, delegations from other parts of Mesoamerica, and workshop neighborhoods where specialists in the manufacture of textiles, pottery, obsidian blades, and other products lived together in early-style apartments.

The biggest center in what is now the United States probably reached its peak about a millennium after Teotihuacán. But it has not been reconstructed, and archaeologists are just beginning to appreciate the scale of what happened there. Known as Cahokia and located east of the Mississippi near St. Louis, it consists of a cluster of some 125 mounds (including a central mound 100 feet high and covering 15 acres) as well as a line of mounds extending six miles to the west.

So surveys and excavations continue, furnishing the sort of data needed to disprove or prove our theories. Emerging patterns—patterns involving the specific locations of different kinds of communities and of buildings and other artifacts within communities—can yield information about the forces that shaped and are still shaping cities and the behavior of people in cities. But one trend stands out above all others: the world was becoming more and more stratified. Every development seemed to favor social distinctions, social classes and elites, and to work against the old hunter-gatherer ways.

Among hunter-gatherers all people are equal. Individuals are recognized as exceptional hunters, healers, or storytellers, and they all have the chance to shine upon appropriate occasions. But it would be unthinkable for one of them, for any one man, to take over as full-time leader. That ethic passed when the nomadic life passed. In fact, a literal explosion of differences accompanied the coming of communities where people lived close together in permanent dwellings and under conditions where moving away was not easy.

The change is reflected clearly in observed changes of settlement patterns.

Hierarchies of settlements imply hierarchies of people. Emerging social levels are indicated by the appearance of villages and towns and cities where only villages had existed before, by different levels of complexity culminating in such centers as Susa and Monte Albán and Cahokia. Circumstances practically drove people to establish class societies. In Mesopotamia, for instance, increasingly sophisticated agricultural systems and intensive concentrations of populations brought about enormous and irreversible changes within a short period. People were clamped in a demographic vise, more and more of them living and depending on less and less land—an ideal setting for the rapid rise of status differences.

Large-scale irrigation was a highly effective centralizing force, calling for new duties and new regularities and new levels of discipline. People still depended on the seasons; but in addition, canals had to be dug and maintained, and periodic cleaning was required to prevent the artificial waterways from filling up with silt and assorted litter. Workers had to be brought together, assigned tasks, and fed, which meant schedules and storehouses and rationing stations and mass-produced pottery to serve as food containers. It took time to organize such activities efficiently. There were undoubtedly many false starts, many attempts by local people to work things out among themselves and their neighbors at a community or village level. Many small centers, budding institutions, were undoubtedly formed and many collapsed, and we may yet detect traces of them in future excavations and analyses of settlement patterns.

The ultimate outcome was inevitable. Survival demanded organization on a regional rather than a local basis. It also demanded high-level administrators and managers, and most of them had to be educated people, mainly because of the need to prepare detailed records of supplies and transactions. Record-keeping has a long prehistory, perhaps dating

back to certain abstract designs engraved on cave walls and bone twenty-five thousand or more years ago. But in Mesopotamia after 4000 B.C. there was a spurt in the art of inventing and utilizing special marks and symbols.

The trend is shown in the stamp and cylinder seals used by officials to place their "signatures" on clay tags and tablets, man's first documents. At first the designs on the stamp seals were uncomplicated, consisting for the most part of single animals or simple geometric motifs. Later, however, there were bigger stamp seals with more elaborate scenes depicting several objects or people or animals. Finally the cylinder seals appeared, which could be rolled to repeat a complex design. These seals indicate the existence of more and more different signatures—and more and more officials and record keepers. Similar trends are evident in potters' marks and other symbols. All these developments precede pictographic writing, which appears around 3200 B.C.

Wherever record keepers and populations were on the rise, in the Near East or Mexico or China, we can be reasonably sure that the need for a police force or the prehistoric equivalent thereof was on the increase, too. Conflict, including everything from fisticuffs to homicide, increases sharply with group size, and people have known this for a long time. The Bushmen have a strong feeling about avoiding crowds: "We like to get together, but we fear fights." They are most comfortable in bands of about twenty-five persons and when they have to assemble in larger groups—which happens for a total of only a few months a year, mainly to conduct initiations, arrange marriages, and be near the few permanent water holes during dry seasons—they form separate small groups of about twenty-five, as if they were still living on their own.

Incidentally, twenty-five has been called a "magic number," because it hints at what may be a universal law of group behavior. There have been many counts of hunter-gatherer bands, not only in the Kalahari Desert, but

also in such diverse places as the forests of Thailand, the Canadian Northwest, and northern India. Although individual bands may vary from fifteen to seventy-five members, the tendency is to cluster around twenty-five, and in all cases a major reason for keeping groups small is the desire to avoid violence. In other words, the association between large groups and conflict has deep roots and very likely presented law-and-order problems during the early days of cities and pre-cities, as it has ever since.

Along with managers and record keepers and keepers of the peace, there were also specialists in trade. A number of factors besides population growth and intensive land use were involved in the origin of cities, and local and long-distance trade was among the most important. Prehistoric centers in the process of becoming urban were almost always trade centers. They typically occupied favored places, strategic points in developing trade networks, along major waterways and caravan routes or close to supplies of critical raw materials.

Archaeologists are making a renewed attempt to learn more about such developments. Wright's current work in southwest Iran, for example, includes preliminary studies to detect and measure changes in the flow of trade. One site about sixty-five miles from Susa lies close to tar pits, which in prehistoric times served as a source of natural asphalt for fastening stone blades to handles and waterproofing baskets and roofs. By saving all the waste bits of this important raw material preserved in different excavated levels, Wright was able to estimate fluctuations in its production over a period of time. In one level, for example, he found that the amounts of asphalt produced increased far beyond local requirements; in fact, a quantitative analysis indicates that asphalt exports doubled at this time. The material was probably being traded for such things as high-quality flint obtained from quarries more than one hundred miles away, since counts of material recovered at the site indicate that imports of the flint doubled during the same period.

In other words, the site was taking its place in an expanding trade network, and similar evidence from other sites can be used to indicate the extent and structure of that network. Then the problem will be to find out what other things were happening at the same time, such as significant changes in cylinder-seal designs and in agricultural and religious practices. This is the sort of evidence that may be expected to spell out just how the evolution of trade was related to the evolution of cities.

Another central problem is gaining a fresh understanding of the role of religion. Something connected with enormous concentrations of people, with population pressures and tensions of many kinds that started building up five thousand or more years ago, transformed religion from a matter of simple rituals carried out at village shrines to the great systems of temples and priesthoods invariably associated with early cities. Sacred as well as profane institutions arose to keep society from splitting apart.

Strong divisive tendencies had to be counteracted, and the reason may involve yet another magic number, another intriguing regularity that has been observed in hunter-gatherer societies in different parts of the world. The average size of a tribe, defined as a group of bands all speaking the same dialect, turns out to be about five hundred persons, a figure that depends to some extent on the limits of human memory. A tribe is a community of people who can identify closely with one another and engage in repeated face-to-face encounters and recognitions; and it happens that five hundred may represent about the number of persons a hunter-gatherer can remember well enough to approach on what would amount to a first-name basis in our society. Beyond that number the level of familiarity declines, and there is an increasing tendency to regard individuals as "they" rather than "we," which is when trouble usually starts. (Architects recommend that an elementary school should not exceed five hundred pupils if the principal is to maintain personal contact with all of them, and the headmaster of one prominent prep school recently used this argument to keep his student body at or below the five-hundred mark.)

Religion of the sort that evolved with the first cities may have helped to "beat" the magic number five hundred. Certainly there was an urgent need to establish feelings of solidarity among many thousands of persons rather than a few hundred. Creating allegiances wider than those provided by direct kinship and person-to-person ties became a most important problem, a task for full-time professionals. In this connection Paul Wheatley of the University of Chicago suggests that "specialized priests were among the first persons to be released from the daily round of subsistence labor." Their role was partly to exhort other workers concerned with the building of monuments and temples, workers who probably exerted greater efforts in the belief that they were doing it not for mere men but for the glory of individuals highborn and close to the gods.

The city evolved to meet the needs of societies under pressure. People were being swept up in a process that had been set in motion by their own activities and that they could never have predicted, for the simple reason that they had no insight into what they were doing in the first place. For example, they did not know, and had no way of knowing, that settling down could lead to population explosions.

There is nothing strange about this state of affairs, to be sure. It is the essence of the human condition and involves us just as intensely today. Then as now, people responded by the sheer instinct of survival to forces that they understood vaguely at best—and worked together as well as they could to organize themselves, to preserve order in the face of accelerating change and complexity and the threat of chaos. They could never know that they were creating what we, its beneficiaries and its victims, call civilization.

IV
Language and Communication

○ ○

All animal species have methods of communication, by which we mean the transfer of information from one organism, or being to another. Information is defined as a stimulus that changes or affects the behavior of an organism.

Of all animal species, humankind has developed the most rich, subtle, and versatile of communication systems: language. But what is *language?* Many anthropologists think of language in terms of the thirteen design features proposed by Charles Hockett. In Hockett's terms, language is characterized by:

1. *Vocal-auditory channel.* It is produced through the nose and mouth and received through the ears.

2. *Broadcast transmission and directional fading.* A speaker can be heard in all directions; a listener can hear a speaker no matter which direction the signal is coming from.

3. *Rapid fading.* As soon as they are spoken, words dissipate and subsequently cannot be retrieved.

4. *Interchangeability.* All speakers of a language can both utter and understand the same words.

5. *Total feedback.* A speaker hears everything she or he says, can monitor it, and can correct or account for mistakes.

6. *Specialization.* Speech serves no other purpose than to communicate; as a specialized system, it can be used even when speaker and listener are engaged in other activities.

7. *Semanticity.* There are systematic connections between spoken words and standardly accepted meanings.

8. *Arbitrariness.* These connections between words and their meanings are a matter of convention; hence it is possible both to create new words with new meanings and to change the meanings of old words.

9. *Discreteness.* Human beings can produce an enormous range of sounds, but each language makes use of only a very small subset of these sounds, far from exhausting the human capacity.

10. *Displacement.* Humans can use language to communicate about things and events that are far removed from the immediate context in which they are interacting. These distant events may be separated by time, distance, or both—and may even include things that have never existed and never will (for example, mermaids).

11. *Productivity.* People regularly utter sentences that have never been said before in exactly the same manner, and they can talk about things (such as inventions or discoveries) that have never been observed.

12. *Traditional transmission.* It appears that human beings are genetically programmed to be predisposed to learn a language (or even more than one). However, the specific language that an individual eventually speaks is acquired solely through learning in a social context—it is not inherited genetically.

13. *Duality of patterning.* Language is patterned on at least two separate levels: *phonemes,* the sounds a language recognizes as significant but which by themselves have no meanings; and *morphemes,* the indivisible units of meaning of a language. The word "dog," for instance, consists of three phonemes ([d], [o], [g]) and one morpheme ([dog]).

The earliest recorded interest in language and its significance for human beings appears in the Old Testament in Genesis. First, Adam names all the creatures of the world—and through this they are placed at his disposal. Later, when through united effort in the land of Shinar humans attempted to build a tower reaching to the very heavens, God scattered them across the face of the earth and caused them to speak different tongues—thereby forever frustrating attempts at pan-human unity.

Both these themes still preoccupy modern linguists: namely, (1) the ways in which words and the categories they represent affect their speakers' experience of, and approach to, the world around them; and (2) the evolutionary tree of language, or the taxonomic relationships among languages, and the ways and rates of linguistic change.

The first recorded rigorous study of a language was accomplished in the fourth century B.C. by the Indian scholar Panini. He analyzed the structure of ancient (Vedic) Sanskrit and condensed its grammatical rules to algebra-like formulas as elegant as those of any modern grammatical analysis. In doing so, he preserved a language that might well otherwise have become extinct, and he set a standard of excellence that still inspires linguistic analysts.

Some 2,000 years later, another student of Sanskrit, Sir William Jones (1746–1794), systematized means to compare and contrast languages and thereby trace the relationships among them. He is considered by some, therefore, to be the modern "father" of comparative linguistics.

Contemporary linguistics is divided into several specialized branches and even more schools of thought. *Structural linguists* analyze individual languages, detailing their phonology (sound system), morphology (meaning representation), and syntax (the organization of language units into sequences). *Comparative (or historical) linguists* compare extant languages, trace their evolution from earlier ("proto") language forms, and attempt to reconstruct the proto-languages from which modern languages evolved. *Sociolinguists* study differences in language uses (or dialectical differences) reflecting socioeconomic groupings. And *psycholinguists* are interested in the mental apparatuses of speech perception, cognitive processes, and so on.

But human communication is not limited to language. Nonverbally, human beings communicate very important messages about many things—including their feelings about (1) themselves, (2) the person they are addressing, and (3) what they are discussing. *Kinesics* is the study of communication through gesturing, and *proxemics* is the study of the meanings of spacial patterns of people and things.

We introduce some of these and also other concerns in Topic Seven, Language, Thought, and Communication.

Language, Thought, and Communication

There is a story, often told in introductory anthropology courses, that the Greek philosopher Plato one day posed to his students the question, "What sets human beings apart from all other creatures?"

One student came up with what seemed to be an irrefutable reply. "Humans," he said, "are featherless bipeds."

While the student was being congratulated by his peers, Plato is said to have slipped away for a while. Upon returning he announced, "Here is our scholar's human being!"—and threw into the crowd of students a freshly plucked chicken.

The question of what exactly does separate human beings as a species from all others has continued to vex philosophers and scientists. Until recently, however, there was at least one thing that most people could agree on: only human beings have language. But was that really saying something meaningful? Does the ability to speak represent fundamental properties of our species, or is it just an epiphenomenon of having the curved tongue, short jaw, and minutely controllable lips that facilitate speech? In other words, is the use of language by humans rooted in unique mental properties, or is it something much more superficial?

Some startling studies conducted in the last two decades have suggested that the answers to these questions were at hand. Various scholars using plastic chips, hand-sign language, and other means to communicate with ape research subjects seemed to be concluding that, using nonlinguistic communication, apes are capable of the mental operations that underlie language use by humans. First, apes could learn an astonishingly large number of "words"—Koko, a female gorilla, has learned more than 500. Second, and more importantly, they could apply rules of grammar to the use of these "words." And third, there even appeared to be evidence that they could combine two "words" to mean something entirely new, as when the chimpanzee Washoe signed *water bird* when, for the first time, her trainer showed her a swan. Thus, it appeared

that although only humans speak, other animals have the mental faculties for language use in media that they are equipped to manipulate. Language no longer was the defining characteristic of our species.

This view of apes, humans, and language captured the popular imagination. And, until very recently, it went relatively unchallenged. The data, after all, were so compelling. However, a general reassessment of these studies is beginning to cast some doubt on the original findings and to dampen some of the enthusiasm with which they were received. This trend is spearheaded by psychologist Herbert Terrace, whose research originally was intended to support the view that apes had language capacities. However, after reviewing his data, Terrace found that serious methodological problems made their interpretation problematical. And when he reviewed the methodologies of other studies, he found similar flaws.

True, these apes did learn large numbers of "words." But it was questionable whether they were using rules of grammar to combine them. For one thing, they may simply have learned sequences of signs just as you learn a telephone number—with no sense that the order *means* anything. Then, Terrace noted that many researchers failed to record sign productions that were out of sequence; some even "corrected" sequences that were "wrong." Further, when camera film showed the humans with whom the apes were communicating, Terrace observed that often the teachers were cueing their ape students unconsciously or leading them through sequences one sign at a time. Thus, the "grammar" of the string of signs produced by the ape was, in fact, created by the human beings interacting with the apes.

Finally, Terrace pointed out that without a full description of the context, it is impossible to assess such episodes as Washoe signing *water bird* when being shown a swan. For instance, did Washoe first sign *water* and then, when her trainer asked her to sign again, sign *bird*? In other words, did Washoe ever make a mental connection between the two "words"? The evidence does not allow us to judge.

So at this point, it is not clear whether or not human beings are the only creatures who can use language. What *is* clear is that linguistic creativity is the birthright of every human being on earth, and that we have elaborated language far beyond the capabilities of any other creature. In "Man the Talker," Peter Farb explores in fascinating detail the nature of language, how it differs from the communications systems of other animals, whether the ability to speak is coded into our genes, and how language may have evolved.

The next article considers the question of what language use means for human beings. In a series of seminal articles published about fifty years ago, Benjamin Whorf proposed that the language a person speaks provides the framework for his or her organization of experiences. Put more formally, Whorf's hypothesis was that "we dissect nature along the lines laid down by our native languages." Reality, far from being objectively discernible, is in Whorf's view a culturally relative thing—constructed according to the categories each language labels, the dimensions of time and space each language incorporates, and the logical relationships expressable in each language's grammar.

This bold hypothesis both stimulated and troubled scholars. Certainly, each culture has its own "world view" fully expressable only in its own language— something that translators of literature always struggle with. But does it therefore follow that, just because the concept of time is encoded differently in English and Hopi (the language of an Indian tribe in the U.S. Southwest), the speakers of these languages *think* differently about time (as Whorf proposes)? Careful research on color perception, for instance, has shown that regardless of the categories of colors labeled by a language, speakers of different languages perceive and remember colors similarly, based on the physiology of color perception.

At present, no definitive proof or disproof of Whorf's ideas exists. His hypothesis explains some facts but not others. We think, however, that his hypothesis merits your careful attention, because it poses both philosophical as well as concrete challenges. Is there an objectively discoverable reality? Whorf's views challenge the empiricist and positivist philosophies that would answer yes. Are all languages equally well adapted for pursuing scientific research? Whorf clearly believes not—and, in fact, suggests that for some kinds of scientific research, the world view of Hopi is better adapted than that of English. In "How Languages Code Reality," Dorothy Lee explores Whorf's hypothesis by showing how the language of the people of the Trobriand Islands emphasizes the nonlineal aspect of reality; in contrast, English emphasizes lineal relationships. One result is that English speakers see patterns that Trobrianders, because their language codes reality differently, literally are unable to understand. Implied in Lee's study is the intriguing notion that there may well be concepts, ideas, and patterns in "reality" to which our language has blinded us.

Alan Dundes's "Seeing Is Believing" is a light article but of interest because it illustrates one aspect of the Whorf hypothesis. Using English, Dundes shows how this language places priority on one sense over the others and, in doing so, affects how we evaluate the information we receive from those other senses.

Of course, human beings do not communicate solely through language. A great amount of information is communicated nonverbally. In "The Sounds of Silence," Edward T. Hall and Mildred R. Hall introduce you to the world of gestures and the use of space in human communication.

15

Man the Talker

BY PETER FARB

Some twenty-five hundred years ago, Psamtik, an Egyptian pharaoh, desired to discover man's primordial tongue. He entrusted two infants to an isolated shepherd and ordered that they should never hear a word spoken in any language. When the children were returned to the pharaoh several years later, he thought he heard them utter *bekos*, which means "bread" in Phrygian, a language of Asia Minor. And so he honored Phrygian as man's "natural" language. Linguists today know that the story of the pharaoh's experiment must be apocryphal. No child is capable of speech until he has heard other human beings speak, and even two infants reared together cannot develop a language from scratch. Nor does any single "natural" language exist. A child growing up anywhere on earth will speak the tongue he hears in his speech community, regardless of the race, nationality, or language of his parents.

Every native speaker is amazingly creative in the various strategies of speech interaction, in word play and verbal dueling, in exploiting a language's total resources to create poetry and literature. Even a monosyllabic *yes*—spoken in a particular speech situation, with a certain tone of voice, and accomplished by an appropriate gesture—might constitute an original use of English. This sort of linguistic creativity is the birthright of every human being on earth, no matter what language he speaks, the kind of community he lives in, or his degree of intelligence. As Edward Sapir pointed out, when it comes to language "Plato walks with the Macedonian swineherd, Confucius with the head-hunting savage of Assam."

And at a strictly grammatical level also, native speakers are unbelievably creative in language. Not every human being can play the violin, do calculus, jump high hurdles, or sail a canoe, no matter how excellent his teachers or how arduous his training—but every person constantly creates utterances never before spoken on earth. Incredible as it may seem at first thought, the sentence you just read possibly appeared in exactly this form for the first time in the history of the English language—and the same thing might be said about the sentence you are reading now. In fact, if conventional remarks—such as greetings, farewells, stock phrases like *thank you*, proverbs, clichés, and so forth—are disregarded, in theory all of a person's speech consists of sentences never before uttered.

A moment's reflection reveals why that may be so. Every language groups its vocabulary into a number of different classes such as nouns, verbs, adjectives, and so on. If English possessed a mere 1,000 nouns (such as *trees, children, horses*) and only 1,000 verbs (*grow, die, change*), the number of possible two-word sentences therefore would be 1,000 × 1,000, or one million. Of course, most of these sentences will be meaningless to a speaker today—yet at one time people thought *atoms split* was a meaningless utterance. The nouns, however, might also serve as the objects of these same verbs in three-word sentences. So with the same meager repertory of 1,000 nouns and 1,000 verbs capable of taking an object, the number of possible three-word sentences increases to 1,000 × 1,000 × 1,000, or one billion. These calculations, of course, are just for minimal sentences and an impoverished vocabulary. Most languages offer their speakers many times a thousand nouns and a thousand verbs, and in addition they possess other classes of words that function as adverbs, adjectives, articles, prepositions, and so on. Think, too, in terms of four-word, ten-word, even fifty-word sentences—and the number of possible grammatical combinations becomes astronomical. One linguist calculated that it would take 10,000,000,000,000 (two thousand times the estimated age of the earth) to utter all the possible English sentences that use exactly twenty words. Therefore, it is improbable that any twenty-word sentence a person speaks was ever spoken previously—and the same thing would hold true, of course, for sentences of greater length, and for most shorter ones as well.

For a demonstration of just why the number of sentences that can be constructed in a language is, at least in theory, infinite, show twenty-five speakers of English a cartoon and ask them to describe in a single sentence what they see. Each of the twenty-five speakers will come up with a different sentence, perhaps examples similar to these:

> I see a little boy entering a magic and practical-joke shop to buy something and not noticing that the owner, a practical joker himself, has laid a booby trap for him.

> The cartoon shows an innocent little kid, who I guess is entering a magic shop because he wants to buy something, about to be captured in a trap by the owner of the shop, who has a diabolical expression on his face.

It has been calculated that the vocabulary and the grammatical structures used in only twenty-five sentences about this cartoon might provide the raw material for nearly twenty *billion* grammatical sentences—a number so great that about forty human life spans would be needed to speak them, even at high speed. Obviously, no one could ever speak, read, or hear in his lifetime more than the tiniest fraction of the possible sentences in his language. That is why almost every sentence in this book—as well as in all the books ever written or to be written—is possibly expressed in its exact form for the first time.

This view of creativity in the grammatical aspects of language is a very recent one. It is part of the revolution in ideas about the structure of language that has taken place since 1957, when Noam Chomsky, of the Massachusetts Institute of Technology, published his *Syntactic Structures*. Since then Chomsky and others have put forth a theory of language that bears little resemblance to the grammar most people learned in "grammar" school. Not all linguists accept Chomsky's theories. But his position, whether it is ultimately shown to be right or wrong, represents an influential school in theoretical linguistics today, one that other schools often measure themselves against.

Chomsky believes that all human beings possess at birth an innate capacity to acquire language. Such a capacity is biologically determined—that is, it belongs to what is usually termed "human nature"—and it is passed from parents to children as part of the offspring's biological inheritance. The innate capacity endows speakers with the general shape of human language, but it is not detailed enough to dictate the precise tongue each child will speak—which accounts for why different languages are spoken in the world. Chomsky states that no one learns a language by learning all of its possible sentences, since obviously that would require countless lifetimes. For example, it is unlikely that any of the speakers who saw the cartoon of the child entering the magic store ever encountered

such a bizarre situation before—yet none of the speakers had any difficulty in constructing sentences about it. Nor would a linguist who wrote down these twenty-five sentences ever have heard them previously—yet he had no difficulty understanding them. So, instead of learning billions of sentences, a person unconsciously acquires a grammar that can generate an infinite number of new sentences in his language.

Such a grammar is innately within the competence of any native speaker of a language. However, no speaker—not even Shakespeare, Dante, Plato, or the David of the Psalms—lives up to his theoretical competence. His actual performance in speaking a language is considerably different, and it consists of numerous errors, hesitations, repetitions, and so forth. Despite these very uneven performances that a child hears all around him, in only a few years—and before he even receives instruction in reading and writing in "grammar" school—he puts together for himself the theoretical rules for the language spoken in his community. Since most sentences that a child hears are not only unique but also filled with errors, how can he ever learn the grammar of his language? Chomsky's answer is that children are born with the capacity to learn only grammars that accord with the innate human blueprint. Children disregard performance errors because such errors result in sentences that could not be described by such a grammar. Strong evidence exists that native speakers of a language know intuitively whether a sentence is grammatical or not. They usually cannot specify exactly what is wrong, and very possibly they make the same mistakes in their own speech, but they know—unconsciously, not as a set of rules they learned in school—when a sentence is incorrect.

The human speaker—born with a capacity for language, infinitely creative in its use, capable of constructing novel utterances in unfamiliar speech situations—shares the globe with a variety of animals that whistle, shriek, squeak, bleat, hoot, coo, call, and howl. And so it has been assumed, ever since Aristotle first speculated about the matter, that human speech is only some superior kind of animal language. Alexander Graham Bell saw nothing odd about his attempts to teach a dog to speak by training it to growl at a steady rate while he manipulated its throat and jaws. The dog finally managed to produce a sequence of syllables which sounded somewhat like *ow ah oo gwah mah*—the closest it could come to "How are you, Grandma?" and Samuel Pepys, in his *Diary* entry for August 24, 1661, noted:

> by and by we are called to Sir W. Batten's to see the strange creature that Captain Holmes hath brought with him from Guiny; it is a great baboon [apparently not a

baboon at all but rather a chimpanzee], but so much like a man in most things, that though they say there is a species of them, yet I cannot believe but that it is a monster got of a man and a she-baboon. I do believe that it already understands much English, and I am of the mind it might be taught to speak or make signs.

Other experimenters concluded that animals could not be taught human languages, but they saw no reason why they themselves should not learn to speak the way animals do. A few enthusiasts have even published dictionaries for various birds and animal languages—among them E. I. Du Pont de Nemours, the French-born founder of the American chemical firm, who in 1807 compiled dictionaries for the languages of such birds as crows and nightingales. These efforts are ludicrous because human speech is quite different from most animal communication. Between the bird's call to its mate and the human utterance *I love you* lie a few hundred million years of evolution, at least one whole day of Biblical Creation. St. Francis of Assisi, talking to the birds, may have had much to say to them, but they had nothing to discuss with him.

Human speech seemingly resembles animal calls in that it employs a small number of sounds, often no more than the number of sounds emitted by many species of birds and mammals. But, unlike animal calls, human sounds are combined to form a vast vocabulary, which in turn is structured into an infinite number of utterances. The number of different units of sound in each human language, such as the *m* in *man* or the *ou* in *house*, varies between about a dozen and a little more than five dozen. English recognizes about 45 units, Italian 24, Hawaiian 13. This range is not notably different from the separate units of sound emitted by many kinds of animals: prairie dog, 10; various species of monkeys, about 20; domestic chicken, 25; chimpanzee, 25; bottle-nosed dolphin, 28; fox, 36.

Chimpanzees, with their 25 units of sound, are incapable of speech, while Hawaiians, with only 13 units, possess a very expressive language. That is because the chimpanzee employs one unit of sound in social play, another when a juvenile is lost, a third when attacked, and so on—but two or more calls cannot be combined to generate additional messages. In contrast, the 13 sounds of Hawaiian can be combined to form 2,197 potential three-sound words, nearly five million six-sound words—and an astronomical number if the full repertory of 13 sounds is used to form longer words. In the same way, a speaker of English can select three units of sound out of his store of 45—such as the sounds represented in writing by *e, n,* and *d*—and then combine them into such meaningful words as *end, den,* and *Ned.* But the chimpanzee cannot combine the three units of sound that mean play, lost

juvenile, and threat of attack to form some other message. Nor can the chimpanzee's call that means "Here is food" ever be changed to talk about the delicacies it consumed yesterday or its expectations about finding certain fruits tomorrow. Generation after generation, as far into the future as the chimpanzee survives as a species, it will use that call solely to indicate the immediate presence of "food."

Certain animals—most notably parrots, mynahs, and other mimicking birds—can emit a wide repertory of sounds, and they also have an uncanny ability to combine them into longer utterances. Nevertheless, they do not exploit their abilities the way human beings do. A trained mynah bird can so unerringly repeat an English sentence that it is scarcely distinguishable on a tape recording from the same sentence spoken by a human being. Parrots also can duplicate human speech with awesome fidelity, and they have been taught vocabularies of more than a hundred words. A parrot can easily enough be trained to mimic the utterance *a pail of water* and also to mimic a variety of nouns such as *sand* and *milk*. But, for all its skill, the parrot will never substitute nouns for each other and on its own say *a pail of sand* or *a pail of milk*.

Even the most vocal animals are utterly monotonous in what they say in a given situation. The well-known nursery rhyme does not reveal what Jack said to Jill when they went up the hill to fetch a pail of water, and in fact no way exists to predict which of the tremendous number of strategies two people will select in such a speech situation. But everyone knows what a male songbird will say when another male enters its territory during the breeding season. It will emit a distinctive series of sounds that signify "Go away!" It cannot negotiate with the intruder, nor can it say "I'm sorry that I must ask you to depart now, but I will be happy to make your acquaintance after the breeding season is concluded." The male defender of the territory is simply responding to the stimulus of an intruder at a certain time of the year by uttering a general statement about the existence of such a stimulus.

Specialists in animal behavior infer the "meaning" of animal sounds from the behavior of the animals at the time they emit the sounds, but it is safe to conclude that the sounds express only indefinable emotions. Individuals belonging to the same animal species emit approximately the same sounds to convey the same emotions. All expressions of pain uttered by any individuals of a monkey species are very much the same, but in the human species the sounds that a speaker uses to communicate his pain are quite arbitrary. A speaker of English says *ouch*, but a Spaniard says *ay* and a Nootka Indian *ishkatakh*. Jill might have emitted an animal-like cry of pain as she came tumbling down the hill—but, as a speaker of English, she also had the choice of saying *I hurt my head* or *Please take me to a doctor.* Even if Jill merely uttered the conventional word, *ouch,* which signifies pain in English, this sound is nevertheless considerably different from an animal's cry of pain. An animal's cry cannot be removed from its immediate context, but Jill's *ouch* can. She could, for example, tell someone the next day about her accident by saying *When I fell down the hill, I cried "ouch."* Or she could utter *ouch* in a completely different context, as when someone makes a feeble pun and she wishes to convey that her sensibilities, not her bones, have been wounded.

An animal, though, has no such choices. As Bertrand Russell remarked about a dog's ability to communicate, "No matter how eloquently a dog may bark, he cannot tell you that his parents were poor but honest." Despite the variety of sounds in the babel of the animal world, nonhuman calls are emotional responses to a very limited number of immediate stimuli. Every other kind of sound made by living things on the planet belongs to human speech alone.

The search for the genesis of speech in the lower animals has not uncovered a single species that can communicate with all the same features found in human speech. The most promising candidates in whom to search for the roots of human language would appear to be man's closest relatives, the apes and monkeys. Many species possess extensive repertories of calls concerned with emotional states, with interpersonal relationships inside the troop or with animals outside of it. The chimpanzee, in particular, has important attributes for learning: intelligence, sociability, and a strong attachment to human beings. The potential for language in chimpanzees seems so great that several attempts have been made to teach them to speak. All such experiments failed, even when the chimpanzees were reared in households on an equal basis with human children. The most successful of these attempts, which involved six years of painstaking attention by a psychologist and his family, resulted in a chimpanzee's learning to speak merely approximations of four English words.

It is now known to be fruitless to teach chimpanzees a spoken language because their vocal apparatus is considerably different from that of human beings. But about 1966 two psychologists at the University of Nevada, Allen and Beatrice Gardner, had the novel idea that chimpanzees might possess a capacity for language even though they lack an apparatus to speak it, a situation similar to that of deaf-mute human children. They decided to attempt to separate the chimpanzee's possible capacity for language from its proven inability to utter the sounds of the language.

Since use of the hands is a prominent feature of chimpanzee behavior, the Gardners employed visual rather than vocal signals by teaching a chimpanzee the American Sign Language system that is used with deaf children in North America. The Gardners theorized that their infant female chimpanzee, Washoe, should see as much sign language as possible, since they knew that merely exposing a human child to speech triggered its language-learning capacity. They took great care to keep her isolated from all other chimpanzees and from most human beings as well. The Gardners always communicated with each other in sign language whenever Washoe was present, and they demanded that anyone in contact with her remain silent and use hand signals.

Their efforts were rewarded almost immediately. Washoe began to repeat the gestures she was taught and also those she noticed the Garnders using between themselves. She built up a vocabulary of thirty-four words in less than two years. Much more important, when she learned a new word she enlarged its application from the specific thing it labeled to an entire class of similar objects. For example, she first learned the sign for *hurt* in reference to scratches and bruises, but later she used the same sign to indicate stains, a decal on the back of a person's hand, and a human navel. And she was able to communicate about things that were not present, as when she heard a distant bark and immediately made the sign for *dog.*

Her proficiency soon went beyond the mere naming of things. She learned verbs and pronouns, and she invented combinations of signs which she used correctly in appropriate speech situations. She combined the signs for *open*, *food*, and *drink* when she wanted something from the refrigerator and the signs for *go* and *sweet* when she wanted to be taken to a raspberry bush. Before she had reached the age of six, she had a vocabulary of 150 signs which she could combine to describe situations entirely new to her. At this writing in early 1973, Washoe is living at the University of Oklahoma with a colony of chimpanzees who are also being trained in sign language. As yet, no sign-language communication has taken place between them. Whether or not Washoe will transmit the signs she has learned to her progeny will not be known until 1974 or 1975, when she becomes old enough to reproduce. She has, however, already demonstrated that she can at least spontaneously communicate with human children who know sign language—even though her status still remains that of an ape. One poignant illustration of that occurred when a mute girl and her parents came to visit the Gardners. Washoe spotted the child and eagerly rushed across the yard to play with her, excitedly giving the sign for *child.* But the human child, seeing a chimpanzee come bounding toward her, responded by tickling her ribs—the sign for *ape*.

Washoe has successfully bridged the barrier between human and nonhuman communication, although she required human help to do so. She progressed from uttering a small number of automatic cries, which referred only to immediate emotions or situations, to learning a language system in which elements could be combined to make further statements. Beyond any doubt, she has learned more of a language, although in visual terms, than any other nonhuman before her. Nevertheless, Washoe's achievement falls far short of the human child's. The fact that a human child at an equivalent stage of development has a vocabulary of thousands of words instead of only 150 is the least significant difference. More important, Washoe apparently does not understand the principles of grammar, as human children do by age three when they construct sentences according to the patterns offered by their languages. An English-speaking child, for example, knows the difference between the subject-predicate-object pattern of *Baby going home* and the question pattern of *Is baby going home?*—but Washoe does not. When Washoe wants to be tickled, she signals any one of several combinations that have no reference at all to sentence structure; *you tickle, tickle you,* or *me tickle*.

The major deficiency in Washoe's accomplishment, though, concerns the relationship of language to human thought. Human beings conceive of their environment as interlocked objects, properties, and actions. A chair is not simply a kind of object, but rather it belongs to a particular category. Because it is inanimate, it can be broken—but it lacks animate characteristics, which means that it cannot drink milk. That is why *chair* can take a verb that refers to inanimate subjects, *break*, but not a verb that refers to animate things, *drink*. A child who unravels a simple statement like *The chair broke* thus must do more than decode a grammatical utterance. He must first master the subtle category of things that *break*, like *chairs* and also *machines* and *windowpanes*. Then he must distinguish the category of things that *break* from things that *tear*, like *paper* and *bedsheets*, or things that *smash*, like *vases* and *cars*. The child must next interpret the influence on the chair of the verb *broke* out of all the possibilities that verb implies, such as that the breaking of a chair is conceptually different from breaking the bank at Monte Carlo or from waves breaking on a beach. To achieve all this, the child unconsciously unravels the sentence into parts that can be analyzed, and then puts the elements together again in a meaningful fashion. Nothing in Washoe's behavior indicates that she uses language in this metaphorical way, which is, after all, the very hallmark of the human mind.

About the time that the Gardners began their experiments with Washoe, David Premack, a psychologist at the University of California, started to teach a chimpanzee named Sarah to read and write by means of a code of variously shaped and colored pieces of plastic, each of which represented a "word." Within six years she had mastered a vocabulary of more than 130 different pieces of plastic; amazingly, she seemed able to understand the grammatical relationships between words which Washoe did not understand. She often makes correct choices between questions, between the concepts of "same" and "different," between the ideas of color and size. She has even shown that she can understand the complex grammatical structure of a compound sentence. When her trainers arranged plastic pieces to mean *Sarah, put the apple in the pail and the banana in the dish,* she responded by the appropriate actions. To do so, she needed to understand that *apple* and *pail* belonged together, but not *apple* and *dish*. Moreover, she had to know the grammatical function of *put*, that it referred to both the *apple* and the *banana*—and she had to interpret the sentence to mean that she was the one who was supposed to do all these things.

Despite Sarah's remarkable responses, serious doubts remain whether or not she has achieved language as human beings know it. Since she performs correctly only about 75 to 80 per cent of the time, the question arises whether or not she has truly internalized the rules of her language. She appears to handle language in somewhat the same way that trained pigeons are able to "play" Ping-Pong. The pigeons, of course, are not truly playing the game of Ping-Pong. They do not unconsciously know the rules of the game even though they go through the motions of it; they lack the desire to win, the satisfaction of a successful play, individual styles, the selection of one strategy in place of another at various stages of the game. Evidence for a lack of internalization is Sarah's failure to generate sentences on her own; she merely accepts those offered by her trainers for her to read and to reply to. A further question that must be raised is whether or not the "Clever Hans Phenomenon" is operative with Sarah. Since she performs better with some experimenters than with others, it is possible that she also is detecting nonverbal cues.

Both Sarah and Washoe had to be taught language by human beings, but the honeybee has on its own evolved a communication system that possesses most of the features of human language—although it does so in a trivial way. When a foraging honeybee locates a source of pollen or nectar, she brings a sample of her find to the hive and thereby informs the other workers about the kind of flowers to look for. She also tells them the exact distance to the source by the tempo of a dance she performs in the form of a figure eight. And the exact direction in which to fly (after, unbelievably, the dancer compensates for wind direction) is indicated by the angle of the dance path. The dance thus conveys two kinds of information: the distance from the hive to the food source and the direction based on the angle of the sun. The other workers use this information to fly unerringly to a source that is sometimes as far away as eight miles.

Strictly speaking, the bee dance meets most of the criteria for a language. It uses arbitrary symbols (the various movements of the dance); it combines them in apparently infinite ways to communicate about something remote in space and time (the food source which the forager recently discovered but can no longer see); and it constantly communicates about situations which the bees have never before experienced (each food source is a unique occurrence at a particular time and place). The bee dance, though, is severely limited as to what it can communicate. It always contains two, and exactly two, components: distance and direction. Some English sentences also contain only two components—such as *Birds fly*—but speakers of English are not forced to construct all their sentences out of a single noun and a single verb. If the other bees in the hive refuse to respond to the communication by the forager, she cannot express the message in any other way. She cannot ask the question *Why don't you fly to the food?* Nor can she issue the imperative *Fly out and forage!* She can only repeat her dance over and over again.

The topics that bees can communicate about—pollen and new locations for hives—are undoubtedly of endless fascination to them but of limited interest to almost all other living things. Bees cannot use their language to explain English grammar, but human beings can talk about the way bees communicate by dancing. Human language is unique in that it can be used as what linguists call a "metalanguage": It can state the rules of any communication system, including its own. In other words, only human language can talk about language. A speaker can discuss the dance of the bees or anything else that he cares to, even when it is foolish or a lie. Because human beings alone possess language, they can handle the barriers of time and space, have a history, speculate about the future, and create in myths beings that never existed and may never exist.

The study of animal communication reveals that human language is not simply a more complex example of a capacity that exists elsewhere in the living world. One animal or another may share a few features with human language, but it is clear that language is based on different principles altogether. So far as is known, people can speak because of their particular kind of vocal apparatus and their specific type of mental organization, not simply because of their higher degree of intelligence. No prototype for language has been found in the apes and monkeys, and no parrot or mynah bird has ever recombined the words it learned into novel utterances. In contrast, every human community in the world possesses a complete language system. Obviously, something happened in evolution to create Man the Talker. But what was it?

Since sentences do not leave anything equivalent to the fossils and pottery shards that allow anthropologists to trace the prehistory of man, linguists can only speculate about the origins of language. Theories have been advanced, have won adherents for a while, then later were shown to be fanciful—and given derisive baby-talk names. Because some of these theories occasionally reappear today in new guises, let me mention several of them as a guide to the wary.

The Bow-Wow Theory states that language arose when man imitated the sounds of nature by the use of onomatopoeic words like *cock-a-doodle-do*, *cuckoo*, *sneeze*, *splash*, and *mumble*. This theory has been thoroughly discredited. It is now known that many onomatopoeic words are of recent, not ancient, origin and that some of them were not derived from natural sounds at all. But the most telling argument against the Bow-Wow Theory is that onomatopoeic words vary from language to language. If the human species had truly based its words on the sounds of nature, these words should be the same in all languages because of the obvious fact that a dog's bark is the same throughout the world. Yet the *bow-wow* heard by speakers of English sounds like *gua-gua* to Spaniards, *af-af* to Russians, and *wan-wan* to Japanese.

The Ding-Dong Theory dates back to Pythagoras and Plato and was long honored, but nowadays it has no support whatsoever. This theory claims a relationship between a word and its sense because everything in nature is supposed to give off a harmonic "ring," which man supposedly detected when he named objects. But the Ding-Dong Theory cannot explain what resonance a small four-footed animal gave off to make Englishmen call it a *dog* rather than any other arbitrary collection of vowels and consonants—and what different resonance it communicated to Frenchmen to make them call it a *chien* or to Japanese to make them call it an *inu*.

Still other explanations for the origin of language are the Pooh-Pooh Theory, which holds that speech originated with man's spontaneous ejaculations of derision, fear, and other emotions; the Yo-Heave-Ho Theory, which claims that language evolved from the grunts and groans evoked by heavy physical labor; the

Sing-Song Theory, which placed the origin of speech in the love songs and the rhythmic chants of early man; and the Ha-Ha Theory; which states that language evolved out of spontaneous laughter. All these speculations have serious flaws, and none can withstand the close scrutiny of present knowledge about the structure of language and about the evolution of our species.

Lately, some anthropologists and linguists have speculated that language originated as a much more recent event than previously believed. Their evidence is largely circumstantial, but it is intriguing. It is based upon the slowness with which human culture evolved over millions of years until its sudden acceleration during the last Ice Age, between about 100,000 and 35,000 years ago. The forerunners of our species arose some five million years ago. Not until about three million years ago did they begin to make crude pebble tools—and they continued to make them in almost the same way, with only a few slight improvements, until the last Ice Age. Then a sudden burst in creativity occurred. This flowering of technology included the increasing diversity of design and materials—and, more important, the use of tools to make other tools by a variety of methods such as boring, scraping, cutting, and polishing. Of all the possible ways to account for this florescence of culture after millions of years of barely perceptible change, the most apparent is the rise of speech as we know it today (but no doubt building upon some earlier system of communication). One vital property of speech is that it can talk about the future; it can plan forward. The flowering of tool manufacture during the last Ice Age demanded just such forward planning, because the succession of different operations, one following the other in precise order, could be achieved only by involved discussions.

Every new discovery in animal behavior, human evolution, or human physiology provides the impetus for scholars to construct new theories about the origins of speech. We can expect that some linguists will continue to search back into the unrecorded past to discover the well-springs of speech, even though most of them today despair of ever finding it. In fact, since 1866 the Linguistic Society of Paris has had a rule that the origin of language is one topic it would not discuss at its meetings. Speculations may be provocative, well reasoned, and based on available evidence—but they never can be demonstrated to be anything more than possibilities. Evidence about language goes back only as far as the earliest written documents, a mere five thousand years or so ago. But by that time languages were already fully developed and not significantly different in kind from those spoken today.

16

How Languages Code Reality

BY DOROTHY LEE

. . . .

The people of the Trobriand Islands codify, and probably apprehend reality, nonlineally in contrast to our own lineal phrasing. Basic to my investigation of the codification of reality in these two societies, is the assumption that a member of a given society not only codifies experienced reality through the use of the specific language and other patterned behavior characteristics of his culture, but that he actually grasps reality only as it is presented to him in this code. The assumption is not that reality itself is relative; rather, that it is differently punctuated and categorized, or that different aspects of it are noticed by, or presented to the participants of different cultures. If reality itself were not absolute, then true communication of course would be impossible. My own position is that there is an absolute reality, and that communication is possible. If, then, that which the different codes refer to is ultimately the same, a careful study and analysis of a different code and of the culture to which it belongs should lead us to concepts which are ultimately comprehensible, when translated into our own code. It may even, eventually, lead us to aspects of reality from which our own code excludes us.

It is a corollary of this assumption that the specific phrasing of reality can be discovered through intensive and detailed analysis of any aspect of culture. My own study was begun with an analysis of linguistic formulation, only because it is in language that I happen to be best able to discover my clues. To show how these clues can be discovered and used as guides to the apprehension of reality, as well as to show what I mean by codification, I shall present at first concrete material from the field of language.

That a word is not the reality, not the thing which it represents, has long been commonplace to all of us. The thing which I hold in my hand as I write, *is* not a pencil; I *call* it a pencil. And it remains the same whether I call it *pencil, molyvi, Bleistift,* or *siwigog.* These words are different sound-complexes applied to the same reality; but is the difference merely one of

sound-complex? Do they refer to the same *perceived* reality? *Pencil* originally meant little tail; it delimited and named the reality according to form. *Molyvi* means lead and refers to the writing element. *Bleistift* refers both to the form and to the writing-element. *Siwigog* means painting-stick and refers to observed function and form. Each culture has phrased the reality differently. To say that *pencil,* for example, applies primarily to form is no idle etymologic statement. When we use this word metaphorically, we refer neither to writing element nor to function, but to form alone; we speak of a pencil of light, or a styptic pencil.

When I used the four words for this object, we all knew what reality was referred to; we knew the meaning of the word. We could visualize the object in my hand, and the words all delimited it in the same way; for example, none of them implied that it was a continuation of my fist. But the student of ethnography often has to deal with words which punctuate reality into different phrasings from the ones with which he is familiar. Let us take, for instance, the words for "brother" and "sister." We go to the islands of Ontong Java to study the kinship system. We ask our informant what he calls his sister and he says *ave;* he calls his brother *kainga.* So we equate *ave* with "sister" and *kainga* with "brother." By way of checking our information we ask the sister what she calls her brother; it turns out that for her *ave* is "brother," not "sister" as we were led to expect; and that it is her sister whom she calls *kainga.*

The same reality, the same actual kinship is present there as with us; but we have chosen a different aspect for naming. We are prepared to account for this; we say that both cultures name according to what we would call a certain type of blood relationship; but whereas we make reference to absolute sex, they refer to relative sex. Further inquiry, however, discloses that in this, also, we are wrong. Because in our own culture we name relatives according to formal definition and biologic relationship, we have thought that

108   Originally published as "Lineal and Nonlineal Codifications of Reality." Reprinted by permission of Elsevier Science Publishing Company, Inc., from *Psychosomatic Medicine* 12, May 1950, pp. 89–97. The bibliography is omitted.

this formulation represents reality; and we have tried to understand the Ontong Javanese relationship terms according to these distinctions which, we believe, are given in nature. But the Ontong Javanese classifies relatives according to a different aspect of reality, differently punctuated. And because of this, he applies *kainga* as well to a wife's sister and a husband's brother; to a man's brother's wife and a woman's sister's husband, as well as to a number of other individuals.

Neither sex nor blood relationship, then, can be basic to this term. The Ontong Javanese name according to formal definition. A man shares the ordinary details of his living with his brothers and their wives for a large part of the year; he sleeps in the same large room, he eats with them, he jokes and works around the house with them; the rest of the year he spends with his wife's sisters and their husbands, in the same easy companionship. All these individuals are *kainga* to one another. The *ave*, on the other hand, names a behavior of great strain and propriety; it is based originally upon the relative sex of siblings, yes, but it does not signify biologic fact alone. It names a social relationship, a behavior, an emotional tone. *Ave* can never spend their adult life together, except on rare and temporary occasions. They can never be under the same roof alone together, cannot chat at ease together, cannot refer even distantly to sex in the presence of each other, not even to one's sweetheart or spouse; more than that, everyone else must be circumspect when the *ave* of someone of the group is present. The *ave* relationship also carries special obligations toward a female *ave* and her children. *Kainga* means a relationship of ease, full of shared living, of informality, gaiety; *ave* names one of formality, prohibition, strain.

These two cultures, theirs and our own, have phrased and formulated social reality in completely different ways, and have given their formulation different names. The word is merely the name of this specific cultural phrasing. From this one instance we might formulate the hypothesis—a very tentative one—that among the Ontong Javanese names describe emotive experiences, not observed forms or functions. But we cannot accept this as fact, unless further investigation shows it to be implicit in the rest of their patterned behavior, in their vocabulary and the morphology of their language, in their ritual and their other organized activity.

One more instance, this time from the language of the Wintu Indians of California, will deal with the varying aspect or segmentation of experience which is used as a basis of classification. To begin with, we take the stem *muk*. On the basis of this stem we form the word *mukeda*, which means: "I turned the basket bottom up"; we form *mukuhara*, which means: "The turtle

is moving along"; and we form *mukurumas*, which means: "automobile." Upon what conceivable principle can an automobile be put in the same category as a turtle and a basket? There is such a principle, however, and it operates also when the Wintu calls the activity of laundering, *to make foam continuously*. According to this principle, he uses only one stem (*puq* or *poq*) to form words for all of the following:

puqeda: I just pushed a peg into the ground.
olpuqal: He is sitting on one haunch.
poqorahara: Birds are hopping along.
olpoqoyabe: There are mushrooms growing.
tunpoqoypoqoya: You walk shortskirted, stifflegged ahead of me.

It is difficult for us to discover the common denominator in the different formations from this one stem, or even to believe that there can be one. Yet, when we discover the principle underlying the classification, the categories themselves are understandable. Basic to the classification is the Wintu view of himself as observer; he stays outside the event. He passes no judgment on essence, and where we would have used kinesthetic or participatory experience as the basis of naming, he names as an observer only, for the shape of the activity or the object. The turtle and the automobile can thus naturally be grouped together with the inverted baskets. The mushroom standing on its stem, the fist grasping a peg against the ground, the stiff leg topped by a short skirt or by the body of a bird or of a man resting on a haunch, obviously all belong together in one category. But the progress of a grasshopper cannot be categorized with that of a hopping bird. We, who classify on a different basis, apprehend the hop of the two kinesthetically and see it as basically the same in both cases; but the Wintu see the difference in recurrent shape, which is all-important to them, and so name the two by means of completely different stems. Again, when we discover this principle, it is easy to see that from the observer's point of view laundering is the making of a lot of foam; and to see why, when beer was introduced to the Wintu, it was named *laundry*.

I have discussed at length the diversity of codification of reality in general, because it is the foundation of the specific study which I am about to present. I shall speak of the formulation of experienced reality among the Trobriand Islanders in comparison to our own; I shall speak of the nature of expectancy, of motivation, of satisfaction, as based upon a reality which is differently apprehended and experienced in two different societies; which is, in fact, for each, a different reality. The Trobriand Islanders were studied by the late Bronislaw Malinowski, who has given us the rich and circumstantial material about them which has made this study possible. I have given a detailed presentation of some implications of their language elsewhere; but since it was in their language that I first noticed the absence of lineality, which led me to this study, I shall give here a summary of the implications of the language.

A Trobriand word refers to a self-contained concept. What we consider an attribute of a predicate, is to the Trobriander an ingredient. Where I would say, for example, "A good gardener," or "The gardener is good," the Trobriand word would include both "gardener" and "goodness"; if the gardener loses the goodness, he has lost a defining ingredient, he is something else, and he is named by means of a completely different word. A *taytu* (a species of yam) contains a certain degree of ripeness, bigness, roundedness, etc.; without one of these defining ingredients, it is something else, perhaps a *bwanawa* or a *yowana*. There are no adjectives in the language; the rare words dealing with qualities are substantivized. The term *to be* does not occur; it is used neither attributively nor existentially, since existence itself is contained; it is an ingredient of being.

Events and objects are self-contained points in another respect; there is a series of beings, but not becoming. There is no temporal connection between objects. The taytu always remains itself; it does not *become* overripe; overripeness is an ingredient of another, a different being. At some point, the taytu *turns into* a yowana, which contains overripeness. And the yowana, overripe as it is, does not put forth shoots, does not *become* a sprouting yowana. When sprouts appear, it ceases to be itself; in its place appears a *silasata*. Neither is there a temporal connection made — or, according to our own premises, perceived — between events; in fact, temporality is meaningless. There are no tenses, no linguistic distinction between past or present. There is no arrangement of activities or events into means and ends, no causal or teleologic relationships. What we consider a causal relationship in a sequence of connected events, is to the Trobriander an ingredient of a patterned whole. He names this ingredient *u'ula*.

There is no automatic relating of any kind in the language. Except for the rarely used verbal it-differents and it-sames, there are no terms of comparison whatever. And we find in an analysis of behavior that the standard for behavior and of evaluation is noncomparative.

These implications of the linguistic material suggest to my mind an absence of axiomatic lineal connection between events or objects in the Trobriand apprehension of reality, and this implication, as I shall attempt to show below, is reinforced in their definition of activity. In our own culture, the line is so basic, that we take it for granted, as given in reality. We see it in visible nature, between material points, and we see it between metaphorical points such as days or acts. It underlies not only our thinking, but also our aesthetic apprehension of the given; it is basic to the emotional climax which has so much value for us, and, in fact, to the meaning of life itself. In our thinking about personality and character, we have taken for granted the presence of the line.

In our academic work, we are constantly acting in terms of an implied line. When we speak of *applying* an *attribute*, for example, we visualize the process as lineal, coming from the outside. If I make a picture of an apple on the board, and want to show that one side is green and the other red I connect these attributes with the pictured apple by means of lines, as a matter of course; how else would I do it? When I organize my data, I *draw* conclusions *from* them. I *trace* a relationship between my facts. I describe a pattern as a *web* of relationships. Look at a lecturer who makes use of gestures; he is constantly making lineal connections in the air. And a teacher with chalk in hand will be drawing lines on the board whether he be a psychologist, a historian, or a paleontologist.

Preoccupation with social facts merely as self-contained facts is mere antiquarianism. In my field, a student of this sort would be an amateur or a dilettante, not an anthropologist. To be an anthropologist, he can arrange his facts in an upward slanting line, in a *unilinear* or *multilinear course* of development; or in *parallel lines* or *converging lines*. Or he may arrange them geographically, with *lines* of diffusion connecting them; or schematically, using *concentric circles*. Or at least, he must indicate what his study *leads to*, what new insights we can *draw from* it. To be accorded status, he must use the guiding line as basic.

The line is found or presupposed in most of our scientific work. It is present in the *induction* and the *deduction* of science and logic. It is present in the philosopher's phrasing of means and ends as lineally connected. Our statistical facts are presented lineally as a *graph* or reduced to a normal *curve*. And all of us, I think, would be lost without our *diagrams*. We *trace* a historical development; we *follow the course* of history and evoluation *down to* the present and *up from* the ape; and it is interesting to note, in passing, that whereas both evolution and history are lineal, the first goes up the blackboard, the second goes down.

Our psychologists picture motivation as external, connected with the act through a line, or, more recently, entering the organism through a lineal channel and emerging transformed, again lineally, as response. I have seen lineal pictures of nervous impulses and heartbeats, and with them I have seen pictured lineally a second of time. These were photographs, you will say, of existing fact, of reality; a proof that the line is present in reality. But I am not convinced, perhaps due to my ignorance of mechanics, that we have not created our recording instruments in such a way that they have to picture time and motion, light and sound, heartbeats and nerve impulses lineally, on the unquestioned assumption of the line as axiomatic. The line is omnipresent and inescapable, and so we are incapable of questioning the reality of its presence.

When we see a *line* of trees, or a *circle* of stones, we assume the presence of a connecting line which is not actually visible. And we assume it metaphorically when we follow a *line* of thought, a *course* of action or the *direction* of an argument; when we *bridge* a gap in the conversation, or speak of the *span* of life or of teaching a *course,* or lament our *interrupted career.* We make children's embroidery cards and puzzle cards on this assumption; our performance tests and even our tests for sanity often assume that the line is present in nature and, at most, to be discovered or given visual existence.

But is the line present in reality? Malinowski, writing for members of our culture and using idiom which would be comprehensible to them, described the Trobriand village as follows: "Concentrically with the circular row of yam houses there runs a ring of dwelling huts." He saw, or at any rate, he represented the village as two circles. But in the texts which he recorded, we find that the Trobrianders at no time mention circles or rings or even rows when they refer to their villages. Any word which they use to refer to a village, such as *a* or *this;* is prefixed by the substantival element *kway* which means *bump* or *aggregate of bumps.* This is the element which they use when they refer to a pimple or a bulky rash; or to canoes loaded with yams. In their terms, a village is an aggregate of bumps; are they blind to the circles? Or did Malinowski create the circles himself, out of his cultural axiom?

Again, for us as well as in Malinowski's description of the Trobrianders, which was written necessarily in terms meaningful to us, all effective activity is certainly not a haphazard aggregate of acts, but a lineally planned series of acts leading to an envisioned end. Their gardening with all its specialized activities, both technical and magical, leading to a rich harvest; their *kula* involving the cutting down of trees, the communal dragging of the tree to the beach, the rebuilding or building of large seaworthy canoes, the provisioning, the magical and ceremonial activities involved— surely all these can be carried through only if they are lineally conceived.

But the Trobrianders do not describe their activity lineally; they do no dynamic relating of acts; they do not use even so innocuous a connective as *and.* Here is part of a description of the planting of coconut: "Thou-approach-there coconut thou-bring-here-we-plant-coconut thou-go-thou-plant our coconut. This-here it-emerge sprout. We-push-away this we-push away this-other coconut-husk-fiber together sprout it-sit together root." We who are accustomed to seek lineal continuity, cannot help supplying it as we read this; but the continuity is not given in the Trobriand text; and all Trobriand speech, according to Malinowski, is "jerky," given in points, not in connecting lines. The only connective I know of in Trobriand is the *pela* which I mentioned above; a kind of preposition which also means "to jump."

I am not maintaining here that the Trobrianders cannot see continuity; rather that lineal connection is not automatically made by them, as a matter of course. At Malinowski's persistent questioning, for example, they did attempt to explain their activities in terms of cause or motivation, by stating possible "results" of uncooperative action. But Malinowski found their answers confused, self-contradictory, inconsistent; their preferred answer was, "It was ordained of old"— pointing to an ingredient value of the act instead of giving an explanation based on lineal connection.

And when they were not trying to find answers to leading questions, the Trobrianders made no such connection in their speech. They assumed, for example, that the validity of a magical spell lay, not in its results, not in proof, but in its very being; in the appropriateness of its inheritance, in its place within the patterned activity, in its being performed by the appropriate person, in its realization of its mythical basis. To seek validity through proof was foreign to their thinking, yet they attempted to do so at the ethnographer's request. I should add here that their names for constellations imply that here they do see lineal figures; I cannot investigate the significance of this, as I have no contextual material. At any rate, I would like to emphasize that, even if the Trobriander does occasionally supply connecting lines between points, his perception and experience do not automatically fall into a lineal framework.

The fact remains that Trobrianders embark on, what is certainly for us, a series of acts which "must require" planning and purposiveness. They engage in acts of gift-giving and gift-receiving which we can certainly see as an exchange of gifts if we want to. When we plot their journeys, we find that they do go from point to point, they do navigate a course, whether they say so or not. Do they merely refrain from giving linguistic expression to something which they actually recognize in nature? On the nonlinguistic level, do they act on an assumption of a lineality which is given no place in their linguistic formulation?

I believe that, where valued activity is concerned, the Trobrianders do not act on an assumption of lineality at any level. There is organization or rather coherence in their acts because Trobriand activity is patterned activity. One act within this pattern brings into existence a preordained cluster of acts. Perhaps one might find a parallel in our culture in the making of a sweater. When I embark on knitting one, the ribbing at the bottom does not *cause* the making of the neckline, nor of the sleeves or the armholes; and it is not part of a lineal series of acts. Rather it is an indispensable part of a patterned activity which includes all of these other acts. Again, when I choose a dress pattern, the acts involved in the making of the dress are already present for me. They are embedded in the pattern which I have chosen.

In this same way, I believe, can be seen the Trobriand insistence that though intercourse is a necessary preliminary to conception, it is not the cause of conception. There are a number of acts in the pattern of procreating; one is intercourse, another the entrance of the spirit of a dead Trobriander into the womb. However, there is a further point here. The Trobrianders, when pressed by the ethnographer or teased by the neighboring Dobuans, showed signs of intense embarrassment, giving the impression that they were trying to maintain unquestioningly a stand in which they had to believe. This, I think, is because pattern is truth and value for them; in fact, acts and being derive value from the embedding pattern.

So the question of the perception of a line remains. It is because they find value in pattern that the Trobrianders act according to nonlinear pattern; not because they cannot perceive lineality.

But all Trobriand activity does not contain value; and when it does not, it assumes lineality, and is utterly despicable. For example, the pattern of sexual intercourse includes the giving of a gift from the boy to the girl; but if a boy gives a gift so as to win the girl's favor, he is despised. Again, the kula pattern includes the eventual reception of a gift from the original recipient; the pattern is such that it keeps the acts physically and temporally completely disparate. In spite of this, however, some men are accused of giving gifts as an inducement to their kula partner to give them a specially good kula gift. Such men are labeled with the vile phrase: he barters. But this means that, unvalued and despised, lineal behavior does exist. In fact, there are villages in the interior whose inhabitants live mainly by bartering manufactured articles for yams. The inhabitants of Omarakana, about whom Malinowski's work and this study are mainly concerned, will barter with them, but consider them pariahs.

This is to say that it is probable that the Trobrianders experience reality in nonlinear pattern because this is the valued reality; and that they are capable of experiencing lineally, when value is absent or destroyed. It is not to say, however, that this in itself means that lineality is given, is present in nature, and that pattern is not. Our own insistence on the line, such as lineal causality, for example, is also often based on unquestioned belief or value. To return to the subject of procreation, the husband in our culture, who has long hoped, and tried in vain, to beget children, will nevertheless maintain that intercourse causes conception; perhaps with the same stubbornness and embarrassment which the Trobrianders exhibited when maintaining the opposite.

The line in our culture not only connects, but it moves. And as we think of a line as moving from point to point, connecting one to the other, so we conceive of roads as *running from* locality to locality. A Trobriander does not speak of roads either as connecting two points, or as *running from* point *to* point. His paths are self-contained, named as independent units; they are not *to* and *from*, they are *at*. And he himself is *at*; he has no equivalent for our *to* or *from*. There is, for instance, the myth of Tudava, who goes—in our view—from village to village and from island to island planting and offering yams. The Trobriand text puts it this way: "Kitava it-shine village already (i.e., completed) he-is-over. 'I-sail I-go Iwa'; Iwa he-anchor he-go ashore. . . . He-sail Digumenu. . . . They-drive (him off) . . . he-go Kwaywata." Point after point is enumerated, but his sailing from and to is given as a discrete event. In our view he is actually following a southeasterly course, more or less; but this is not given as course or line, and no directions are even mentioned. In fact, in the several texts referring to journeyings in the Archipelago, no words occur for the cardinal directions. In sailing, the "following" winds are named according to where they are *at*, the place where they strike the canoe, such as wind-striking-the-outrigger-beam; not according to where they *come from*. Otherwise, we find names for the southwest wind (*youyo*), and the northwest wind (*bombatu*), but these are merely substantival names which have nothing to do with direction; names for kinds of wind.

When a member of our society gives an unemotional description of a person, he follows an imaginary line, usually downward: from head to foot, from tip to toe, from hair to chin. The Navaho do the opposite, following a line upward. The Trobriander follows no line, at least none that I can see. "My head boils," says a kula spell; and it goes on to enumerate the parts of the head as follows: nose, occiput, tongue, larynx, speech, mouth. Another spell casting a protective fog, runs as follows: "I befog the hand, I befog the foot, I befog the head, I befog the shoulders . . ." There is a magic formula where we do recognize a line, but it is one which Malinowski did not record verbatim at the time, but which he put down later from memory; and it is not improbable that his memory edited the formula according to the lineality of his culture.

When the Trobriander enumerates the parts of a canoe, he does not follow any recognizable lineal order: "Mist . . . surround me my mast . . . the nose of my canoe . . . my sail . . . my steering oar . . . my canoe-gunwale . . . my canoe-bottom . . . my prow . . . my rib . . . my threading-stick . . . my prow-board . . . my transverse stick . . . my canoe-side."

Malinowski diagrams the garden site as a square piece of land subdivided into squares; the Trobrianders refer to it in the same terms as those which they use in referring to a village—a bulky object or an aggregate of bumps. When the plots in the garden site are apportioned to the gardeners, the named plots are assigned by name, the others by location along each named side of the garden. After this, the inner plots, the "belly" of the garden, are apportioned. Following along a physical rim is a procedure which we find elsewhere also. In a spell naming villages on the main island, there is a long list of villages which lie along the coast northward, then westward around the island, then south. To us, of course, this is lineal order. But we have no indication that the Trobrianders see other than geographical location, point after point, as they move over a physically continuous area; the line as a guide to procedure is not necessarily implied. No terms are used here which might be taken as an implication of continuity, no "along the coast" or "around" or "northward."

When we in our culture deal with events or experiences of the self, we use the line as guide for various reasons, two of which I shall take up here. First, we feel we must arrange events chronologically in a lineal order; how else could our historians discover the causes of a war or a revolution or a defeat? Among the Trobrianders, what corresponds to our history is an aggregate of anecdotes, that is, unconnected points, told without respect to chronological sequence, or development, or causal relationship; with no grammatical distinction made between words referring to past events, or to present or contemplated ones. And in telling an anecdote, they take no care that a temporal sequence should be followed. For instance, they said to Malinowski, "They-eat-taro, they-spew-taro, they-disgusted-taro"; but if time, as we believe, is a moving line, then the revulsion came first in time, the vomiting was the result, coming afterward. Again, they say, "This-here . . . ripes . . . falls-down truly gives-birth . . . sits seed in belly-his"; but certainly the seed is there first, and the birth follows in time, if time is lineal.

Secondly, we arrange events and objects in a sequence which is climactic, in size and intensity, in emotional meaning, or according to some other principle. We often arrange events from earlier to later, not because we are interested in historical causation, but because the present is the climax of our history. But when the Trobriander relates happenings, there is no developmental arrangement, no building up of emotional tone. His stories have no plot, no lineal development, no climax. And when he repeats his garden spell, his list is neither climactic, not anticlimactic; it sounds merely untidy to us:

> The belly of my garden lifts
> The belly of my garden rises
> The belly of my garden reclines
> The belly of my garden is-a-bushhen's-nest-in-lifting
> The belly of my garden is-an-anthill
> The belly of my garden lifts-bends
> The belly of my garden is-an-ironwood-tree-in-lifting
> The belly of my garden lies-down
> The belly of my garden burgeons.

When the Trobrianders set out on their great ceremonial kula expedition, they follow a preestablished order. First comes the canoe of the Tolab wage, an obscure subclan. Next comes the canoes of the great chiefs. But this is not climactic; after the great chiefs come the commoners. The order derives meaning not from lineal sequence, but from correspondence with a present, experienced, meaningful pattern, which is the recreation or realization of the mythical pattern; that which has been ordained of old and is forever. Its meaning does not lie in an item-to-item relationship, but in fitness, in the repetition of an established unit.

An ordering of this sort gives members of our society a certain esthetic dysphoria except when, through deliberate training, we learn to go beyond our cultural expectation; or, when we are too young to have taken on the phrasings of our culture. When we manipulate objects naively, we arrange them on some climactic lineal principle. Think of a college commencement, with the faculty arranged in order of rank or length of tenure or other mark of importance; with the students arranged according to increasing physical height, from shortest to tallest, actually the one absolutely irrelevant principle as regards the completion of their college education, which is the occasion for the celebration. Even when the sophisticated avoid this principle, they are not unconscious of it; they are deliberately avoiding something which is there.

And our arrangement of history, when we ourselves are personally involved, is mainly climactic. My great grandmother sewed by candle light, my grandmother used a kerosene lamp, my mother did her studying by gaslight, I did it by a naked electric ceiling light, and my children have diffused fluorescent lighting. This is progress; this is the meaningful sequence. To the Trobriander, climax in history is abominable, a denial of all good, since it would imply not only the presence of change, but also that change increases the good; but to him value lies in sameness, in repeated pattern, in the incorporation of all time within the same point. What is good in life is exact identity with all past Trobriand experience, and all mythical experience.

There is no boundary between past Trobriand existence and the present; he can indicate that an action is completed, but this does not mean that the action is past; it may be completed and present or timeless. Where we would say "many years ago" and use the past tense, the Trobriander will say "in my father's childhood" and use non-temporal verbs; he places the event situationally, not temporally. Past, present, and future are presented linguistically as the same, are present in his existence, and sameness with what we call the past and with myth, represents value to the Trobriander. Where we see a developmental line, the Trobriander sees a point, at most a swelling in value. Where we find pleasure and satisfaction in moving away from the point, in change as variety or progress, the Trobriander finds it in the repetition of the known, in maintaining the point; that is, in what we call monotony.

Esthetic validity, dignity, and value come to the Trobriander not through arrangement into a climactic line, but rather in the undisturbed incorporation of the events within their original, nonlineal order. The only history which has meaning for him is that which evokes the value of the point, or which, in the repetition, swells the value of the point. For example, every occasion in which a kula object participates becomes an ingredient of its being and swells its value; all these occasions are enumerated with great satisfaction, but the lineal course of the traveling kula object is not important.

As we see our history climactically, so do we plan future experiences climactically, leading up to future satisfaction or meaning. Who but a very young child would think of starting a meal with strawberry shortcake and ending it with spinach? We have come to identify the end of the meal with the height of satisfaction, and we identify semantically the words dessert and reward, only because of the similarity of their position in a climactic line. The Trobriand meal has no dessert, no line, no climax. The special bit, the relish, is eaten *with* the staple food; it is not something to "look *forward* to," while disposing of a meaningless staple.

None of the Trobriand activities is fitted into a climactic line. There is no job, no labor, no drudgery, which finds its reward outside the act. All work con-

tains its own satisfaction. We cannot speak of S–R here, as all action contains its own immanent "stimulus." The present is not a means to future satisfaction, but good in itself, as the future is also good in itself; neither better nor worse, neither climactic nor anticlimactic, in fact, not lineally connected nor removed.

It follows that the present is not evaluated in terms of its place within a course of action leading upward to a worthy end. In our culture, we can rarely evaluate the present in itself. I tell you that Sally is selling notions at Woolworth's, but this in itself means nothing. It acquires some meaning when I add that she has recently graduated from Vassar. However, I go on to tell you that she has been assistant editor of *Vogue*, next a nursemaid, a charwoman, a public school teacher. But this is a mere jumble; it makes no sense and has no meaning, because the series leads to nothing. You cannot relate one job to another, and you are unable to see them discretely simply as part of her being. However, I now add that she is gathering material for a book on the working mother. Now all this falls in line, it makes sense in terms of a career. Now her job is good and it makes her happy, because it is part of a planned climactic line leading to more pay, increased recognition, higher rank. There was a story in a magazine about the college girl who fell in love with the milkman one summer; the reader felt tense until it was discovered that this was just a summer job, that it was only a means for the continuation of the man's education in the Columbia Law School. Our evaluation of happiness and unhappiness is bound with this motion along an envisioned line leading to a desired end. In the fulfillment of this course or career—not in the fulfillment of the self as point—do we find value. Our conception of freedom rests on the principle of noninterference with this moving line, noninterruption of the intended course of action.

It is difficult to tell whether climax is given in experience at all, or whether it is always imposed on the given. At a time when progress and evolution were assumed to be implicit in nature, our musicians and writers gave us climactic works. Nowadays, our more reflective art does not present experience climactically. Then, is emotion itself climactic? Climax, for us, evokes "thrill" or "drama." But we have cultures, like the Tikopia, where life is lived, to our perception, on an even emotive plane without thrill or climax. Experiences which "we know to be" climactic, are described without climax by them. For example, they, as well as the Trobrianders, described intercourse as an aggregate of pleasurable experiences. But Malinowski is disturbed by this; he cannot place the erotic kiss in Trobriand experience, since it has no climactic function.

In our culture, childbearing is climactic. Pregnancy is represented by the usual obstetrician as an uncomfortable means to a dramatic end. For most women, all intensity of natural physical experience is nowadays removed from the actual birth itself; but the approach of birth nevertheless is a period of mounting tension, and drama is supplied by the intensive social recognition of the event, the dramatic accumulation of gifts, flowers, telegrams. A pregnancy is not formally announced since, if it does not eventuate in birth, it has failed to achieve its end; and failure to reach the climax brings shame. In its later stages it may be marked with a shower; but the shower looks forward to the birth, it does not celebrate the pregnancy itself. Among the Trobrianders, pregnancy has meaning in itself, as a state of being. At a first pregnancy, there is a long ceremonial involving "preparatory" work on the part of many people, which merely celebrates the pregnancy. It does not anchor the baby, it does not *have as its purpose* a more comfortable time during the pregnancy, it does not *lead to* an easier birth or a healthy baby. It makes the woman's skin white, and makes her be at her most beautiful; yet this *leads* to nothing, since she must not attract men, not even her own husband.

Are we then right in accepting without question the presence of a line in reality? Are we in a position to say with assurance that the Trobrianders are wrong and we are right? Much of our present-day thinking, and much of our evaluation, are based on the premise of the line and of the line as good. Students have been refused admittance to college because the autobiographic sketch accompanying their application showed absence of the line; they lacked purposefulness and ability to plan; they were inadequate as to character as well as intellectually. Our conception of personality formation, our stress on the significance of success and failure and of frustration in general, is based on the axiomatically postulated line. Yet can there be blocking without presupposed lineal motion or effort? If I walk along a path because I like the country, or if it is not important to get to a particular point at a particular time, then the insuperable puddle from the morning's shower is not frustrating; I throw stones into it and watch the ripples, and then choose another path. If the undertaking is of value in itself, a point good in itself, and not because it leads to something, then failure has no symbolic meaning; it merely results in no cake for supper, or less money in the family budget; it is not personally destructive. But failure is devastating in our culture, because it is not failure of the undertaking alone; it is the moving, becoming, lineally conceived self which has failed.

Ethnographers have occasionally remarked that the people whom they studied showed no annoyance when interrupted. Is this an indication of mild temper, or might it be the case that they were not interrupted at all, as there was no expectation of lineal continuity? Such questions are new in anthropology and most ethnographers therefore never thought of recording material to make us question the line as basic to all experience; whether it is actually present in given reality or not, it is not always present in experienced reality. We cannot even take it for granted as existing among those members of our society who are not completely or naively steeped in their culture, such as many of our artists, for example. And we should be very careful, in studying other cultures, to avoid the unexamined assumption that their actions are based on the predication of a lineal reality.

Seeing Is Believing

BY ALAN DUNDES

Whether from early memories of playing "peek-a-boo," "showing and telling" in school, or learning the opening phrase of the national anthem—"Oh, say can you see"—the primacy of vision in American culture is affirmed again and again as infants grow to adulthood. Americans are conditioned from childhood to believe that "what you see is what you get."

There is more to such a phenomenon than immediately meets the eye. That Americans rely more on vision than on other senses doesn't mean that they are aware of it. Nor does it mean that it is a peculiarly American trait. People everywhere rely on their senses to perceive their world and order their experiences, but since my data are derived from American folk speech, I cannot speak about others. In any case, because I have been taught to mistrust hearsay, I have decided to take a look at the evidence for a visual bias and to see for myself.

In Western thought, a distinction has commonly been made between sensory perception and reasoning. The power of reason is presumably the superior of the two. According to Aristotle, there are five senses—sight, hearing, smell, taste, and touch—which provide data generally deemed less trustworthy or, at least, frequently illusory, compared to the information that is provided by the faculties of rational thought. Subjective versus objective and body versus mind are other expressions of this distinction between the sensory and the rational. If we assume, however, that reasoning cannot take place without some reference to metaphor, then it is certainly possible that much American logic and reasoning is closely tied to metaphor in general and to visual metaphor in particular.

The allegedly inferior sensory experiences seem to be ranked according to how effective or reliable a given sense is assumed to be. In American culture, the sense of sight is normally the first of the five senses to be listed. However, whether sight is actually more useful or crucial for perception than the other senses is a moot question and, in fact, does not require an answer to show that a cultural bias for the sense of sight really exists. In the present context, it is not the literal meaning of sight that is important, but the metaphorical. I believe that, metaphorically speaking, Americans tend to *see* the world around them, rather than hear, feel, smell, or taste it. It may be no accident that Americans *observe* laws and holidays.

American speech provides persuasive evidence to support the notion that "vision" is used as a metaphor for "understanding." Consider, for example, the classic punning proverb, " 'I see,' said the blind man, as he picked up his hammer and saw." The oppositional structure in this text is produced by the juxtaposition of sight and blindness. Here is a clear distinction between literal and metaphorical seeing. Literally a blind man cannot see, but figuratively he certainly can.

Americans consistently speak of "seeing" the point of an argument when, in fact, an argument is not really seen but comprehended. Intellectual positions, or "perspectives," are frequently referred to as points of *view*. When articulated, they may be introduced by such formulas as, "As I see it" or "It all depends on how you look at it."

American culture is pronouncedly concerned with empiricism, and this empiricism is explicitly visual. "Seeing is believing" and "I'm from Missouri" (which means "you've got to show me") are indications of the emphasis on seeing something for oneself and the tendency to distrust anyone else's report of a given event. "I saw it with my own (two) eyes" is a common authenticating formula, as is the invitation to "see for yourself."

Without sight, there may be disbelief or lack of faith: "I'll believe it when I see it," "That I've got to see," or "I can't picture that." Even though the reliability of vision may be questioned—"There's more to this than meets the eye"—in general, people tend to believe what they see. Thus, when something is really out of the ordinary, we say,

"I couldn't believe my eyes." Something that is incredible or unbelievable is termed "out of sight," a phrase dating from before the end of the nineteenth century.

Imagination is sometimes called "the mind's eye," but why should the mind have an eye? Probably for the same reason that patients want doctors "to see them." Telephone conversations or other purely oral–aural channels are not considered entirely satisfactory. Actually, the patient is probably relieved by *his* seeing the doctor. Seeing the doctor, in turn, is part of the widespread cultural insistence upon interviews. Literally, the word *interview* refers to A seeing B and B seeing A.

Consider the nature of American tourist philosophy—sightseeing. To "see the sights" is a common goal of tourists, a goal also reflected in the mania for snapping pictures as permanent records of what was seen. Typical travel boasting consists of inflicting an evening of slide viewing on unwary friends so that they may see what their hosts saw.

This is surely a strange way of defining tourism. Visiting a foreign locale certainly involves all of the sensory apparatus. There are exotic smells and tastes, and the opportunity to savor new foods and experience the "feel" of a foreign setting is as important in understanding a country and its people as seeing them. One reason Americans frequently fail to enjoy touring as much as they might may be their almost compulsive tendency to see as many sights as possible. The seeing of many sights is, of course, consistent with a tendency to quantify living, and, specifically, with the desire to get one's money's worth.

When shopping, whether in foreign countries or at home, Americans are reluctant to buy anything "sight unseen." They prefer "to look something over," "to walk into something with their eyes open." A thorough inspection theoretically allows one to "see through" a pretense or fake. And obviously, a product can only "catch a person's eye" if he sees it.

Public "images," too, are part of

the visual pattern. But why, after all, should a person have to be depicted in a term such as image? Even though looks may be deceiving ("Never judge a book by its cover"), it seems clear that packaging that appeals to visual esthetics is equally effective whether one is hawking cigarettes or automobiles or selling political candidates.

The reduction of persons or events to purely visual terms is also evident in the use of the popular slang phrase for a detective: "private eye." By the same token, sleep is commonly referred to as "shut-eye," which obviously singles out only one aspect of the dormant state. Furthermore, this suggestion that sleep is shut-eye also implies that the waking state is marked chiefly by having one's eyes open.

As I collected examples of folk speech, I soon found that comparison of vision with the other senses reaffirmed the superiority of sight. That a "seer" can make predictions by gazing into a crystal ball, for example, suggests that vision is more effective than the other senses in fore*seeing* future events.

The same bias in favor of the visual is found in American greeting and leave-taking formulas. Examples include: "See you around," "I'll be seeing you," or "I haven't seen so-and-so in ages." Greetings may also be couched in visual terms. "It's good to see you," Americans say, rather than, "It's good to hear, smell, or feel you."

There seem to be relatively few complimentary references to hearers, smellers, talkers, and touchers. "Look, but don't touch" hints at a delight in gawking (girl-watching), and possibly at a cultural distaste for body contact. Someone who is "touchy" is not pleasant to have around. A "soft touch," which sounds as if it should have a positive connotation, is a slang term for a dupe or easy mark.

One of the most interesting pieces of evidence supporting the notion of visual superiority over the other senses is that the original version of "Seeing's believing" was presumably "Seeing's believing, but feeling's the truth." That most Americans have dropped the second portion of the proverb does not seem to be an accident. Rather, it reflects a definite penchant for the visual in contrast to the tactual. Originally, the proverb denigrated "seeing" in favor of "feeling."

Comparisons between the visual and the aural are the most common, however, with hearing considered second best. Consider "Believe nothing of what you hear and only half of what you see." Although caution is urged against believing everything one sees, seeing is surely depicted as being more reliable and trustworthy than hearing. Compare the following two statements: "I hear that X has just moved to Miami," and "I see that X has just moved to Miami." The first statement is possibly true, possibly not true: there is an element of doubt. The second, in contrast, seems to be a statement of fact.

Other instances are found in legal parlance. Although judges hear cases, there is no doubt that *hearsay*, that is, aural–oral, evidence is not in the same league as that offered by an eyewitness. Actually, the word *witness* indicates that the person was physically present during an event and saw with his own eyes the activities in question. If so, then the term *eyewitness* is redundant. Strangely enough, at *hearings* there is an insistence that *hearsay* evidence be rejected and that only *eyewitness* testimony be accepted.

On the other hand, it is interesting to recall that Justice is depicted as being blind. Justice cannot see and presumably blindness guarantees fairness. But of course, sometimes even an innocent man may be guilty "in the eyes of the law."

The eye is also more powerful than the ear insofar as it is regarded as an active rather than a passive agent. The eye looks, peers, or gazes. There is seductive power in the eye, as in "giving a girl the eye," and the malevolent power of the eye is manifested in "the evil eye." The ear, by contrast, is a passive receptacle. There is little evidence of evil ears. Remember also that "big brother is watching you," not listening to you, although bugging rooms with microphones makes listening more likely than watching. Note also that voyeurs, such as Peeping Toms, are considered to be worse than eavesdroppers. The active versus passive with respect to seeing and hearing may also be implied by the connotative differences between "spectators" and "audience."

Marshall McLuhan and his followers have suggested that the oral–aural channels of preliterate, or rather, nonliterate man may be enjoying a renaissance. According to this view, as man becomes literate, written language—which must be seen to be read—takes priority over the oral. Recently, however, radio and television have created postliterate man, whose world is once more primarily oral–aural. Many Americans learn the news of the day by hearing it on the radio rather than by reading it in newspapers. Even on television, the argument says, the news is mainly told, not shown. Then, too, telephone conversations are replacing letter writing more and more.

One can contend, however, that television has replaced radio, and thus the visual still supersedes the purely aural. Americans still prefer to get agreements in writing rather than to trust a gentleman's handshake (a tactile sign) or take someone's word or say-so (oral sign) for a contract. Once an agreement is

down in black and white, Americans watch out for, and read, the small print, with an "eye" toward avoiding an unfavorable set of conditions.

If Americans do have a deep-seated penchant for the visual sense, as I have tried to suggest by examining American folk speech, the question of what it means remains to be answered. It is not just a matter of being able to see more clearly why Americans tend to look for men of vision to lead them. Much more important is the influence of folk metaphors on scientific thought. American science is not culture-free, no matter how devoutly American scientists wish that it were or think that it is.

As an anthropologist, I am struck by the fact that American anthropologists insist upon being participant observers (not voyeurs!) when they go into the field so as to gain insight into the world-views of other cultures. Why "insight"? Do all examples of problem solving by insight actually involve visual perception? And why world-view?

Anthropologists do not always agree whether man is active or passive with regard to world-view. Bronislaw Malinowski, for example, tended to consider man passive: he depicted man as being molded by the impress of a culturally patterned, cookie cutter kind of world-view, which imposed its structure upon human minds. "What interests me really in the study of the native," Malinowski said, "is his outlook on things, his *Weltanschauung*. Every human culture gives its members a definite vision of the world." In contrast, Robert Redfield, by defining world-view as "the way a people characteristically look outward upon the universe," suggested that man was a more active participant. In any case, whether man passively accepts a culturally determined world-view or actively creates a world-view system, the visual bias in the very search by anthropologists for world-view is evident.

It has been observed that for Americans the universe is essentially something they can draw a picture or diagram of. But surely a person's world is felt, smelled, tasted, and heard as well. This propensity for visual metaphorical categories may produce distortion in attempts to describe facets of American culture. It is unlikely that such distortion would even be noticed, since the distortion, like beauty, is strictly in the subjective eye of the beholder. But what happens when Americans or American scientists seek to describe features of other cultures or the features of the natural world?

It is at least possible that by looking for the world-view of other peoples, we run the risk of imposing our own rank-ordering of the senses upon data that may not be perceived in the same way by the people whose cultures are being described. If we are truly interested in understanding how other peoples perceive reality, we must recognize their cognitive categories and try to escape the confines of our own.

The history of man is full of instances of one group's conscious or unconscious attempts to impose its particular set of cognitive categories upon another group. The imposing group typically claims that its categories represent the true nature of reality (as opposed to the categories of the victimized group, which are deemed odd at best and false at

worst). Whether it is nineteenth-century American linguists searching in vain for Latin cases (for example, the dative or accusative) in American Indian languages, or a modern Western physician, imbued with the number three, trying to persuade an American Indian, who believes in the sacredness of the number four, that only three doses or inoculations are sufficient (as in a series of three polio shots), the issue is the same.

This is why it is essential for Americans (and for other peoples as well) to become aware of their dependence upon cognitive categories such as the visual metaphorical mode I have been talking about. Armed with this awareness, it is possible to appreciate more fully the aptness of the visual metaphor Ruth Benedict used to explain why so many social theorists failed to notice custom or culture: "We do not see the lens through which we look." A conscious recognition of our visual bias may help make the lens visible. We must never forget the possible relativity of our own sensory perception categories.

Inventories of the same or similar sense categories found in other cultures may help. Clifford Geertz reports, for example, that the Javanese have five senses (seeing, hearing, *talking*, smelling, and feeling), which do not coincide exactly with

our five. The delineation of such differences may teach us just how culture-bound or culture-specific our own observations of nature may be. We tend to delude ourselves into thinking we are studying the nature of nature, foolishly forgetting that we cannot observe raw or pure nature. We can perceive nature only through the mediation of culture, with its panoply of culturally relative cognitive categories.

Much of the study of "natural history" often turns out to be "cultural history" in disguise. Theories and ideas about the natural world are invariably couched in terms of a specific human language and are based upon data obtained from human observation. With human observation expressed in human language, one simply cannot avoid cultural bias. Searching for culture-free descriptions of nature may be a worthwhile goal, and perhaps man will one day succeed in achieving it. In the meantime, we must be wary of mistaking relatives for absolutes, of mistaking culture for nature. Cross-cultural comparisons of sense categories may not only reveal critical differences in the specific senses, but also whether or not the apparent priority of vision over the other senses is a human universal. For the moment, we can do little more than wait and *see*.

18

The Sounds of Silence

BY EDWARD T. HALL AND MILDRED REED HALL

....

Bob leaves his apartment at 8:15 A.M. and stops at the corner drugstore for breakfast. Before he can speak, the counterman says, ''The usual?'' Bob nods yes. While he savors his Danish, a fat man pushes onto the adjoining stool and overflows into his space. Bob scowls and the man pulls himself in as much as he can. Bob has sent two messages without speaking a syllable.

Henry has an appointment to meet Arthur at 11 o'clock; he arrives at 11:30. Their conversation is friendly, but Arthur retains a lingering hostility. Henry has unconsciously communicated that he doesn't think the appointment is very important or that Arthur is a person who needs to be treated with respect.

George is talking to Charley's wife at a party. Their conversation is entirely trivial, yet Charley glares at them suspiciously. Their physical proximity and the movements of their eyes reveal that they are powerfully attracted to each other.

José Ybarra and Sir Edmund Jones are at the same party and it is important for them to establish a cordial relationship for business reasons. Each is trying to be warm and friendly, yet they will part with mutual distrust and their business transaction will probably fall through. José, in Latin fashion, moved closer and closer to Sir Edmund as they spoke, and this movement was miscommunicated as pushiness to Sir Edmund, who kept backing away from this intimacy, and this was miscommunicated to José as coldness. The silent languages of Latin and English cultures are more difficult to learn than their spoken languages.

In each of these cases, we see the subtle power of nonverbal communication. The only language used throughout most of the history of humanity (in evolutionary terms, vocal communication is relatively recent), it is the first form of communication you learn. You use this preverbal language, consciously and unconsciously, every day to tell other people how you feel about yourself and them. This language includes your posture, gestures, facial expressions, costume, the way you walk, even your treatment of time and space and

material things. All people communicate on several different levels at the same time but are usually aware of only the verbal dialog and don't realize that they respond to nonverbal messages. But when a person says one thing and really believes something else, the discrepancy between the two can usually be sensed. Nonverbal-communication systems are much less subject to the conscious deception that often occurs in verbal systems. When we find ourselves thinking, ''I don't know what it is about him, but he doesn't seem sincere,'' it's usually this lack of congruity between a person's words and his behavior that makes us anxious and uncomfortable.

Few of us realize how much we all depend on body movement in our conversation or are aware of the hidden rules that govern listening behavior. But we know instantly whether or not the person we're talking to is ''tuned in'' and we're very sensitive to any breach in listening etiquette. In white middle-class American culture, when someone wants to show he is listening to someone else, he looks either at the other person's face or, specifically, at his eyes, shifting his gaze from one eye to the other.

If you observe a person conversing, you'll notice that he indicates he's listening by nodding his head. He also makes little ''Hmm'' noises. If he agrees with what's being said, he may give a vigorous nod. To show pleasure or affirmation, he smiles; if he has some reservations, he looks skeptical by raising an eyebrow or pulling down the corners of his mouth. If a participant wants to terminate the conversation, he may start shifting his body position, stretching his legs, crossing or uncrossing them, bobbing his foot or diverting his gaze from the speaker. The more he fidgets, the more the speaker becomes aware that he has lost his audience. As a last measure, the listener may look at his watch to indicate the imminent end of the conversation.

Talking and listening are so intricately intertwined that a person cannot do one without the other. Even when one is alone and talking to oneself, there is part of the brain that speaks while another part listens. In all conversations, the listener is positively or negatively reinforcing the speaker all the time. He may even guide the conversation without knowing it, by laughing or frowning or dismissing the argument with a wave of his hand.

The language of the eyes—another age-old way of exchanging feelings—is both subtle and complex. Not only do men and women use their eyes differently but there are class, generation, regional, ethnic and national cultural differences. Americans often complain about the way foreigners stare at people or hold a glance too long. Most Americans look away from someone who is using his eyes in an unfamiliar way because it makes them self-conscious. If a man looks at another man's wife in a certain way, he's asking for trouble, as indicated earlier. But he might not be ill-mannered or seeking to challenge the husband. He might be a European in this country who hasn't learned our visual mores. Many American women visiting France or Italy are acutely embarrassed because, for the first time in their lives, men really look at them—their eyes, hair, nose, lips, breasts, hips, legs, thighs, knees, ankles, feet, clothes, hairdo, even their walk. These same women, once they have become used to being looked at, often return to the United States and are overcome with the feeling that "No one ever really looks at me anymore."

Analyzing the mass of data on the eyes, it is possible to sort out at least three ways in which the eyes are used to communicate: dominance vs. submission, involvement vs. detachment and positive vs. negative attitude. In addition, there are three levels of consciousness and control, which can be categorized as follows: (1) conscious use of the eyes to communicate, such as the flirting blink and the intimate nose-wrinkling squint; (2) the very extensive category of unconscious but learned behavior governing where the eyes are directed and when (this unwritten set of rules dictates how and under what circumstances the sexes, as well as people of all status categories, look at each other); and (3) the response of the eye itself, which is completely outside both awareness and control—changes in the cast (the sparkle) of the eye and the pupillary reflex.

The eye is unlike any other organ of the body, for it is an extension of the brain. The unconscious pupillary reflex and the cast of the eye have been known by people of Middle Eastern origin for years—although most are unaware of their knowledge. Depending on the context, Arabs and others look either directly at the eyes or deeply *into* the eyes of their interlocutor. We became aware of this in the Middle East several years ago while looking at jewelry. The merchant suddenly started to push a particular bracelet at a customer and said, "You buy this one." What interested us was that the bracelet was not the one that had been consciously selected by the purchaser. But the merchant, watching the pupils of the eyes, knew what the purchaser really wanted to buy. Whether he specifically knew *how* he knew is debatable.

A psychologist at the University of Chicago, Eckhard Hess, was the first to conduct systematic studies of the pupillary reflex. His wife remarked one evening, while watching him reading in bed, that he must be very interested in the text because his pupils were dilated. Following up on this, Hess slipped some pictures of nudes into a stack of photographs that he gave to his male assistant. Not looking at the photographs but watching his assistant's pupils, Hess was able to tell precisely when the assistant came to the nudes. In further experiments, Hess retouched the eyes in a photograph of a woman. In one print, he made the pupils small, in another, large; nothing else was changed. Subjects who were given the photographs found the woman with the dilated pupils much more attractive. Any man who has had the experience of seeing a woman look at him as her pupils widen with reflex speed knows that she's flashing him a message.

The eye-sparkle phenomenon frequently turns up in our interviews of couples in love. It's apparently one of the first reliable clues in the other person that love is genuine. To date, there is no scientific data to explain eye sparkle; no investigation of the pupil, the cornea or even the white sclera of the eye shows how the sparkle originates. Yet we all know it when we see it.

One common situation for most people involves the use of the eyes in the street and in public. Although eye behavior follows a definite set of rules, the rules vary according to the place, the needs and feelings of the people, and their ethnic background. For urban whites, once they're within definite recognition distance (16–32 feet for people with average eyesight), there is mutual avoidance of eye contact—unless they want something specific: a pickup, a handout or information of some kind. In the West and in small towns generally, however, people are much more likely to look at and greet one another, even if they're strangers.

It's permissible to look at people if they're beyond recognition distance; but once inside this sacred zone, you can only steal a glance at strangers. You *must* greet friends, however; to fail to do so is insulting. Yet, to stare too fixedly even at them is considered rude and hostile. Of course, all of these rules are variable.

A great many blacks, for example, greet each other in public even if they don't know each other. To blacks, most eye behavior of whites has the effect of giving the impression that they aren't there, but this is due to white avoidance of eye contact with *anyone* in the street.

Another very basic difference between people of different ethnic backgrounds is their sense of territoriality and how they handle space. This is the silent communication, or miscommunication, that caused friction between Mr. Ybarra and Sir Edmund Jones in our earlier example. We know from research that everyone has around himself an invisible bubble of space that contracts and expands depending on several factors: his emotional state, the activity he's performing at the time and his cultural background. This bubble is a kind of mobile territory that he will defend against intrusion. If he is accustomed to close personal distance between himself and others, his bubble will be smaller than that of someone who's accustomed to greater personal distance. People of North European heritage—English, Scandinavian, Swiss and German—tend to avoid contact. Those whose heritage is Italian, French, Spanish, Russian, Latin American or Middle Eastern like close personal contact.

People are very sensitive to any intrusion into their spatial bubble. If someone stands too close to you, your first instinct is to back up. If that's not possible, you lean away and pull yourself in, tensing your muscles. If the intruder doesn't respond to these body signals, you may then try to protect yourself, using a briefcase, umbrella or raincoat. Women—especially when traveling alone—often plant their pocketbook in such a way that no once can get very close to them. As a last resort, you may move to another spot and position yourself behind a desk or a chair that provides screening. Everyone tries to adjust the space around himself in a way that's comfortable for him; most often, he does this unconsciously.

Emotions also have a direct effect on the size of a person's territory. When you're angry or under stress, your bubble expands and you require more space. New York psychiatrist Augustus Kinzel found a difference in what he calls Body-Buffer Zones between violent and nonviolent prison inmates. Dr. Kinzel conducted experiments in which each prisoner was placed in the center of a small room and then Dr. Kinzel slowly walked toward him. Nonviolent prisoners allowed him to come quite close, while prisoners with a history of violent behavior couldn't tolerate his proximity and reacted with some vehemence.

Apparently, people under stress experience other people as looming larger and closer than they actually are. Studies of schizophrenic patients have indicated that they sometimes have a distorted perception of space, and several psychiatrists have reported patients who experience their body boundaries as filling up an entire room. For these patients, anyone who comes into the room is actually inside their body, and such an intrusion may trigger a violent outburst.

Unfortunately, there is little detailed information about normal people who live in highly congested urban areas. We do know, of course, that the noise, pollution, dirt, crowding and confusion of our cities induce feelings of stress in most of us, and stress leads to a need for greater space. The man who's packed into a subway, jostled in the street, crowded into an elevator and forced to work all day in a bull pen or in a small office without auditory or visual privacy is going to be very stressed at the end of his day. He needs places that provide relief from constant overstimulation of his nervous system. Stress from overcrowding is cumulative and people can tolerate more crowding early in the day than later; note the increased bad temper during the evening rush hour as compared with the morning melee. Certainly one factor in people's desire to commute by car is the need for privacy and relief from crowding (except, often, from other cars); it may be the only time of the day when nobody can intrude.

In crowded public places, we tense our muscles and hold ourselves stiff, and thereby communicate to others our desire not to intrude on their space and, above all, not to touch them. We also avoid eye contact, and the total effect is that of someone who has "tuned out." Walking along the street, our bubble expands slightly as we move in a stream of strangers, taking care not to bump into them. In the office, at meetings, in restaurants, our bubble keeps changing as it adjusts to the activity at hand.

Most white middle-class Americans use four main distances in their business and social relations: intimate, personal, social and public. Each of these distances has a near and a far phase and is accompanied by changes in the volume of the voice. Intimate distance varies from direct physical contact with another person to a distance of six to eighteen inches and is used for our most private activities—caressing another person or making love. At this distance, you are overwhelmed by sensory inputs from the other person—heat from the body, tactile stimulation from the skin, the fragrance of perfume, even the sound of breathing—all of which literally envelop you. Even at the far phase, you're still within easy touching distance. In general, the use of intimate distance in public between adults is frowned on. It's also much too close for strangers, except under conditions of extreme crowding.

In the second zone—personal distance—the close phase is one and a half to two and a half feet; it's at this distance that wives usually stand from their husbands in public. If another woman moves into this zone, the wife will most likely be disturbed. The far phase—two and a half to four feet—is the distance used to "keep someone at arm's length" and is the most common spacing used by people in conversation.

The third zone—social distance—is employed during business transactions or exchanges with a clerk or repairman. People who work together tend to use close social distance—four to seven feet. This is also the distance for conversation at social gatherings. To stand at this distance from someone who is seated has a dominating effect (e.g., teacher to pupil, boss to secretary). The far phase of the third zone—seven to twelve feet—is where people stand when someone says, "Stand back so I can look at you." This distance lends a formal tone to business or social discourse. In an executive office, the desk serves to keep people at this distance.

The fourth zone—public distance—is used by teachers in classrooms or speakers at public gatherings. At its farthest phase—25 feet and beyond—it is used for important public figures. Violations of this distance can lead to serious complications. During his 1970 U.S. visit, the president of France, Georges Pompidou, was harassed by pickets in Chicago, who were permitted to get within touching distance. Since pickets in France are kept behind barricades a block or more away, the president was outraged by this insult to his person, and President Nixon was obliged to communicate his concern as well as offer his personal apologies.

It is interesting to note how American pitchmen and panhandlers exploit the unwritten, unspoken conventions of eye and distance. Both take advantage of the fact that once explicit eye contact is established, it is rude to look away, because to do so means to brusquely dismiss the other person and his needs. Once having caught the eye of his mark, the panhandler then locks on, not letting go until he moves through the public zone, the social zone, the personal zone and, finally, into the intimate sphere, where people are most vulnerable.

Touch also is an important part of the constant stream of communication that takes place between people. A light touch, a firm touch, a blow, a caress are all communications. In an effort to break down barriers among people, there's been a recent upsurge in group-encounter activities, in which strangers are encouraged to touch one another. In special situations such as these, the rules for not touching are broken with group approval and people gradually lose some of their inhibitions.

Although most people don't realize it, space is perceived and distances are set not by vision alone but with all the senses. Auditory space is perceived with the ears, thermal space with the skin, kinesthetic space with the muscles of the body and olfactory space with the nose. And, once again, it's one's culture that determines how his senses are programmed—which sensory information ranks highest and lowest. The important thing to remember is that culture is very persistent. In this country, we've noted the existence of culture patterns that determine distance between people in the third and fourth generations of some families, despite their prolonged contact with people of very different cultural heritages.

Whenever there is great cultural distance between two people, there are bound to be problems arising from differences in behavior and expectations. An example is the American couple who consulted a psychiatrist about their marital problems. The husband was from New England and had been brought up by reserved parents who taught him to control his emotions and to respect the need for privacy. His wife was from an Italian family and had been brought up in close contact with all the members of her large family, who were extremely warm, volatile and demonstrative.

When the husband came home after a hard day at the office, dragging his feet and longing for peace and quiet, his wife would rush to him and smother him. Clasping his hands, rubbing his brow, crooning over his weary head, she never left him alone. But when the wife was upset or anxious about her day, the husband's response was to withdraw completely and leave her alone. No comforting, no affectionate embrace, no attention—just solitude. The woman became convinced her husband didn't love her and, in desperation, she consulted a psychiatrist. Their problem wasn't basically psychological but cultural.

Why has man developed all these different ways of communicating messages without words? One reason is that people don't like to spell out certain kinds of messages. We prefer to find other ways of showing our feelings. This is especially true in relationships as sensitive as courtship. Men don't like to be rejected and most women don't want to turn a man down bluntly. Instead, we work out subtle ways of encouraging or discouraging each other that save face and avoid confrontations.

How a person handles space in dating others is an obvious and very sensitive indicator of how he or she feels about the other person. On a first date, if a woman sits or stands so close to a man that he is acutely conscious of her physical presence—inside the intimate-distance zone—the man usually construes it to mean that she is encouraging him. However, before the man starts moving in on the woman, he should be sure what message she's really sending; otherwise, he risks bruising his ego. What is close to someone of North European background may be neutral or distant to someone of Italian heritage. Also, women sometimes use space as a way of misleading a man and there are few things that put men off more than women who communicate contradictory messages—such as women who cuddle up and then act insulted when a man takes the next step.

How does a woman communicate interest in a man? In addition to such familiar gambits as smiling at him, she may glance shyly at him, blush and then look away. Or she may give him a real come-on look and move in very close when he approaches. She may touch his arm and ask for a light. As she leans forward to light her cigarette, she may brush him lightly, enveloping him in her perfume. She'll probably continue to smile at him and she may use what ethologists call preening gestures—touching the back of her hair, thrusting her breasts forward, tilting her hips as she stands or crossing her legs if she's seated, perhaps even exposing one thigh or putting a hand on her thigh and stroking it. She may also stroke her wrists as she converses or show the palm of her hand as a way of gaining his attention. Her skin may be unusually flushed or quite pale, her eyes brighter, the pupils larger.

If a man sees a woman whom he wants to attract, he tries to present himself by his posture and stance as someone who is self-assured. He moves briskly and confidently. When he catches the eye of the woman, he may hold her glance a little longer than normal. If he gets an encouragaing smile, he'll move in close and engage her in small talk. As they converse, his glance shifts over her face and body. He, too, may make preening gestures—straightening his tie, smoothing his hair or shooting his cuffs.

How do people learn body language? The same way they learn spoken language—by observing and imitating people around them as they're growing up. Little girls imitate their mothers or an older female. Little boys imitate their fathers or a respected uncle or a character on television. In this way, they learn the gender signals appropriate for their sex. Regional, class and ethnic patterns of body behavior are also learned in childhood and persist throughout life.

Such patterns of masculine and feminine body behavior vary widely from one culture to another. In America, for example, women stand with their thighs together. Many walk with their pelvis tipped slightly forward and their upper arms close to their body. When they sit, they cross their legs at the knee or, if they are well past middle age, they may cross their ankles. American men hold their arms away from their body, often swinging them as they walk. They stand with their legs apart (an extreme example is the cowboy, with legs apart and thumbs tucked into his belt). When they sit, they put their feet on the floor with legs apart and, in some parts of the country, they cross their legs by putting one ankle on the other knee.

Leg behavior indicates sex, status and personality. It also indicates whether or not one is at ease or is showing respect or disrespect for the other person. Young Latin-American males avoid crossing their legs. In their world of *machismo* the preferred position for young males when with one another (if there is no older dominant male present to whom they must show respect) is to sit on the base of their spine with their leg muscles relaxed and their feet wide apart. Their respect position is like our military equivalent; spine straight, heels and ankles together—almost identical to that displayed by properly brought up young women in New England in the early part of this century.

American women who sit with their legs spread apart in the presence of males are *not* normally signaling a come-on—they are simply (and often unconsciously) sitting like men. Middle-class women in the presence of other women to whom they are very close may on occasion throw themselves down on a soft chair or sofa and let themselves go. This is a signal that nothing serious will be taken up. Males, on the other hand, lean back and prop their legs up on the nearest object.

The way we walk, similarly, indicates status, respect, mood and ethnic or cultural affiliation. The many variants of the female walk are too well known to go into here, except to say that a man would have to be blind not to be turned on by the way some women walk—a fact that made Mae West rich before scientists ever studied these matters. To white Americans, some French middle-class males walk in a way that is both humorous and suspect. There is a bounce and looseness to the French walk, as though the parts of the body were somehow unrelated. Jacques Tati, the French movie actor, walks this way; so does the great mime, Marcel Marceau.

Blacks and whites in America—with the exception of middle- and upper-middle-class professionals of both groups—move and walk very differently from each other. To the blacks, whites often seem incredibly stiff, almost mechanical in their movements. Black males, on the other hand, have a looseness and coordination that frequently makes whites a little uneasy; it's too different, too integrated, too alive, too male. Norman Mailer has said that squares walk from the shoulders, like bears, but blacks and hippies walk from the hips, like cats.

All over the world people walk not only in their own characteristic way but have walks that communicate the nature of their involvement with whatever it is they're doing. The purposeful walk of North Europeans is an important component of proper behavior on the job. Any male who has been in the military knows how essential it is to walk properly (which makes for a continuing source of tension between blacks and whites in the Service). The quick shuffle of servants in the Far East in the old days was a show of respect. On the island of Truk, when we last visited, the inhabitants even had a name for the respectful walk that one used when in the presence of a chief or when walking past a chief's house. The term was *sufan*, which meant to be humble and respectful.

The notion that people communicate volumes by their gestures, facial expressions, posture and walk is not new; actors, dancers, writers and psychiatrists have long been aware of it. Only in recent years, however, have scientists begun to make systematic observations of body motions. Ray L. Birdwhistell of the University of Pennsylvania is one of the pioneers in body-motion research and coined the term kinesics to describe this field. He developed an elaborate notation system to record both facial and body movements, using an approach similar to that of the linguist, who studies the basic elements of speech. Birdwhistell and other kinesicists such as Albert Sheflen, Adam Kendon and William Condon take movies of people interacting. They run the film over and over again, often at reduced speed for frame-by-frame analysis, so that they can observe even the slightest body movements not perceptible at normal interaction speeds. These movements are then recorded in notebooks for later analysis.

To appreciate the importance of nonverbal-communication systems, consider the unskilled inner-city black looking for a job. His handling of time and space alone is sufficiently different from the white middle-class pattern to create great misunderstandings on both sides. The black is told to appear for a job interview at a certain time. He arrives late. The white interviewer concludes from his tardy arrival that the black is irresponsible and not really interested in the job. What the interviewer doesn't know is that the black time system (often referred to by blacks as C.P.T.— colored people's time) isn't the same as that of whites. In the words of a black student who had been told to make an appointment to see his professor: "Man, you *must* be putting me on. I never had an appointment in my life."

The black job applicant, having arrived late for his interview, may further antagonize the white interviewer by his posture and his eye behavior. Perhaps he slouches and avoids looking at the interviewer; to him, this is playing it cool. To the interviewer, however, he may look shifty and sound uninterested. The interviewer has failed to notice the actual signs of interest and eagerness in the black's behavior, such as the subtle shift in the quality of the voice—a gentle and tentative excitement—an almost imperceptible change in the cast of the eyes and a relaxing of the jaw muscles.

Moreover, correct reading of black-white behavior is continually complicated by the fact that both groups are comprised of individuals—some of whom try to accommodate and some of whom make it a point of pride *not* to accommodate. At present, this means that many Americans, when thrown into contact with one another, are in the precarious position of not knowing which pattern applies. Once identified and analyzed, nonverbal-communications systems can be taught, like a foreign language. Without this training, we respond to nonverbal communications in terms of our own culture; we read everyone's behavior as if it were our own, and thus we often misunderstand it.

Several years ago in New York City, there was a program for sending children from predominantly black and Puerto Rican low-income neighborhoods to summer school in a white upper-class neighborhood on the East Side. One morning, a group of young black and Puerto Rican boys raced down the street, shouting and screaming and overturning garbage cans on their way to school. A doorman from an apartment building nearby chased them and cornered one of them inside a building. The boy drew a knife and attacked the doorman. This tragedy would not have occurred if the doorman had been familiar with the behavior of boys from low-income neighborhoods, where such antics are routine and socially acceptable and where pursuit would be expected to invite a violent response.

The language of behavior is extremely complex. Most of us are lucky to have under control one subcultural system—the one that reflects our sex, class, generation and geographic region within the United States. Because of its complexity, efforts to isolate bits of nonverbal communication and generalize from them are in vain; you don't become an instant expert of people's behavior by watching them at cocktail parties. Body language isn't something that's independent of the person, something that can be donned and doffed like a suit of clothes.

Our research and that of our colleagues has shown that, far from being a superficial form of communication that can be consciously manipulated, nonverbal-communication systems are interwoven into the fabric of the personality and, as sociologist Erving Goffman has demonstrated, into society itself. They are the warp and woof of daily interaction with others and they influence how one expresses oneself, how one experiences oneself as a man or a woman.

Nonverbal communications signal to members of your own group what kind of person you are, how you feel about others, how you'll fit into and work in a group, whether you're assured or anxious, the degree to which you feel comfortable with the standards of your own culture, as well as deeply significant feelings about the self, including the state of your own psyche. For most of us, it's difficult to accept the reality of another's behavioral system. And, of course, none of us will ever become fully knowledgeable of the importance of every nonverbal signal. But as long as each of us realizes the power of these signals, this society's diversity can be a source of great strength rather than a further—and subtly powerful—source of division.

V
Cultural Anthropology

○ ○

Cultural anthropolgy has two main areas of study. One, termed *ethnography*, is the intensive study, description, and analysis of a specific group of people and their culture. The other, *ethnology*, is the systematic comparison of materials across cultural boundaries, with the aim of detecting and specifying accurate generalizations (formerly called laws) about human behavior and culture. The concept of *culture* is central to both ethnography and ethnology.

What is *culture?* Surprisingly, although it is the central concept of anthropology, it is difficult to find exact agreement on the meaning of the term among anthropologists. Depending on their interests, some scholars emphasize the symbolic nature of culture; others, its function as a mechanism of adaptation; still others, the ways in which it structures our perception of the world; and yet others, on the ways it patterns behavior. Nevertheless, it is possible to find agreement among anthropologists with regard to some basic aspects of culture:

1. Culture is central to human existence. The biological and cultural sides of humankind evolved together, constantly affecting each other's course. The concept *human being* and the concept *culture* are thus inseparable.

2. Culture is not inherited through the genes. Each person acquires his or her culture through interaction with other members of the group(s) into which she or he is born. In other words, culture is learned.

3. Not only is culture learned, but also everything that is learned is culture. All human knowledge, all activities, all beliefs, values, mores, schemes for organizing information about the world, languages, philosophical systems, technologies, arts, and major behavioral patterns are learned and hence are aspects of culture.

4. Culture is a group phenomenon. The growing infant does not invent a culture for itself; it learns the culture of its society. Left all alone to its own devices, an infant *cannot* invent culture. Indeed, if a child is deprived of the opportunity to learn a language by the time it is five or six, it is probably unlikely ever to be able to learn one afterward.

5. Culture is patterned. All cultures of the world consist of many facets and elements. But theses are not randomly thrown together like marbles in a bag or patches on a quilt. There are systematic relationships among the elements of a culture, and change in one area is likely to cause stress or change in other areas.

6. Culture is symbolic. This means that all cultural phenomena have meanings beyond their own existence. (A cat, in American culture, is not just an animal with the label "cat." It "has nine lives," is "stealthy," and is "independent." A cat, then, as a part of our culture, represents a set of meanings; in other words, it is a symbol.) Culture, therefore, provides the backdrop of shared meanings against which all things are experienced.

As you can appreciate, the subject of cultural anthropology is vast. It embodies the study of virtually every aspect of human behavior—from how you nourish yourself to how you feel about yourself and others, from your religion (or lack of one) to how you drive a car. For convenience, we have organized the articles in this section into seven topics. Although we certainly have not come close to covering all areas of cultural anthropology. Nevertheless, we offer you interesting reading in some of the most important areas.

Fieldwork

. . . .

For most anthropologists, fieldwork is one of the more significant experiences of their lives. Few anthropologists return home from the field unchanged, and for many the personal changes are quite deep and enduring. In a distant place among strangers, the fieldworker is cut off from the people and patterns that gave his or her life meaning and in terms of which she or he built a sense of self. In a very real sense, one becomes childlike: understanding little, incompetent to perform any locally valued tasks, utterly dependent on the good will of others for virtually everything. Like a child the fieldworker starts to build a social identity; to a great measure, the success of the research will depend upon how well she or he succeeds in accomplishing this task. Not the least of one's challenges is to come to terms with the world view of one's hosts and research subjects—which frequently is at significant variance with one's own.

Napoleon A. Chagnon is very candid about the emotional stress he endured in the course of "Doing Fieldwork among the Yąnomamö." One can hardly imagine a society more different from our own. However, a word of caution is in order. Without giving away the whole story, we wish to indicate that one point made by Horace Miner's "Body Ritual among the Nacirema" is that the language used by the researcher in reporting on the behavior of his or her subjects can make them seem much more foreign than they really are.

"Shakespeare in the Bush," by Laura Bohannan, and "Eating Christmas in the Kalahari," by Richard B. Lee, both deal with the problem of cross-cultural (mis)understanding. It is inevitable that the fieldworker will misunderstand—and be misunderstood by—the people she or he is studying. Good researchers, however, use instances of misunderstanding as instruments of investigation into the divergent premises of the culture of their subjects, and their own culture as well. The result can be a much deeper understanding of both.

A better understanding of one's own culture is the focus of Joan Ablon's "Doing Fieldwork in Middle Class America." Ablon describes a host of relatively new problems encountered by anthropologists studying people very much like themselves. If anthropology is to maintain its traditional personalized format for fieldwork, she argues, new ways for dealing with informants and the interpersonal complexities of modern society must be developed.

19

Doing Fieldwork Among the Yąnomamö

BY NAPOLEON A. CHAGNON

The Yąnomamö[1] Indians live in southern Venezuela and the adjacent portions of northern Brazil. Some 125 widely scattered villages have populations ranging from 40 to 250 inhabitants, with 75 to 80 people the most usual number. In total numbers their population probably approaches 10,000 people, but this is merely a guess. Many of the villages have not yet been contacted by outsiders, and nobody knows for sure exactly how many uncontacted villages there are, or how many people live in them. By comparison to African or Melanesian tribes, the Yąnomamö population is small. Still, they are one of the largest unacculturated tribes left in all of South America.

But they have a significance apart from tribal size and cultural purity: the Yąnomamö are still actively conducting warfare. It is in the nature of man to fight, according to one of the myths, because the blood of "Moon" spilled on this layer of the cosmos, causing men to become fierce. I describe the Yąnomamö as "the fierce people" because that is the most accurate single phrase that describes them. That is how they conceive themselves to be, and that is how they would like others to think of them.

I spent nineteen months with the Yąnomamö,[2] during which time I acquired some proficiency in their language and, up to a point, submerged myself in their culture and way of life. The thing that impressed me most was the importance of aggression in their culture. I had the opportunity to witness a good many incidents that expressed individual vindictiveness on the one hand and collective bellicosity on the other. These ranged in seriousness from the ordinary incidents of wife beating and chest pounding to dueling and organized raiding by parties that set out with the intention of ambushing and killing men from enemy villages (Fig. 1). One of the villages discussed in the chapters that follow was raided approximately twenty-five times while I conducted the fieldwork, six times by the group I lived among.

The fact that the Yąnomamö live in a state of chronic warfare is reflected in their mythology, values, settlement pattern, political behavior and marriage practices. Accordingly, I have organized this case study in such a way that students can appreciate the effects of warfare on Yąnomamö culture in general and on their social organization and politics in particular (Fig. 1).

I collected the data under somewhat trying circumstances, some of which I will describe in order to give the student a rough idea of what is generally meant when anthropologists speak of "culture shock" and "fieldwork." It should be borne in mind, however, that each field situation is in many respects unique, so that the problems I encountered do not necessarily exhaust the range of possible problems other anthropologists have confronted in other areas. There are a few problems, however, that seem to be nearly universal among anthropological fieldworkers, particularly those having to do with eating, bathing, sleeping, lack of privacy and loneliness, or discovering that primitive man is not always as noble as you originally thought.

This is not to state that primitive man everywhere is unpleasant. By way of contrast, I have also done limited

1. The word Yąnomamö is nasalized through its entire length, indicated by the diacritical mark [ą]. When this mark appears on a word, the entire word is nasalized. The terminal vowel [-ö] represents a sound that does not occur in the English language. It corresponds to the phone [+] of linguistic orthography. In normal conversation, Yąnomamö is pronounced like "Yah-no-mama," except that it is nasalized. Finally, the words having the [-ä] vowel are pronounced at that vowel with the "uh" sound of "duck." Thus, the name Kąobawä would be pronounced "cow-ba-wuh," again nasalized.

2. I spent a total of twenty-three months in South America of which nineteen were spent among the Yąnomamö on three separate field trips. The first trip, November 1964 through February 1966, was to Venezuela. During this time I spent nineteen months in direct contact with the Yąnomamö, using my periodic trips back to Caracas to visit my family and to collate the genealogical data I had collected up to that point. On my second trip, January through March 1967, I spent two months among Brazilian Yąnomamö and one more month with Venezuelan Yąnomamö. Finally, I returned to Venezuela for three more months among the Yąnomamö, January through April 1968.

fieldwork among the Yąnomamö's northern neighbors, the Carib-speaking Makiritare Indians. This group was very pleasant and charming, all of them anxious to help me and honor bound to show any visitor the numerous courtesies of their system of etiquette. In short, they approached the image of primitive man that I had conjured up, and it was sheer pleasure to work with them. The recent work by Colin Turnbull (1966) brings out dramatically the contrast in personal characteristics of two African peoples he has studied.

Hence, what I say about some of my experiences is probably equally true of the experiences of many fieldworkers. I write about my own experiences because there is a conspicuous lack of fieldwork descriptions available to potential fieldworkers. I think I could have profited by reading about the private misfortunes of my own teachers; at least I might have been able to avoid some of the more stupid errors I made. In this regard there are a number of recent contributions by fieldworkers describing some of the discomforts and misfortunes they themselves sustained.[3] Students planning to conduct fieldwork are urged to consult them.

My first day in the field illustrated to me what my teachers meant when they spoke of "culture shock." I had traveled in a small, aluminum rowboat propelled by a large outboard motor for two and a half days. This took me from the Territorial capital, a small town on the Orinoco River, deep into Yąnomamö country. On the morning of the third day we reached a small mission settlement, the field "headquarters" of a group of Americans who were working in two Yąnomamö villages. The missionaries had come out of these villages to hold their annual conference on the progress of their mission work, and were conducting their meetings when I arrived. We picked up a passenger at the mission station, James P. Barker, the first non-Yąnomamö to make a sustained, permanent contact with the tribe (in 1950). He had just returned from a year's furlough in the United States, where I had earlier visited him before leaving for Venezuela. He agreed to accompany me to the village I had selected for my base of operations to introduce me to the Indians. This village was also his own home base, but he had not been there for over a year and did not plan to join me for another three months. Mr. Barker had been living with this particular group about five years.

We arrived at the village, Bisaasi-teri, about 2:00 P.M. and docked the boat along the muddy bank at the ter-

minus of the path used by the Indians to fetch their drinking water. It was hot and muggy, and my clothing was soaked with perspiration. It clung uncomfortably to my body, as it did thereafter for the remainder of the work. The small, biting gnats were out in astronomical numbers, for it was the beginning of the dry season. My face and hands were swollen from the venom of their numerous stings. In just a few moments I was to meet my first Yąnomamö, my first primitive man. What would it be like? I had visions of entering the village and seeing 125 social facts running about calling each other kinship terms and sharing food, each waiting and anxious to have me collect his genealogy. I would wear them out in turn. Would they like me? This was important to me; I wanted them to be so fond of me that they would adopt me into their kinship system and way of life, because I had heard that successful anthropologists always get adopted by their people. I had learned during my seven years of anthropological training at the University of Michigan that kinship was equivalent to society in primitive tribes and that it was a moral way of life, "moral" being something "good" and "desirable." I was determined to work my way into their moral system of kinship and become a member of their society.

My heart began to pound as we approached the village and heard the buzz of activity within the circular compound. Mr. Barker commented that he was anxious to see if any changes had taken place while he was away and wondered how many of them had died during his absence. I felt into my back pocket to make sure that my notebook was still there and felt personally more secure when I touched it. Otherwise, I would not have known what to do with my hands.

The entrance to the village was covered over with brush and dry palm leaves. We pushed them aside to expose the low opening to the village. The excitement of meeting my first Indians was almost unbearable as I duck-waddled through the low passage into the village clearing.

I looked up and gasped when I saw a dozen burly, naked, filthy, hideous men staring at us down the shafts of their drawn arrows! Immense wads of green tobacco were stuck between their lower teeth and lips making them look even more hideous, and strands of dark-green slime dripped or hung from their noses. We arrived at the village while the men were blowing a hallucinogenic drug up their noses. One of the side effects of the drug is a runny nose. The mucus is always saturated with the green powder and the Indians usually let it run freely from their nostrils. My next discovery was that there were a dozen or so vicious, underfed dogs snapping at my legs, circling me as if I were going to be their next meal. I just stood there holding my notebook, helpless and pathetic. Then the stench of the decaying vegetation and filth struck me and I almost

Fig. 1. Members of allied villages engaged in a chest-pounding duel which followed a feast.

got sick. I was horrified. What sort of a welcome was this for the person who came here to live with you and learn your way of life, to become friends with you? They put their weapons down when they recognized Barker and returned to their chanting, keeping a nervous eye on the village entrances.

We had arrived just after a serious fight. Seven women had been abducted the day before by a neighboring group, and the local men and their guests had just that morning recovered five of them in a brutal club fight that nearly ended in a shooting war. The abductors, angry because they lost five of the seven captives, vowed to raid the Bisaasi-teri. When we arrived and entered the village unexpectedly, the Indians feared that we were the raiders. On several occasions during the next two hours the men in the village jumped to their feet, armed themselves, and waited nervously for the noise outside the village to be identified. My enthusiasm for collecting ethnographic curiosities diminished in proportion to the number of

times such an alarm was raised. In fact, I was relieved when Mr. Barker suggested that we sleep across the river for the evening. It would be safer over there.

As we walked down the path to the boat, I pondered the wisdom of having decided to spend a year and a half with this tribe before I had even seen what they were like. I am not ashamed to admit, either, that had there been a diplomatic way out, I would have ended my fieldwork then and there. I did not look forward to the next day when I would be left alone with the Indians; I did not speak a word of their language, and they were decidedly different from what I had imagined them to be. The whole situation was depressing, and I wondered why I ever decided to switch from civil engineering to anthropology in the first place. I had not eaten all day, I was soaking wet from perspiration, the gnats were biting me, and I was covered with red pigment, the result of a dozen or so complete examinations I had been given by as many burly Indians. These examinations capped an otherwise grim day. The In-

Fig. 2. One way that warfare affects other aspects of Yạnomamö social organization is in the great significance of intervillage alliances. Here members of an allied village dance excitedly in their hosts' village in anticipation of the feast and chest-pounding duel that will follow.

dians would blow their noses into their hands, flick as much of the mucus off that would separate in a snap of the wrist, wipe the residue into their hair, and then carefully examine my face, arms, legs, hair, and the contents of my pockets. I asked Mr. Barker how to say "Your hands are dirty"; my comments were met by the Indians in the following way: They would "clean" their hands by spitting a quantity of slimy tobacco juice into them, rub them together, and then proceed with the examination.

Mr. Barker and I crossed the river and slung our hammocks. When he pulled his hammock out of a rubber bag, a heavy, disagreeable odor of mildewed cotton came with it. "Even the missionaries are filthy," I thought to myself. Within two weeks, everything I owned smelled the same way, and I lived with that odor for the remainder of the fieldwork. My own habits of personal cleanliness reached such levels that I didn't

even mind being examined by the Indians, as I was not much cleaner than they were after I had adjusted to the circumstances.

So much for my discovery that primitive man is not the picture of nobility and sanitation I had conceived him to be. I soon discovered that it was an enormously time-consuming task to maintain my own body in the manner to which it had grown accustomed in the relatively antiseptic environment of the northern United States. Either I could be relatively well fed and relatively comfortable in a fresh change of clothes and do very little fieldwork, or, I could do considerably more fieldwork and be less well fed and less comfortable.

It is appalling how complicated it can be to make oatmeal in the jungle. First, I had to make two trips to the river to haul the water. Next, I had to prime my kerosene stove with alcohol and get it burning, a tricky procedure when you are trying to mix powdered milk and fill a coffee pot at the same time: the alcohol prime always burned out before I could turn the kerosene on, and I would have to start all over. Or, I would turn the kerosene on, hoping that the element was still hot enough to vaporize the fuel, and start a small fire in my palm-thatched hut as the liquid kerosene squirted all over the table and walls and ignited. It was safer to start over with the alcohol. Then I had to boil the oatmeal and pick the bugs out of it. All my supplies, of course, were carefully stored in Indian-proof, rat-proof, moisture-proof, and insect-proof containers, not one of which ever served its purpose adequately. Just taking things out of the multiplicity of containers and repacking them afterward was a minor project in itself. By the time I had hauled the water to cook with, unpacked my food, prepared the oatmeal, milk, and coffee, heated water for the dishes, washed and dried the dishes, repacked the food in the containers, stored the containers in locked trunks and cleaned up my mess, the ceremony of preparing breakfast had brought me almost up to lunch time!

Eating three meals a day was out of the question. I solved that problem by eating a single meal that could be prepared in a single container, or, at most, in two containers, washed my dishes only when there were no clean ones left, using cold river water, and wore each change of clothing at least a week to cut down on my laundry problem, a courageous undertaking in the tropics. I was also less concerned about sharing provisions with the rats, insects, Indians, and the elements, thereby eliminating the need for my complicated storage process. I was able to last most of the day on *café con leche*, heavily sugared espresso coffee diluted about five to one with hot milk. I would prepare this in the evening and store it in a thermos. Frequently, my single meal was no more complicated than a can of sardines and a package of crackers. But at least two or three times a week I would do something sophisticated, like make oatmeal or boil rice and add a can of tuna fish or tomato paste to it. I even saved time by devising a water system that obviated the trips to the river. I had a few sheets of zinc roofing brought in and made a rain-water trap; I caught the water on the zinc surface, funneled it into an emply gasoline drum, and then ran a plastic hose from the drum to my hut. When the drum was exhausted in the dry season, I hired the Indians to fill it with water from the river.

I ate much less when I traveled with the Indians to visit other villages. Most of the time my travel diet consisted of roasted or boiled green plantains that I obtained from the Indians, but I always carried a few cans of sardines with me in case I got lost or stayed away longer than I had planned. I found peanut butter and crackers a very nourishing food, and a simple one to prepare on trips. It was nutritious and portable, and

only one tool was required to prepare the meal, a hunting knife that could be cleaned by wiping the blade on a leaf. More importantly, it was one of the few foods the Indians would let me eat in relative peace. It looked too much like animal feces to them to excite their appetites.

I once referred to the peanut butter as the dung of cattle. They found this quite repugnant. They did not know what "cattle" were, but were generally aware that I ate several canned products of such an animal. I perpetrated this myth, if for no other reason than to have some peace of mind while I ate. Fieldworkers develop strange defense mechanisms, and this was one of my own forms of adaptation. On another occasion I was eating a can of frankfurters and growing very weary of the demands of one of my guests for a share in my meal. When he asked me what I was eating, I replied: "Beef." He then asked, "What part of the animal are you eating?" to which I replied, "Guess!" He stopped asking for a share.

Meals were a problem in another way. Food sharing is important to the Yąnomamö in the context of displaying friendship. "I am hungry," is almost a form of greeting with them. I could not possibly have brought enough food with me to feed the entire village, yet they seemed not to understand this. All they could see was that I did not share my food with them at each and every meal. Nor could I enter into their system of reciprocities with respect to food; every time one of them gave me something "freely," he would dog me for months to pay him back, not with food, but with steel tools. Thus, if I accepted a plantain from someone in a different village while I was on a visit, he would most likely visit me in the future and demand a machete as payment for the time that he "fed" me. I usually reacted to these kinds of demands by giving a banana, the customary reciprocity in their culture—food for food—but this would be a disappointment for the individual who had visions of that single plantain growing into a machete over time.

Despite the fact that most of them knew I would not share my food with them at their request, some of them always showed up at my hut during mealtime. I gradually became accustomed to this and learned to ignore their persistent demands while I ate. Some of them would get angry because I failed to give in, but most of them accepted it as just a peculiarity of the subhuman foreigner. When I did give in, my hut quickly filled with Indians, each demanding a sample of food that I had given one of them. If I did not give all a share, I was that much more despicable in their eyes.

A few of them went out of their way to make my meals unpleasant, to spite me for not sharing; for example, one man arrived and watched me eat a cracker with honey on it. He immediately recognized the honey, a particularly esteemed Yąnomamö food. He knew that I would not share my tiny bottle and that it would be futile to ask. Instead, he glared at me and queried icily, "Shaki!⁴ What kind of animal semen are you eating on that cracker?" His question had the desired effect, and my meal ended.

Finally, there was the problem of being lonely and separated from your own kind, especially your family. I tried to overcome this by seeking personal friendships among the Indians. This only complicated the matter because all my friends simply used my confidence to gain privileged access to my cache of steel tools and trade goods, and looted me. I would be bitterly disappointed that my "friend" thought no more of me than to finesse our relationship exclusively with the intention of getting at my locked up possessions, and my depression would hit new lows every time I discovered this. The loss of the possession bothered me much less than the shock that I was, as far as most of them were concerned, nothing more than a source of desirable items; no holds were barred in relieving me of these, since I was considered something subhuman, a non-Yąnomamö.

The thing that bothered me most was the incessant, passioned, and aggressive demands the Indians made. It would become so unbearable that I would have to lock myself in my mud hut every once in a while just to escape from it: Privacy is one of Western culture's greatest achievements. But I did not want privacy for its own sake; rather, I simply had to get away from the begging. Day and night for the entire time I lived with the Yąnomamö I was plagued by such demands as "Give me a knife, I am poor!"; "If you don't take me with you on your next trip to Widokaiya-teri I'll chop a hole in your canoe!"; "Don't point your camera at me or I'll hit you!"; "Share your food with me!"; "Take me across the river in your canoe and be quick about it!"; "Give me a cooking pot!"; "Loan me your flashlight so I can go hunting tonight!"; "Give me medicine . . . I itch all over!"; "Take us on a week-long hunting trip with your shotgun!"; and "Give me an axe or I'll break into your hut when you are away visiting and steal one!" And so I was bombarded by such demands day after day, months on end, until I could not bear to see an Indian.

It was not as difficult to become calloused to the incessant begging as it was to ignore the sense of urgency, the impassioned tone of voice, or the intimida-

tion and aggression with which the demands were made. It was likewise difficult to adjust to the fact that the Yąnomamö refused to accept "no" for an answer until or unless it seethed with passion and intimidation—which it did after six months. Giving in to a demand always established a new threshold; the next demand would be for a bigger item or favor, and the anger of the Indians even greater if the demand was not met. I soon learned that I had to become very much like the Yąnomamö to be able to get along with them on their terms: sly, aggressive, and intimidating.

Had I failed to adjust in this fashion I would have lost six months of supplies to them in a single day or would have spent most of my time ferrying them around in my canoe or hunting for them. As it was, I did spend a considerable amount of time doing these things and did succumb to their outrageous demands for axes and machetes, at least at first. More importantly, had I failed to demonstrate that I could not be pushed around beyond a certain point, I would have been the subject of far more ridicule, theft, and practical jokes than was the actual case. In short, I had to acquire a certain proficiency in their kind of interpersonal politics and to learn how to imply subtly that certain potentially undesirable consequences might follow if they did such and such to me. They do this to each other in order to establish precisely the point at which they cannot goad an individual any further without precipitating retaliation. As soon as I caught on to this and realized that much of their aggression was stimulated by their desire to discover my flash point, I got along much better with them and regained some lost ground. It was sort of like a political game that everyone played, but one in which each individual sooner or later had to display some sign that his bluffs and implied threats could be backed up. I suspect that the frequency of wife beating is a component of this syndrome, since men can display their ferocity and show others that they are capable of violence. Beating a wife with a club is considered to be an acceptable way of displaying ferocity and one that does not expose the male to much danger. The important thing is that the man has displayed his potential for violence and the implication is that other men better treat him with respect and caution.

After six months, the level of demand was tolerable in the village I used for my headquarters. The Indians and I adjusted to each other and knew what to expect with regard to demands on their part for goods, favors, and services. Had I confined my fieldwork to just that village alone, the field experience would have been far more enjoyable. But, as I was interested in the demographic pattern and social organization of a much larger area, I made regular trips to some dozen different villages in order to collect genealogies or to recheck those I already had. Hence, the intensity of begging and in-

4. "Shaki," or, rather, "Shakiwa," is the name they gave me because they could not pronounce "Chagnon." They like to name people for some distinctive feature when possible. *Shaki* is the name of a species of noisome bee; they accumulate in large numbers around ripening bananas and make pests of themselves by eating into the fruit, showering the people below with the debris. They probably adopted this name for me because I was also a nuisance, continuously prying into their business, taking pictures of them, and, in general, being where they did not want me.

Fig. 3. Kąobawä, the wise leader, listens to identify a strange noise in the jungle.

timidation was fairly constant for the duration of the fieldwork. I had to establish my position in some sort of pecking order of ferocity at each and every village.

For the most part, my own "fierceness" took the form of shouting back at the Yąnomamö as loudly and as passionately as they shouted at me, especially at first, when I did not know much of their language. As I became more proficient in their language and learned more about their political tactics, I became more sophisticated in the art of bluffing. For example, I paid one young man a machete to cut palm trees and make boards from the wood. I used these to fashion a platform in the bottom of my dugout canoe to keep my possessions dry when I traveled by river. That afternoon I was doing informant work in the village; the

long-awaited mission supply boat arrived, and most of the Indians ran out of the village to beg goods from the crew. I continued to work in the village for another hour or so and went down to the river to say "hello" to the men on the supply boat. I was angry when I discovered that the Indians had chopped up all my palm boards and used them to paddle their own canoes[5] across the river. I knew that if I overlooked this incident I would have invited them to take greater liberties with my goods in the future. I crossed the river, docked amidst their dugouts, and shouted for the Indians to come out and see me. A few of the culprits appeared, mischievous grins on their faces. I gave a spirited lecture about

5. The canoes were obtained from missionaries, who, in turn, got them from a different tribe.

Fig. 4. Koamashima, Kąobawä's youngest wife, playing with her son, who is holding a tree frog.

how hard I had worked to put those boards in my canoe, how I had paid a machete for the wood, and how angry I was that they destroyed my work in their haste to cross the river. I then pulled out my hunting knife and, while their grins disappeared, cut each of their canoes loose, set it into the current, and let them float away. I left without further ado and without looking back.

They managed to borrow another canoe and, after some effort, recovered their dugouts. The headman of the village later told me with an approving chuckle that I had done the correct thing. Everyone in the village, except, of course, the culprits, supported and defended my action. This raised my status.

Whenever I took such action and defended my rights, I got along much better with the Yąnomamö. A good deal of their behavior toward me was directed with the forethought of establishing the point at which I would react defensively. Many of them later reminisced about the early days of my work when I was "timid" and a little afraid of them, and they could bully me into giving goods away.

Theft was the most persistent situation that required me to take some sort of defensive action. I simply could not keep everything I owned locked in trunks, and the Indians came into my hut and left at will. I developed a very effective means for recovering almost all the stolen items. I would simply ask a child who took the item and then take the person's hammock when he was not around, giving a spirited lecture to the others as I

Fig. 5. Rerebawä during an ebene *session sitting on the sidelines in an hallucinogenic stupor.*

marched away in a faked rage with the thief's hammock. Nobody ever attempted to stop me from doing this, and almost all of them told me that my technique for recovering my possessions was admirable. By nightfall the thief would either appear with the stolen object or send it along with someone else to make an exchange. The others would heckle him for getting caught and being forced to return the item.

With respect to collecting the data I sought, there was a very frustrating problem. Primitive social organization is kinship organization, and to understand the Yąnomamö way of life I had to collect extensive genealogies. I could not have deliberately picked a more difficult group to work with in this regard: They have very stringent name taboos. They attempt to name people in such a way that when the person dies and they can no longer use his name, the loss of the word in the language is not inconvenient. Hence, they name people for specific and minute parts of things, such as "toenail of some rodent," thereby being able to retain the words "toenail" and "(specific) rodent," but not being able to refer directly to the toenail of that rodent. The taboo is

maintained even for the living: One mark of prestige is the courtesy others show you by not using your name. The sanctions behind the taboo seem to be an unusual combination of fear and respect.

I tried to use kinship terms to collect genealogies at first, but the kinship terms were so ambiguous that I ultimately had to resort to names. They were quick to grasp that I was bound to learn everybody's name and reacted, without my knowing it, by inventing false names for everybody in the village. After having spent several months collecting names and learning them, this came as a disappointment to me: I could not cross-check the genealogies with other informants from distant villages.

They enjoyed watching me learn these names. I assumed, wrongly, that I would get the truth to each question and that I would get the best information by working in public. This set the stage for converting a serious project into a farce. Each informant tried to outdo his peers by inventing a name even more ridiculous than what I had been given earlier, or by asserting that the individual about whom I inquired was married to his mother or daughter, and the like. I would have the informant whisper the name of the individual in my ear, noting that he was the father of such and such a child. Everybody would then insist that I repeat the name aloud, roaring in hysterics as I clumsily pronounced the name. I assumed that the laughter was in response to the violation of the name taboo or to my pronunciation. This was a reasonable interpretation, since the individual whose name I said aloud invariably became angry. After I learned what some of the names meant, I began to understand what the laughter was all about. A few of the more colorful examples are: "hairy vagina," "long penis," "feces of the harpy eagle," and "dirty rectum." No wonder the victims were angry.

I was forced to do my genealogy work in private because of the horseplay and nonsense. Once I did so, my informants began to agree with each other and I managed to learn a few new names, real names. I could then test any new informant by collecting a genealogy from him that I knew to be accurate. I was able to weed out the more mischievous informants this way. Little by little I extended the genealogies and learned the real names. Still, I was unable to get the names of the dead and extend the genealogies back in time, and even my best informants continued to deceive me about their own close relatives. Most of them gave me the name of a living man as the father of some individual in order to avoid mentioning that the actual father was dead.

The quality of a genealogy depends in part on the number of generations it embraces, and the name taboo prevented me from getting any substantial information about deceased ancestors. Without this information, I could not detect marriage patterns through time. I had to rely on older informants for this information, but these were the most reluctant of all. As I became more proficient in the language and more skilled at detecting lies, my informants became better at lying. One of them in particular was so cunning and persuasive that I was shocked to discover that he had been inventing his information. He specialized in making a ceremony out of telling me false names. He would look around to make sure nobody was listening outside my hut, enjoin me to never mention the name again, act very nervous and spooky, and then grab me by the head to whisper the name very softly into my ear. I was always elated after an informant session with him, because I had several generations of dead ancestors for the living people. The others refused to give me this information. To show my gratitude, I paid him quadruple the rate I had given the others. When word got around that I had increased the pay, volunteers began pouring in to give me genealogies.

I discovered that the old man was lying quite by accident. A club fight broke out in the village one day, the result of a dispute over the possession of a woman. She had been promised to Rerebawä, a particularly

aggressive young man who had married into the village. Rerebawä had already been given her older sister and was enraged when the younger girl began having an affair with another man in the village, making no attempt to conceal it from him. He challenged the young man to a club fight, but was so abusive in his challenge that the opponent's father took offense and entered the village circle with his son, wielding a long club. Rerebawä swaggered out to the duel and hurled insults at both of them, trying to goad them into striking him on the head with their clubs. This would have given him the opportunity to strike them on the head. His opponents refused to hit him, and the fight ended. Rerebawä had won a moral victory because his opponents were afraid to hit him. Thereafter, he swaggered around and insulted the two men behind their backs. He was genuinely angry with them, to the point of calling the older man by the name of his dead father. I quickly seized on this as an opportunity to collect an accurate genealogy and pumped him about his adversary's ancestors. Rerebawä had been particularly nasty to me up to this point, but we became staunch allies: We were both outsiders in the local village. I then asked about other dead ancestors and got immediate replies. He was angry with the whole group and not afraid to tell me the names of the dead. When I compared his version of the genealogies to that of the old man, it was obvious that one of them was lying. I challenged his information, and he explained that everybody knew that the old man was deceiving me and bragging about it in the same village. The names the old man had given me were the dead ancestors of the members of a village so far away that he thought I would never have occasion to inquire about them. As it turned out, Rerebawä knew most of the people in that village and recognized the names.

I then went over the complete genealogical records with Rerebawä, genealogies I had presumed to be in final form. I had to revise them all because of the numerous lies and falsifications they contained. Thus, after five months of almost constant work on the genealogies of just one group, I had to begin almost from scratch!

Discouraging as it was to start over, it was still the first real turning point in my fieldwork. Thereafter, I began taking advantage of local arguments and animosities in selecting my informants, and used more extensively individuals who had married into the group. I began traveling to other villages to check the genealogies, picking villages that were on strained terms with the people about whom I wanted information. I would then return to my base camp and check with local informants the accuracy of the information. If the informants became angry when I mentioned the new names I acquired from the unfriendly group, I was almost certain that the information was accurate. For this kind of checking I had to use informants whose genealogies I knew rather well: they had to be distantly enough related to the dead person that they would not go into a rage when I mentioned the name, but not so remotely related that they would be uncertain of the accuracy of the information. Thus, I had to make a list of names I dared not use in the presence of each and every informant. Despite the precautions, I occasionally hit a name that put the informant into a rage, such as that of a dead brother or sister that other informants had not reported. This always terminated the day's work with that informant, for he would be too touchy to continue any further, and I would be reluctant to take a chance on accidentally discovering another dead kinsman so soon after the first.

These were always unpleasant experiences, and occasionally dangerous ones, depending on the temperament of the informant. On one occasion I was planning to visit a village that had been raided about a week earlier. A woman whose name I had on my list had been killed by the raiders. I planned to check each individual on the list one by one to estimate ages, and I wanted to remove her name so that I would not say it aloud in the village. I knew that I would be in considerable difficulty if I said this name aloud so soon after her death. I called on my original informant and asked him to tell me the name of the woman who had been killed. He refused, explaining that she was a close relative of his. I then asked him if he would become angry if I read off all the names on the list. This way he did not have to say her name and could merely nod when I mentioned the right one. He was a fairly good friend of mine, and I thought I could predict his reaction. He assured me that this would be a good way of doing it. We were alone in my hut so that nobody could overhear us. I read the names softly, continuing to the next when he gave a negative reply. When I finally spoke the name of the dead woman he flew out of his chair, raised his arm to strike me, and shouted: "You son-of-a-bitch! If you ever say that name again, I'll kill you!" He was shaking with rage, but left my hut quietly. I shudder to think what might have happened if I had said the name unknowingly in the woman's village. I had other, similar experiences in different villages, but luckily the dead person had been dead for some time and was not closely related to the individual into whose ear I whispered the name. I was merely cautioned to desist from saying any more names, lest I get people angry with me.

I had been working on the genealogies for nearly a year when another individual came to my aid. It was Kạobawä, the headman of Upper Bisaasi-teri, the group in which I spent most of my time. He visited me one day after the others had left the hut and volunteered to help me on the genealogies. He was poor, he explained, and needed a machete. He would work only on the condition that I did not ask him about his own parents and

other very close kinsmen who were dead. He also added that he would not lie to me as the others had done in the past. This was perhaps the most important single event in my fieldwork, for out of this meeting evolved a very warm friendship and a very profitable informant-fieldworker relationship.

Kạobawä's familiarity with his group's history and his candidness were remarkable. His knowledge of details was almost encyclopedic. More than that, he was enthusiastic and encouraged me to learn details that I might otherwise have ignored. If there were things he did not know intimately, he would advise me to wait until he could check things out with someone in the village. This he would do clandestinely, giving me a report the next day. As I was constrained by my part of the bargain to avoid discussing his close dead kinsmen, I had to rely on Rerebawä for this information. I got Rerebawä's genealogy from Kạobawä.

Once again I went over the genealogies with Kạobawä to recheck them, a considerable task by this time: they included about two thousand names, representing several generations of individuals from four different villages. Rerebawä's information was very accurate, and Kạobawä's contribution enabled me to trace the genealogies further back in time. Thus, after nearly a year of constant work on genealogies, Yąnomamö demography and social organization began to fall into a pattern. Only then could I see how kin groups formed and exchanged women with each other over time, and only then did the fissioning of larger villages into smaller ones show a distinct pattern. At this point I was able to begin formulating more intelligent questions because there was now some sort of pattern to work with. Without the help of Rerebawä and Kạobawä I could not have made very much sense of the plethora of details I had collected from dozens of other informants.

I spent a good deal of time with these two men and their families and got to know them well. They frequently gave their information in a way which related themselves to the topic under discussion. We became very close friends. I will speak of them frequently in the following chapters, using them as "typical" Yąnomamö, if, indeed, one may speak of typical anything. I will briefly comment on what these men are like and their respective statuses in the village.

Kạobawä is about 40 years old (Fig. 3). I say "about" because the Yąnomamö numeration system has only three numbers: one, two, and more-than-two. He is the headman of Upper Bisaasi-teri. He has had five or six wives so far and temporary affairs with as many more women, one of which resulted in a child. At the present time he has just two wives, Bahimi and Koamashima. He has had a daughter and a son by Bahimi, his eldest and favorite wife. Koamashima, about 20 years old, recently had her first child, a boy (Fig. 4). Kạobawä may give Koamashima to his youngest brother. Even now the brother shares in her sexual services. Kąobawä recently gave his third wife to another of his brothers because she was beshi: "horny." In fact, this girl had been married to two other men, both of whom discarded her because of her infidelity. Kąobawä had one daughter by her; she is being raised by his brother.

Kąobawä's eldest wife, Bahimi, is about thirty-five years old. She is his first cross-cousin. Bahimi was pregnant when I began my fieldwork, but she killed the new baby, a boy, at birth, explaining tearfully that it would have competed with Ariwari, her nursing son, for milk. Rather than expose Ariwari to the dangers and uncertainty of an early weaning, she killed the new child instead. By Yąnomamö standards, she and Kąobawä have a very tranquil household. He only beats her once in a while, and never very hard. She never has affairs with other men.

Kąobawä is quiet, intense, wise, and unobtrusive. He leads more by example than by threats and coercion. He can afford to be this way as he established his reputation for being fierce long ago, and other men respect him. He also has five mature brothers who support him, and he has given a number of his sisters to other men in the village, thereby putting them under some obligation to him. In short, his "natural" following (kinsmen) is large, and he does not have to constantly display his ferocity. People already respect him and take his suggestions seriously.

Rerebawä is much younger, only about twenty-two years old. (See Fig. 5.) He has just one wife by whom he has had three children. He is from Karohi-teri, one of the villages to which Kąobawä's is allied. Rerebawä left his village to seek a wife in Kąobawä's group because there were no eligible women there for him to marry.

Rerebawä is perhaps more typical than Kąobawä in the sense that he is concerned about his reputation for ferocity and goes out of his way to act tough. He is, however, much braver than the other men his age and backs up his threats with action. Moreover, he is concerned about politics and knows the details of intervillage relationships over a large area. In this respect he shows all the attributes of a headman, although he is still too young and has too many competent older brothers in his own village to expect to move easily into the position of leadership there.

He does not intend to stay in Kąobawä's group and has not made a garden. He feels that he has adequately discharged his obligations to his wife's parents by providing them with fresh game for three years. They should let him take the wife and return to his own village with her, but they refuse and try to entice him to remain permanently in Bisaasi-teri to provide them with game when they are old. They have even promised to give him their second daughter if he will stay permanently.

Although he has displayed his ferocity in many ways, one incident in particular shows what his character is like. Before he left his own village to seek a wife, he had an affair with the wife of an older brother. When he was discovered, his brother attacked him with a club. Rerebawä was infuriated so he grabbed an axe and drove his brother out of the village after soundly beating him with the flat of the blade. The brother was so afraid that he did not return to the village for several days. I recently visited his village with him. He made a point to introduce me to this brother. Rerebawä dragged him out of his hammock by the arm and told me, "This is the brother whose wife I had an affair with," a deadly insult. His brother did nothing and slunk back into his hammock, shamed, but relieved to have Rerebawä release the vise-grip on his arm.

Despite the fact that he admires Kąobawä, he has a low opinion of the others in Bisaasi-teri. He admitted confidentially that he thought Bisaasi-teri was an abominable group: "This is a terrible neighborhood! All the young men are lazy and cowards and everybody is committing incest! I'll be glad to get back home." He also admired Kąobawä's brother, the headman of Monou-teri. This man was killed by raiders while I was doing my fieldwork. Rerebawä was disgusted that the others did not chase the raiders when they discovered the shooting: "He was the only fierce one in the whole group; he was my close friend. The cowardly Monou-teri hid like women in the jungle and didn't even chase the raiders!"

Even though Rerebawä is fierce and capable of being quite nasty, he has a good side as well. He has a very biting sense of humor and can entertain the group for hours on end with jokes and witty comments. And he is one of few Yąnomamö that I feel I can trust. When I returned to Bisaasi-teri after having been away for a year, Rerebawä was in his own village visiting his kinsmen. Word reached him that I had returned, and he immediately came to see me. He greeted me with an immense bear hug and exclaimed, "Shaki! Why did you stay away so long? Did you know that my will was so cold while you were gone that at times I could not eat for want of seeing you?" I had to admit that I missed him, too.

Of all the Yąnomamö I know, he is the most genuine and the most devoted to his culture's ways and values. I admire him for that, although I can't say that I subscribe to or endorse these same values. By contrast, Kąobawä is older and wiser. He sees his own culture in a different light and criticizes aspects of it he does not like. While many of his peers accept some of the superstitions and explanatory myths as truth and as the way things ought to be, Kąobawä questions them and privately pokes fun at some of them. Probably, more of the Yąnomamö are like Rerebawä, or at least try to be.

Shakespeare in the Bush

BY LAURA BOHANNAN

. . . .

Just before I left Oxford for the Tiv in West Africa, conversation turned to the season at Stratford. "You Americans," said a friend, "often have difficulty with Shakespeare. He was, after all, a very English poet, and one can easily misinterpret the universal by misunderstanding the particular."

I protested that human nature is pretty much the same the whole world over; at least the general plot and motivation of the greater tragedies would always be clear—everywhere—although some details of custom might have to be explained and difficulties of translation might produce other slight changes. To end an argument we could not conclude, my friend gave me a copy of *Hamlet* to study in the African bush: it would, he hoped, lift my mind above its primitive surroundings, and possibly I might, by prolonged meditation, achieve the grace of correct interpretation.

It was my second field trip to that African tribe, and I thought myself ready to live in one of its remote sections—an area difficult to cross even on foot. I eventually settled on the hillock of a very knowledgeable old man, the head of a homestead of some hundred and forty people, all of whom were either his close relatives or their wives and children. Like the other elders of the vicinity, the old man spent most of his time performing ceremonies seldom seen these days in the more accessible parts of the tribe. I was delighted. Soon there would be three months of enforced isolation and leisure, between the harvest that takes place just before the rising of the swamps and the clearing of new farms when the water goes down. Then, I thought, they would have even more time to perform ceremonies and explain them to me.

I was quite mistaken. Most of the ceremonies demanded the presence of elders from several homesteads. As the swamps rose, the old men found it too difficult to walk from one homestead to the next, and the ceremonies gradually ceased. As the swamps rose even higher, all activities but one came to an end. The women brewed beer from maize and millet. Men, women, and children sat on their hillocks and drank it.

People began to drink at dawn. By midmorning the whole homestead was singing, dancing, and drumming. When it rained, people had to sit inside their huts: there they drank and sang or they drank and told stories. In any case, by noon or before, I either had to join the party or retire to my own hut and my books. "One does not discuss serious matters when there is beer. Come, drink with us." Since I lacked their capacity for the thick native beer, I spent more and more time with *Hamlet*. Before the end of the second month, grace descended on me. I was quite sure that *Hamlet* had only one possible interpretation, and that one universally obvious.

Early every morning, in the hope of having some serious talk before the beer party, I used to call on the old man at his reception hut—a circle of posts supporting a thatched roof above a low mud wall to keep out wind and rain. One day I crawled through the low doorway and found most of the men of the homestead sitting huddled in their ragged cloths on stools, low plank beds, and reclining chairs, warming themselves against the chill of the rain around a smoky fire. In the center were three pots of beer. The party had started.

The old man greeted me cordially. "Sit down and drink." I accepted a large calabash full of beer, poured some into a small drinking gourd, and tossed it down. Then I poured some more into the same gourd for the man second in seniority to my host before I handed my calabash over to a young man for further distribution. Important people shouldn't ladle beer themselves.

"It is better like this," the old man said, looking at me approvingly and plucking at the thatch that had caught in my hair. "You should sit and drink with us more often. Your servants tell me that when you are not with us, you sit inside your hut looking at a paper."

The old man was acquainted with four kinds of "papers": tax receipts, bride price receipts, court fee receipts, and letters. The messenger who brought him letters from the chief used them mainly as a badge of office, for he always knew what was in them and told the old man. Personal letters for the few who had relatives in the government or mission stations were kept until someone went to a large market where there was a letter writer and reader. Since my arrival, letters were brought to me to be read. A few men also brought me bride price receipts, privately, with requests to change the figures to a higher sum. I found moral arguments were of no avail, since in-laws are fair game, and the technical hazards of forgery difficult to explain to an illiterate people. I did not wish them to think me silly enough to look at any such papers for days on end, and I hastily explained that my "paper" was one of the "things of long ago" of my country.

"Ah," said the old man. "Tell us."

I protested that I was not a storyteller. Storytelling is a skilled art among them; their standards are high, and the audiences critical—and vocal in their criticism. I protested in vain. This morning they wanted to hear a story while they drank. They threatened to tell me no more stories until I told them one of mine. Finally, the old man promised that no one would criticize my style "for we know you are struggling with our language." "But," put in one of the elders, "you must explain what we do not understand, as we do when we tell you our stories." Realizing that here was my chance to prove *Hamlet* universally intelligible, I agreed.

The old man handed me some more beer to help me on with my storytelling. Men filled their long wooden pipes and knocked coals from the fire to place in the pipe bowls; then, puffing contentedly, they sat back to listen. I began in the proper style, "Not yesterday, not yesterday, but long ago, a thing occurred. One night three men were keeping watch outside the homestead of the great chief, when suddenly they saw the former chief approach them."

"Why was he no longer their chief?"

"He was dead," I explained. "That is why they were troubled and afraid when they saw him."

"Impossible," began one of the elders, handing his pipe on to his neighbor, who interrupted, "Of course it wasn't the dead chief. It was an omen sent by a witch. Go on."

Slightly shaken, I continued. "One of these three was a man who knew things"—the closest translation for scholar, but unfortunately it also meant witch. The second elder looked triumphantly at the first. "So he spoke to the dead chief saying, 'Tell us what we must do so you may rest in your grave,' but the dead chief did not answer. He vanished, and they could see him no more. Then the man who knew things—his name was Horatio—said this event was the affair of the dead chief's son, Hamlet."

There was a general shaking of heads round the circle. "Had the dead chief no living brothers? Or was this son the chief?"

"No," I replied. "That is, he had one living brother who became the chief when the elder brother died."

The old men muttered: such omens were matters for chiefs and elders, not for youngsters; no good could come of going behind a chief's back; clearly Horatio was not a man who knew things.

"Yes, he was," I insisted, shooing a chicken away from my beer. "In our country the son is next to the father. The dead chief's younger brother had become the great chief. He had also married his elder brother's widow only about a month after the funeral."

"He did well," the old man beamed and announced to the others, "I told you that if we knew more about Europeans, we would find they really were very like us. In our country also," he added to me, "the younger brother marries the elder brother's widow and becomes the father of his children. Now, if your uncle, who married your widowed mother, is your father's full brother, then he will be a real father to you. Did Hamlet's father and uncle have one mother?"

His question barely penetrated my mind; I was too upset and thrown too far off balance by having one of the most important elements of *Hamlet* knocked straight out of the picture. Rather uncertainly I said that I thought they had the same mother, but I wasn't sure—the story didn't say. The old man told me severely that these genealogical details made all the difference and that when I got home I must ask the elders about it. He shouted out the door to one of his younger wives to bring his goatskin bag.

Determined to save what I could of the mother motif, I took a deep breath and began again. "The son Hamlet was very sad because his mother had married again so quickly. There was no need for her to do so, and it is our custom for a widow not to go to her next husband until she has mourned for two years."

"Two years is too long," objected the wife, who had appeared with the old man's battered goatskin bag. "Who will hoe your farms for you while you have no husband?"

"Hamlet," I retorted without thinking, "was old enough to hoe his mother's farms himself. There was no need for her to remarry." No one looked convinced. I gave up. "His mother and the great chief told Hamlet not to be sad, for the great chief himself would be a father to Hamlet. Furthermore, Hamlet would be the next chief: therefore he must stay to learn the things of a chief. Hamlet agreed to remain, and all the rest went off to drink beer."

While I paused, perplexed at how to render Hamlet's disgusted soliloquy to an audience convinced that Claudius and Gertrude had behaved in the best possible manner, one of the young men asked me who had married the other wives of the dead chief.

"He had no other wives," I told him.

"But a chief must have many wives! How else can he brew beer and prepare food for all his guests?"

I said firmly that in our country even chiefs had only one wife, that they had servants to do their work, and that they paid them from tax money.

It was better, they returned, for a chief to have many wives and sons who would help him hoe his farms and feed his people; then everyone loved the chief who gave much and took nothing—taxes were a bad thing.

I agreed with the last comment, but for the rest fell back on their favorite way of fobbing off my questions: "That is the way it is done, so that is how we do it."

I decided to skip the soliloquy. Even if Claudius was here thought quite right to marry his brother's widow, there remained the poison motif, and I knew they would disapprove of fratricide. More hopefully I resumed, "That night Hamlet kept watch with the three who had seen his dead father. The dead chief again appeared, and although the others were afraid, Hamlet followed his dead father off to one side. When they were alone, Hamlet's dead father spoke."

"Omens can't talk!" The old man was emphatic.

"Hamlet's dead father wasn't an omen. Seeing him might have been an omen, but he was not." My audience looked as confused as I sounded. "It *was* Hamlet's dead father. It was a thing we call a 'ghost.'" I had to use the English word, for unlike many of the neighboring tribes, these people didn't believe in the survival after death of any individuating part of the personality.

"What is a 'ghost'? An omen?"

"No, a 'ghost' is someone who is dead but who walks around and can talk, and people can hear him and see him but not touch him."

They objected. "One can touch zombis."

"No, no! It was not a dead body the witches had animated to sacrifice and eat. No one else made Hamlet's dead father walk. He did it himself."

"Dead men can't walk," protested my audience as one man.

I was quite willing to comprise. "A 'ghost' is the dead man's shadow."

But again they objected. "Dead men cast no shadows."

"They do in my country," I snapped.

The old man quelled the babble of disbelief that arose immediately and told me with that insincere, but courteous, agreement one extends to the fancies of the young, ignorant, and superstitious, "No doubt in your country the dead can also walk without being zombis." From the depths of his bag he produced a withered fragment of kola nut, bit off one end to show it wasn't poisoned, and handed me the rest as a peace offering.

"Anyhow," I resumed, "Hamlet's dead father said that his own brother, the one who became chief, had poisoned him. He wanted Hamlet to avenge him. Hamlet believed this in his heart, for he did not like his father's brother." I took another swallow of beer. "In the country of the great chief, living in the same homestead, for it was a very large one, was an important elder who was often with the chief to advise and to help him. His name was Polonius. Hamlet was courting his daughter, but her father and her brother . . . [I cast hastily about for some tribal analogy] warned her not to let Hamlet visit her when when was alone on her farm, for he would be a great chief and so could not marry her."

"Why not!" asked the wife, who had settled down on the edge of the old man's chair. He frowned at her for asking stupid questions and growled, "They lived in the same homestead."

"That was not the reason," I informed them. "Polonius was a stranger who lived in the homestead because he helped the chief, not because he was a relative."

"Then why couldn't Hamlet marry her!"

"He could have," I explained, "but Polonius didn't think he would. After all, Hamlet was a man of great importance who ought to marry a chief's daughter, for in his country a man could have only one wife. Polonius was afraid that if Hamlet made love to his daughter, then no one else would give a high price for her."

"That might be true" remarked one of the shrewder elders, "but a chief's son would give his mistress's father enough presents and patronage to more than make up the difference. Polonius sounds like a fool to me."

"Many people think he was," I agreed. "Meanwhile Polonius sent his son Laertes off to Paris to learn the things of that country, for it was the homestead of a very great chief indeed. Because he was afraid that Laertes might waste a lot of money on beer and women and gambling, or get into trouble by fighting, he sent one of his servants to Paris secretly, to spy out what Laertes was doing. One day Hamlet came upon Polonius's daughter Ophelia. He behaved so oddly he frightened her. "Indeed,"—I was fumbling for words to express the dubious quality of Hamlet's madness—"the chief and many others had also noticed that when Hamlet talked one could understand the words but not what they meant. Many people thought that he had become mad." My audience suddenly became much more attentive. "The great chief wanted to know what was wrong with Hamlet, so he sent for two of Hamlet's age mates [school friends would have taken long explanation] to talk to Hamlet and find out what troubled his heart. Hamlet, seeing that they had been bribed by the chief to betray him, told them nothing. Polonius, however, insisted that Hamlet was mad because he had been forbidden to see Ophelia, whom he loved."

"Why," inquired a bewildered voice, "should anyone bewitch Hamlet on that account?"

"Bewitch him?"

"Yes, only witchcraft can make anyone mad, unless of course, one sees the beings that lurk in the forest."

I stopped being a storyteller, took out my notebook and demanded to be told more about these two causes of madness. Even while they spoke and I jotted notes, I tried to calculate the effect of this new factor on the plot. Hamlet had not been exposed to the beings that lurk in the forest. Only his relatives in the male line could bewitch him. Barring relatives not mentioned by Shakespeare, it had to be Claudius who was attempting to harm him. And, of course, it was.

For the moment I staved off questions by saying that the great chief also refused to believe that Hamlet was mad for the love of Ophelia and nothing else. "He was sure that something much more important was troubling Hamlet's heart."

"Now Hamlet's age mates," I continued, "had brought with them a famous storyteller. Hamlet decided to have this man tell the chief and all his homestead a story about a man who had poisoned his brother because he desired his brother's wife and wished to be chief himself. Hamlet was sure the great chief could not hear the story without making a sign if he was indeed guilty, and then he would discover whether his dead father had told him the truth."

The old man interrupted, with deep cunning, "Why should a father lie to his son?" he asked.

I hedged: "Hamlet wasn't sure that it really was his dead father." It was impossible to say anything, in that language, about devil-inspired visions.

"You mean," he said, "it actually was an omen, and he knew witches sometimes send false ones. Hamlet was a fool not to go to one skilled in reading omens and divining the truth in the first place. A man-who-sees-the-truth could have told him how his father died, if he really had been poisoned, and if there was witchcraft in it; then Hamlet could have called the elders to settle the matter."

The shrewd elder ventured to disagree. "Because his father's brother was a great chief, one-who-sees-the-truth might therefore have been afraid to tell it. I think it was for that reason that a friend of Hamlet's father—a witch and an elder—sent an omen so his friend's son would know. Was the omen true?"

"Yes," I said, abandoning ghosts and the devil; a witch-sent omen it would have to be. "It was true, for when the storyteller was telling his tale before all the homestead, the great chief rose in fear. Afraid that Hamlet knew his secret he planned to have him killed."

The stage set of the next bit presented some difficulties of translation. I began cautiously. "The great chief told Hamlet's mother fo find out from her son what he knew. But because a woman's children are always first in her heart, he had the important elder Polonius hide behind a cloth that hung against the wall of Hamlet's mother's sleeping hut. Hamlet started to scold his mother for what she had done."

There was a shocked murmur from everyone. A man should never scold his mother.

"She called out in fear, and Polonius moved behind the cloth. Shouting, 'A rat!' Hamlet took his machete and slashed through the cloth." I paused for dramatic effect. "He had killed Polonius!"

The old men looked at each other in supreme disgust. "That Polonius truly was a fool and a man who knew nothing! What child would not know enough to shout, 'It's me!'" With a pang, I remembered that these people are ardent hunters, always armed with bow, arrow, and machete; at the first rustle in the grass an arrow is aimed and ready, and the hunter shouts "Game!" If no human voice answers immediately, the arrow speeds on its way. Like a good hunter Hamlet had shouted, "A rat!"

I rushed in to save Polonius's reputation. "Polonius did speak. Hamlet heard him. But he thought it was the chief and wished to kill him to avenge his father. He had meant to kill him earlier that evening..." I broke down, unable to describe to these pagans, who had no belief in individual afterlife, the difference between dying at one's prayers and dying "unhousell'd, disappointed, unaneled."

This time I had shocked by audience seriously. "For a man to raise his hand against his father's brother and the one who has become his father—that is a terrible thing. The elders ought to let such a man be bewitched."

I nibbled at my kola nut in some perplexity, then pointed out that after all the man had killed Hamlet's father.

"No," pronounced the old man, speaking less to me than to the young men sitting behind the elders. "If your father's brother has killed your father, you must appeal to your father's age mates; *they* may avenge him. No man may use violence against his senior relatives." Another thought struck him. "But if his father's brother had indeed been wicked enough to bewitch Hamlet and make him mad that would be a good story indeed, for it would be his fault that Hamlet, being mad, no longer had any sense and thus was ready to kill his father's brother."

There was a murmur of applause. *Hamlet* was again a good story to them, but it no longer seemed quite the same story to me. As I thought over the coming complications of plot and motive, I lost courage and decided to skim over dangerous ground quickly.

"The great chief," I went on, "was not sorry that Hamlet had killed Polonius. It gave him a reason to send Hamlet away, with his two treacherous age mates, with letters to a chief of a far country, saying that Hamlet should be killed. But Hamlet changed the writing on their papers, so that the chief killed his age mates instead." I encountered a reproachful glare from one of the men whom I had told undetectable forgery was not merely immoral but beyond human skill. I looked the other way.

"Before Hamlet could return, Laertes came back for his father's funeral. The great chief told him Hamlet had killed Polonius. Laertes swore to kill Hamlet because of this, and because his sister Ophelia, hearing her father had been killed by the man she loved, went mad and drowned in the river."

"Have you already forgotten what we told you?" The old man was reproachful. "One cannot take vengeance on a madman; Hamlet killed Polonius in his madness. As for the girl, she not only went mad, she was drowned. Only witches can make people drown. Water itself can't hurt anything. It is merely something one drinks and bathes in."

I began to get cross. "If you don't like the story, I'll stop."

The old man made soothing noises and himself poured me some more beer. "You tell the story well, and we are listening. But is clear that the elders of your country have never told you what the story really means. No, don't interrupt! We believe you when you say your marriage customs are different, or your clothes and weapons. But people are the same everywhere; therefore, there are always witches and it is we, the elders, who know how witches work. We told you it was the great chief who wished to kill Hamlet, and now your own words have proved us right. Who were Ophelia's male relatives?"

"There were only her father and her brother." Hamlet was clearly out of my hands.

"There must have been many more; this also you must ask of your elders when you get back to your country. From what you tell us, since Polonius was dead, it must have been Laertes who killed Ophelia, although I do not see the reason for it."

We had emptied one pot of beer, and the old men argued the point with slightly tipsy interest. Finally one of them demanded of me, "What did the servant of Polonius say on his return?"

With difficulty I recollected Reynaldo and his mission. "I don't think he did return before Polonius was killed."

"Listen," said the elder, "and I will tell you how it was and how your story will go, then you may tell me if I am right. Polonius knew his son would get into trouble,

and so he did. He had many fines to pay for fighting, and debts from gambling. But he had only two ways of getting money quickly. One was to marry off his sister at once, but it is difficult to find a man who will marry a woman desired by the son of a chief. For if the chief's heir commits adultery with your wife, what you do? Only a fool calls a case against a man who will someday be his judge. Therefore Laertes had to take the second way: he killed his sister by witchcraft, drowning her so he could secretly sell her body to the witches."

I raised an objection. "They found her body and buried it. Indeed Laertes jumped into the grave to see his sister once more—so, you see, the body was truly there. Hamlet, who had just come back, jumped in after him."

"What did I tell you?" The elder appealed to the others. "Laertes was up to no good with his sister's body. Hamlet prevented him, because the chief's heir, like a chief, does not wish any other man to grow rich and powerful. Laertes would be angry, because he would have killed his sister without benefit to himself. In our country he would try to kill Hamlet for that reason. Is this not what happened?"

"More or less," I admitted. "When the great chief found Hamlet was still alive, he encouraged Laertes to try to kill Hamlet and arranged a fight with machetes between them. In the fight both the young men were wounded to death. Hamlet's mother drank the poisoned beer that the chief meant for Hamlet in case he won the fight. When he saw his mother die of poison, Hamlet, dying, managed to kill his father's brother with his machete."

"You see, I was right!" exclaimed the elder.

"That was a very good story," added the old man, "and you told it with very few mistakes. There was just one more error, at the very end. The poison Hamlet's mother drank was obviously meant for the survivor of the fight, whichever it was. If Laertes had won, the great chief would have poisoned him, for no one would know that he arranged Hamlet's death. Then, too, he need not fear Laertes' witchcraft; it takes a strong heart to kill one's only sister by witchcraft.

"Sometime," concluded the old man, gathering his ragged toga about him, "you must tell us some more stories of your country. We, who are elders, will instruct you in their true meaning, so that when you return to your own land your elders will see that you have not been sitting in the bush, but among those who know things and who have taught you wisdom."

Eating Christmas in the Kalahari

BY RICHARD BORSHAY LEE

The !Kung Bushmen's knowledge of Christmas is thirdhand. The London Missionary Society brought the holiday to the southern Tswana tribes in the early nineteenth century. Later, native catechists spread the idea far and wide among the Bantu-speaking pastoralists, even in the remotest corners of the Kalahari Desert. The Bushmen's idea of the Christmas story, stripped to its essentials, is "praise the birth of white man's god-chief"; what keeps their interest in the holiday high is the Tswana-Herero custom of slaughtering an ox for his Bushmen neighbors as an annual goodwill gesture. Since the 1930's, part of the Bushmen's annual round of activities has included a December congregation at the cattle posts for trading, marriage brokering, and several days of trance-dance feasting at which the local Tswana headman is host.

As a social anthropologist working with !Kung Bushmen, I found that the Christmas ox custom suited my purposes. I had come to the Kalahari to study the hunting and gathering subsistence economy of the !Kung, and to accomplish this it was essential not to provide them with food, share my own food, or interfere in any way with their food-gathering activities. While liberal handouts of tobacco and medical supplies were appreciated, they were scarcely adequate to erase the glaring disparity in wealth between the anthropologist, who maintained a two-month inventory of canned goods, and the Bushmen, who rarely had a day's supply of food on hand. My approach, while paying off in terms of data, left me open to frequent accusations of stinginess and hard-heartedness. By their lights, I was a miser.

The Christmas ox was to be my way of saying thank you for the cooperation of the past year; and since it was to be our last Christmas in the field, I determined to slaughter the largest, meatiest ox that money could buy, insuring that the feast and trance dance would be a success.

Through December I kept my eyes open at the wells as the cattle were brought down for watering. Several animals were offered, but none had quite the grossness that I had in mind. Then, ten days before the holiday, a Herero friend led an ox of astonishing size and mass up to our camp. It was solid black, stood five feet high at the shoulder, had a five-foot span of horns, and must have weighed 1,200 pounds on the hoof. Food consumption calculations are my specialty, and I quickly figured that bones and viscera aside, there was enough meat—at least four pounds—for every man, woman, and child of the 150 Bushmen in the vicinity of /ai/ai who were expected at the feast.

Having found the right animal at last, I paid the Herero £20 ($56) and asked him to keep the beast with his herd until Christmas day. The next morning word spread among the people that the big solid black one was the ox chosen by /ontah (my Bushman name; it means. roughly, "whitey") for the Christmas feast. That afternoon I received the first delegation. Ben!a, an outspoken sixty-year-old mother of five, came to the point slowly.

"Where were you planning to eat Christmas?"

"Right here at /ai/ai," I replied.

"Alone or with others?"

"I expect to invite all the people to eat Christmas with me."

"Eat what?"

"I have purchased Yehave's black ox, and I am going to slaughter and cook it."

"That's what we were told at the well but refused to believe it until we heard it from yourself."

"Well, it's the black one," I replied expansively, although wondering what she was driving at.

"Oh, no!" Ben!a groaned, turning to her group. "They were right." Turning back to me she asked, "Do you expect us to eat that bag of bones?"

"Bag of bones! It's the biggest ox at /ai/ai."

"Big, yes, but old. And thin.

EDITOR'S NOTE: *The !Kung and other Bushmen speak click languages. In the story, three different clicks are used:*

1. The dental click (/), as in /ai/ai, /ontah, and /gaugo. The click is sometimes written in English as tsk-tsk.

2. The alveopalatal click (!), as in Ben!a and !Kung.

3. The lateral click (//), as in //gom. Clicks function as consonants; a word may have more than one, as in /n!au.

Everybody knows there's no meat on that old ox. What did you expect us to eat off it, the horns?"

Everybody chuckled at Ben!a's one-liner as they walked away, but all I could manage was a weak grin.

That evening it was the turn of the young men. They came to sit at our evening fire. /gaugo, about my age, spoke to me man-to-man.

"/ontah, you have always been square with us," he lied. "What has happened to change your heart? That sack of guts and bones of Yehave's will hardly feed one camp, let alone all the Bushmen around /ai/ai." And he proceeded to enumerate the seven camps in the /ai/ai vicinity, family by family. "Perhaps you have forgotten that we are not few, but many. Or are you too blind to tell the difference between a proper cow and an old wreck? That ox is thin to the point of death."

"Look, you guys," I retorted, "that is a beautiful animal, and I'm sure you will eat it with pleasure at Christmas."

"Of course we will eat it; it's food. But it won't fill us up to the point where we will have enough strength to dance. We will eat and go home to bed with stomachs rumbling."

That night as we turned in, I asked my wife, Nancy: "What did you think of the black ox?"

"It looked enormous to me. Why?"

"Well, about eight different people have told me I got gypped; that the ox is nothing but bones."

"What's the angle?" Nancy asked. "Did they have a better one to sell?"

"No, they just said that it was going to be a grim Christmas because there won't be enough meat to go around. Maybe I'll get an independent judge to look at the beast in the morning."

Bright and early, Halingisi, a Tswana cattle owner, appeared at our camp. But before I could ask him to give me his opinion on Yehave's black ox, he gave me the eye signal that indicated a confidential chat. We left the camp and sat down.

"/ontah, I'm surprised at you;

you've lived here for three years and still haven't learned anything about cattle."

"But what else can a person do but choose the biggest, strongest animal one can find?" I retorted.

"Look, just because an animal is big doesn't mean that it has plenty of meat on it. The black one was a beauty when it was younger, but now it is thin to the point of death."

"Well I've already bought it. What can I do at this stage?"

"Bought it already? I thought you were just considering it. Well, you'll have to kill it and serve it, I suppose. But don't expect much of a dance to follow."

My spirits dropped rapidly. I could believe that Ben!a and /gaugo just might be putting me on about the black ox, but Halingisi seemed to be an impartial critic. I went around that day feeling as though I had bought a lemon of a used car.

In the afternoon it was Tomazo's turn. Tomazo is a fine hunter, a top trance performer (see "The Trance Cure of the !Kung Bushmen," NATURAL HISTORY, November, 1967), and one of my most reliable informants. He approached the subject of the Christmas cow as part of my continuing Bushmen education.

"My friend, the way it is with us Bushmen," he began, "is that we love meat. And even more than that, we love fat. When we hunt we always search for the fat ones, the ones dripping with layers of white fat: fat that turns into a clear, thick oil in the cooking pot, fat that slides down your gullet, fills your stomach and gives you a roaring diarrhea," he rhapsodized.

"So, feeling as we do," he continued, "it gives us pain to be served such a scrawny thing as Yehave's black ox. It is big, yes, and no doubt its giant bones are good for soup, but fat is what we really crave and so we will eat Christmas this year with a heavy heart."

The prospect of a gloomy Christmas now had me worried, so I asked Tomazo what I could do about it.

"Look for a fat one, a young one . . . smaller, but fat. Fat enough

to make us //gom ('evacuate the bowels'), then we will be happy."

My suspicions were aroused when Tomazo said that he happened to know of a young, fat, barren cow that the owner was willing to part with. Was Toma working on commission, I wondered? But I dispelled this unworthy thought when we approached the Herero owner of the cow in question and found that he had decided not to sell.

The scrawny wreck of a Christmas ox now became the talk of the /ai/ai water hole and was the first news told to the outlying groups as they began to come in from the bush for the feast. What finally convinced me that real trouble might be brewing was the visit from u!au, an old conservative with a reputation for fierceness. His nickname meant spear and referred to an incident thirty years ago in which he had speared a man to death. He had an intense manner; fixing me with his eyes, he said in clipped tones:

"I have only just heard about the black ox today, or else I would have come here earlier. /ontah, do you honestly think you can serve meat like that to people and avoid a fight?" He paused, letting the implications sink in. "I don't mean fight you, /ontah; you are a white man. I mean a fight between Bushmen. There are many fierce ones here, and with such a small quantity of meat to distribute, how can you give everybody a fair share? Someone is sure to accuse another of taking too much or hogging all the choice pieces. Then you will see what happens when some go hungry while others eat."

The possibility of at least a serious argument struck me as all too real. I had witnessed the tension that surrounds the distribution of meat from a kudu or gemsbok kill, and had documented many arguments that sprang up from a real or imagined slight in meat distribution. The owners of a kill may spend up to two hours arranging and rearranging the piles of meat under the gaze of a circle of recipients before handing them out. And I also knew that the

Christmas feast at /ai/ai would be bringing together groups that had feuded in the past.

Convinced now of the gravity of the situation, I went in earnest to search for a second cow; but all my inquiries failed to turn one up.

The Christmas feast was evidently going to be a disaster, and the incessant complaints about the meagerness of the ox had already taken the fun out of it for me. Moreover, I was getting bored with the wisecracks, and after losing my temper a few times, I resolved to serve the beast anyway. If the meat fell short, the hell with it. In the Bushmen idiom, I announced to all who would listen:

"I am a poor man and blind. If I have chosen one that is too old and too thin, we will eat it anyway and see if there is enough meat there to quiet the rumbling of our stomachs."

On hearing this speech, Ben!a offered me a rare word of comfort. "It's thin," she said philosophically, "but the bones will make a good soup."

At dawn Christmas morning, instinct told me to turn over the butchering and cooking to a friend and take off with Nancy to spend Christmas alone in the bush. But curiosity kept me from retreating. I wanted to see what such a scrawny ox looked like on butchering, and if there *was* going to be a fight, I wanted to catch every word of it. Anthropologists are incurable that way.

The great beast was driven up to our dancing ground, and a shot in the forehead dropped it in its tracks. Then, freshly cut branches were heaped around the fallen carcass to receive the meat. Ten men volunteered to help with the cutting. I asked /gaugo to make the breast bone cut. This cut, which begins the butchering process for most large game, offers easy access for removal of the viscera. But it also allows the hunter to spot-check the amount of fat on the animal. A fat game animal carries a white layer up to an inch thick on the chest, while in a thin one, the knife will quickly cut to bone. All eyes fixed on his hand as /gaugo, dwarfed by the great car-

cass, knelt to the breast. The first cut opened a pool of solid white in the black skin. The second and third cut widened and deepened the creamy white. Still no bone. It was pure fat; it must have been two inches thick.

"Hey /gau," I burst out, "that ox is loaded with fat. What's this about the ox being too thin to bother eating? Are you out of your mind?"

"Fat?" /gau shot back, "You call that fat? This wreck is thin, sick, dead!" And he broke out laughing. So did everyone else. They rolled on the ground, paralyzed with laughter. Everybody laughed except me; I was thinking.

I ran back to the tent and burst in just as Nancy was getting up. "Hey, the black ox. It's fat as hell! They were kidding about it being too thin to eat. It was a joke or something. A put-on. Everyone is really delighted with it!"

"Some joke," my wife replied. "It was so funny that you were ready to pack up and leave /ai/ai."

If it had indeed been a joke, it had been an extraordinarily convincing one, and, tinged, I thought, with more than a touch of malice as many jokes are. Nevertheless, that it was a joke lifted my spirits considerably, and I returned to the butchering site where the shape of the ox was rapidly disappearing under the axes and knives of the butchers. The atmosphere had become festive. Grinning broadly, their arms covered with blood well past the elbow, men packed chunks of meat into the big cast-iron cooking pots, fifty pounds to the load, and muttered and chuckled all the while about the thinness and worthlessness of the animal and /ontah's poor judgment.

We danced and ate that ox two days and two nights; we cooked and distributed fourteen potfuls of meat and no one went home hungry and no fights broke out.

But the "joke" stayed in my mind. I had a growing feeling that something important had happened in my relationship with the Bushmen and that the clue lay in the meaning of the joke. Several days later, when most of the people had dispersed back to the bush camps, I raised the

question with Hakekgose, a Tswana man who had grown up among the !Kung, married a !Kung girl, and who probably knew their culture better than any other non-Bushman.

"With us whites," I began, "Christmas is supposed to be the day of friendship and brotherly love. What I can't figure out is why the Bushmen went to such lengths to criticize and belittle the ox I had bought for the feast. The animal was perfectly good and their jokes and wisecracks practically ruined the holiday for me."

"So it really did bother you," said Hakekgose. "Well, that's the way they always talk. When I take my rifle and go hunting with them, if I miss, they laugh at me for the rest of the day. But even if I hit and bring one down, it's no better. To them, the kill is always too small or too old or too thin; and as we sit down on the kill site to cook and eat the liver, they keep grumbling, even with their mouths full of meat. They say things like, 'Oh this is awful! What a worthless animal! Whatever made me think that this Tswana rascal could hunt!'"

"Is this the way outsiders are treated?" I asked.

"No, it is their custom; they talk that way to each other too. Go and ask them."

/gaugo had been one of the most enthusiastic in making me feel bad about the merit of the Christmas ox. I sought him out first.

"Why did you tell me the black ox was worthless, when you could see that it was loaded with fat and meat?"

"It is our way," he said smiling. "We always like to fool people about that. Say there is a Bushman who has been hunting. He must not come home and announce like a braggard, 'I have killed a big one in the bush!' He must first sit down in silence until I or someone else comes up to his fire and asks, 'What did you see today?' He replies quietly, 'Ah, I'm no good for hunting. I saw nothing at all [pause] just a little tiny one.' Then I smile to myself," /gaugo continued, "because I know he has killed something big.

"In the morning we make up a party of four or five people to cut up and carry the meat back to the camp. When we arrive at the kill we examine it and cry out, 'You mean to say you have dragged us all the way out here in order to make us cart home your pile of bones? Oh, if I had known it was this thin I wouldn't have come.' Another one pipes up, 'People, to think I gave up a nice day in the shade for this. At home we may be hungry but at least we have nice cool water to drink.' If the horns are big, someone says, 'Did you think that somehow you were going to boil down the horns for soup?'

"To all this you must respond in kind. 'I agree,' you say, 'this one is not worth the effort; let's just cook the liver for strength and leave the rest for the hyenas. It is not too late to hunt today and even a duiker or a steenbok would be better than this mess.'

"Then you set to work nevertheless; butcher the animal, carry the meat back to the camp and everyone eats," /gaugo concluded.

Things were beginning to make sense. Next, I went to Tomazo. He corroborated /gaugo's story of the obligatory insults over a kill and added a few details of his own.

"But," I asked, "why insult a man after he has gone to all that trouble to track and kill an animal and when he is going to share the meat with you so that your children will have something to eat?"

"Arrogance," was his cryptic answer.

"Arrogance?"

"Yes, when a young man kills much meat he comes to think of himself as a chief or a big man, and he thinks of the rest of us as his servants or inferiors. We can't accept this. We refuse one who boasts, for someday his pride will make him kill somebody. So we always speak of his meat as worthless. This way we cool his heart and make him gentle."

"But why didn't you tell me this before?" I asked Tomazo with some heat.

"Because you never asked me," said Tomazo, echoing the refrain that has come to haunt every field ethnographer.

The pieces now fell into place. I had known for a long time that in situations of social conflict with Bushmen I held all the cards. I was the only source of tobacco in a thousand square miles, and I was not incapable of cutting an individual off for noncooperation. Though my boycott never lasted longer than a few days, it was an indication of my strength. People resented my presence at the water hole, yet simultaneously dreaded my leaving. In short I was a perfect target for the charge of arrogance and for the Bushmen tactic of enforcing humility.

I had been taught an object lesson by the Bushmen; it had come from an unexpected corner and had hurt me in a vulnerable area. For the big black ox was to be the one totally generous, unstinting act of my year at /ai/ai, and I was quite unprepared for the reaction I received.

As I read it, their message was this: There are no totally generous acts. All "acts" have an element of calculation. One black ox slaughtered at Christmas does not wipe out a year of careful manipulation of gifts given to serve your own ends. After all, to kill an animal and share the meat with people is really no more than Bushmen do for each other every day and with far less fanfare.

In the end, I had to admire how the Bushmen had played out the farce—collectively straight-faced to the end. Curiously, the episode reminded me of the *Good Soldier Schweik* and his marvelous encounters with authority. Like Schweik, the Bushmen had retained a thoroughgoing skepticism of good intentions. Was it this independence of spirit, I wondered, that had kept them culturally viable in the face of generations of contact with more powerful societies, both black and white? The thought that the Bushmen were alive and well in the Kalahari was strangely comforting. Perhaps, armed with that independence and with their superb knowledge of their environment, they might yet survive the future.

Body Ritual Among the Nacirema

BY HORACE MINER

The anthropologist has become so familiar with the diversity of ways in which different peoples behave in similar situations that he is not apt to be surprised by even the most exotic customs. In fact, if all of the logically possible combinations of behavior have not been found somewhere in the world, he is apt to suspect that they must be present in some yet undescribed tribe. This point has, in fact, been expressed with respect to clan organization by Murdock (1949:71). In this light, the magical beliefs and practices of the Nacirema present such unusual aspects that it seems desirable to describe them as an example of the extremes to which human behavior can go.

Professor Linton first brought the ritual of the Nacirema to the attention of anthropologists twenty years ago (1936:326), but the culture of this people is still very poorly understood. They are a North American group living in the territory between the Canadian Cree, the Yaqui and Tarahumare of Mexico, and the Carib and Arawak of the Antilles. Little is known of their origin, although tradition states that they came from the east. According to Nacirema mythology, their nation was originated by a culture hero, Notgnihsaw, who is otherwise known for two great feats of strength—the throwing of a piece of wampum across the river Pa-To-Mac and the chopping down of a cherry tree in which the Spirit of Truth resided.

Nacirema culture is characterized by a highly developed market economy which has evolved in a rich natural habitat. While much of the people's time is devoted to economic pursuits, a large part of the fruits of these labors and a considerable portion of the day are spent in ritual activity. The focus of this activity is the human body, the appearance and health of which loom as a dominant concern in the ethos of the people. While such a concern is certainly not unusual, its ceremonial aspects and associated philosophy are unique.

The fundamental belief underlying the whole system appears to be that the human body is ugly and that its natural tendency is to debility and disease. Incarcerated in such a body, man's only hope is to avert these characteristics through the use of the powerful influences of ritual and ceremony. Every household has one or more shrines devoted to this purpose. The more powerful individuals in the society have several shrines in their houses and, in fact, the opulence of a house is often referred to in terms of the number of such ritual centers it possesses. Most houses are of wattle and daub construction, but the shrine rooms of the more wealthy are walled with stone. Poorer families imitate the rich by applying pottery plaques to their shrine walls.

While each family has at least one such shrine, the rituals associated with it are not family ceremonies but are private and secret. The rites are normally only discussed with children, and then only during the period when they are being initiated into these mysteries. I was able, however, to establish sufficient rapport with the natives to examine these shrines and to have the rituals described to me.

The focal point of the shrine is a box or chest which is built into the wall. In this chest are kept the many charms and magical potions without which no native believes he could live. These preparations are secured from a variety of specialized practioners. The most powerful of these are the medicine men, whose assistance must be rewarded with substantial gifts. However, the medicine men do not provide the curative potions for their clients, but decide what the ingredients should be and then write them down in an ancient and secret language. This writing is understood only by the medicine men and by the herbalists who, for another gift, provide the required charm.

The charm is not disposed of after it has served its purpose, but is placed in the charm-box of the household shrine. As these magical materials are specific for certain ills, and the real or imagined maladies of the people are many, the charm-box is usually full to overflowing. The magical packets are so numerous that people forget what their purposes were and fear to use them again. While the natives are very vague on this

Reproduced by permission of the American Anthropological Association from *American Anthropologist*, 58(3): 503–507, 1956.

point, we can only assume that the idea in retaining all the old magical materials is that their presence in the charm-box, before which the body rituals are conducted, will in some way protect the worshipper.

Beneath the charm-box is a small font. Each day every member of the family, in succession, enters the shrine room, bows his head before the charm-box, mingles different sorts of holy water in the font, and proceeds with a brief rite of ablution. The holy waters are secured from the Water Temple of the community, where the priests conduct elaborate ceremonies to make the liquid ritually pure.

In the hierarchy of magical practitioners, and below the medicine men in prestige, are specialists whose designation is best translated "holy-mouth-men." The Nacirema have an almost pathological horror of and fascination with the mouth, the condition of which is believed to have a supernatural influence on all social relationships. Were it not for the rituals of the mouth, they believe that their teeth would fall out, their gums bleed, their jaws shrink, their friends desert them, and their lovers reject them. They also believe that a strong relationship exists between oral and moral characteristics. For example, there is a ritual ablution of the mouth for children which is supposed to improve their moral fiber.

The daily body ritual performed by everyone includes a mouth-rite. Despite the fact that these people are so punctilious about care of the mouth, this rite involves a practice which strikes the uninitiated stranger as revolting. It was reported to me that the ritual consists of inserting a small bundle of hog hairs into the mouth, along with cer'ain magical powders, and then moving the bundle in a highly formalized series of gestures.

In addition to the private mouth-rite, the people seek out a holy-mouth-man once or twice a year. These practitioners have an impressive set of paraphernalia, consisting of a variety of augers, awls, probes, and prods. The use of these objects in the exorcism of the evils of the mouth involves almost unbelievable ritual torture of the client. The holy-mouth-man opens the client's mouth and, using the above mentioned tools, enlarges any holes which decay may have created in the teeth. Magical materials are put into these holes. If there are no naturally occurring holes in the teeth, large sections of one or more teeth are gouged out so that the supernatural substance can be applied. In the client's view, the purpose of these ministrations is to arrest decay and to draw friends. The extremely sacred and traditional character of the rite is evident in the fact that the natives return to the holy-mouth-men year after year, despite the fact that their teeth continue to decay.

It is to be hoped that, when a thorough study of the Nacirema is made, there will be careful inquiry into the personality structure of these people. One has but to watch the gleam in the eye of a holy-mouth-man, as he jabs an awl into an exposed nerve, to suspect that a certain amount of sadism is involved. It this can be established, a very interesting pattern emerges, for most of the population shows definite masochistic tendencies. It was to these that Professor Linton referred in discussing a distinctive part of the daily body ritual which is performed only by men. This part of the rite involves scraping and lacerating the surface of the face with a sharp instrument. Special women's rites are performed only four times during each lunar month, but what they lack in frequency is made up in barbarity. As part of this ceremony, women bake their heads in small ovens for about an hour. The theoretically interesting point is that what seems to be a preponderantly masochistic people have developed sadistic specialists.

The medicine men have an imposing temple, or *latipso*, in every community of any size. The more elaborate ceremonies required to treat very sick patients can only be performed at this temple. These ceremonies involve not only the thaumaturge but a permanent group of vestal maidens who move sedately about the temple chambers in distinctive costume and headdress.

The *latipso* ceremonies are so harsh that it is phenomenal that a fair proportion of the really sick natives who enter the temple ever recover. Small children whose indoctrination is still incomplete have been known to resist attempts to take them to the temple because "that is where you go to die." Despite this fact, sick adults are not only willing but eager to undergo the protracted ritual purification, if they can afford to do so. No matter how ill the supplicant or how grave the emergency, the guardians of many temples will not admit a client if he cannot give a rich gift to the custodian. Even after one has gained admission and survived the ceremonies, the guardians will not permit the neophyte to leave until he makes still another gift.

The supplicant entering the temple is first stripped of all his or her clothes. In every-day life the Nacirema avoids exposure of his body and its natural functions. Bathing and excretory acts are performed only in the secrecy of the household shrine, where they are ritualized as part of the body-rites. Psychological shock results from the fact that body secrecy is suddenly lost upon entry into the *latipso*. A man, whose own wife has never seen him in an excretory act, suddenly finds himself naked and assisted by a vestal maiden while he performs his natural functions into a sacred vessel. This sort of ceremonial treatment is necessitated by the fact that the excreta are used by a diviner to ascertain the course and nature of the client's sickness. Female clients, on the other hand, find their naked bodies are subjected to the scrutiny, manipulation and prodding of the medicine men.

Few supplicants in the temple are well enough to do anything but lie on their hard beds. The daily ceremonies, like the rites of the holy-mouth-men, involve discomfort and torture. With ritual precision, the vestals awaken their miserable charges each dawn and roll them about on their beds of pain while performing ablutions, in the formal movements of which the maidens are highly trained. At other times they insert magic wands in the supplicant's mouth or force him to eat substances which are supposed to be healing. From time to time the medicine men come to their clients and jab magically treated needles into their flesh. The fact that these temple ceremonies may not cure, and may even kill the neophyte, in no way decreases the people's faith in the medicine men.

There remains one other kind of practitioner, known as a "listener." This witch-doctor has the power to exorcise the devils that lodge in the heads of people who have been bewitched. The Nacirema believe that parents bewitch their own children. Mothers are particularly suspected of putting a curse on children while teaching them the secret body rituals. The counter-magic of the witch-doctor is unusual in its lack of ritual. The patient simply tells the "listener" all his troubles and fears, beginning with the earliest difficulties he can remember. The memory displayed by the Nacirema in these exorcism sessions is truly remarkable. It is not uncommon for the patient to bemoan the rejection he felt upon being weaned as a babe, and a few individuals even see their troubles going back to the traumatic effects of their own birth.

In conclusion, mention must be made of certain practices which have their base in native esthetics but which depend upon the pervasive aversion to the natural body and its functions. There are ritual fasts to make fat people thin and ceremonial feasts to make thin people fat. Still other rites are used to make women's breasts larger if they are small, and smaller if they are large. General dissatisfaction with breast shape is symbolized in the fact that the ideal form is virtually outside the range of human variation. A few women afflicted with almost inhuman hypermammary development are so idolized that they make a handsome living by simply going from village to village and permitting the natives to stare at them for a fee.

Reference has already been made to the fact that excretory functions are ritualized, routinized, and relegated to secrecy. Natural reproductive functions are similarly distorted. Intercourse is taboo as a topic and scheduled as an act. Efforts are made to avoid pregnancy by the use of magical materials or by limiting intercourse to certain phases of the moon. Conception is actually very infrequent. When pregnant, women dress so as to hide their condition. Parturition takes place in secret, without friends or relatives to assist, and the majority of women do not nurse their infants.

Our review of the ritual life of the Nacirema has certainly shown them to be a magic-ridden people. It is hard to understand how they have managed to exist so long under the burdens which they have imposed upon themselves. But even such exotic customs as these take on real meaning when they are viewed with the insight provided by Malinowski when he wrote (1948:70):

> Looking from far and above, from our high places of safety in the developed civilization, it is easy to see all the crudity and irrelevance of magic. But without its power and guidance early man could not have mastered his practical difficulties as he has done, nor could man have advanced to the higher stages of civilization.

References

Linton, Ralph
　　1936 The Study of Man. New York, D. Appleton-Century Co.
Malinowski, Bronislaw
　　1948 Magic, Science, and Religion. Glencoe, The Free Press.
Murdock, George P.
　　1949 Social Structure. New York, The Macmillan Co.

Doing Fieldwork in Middle Class America

BY JOAN ABLON

During the past decade anthropologists have discovered that the urban area is a rich as well as convenient arena for fieldwork. The intricacies and implications of urban research are only beginning to be felt as the potential of diversified field scenes is being realized. Urban anthropologists characteristically have chosen as the subjects of their research minority groups or disenfranchised inner city poor who retain trappings of exotica (or poverty) congenial to the anthropologist's historical proclivity and bias for work with the culturally different and, now, the underdog in modern society, thereby retaining what Mitchell (1970) has termed "The Blue Lagoon Personality." Few anthropologists have heeded Nader's exhortation (1972) to "study up" and to investigate the powerful or wealthy who constitute the power structure of American society. Neither have anthropologists chosen to study horizontally those closer to their own social and economic status—the middle class. Anthropologists who study middle class or other populations of nonexotic Americans, now have the opportunity to define and contribute to the interface between anthropology and other social sciences. Sociologists and political scientists have focused on many of the same areas of interest in this country as have anthropologists in culturally dissimilar settings. For example, my own research experiences suggest that our conceptual designs and field methods can offer unique, in-depth qualitative materials to complement the broad gauged and statistical urban sociological studies.

Further, I contend that applied anthropologists have a special responsibility to understand and deal with these populations which determine much of the basic character and detail of our daily lives by the products of their voting prerogatives and their daily work activities. The political "buck" both starts and stops here. We and others may work till doomsday with the impoverished and politically impotent but accomplish very little for general economic or social reform until middle and upper class populations are understood

and moved to social and political action. Therefore, it can be argued that the mandate to work with these populations is our calling at this time.

I will discuss here a number of new field problems which I see arising as anthropologists begin to work with American middle class populations. These problems deal with the essence of the dyadic relationship between the anthropologist and informant and involve the personalities, values, and individual human needs of each.

We must anticipate and manage potential areas of value conflict between the anthropologist and his informants. In studies with non-Western peoples far afield or minority groups in the inner city, despite specific characteristics unpleasant to the anthropologist personally or professionally, the exotic nature of the culture and our basic philosophy of cultural relativism have made objectionable characteristics curious, even lovable or, at the least, bearable because of their distinctiveness. The potential of actual value conflicts with our informants becomes more real when we deal with persons who live and interact within our own cultural world. For example, some anthropologists personally might feel there is no redeeming dimension to the reality of certain values within their own mainstream culture which are at odds with the anthropological premise of "freedom and equality" for all peoples as a premium ethical and professional principle.

Gulick (1973:1013, 1017–1018), in one of the rare statements in the anthropological literature that speaks to this issue commented on both the lack of studies by anthropologists of mainstream American society, and on, in fact, anthropologists' apparent distaste for American cultural patterns. Says Gulick:

> . . . many American anthropologists hate American middle-class culture and therefore react emotionally to such questions as whether the culture of poverty is middle-class *manque* or whether it is a viable culture in its own right.

If my guess is correct, then we are faced with the

very serious question of whether American anthropology as presently constituted is qualified to study American cultures reasonably objectively. If it is not, then we must face the possibility that would-be recruits to professional anthropology who want to study their own culture would be best advised by *anthropologists* to become political scientists, psychologists, or sociologists, since these professionals for a long time have claimed to have objective techniques for studying their own culture [p. 1013].

If anthropologists are unwilling to study mainstream urban United States culture, they can hardly contribute, responsibly and professionally, to the reordering of that culture's priorities that many people feel is needed. "The anthropological perspective," according to two reform-minded educators, "allows one to be part of his own culture and, at the same time, to be out of it" (Postman and Weingartner 1970:4). The irony is that middle-class American anthropologists are apparently unable or unwilling to apply this perspective in participant-observer research of the sort undertaken by Gans.

North American urban anthropology is part of anthropology's general identity problem . . . because it brings this paradoxical situation to the fore. The opportunity, however, for it to establish its relevance by recruiting professionals who are willing to undertake such research is obvious, as is the likelihood that the character of anthropology would undergo some changes as the result of such a development [pp. 1017–18].

The diminution of cultural barriers leads to increased personal visibility of the anthropologist. Not only the personal values of the anthropologist may be challenged in relating to our own mainstream middle class informants, but also the nature of language or cultural differences. The nuances of the anthropologist's personality may be scanned and if he is not deemed likable, his fieldwork may suffer. Obviously, anthropologists in all settings are, in broad stroke, examined for their acceptability by prevailing cultural standards, but the scanning often is much more broadly gauged or impressionistic.

Moreover, there is the likelihood that the questions of the anthropologist will be turned back on him. Despite deep affection, concern, and camaraderie which most anthropologists have had in their relationships with informants in traditional settings, strong ethnic identity maintenance boundaries and explicit cultural and life style differences between anthropologists and native informants existed that precluded the demand for certain kinds of intimate sharing of personal information by the anthropologist—who, of course, got from his informants much of the same sort of information that he could withhold—almost to the degree of a therapist who withholds the personal details of his life from his patients, about whom he knows "everything." Middle class Americans who are the anthro-

pologist's economic and social peers may indeed want to know and do ask, a great many things about the the life style of the investigator, particularly if he has taken on a participant-observer role. Questions concerning the anthropologist's salary, sex life, and daily (and nightly activities) are quite likely to be asked of him. The intimate nature of these kinds of questions might be contrasted to that of questions asked of anthropologists by informants more culturally and geographically removed. For example, representative of the most personal questions asked of me during my first field experience in a Mayan village was, "How large is your father's cornfield?" Intimate details of the anthropologist's normal life style when at home are less likely to be elicited for scrutiny by informants who live even a thousand miles distant, as opposed to a mile or two miles away.

Let us now explore several topics of ethical concern to us when we deal as anthropologists with human subjects. I shall discuss the right to private personality and the nature of privacy.

The anthropologist must effectively deal with being the insider and outsider in his own culture. The activities of subjects in a culturally dissimilar setting provide relatively discrete, distinctive phenomena which the sensitive observer will carefully note and chronicle to develop a body of data. The objective, systematic recording of familiar, everyday activities in the lives of urban dwellers who may exhibit behavior patterns very similar to those of the anthropologist, may become more problematical. For example, do we remember to record in our notes the offering of a cup of coffee, to describe the china cup and saucer (so similar to our mother-in-law's) in the same manner as we would record the serving of more unusual foods offered us in a remote village? Many of us who learned field methods in communities far away now worry about the pitfalls in training a new generation of students who will "cut their teeth" on social and cultural phenomena a scant mile from our classroom. Can these students really become first-rate anthropologists without the classic rural, non-Western field experience which has become the hallmark of our trade? I suggest they can, directed by more specific, analytic guidelines for the gathering of data and the conceptualization of cultural materials. Spradley and McCurdy's methodology (1972) for observing "cultural scenes" and capturing the insider's view provides one schema to overcome the seductive dangers of taking for granted familiar-appearing behavior and motives within our own cultural setting.

The anthropologist must be alert and open to new and different opportunities for reciprocity in the field situation. Anthropologists are increasingly concerned with reciprocity in the field situation. What are we giving to our informants that will in some way pay them back for all they are giving to us? How can we contribute to better their lives? Most of us, in our studies of more traditional people, become involved in the daily problems of our informants' lives. Even the "purest" of us dispense aspirin, drive informants to doctors, loan them money, or put them up for a night or a week.

Schensul (1974) and Jacobs (1974) have described in some detail how they involved themselves in significant practical activities of neighborhood health centers. Such practical activities are much more appropriate in working with politically and economically alienated Chicano and Black populations than with middle class or upper class Whites who often have skills in social organization and may even have lawyers and grants and budget experts as part of their community organizations. Many of the opportunities for personal gratification we received from working with culturally or economically different people are no longer available. Models for more sophisticated partnerships will have to be developed for anthropologists who wish to be involved in community action with the middle class.

We are now encountering a population that, on the face of it, does not *need* an anthropologist around. Many poor and isolated peoples have used our presence and equipment to good advantage. They *needed us* to complain to about insensitive government bureaucracies; they *needed* our car to get to the doctor or the store. Now we may be finding ourselves useless logistically, but still needed psychologically. In the past, our informants' problems almost always have been inextricably involved with poverty. For this anthropologist, it has been something of a jolt to work with a population that has none of the stresses related to inadequate income, poor housing or schools, or acute health conditions, but has another order of personal problems that cannot be directly laid to the door of economics. Despite their affluence, the lot of middle class individuals is not necessarily a particularly happy one for them. Many have dramatic personal problems that frequently have their origins within the confines of the family culture and structure. These problems are as severe and urgent to the persons involved as are the kinds of problems we have tended to link to economic need. Some anthropologists would object to a concern with the "happiness" or "unhappiness" of informants. They feel that is not the business of the anthropologist. I am convinced that if we are to provide an understanding of the reality of a person's life we cannot ignore his joys or his sorrows. The emotional need and propensity of middle class Americans to talk easily about their personal problems may offer one of the most significant areas in which the anthropologist can reciprocate. He can be a good listener. Most persons do not easily take advantage of a referral to a clinician who might help them. The anthropologist may constitute the only sympathetic and nonjudgmental listener the informant will experience. Yet anthropologists may be little equipped personally or professionally to listen to hours of personal and family problems.

Many difficulties shared by various minorities are related to the inequalities and ravages of history and bureaucracy, and hostility and partisan activities can be directed toward these relatively impersonal forces. Middle class family problems cannot be handled in this way. While anthropologists might work to change the policies of an agency, few are clinically trained to aid people in working out their personal or emotional problems. Perhaps we should consider as one new element of our training experience courses dealing with how to listen carefully to personal problems and devise non-"clinical" and nondirective yet supportive modes of responding to expressed problems which require on-the-spot, helpful responses. This capability will provide one immediate and often called for dimension of reciprocity in field relationships.

In sum, I suggest that anthropologists, who choose to work with middle class populations, may have to develop thoughtful new models for relating to informants. If we are to maintain our traditional anthropological personalized format for fieldwork, we may indeed have to modify certain significant elements within this format to give cognizance to the new interpersonal complexities of the urban field scene.

References

Gulick, J.
  1973 Urban Anthropology. *In* Handbook of Social and Cultural Anthropology. John G. Honigmann, ed. New York: Rand McNally.
Jacobs, S.
  1974 Action and Advocacy Anthropology. Human Organization 33:209–215.
Mitchell, J. C.
  1970 Urban Anthropology: Its Perspectives and Problems. Unpublished paper. University of Wisconsin at Milwaukee Conference on Anthropological Research in Cities.
Nader, L.
  1969 Up the Anthropologist: Perspectives Gained from Studying Up. *In* Reinventing Anthropology. Dell Hymes, ed. New York: Random House.
Postman, N., and C. Weingartner
  1970 Teaching as a Subversive Activity. New York: Delacorte Press.
Schensul, S. L.
  1974 Skills Needed in Action Anthropology: Lessons from El Centro de la Causa. Human Organization 33:203–209.
Spradley, J. P., and D. W. McCurdy
  1972 The Cultural Experience. Chicago: Science Research Associates.

TOPIC NINE

Kinship and Marriage

....

Each culture provides an accepted range of options for human activities. It thus sets limits on human behavior as well as creating its potential. Although the spectrum of accepted activities and behavior in human groups around the world is vast, there are nevertheless certain patterns that reappear in virtually every culture. These are termed *cultural universals.*

The regulation of sexual behavior is one such cultural universal. Sexual mores vary enormously from one culture to another, but all cultures apparently share one basic value—namely, that sexual intercourse between parents and their children is to be avoided. In addition, most cultures also prohibit sexual contact between brothers and sisters. The term for prohibited sex among relatives is *incest,* and because most cultures attach very strong feelings of revulsion and horror to incest, it is said to be forbidden by *taboo.*

The universal presence of the incest taboo means that individuals must seek socially acceptable sexual relationships outside their own families. All cultures provide definitions of the categories of persons who are eligible and ineligible to have sex with each other. These definitions vary greatly cross-culturally. In our society, for instance, the incest taboo covers only the nuclear family and direct linear relatives and their siblings (parents, aunts and uncles, grandparents, and so on). However, in societies organized primarily in terms of kinship ties, the categories of sexually ineligible individuals can be very large indeed, reaching out to include almost all of a person's relatives linked through either male (patrilineal) or female (matrilineal) kinship. The Lepcha of Sikkim are such a society.

Cultures do more, however, than simply prohibit sex between categories of individuals. They also provide for institutionalized marriages, the ritualized means for publically legitimizing sexual partnerships and designating social positions for their offspring. The interaction of these two universals—the incest taboo and institutionalized marriage—creates a third universal: the social institution known as the family. But "Is the Family Universal?" asks Melford E. Spiro in

a seminal article published more than thirty years ago. Spiro uses the Israeli *kibbutz* as a means to reexamine the concept of the family. Though his article is somewhat dated now, it is considered a classic because it forced anthropologists to rethink many of their assumptions about the forms and functions of the family. Spiro has continued his study of the same *kibbutzim* for over three decades, observing them and their members as they have grown, developed, and reacted to the vast changes that have overtaken Israeli society during that period. As his latest book, *Gender and Culture: Kibbutz Women Revisited* (Columbia Univ. Press, 1980), makes clear, Spiro himself has rethought many of his original ideas.

The remaining two articles, by Charles and Cherry Lindholm, look at two societies in which patterns of relationships in marriage are very different indeed. In "What Price Freedom?" the Lindholms describe the Lepcha of Sikkim, a small Himalayan kingdom north of India. Lepcha culture has two very remarkable features: total freedom from sexual jealousy (in fact, there is no word for jealousy in the Lepcha language) and a great degree of sexual freedom. Among the Lepcha, for example, certain relatives have an absolute right to sleep with a man's wife. Similarly, if a visitor even speaks with a Lepcha woman or pays her any attention at all, she assumes he is trying to seduce her—an attempt she is more than happy to encourage. Unfortunately, there is a price to be paid for all of this sexual freedom.

In "Marriage as Warfare," the Lindholms examine the impact of an enduring "marital war" on personal relationships, especially on those between spouses. Among the Pakhtun of Pakistan, the family clearly is far from being a "haven in a heartless world," as Christopher Lasch describes the family in America. Instead, it is a microcosm in which the violence of the society is mirrored and engendered and in which men dream, not of mistresses, but of unobtainable friendship. Charles Lindholm has elaborated on this study of Pakhtun society in his book *Generosity and Jealousy:*

Emotional Structures in a Competitive Society (Columbia Univ. Press, 1982). The book describes the pervasive effects of Pakhtun social structure on child rearing, politics, residence patterns, and interpersonal relations. Lindholm holds that the values of generosity and hospitality, for which the Pakhtun are justly famous, cannot be understood within this structure, which impels people toward relations based on enmity and jealousy. Instead, he argues, these values are expressions of underlying universal human needs for attachment—needs that the harsh Pakhutun social order reveres in its ideology and rituals but prohibits in normal daily interactions.

What Price Freedom?

BY CHARLES LINDHOLM AND CHERRY LINDHOLM

The two-day marriage ceremony is almost over. The oxen have been sacrificed, the Buddhist priests have said their prayers, the guests have presented their gifts of cloth and money and have been given proportionate amounts of meat in return. The bride and her relatives, who have come from a far-distant village, are sitting against the left wall of her new family's house, facing the groom and his family in customary fashion. The girl, though only 14, is slightly older than her young husband and is considered quite mature to be a new bride. She covers her face with her headcloth to hide her expression as the ritual discussion of her qualities begins between the families.

"We are giving you," announces her uncle, addressing the groom's family, "the yolk of this egg that we have peeled for you."

One of the groom's party replies, "Thank you very much. It is very kind of you. But it seems to us as if this egg has been nibbled at! And we would not be surprised if her pubic hair were not as long as that of a female devil or in appearance rather like a field of fresh corn!"

"We assure you," retorts the bride's uncle, "that the egg has been freshly peeled to make it easy for you to eat."

"Well, it seems to us that the shell has been off for a very considerable time!"

"And what does it matter if her pubic hair is like a tangled bush? A clever goat can find its way through any bramble!"

This sexual joking during a solemn ritual occurs among the Lepcha people of Sikkim, a small Himalayan kingdom north of India. Since 1974, it has been an "associate state" of India, and the power of the *chogyal*, or king, is purely nominal. The Lepchas live primarily on a royal preserve set aside for them by ancestors of today's *chogyal*. There, the Lepchas are relatively free to pursue their ancient culture. The preserve, Jongu, is located in

the precipitous valleys of the high Himalayas. Towering over all else is snow-capped, 28,208-foot Kanchenjunga, which ironically enough is worshipped as a war god by the peace-loving Lepchas.

There is probably not a 100-foot-square piece of flatland in the whole region, and cultivation often takes place at a 60-degree angle. The Lepchas find it impossible to use even mules for porterage and are obliged to carry all baggage on their own backs. But in spite of their harsh environment, the industrious Lepchas manage to grow rice, wheat, millet and maize, as well as a variety of fruits, vegetables and spices, including the spice cardamom, their only cash crop.

The climate is extremely wet, with occasional ruinous hailstorms. Famine is greatly feared, and most of the Lepcha religious rituals are designed to ward off hunger and disease.

They were first studied in 1876 by Colonel G. G. Mainwaring, a British officer. He was so impressed by their gentleness that he thought they were the original sinless children of Eve. Halfdan Siiger, who visited them in 1949, wrote that "they are by nature extremely kind, and when they lose their immediate fear of a stranger and gain confidence in him, they meet him with a lovely smile and an open mind, and above all with friendliness." The major anthropological work— *Himalayan Village*—was written by Geoffrey Gorer, who visited them in 1937 and was struck not only by their shyness and peaceful ways but also by their humorous verbal preoccupation with sex.

Indeed, to the Lepchas sex is continually and inexhaustibly funny. During village feasts, they spend their time eating, drinking *chi* (the very formidable local millet beer), and laughing heartily at the never-ending flow of sexual jokes and innuendos. In addition to the feasts given at births, marriages, deaths, and when

visiting relatives arrive from distant villages, there are the monthly Lamaist festivals and large bimonthly monastery feasts. At such a feast, 80 or 90 people may be present and the merrymaking may even continue into the next day, with people catnapping intermittently. A dozen or so lamas (Buddhist priests) will be sitting in the main prayer room of the monastery, while the smaller prayer room will be occupied by six or seven nuns and a great number of other women, old men and young children. In the monastery yard, the wives of the feast-givers and anyone else who wishes will be busy with the large cook pots, preparing the vegetables, cereal, meat and *chi*.

The younger men and women and the older boys sit about on the grass and stones outside, chatting, joking, and occasionally fetching water or firewood for the cooking. The younger boys may hang about with them and listen to the conversations, but more often they either sit quietly on the grass or else play on the hill outside the monastery grounds, chasing hens or imitating birdcalls. The girls generally tag along with their parents or an older sister and will often be carrying a younger sibling. Small groups of toddlers sit some distance from the grown-ups, clustering silently around pots of *chi*, which they drink through bamboo straws; after a time, they become quite tipsy and noticeably less quiet; they stagger around for a while and then fall asleep. No one pays them any attention.

As the night wears on, people become more and more mellow, voices become louder, gestures more expansive, and there is much laughter at the obscene remarks that fly back and forth among the guests. Full of food and drink, some guests happily doze, while others occupy themselves with braiding one another's hair. Couples may wander off into the forest or to a nearby shed from time to

Reprinted from *Science Digest*, November/December 1980, by permission of the authors.

time. Occasionally, there will be some lighthearted sexual byplay as a young man, or sometimes a young woman, grabs at another young man's penis, to the delight of the onlookers. Or an old man, having become quite drunk, will expose himself to the laughing throng. But for the most part, the sexual joking is verbal, and the ability to talk well and tell good stories is much admired among the Lepcha people.

It is generally thought that such sexual joking is the result of sexual frustration and inhibition, but among the Lepchas this is certainly not the case. Their sex lives are notoriously active. Impotence is unheard of and sexual activity continues until quite late in life for both men and women. There is no language of seduction or foreplay employed, since the Lepchas consider that anticipation alone guarantees sufficient stimulation; one simply makes a straightforward proposition, which is usually accepted. As Gorer notes, "Sexual activity is practically divorced from emotion; it is a pleasant and amusing experience, and as much a necessity as food and drink; and like food and drink it does not matter from whom you receive it, as long as you get it, though you are naturally grateful to the people who provide you with either item regularly."

Sexual jealousy is not considered a normal emotion and there is no word for jealousy in the language. In fact, certain relatives have an absolute right to sleep with one's wife, and as Chudo, a Lepcha man, told Gorer, "If I caught my elder brother's son sleeping with my wife, I shouldn't be cross at all; on the contrary, I should be very pleased, for she would be teaching him how to do it properly, and I would know that he had a good teacher."

Aside from nephews, a man's younger brothers also have free access to his wife, and boys are usually initiated into sex by an uncle's or brother's wife. Other men are also permitted to sleep with her, providing that they are not too blatant about it and do not have sex with her in the house unless the husband is away and unlikely to come home and witness the act.

INCEST TABOOS

This is not to say that Lepcha society is totally promiscuous. In fact, the range of partners prohibited by incest taboos is extremely wide: sex is forbidden with a partner related back at least seven generations on the father's side and at least four on the mother's. Ideally, the prohibitions should reach back nine generations on both sides, but this would render marriage almost impossible. It is also forbidden to sleep with a woman one's father has had sex with; this is considered incestuous, and fathers instruct their young sons early as to their permitted and prohibited sexual partners. The choices are limited by the rules of exogamy (marriage outside a group of lineal relatives), the wide range of incest prohibitions, and the fact that the Lepchas are mainly patrilocal (the wife moving in with the husband's family). Hence, sex with most girls who have grown up in the village is forbidden. (A large village consists of 50 to 60 houses.) Marriage and sex partners must come from some distance away. Siiger notes that "real ingenuity has to be exercised in order to find a suitable partner for one's son or daughter," and perhaps this is the reason for allowing the sharing of women within the village. Indeed, the fact that most people at any gathering will be sexually taboo might account for the extraordinary amount of sexual joking.

Girls usually have their first sexual encounters before puberty, as it is believed that a virgin girl will not normally grow breasts or begin menstruating but must have sexual intercourse in order for these transformations to occur. There is no stigma attached to a grown man forcing a little girl of 9 or 10 to have sex with him; such an occurrence, in fact, is considered quite amusing and is a subject for joking and laughter. If a girl starts menstruating while still a virgin—as does happen occasionally—it is thought that she has been visited by a supernatural, and this is considered an extremely lucky sign. Dreams of copulating with a supernatural being are supposed to come to a woman during every menstrual period; if, one month, she fails to have this dream, it signifies that she is shortly to die. This is the only sexual dream that the Lepchas admit to having.

Since most men in the home village are prohibited, women often have their first sexual experience with a visitor, and unrelated guests can therefore be quite popular. Gorer reports that his difficulty in obtaining information about sex from the women was not due to the jealousy of the husbands, as might be the case in many societies, but to "the fact that almost every woman from eight to eighty interpreted any sort of special attention as an attempt at seduction, an attempt which—no matter what their youth or age—they had no intention of repelling."

Marriages are not arranged by the parents but by the village headman. The partners must be the correct genealogical distance and have complementary horoscopes. Girls are usually engaged around the age of 9 and boys around the age of 12. No attention is paid to the desires of the young couple, and girls especially will often resist marriage, no doubt largely because it means leaving their home village. After the pair is engaged and the bride-price given, the boy and girl are expected to copulate under the watchful eyes of their uncles; this is thought to ensure the stability of the marriage. The period of greatest sexual adventuring for the Lepcha boy and girl occurs during the engagement, especially if the couple do not particularly like each other or if their villages are far apart.

After the engagement, the boy must perform bride-service during visits to his in-laws' house, where he is treated as a servant and subjected to a great deal of sexual teasing. He is not allowed to retaliate in kind, and if he is provoked into doing so, he will be humiliated by his fiancée's family. The relationship with in-laws is one of the utmost respect; one should not direct obscene jokes toward them nor make such jokes in their presence, though when the engagement period is over this latter proscription is often ignored. Ideally, one should also behave with similar decorum toward one's parents and siblings of the opposite sex, but in Jongu the Lepchas are rather lax on this point of etiquette. The major prohibition is one that disallows adult brothers and sisters from touching one another, except during times of illness, and the brother-sister incest taboo is the most stringent of all. (Interestingly enough, the Lepcha creation myth claims that the original mother and father of the Lepcha people were brother and sister.) The breaking of an incest taboo has extremely serious consequences: it is believed to result in a year of disaster, not only for the man and woman involved but for the entire community in which they live.

This belief illustrates the structure of Lepcha society, for the Lepcha life-style is communal. People find their identity in their *ptso* (patriline) and village membership, and the ideal of cooperation, unselfishness and sharing comes close to being a reality. The Lepchas redistribute their resources to alleviate poverty, and sharing with the poor is considered a very good custom because, as one village headman explained, "It makes everybody realize that they are part of one group and the happiness of one is the happiness of all." Both children and adults are extraordinarily unselfish and always share things. Children are taught to help others, so that others in their turn will help them, and they are told that no one will help a thief. They are instructed to receive a

THE LEPCHA

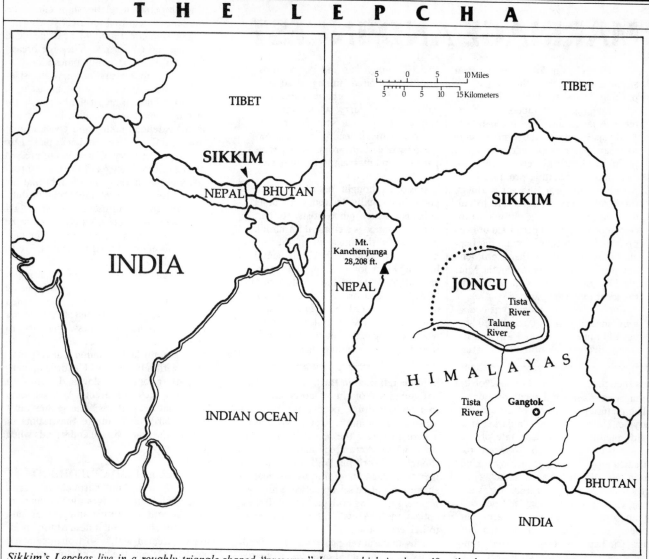

Sikkim's Lepchas live in a roughly triangle-shaped "preserve," Jongu, which is about 40 miles long on each side. The precipitous countryside includes tropical river valleys and 12,000-foot cliffs, and trails off (dotted line) into barren, freezing highlands.

gift in cupped hands and always to give a small gift in return. Gift-giving, which is a continuing motif in Lepcha life, is always an exchange, never simply one-sided receiving.

Among the Lepchas, relations are based on exact reciprocity and mutual obligations, and the individual who fulfills those obligations is automatically a good person and will be well liked. People express their liking for others. "I care for my parents because they gave me food," said one man. Another explained that "When I go out to work and come back tired, my wife has a good meal ready for me and looks after me; then I think 'This is my wife, and I am pleased in my belly.'" It is interesting to note that the stomach, not the heart, is considered to

be the center of the emotions, and that past events are often remembered in terms of menus.

Life takes place within the range of the extended family. A man hopes to get responsibility for his family in his mid-thirties and to give up responsibility when he reaches 60. Children are therefore greatly desired, and adoption by childless couples is common. It is expected that the child will help his parents in their old age. Boys and girls, like men and women, are considered alike in their basic natures. The same rules of behavior apply to both sexes. Male and female work roles are not greatly differentiated; both sexes work in the fields, and men will take over the cooking if necessary. Although the society is patrilineal, with women unable to

inherit land, the only real difference the Lepchas see between men and women is in the genitals, which are considered to have a sort of independent life very much of their own.

NO AUTHORITY FIGURES

The Lepchas dislike anyone who tries to show authority. They work together in gangs, but no one tells another what to do and the headman leads by suggestion and example. Deviants are those who are aggressive, domineering and violent, and people who attempt to dominate will be excluded from the communal feasting cycle. However, such individuals, and even those who commit sodomy (which is thought to be like incest), are not considered personally responsible. Their behav-

MARRIAGE AND INCEST

The Lepchas of Sikkim enjoy great sexual freedom, but their choice of partners is strictly limited by a very wide-ranging incest taboo, which extends as far as the seventh generation. Anthropologists use the term *exogamy* to mean marriage outside a group of prohibited kin. While every human society has rules stating prohibited and permitted marriage and sex partners, these rules vary from culture to culture, and what may be considered incest in one society is permitted or even preferred in another. Among the Lepchas, sex with the father's brother's daughter is incestuous, but in the Middle East this cousin is thought to be the ideal marriage partner.

The converse of exogamy is *endogamy*, meaning that marriage and sexual life must be pursued *within* a defined circle of people. In Western society, though sex and marriage are legally prohibited among close relatives, everyone is otherwise theoretically free to marry whomever they choose. Many other societies, however, are specifically endogamous, allowing only a certain group of marriage partners, and marriage with an outsider is frowned upon.

It is often thought that the incest taboo is biologically derived, but among animals no such taboo exists. Rather, the incest taboo is a cultural formation maintaining the integrity of the human family, which is the fundamental building block for all human social organization. Without the family structure, the social order would collapse upon itself in confusion. This is especially true in less complex societies, where kinship is the key to all economic and political relationships.

ior is thought to be a result of malevolent action by devils of the Lepcha religion.

The picture given so far of Lepcha life is idyllic. However, there is a darker side to this picture. The suicide rate of the Lepchas is extremely high. Women commit suicide by drowning, men by taking poison, and nearly all suicides occur directly after a public reproof for such transgressions as being lazy and neglecting one's work or failing to carry out properly one's obligations toward another. The Lepchas possess an overly sensitive sense of shame, and it is very easy to shame someone. While the rules of the society are somewhat flexible, antisocial behavior leads to exclusion, and a public shaming can often result in suicide, even when a person is wrongly accused. Not having a strongly developed sense of self, such as prevails in other cultures, a Lepcha cannot withstand the disapproval of the community. His feelings of aggression in this situation find their expression in self-destruction, just as in lesser cases a Lepcha who is angry will destroy his or her own possessions.

Communal life among the Lepchas ignores individual differences and stresses obligation rather than affect, or feeling. People exist only as a part of a larger whole. They are liked and accepted according to their fulfillment of obligations, not according to their individual personalities, which are not really recognized among the Lepchas. This lack of individuality is reflected in the fact that individual names are of almost no consequence in Lepcha culture; people are called by kinship terms, and it is even possible for a man to forget the actual name of his own wife. Arranged marriages are thought to work out well since they are merely a relation of mutual obligation such as might be set up between any two people. Providing both parties fulfill these obligations, they will automatically grow to like each other.

This underdeveloped sense of individuality is accompanied by a lack of creativity. There are no local arts and crafts except storytelling, and it is forbidden to invent new stories to enlarge the traditional stock. Individual inventiveness is seen mainly in the Lepchas' sexual joking. A general sense of lack of affect is apparent in the society, since all strong emotions are suppressed as threatening to the cooperative structure of the community. Relationships tend to be cut-and-dried, without much personal content. The basic cultural stance is one of indifference, and the most commonly heard phrase is *ket ma-nin*, "it doesn't matter." The Lepchas are easily taken advantage of by unscrupulous Hindu merchants, who place them deeply in debt. Their culture requires specific protection by the state, for it soon disappears among Lepchas who leave the preserve. The concreteness and absolute quality of all relationships make the Lepchas extremely weak at working with abstract concepts, and the stress on smooth personal relationships eliminates the tension required for creative effort.

Children are raised to be dependent, passive and conformist. They are breast-fed until the next child comes along, an average of four years, but a youngest or only child may be given the breast until puberty. Though breast-fed by the mother only, infants are handled by everyone in the extended family and given a great deal of diffuse attention, being picked up as soon as they cry. Gorer was impressed by the lack of crying and the general passivity of the children and thought that the passionless quality of adult relationships was due to the diffuseness of childhood relationships. There does not seem to be a very strong emotional tie with the parents, and children tend to relate more to their older siblings.

Though children begin participating in adult labor at a very early age, no specific tasks, such as herding cattle, are assigned them, and Gorer attributes the young men's extreme boyishness, inability to stand alone and lack of self-reliance to their general lack of individual responsibility within the family. The developmental pattern for men is slow and even, with no great life-crisis events. Women seem more mature, perhaps because they must adjust early on in life to the trauma of leaving the home village and friends when they marry.

BEDEVILED CHILDHOOD

Family life is not particularly warm. Though infants are given much attention, that attention is rather impersonal, and the older child, though desired for his labor, is treated with a sort of impersonal neglect. Despite the lack of violence in the society, children are often beaten for getting in the way or interfering with adults, though the beatings are given without anger. Children are offered violence or succor with equal impersonality. They are trained by fear, and the most common way to gain obedience is to threaten a child with the vengeance of a devil. A child who still wants the breast after a new infant has been born will be told that the infant is a devil. Children who die are thought to become devils and are considered dangerous; hence, the adults' attitude toward children is ambiguous from the start. For the child, the world is a place of pervasive anxiety, and adults remember their childhoods as times of fear, hurt and obscurity. Children are, quite simply, miniature and relatively incompetent adults who do not even have the recompense of receiving respect for their work in the household.

Anxiety does not vanish with adulthood. The world is not beautiful, it is frightening, and the Lepcha pays no attention to the mountains that rise in splendor all around him but walks instead with his eyes on the ground. The religion of the Lepchas is primarily a religion of fear. Spirits of nature and of the dead are terrifying, and the aim of ritual is to keep them at bay. It may seem contradictory that such a peaceful people should have a religion with such violent and frightening iconography, but the human emotional makeup demands a balance. What cannot be expressed within society finds its expression in ritual, and the aggression the Lepchas deny in their daily lives is encountered in the threatening gods and devils of their religion.

UNNEUROTIC ADULTS

Gorer ascribed the Lepcha character to the infants' toilet training, which is out of phase with psychosexual development, combined with diffuse and impersonal attention from many adults. Such a pattern will tend to produce "a society in which the great majority of adults will be unneurotic, unaggressive, generous, with undisturbed sexual potency. . . . they will also be uninventive, with no high art and little development of the crafts; no complexity will be meaningful. There will be little intensity in adult relations, and little passion in either life or art."

This picture may be oversimplifying the factors behind the development of the Lepcha personality. It must also be remembered that the Lepchas have a long history of oppression and have been enslaved several times in the past few hundred years by their more warlike neighbors of Nepalese extraction. The word *Lepcha*, in fact, indicates the people's low status, since it is a derogatory Nepalese term meaning "nonsense speakers." The Lepchas call themselves the Rong. Furthermore, their entire relation with their ecology has totally changed from the freedom of hunting and gathering to the restrictions of intensive agriculture.

The Lepchas—there are perhaps 20,000 of them in Sikkim at this time— are a dying culture. One authority notes that the decade 1961–71 "reveals the dismal fact that the Lepchas have a negative growth rate." They have a low birthrate and a high incidence of sterility, suicide, disease and out-migration. Struggling to protect their cultural integrity, the Lepchas have evolved a complex and inwardly turned social order in which the aggressions of the outer world are countered by cooperation and sharing within the community.

Marriage as Warfare

BY CHARLES LINDHOLM AND CHERRY LINDHOLM

The rapid beating of the war drums reverberates along the narrow winding streets of a Pakhtun village, isolated in the remote mountain valley of Swat in northwestern Pakistan. However, it is not a battle that the drums are heralding. It is a marriage.

The Yusufzai Pakhtun of Swat are members of the great Pakhtun (or Pathan) tribe, which dominates Afghanistan and northern Pakistan. They have long been famous for their aggressive daring and bravery in warfare, their fiery pride and individualism, and their refusal to accept defeat or domination. Historically, they have always been the conquerors, never the conquered.

The nomadic Yusufzai migrated to the fertile valley of Swat from Kabul in the early sixteenth century. After defeating the local population and reducing them to landless servants, the Yusufzai settled down and became small farmers (any Yusufzai Pakhtun who lost his land joined the despised servant class and was stripped of his rights and his honor as a Pakhtun). In the nineteenth century the Swat Pakhtun won the admiration of the British for their successful resistance to colonial invasion, and they acceded to Pakistan only when assured of local autonomy. Even today, the valley of Swat is relatively free from the influence of the state, and order is maintained by personal strength and the force of custom.

Swat's climate is suitable for double cropping (wheat and clover in the spring, rice and corn in the fall), and the sparkling Swat River, which bisects the valley, provides an adequate water supply. There is an extensive irrigation system, and the hillsides are well terraced. But despite the lush appearance of the valley, overpopulation has placed a terrible strain on the resource base, and competition for control of land is fierce and sometimes deadly. Innumerable bloody battles have been waged since the Yusufzai established their rule in Swat.

Inside her house, a girl of twelve, hearing the war drums' energetic tattoo, cowers in fear on a string cot. She cries silently behind the folds of her voluminous embroidered shawl, while her relatives gather about her, their faces long and mournful. Even the bright luster of the girl's golden jewelry does little to alleviate the atmosphere of tension and distress in the household.

The girl on the cot is the new bride, and she and her family are waiting for the moment when she must leave her natal home forever and take up residence in her husband's house. The use of the war drums for a wedding is actually far from ludicrous, for marriage in Swat is very much like a prolonged combat and is recognized as such by both men and women. The relationship resembles that between two opposing countries where an ever present cold war frequently erupts into skirmishes and open conflict.

During our nine-month stay in a Swat village in 1977, we witnessed such relationships firsthand. With our twelve-year-old daughter, we lived with a Pakhtun family in three small rooms that had been constructed on the roof of their house. As friends, guests, and adopted relatives, we were accepted into the life of the village with the warmhearted generosity and hospitality for which the Pakhtun are deservedly renowned.

This remarkable hospitality, combined with an idealized notion of male friendship, is one of the three cornerstones of *Pakhtunwali*, the Pakhtun code of honor, the other two being refuge and blood revenge. This code is older than Islam and often supersedes Islamic tenets. For example, Islam allows divorce, *Pakhtunwali* does not; also, sometimes a man will swear falsely, his hand on the Holy Koran, in order to save a friend.

Although the Pakhtun are strict Sunni Muslims, they derive their identity and self-respect from the zealous observance of *Pakhtunwali*, land ownership, and tight control over women by means of a rigorous system of purdah (female seclusion). The worst insult one can offer a man is to call him *begherata*, man without honor. This pejorative has three meanings: someone who is lazy and weak, someone who has lost his land, and someone who has no control over his women. To the proud Pakhtun, loss of honor is worse than death, since it renders him unworthy of the name "Pakhtun."

The Pakhtun's liberal hospitality is generally demonstrated on the stage of the *hujera*, or men's house, where the guest is enthusiastically welcomed, made comfortable on a cot with fat cushions behind his head, served tea and the best food available, and showered with his proud host's unstinting attentions. To entertain a guest is a great honor, and the host will spare no effort to make the occasion as lavish and enjoyable as possible. Nor is this ritualized hospitality mere etiquette or a means of swelling the host's self-esteem. The warm friendliness that accompanies the ritual is genuine, deeply felt, and extremely moving. In the *hujera*, the violent Pakhtun of the battlefield, who will fight to the death for his land, for someone else's land, or to avenge any slight on his honor, becomes the epitome of cordiality, gentle dignity, and brotherly affection.

This metamorphosis is not altogether surprising. In a society where survival depends upon a man's physical and psychological toughness, there is little chance to express such emotions as affection and tenderness. The guest in the *hujera* fulfills in ritual fashion the role of the idealized friend who, according to one Pakhtun proverb,

"without invitation, will assure me of his love." This dream of the perfect friend, always a man, which has been honored in countless proverbs and poems over the centuries, is the beloved fantasy of every Pakhtun male. The friend, however, must necessarily be a stranger, for all Swat Pakhtun are, by the very nature of their harsh and competitive society, rivals and potential enemies. Naturally, given these qualifications, friendship in Swat is very rare indeed. Yet the dream persists and is acted out in the rite of hospitality whenever the opportunity arises.

In sharp contrast to the romantic image of the friend and public display of hospitality, the Pakhtun's domestic

arena, concealed behind the impenetrable walls of the purdah household, is the site of confrontations more akin to those of the battlefield.

As the drumming grows louder, the trembling bride remembers her mother's advice for a successful marriage: "You must keep power over your husband. Always speak first when he enters, even if only to cough. Sleep with your hand behind his head. Then he will miss you and never be satisfied with any other."

The girl prays that her husband will like her and that he will not humiliate her and her family by taking a second wife. That would be the worst possible catastrophe. She is of a good family and her family pride is strong.

Now the time has come for her to leave. She clutches at the cot, but her elder brother pulls her hands free and lifts her onto the palanquin that will carry her to her husband's house. The embroidered cover is dropped into place, and the girl is carried into the narrow street. Men of the husband's house are waiting to join the procession. They help with the palanquin and triumphantly bounce it about. Village boys line the route and throw stones, hoping to overturn the bride into the muddy alley. In the past, serious fights sometimes erupted because of injuries caused by this ritual stoning, but in recent years the violence has lessened.

The procession continues through the village, led by the men carrying the bride and followed by a supply of household goods from her father's house. The drums of the groom are now heard as the procession approaches his compound. Men of his family gleefully fire their rifles, and small boys toss sweets to the crowd from the low rooftops. The drumming reaches a crescendo as the party enters the groom's house. This is a tense moment. Sometimes, the groom's family tries to deny entry to the men of the bride's party, and a fight breaks out. But today everything goes smoothly, and men of both houses carry the palanquin into the inner courtyard.

Strong hands lift the bride onto a cot in the corner of the single room where she will live with her husband. The men then leave the house to begin feasting in the *hujera*. Totally enclosed in her shawl, the new bride presses

In a Swat village, a palanquin transports a bride to her new home.

Cherry Lindholm

tightly to her chest the Koran her father has given her. The women of the household surround her, talking incessantly and cajoling her to show her face. A young girl begins the drumbeat for women, and the groom's female relatives start dancing in the courtyard, celebrating the newcomer's arrival. Later, they will give her money, and in return, she will bow before them and touch their feet in token of future subservience. But, for the moment, the bride remains motionless on the cot. She will stay in this position for three days, rising only to relieve herself. On the third night her husband will creep into the house to consummate the marriage.

While the bride huddles nervously in her new home, the groom, a green-eyed man of twenty-five, is fingering his mustache in the *hujera* of a relative, a different *hujera* from the one where the feasting is taking place. He is not permitted to join in the festivities of the marriage but must hide in shame at losing his bachelor status. Twenty years ago, young grooms sometimes ran away from their home villages and had to be coaxed back to their wives. But men's shame is no longer so acute. In those days, all men slept in the *hujera* and only slipped out to visit their wives secretly at night. Women also were shyer then, and a man might not see his wife's face for a year or more. But nowadays, with the curtailment of warfare and the weakening of the village khans, or leaders, most men sleep at home with their wives.

The groom is speculating about his new wife's appearance. He has never seen her, but he has heard reports that she is light skinned and fat—an ideal beauty. His own sexual experience has been with boys his own age who played the passive role and with girls of the servant class. For him, sexual dominance is an expression of power. He hopes that the youth and innocence of his bride will render her docile and respectful. However, he fears that the marriage will be a contentious one. That is how all marriages end up. "It is because our women are no good," he muses.

For two more nights the groom stays in the *hujera*, pretending indifference to his marriage. Then, on the third night, he steals into his family's com-

pound and opens the door of the room where his bride is waiting. He is slightly inebriated from smoking hashish. She is unveiled and afraid to look at him. Sometimes, the groom finds his bride repulsive and cannot have sex with her. Or he may have been enchanted by a male lover and rendered incapable of heterosexual intercourse. The bride has no recourse, for Pakhtun marriage is a lifetime contract. Moreover, the wife even follows her husband to heaven or hell, so that they are united for eternity.

In the room adjoining the nuptial chamber, the groom's sisters have bored a hole in the wall and are spying on the couple. The groom gives the girl a gold watch and some sweets. He begins to caress and tease her, but she is too terrified to respond, and the sexual act is rough and hasty. Thus the couple enter into married life.

The giving of a woman in marriage is a touchy business for the Swat Pakhtun. Historically, a weak lineage gave women to its stronger neighbors in order to form alliances, and victors in war expressed their triumph by taking women from the conquered. As a result, there is the suggestion that the wife givers are inferior to the wife takers—and any hint of inferiority is intolerable to a Pakhtun. Hostility toward marriage as an institution is seen in the ritual stoning of the bride's palanquin and in the fights between the bride's party and the groom's party. If divorce were allowed, no marriage would last for long.

The groom feels shame at his marriage because every Pakhtun man, not unlike the mythical American cowboy, seeks to present himself as completely self-reliant, independent, and free of obligation. But the cowboy can always reject home and family and ride away into the sunset—an option the Pakhtun man does not have. Instead, he effectively hides his wife inside the privacy of the purdah household. Her presence is known to an outsider only through the tea she prepares. The Pakhtun woman must never be seen by men who are not close family members. She must never leave the compound walls without her husband's permission. By remaining a virtual prisoner inside her husband's house, she helps to uphold his honor, for she is a part of all he

possesses and her behavior is a direct reflection of his power and control.

Years ago, if a Pakhtun woman was seen by a man who was not her relative, her enraged husband would cut off her nose as a punishment and as a means of cleansing his family honor, which her carelessness had sullied. While this custom has been abandoned, severe beatings are common. And a woman found alone with a man who is not a relative has committed a killing offense, for it will be assumed that the liaison is sexual. In such a case, although the husband may not actually desire her death, the pressure of public opinion, the code of *Pakhtunwali*, which demands vengeance, and his own sense of acute shame, would all push him to take action.

Because they are able to dishonor men, women are feared. On the other hand, the woman has only physical violence to fear from her husband. Even more than the male, she is accustomed to violence from childhood. Her personal pride is far more powerful than her fear of a beating. Although she is a prisoner in her husband's house, her position is in some ways stronger than his, for she holds the weaponry for his dishonoring, whereas he holds merely a stick with which to beat her. While the wife must live with her jailer, the husband is obliged to share his house with an enemy—and an extremely tenacious and able one.

Marriage thus begins as a hostile relationship. The young bride's apprehension and the groom's shame accompany the determination of each to dominate the other. Pakhtun marriage demands a precarious balance of power, and the young partners are ready from the start to fight each other to avoid being dominated and shamed.

It is now a year after the marriage—the bride has her place within her husband's household. In her eyes, she is treated like a slave. Her mother-in-law is impossibly demanding; the girl can do nothing right. Her husband takes no notice of her beyond the servicing of his sexual needs. Recently, she has begun having fits in which she is possessed by demons. During these fits, she rolls in the dirt and must be restrained from throwing herself into the well or the fire. From her mouth, demonic voices hurl abuse at her husband

and his family. Exorcisms by a holy man, who puts sticks between her fingers and squeezes her hand painfully, are only temporarily effective. Finally, her father is asked to intervene. "If this happens again," he warns her, "I'll shoot you." The demons stop appearing.

Shortly afterward, she gives birth to a son, and her position in her husband's household improves. She is now respected, for she has contributed to perpetuating her husband's line. But her relations with her mother-in-law continue to be as unpleasant as ever.

As time goes by, the marriage proves to be as difficult as the young groom feared. Fighting goes on daily, over the wife's poorly made milk curd or over a piece of rotten meat the husband has foolishly purchased. The husband may strike out because his wife is nagging him to buy another piece of jewelry that she can show off to her neighbor; the wife may be irate because the husband, in a display of generosity, has depleted the family larder. Anything can cause a serious fight, and several times the bruised wife returns, with injured pride, to her father's house. There she is pampered by her relatives for a time, but she must go back to her husband upon his demand. She returns, and the fights continue.

Like all Pakhtun husbands, he severely beats his wife to break her of bad habits and make her submissive. The young woman nonetheless remains proud and fearless; far from becoming meek, she defends herself aggressively, clawing at her husband's face and tearing the shirt from his back. He strikes out, especially at her face, and sometimes uses a club or throws a stone at her. This is considered perfectly normal, and the wife is even somewhat proud of her battle scars. She abuses her elder sister's husband, who rarely hits his wife, as "a man with no penis." Yet her own husband fares no better, as she frequently calls curses down upon him and abuses his lineage: "Your ancestor was nothing and my ancestor was great!"

The husband, becoming wearied with the constant effort to subdue and control his defiant female adversary, dreams of defeating her once and for all by bringing in another, more tractable wife. He frequently threatens her

with this ultimate humiliation, but is unable to implement his plan because he lacks funds. Despite the proverb that "a fool can be recognized by his two wives," most men dream of a second marriage. Those few who can afford it, however, inevitably regret it, for with the arrival of a second wife, warfare begins in earnest. Each woman seeks, with magical spells and sheer contentiousness, to drive the other out. Sometimes, one wife will poison the other or, more commonly, the husband; sometimes the husband's throat is slit while he sleeps. The first wife continually badgers the husband to bring in yet a third wife, in order to humiliate the second wife as she has been humiliated. The besieged husband, who has found the second wife as irritating as the first, futilely wishes he could turn back the clock.

Although they continue to squabble, the husband and wife are actually quite fond of each other. Each admires the other's resolute pride and fighting ability. But the man cannot show his affection, for to do so would give the wife courage to dishonor him. A man who displays affection to his wife is indicating weakness, which the woman will immediately exploit in the battle for domination. She may begin leaving the house without permission, confident that the loving husband will not punish her. Then she will start having affairs with other men, thoroughly dishonoring her weakling spouse. Therefore, a man must avoid laughing with his wife or showing her any tenderness, in spite of his feelings for her. "Instead of a kiss, he gives me a bite," says the wife, baring her teeth. But if he did give her a kiss, she would begin to feel he had become emasculated.

The husband carries his feigned indifference to his wife into public life, never mentioning her to his friends. Nor do they inquire after her; to do so would be a breach of etiquette. Instead, they merely ask him, "How is your house?"

The wife is not so constrained. Confined to the compound, she spends much of her time complaining to visitors, to servants, and even to her children about the activities of her husband. Gossip about the wrongdoings of their men is the major subject of women's conversations. "All Swat

men are rotten," they say. That is the nature of men. The wife's solace is hearing the tribulations of other women and anticipating the power she will wield in her later years. By that time, her husband will be a tired old man, without the energy for fighting, her sons will be grown, and their wives will be living in her house under her rule. She will control her domestic sphere like a real matriarch, and the purdah compound, her former prison, will become her court. Indeed, the Western image of the docile purdah female is an inaccurate picture of the Pakhtun woman of Swat.

This story is representative of the marriage relations among the Yusufzai Pakhtun. Perhaps a particular couple will fight less than usual because of extraordinary meekness or compatibility. Fortunate couples may reach a sort of wary, joking understanding in old age. But, in general, the marriage relation is one of strife, violence, and struggle.

This pattern of hostility and rivalry derives from the social model of the society, which is technically termed a segmentary lineage system. This means that the Yusufzai Pakhtun trace themselves, through the male line, to a common ancestor, Yusuf, the progenitor of the entire clan. All consider themselves equal, and all have rights in the family land. Despite this ideology of equality, however, those who are strong force the weak from their land. To be a landless Pakhtun is to lose one's birthright and become a member of the servant class. Thus, each family seeks to protect itself and subordinate others.

Life in the Yusufzai village is largely a contest to determine dominance. A man's chief rival is his father's brother's son, who has a claim on the land of the common grandfather. This cousin is often one's in-law as well, since marriage with the father's brother's daughter is greatly favored in Swat. By marrying their female patrilineal cousin, the Yusufzai hope to gain control over their main political rival, but to no avail, since such marriages are notoriously hostile.

The term for the father's brother's son is *tarbur*, a word that means enemy. But the *tarbur* is also an ally, for only he can be counted upon to come to one's aid in case of an attack by a more genealogically distant adversary. Groupings occur on the basis of patrilineal kinship and only take place when there is an external threat. When the British attacked them, the Yusufzai Pakhtun forgot their internal enmities and united to expel the invader.

In this system, men constantly maneuver for power and honor. Loyalties shift easily. As one family becomes strong, others unite against it. Some families rise, but are soon torn apart by internal dissension. As the modern Pakhtun writer Ghani Khan has observed, ''The Pakhtun have not become a great nation because a man would rather burn his house than see his elder brother rule it.''

In such an environment, a martial air and genuine willingness to fight are absolute necessities for survival. Even hospitality, the most loving relationship found in the society, is tinged with rivalry, as hosts express their strength and dominance through lavish entertainment. The assertion of one's own pride and the denigration of other lineages is therefore the primary emotional stance of the Pakhtun. This stance is not confined to men. The

women also consider all men not of their patrilineage to be of inferior quality. Every marriage is thus with an inferior, and the partners are well prepared to fight each other to uphold the honor of their respective houses.

Although the husband tries to ignore his wife, she refuses to be overlooked. Her own pride, instilled by her lineage, demands that she assert herself. The woman's place is in the house, however—patrilineal descent prevents her from inheriting land or from participating in struggles over land. Where a man's pride and identity rest in his landholdings, her honor is found in vindicating her superiority in the household. The bruises that inevitably result she regards as marks of honor. If her health is good, if she can avoid being expelled by another wife, and if she has sons, her struggle is likely to end in victory. The aging husband, beset by rivals on all sides, and even besieged by his own sons demanding their share of his land, will accept his wife's rule in exchange for relative peace in the compound.

Small wonder that the Pakhtun man dreams of the mythical friend. This

dream, and the ritual of hospitality in which it finds expression, derives from the stern social order, which sets every man against every other, and which prevents any amicable relationship within the family. Deprived of any real opportunity to be affectionate and generous, the Pakhtun male releases these suppressed feelings in the rite of hospitality.

Women, on the other hand, have no great interest in hospitality, although they cook for guests for the sake of their own pride. Unlike the man, who seeks to dominate in a world of opponents, the woman strives only to dominate in the house. The man's goal is impossible, but the woman's is fairly attainable. Women are also united in a community of complaint against their husbands. They do not engage in life and death struggles over land, and in consequence, their enmities are less deep than the men's. Despite the travails and bruises of marriage, women tend to succeed in their goals, while men spend their time pursuing a chimera of friendship.

Is the Family Universal?

BY MELFORD E. SPIRO

....

INTRODUCTION

The universality of the family has always been accepted as a sound hypothesis in anthropology; recently, Murdock has been able to confirm this hypothesis on the basis of his important cross-cultural study of kinship. Moreover, Murdock reports that the "nuclear" family is also universal, and that typically it has four functions: sexual, economic, reproductive, and educational. What is more important is his finding that no society "has succeeded in finding an adequate substitute for the nuclear family, to which it might transfer these functions" (1949:11). In the light of this evidence there would be little reason to question his prediction that "it is highly doubtful whether any society ever will succeed in such an attempt, utopian proposals for the abolition of the family to the contrary notwithstanding" (p. 11).

The functions served by the nuclear family are, of course, universal prerequisites for the survival of any society; and it is on this basis that Murdock accounts for its universality.

> Without provision for the first and third [sexual and reproductive], society would become extinct; for the second [economic], life itself would cease; for the fourth [educational], culture would come to an end. The immense social utility of the nuclear family and the basic reason for its universality thus begins to emerge in strong relief [p. 10].

Although sexual, economic, reproductive, and educational activities are the functional prerequisites of any society, it comes as somewhat of a surprise, nevertheless, that all four functions are served by the same social group. One would normally assume, on purely a priori grounds, that within the tremendous variability to be found among human cultures, there would be some cultures in which these four functions were distributed among more than one group. Logically, at least, it is entirely possible for these functions to be divided among various social groups within a society; and it is, indeed, difficult to believe that somewhere man's in-

ventive ingenuity should not have actualized this logical possibility. As a matter of fact this possibility has been actualized in certain utopian communities—and it has succeeded within the narrow confines of these communities. The latter, however, have always constituted subgroups within a larger society, and the basic question remains as to whether such attempts could succeed when applied to the larger society.

Rather than speculate about the answer to this question, however, this paper presents a case study of a community which, like the utopian communities, constitutes a subgroup within a larger society and which, like some utopian communities, has also evolved a social structure which does not include the family. It is hoped that an examination of this community—the Israeli *kibbutz*—can shed light on this question.

MARRIAGE AND THE FAMILY IN THE *KIBBUTZ*

A *kibbutz* (plural, *kibbutzim*) is an agricultural collective in Israel, whose main features include communal living, collective ownership of all property (and, hence, the absence of "free enterprise" and the "profit motive"), and the communal rearing of children. *Kibbutz* culture is informed by its explicit, guiding principle of: "from each according to his ability, to each according to his needs." The "family," as that term is defined in *Social Structure*, does not exist in the *kibbutz*, in either its nuclear, polygamous, or extended forms. It should be emphasized, however, that the *kibbutzim* are organized into three separate national federations, and though the basic structure of *kibbutz* society is similar in all three, there are important differences among them. Hence, the term *kibbutz*, as used in this paper, refers exclusively to those *kibbutzim* that are members of the federation studied by the author.[1]

1. The field work, on which statements concerning the *kibbutz* are based, was conducted in the year 1951–1952, and was made possible by a postdoctoral fellowship awarded by the Social Science Research Council.

Reproduced by permission of the American Anthropological Association from *American Anthropologist*, 56(5): 839–846, 1954. The Addendum is reprinted from *A Modern Introduction to the Family*, Norman W. Bell and Ezra F. Vogel, eds., copyright © The Free Press (The Macmillan Company) 1960.

As Murdock defines it (p. 1), the "family":

> is a social group characterized by common residence, economic cooperation, and reproduction. It includes adults of both sexes, at least two of whom maintain a socially approved sexual relationship, and one or more children, own or adopted, of the sexually cohabiting adults.

The social group in the *kibbutz* that includes adults of both sexes and their children, although characterized by reproduction, is not characterized by common residence or by economic co-operation. Before examining this entire social group, however, we shall first analyze the relationship between the two adults in the group who maintain a "socially approved sexual relationship," in order to determine whether their relationship constitutes a "marriage."

Murdock's findings reveal that marriage entails an interaction of persons of opposite sex such that a relatively permanent sexual relationship is maintained and an economic division of labor is practised. Where either of these behavior patterns is absent, there is no marriage. As Murdock puts it (p. 8):

> Sexual unions without economic cooperation are common, and there are relationships between men and women involving a division of labor without sexual gratification... but marriage exists only when the economic and the sexual are united in one relationship, and this combination occurs only in marriage.

In examining the relationship of the couple in the *kibbutz* who share a common marriage, and whose sexual union is socially sanctioned, it is discovered that only one of these two criteria—the sexual—applies. Their relationship does not entail economic co-operation. If this be so—and the facts will be examined in a moment—there is no marriage in the *kibbutz*, if by "marriage" is meant a relationship between adults of opposite sex, characterized by sexual and economic activities. Hence, the generalization that, "marriage, thus defined, exists in every known society" (p. 8), has found an exception.

A *kibbutz* couple lives in a single room, which serves as a combined bedroom-living room. Their meals are eaten in a communal dining room, and their children are reared in a communal children's dormitory. Both the man and woman work in the *kibbutz*, and either one may work in one of its agricultural branches or in one of the "service" branches. The latter include clerical work, education, work in the kitchen, laundry, etc. In actual fact, however, men preponderate in the agricultural branches, and women, in the service branches of the economy. There are no men, for example, in that part of the educational system which extends from infancy to the junior-high level. Nor do women work in those agricultural branches that require the use of heavy machinery, such as trucks, tractors, or combines. It should be noted, however, that some women play major roles in agricultural branches, such as the vegetable garden and the fruit orchards; and some men are indispensable in service branches such as the high school. Nevertheless, it is accurate to state that a division of labor based on sex is characteristic of the *kibbutz* society as a whole. This division of labor, however, does not characterize the relationship that exists between couples. Each mate works in some branch of the *kibbutz* economy and each, as a member (*chaver*) of the *kibbutz* receives his equal share of the goods and services that the *kibbutz* distributes. Neither, however, engages in economic activities that are exclusively directed to the satisfaction of the needs of his mate. Women cook, sew, launder, etc., for the entire *kibbutz*, and not for their mates exclusively. Men produce goods, but the economic returns from their labor go to the *kibbutz*, not to their mates and themselves, although they, like all members of the *kibbutz* share in these economic returns. Hence, though there is economic co-operation between the sexes within the community as a whole, this co-operation does not take place between mates because the social structure of this society precludes the necessity for such co-operation.

What then is the nature of the relationship of the *kibbutz* couple? What are the motives for their union? What functions, other than sex, does it serve? What distinguishes such a union from an ordinary love affair?

In attempting to answer these questions it should first be noted that premarital sexual relations are not taboo. It is expected, however, that youth of high-school age refrain from sexual activity; sexual intercourse between high-school students is strongly discouraged. After graduation from high school, however, and their election to membership in the *kibbutz*, there are no sanctions against sexual relations among these young people. While still single, *kibbutz* members live in small private rooms, and their sexual activities may take place in the room of either the male or the female, or in any other convenient location. Lovers do not ask the *kibbutz* for permission to move into a (larger) common room, nor, if they did, would this permission be granted if it were assumed that their relationship was merely that of lovers. When a couple asks for permission to share a room, they do so—and the *kibbutz* assumes that they do so—not because they are lovers, but because they are in love. The request for a room, then, is the sign that they wish to become a "couple" (*zug*), the term the *kibbutz* has substituted for the traditional "marriage." This union does not require the sanction of a marriage ceremony, or of any other event. When a couple requests a room, and the *kibbutz* grants the request, their union is *ipso facto* sanctioned by society. It should be noted, however, that all *kibbutz* "couples" eventually "get married" in accordance with the marriage laws of the state—usually just before, or soon after, their first child is born—because children born out of wedlock have no legal rights according to state law.

But becoming a "couple" affects neither the status nor the responsibilities of either the male or the female in the *kibbutz*. Both continue to work in whichever branch of the economy they had worked in before their union. The legal and social status of both the male and the female remain the same. The female retains her maiden name. She not only is viewed as a member of the *kibbutz* in her own right, but her official registration card in the *kibbutz* files remains separate from that of her "friend" (*chaver*)—the term used to designate spouses.[2]

But if sexual satisfaction may be obtained outside of this union, and if the union does not entail economic co-operation, what motivates people to become "couples"? It seems that the motivation is the desire to satisfy certain needs for intimacy, using that term in both its physical and psychological meanings. In the first place, from the sexual point of view, the average *chaver* is not content to engage in a constant series of casual affairs. After a certain period of sexual experimentation, he desires to establish a relatively permanent relationship with one person. But in addition to the physical intimacy of sex, the union also provides a psychological intimacy that may be expressed by notions such as "comradeship," "security," "dependency," "succorance," etc. And it is this psychological intimacy, primarily, that distinguishes "couples" from lovers. The criterion of the "couple" relationship, then, that which distinguishes it from a relationship between adults of the same sex who enjoy psychological intimacy, or from that of adults of opposite sex who enjoy physical intimacy, is love. A "couple" comes into being when these two kinds of intimacy are united in one relationship.

Since the *kibbutz* "couple" does not constitute a marriage because it does not satisfy the economic criterion of "marriage," it follows that the "couple" and their children do not constitute a family, economic co-operation being part of the definition of the "family." Furthermore, as has already been indicated, this group of adults and children does not satisfy the criterion of "common residence." For though the children visit their parents in the latter's room every day, their residence is in one of the "children's houses" (*bet yeladim*), where they sleep, eat, and spend most of their time.

More important, however, in determining whether or not the family exists in the *kibbutz* is the fact that the "physical care" and the "social rearing" of the children are not the responsibilities of their own parents. But these responsibilities, according to Murdock's findings, are the most important functions that the adults in the "family" have with respect to the children.

Before entering into a discussion of the *kibbutz* system of "collective education" (*chinuch meshutaf*), it should be emphasized that the *kibbutz* is a child-centered society, *par excellence*. The importance of children, characteristic of traditional Jewish culture, has been retained as one of the primary values in this avowedly antitraditional society. "The Parents Crown" is the title given to the chapter on children in an ethnography of the Eastern European Jewish village. The authors of this enthnography write (Zborowski and Herzog 1952:308):

> Aside from the scriptural and social reasons, children are welcomed for the joy they bring beyond the gratification due to the parents—the pleasure of having a child in the house. A baby is a toy, the treasure, and the pride of the house.

This description, except for the scriptural reference, applies without qualification to the *kibbutz*.

But the *kibbutz* has still another reason for cherishing its children. The *kibbutz* views itself as an attempt to revolutionize the structure of human society and its basic social relations. Its faith in its ability to achieve this end can be vindicated only if it can raise a generation that will choose to live in this communal society, and will, thus, carry on the work that was initiated by the founders of this society—their parents.

For both these reasons the child is king. Children are lavished with attention and with care to the point where many adults admit that the children are "spoiled." Adult housing may be poor, but the children live in good houses; adult food may be meager and monotonous, but the children enjoy a variety of excellent food; there may be a shortage of clothes for adults, but the children's clothing is both good and plentiful.

Despite this emphasis on children, however, it is not their own parents who provide directly for their physical care. Indeed, the latter have no responsibilities in this regard. The *kibbutz* as a whole assumes this responsibility for all its children. The latter sleep and eat in special "children's houses"; they obtain their clothes from a communal store; when ill, they are taken care of by their "nurses." This does not mean that parents are not concerned about the physical welfare of their own children. On the contrary, this is one of their primary concerns. But it does mean that the active responsibility for their care has been delegated to a community institution. Nor does it mean that parents do not work for the physical care of their children, for this is one of their strongest drives. But the fruits of their labor are not given directly to their children; they are given instead to

---

2. Other terms, "young man" (*bachur*) and "young woman" (*bachura*), are also used in place of "husband" and "wife." If more than one person in the *kibbutz* has the same proper name, and there is some question as to who is being referred to when the name is mentioned in conversation, the person is identified by adding, "the *bachur* of so-and-so," or "the *bachura* of so-and-so."

the community which, in turn, provides for all the children. A bachelor or a "couple" without children contribute as much to the children's physical care as a "couple" with children of their own.

The family's responsibility for the socialization of children, Murdock reports, is "no less important than the physical care of the children."

> The burden of education and socialization everywhere falls primarily upon the nuclear family.... Perhaps more than any other single factor collective responsibility for education and socialization welds the various relationships of the family firmly together [p. 10].

But the education and socialization of *kibbutz* children are the function of their "nurses" and teachers, and not of their parents. The infant is placed in the "infants' house" upon the mother's return from the hospital, where it remains in the care of nurses. Both parents see the infant there; the mother when she feeds it, the father upon return from work. The infant is not taken to its parents' room until its sixth month, after which it stays with them for an hour. As the child grows older, the amount of time he spends with his parents increases, and he may go to their room whenever he chooses during the day, though he must return to his "children's house" before lights-out. Since the children are in school most of the day, however, and since both parents work during the day, the children—even during their school vacations—are with their parents for a (approximately) two-hour period in the evening—from the time that the parents return from work until they go to eat their evening meal. The children may also be with the parents all day Saturday—the day of rest—if they desire.

As the child grows older he advances through a succession of "children's houses" with children of his own age, where he is supervised by a "nurse." The "nurse" institutes most of the disciplines, teaches the child his basic social skills, and is responsible for the "socialization of the instincts." The child also learns from his parents, to be sure, and they too are agents in the socialization process. But the bulk of his socialization is both entrusted, and deliberately delegated, to the "nurses" and teachers. There is little doubt but that a *kibbutz* child, bereft of the contributions of his parents to his socialization, would know his culture; deprived of the contributions of his "nurses" and teachers, however, he would remain an unsocialized individual.

As they enter the juvenile period, pre-adolescence, and adolescence, the children are gradually inducted into the economic life of the *kibbutz*. They work from an hour (grade-school students) to three hours (high school seniors) a day in one of the economic branches under the supervision of adults. Thus, their economic skills, like most of their early social skills, are taught

them by adults other than their parents. This generalization applies to the learning of values, as well. In the early ages, the *kibbutz* values are inculcated by "nurses," and later by teachers. When the children enter junior high, this function, which the *kibbutz* views as paramount in importance, is delegated to the "homeroom teacher," known as the "educator" (*mechanech*), and to a "leader" (*madrich*) of the inter-*kibbutz* youth movement. The parents, of course, are also influential in the teaching of values, but the formal division of labor in the *kibbutz* has delegated this responsibility to other authorities.

Although the parents do not play an outstanding role in the socialization of their children, or in providing for their physical needs, it would be erroneous to conclude that they are unimportant figures in their children's lives. Parents are of crucial importance in the *psychological* development of the child. They serve as the objects of his most important identifications, and they provide him with a certain security and love that he obtains from no one else. If anything, the attachment of the young children to their parents is greater than it is in our own society. But this is irrelevant to the main consideration of this paper. Its purpose is to call attention to the fact that those functions of parents that constitute the *conditio sine qua non* for the existence of the "family"—the physical care and socialization of children—are not the functions of the *kibbutz* parents. It can only be concluded that in the absence of the economic and educational functions of the typical family, as well as of its characteristic of common residence, that the family does not exist in the *kibbutz*.

INTERPRETATION

It is apparent from this brief description of the kibbutz that most of the functions characteristic of the typical nuclear family have become the functions of the entire *kibbutz* society. This is so much the case that the *kibbutz* as a whole can almost satisfy the criteria by which Murdock defines the "family." This observation is not meant to imply that the *kibbutz* is a nuclear family. Its structure and that of the nuclear family are dissimilar. This observation does suggest, however, that the *kibbutz* can function without the family because it functions as if it, itself, were a family; and it can so function because its members perceive each other as kin, in the psychological implications of that term. The latter statement requires some explanation.

The members of the *kibbutz* do not view each other merely as fellow citizens, or as co-residents in a village, or as co-operators of an agricultural economy. Rather do they view each other as *chaverim*, or comrades, who comprise a group in which each is intimately related to the other, and in which the welfare of the one is bound up with the welfare of the other. This is a society in which the principle, "from each according to his ability, to each according to his needs," can be practised not because its members are more altruistic than the members of other societies, but because each member views his fellow as a kinsman, psychologically speaking. And just as a father in the family does not complain because he works much harder than his children, and yet he may receive no more, or even less, of the family income than they, so the *kibbutz* member whose economic productivity is high does not complain because he receives no more, and sometimes less, than a member whose productivity is low. This "principle" is taken for granted as the normal way of doing things. Since they are all *chaverim*, "it's all in the family," psychologically speaking.

In short, the *kibbutz* constitutes a *gemeinschaft*. Its patterns of interaction are interpersonal patterns; its ties are kin ties, without the biological tie of kinship. In this one respect it is the "folk society," in almost its pure form. The following quotation from Redfield (1947) could have been written with the *kibbutz* in mind, so accurately does it describe the social-psychological basis of *kibbutz* culture.

> The members of the folk society have a strong sense of belonging together. The group ... see their own resemblances and feel correspondingly united. Communicating intimately with each other, each has a strong claim on the sympathies of the others [p. 297]. ... the personal and intimate life of the child in the family is extended, in the folk society, into the social world of the adults. ... It is not merely that relations in such a society are personal; it is also that they are familial. ... the result is a group of people among whom prevail the personal and categorized relationships that characterize families as we know them, and in which the patterns of kinship tend to be extended outward from the group of genealogically connected individuals into the whole society. The kin are the type persons for all experience [p. 301].

Hence it is that the bachelor and the childless "couple" do not feel that an injustice is being done them when they contribute to the support of the children of others. The children *in* the *kibbutz* are viewed as the children *of* the *kibbutz*. Parents (who are much more attached to their own children than they are to the children of others) and bachelors, alike, refer to all the *kibbutz* children as "our children."

The social perception of one's fellows as kin, psychologically speaking, is reflected in another important aspect of *kibbutz* behavior. It is a striking and significant fact that those individuals who were born and raised in the *kibbutz* tend to practise group exogamy, although there are no rules that either compel or encourage them to do so. Indeed, in the *kibbutz* in which our field work was carried out, all such individuals

married outside their own *kibbutz*. When they are asked for an explanation of this behavior, these individuals reply that they cannot marry those persons with whom they have been raised and whom they, consequently, view as siblings. This suggests, as Murdock has pointed out, that "the *kibbutz* to its members *is* viewed psychologically as a family to the extent that it generates the same sort of unconscious incest-avoidance tendencies" (private communication).

What is suggested by this discussion is the following proposition: although the *kibbutz* constitutes an exception to the generalization concerning the universality of the family, structurally viewed, it serves to confirm this generalization, functionally and psychologically viewed. In the absence of a specific social group—the family—to whom society delegates the functions of socialization, reproduction, etc., it has become necessary for the entire society to become a large extended family. But only in a society whose members perceive each other psychologically as kin can it function as a family. And there would seem to be a population limit beyond which point individuals are no longer perceived as kin. That point is probably reached when the interaction of its members is no longer face-to-face; in short, when it ceases to be a primary group. It would seem probable, therefore, that only in a "familial" society, such as the *kibbutz*, is it possible to dispense with the family.

References

Murdock, G. P.
  1949 Social structure. New York, Macmillan.
Redfield, R.
  1947 The folk society. The American Journal of Sociology 52:293–308.
Zborowski, M. and E. Herzog
  1952 Life is with people. New York, International Universities Press.

ADDENDUM, 1958

This is, quite obviously, an essay in the interpretation, rather than in the reporting of data. After rereading the paper in 1958, I realized that the suggested interpretation follows from only one conception of the role which definitions play in science. Starting with Murdock's inductive—based on a sample of 250 societies—definitions of marriage and family, I concluded that marriage and the family do not exist in the *kibbutz*, since no single group or relationship satisfies the conditions stipulated in the definitions. If I were writing this essay today, I would wish to explore alternative interpretations, as well—interpretations which, despite Murdock's definitions, would affirm the existence of marriage and the family in the *kibbutz*. Hence, I shall here very briefly outline the direction which one alternative interpretation would take.

The *kibbutz*, it should be noted first, does not practice—nor does it sanction—sexual promiscuity. Each adult member is expected to form a more-or-less permanent bisexual union; and this union is socially sanctioned by the granting of a joint room to the couple. The resulting relationship is different from any other adult relationship in the *kibbutz* in a number of significant features. (1) It alone includes common domicile for persons of opposite sex. (2) It entails a higher rate of interaction than is to be found in any other bisexual relationship. (3) It involves a higher degree of emotional intimacy than is to be found in any other relationship. (4) It establishes (ideally) an exclusive sexual relationship. (5) It leads to the deliberate decision to have children. These characteristics which, separately and severally, apply uniquely to this relationship, not only describe its salient features but also comprise the motives for those who enter into it. The couple, in short, viewed either objectively or phenomenologically, constitutes a unique social group in the *kibbutz*.

What, then, are we to make of this group? Since economic co-operation is not one of its features, we can, using Murdock's cross-cultural indices, deny that the relationship constitutes marriage. This is the conclusion of the foregoing paper. In retrospect, however, this conclusion does not leave me entirely satisfied. First, although we deny that the relationship constitutes a marriage, it nevertheless remains, both structurally and psychologically, a unique relationship within the *kibbutz*. Moreover, it is, with the exception of the economic variable, similar to those distinctive relationships in other societies to which the term marriage is applied. Hence, if I were writing this paper today, I should want to ask, before concluding that marriage is not universal, whether Murdock's inductive definition of marriage is, in the light of the *kibbutz* data, the most fruitful, even for his large sample; and if it were agreed that it is, whether it ought not to be changed or qualified so as to accommodate the relationship between *kibbutz* "spouses." Here I can only briefly explore the implications of these questions.

If the stated characteristics of the *kibbutz* relationship are found in the analogous relationship (marriage) in other societies—and I do not know that they are—it is surely apposite to ask whether Murdock's definition could not or should not stipulate them, as well as those already stipulated. For if they are found in other societies, on what theoretical grounds do we assign a higher priority to sex or economics over emotional intimacy, for example? Hence, if this procedure were adopted (and assuming that the characteristics of the

kibbutz relationship were to be found in the marriage relationship in other societies), we would, since the *kibbutz* relationship satisfies all but one of the cross-cultural criteria, term the *kibbutz* relationship "marriage."

Alternatively, we might suggest that Murdock's definition of marriage, as well as the one suggested here, are unduly specific; that cross-cultural research is most fruitfully advanced by means of analytic, rather than substantive or enumerative, definitions. Thus, for example, we might wish to define marriage as "any socially sanctioned relationship between nonsanguineally-related cohabiting adults of opposite sex which satisfied felt needs—mutual, symmetrical, or complementary." A non-enumerative definition of this type would certainly embrace all known cases now termed "marriage" and would, at the same time, include the *kibbutz* case as well.

In the same vein, and employing similar definitional procedures, alternative conclusions can be suggested with respect to the family in the *kibbutz*. Although parents and children do not comprise a family, as Murdock defines family, they nevertheless constitute a unique group within the *kibbutz*, regardless of the term with which we may choose to designate it. (1) Children are not only desired by *kibbutz* parents, but, for the most part, they are planned. (2) These children—and no others—are called by their parents "sons" and "daughters"; conversely, they call their parents—and no other adults—"father" and "mother." (3) Parents and children comprise a social group in both an interactional and an emotional, if not in a spatial, sense. That is, though parents and children do not share a common domicile, they are identified by themselves and by others as a uniquely cohesive unit within the larger *kibbutz* society; this unit is termed a *mishpacha* (literally, "family"). (4) The nature of their interaction is different from that which obtains between the children and any other set of adults. (5) The rate of interaction between parents and children is greater than that between the children and any other set of adults of both sexes. (6) The psychological ties that bind them are more intense than those between the children and any other set of adults of both sexes.

Here, then, we are confronted with the same problem we encountered with respect to the question of *kibbutz* marriage. Because the parent-child relationship in the *kibbutz* does not entail a common domicile, physical care, and social rearing—three of the stipulated conditions in Murdock's definition of family—we concluded that the family does not exist in the *kibbutz*. But, since parents and children comprise a distinct and differentiated social group within the *kibbutz*, I am now not entirely satisfied with a conclusion which seems, at least by implication, to ignore its presence. For, surely, regardless of what else we might do with this group, we cannot simply ignore it. We can either perceive it, in cross-cultural perspective, as a unique group, and invent a new term to refer to it, or we can revise Murdock's definition of family in order to accommodate it.

Should the latter alternative be preferred, it could be effected in the following way. The stipulation of "common residence" could be qualified to refer to a reference, rather than to a membership, residence; and this is what the parental room is, for children as well as parents. When, for example, they speak of "my room" or "our room," the children almost invariably refer to the parental room, not to their room in the communal children's house. If, moreover, the educational and economic functions of the family were interpreted as responsibilities for which parents were either immediately or ultimately responsible, the *kibbutz* parent-child unit would satisfy these criteria as well. For, though parents do not provide immediately for the physical care of their children, neither do they renounce their responsibility for them. Rather, they seek to achieve this end by working jointly rather than separately for the physical welfare of all the children—including, of course, their own.

Similarly, though the parents have only a minor share in the formal socialization process, they do not simply give their children to others to be raised as the latter see fit. Rather, socialization is entrusted to specially designated representatives, nurses and teachers, who rear children, not according to their own fancy, but according to rules and procedures established by the parents. In short, though parents do not themselves socialize their children, they assume the ultimate responsibility for their socialization. Interpreted in this way, the relationship between *kibbutz* parents and children satisfies Murdock's definition of family.

To conclude, this addendum represents an alternative method of interpreting the *kibbutz* data concerning the relationship between spouses, and among parents and children. I am not suggesting that this interpretation is necessarily more fruitful than the one adopted in the paper. Certainly, however, I should want to examine it carefully before concluding, as I previously did, that marriage and the family are not universal.

Political and Economic Organization

All societies have means of molding their members' behavior to conform to group values (general orientations toward "good" and "bad," "right" and "wrong") and group norms (specific expectations of behavior depending on who the actor is and the social context in which the behavior is taking place). Anthropologists call such means the mechanisms of social control, and they distinguish between internal means and external means.

Internal mechanisms of control rely on the individual's personal acceptance—through enculturation and socialization—of his or her culture's values and norms. In other words, the individual will feel uncomfortable when the moral order of the society is violated and, therefore, will be motivated not to transgress the society's moral code or expectations. External means of control are the responses of the society or its representatives to a specific actions—either to reinforce (reward) them or to diminish the likelihood of their repetition by the culprit or by others. The former, reinforcing responses, are termed *positive sanctions*. The latter, punishments, are termed *negative sanctions*. Internalized values and norms, together with positive and negative sanctions, operate in all societies. However, there is enormous cross-cultural variation in the behaviors that are reinforced or punished and in the specific forms that the means of social control take.

One of the critical issues with regard to social control is which individuals or groups within a society have access to its mechanisms outside the family unit. For social control is a primary function of all political systems—that is, those social institutions organizing the application of power to the solution of public problems. (Power, after all, is the ability to compel others to do what one wants them to, and the mechanisms of social control are central to this undertaking.) In "Poor Man, Rich Man, Big-Man, Chief," Marshall Sahlins compares and contrasts Melanesian and Polynesian forms of political authority and discovers that the critical factor in each is the degree to which political institutions can control the economies (production and consumption) of individual households.

In "Cannibalistic Revenge in Jalé Warfare," Klaus-Friedrich Koch examines intervillage feuding and its by-product—ritualistic cannibalism—as a means (among other things) to channel aggressive behavior into culturally acceptable patterns. Here, internalized means of social control seem quite prominent.

Just as all societies have mechanisms of social control, so too have all societies institutionalized the production, distribution, and consumption of material goods and services. That is, they have an *economic system.* The form a society's economy takes will have a profound impact on many other social institutions, a point well made in Marshall Sahlin's study. In "Subsistence Strategies and the Organization of Social Life," David E. K. Hunter reviews data from archaeology and ethnology to indicate ways in which economies influence other aspects of social life. In doing so, he begins with an examination of the simplest hunting and food-gathering societies and ends with a sketch of modern industrial society. As you will see, one of the critical factors is not so much the specific subsistence strategy employed by a society, but whether or not the economy is organized around the production and distribution of surpluses.

The popular view of early human societies is that they were barely able to eke out a meager existence from a harsh and inhospitable environment. In "Murders in Eden," Marvin Harris argues that in fact, early hunting-and-gathering societies enjoyed an enviable standard of living and a great deal of leisure time—so long as they kept their population relatively stable, which they did through the practice of infanticide.

Allen Johnson, in his article "In Search of the Affluent Society," focuses on consumption rather than on production. He argues that the narrow economist's view is inadequate for assessing economic systems—that a critical variable is the quality of life an economic system permits its participants. In comparing a "simple" Amazonian society to French society, Johnson emphasizes a point made by Harris in the previous article: that the simple society provides its members with more time for visiting, play, conversation, and rest than does French society. And he shares with us some personal questions this raises for him.

27

Subsistence Strategies and the Organization of Social Life

BY DAVID E. K. HUNTER

The sun beats down on the parched grasses, and its heat radiates from the rocky soil of the Kalahari Desert in southern Africa. Across the bleached landscape three men move slowly, in single file, keeping a line of thorny bushes between them and the herd of grazing giraffes. They have prayed and they have prepared their hunting arrows with poison freshly made from beetle paste. Now, with luck, one of them will wound a giraffe and they will follow it—for days, if necessary—until the poison works itself throughout the giant creature's bloodstream and slowly numbs and paralyzes it. Carefully avoiding its desperate last kicks, the men will use their clubs and spears to kill the animal. They will butcher it wherever it has fallen, cutting the meat into strips to dry in the sun. Then, finally, the men will return to their families camped in brush-and-hide windbreaks around a waterhole. The bones, the hide, and the meat will be passed from hand to hand, divided according to ancient customs, distributed along lines of family and kinship.

The people described here belong to the !Kung San (formerly known as the Bushmen); about 45,000 still live a semi-nomadic hunting and food-gathering existence in the Kalahari Desert. Their camps are small, numbering ten to thirty members, and they are communal and egalitarian. The sharing of food is fundamental to their way of life, and when, for whatever reasons, food sharing breaks down, the camp ceases to be a meaningful social unit: people pack their few belongings and move elsewhere, to camps of their relatives.

ECONOMY, SOCIETY, AND THE COMPARATIVE METHOD

In its most general sense, *economy* refers to the organized ways in which a society produces (or otherwise secures), distributes, and consumes its material goods (raw materials, products, and so on) and its services (that is, the patterns of behavior that supply individuals with their needs). Economic institutions are interlaced with the other social institutions of a society—indeed,

so much so, that separating them out for study is quite difficult. In order to do so here, and to indicate some of the ways in which economy and society are interwoven, this article focuses on strategies of subsistence and the ways in which such strategies affect and are affected by the organization of social groupings.

In order to keep this discussion reasonably brief and to the point, subsistence strategies will be considered under five main categories: hunting and food gathering, horticulture, pastoralism, agriculture, and industrialism. Inevitably, this classification has meant doing some violence to the actual facts—overlooking the ways in which the different strategies actually blend into or overlap with each other and stereotyping various social groups in terms of predominant features while downplaying (or even overlooking) other facets of their economic lives. This is the price one pays for using the comparative method; it is justified, however, if the main patterns it highlights nevertheless have something important to teach.

Anthropologists, in attempting to study and compare societies (both past and present) around the world, must take into account the tremendous impact of European imperialism and colonialism on the societies of Africa, Asia, and the Americas. Those societies that managed to survive into modern times often are distorted versions of their ancestral forms. Their populations were decimated by European diseases, their diversified subsistence systems were subordinated to the single cash-crop demands of European markets, their social life and political systems were torn apart by a tremendous increase in organized warfare (Sahlins 1972). However, while keeping these facts in mind, anthropologists have been able to note certain recurring patternings of social life that seem to be tightly tied to basic subsistence strategies.

Hunting and Food-Gathering Societies

The earliest human societies subsisted by foraging for vegetable foods and small game, fishing, collecting shellfish, and hunting larger animals. In modern times, the world's simplest and most marginal societies still subsist using these methods. They depend to a large degree on tools made of stone, wood, and bone.

Similarities among Hunting and Food-Gathering Societies. Although there are significant cultural differences among such groups, and in spite of the fact that they occupy environments varying from deserts to frozen wastelands, nevertheless there are certain recurring features of economic and social organizations that hunters and food-gatherers share—features that set them off from other kinds of societies. Contrary to both popular and scholarly preconceptions, hunting and food-gathering peoples do not work very hard. In fact, more time is spent socializing than in procuring food, which occupies perhaps some five hours per day (Sahlins 1972:1–39). Their communities are mobile and small. On the whole, social relationships among individuals tend to be quite egalitarian, at least in part because there is little private property. There is no social class differentiation, nor even institutionalized positions of prestige that are limited to favored subgroups.

In general, men are primarily responsible for hunting and for protecting the group. The women often hunt smaller game and forage for food (both animal and vegetable), typically providing some 60 to 70 percent of the total calories consumed by the group (Lee 1969). Women also take primary responsibility for raising the children. Marriage, in one or another form, in universally present, with monogamy the dominant form. Most social life is organized in terms of people's kinship relations. That is, the ways in which people are related to each other determines whether or not they may marry, what kinds of food or material goods they will exchange with each other, whether they observe the same taboos, and so on.

Differences among Hunting and Food-Gathering Societies. In spite of all these similarities, significant differences in societal organization do exist among contemporary hunting and food-gathering societies (Martin 1974). For one thing, political organization takes several forms, including male-centered kinship groups, female-centered kinship groups, and groups organized along kinship lines irrespective of gender. Those groups living in harsh climates and with a correspondingly low productivity are quite small, often numbering less than a few hundred individuals. But where nature is bountiful or affords special means of accumulating food surpluses (as on the Northwest Coast of North America, where annual salmon runs provided abundant food that could be stored for year-round consumption), hunting and food-gathering societies grew large, numbering into the thousands. Similarly, whereas most such groups are semi-nomadic because of their

need to search for food, those who inhabit rich environments have developed sedentary village settlements. And with surplus food production and a sedentary life-style, social inequality is institutionalized among hunting and food-gathering groups just as it is in more technologically advanced societies (Martin and Voorhies 1975).

Horticultural Societies

Some 12,000 to 15,000 years ago, coinciding with the retreat of the last glaciers, a drying trend occurred in what previously had been rich, subtropical climates. The giant deserts of Africa, Asia, and the Middle East took shape. Even beyond their constantly expanding borders, new arid conditions made the age-old hunting and food-gathering way of life precarious. Some groups continued to eke out an existence using the old subsistence techniques. Others crowded together in the more abundant regions, harvesting wild grains until population pressures drove them out into less favorable environments. There they attempted to recreate the rich environments they had left. And in doing so, they created a whole new way of subsisting: the domestication of plants and animals (Flannery 1965, 1968). This process seems to have repeated itself at least three times in three different places: in the Far East in Thailand some 11,000 years ago; in the Middle East, about 10,000 years ago; and in Mesoamerica, some 6,000 to 9,000 years ago. From these three centers of origin, the domestication of plants and animals spread outward, until it became the most widespread means of subsistence and the economic base upon which all civilizations were built.

Recent research, reported in 1980 and 1981, indicates that people living in widely scattered areas of the world may well have domesticated some plant and animal species as early as 19,000 years ago. Wheat and barley, for example, apparently were being grown along the Nile fully 8,000 years before these grains were domesticated in Mesopotamia. And Charles Nelson, an anthropologist at the University of Massachusetts at Boston, reports evidence of early domestication of cattle in Kenya, southern Europe, and southwestern Egypt. But these societies did not develop civilizations on their own. Nelson theorizes that for civilization to arise, several elements must combine in a fertile environment. First, plants and animals must be domesticated, and the technology for harvesting and storing crops must be developed. Then, a society must come into contact with other societies, diversifying its domesticated plant and animal species and opening itself both to trade and to the new ideas that inevitably come with commerce. When this happens, food becomes more abundant and overpopulation ensues. The result, Nelson argues, is the birth of civilization. Apparently, though plants and animals were domesticated in many places, the *combination* of elements leading to the birth of civilization occurred in only three places: the Far East, the Middle East, and Mesoamerica.

You should not imagine that the domestication of plants and animals brought an easier work load or more leisure time to its inventors. Whereas hunting and food-foraging peoples work perhaps three to four days (averaging five hours per day) out of every week to secure their food, food *producers* (domesticators) must work every day—and long hours at that! Marvin Harris (1975:233–255), after comparing research on the energy spent and calories produced by five societies, concludes that the advantage of food production over hunting and food gathering lies in the ability of food producers to sustain settlements, rather than in any labor-saving improvements in productivity or in increased leisure time.

Horticulture is a technical term referring to the planting of gardens and fields using only human muscle power and the mechanical advantage of handheld tools (such as digging sticks and hoes), whereas *agriculture* refers to the use of an animal-drawn plow. There are two distinct approaches to horticulture: subsistence farming (producing only enough to feed the group) and surplus farming. The differences between the two are quite profound.

Subsistence Farming.   Subsistence farmers live in environments that are unfavorable to cultivation. They are most often found in tropical or subtropical jungles where the forest constantly must be cleared away and always threatens to overgrow the fields. Every few years subsistence farmers must move their settlements when new fields have to be cleared. Their settlements are small, and competition among neighboring villages typically is high. In fact, ongoing feuding, raiding, and even prescheduled battles between the forces of nearby villages are not uncommon. Political organization rarely extends beyond the village, and usually it is based on positions that are inherited by males through the kinship system.

Where the environment is less difficult, competition and fighting among villages drop remarkably, and the political system frequently is organized around kinship-related women rather than men (Otterbein and Otterbein 1965). In this context, few differences in power and prestige exist between men and women. In fact, relationships between the sexes approach the egalitarian qualities generally found in hunting and food-gathering societies.

Although, in the richer environments, the production of surplus food is technologically possible, surplus production simply is not a culturally valued norm. Hence role specialization is relatively undeveloped—

not very much greater than among hunting and food-gathering groups. It seems, therefore, that with an abundant environment and little by way of tradable surpluses, social stratification and the institutionalization of prestige ranking are minimal.

Surplus Farming.   Surplus farmers live in densely populated, permanent settlements. They have highly elaborated political institutions that tend to be male-dominated and structured by kinship relations. There is occupational specialization with the institutionalization of prestige differences, and social stratification is well established. Because the production of surpluses is a culturally valued norm, such societies often are expansionistic, with differentiated military force. Expansion means more land and more (captured) labor, which in turn allows the centralized accumulation of greater surpluses that can be used to pay for political support, specialized craftspeople, and conspicuous consumption.

As in hunting and food-gathering societies, women in horticultural societies perform most of the productive work associated with securing food. Although the men will do the heaviest work, such as clearing the fields, it is usually the women who prepare the fields, plant the crops, tend and harvest them, and share the food with their husbands and extended families (D'Andrade 1966, Murdock 1937).

Pastoralist Societies

Pastoralism is an approach to food production that relies on herding and animal husbandry to satisfy the bulk of a group's needs. Animal herds provide milk, dung (for fuel), skin, sheared fur, and even blood (which is drunk as a major source of protein in East Africa).

Pastoralist societies have flourished in many regions that are not suitable for plant domestication, such as semi-arid desert regions and the northern tundra plains of Europe and Asia. They are also found in less severe climates, including East African savannas and mountain grasslands. However, pastoralism almost never occurs in forest or jungle regions. It is an interesting fact, which scholars have not been able to explain, that no true pastoralist societies ever emerged in the Americas prior to the arrival of the Europeans.

Although many pastoralist groups rely partly on horticulture to subsist, most are nomads (or semi-nomads) who follow their herds in a never-ending quest for pasture lands and water. Hence, such societies typically consist of relatively small, mobile communities. When needed resources are predictable, pastoralist societies typically are composed of stable groups united under strong political figures. When resources are not predictable, they are quick to split apart and compete with each other. Hence, centralized political leadership does not appear (Salzman 1967). To the extent that political organization does exist, pastoralist societies generally are organized around male-centered kinship groups.

Pastoralism rests on three strategic resources: animal herds, pasture lands, and water. Animals usually are more or less equally available to all families in pastoralist groups. But access to the latter two resources often varies widely among families in such societies. Hence, although there are great differences of wealth in some pastoralist groups, rarely is there institutionalized stratification. When social classes and centralized political organization do develop, they appear to be responses to expansionist pressures from neighboring state-level societies.

When, through bonds of kinship, pastoralist societies have organized into those enormous sociopolitical entities called hordes, their extreme mobility, fierceness, and kinship-based fanatic loyalty have made them into extraordinary military powers. As such, nomadic pastoralists have influenced the course of civilization far more than their numbers alone would suggest. It was to keep out Central Asian hordes that the emperors of the Chou dynasty in China built the Great Wall in the third and fourth centuries B.C. And it was nomadic pastoralist armies who, in the fourth and fifth centuries A.D., drove the final nails into the coffin of the Roman Empire in the West. In fact, many of the states of ancient Asia, the Middle East, and Eastern Europe arose partly in protective response to pastoralist raids. But in fairness it must be said that pastoralists influenced civilizations not only through their destructiveness. In what is now Hungary, for example, the nomads themselves first established some of the oldest politically centralized societies in Europe (Cohen 1974).

Agricultural Societies

Agriculture, as we noted before, is plant cultivation that makes use of the plow. Agriculture is more efficient than horticulture. Plowing makes use of the far greater muscle power of draft animals, and it also turns the topsoil much deeper than does hoeing, allowing for better airing and fertilizing of the ground and thus improving the yield. Nevertheless, early agriculture probably did not yield much more than food gatherers in bountiful environments were able to harvest. However, by around 5500 B.C., farmers in the Middle East not only were using the plow, but *irrigation* as well. With irrigation, farming became capable of producing vast surpluses—enough to feed large numbers of people who did not produce food themselves.

Reliance on irrigated agriculture had several drastic and interrelated consequences for society. It pulled ever-growing populations together into those areas where irrigation could be practiced—into broad river valleys like those of the Nile in Egypt, the Tigris and Euphrates in the Middle East, the Huangho (Yellow River) in China, and the Danube and Rhine in Europe. This rapidly rising and geographically compressed population density gave rise to cities and to new social forms. For the first time, society was *not* organized principally in terms of kinship. Rather, occupational diversity and institutional specialization (including differentiated political, economic, and religious institutions) predominated.

Dependence on irrigation had additional, even more far-reaching, consequences. Irrigation projects are large and complicated. They consist of dams, canals and elaborate systems of ditches whose use must be carefully coordinated. The planning and building of such projects takes experts with the time and authority to direct the efforts of hundreds and even thousands of specialized laborers and farmers. This can be accomplished only by a society with centralized political organization. And it is clear that at least in the case of Chinese civilization, the organizational demands of irrigation farming led to the emergence of the centralized state (Wittfogel 1957).

Irrigated agriculture also made land that was suitable for farming into a scarce resource. Those who controlled access to arable land and its use soon were rich and powerful. They could command the payment of taxes and political support. By taxing the bulk of agricultural surpluses, political leaders could employ bureaucracies to implement their plans and armies to protect their privileges—both from external enemies and internal rebels. Thus social classes became entrenched, and the State evolved. Not surprisingly, the State is the most warlike of all sociopolitical forms (Otterbein 1970). For agricultural (and industrial) societies, conquest makes economic sense because it brings new farmlands and food producers under the State's control, increasing the surpluses at its disposal and thereby making possible ever more ambitious undertakings.

Industrial Society

The industrial revolution was a European and American phenomenon. Industrialism consists of the use of mechanical means (machines and chemical processes) for the production of goods. Contrary to its name the industrial "revolution" at first developed slowly. It had begun primarily in England early in the eighteenth century and gained momentum by the turn of the nineteenth century (Eli Whitney built a factory for the mass production of guns near New Haven, Connecticut in 1798). By the mid-1800s, it had swung into high gear with the invention of the steam locomotive and Henry Bessemer's development of large-scale production techniques at his steel works in England in 1858. It is called a "revolution" because of the enormous changes industrialism brought about in society.

Industrial society is characterized by more than just the use of mechanical means for production. It is an entirely new form of society that requires an immense, mobile, diversely specialized, highly skilled, and well-coordinated labor force. Among other things, this means that the labor force must be educated. Imagine the difficulties facing even the least skilled factory worker who cannot read. Hence an educational system open to all is a hallmark of industrial society—something that was not necessary in pre-industrial times. Industrialism also requires the creation of highly organized systems of exchange between the suppliers of raw materials and industrial manufacturers on the one hand, and between the manufacturers and consumers on the other.

Like agricultural societies, industrial societies inevitably are stratified. The nature of the stratification varies, depending on whether the society allows private ownership of capital (capitalism) or puts all capital in the hands of the State (socialism). However, all industrial societies may be said to have at least two social classes: (1) a large labor force that produces goods and services but has no say in what is done with them; and (2) a much smaller class that determines what shall be produced and how it shall be distributed.

Industrialism brought about a tremendous shift of populations. Over the past century and a half, vast numbers of rural peasants and farmers have migrated from the countryside to the cities, transforming themselves into what is called an urban proletariate. Kinship, which still played an important role in the organization of preindustrial agricultural society, now plays a much smaller role in patterning public affairs. (Some newly emergent industrial societies, such as those Arab states like Saudi Arabia that grew into existence from a nomadic pastoralist base, still are organized sociopolitically in terms of kinship relations.) Similarly, religious institutions, which in preindustrial society were very closely tied to political institutions, no longer dominate the scene—industrial society is highly secularized. (An exception to this generalization is the existence of so-called civil religions, such as Marxist-Leninism in socialist countries; another is the recent creation of a new Islamic state in Iran by followers of the Ayatollah Khomeini.) In general, the predominant form of social and political organization in industrial society is the bureaucracy—that least personal of all formal organizations, itself having been inspired by the model of the efficiently functioning machine the symbol of industrial production and of industrial society as a way of life.

SOCIETY AND ECONOMY

This article attempts to indicate some of the ways in which the economy and other social institutions are interwoven to make up the fabric of society. To accomplish this, it has focused on one aspect of economy—namely, the major strategies of subsistence that societies around the world employ. This is not meant to suggest that all social institutions are created only in response to—or caused by—subsistence strategies (or other aspects of the economy). That kind of a simplistic, one-way causal view, called economic determinism, enjoyed a vogue around the turn of this century before it was thoroughly refuted by careful research. Even those anthropologists who study cultural ecology—that is, the ways in which peoples' cultures adapt them to their environments—do not propose that environments or even subsistence strategies directly cause specific sociocultural forms to emerge. Rather, anthropologists recognize that human groups exist in dynamic relationships with the environment, that they both respond to and act upon the environment, and that the ways in which they interact with the environment have consequences for their social lives individually and as social groups.

Within this set of interdependent relationships, each society picks its way making use of culturally inherited patterns and also newly acquired, invented, or discovered techniques of production and distribution. Hence, in every generation, each society recreates and also modifies (to whatever degree) its design for living, its particular solutions to the problems of existence. Using the comparative method, anthropologists are able to point to some of the patterned commonalities and differences among societies. Here, I have highlighted these by organizing them in terms of the five major approaches to, or strategies for, subsistence.

References

Cohen, Yehudi A.
1974 "Pastoralism," in Yehudi A. Cohen (ed.), *Man in Adaptation: The Cultural Present* (2nd ed.), Chicago: Aldine.

D'Andrade, Roy
1966 "Sex differences and cultural institutions," in Eleanor Maccoby (ed.), *The Development of Sex Differences*, Stanford: Stanford University Press.

Flannery, Kent V.
1965 "The ecology of early food production in Mesoamerica," *Science*, vol. 147:1247–1256.
1968 "Archaeological systems theory and early Mesopotamia," in Betty J. Meggars (ed.), *Anthropological Archaeology in the Americas*, Washington, D.C.: The Anthropological Society of Washington.

Harris, Marvin
1975 *Culture, People, Nature*, New York: Thomas Y. Crowell.

Martin, M. Kay, and Barbara Voorhies
1975 *The Female of the Species*, New York: Columbia University Press.

Murdock, George Peter
1937 "Comparative data on the division of labor by sex," *Social Forces*, vol. 16:551–553.

Otterbein, Keith
1970 *The Evolution of War*, New Haven, Conn.: Human Relations Area Files.

Otterbein, Keith, and Charlotte Swanson Otterbein
1965 "An eye for an eye, a tooth for a tooth: a cross-cultural study of feuding, "*American Anthropologist*, vol. 67:1470–1482.

Sahlins, Marshall
1972 *Stone Age Economics*, Chicago: Aldine

Salzman, Philip C.
1967 "Political organization among nomadic peoples," *Proceedings of the American Philosophical Society*, vol. 3:115–131.

Wittfogel, Karl
1957 *Oriental Despotism,* New Haven, Conn.: Yale University Press.

Poor Man, Rich Man, Big-Man, Chief

BY MARSHALL D. SAHLINS

With an eye to their own life goals, the native peoples of Pacific Islands unwittingly present to anthropologists a generous scientific gift: an extended series of experiments in cultural adaptation and evolutionary development. They have compressed their institutions within the confines of infertile coral atolls, expanded them on volcanic islands, created with the means history gave them cultures adapted to the deserts of Australia, the mountains and warm coasts of New Guinea, the rain forests of the Solomon Islands. From the Australian Aborigines, whose hunting and gathering existence duplicates in outline the cultural life of the later Paleolithic, to the great chiefdoms of Hawaii, where society approached the formative levels of the old Fertile Crescent civilizations, almost every general phase in the progress of primitive culture is exemplified.

Where culture so experiments, anthropology finds its laboratories — makes its comparisons.

In the southern and eastern Pacific two contrasting cultural provinces have long evoked anthropological interest: *Melanesia*, including New Guinea, the Bismarcks, Solomons, and island groups east to Fiji; and *Polynesia*, consisting in its main portion of the triangular constellation of lands between New Zealand, Easter Island, and the Hawaiian Islands. In and around Fiji, Melanesia and Polynesia intergrade culturally, but west and east of their intersection the two provinces pose broad contrasts in several sectors: in religion, art, kinship groupings, economics, political organization. The differences are the more notable for the underlying similarities from which they emerge. Melanesia and Polynesia are both agricultural regions in which many of the same crops—such as yams, taro, breadfruit, bananas, and coconuts—have long been cultivated by many similar techniques. Some recently presented linguistic and archaeological studies suggest that Polynesian cultures originated from an eastern Melanesian hearth during the first millennium B.C. Yet in anthropological annals the Polynesians were to become famous for elaborate forms of rank and chieftainship, whereas most Melanesian societies broke off advance on this front at more rudimentary levels.

It is obviously imprecise, however, to make out the political contrast in broad culture-area terms. Within Polynesia, certain of the islands, such as Hawaii, the Society Islands and Tonga, developed unparalleled political momentum. And not all Melanesian polities, on the other side, were constrained and truncated in their evolution. In New Guinea and nearby areas of western Melanesia small and loosely ordered political groupings are numerous, but in eastern Melanesia, New Caledonia and Fiji for example, political approximations of the Polynesian condition become common. There is more of an upward west to east slope in political development in the southern Pacific than a step-like, quantum progression. It is quite revealing, however, to compare the extremes of this continuum, the western Melanesian underdevelopment against the greater Polynesian chiefdoms. While such comparison does not exhaust the evolutionary variations, it fairly establishes the scope of overall political achievement in this Pacific phylum of cultures.

Measurable along several dimensions, the contrast between developed Polynesian and underdeveloped Melanesian polities is immediately striking for differences in scale. H. Ian Hogbin and Camilla Wedgwood concluded from a survey of Melanesian (most western Melanesian) societies that ordered, independent political bodies in the region typically include seventy to three hundred persons; more recent work in the New Guinea Highlands suggests political groupings of up to a thousand, occasionally a few thousand, people.[1] But in Polynesia sovereignties of two thousand or three thousand are run-of-the-mill, and the most advanced chiefdoms, as in Tonga or Hawaii, might claim ten thousand, even tens of thousands. Varying step by step with such differences in size of the polity are differences in territorial extent: from a few square miles in western

1. H. Ian Hogbin and Camilla H. Wedgwood, "Local Groupings in Melanesia," *Oceania* 23 (1952–53) : 241–276; 24 (1953–54) : 58–76.

Reprinted from "Poor Man, Rich Man, Big-Man, Chief: Political Types in Melanesia and Polynesia," *Comparative Studies in Society and History*, Vol. 5, No. 3, pp. 285–303, by Marshall D. Sahlins, by permission of Cambridge University Press.

Melanesia to tens or even hundreds of square miles in Polynesia.

The Polynesian advance in political scale was supported by advance over Melanesia in political structure. Melanesia presents a great array of social-political forms: here political organization is based upon patrilineal descent groups, there on cognatic groups, or men's club-houses recruiting neighborhood memberships, on a secret ceremonial society, or perhaps on some combination of these structural principles. Yet a general plan can be discerned. The characteristic western Melanesian "tribe," that is, the ethnic-cultural entity, consists of many autonomous kinship-residential groups. Amounting on the ground to a small village or a local cluster of hamlets, each of these is a copy of the others in organization, each tends to be economically self-governing, and each is the equal of the others in political status. The tribal plan is one of politically unintegrated segments—segmental. But the political geometry in Polynesia is pyramidal. Local groups of the order of self-governing Melanesian communities appear in Polynesia as subdivisions of a more inclusive political body. Smaller units are integrated into larger through a system of intergroup ranking, and the network of representative chiefs of the subdivisions amounts to a coordinating political structure. So instead of the Melanesian scheme of small, separate, and equal political blocs, the Polynesian polity is an extensive pyramid of groups capped by the family and following of a paramount chief. (This Polynesian political upshot is often, although not always, facilitated by the development of ranked lineages. Called *conical clan* by Kirchhoff, at one time *ramage* by Firth and *status lineage* by Goldman, the Polynesian ranked lineage is the same in principle as the so-called *obok* system widely distributed in Central Asia, and it is at least analogous to the Scottish clan, the Chinese clan, certain Central African Bantu lineage systems, the house-groups of Northwest Coast Indians, perhaps even the "tribes" of the Israelites. Genealogical ranking is its distinctive feature: members of the same descent unit are ranked by genealogical distance from the common ancestor; lines of the same group become senior and cadet branches on this principle; related corporate lineages are relatively ranked, again by genealogical priority.)

Here is another criterion of Polynesian political advance: historical performance. Almost all of the native peoples of the South Pacific were brought up against intense European cultural pressure in the late eighteenth and the nineteenth centuries. Yet only the Hawaiians, Tahitians, Tongans, and to a lesser extent the Fijians, successfully defended themselves by evolving countervailing, native-controlled states. Complete with public governments and public law, monarchs and taxes, ministers and minions, these nineteenth-century states are testimony to the native Polynesian political genius, to the level and the potential of indigenous political accomplishments.

Embedded within the grand differences in political scale, structure and performance is a more personal contrast, one in quality of leadership. An historically particular type of leader-figure, the "big-man" as he is often locally styled, appears in the underdeveloped settings of Melanesia. Another type, a chief properly so-called, is associated with the Polynesian advance. Now these are distinct sociological types, that is to say, differences in the powers, privileges, rights, duties, and obligations of Melanesian big-men and Polynesian chiefs are given by the divergent societal contexts in which they operate. Yet the institutional distinctions cannot help but be manifest also in differences in bearing and character, appearance and manner—in a word, personality. It may be a good way to begin the more rigorous sociological comparison of leadership with a more impressionistic sketch of the contrast in the human dimension. Here I find it useful to apply characterizations—or is it caricature?—from our own history to big-men and chiefs, however much injustice this does to the historically incomparable backgrounds of the Melanesians and Polynesians. The Melanesian big-man seems to thoroughly bourgeois, so reminiscent of the free-enterprising rugged individual of our own heritage. He combines with an ostensible interest in the general welfare a more profound measure of self-interested cunning and economic calculation. His gaze, as Veblen might have put it, is fixed unswervingly to the main chance. His every public action is designed to make a competitive and invidious comparison with others, to show a standing above the masses that is product of his own personal manufacture. The historical caricature of the Polynesian chief, however, is feudal rather than capitalist. His appearance, his bearing is almost regal; very likely he just *is* a big man—"'Can't you see he is a chief? See how big he is?'"[2] In his every public action is a display of the refinements of breeding, in his manner always that *noblesse oblige* of true pedigree and an incontestable right of rule. With his standing not so much a personal achievement as a just social due, he can afford to be, and he is, every inch a chief.

In the several Melanesian tribes in which big-men have come under anthropological scrutiny, local cultural differences modify the expression of their personal powers. But the indicative quality of big-man authority is everywhere the same: it is *personal* power. Big-men do not come to office; they do not succeed to, nor are they installed in, existing positions of leadership over political groups. The attainment of big-man status is rather the outcome of a series of acts which elevate a person

2. Edward Winslow Gifford, *Tongan Society* (Honolulu: Bernice P. Bishop Museum Bulletin 61, 1926).

above the common herd and attract about him a coterie of loyal, lesser men. It is not accurate to speak of "big-man" as a political title, for it is but an acknowledged standing in interpersonal relations—a "prince among men" so to speak as opposed to "The Prince of Danes." In particular Melanesian tribes the phrase might be "man of importance" or "man of renown," "generous rich-man," or "center-man," as well as "big-man."

A kind of two-sidedness in authority is implied in this series of phrases, a division of the big-man's field of influence into two distinct sectors. "Center-man" particularly connotes a cluster of followers gathered about an influential pivot. It socially implies the division of the tribe into political in-groups dominated by outstanding personalities. To the in-group, the big-man presents this sort of picture:

> The place of the leader in the district group [in northern Malaita] is well summed up by his title, which might be translated as "center-man." . . . He was like a banyan, the natives explain, which, though the biggest and tallest in the forest, is still a tree like the rest. But, just because it exceeds all others, the banyan gives support to more lianas and creepers, provides more food for the birds, and gives better protection against sun and rain.[3]

But "man of renown" connotes a broader tribal field in which a man is not so much a leader as he is some sort of hero. This is the side of the big-man facing outward from his own faction, his status among some or all of the other political clusters of the tribe. The political sphere of the big-man divides itself into a small internal sector composed of his personal satellites—rarely over eighty men—and a much larger external sector, the tribal galaxy consisting of many similar constellations.

As it crosses over from the internal into the external sector, a big-man's power undergoes qualitative change. Within his faction a Melanesian leader has true command ability, outside of it only fame and indirect influence. It is not that the center-man rules his faction by physical force, but his followers do feel obliged to obey him, and he can usually get what he wants by haranguing them—public verbal suasion is indeed so often employed by center-men that they have been styled "harangue-utans." The orbits of outsiders, however, are set by their own center-men. "'Do it yourself. I'm not *your* fool,'" would be the characteristic response to an order issued by a center-man to an outsider among the Siuai.[4] This fragmentation of true authority presents special political difficulties, particularly in organizing large masses of people for the prosecution of such collective ends as warfare or ceremony. Big-men do instigate mass action, but only by establishing both extensive re-

nown and special personal relations of complusion or reciprocity with other center-men.

Politics is in the main personal politicking in these Melanesian societies, and the size of a leader's faction as well as the extent of his renown are normally set by competition with other ambitious men. Little or no authority is given by social ascription: leadership is a creation—a creation of followership. "Followers," as it is written of the Kapauku of New Guinea, "stand in various relations to the leader. Their obedience to the headman's decisions is caused by motivations which reflect their particular relations to the leader."[5]

So a man must be prepared to demonstrate that he possesses the kinds of skills that command respect—magical powers, gardening prowess, mastery of oratorical style, perhaps bravery in war and feud. Typically decisive is the deployment of one's skills and efforts in a certain direction: towards amassing goods, most often pigs, shell monies and vegetable foods, and distributing them in ways which build a name for cavalier generosity, if not for compassion. A faction is developed by informal private assistance to people of a locale. Tribal rank and renown are developed by great public giveaways sponsored by the rising big-man, often on behalf of his faction as well as himself. In different Melanesian tribes, the renown-making public distribution may appear as one side of a delayed exchange of pigs between corporate kinship groups; a marital consideration given a bride's kinfolk; a set of feasts connected with the erection of the big-man's dwelling, or of a clubhouse for himself and his faction, or with the purchase of higher grades of rank in secret societies; the sponsorship of a religious ceremony; a payment of subsidies and blood compensations to military allies; or perhaps the giveaway in a ceremonial challenge bestowed on another leader in the attempt to outgive and thus outrank him (a potlatch).

The making of the faction, however, is the true making of the Melanesian big-man. It is essential to establish relations of loyalty and obligation on the part of a number of people such that their production can be mobilized for renown-building external distribution. The bigger the faction the greater the renown; once momentum in external distribution has been generated the opposite can also be true. Any ambitious man who can gather a following can launch a societal career. The rising big-man necessarily depends initially on a small core of followers, principally his own household and his closest relatives. Upon these people he can prevail economically: he capitalizes in the first instance on kinship dues and by finessing the relation of reciprocity appropriate among close kinsmen. Often it becomes necessary at an early phase to enlarge one's household.

3. H. Ian Hogbin, "Native Councils and Courts in the Solomon Islands," *Oceania* 14 (1943–44) : 258–283.

4. Douglas Oliver, *Solomon Islands Society* (Cambridge: Harvard University Press, 1955).

5. Leopold Pospisil, *Kapauku Papuans and Their Law* (New Haven: Yale University Press, Yale University Publications in Anthropology, no. 54, 1958).

The rising leader goes out of his way to incorporate within his family "strays" of various sorts, people without familial support themselves, such as widows and orphans. Additional wives are especially useful. The more wives a man has the more pigs he has. The relation here is functional, not identical: with more women gardening there will be more food for pigs and more swineherds. A Kiwai Papuan picturesquely put to an anthropologist in pidgin the advantages, economic and political, of polygamy:"'Another woman go garden, another woman go take firewood, another woman go catch fish, another woman cook him—husband he sing out plenty people come kaikai [i.e., come to eat].' "[6] Each new marriage, incidentally, creates for the big-man an additional set of in-laws from whom he can exact economic favors. Finally, a leader's career sustains its upward climb when he is able to link other men and their families to his faction, harnessing their production to his ambition. This is done by calculated generosities, by placing others in gratitude and obligation through helping them in some big way. A common technique is payment of bridewealth on behalf of young men seeking wives.

The great Malinowski used a phrase in analyzing primitive political economy that felicitously describes just what the big-man is doing: amassing a "fund of power." A big-man is one who can create and use social relations which give him leverage on others' production and the ability to siphon off an excess product—or sometimes he can cut down their consumption in the interest of the siphon. Now although his attention may be given primarily to short-term personal interests, from an objective standpoint the leader acts to promote long-term societal interests. The fund of power provisions activities that involve other groups of society at large. In the greater perspective of that society at large, big-men are indispensable means of creating supralocal organization: in tribes normally fragmented into small independent groups, big-men at least temporarily widen the sphere of ceremony, recreation and art, economic collaboration, of war too. Yet always this greater societal organization depends on the lesser factional organization, particularly on the ceilings on economic mobilization set by relations between center-men and followers. The limits and the weaknesses of the political order in general are the limits and weaknesses of the factional in-groups.

And the personal quality of subordination to a center-man is a serious weakness in factional structure. A personal loyalty has to be made and continually reinforced; if there is discontent it may well be severed. Merely to create a faction takes time and effort, and to hold it, still more effort. The potential rupture of per-

sonal links in the factional chain is at the heart of two broad evolutionary shortcomings of western Melanesian political orders. First, a comparative instability. Shifting dispositions and magnetisms of ambitious men in a region may induce fluctuations in factions, perhaps some overlapping of them, and fluctuations also in the extent of different renowns. The death of a center-man can become a regional political trauma: the death undermines the personally cemented faction, the group dissolves in whole or in part, and the people re-group finally around rising pivotal big-men. Although particular tribal structures in places cushion the disorganization, the big-man political system is generally unstable over short terms: in its superstructure it is a flux of rising and falling leaders, in its substructure of enlarging and contracting factions. Secondly, the personal political bond contributes to the containment of evolutionary advance. The possibility of their desertion, it is clear, often inhibits a leader's ability to forceably push up his followers' output, thereby placing constraints on higher political organization, but there is more to it than that. If it is to generate great momentum, a big-man's quest for the summits of renown is likely to bring out a contradiction in his relations to followers, so that he finds himself encouraging defection—or worse, an egalitarian rebellion—by encouraging production.

One side of the Melanesian contradiction is the initial economic reciprocity between a center-man and his followers. For his help they give their help, and for goods going out through his hands other goods (often from outside factions) flow back to his followers by the same path. The other side is that a cumulative build-up of renown forces center-men into economic extortion of the faction. Here it is important that not merely his own status, but the standing and perhaps the military security of his people depend on the big-man's achievements in public distribution. Established at the head of a sizeable faction, a center-man comes under increasing pressure to extract goods from his followers, to delay reciprocities owing them, and to deflect incoming goods back into external circulation. Success in competition with other big-men particularly undermines internal-factional reciprocities: such success is precisely measurable by the ability to give outsiders more than they can possibly reciprocate. In well delineated big-man polities, we find leaders negating the reciprocal obligations upon which their following had been predicated. Substituting extraction for reciprocity, they must compel their people to "eat the leader's renown," as one Solomon Island group puts it, in return for productive efforts. Some center-men appear more able than others to dam the inevitable tide of discontent that mounts within their factions, perhaps because of charismatic personalities, perhaps because of the particular social organizations in which they operate. But

6. Gunnar Landtman, *The Kiwai of British New Guinea* (London: Macmillan, 1927).

paradoxically the ultimate defense of the center-man's position is some slackening of his drive to enlarge the funds of power. The alternative is much worse. In the anthropological record there are not merely instances of big-man chicanery and of material deprivation of the faction in the interests of renown, but some also of overloading of social relations with followers: the generation of antagonisms, defections, and in extreme cases the violent liquidation of the center-man. Developing internal contraints, the Melanesian big-man political order brakes evolutionary advance at a certain level. It sets ceilings on the intensification of political authority, on the intensification of household production by political means, and on the diversion of household outputs in support of wider political organization. But in Polynesia these constraints were breached, and although Polynesian chiefdoms also found their developmental plateau, it was not before political evolution had been carried above the Melanesian ceilings. The fundamental defects of the Melanesian plan were overcome in Polynesia. The division between small internal and larger external political sectors, upon which all big-man politics hinged, was suppressed in Polynesia by the growth of an enclaving chiefdom-at-large. A chain of command subordinating lesser chiefs and groups to greater, on the basis of inherent societal rank, made local blocs or personal followings (such as were independent in Melanesia) merely dependent parts of the larger Polynesian chiefdom. So the nexus of the Polynesian chiefdom became an extensive set of offices, a pyramid of higher and lower chiefs holding sway over larger and smaller sections of the polity. Indeed the system of ranked and subdivided lineages (conical clan system), upon which the pyramid was characteristically established, might build up through several orders of inclusion and encompass the whole of an island or group of islands. While the island or the archipelago would normally be divided into several independent chiefdoms, high-order lineage connections between them, as well as kinship ties between their paramount chiefs, provided structural avenues for at least temporary expansion of political scale, for consolidation of great into even greater chiefdoms.

The pivotal paramount chief as well as the chieftains controlling parts of a chiefdom were true office holders and title holders. They were not, like Melanesian bigmen, fishers of men: they held positions of authority over permanent groups. The honorifics of Polynesian chiefs likewise did not refer to a standing in interpersonal relations, but to their leadership of political divisions—here "The Prince of Danes" *not* "the prince among men." In western Melanesia the personal superiorities and inferiorities arising in the intercourse of particular men largely defined the political bodies. In Polynesia there emerged suprapersonal structures of leadership and followership, organizations that continued independently of the particular men who occupied positions in them for brief mortal spans.

And these Polynesian chiefs did not make their positions in society—they were installed in societal positions. In several of the islands, men did struggle to office against the will and strategems of rival aspirants. But then they came *to* power. Power resided in the office; it was not made by the demonstration of personal superiority. In other islands, Tahiti was famous for it, succession to chieftainship was tightly controlled by inherent rank. The chiefly lineage ruled by virtue of its genealogical connections with divinity, the chiefs were succeeded by first sons, who carried "in the blood" the attributes of leadership. The important comparative point is this: the qualities of command that had to reside in men in Melanesia, that had to be personally demonstrated in order to attract loyal followers, were in Polynesia socially assigned to office and rank. In Polynesia, people of high rank and office *ipso facto* were leaders, and by the same token the qualities of leadership were automatically lacking—theirs was not to question why—among the underlying population. Magical powers such as a Melanesian big-man might acquire to sustain his position, a Polynesian high chief inherited by divine descent as the *mana* which sanctioned his rule and protected his person against the hands of the commonalty. The productive ability the big-man laboriously had to demonstrate was effortlessly given Polynesian chiefs as religious control over agricultural fertility, and upon the ceremonial implementation of it the rest of the people were conceived dependent. Where a Melanesian leader had to master the compelling oratorical style, Polynesian paramounts often had trained "talking chiefs" whose voice was the chiefly command.

In the Polynesian view, a chiefly personage was in the nature of things powerful. But this merely implies the objective observation that his power was of the group rather than of himself. His authority came from the organization, from an organized acquiescence in his privileges and organized means of sustaining them. A kind of paradox resides in evolutionary developments which detach the exercise of authority from the necessity to demonstrate personal superiority: organizational power actually extends the role of personal decision and conscious planning, gives it greater scope, impact, and effectiveness. The growth of a political system such as the Polynesian constitutes advance over Melanesian orders of interpersonal dominance in the human control of human affairs. Especially significant for society at large were privileges accorded Polynesian chiefs which made them greater architects of funds of power than ever was any Melanesian big-man.

Masters of their people and "owners" in a titular

sense of group resources, Polynesian chiefs had rights of call upon the labor and agricultural produce of households within their domains. Economic mobilization did not depend on, as it necessarily had for Melanesian big-men, the *de novo* creation by the leader of personal loyalties and economic obligations. A chief need not stoop to obligate this man or that man, need not by a series of individual acts of generosity induce others to support him, for economic leverage over a group was the inherent chiefly due. Consider the implications for the fund of power of the widespread chiefly privilege, related to titular "ownership" of land, of placing an interdiction, a tabu, on the harvest of some crop by way of reserving its use for a collective project. By means of the tabu the chief directs the course of production in a general way: households of his domain must turn to some other means of subsistence. He delivers a stimulus to household production: in the absence of the tabu further labors would not have been necessary. Most significantly, he has generated a politically utilizable agricultural surplus. A subsequent call on this surplus floats chieftainship as a going concern, capitalizes the fund of power. In certain islands, Polynesian chiefs controlled great storehouses which held the goods congealed by chiefly pressures on the commonalty. David Malo, one of the great native custodians of old Hawaiian lore, felicitously catches the political significance of the chiefly magazine in his well-known *Hawaiian Antiquities*:

> It was the practice for kings [i.e., paramount chiefs of individual islands to build store-houses in which to collect food, fish, tapas [bark cloth], malos [men's loin cloths] pa-us [women's loin shirts], and all sorts of goods. These store-houses were designed by the Kalaimoku [the chief's principal executive] as a means of keeping the people contented, so they would not desert the king. They were like the baskets that were used to entrap the *hinalea* fish. The *hinalea* thought there was something good within the basket, and he hung round the outside of it. In the same way the people thought there was food in the storehouses, and they kept their eyes on the king. As the rat will not desert the pantry . . . where he thinks food is, so the people will not desert the king while they think there is food in his store-house.[7]

Redistribution of the fund of power was the supreme art of Polynesian politics. By well-planned *noblesse oblige* the large domain of a paramount chief was held together, organized at times for massive projects, protected against other chiefdoms, even further enriched. Uses of the chiefly fund included lavish hospitality and entertainments for outside chiefs and for the chief's own people, and succor of individuals or the underlying population at large in times of scarcities—bread and circuses. Chiefs subsidized craft production, promoting

in Polynesia a division of technical labor unparalleled in extent and expertise in most of the Pacific. They supported also great technical construction, as of irrigation complexes, the further returns to which swelled the chiefly fund, They initiated large-scale religious construction too, subsidized the great ceremonies, and organized logistic support for extensive military campaigns. Larger and more easily replenished than their western Melanesian counterparts, Polynesian funds of power permitted greater political regulation of a greater range of social activities on greater scale.

In the most advanced Polynesian chiefdoms, as in Hawaii and Tahiti, a significant part of the chiefly fund was deflected away from general redistribution towards the upkeep of the institution of chieftainship. The fund was siphoned for the support of a permanent administrative establishment. In some measure, goods and services contributed by the people precipitated out as the grand houses, assembly places and temple platforms of chiefly precincts. In another measure, they were appropriated for the livelihood of circles of retainers, many of them close kinsmen of the chief, who clustered about the powerful paramounts, These were not all useless hangers-on. They were political cadres: supervisors of the stores, talking chiefs, ceremonial attendants, high priests who were intimately involved in political rule, envoys to transmit directives through the chiefdom. There were men in these chiefly retinues—in Tahiti and perhaps Hawaii, specialized warrior corps—whose force could be directed internally as a buttress against fragmenting or rebelling elements of the chiefdom. A Tahitian or Hawaiian high chief had more compelling sanctions than the harangue. He controlled a ready physical force, an armed body of executioners, which gave him mastery particularly over the lesser people of the community. While it looks a lot like the big-man's faction again, the differences in functioning of the great Polynesian chief's retinue are more significant than the superficial similarities in appearance. The chief's coterie, for one thing, is economically dependent upon him rather than he upon them. And in deploying the cadres politically in various sections of the chiefdom, or against the lower orders, the great Polynesian chiefs sustained command where the Melanesian big-man, in his external sector, had at best renown.

This is not to say that the advanced Polynesian chiefdoms were free of internal defect, of potential or actual malfunctioning. The large political-military apparatus indicates something of the opposite. So does the recent work of Irving Goldman[8] on the intensity of "status rivalry" in Polynesia, especially when it is considered that much of the status rivalry in developed chiefdoms,

---

7. David Malo, *Hawaiian Antiquities* (Honolulu: Hawaiian Gazette Co., 1903).

8. Irving Goldman, "Status Rivalry and Cultural Evolution in Polynesia," *American Anthropologist* 57 (1957) : 680–697; "Variations in Polynesian Social Organization," *Journal of the Polynesian Society* 66 (1957) : 374–390.

as the Hawaiian, amounted to popular rebellion against chiefly despotism rather than mere contest for position within the ruling-stratum. This suggests that Polynesian chiefdoms, just as Melanesian big-man orders, generate along with evolutionary development countervailing anti-authority pressures, and that the weight of the latter may ultimately impede further development.

The Polynesian contradiction seems clear enough. On one side, chieftainship is never detached from kinship moorings and kinship economic ethics. Even the greatest Polynesian chiefs were conceived superior kinsmen to the masses, fathers of their people, and generosity was morally incumbent upon them. On the other side, the major Polynesian paramounts seemed inclined to "eat the power of the government too much," as the Tahitians put it, to divert an undue proportion of the general wealth toward the chiefly establishment. The diversion could be accomplished by lowering the customary level of general redistribution, lessening the material returns of chieftainship to the community at large—tradition attributes the great rebellion of Mangarevan commoners to such cause. Or the diversion might—and I suspect more commonly did—consist in greater and more forceful exactions from lesser chiefs and people, increasing returns to the chiefly apparatus without necessarily affecting the level of general redistribution. In either case, the well-developed chiefdom creates for itself the dampening paradox of stoking rebellion by funding its authority.

In Hawaii and other islands cycles of political centralization and decentralization may be abstracted from traditional histories. That is, larger chiefdoms periodically fragmented into smaller and then were later reconstituted. Here would be more evidence of a tendency to overtax the political structure. But how to explain the emergence of a developmental stymie, of an inability to sustain political advance beyond a certain level? To point to a chiefly propensity to consume or a Polynesian propensity to rebel is not enough: such propensities are promoted by the very advance of chiefdoms. There is reason to hazard instead that Parkinson's notable law is behind it all: that progressive expansion in political scale entailed more-than-proportionate accretion in the ruling apparatus, unbalancing the flow of wealth in favor of the apparatus. The ensuing unrest then curbs the chiefly impositions, sometimes by reducing chiefdom scale to the nadir of the periodic cycle. Comparison of the requirements of administration in small and large Polynesian chiefdoms helps make the point.

A lesser chiefdom, confined say as in the Marquesas Islands to a narrow valley, could be almost personally ruled by a headman in frequent contact with the relatively small population. Melville's partly romanticized—also for its ethnographic details, partly cribbed—account in *Typee* makes this clear enough. But the great Polynesian chiefs had to rule much larger, spatially dispersed, internally organized populations. Hawaii, an island over four thousand square miles with an aboriginal population approaching one hundred thousand, was at times a single chiefdom, at other times divided into two to six independent chiefdoms, and at all times each chiefdom was composed of large subdivisions under powerful subchiefs. Sometimes a chiefdom in the Hawaiian group extended beyond the confines of one of the islands, incorporating part of another through conquest. Now, such extensive chiefdoms would have to be coordinated; they would have to be centrally tapped for a fund of power, buttressed against internal disruption, sometimes massed for distant, perhaps overseas, military engagements. All of this to be implemented by means of communication still at the level of word-of-mouth, and means of transportation consisting of human bodies and canoes. (The extent of certain larger chieftainships, coupled with the limitations of communication and transportation, incidentally suggests another possible source of political unrest: that the burden of provisioning the governing apparatus would tend to fall disproportionately on groups within easiest access of the paramount.) A tendency for the developed chiefdom to proliferate in executive cadres, to grow top-heavy, seems in these circumstances altogether functional, even though the ensuing drain on wealth proves the chiefdom's undoing. Functional also, and likewise a material drain on the chiefdom at large, would be widening distinctions between chiefs and people in style of life. Palatial housing, ornamentation and luxury, finery and ceremony, in brief, conspicuous consumption, however much it seems mere self-interest always has a more decisive social significance. It creates those invidious distinctions between rulers and ruled so conducive to a passive—hence quite economical!—acceptance of authority. Throughout history, inherently more powerful political organizations than the Polynesian, with more assured logistics of rule, have turned to it—including in our time some ostensibly revolutionary and proletarian governments, despite every pre-revolutionary protestation of solidarity with the masses and equality for the classes.

In Polynesia then, as in Melanesia, political evolution is eventually shortcircuited by an overload on the relations between leaders and their people. The Polynesian tragedy, however, was somewhat the opposite of the Melanesian. In Polynesia, the evolutionary ceiling was set by extraction from the population at large in favor of the chiefly faction, in Melanesia by extraction from the big-man's faction in favor of distribution to the population at large. Most importantly, the Polynesian ceiling was higher. Melanesian big-men and Polynesian chiefs not only reflect different varieties and levels of political lution, they display in different degrees the capacity to generate and to sustain political progress.

Especially emerging from their juxtaposition is the more decisive impact of Polynesian chiefs on the economy, the chief's greater leverage on the output of the several households of society. The success of any primitive political organization is decided here, in the control that can be developed over household economies. For the household is not merely the principal productive unit in primitive societies, it is often quite capable of autonomous direction of its own production, and it is oriented towards production for its own, not societal consumption. The greater potential of Polynesian chieftainship is precisely the greater pressure it could exert on household output, its capacity both to generate a surplus and to deploy it out of the household towards a broader division of labor, coopera-

tive construction, and massive ceremonial and military action. Polynesian chiefs were the more effective means of societal collaboration on economic, political, indeed all cultural fronts. Perhaps we have been too long accustomed to perceive rank and rule from the standpoint of the individuals involved, rather than from the perspective of the total society, as if the secret of the subordination of man to man lay in the personal satisfactions of power. And then the breakdowns too, or the evolutionary limits, have been searched out in men, in "weak" kings or megalomaniacal dictators—always, "who is the matter?" An excursion into the field of primitive politics suggests the more fruitful conception that the gains of political developments accrue more decisively to society than to individuals, and the failings as well are of structure not men.

29

Cannibalistic Revenge in Jalé Warfare

BY KLAUS-FRIEDRICH KOCH

In October, 1968, two white missionaries on a long trek between two stations were killed in a remote valley in the Snow Mountains of western New Guinea, and their bodies were eaten. A few days later, warriors armed with bows and arrows gave a hostile reception to a group of armed police flown to the site by helicopter. These people, described by the newspapers as "savages living in a stone-age culture," belong to a large population of Papuans among whom I lived for nearly two years, from 1964 to 1966.

People living to the west, in the high valley of the Balim River, call them "Jalé," and this is the name that I use for them. When I read of the killing of the missionaries I was reminded of how I had first heard that the people whom I had selected for ethnographic study had anthropophagic (man-eating) predilections. After arriving at Sentani airport on the north coast, I began negotiations for transport to a mission airstrip located in the Jalémó, the country of the Jalé. "I hope the Jalé will give us permission to land," one pilot said to me. "Just a few weeks ago the airstrip was blocked because the Jalé needed the ground for a dance and a cannibalistic feast to celebrate a military victory."

Our cultural heritage predisposes many people to view the eating of human meat with extreme horror. No wonder then that the literature on the subject is permeated with grossly erroneous and prejudicial ideas about the practice. Few anthropologists have been able to study cannibalism because missions and colonial governments have generally succeeded in eradicating a custom considered to epitomize, more than any other, the alleged mental primitiveness and diabolical inspirations of people with simple technologies. However, the Jalé, completely isolated from foreign influences until 1961, still practice cannibalism as an institutionalized form of revenge in warfare, which is itself an integral aspect of their life.

The Jalé live in compact villages along several valleys north and south of the Snow Mountains in east-central West New Guinea. Until the first missionaries entered the Jalémó in 1961, the Jalé were ignorant of the "outside" world. Five years later, when I left the area, many Jalé villages still had never been contacted, and culture change among the people living close to a mission station was largely limited to the acceptance of a few steel tools and to an influx of seashells imported by the foreigners.

Two weeks after I had set up camp in the village of Pasikni. a year-long truce with a neighboring village came to an end. Three days of fierce fighting ensued, during which the Pasikni warriors killed three enemies (among them a small boy), raided the defeated settlement, and drove its inhabitants into exile with friends and relatives in other villages of the region. At that time I understood little of the political realities of Jalé society, where neither formal government nor forensic institutions exist for the settlement of conflicts. Later, when I had learned their language, I began to comprehend the conditions that make military actions an inevitable consequence of the absence of an effective system of political control.

From an anthropological perspective any kind of war is generally a symptom of the absence, inadequacy, or breakdown of other procedures for resolving conflicts. This view is especially applicable to Jalé military operations, which aim neither at territorial gains and the conquest of resources nor at the suppression of one political or religious ideology and its forceful replacement by another. All armed conflicts in Jalémó occur as a result of bodily injury or killing suffered in retaliation for the infliction of a wrong. Violent redress may be exacted for adultery or theft or for a breach of obligation—usually a failure to make a compensatory payment of pigs.

Jalé warfare is structured by a complex network of kin relationships. The Jalé conceptually divide their society into two parts (moieties) whose members must marry someone from the opposite side. By a principle of patrilineal descent a person always belongs to

Opposite page: By the time these young boys become warriors, they will be expert archers. Training begins early; boys who can hardly walk carry bows made by their fathers. Practice games perfect the proper stance.

the moiety of his father. Links between kin groups created by intervillage marriages—about half the wives in a village were born elsewhere—provide the structure of trade networks and alliance politics.

Most villages contain two or more residential compounds, or wards. One hut among the group of dwellings forming a ward is considerably bigger than all the others. This is the men's house, a special domicile for men and for boys old enough to have been initiated. Women and uninitiated boys live in the smaller huts, each of which usually houses the family of one man. The residents of a men's house constitute a unified political and ritual community, and it is this community, not the village as a whole, that is the principal war-making unit.

As in all societies, there are some individuals who have more influence over the affairs of their fellows than most. In Jalémó a man gains a position of authority (which never extends much beyond the immediate kin group) through his acquisition of an esoteric knowledge of performing rituals and through the clever management of his livestock to the benefit of his relatives, for every important event demands the exchange of pigs—to solemnify or legitimate the creation of a new status or to settle a conflict. Most disputes are over women, pigs, or gardens, and any one of them may generate enough political enmity to cause a war in which many people may lose their lives and homes.

In every Jalé war one person on either side, called the "man-at-the-root-of-the-arrow," is held responsible for the outbreak of hostilities. These people are the parties to the original dispute, which ultimately escalates into armed combat. Being a man-at-the-root-of-the-arrow carries the liability of providing compensation for all injuries and deaths suffered by supporters on the battlefield as well as by all others—including women and children—victimized in clandestine revenge raids. This liability acts as a built-in force favoring an early end of hostilities.

On rare occasions blood revenge

WEST NEW GUINEA

has been prevented by delivery of wergild compensation, in the form of a pig to the kinsmen of a slain person. But only those people who, for one reason or another, cannot rally support for a revenge action and who shy away from solitary, surreptitious ambush attacks will accept such an offer if it is made at all. A negotiated peace settlement of this nature is most likely if the disputants are from the same village or if the whole settlement is at war with a common outside enemy.

When two villages are at war with each other, periods of daily combat are interrupted by short "cease-fires" during which the warriors attend to the more mundane task of garden work, but they are always prepared to counter a surprise attack launched by the enemy. After several weeks of discontinuous fighting, however, the threat of famine due to the prolonged neglect of proper cultivation induces the belligerents to maintain an informal and precarious truce. During this time small bands of kinsmen and members of the men's house of a victim whose death could not be avenged on the battlefield will venture clandestine expeditions into enemy territory, from which a successful raiding party may bring back

a pig as well. It is a revenge action of this kind that often precipitates a resumption of open warfare.

Fighting on the battlefield follows a pattern of haphazardly coordinated individual engagements, which rely on the tactic of "shoot-and-run." This technique requires a warrior to advance as far as the terrain affords him cover, discharge an arrow or two, and then run back to escape from the reach of enemy shots. When one side has been forced to retreat to its village, the fighting turns into sniping from behind huts and fences. Women and children always leave the village if an invasion is imminent and take refuge with friends and relatives in other villages. As a last resort the men retreat into the men's house, which a taboo protects from being burned. When a battle reaches this stage, the victorious warriors often plunder and burn family huts. Following a catastrophe of this extent the defeated side usually elects to abandon their village, and the warfare ceases, but the hostilities linger on until a formal peace ceremony reconciles the principal parties. Arranging the ceremony, which features the ritual slaughter and consumption of a pig, may take years of informal negotia-

Treacherous unbridged rivers are one of the obstacles the Jalé must surmount on revenge raids in distant valleys. Jalemo terrain is among the most rugged in New Guinea.

tions between people who have relatives on both sides. Afterward, dances in both villages and pig exchanges on a large scale consolidate the termination of the conflict.

"People whose face is known must not be eaten," say the Jalé. Consequently, cannibalism is normally not tolerated in wars between neighboring villages, and the few incidents that did occur during the lifetime of the oldest Pasikni men are remembered as acts of tragic perversion. In wars between villages separated by a major topographic boundary such as a mountain ridge, however, cannibalistic revenge is an integral part of the conflict.

While territorially confined hostilities usually end within a few years, interregional wars may last for more than a generation. During this long period revenge parties from either side venture sporadic expeditions into hostile areas, keenly avoiding any confrontation in battle and seeking instead to surprise lone hunters or small groups of women working in distant gardens. The geography of interregional wars favors long-lasting military alliances that have a stability quite unlike the temporary and shifting allegiances that personal kin connections and trading partner-ships create in local conflicts.

If an enemy is killed during a foray into hostile territory, the raiders will make every effort to bring the body home. If tactical exigencies demand that the revenge party retreat without the victim, an attempt is made to retrieve at least a limb. The avengers always present the body to an allied kin group that has lost a member in the war. In return they receive pigs and are feted at a victory dance, during which the victim's body is steam-cooked in an earth oven dug near the village. Before the butchering begins, the head is specially treated by ritual experts: eyelids and lips are clamped with the wing bones of a bat to prevent the victim's ghost from seeing through these apertures. Thus blinded, it will be unable to guide a revenge expedition against its enemies.

After the head has been severed, it is wrapped in leaves. To insure more revenge killings in the future, some men shoot reed arrows into the head while it is dragged on the ground by a piece of vine. Then the head is unwrapped and swung through the fire to burn off the hair. This is accompanied by loud incantations meant to lure the victim's kinsmen into sharing his fate.

Following this ritual overture the butchers use stone adzes and bamboo knives to cut the body apart. The fleshy portions are removed from the skull, and in an established order of step-by-step incisions, the limbs are separated from the trunk, which is split open to allow removal of the gastronomically highly prized entrails. Some small, choice cuts, especially rib sections, are roasted over the fire, but the bulk of the meat is cooked with a variety of leafy vegetables.

Before and during the operation, people who are preparing the oven, tending the fire, or just standing around appraise the victim. A healthy, muscular body is praised with ravenous exclamations, but a lesser grade body is also applauded.

When the meat is done, the pit is opened and the "owners of the body," as the Jalé call the recipients of a slain enemy, distribute much of the food among the attending relatives of the person whose death the killing has avenged. It is also distributed to the allied kin groups of a person maimed or killed in the war. Eligible people from other villages who could not participate in the celebrations are later sent pieces reserved for them. If mood so moves the Jalé, they may place some of the victim's bones in a tree near the cooking site to tell travelers of their brave deed.

In the course of the dancing and singing, a poetically gifted man may introduce a new song. If the lyrics appeal to others, it becomes a standard piece in the repertoire. The songs commemorate fortunate and tragic events from past wars, and a typical verse goes like this:

Ngingi, your mother
bakes only tiny potatoes for you.
Isel, your mother too
bakes only the ends of potatoes
for you.
We shall bake big potatoes for you
On the day of Kingkaen's return.

Several hundred loops of split liana vine are worn by Jalé men day and night. As an expression of masculinity, younger men wear more loops than their elders. Penis sheaths, cut from gourds, are tied around the body.

Three-day battle culminates in plunder of an enemy village and burning of selected huts, as victorious warriors watch from a nearby ridge. After such a drastic defeat, a village is usually abandoned and open hostilities cease.

Killed from ambush as he returned from battle, the victim, below, is carried to his funeral by members of his own village. The body will be cremated.

Ngingi and Isel are the names of two men from a hostile village, the home of a young woman named Kingkaen who was killed in an ambush attack in September, 1964. The lines make fun of the men who, because of Kingkaen's death, have to eat poor food prepared by the inept hands of senile women.

When the festival of revenge is over, the members of the men's house group of the owners of the body arrange for the ritual removal of the victim's ghost from their village. Rhythmically voicing efficacious formulas and whistling sounds, a ceremonial procession of men carries a special arrow into the forest, as far into enemy territory as is possible without risk. A small lump of pig's fat is affixed to the arrow by an expert in esoteric lore. (Pig's fat used for ritual purposes becomes a sacred substance that is applied in many different contexts.) The arrow is finally shot toward the enemy village. This, the Jalé believe, will make the ghost stay away from their own village, but as a further precaution they block the path with branches and plants over which spells are said.

Protective rites of this kind, and the vengeance ritual described above, are the only aspects of Jalé cannibalism that may be viewed as "religious." The actual consumption of human meat and organs does not constitute an act with intrinsic "supernatural" effects. Instead, as my Jalé friends repeatedly assured me, their reason for eating an enemy's body is that man tastes as good as pork, if not better. And they added that the bad enemies in the other valley had eaten some of their people.

These descriptions of Jalé rituals and beliefs do not sufficiently explain the practice of cannibalism. To do so would necessitate the compilation of all available information about this custom from every part of the world. On the basis of these data an extensive study would have to be made of the ecological and cultural variables found to be associated with institutionalized cannibalism. Perhaps it would then be possible to recognize specific ecological and sociological

features that appear to be correlated with the consumption of human meat, but the task of interpreting the custom as a sociopsychological phenomenon would still remain.

It is obvious that the enigmatic nature of cannibalism has invited many writers to speculate about its origin and its biopsychic basis. Aristotle attributed anthropophagy among tribes around the Black Sea to their feral bestiality and morbid lust. In 1688 a treatise was published in Holland entitled *De natura et moribus anthropophagorum* ("On the Nature and Customs of Anthropophagi"), and some ethnographers writing in the nineteenth century still regarded the rejection of cannibalism as the "first step into civilization." Certainly, the consumption by man of a member of his own species is as much a problem for evolutionary bioanthropology as it is for ethnology and psychology. I have made an extensive survey of the various theories proposed by earnest scholars to elucidate the phenomenon, and I have found that, at best, a few hypotheses appear plausible for the interpretation of certain aspects of some cannibalistic practices.

In Jalémó the eating of a slain enemy, in addition to its dietary value, certainly indicates a symbolic expression of spite incorporated into an act of supreme vengeance. Violent retaliation, in turn, must be seen as a consequence of certain sociopsychological conditions that determine the degree of aggressive behavior expected and tolerated in their culture. Cross-cultural studies by anthropologists have supported theories that are applicable to Jalé society. An accepted model of personality development demonstrates that societies in which boys grow up in intimate association with their mothers, who dominate a household situation in which the boy's male elders, especially their fathers, do not take part, are characterized by a high level of physical violence. Sociological models developed from large-scale comparative research predict that in societies in which small kin groups operate as relatively independent

political units, warfare within the society is a common means of resolving conflict.

Both models squarely apply to Jalé society. First, young boys, separated from the community of the men's house until their initiation, are socialized in a female environment. Second, the wards of a village are not integrated by a centralized system of headmanship, and no political cooperation exists between them until they are threatened by, or faced with, actual hostility from other villages. These are the critical variables that partially determine the bellicosity and violence I have observed.

No specific hypothesis can be given to explain the cannibalism that the Jalé incorporate in their vengeance. It is certain, however, that no understanding can be achieved by applying precepts of Western thought. In a missionary's travelogue published seventy years ago, the author, speaking of an African tribe, recounted:

Once, when told by a European that the practice of eating human flesh was a most degraded habit, the cannibal answered, "Why degraded? You people eat sheep and cows and fowls, which are all animals of a far lower order, and we eat man, who is great and above all; it is you who are degraded!"

Jalé warriors celebrate a battlefield triumph with a victory dance. Brilliant bird of paradise feathers punctuate the scene.

Murders in Eden

BY MARVIN HARRIS

The accepted explanation for the transition from band life to farming villages used to go like this: Hunter-collectors had to spend all their time getting enough to eat. They could not produce a "surplus above subsistence," and so they lived on the edge of extinction in chronic sickness and hunger. Therefore, it was natural for them to want to settle down and live in permanent villages, but the idea of planting seeds never occurred to them. One day an unknown genius decided to drop some seeds in a hole, and soon planting was being done on a regular basis. People no longer had to move about constantly in search of game, and the new leisure gave them time to think. This led to further and more rapid advances in technology and thus more food—a "surplus above subsistence"—which eventually made it possible for some people to turn away from farming and become artisans, priests, and rulers.

The first flaw in this theory is the assumption that life was exceptionally difficult for our stone age ancestors. Archaeological evidence from the upper paleolithic period—about 30,000 B.C. to 10,000 B.C.—makes it perfectly clear that hunters who lived during those times enjoyed relatively high standards of comfort and security. They were no bumbling amateurs. They had achieved total control over the process of fracturing, chipping, and shaping

crystalline rocks, which formed the basis of their technology, and they have aptly been called the "master stoneworkers of all times." Their remarkably thin, finely chipped "laurel leaf" knives, eleven inches long but only four-tenths of an inch thick, cannot be duplicated by modern industrial techniques. With delicate stone awls and incising tools called burins, they created intricately barbed bone and antler harpoon points, well-shaped antler throwing boards for spears, and fine bone needles presumably used to fashion animal-skin clothing. The items made of wood, fibers, and skins have perished, but these too must have been distinguished by high craftsmanship.

Contrary to popular ideas, "cave men" knew how to make artificial shelters, and their use of caves and rock overhangs depended on regional possibilities and seasonal needs. In southern Russia archaeologists have found traces of a hunter's animal-skin dwelling set in a shallow pit forty feet long and twelve feet wide. In Czechoslovakia winter dwellings with round floor plans twenty feet in diameter were already in use more than 20,000 years ago. With rich furs for rugs and beds, as well as plenty of dried animal dung or fat-laden bones for the hearth, such dwellings can provide a quality of shelter superior in many respects to contemporary inner-city apartments.

As for living on the edge of starvation, such a picture is hard to reconcile with the enormous quantities of animal bones accumulated at various paleolithic kill sites. Vast herds of mammoth, horses, deer, reindeer, and bison roamed across Europe and Asia. The bones of over a thousand mammoth, excavated from one site in Czechoslovakia, and the remains of 10,000 wild horses that were stampeded at various intervals over a high cliff near Solutré, France, testify to the ability of paleolithic peoples to exploit these herds systematically and efficiently. Moreover, the skeletal remains of the hunters themselves bear witness to the fact that they were unusually well-nourished.

The notion that paleolithic populations worked round the clock in order to feed themselves now also appears ludicrous. As collectors of food plants they were certainly no less effective than chimpanzees. Field studies have shown that in their natural habitat the great apes spend as much time grooming, playing, and napping as they do foraging and eating. And as hunters our upper paleolithic ancestors must have been at least as proficient as lions—animals which alternate bursts of intense activity with long periods of rest and relaxation. Studies of how present-day hunters and collectors allocate their time have shed more light on this issue. Richard Lee of the University of

Toronto kept a record of how much time the modern Bushman hunter-collectors spend in the quest for food. Despite their habitat—the edge of the Kalahari, a desert region whose lushness is hardly comparable to that of France during the upper paleolithic period—less than three hours per day per adult is all that is needed for the Bushmen to obtain a diet rich in proteins and other essential nutrients.

The Machiguenga, simple horticulturalists of the Peruvian Amazon studied by Allen and Orna Johnson, spend a little more than three hours per day per adult in food production and get less animal protein for this effort than do the Bushmen. In the rice-growing regions of eastern Java, modern peasants have been found to spend about forty-four hours per week in productive farm work—something no self-respecting Bushman would ever dream of doing—and Javanese peasants seldom eat animal proteins. American farmers, for whom fifty-and-sixty-hour work weeks are commonplace, eat well by Bushman standards but certainly cannot be said to have as much leisure.

I do not wish to minimize the difficulties inherent in comparisons of this sort. Obviously the work associated with a particular food-production system is not limited to time spent in obtaining the raw product. It also takes time to process the plants and animals into forms suitable for consumption, and it takes still more time to manufacture and maintain such instruments of production as spears, nets, digging sticks, baskets, and plows. According to the Johnsons' estimates, the Machiguenga devote about three additional hours per day to food preparation and the manufacture of essential items such as clothing, tools, and shelter. In his observations of the Bushmen, Lee found that in one day a woman could gather enough food to feed her family for three days and that

she spent the rest of her time resting, entertaining visitors, doing embroidery, or visiting other camps. "For each day at home, kitchen routines, such as cooking, nut cracking, collecting firewood, and fetching water, occupy one to three hours of her time."

The evidence I have cited above leads to one conclusion: The development of farming resulted in an increased work load per capita. There is a good reason for this. Agriculture is a system of food production that can absorb much more labor per unit of land than can hunting and collecting. Hunter-collectors are essentially dependent on the natural rate of animal and plant reproduction; they can do very little to raise output per unit of land (although they can easily decrease it). With agriculture, on the other hand, people control the rate of plant reproduction. This means that production can be intensified without immediate adverse consequences, especially if techniques are available for combating soil exhaustion.

The key to how many hours people like the Bushmen put into hunting and collecting is the abundance and accessibility of the animal and plant resources available to them. As long as population density—and thus exploitation of these resources—is kept relatively low, hunter-collectors can enjoy both leisure and high-quality diets. Only if one assumes that people during the stone age were unwilling or unable to limit the density of their populations does the theory of our ancestors' lives as "short, nasty, and brutish" make sense. But that assumption is unwarranted. Hunter-collectors are strongly motivated to limit population, and they have effective means to do so. Another weakness in the old theory of the transition from hunting and collecting to agriculture is the assumption that human beings

naturally want to "settle down." This can scarcely be true given the tenacity with which people like the Bushmen, the aborigines of Australia, and the Eskimo have clung to their old "walk-about" way of life despite the concerted efforts of government and missionaries to persuade them to live in villages.

Each advantage of permanent village life has a corresponding disadvantage. Do people crave company? Yes, but they also get on each other's nerves. As Thomas Gregor has shown in a study of the Mehinacu Indians of Brazil, the search for personal privacy is a pervasive theme in the daily life of people who live in small villages. The Mehinacu apparently know too much about each other's business for their own good. They can tell from the print of a heel or a buttock where a couple stopped and had sexual relations off the path. Lost arrows give away the owner's prize fishing spot; an ax resting against a tree tells a story of interrupted work. No one leaves or enters the village without being noticed. One must whisper to secure privacy—with walls of thatch there are no closed doors. The village is filled with irritating gossip about men who are impotent or who ejaculate too quickly, and about women's behavior during coitus and the size, color and odor of their genitalia.

Is there physical security in numbers? Yes, but there is also security in mobility, in being able to get out of the way of aggressors. Is there an advantage in having a larger, cooperative labor pool? Yes, but larger concentrations of people lower the game supply and deplete natural resources.

As for the haphazard discovery of the planting process, hunter-collectors are not so dumb as this sequence in the old theory would suggest. The anatomical details in the paintings of animals found on the walls of caves in France and Spain bear witness to a people whose powers of observation were honed to great accuracy. And our admiration for their intellects has been forced to new heights by Alexander Marshak's discovery that the faint scratches on the surface of 20,000-year-old bone and antler artifacts were put there to keep track of the phases of the moon and other astronomical events. It is unreasonable to suppose that the people who made the great murals on the walls of Lascaux, and who were intelligent enough to make calendrical records, could have been ignorant of the biological significance of tubers and seeds.

Studies of hunter-collectors of the present and recent past reveal that the practice of agriculture is often forgone not for lack of knowledge but as a matter of convenience. Simply by gathering acorns, for example, the Indians of California probably obtained larger and more nutritious harvests than they could have derived from planting maize. And on the Northwest coast the great annual migrations of salmon and candlefish rendered agricultural work a relative waste of time. Hunter-collectors often display all the skills and techniques necessary for practicing agriculture minus the step of deliberate planting. The Shoshoni and Paiute of Nevada and California returned year after year to the same strands of wild grains and tubers, carefully refrained from stripping them bare, and sometimes even weeded and watered them. Many other hunter-collectors use fire to deliberately promote the growth of preferred species and to retard the growth of trees and weeds.

Finally, some of the most important archaeological discoveries of recent years indicate that in the Old World the earliest villages were built 1,000 to 2,000 years before the development of a farming economy, whereas in the New World plants were domesticated long before village life began. Since

the early Americans had the idea for thousands of years before they made full use of it, the explanation for the shift away from hunting and collection must be sought outside their heads. I'll have more to say about these archaeological discoveries later on.

What I've shown so far is that as long as hunter-collectors kept their population low in relation to their prey, they could enjoy an enviable standard of living. But how did they keep their population down? This subject is rapidly emerging as the most important missing link in the attempt to understand the evolution of cultures.

Even in relatively favorable habitats, with abundant herd animals, stone age peoples probably never let their populations rise above one or two persons per square mile. Alfred Kroeber estimated that in the Canadian plains and prairies the bison-hunting Cree and Assiniboin, mounted on horses and equipped with rifles, kept their densities below two persons per square mile. Less favored groups of historic hunters in North America, such as the Labrador Naskapi and the Nunamuit Eskimo, who depended on caribou, maintained densities *below* .3 persons per square mile. In all of France during the late stone age there were probably no more than 20,000 and possibly as few as 1,600 human beings.

"Natural" means of controlling population growth cannot explain the discrepancy between these low densities and the potential fertility of the human female. Healthy populations interested in maximizing their rate of growth average eight pregnancies brought to term per woman. Childbearing rates can easily go higher. Among the Hutterites, a sect of thrifty farmers living in western Canada, the average is 10.7 births per woman. In order to maintain the estimated .001 percent annual rate of growth for the old stone age, each woman must

have had on the average less than 2.1 children who survived to reproductive age. According to the conventional theory such a low rate of growth was achieved, despite high fertility, by disease. Yet the view that our stone age ancestors led disease-ridden lives is difficult to sustain.

No doubt there were diseases. But as a mortality factor they must have been considerably less significant during the stone age than they are today. The death of infants and adults from bacterial and viral infections—dysenteries, measels, tuberculosis, whooping cough, colds, scarlet fever—is strongly influenced by diet and general body vigor, so stone age hunter-collectors probably had high recovery rates from these infections. And most of the great lethal epidemic diseases—smallpox, typhoid fever, flu, bubonic plague, cholera—occur only among populations that have high densities. These are the diseases of state-level societies; they flourish amid poverty and crowded, unsanitary urban conditions. Even such scourges as malaria and yellow fever were probably less significant among the hunter-collectors of the old stone age. As hunters they would have preferred dry, open habitats to the wetlands where these diseases flourish. Malaria probably achieved its full impact only after agricultural clearings in humid forests had created better breeding conditions for mosquitoes.

What is actually known about the physical health of paleolithic populations? Skeletal remains provide important clues. Using such indices as average height and the number of teeth missing at time of death, J. Lawrence Angel has developed a profile of changing health standards during the last 30,000 years. Angel found that at the beginning of this period adult males averaged 177 centimeters (5' 11") and adult females about 165 centimeters (5' 6").

Twenty thousand years later the males grew no taller than the females formerly grew—165 centimeters—whereas the females averaged no more than 153 centimeters (5' 0"). Only in very recent times have populations once again attained statures characteristic of the old stone age peoples. American males, for example, averaged 175 centimeters (5' 9") in 1960. Tooth loss shows a similar trend. In 30,000 B.C. adults died with an average of 2.2 teeth missing; in 6500 B.C., with 3.5 missing; during Roman times, with 6.6 missing. Although genetic factors may also enter into these changes, stature and the condition of teeth and gums are known to be strongly influenced by protein intake, which in turn is predictive of general well-being. Angel concludes that there was "a real depression of health" following the "high point" of the upper paleolithic period.

Angel has also attempted to estimate the average age of death for the upper paleolithic, which he places at 28.7 years for females and 33.3 years for males. Since Angel's paleolithic sample consists of skeletons found all over Europe and Africa, his longevity estimates are not necessarily representative of any actual band of hunters. If the vital statistics of contemporary hunter-collector bands can be taken as representative of paleolithic bands, Angel's calculations err on the low side. Studies of 165 !Kung Bushman women by Nancy Howell show that life expectancy at birth is 32.5 years, which compares favorably with the figures for many modern developing nations in Africa and Asia. To put these data in proper perspective, according to the Metropolitan Life Insurance Company the life expectancy at birth for non-white males in the United States in 1900 was also 32.5 years. Thus, as paleodemographer Don Dumond has suggested, there are hints that "mortality was effectively no higher

under conditions of hunting than under those of a more sedentary life, including agriculture." The increase in disease accompanying sedentary living "may mean that the mortality rates of hunters were more often significantly lower" than those of agricultural peoples.

Although a life span of 32.5 years may seem very short, the reproductive potential even of women who live only to Angel's 28.7 years of age is quite high. If a stone age woman had her first pregnancy when she was sixteen years old, and a live baby every two and a half years thereafter, she could easily have had over five live births by the time she was twenty-nine. This means that approximately three-fifths of stone age children could not have lived to reproductive age if the estimated rate of less than .001 percent population growth was to be maintained. Using these figures, anthropological demographer Ferki Hassan concludes that even if there was 50 percent infant mortality due to "natural" causes, another 23 to 35 percent of all potential offspring would have to be "removed" to achieve zero growth population.

If anything, these estimates appear to err in exaggerating the number of deaths from "natural" causes. Given the excellent state of health the people studied by Angel seemed to enjoy before they became skeletons, one suspects that many of the deceased died of "unnatural" causes.

Infanticide during the paleolithic period could very well have been as high as 50 percent—a figure that corresponds to estimates made by Joseph Birdsell of the University of California in Los Angeles on the basis of data collected among the aboriginal populations of Australia. And an important factor in the short life span of paleolithic women may very well have been the attempt to induce abortions in order to lengthen the interval between births.

Contemporary hunter-collectors in general lack effective chemical or mechanical means of preventing pregnancy—romantic folklore about herbal contraceptives notwithstanding. They do, however, possess a large repertory of chemical and mechanical means for inducing abortion. Numerous plant and animal poisons that cause generalized physical traumas or that act directly on the uterus are used throughout the world to end unwanted pregnancies. Many mechanical techniques for inducing abortion are also employed, such as tying tight bands around the stomach, vigorous massages, subjection to extremes of cold and heat, blows to the abdomen, and hopping up and down on a plank placed across a woman's belly "until blood spurts out of the vagina." Both the mechanical and chemical approaches effectively terminate pregnancies, but they are also likely to terminate the life of the pregnant woman. I suspect that only a group under severe economic and demographic stress would resort to abortion as its principal method of population regulation.

Hunter-collectors under stress are much more likely to turn to infanticide and geronticide (the killing of old people). Geronticide is effective only for short-run emergency reductions in group size. It cannot lower long-term trends of population growth. In the case of both geronticide and infanticide, outright conscious killing is probably the exception. Among the Eskimo, old people too weak to contribute to their own subsistence may "commit suicide" by remaining behind when the group moves, although children actively contribute to their parents' demise by accepting the cultural expectation that old people ought not to become a burden when food is scarce. In Australia, among the Murngin of Arnhem Land, old people are helped along toward their fate by being treated as if they were already dead when they become sick; the group begins to perform its last rites, and the old person responds by getting sicker. Infanticide runs a complex gamut from outright murder to mere neglect. Infants may be strangled, drowned, bashed against a rock, or exposed to the elements. More commonly, an infant is "killed" by neglect; the mother gives less care than is needed when it gets sick, nurses it less often, refrains from trying to find supplementary foods, or "accidentally" lets it fall from her arms. Hunter-collector women are strongly motivated to space out the age difference between their children since they must expend a considerable amount of effort merely lugging them about during the day. Richard Lee has calculated that over a four-year period of dependency a Bushman mother will carry her child a total of 4,900 miles on collecting expeditions and campsite moves. No Bushman woman wants to be burdened with two or three infants at a time as she travels that distance.

The best method of population control available to stone age hunter-collectors was to prolong the span of years during which a mother nursed her infant. Recent studies of menstrual cycles carried out by Rose Frisch and Janel McArthur have shed light on the physiological mechanism responsible for lowering the fertility of lactating women. After giving birth, a fertile woman will not resume ovulation until the percentage of her body weight that consists of fat has passed a critical threshold. This threshold (about 20–25 percent) represents the point at which a woman's body has stored enough reserve energy in the form of fat to accommodate the demands of a growing fetus. The average energy cost of a normal pregnancy is 27,000 calories—just about the amount of energy that must be stored before a woman can conceive. A nursing infant drains about 1,000 extra

calories from its mother per day, making it difficult for her to accumulate the necessary fatty reserve. As long as the infant is dependent on its mother's milk, there is little likelihood that ovulation will resume. Bushman mothers, by prolonging lactation, appear to be able to delay the possibility of pregnancy for more than four years. The same mechanism appears to be responsible for delaying menarche—the onset of menstruation. The higher the ratio of body fat to body weight, the earlier the age of menarche. In well-nourished modern populations menarche has been pushed forward to about twelve years of age, whereas in populations chronically on the edge of caloric deficits it may take eighteen or more years for a girl to build up the necessary fat reserves.

What I find so intriguing about this discovery is that it links low fertility with diets that are high in proteins and low in carbohydrates. On the one hand, if a woman is to nurse a child successfully for three or four years she must have a high protein intake to sustain her health, body vigor, and the flow of milk. On the other hand, if she consumes too many carbohydrates she will begin to put on weight, which will trigger the resumption of ovulation. A demographic study carried out by J. K. Van Ginneken indicates that nursing women in underdeveloped countries, where the diet consists mostly of starchy grains and root crops, cannot expect to extend the interval between births beyond eighteen months. Yet nursing Bushman women, whose diet is rich in animal and plant proteins and who lack starchy staples, as I have said, manage to keep from getting pregnant four or more years after each birth. This relationship suggests that during good times hunter-collectors could rely on prolonged lactation as their principal defense against overpopulation. Conversely, a decline in the quality of food supply would tend to bring about

an increase in population. This in turn would mean either that the rate of abortion and infanticide would have to be accelerated or that still more drastic cuts in the protein ration would be needed.

I am not suggesting that the entire defense against overpopulation among our stone age ancestors rested with the lactation method. Among the Bushmen of Botswana the present rate of population growth is .5 percent per annum. This amounts to a doubling every 139 years. Had this rate been sustained for only the last 10,000 years of the old stone age, by 10,000 B.C. the population of the earth would have reached 604,463,000,000,000,-000,000,000.

Suppose the fertile span were from sixteen years of age to forty-two. Without prolonged nursing, a woman might experience as many as twelve pregnancies. With the lactation method, the number of pregnancies comes down to six. Lowered rates of coitus in older women might further reduce the number to five. Spontaneous abortions and infant mortality caused by disease and accidents might bring the potential reproducers down to four— roughly two more than the number permissible under a system of zero population growth. The "extra" two births could then be controlled through some form of infanticide based on neglect. The optimal method would be to neglect only the girl babies, since the rate of growth in populations that do not practice monogamy is determined almost entirely by the number of females who reach reproductive age.

Our stone age ancestors were thus perfectly capable of maintaining a stationary population, but there was a cost associated with it— the waste of infant lives. This cost lurks in the background of prehistory as an ugly blight in what might otherwise be mistaken for a Garden of Eden.

In Search of the Affluent Society

BY ALLEN JOHNSON

One of the paradoxes of modern life is the persistence of suffering and deep dissatisfaction among people who enjoy an unparalleled abundance of material goods. The paradox is at least as old as our modern age. Ever since the benefits and costs of industrial technology became apparent, opinion has been divided over whether we are progressing or declining.

The debate grows particularly heated when we compare our civilization with the cultures of "primitive" or "simpler" peoples. At the optimistic extreme, we are seen as the beneficiaries of an upward development that has brought us from an era in which life was said to be "nasty, brutish, and short," into one of ease, affluence, and marvelous prospects for the future. At the other extreme, primitives are seen as enjoying idyllic lives of simplicity and serenity, from which we have descended dangerously through an excess of greed. The truth is a complex mix of these two positions, but it is striking how difficult it is to take a balanced view. We are attracted irresistibly to either the optimistic or the pessimistic position.

The issue is of more than academic interest. The modern world is trying to come to grips with the idea of "limits to growth" and the need to redistribute wealth. Pressures are mounting from the environment on which we depend and from the people with whom we share it. Scientists, planners, and policy makers are now talking about "alternative futures," trying to marshal limited resources for the greater good of humanity. In this context it is useful to know whether people living in much simpler economies than our own really do enjoy advantages we have lost.

In his book *The Affluent Society*, economist John Kenneth Galbraith accepts the optimistic view, with some reservations. According to him, the modern trend has been toward an increase in the efficiency of production; working time has decreased while the standard of living has risen through a growth in purchasing power. One of Galbraith's reservations is that he does not see this growth as an unmitigated good. He sees our emphasis on acquiring goods as left over from times when the experience of poverty was still real and thinks we are ready to acknowledge our wealth and reduce our rates of consumption. The trend over the last 100 years toward a shorter work week, he argues, demonstrates that we are relinquishing some of our purchasing power in exchange for greater leisure.

Galbraith's view that modern affluence both brings us greater leisure and fills our basic needs better than any previous economic system is widespread. Yet the first part of this view is almost certainly wrong, and the second is debatable. Anthropologist Marshall Sahlins has shown that hunting-and-gathering economies, such as those found among the Australian aborigines and the San of southern Africa, require little work (three to four hours per adult each day) to provide ample and varied diets. Although they lack our abundance of goods, material needs are satisfied in a leisurely way, and in their own view, people are quite well off.

Sahlins points out that there are two roads to affluence: our own, which is to produce more, and what he calls the Buddhist path, which is to be satisfied with less. Posing the problem of affluence in this way makes it clear that affluence depends not only on material wealth but also on subjective satisfaction. There is apparently plenty of room for choice in designing a life of affluence.

Recent studies of how people in different societies spend their time allow us to make a fairly objective comparison of primitive and modern societies. In one analysis, Alexander Szalai studied middle-class French couples residing in six cities in France—Arras, Besançon, Chalon-sur-Saône, Dunkerque, Épinal, and Metz. Orna Johnson and I, both of us anthropologists, collected similar data when we lived among the Machiguenga Indians of Peru for some 18 months, which were spread over one long and two shorter visits.

The Machiguenga live in extended family groups scattered throughout the Amazon rain forest. They spend approximately equal amounts of time growing food in gardens carved out of the surrounding forest and in hunting, fishing, and collecting wild foods. They are self-sufficient; almost everything they consume is produced by their own labors using materials that are found close at hand. Despite some similarities in how the French and the Machiguenga spend their time (for instance, in the way work is apportioned between the sexes), the differences between the societies are applicable to our purposes.

For reasons that will become clear, we divide ways of spending time into three categories: production time, consumption time, and free time. Production time refers to what we normally think of as work, in which goods and services are produced either for further production (capital goods) or for direct consumption (consumption goods). Consumption time refers to time spent using consumption goods. Eating, and what we think of as leisure time — watching television, visiting amusement parks, playing tennis — is spent this way. Free time is spent in neither production nor consumption; it includes sheer idleness, rest, sleep, and chatting.

Of course, these three categories of time are arbitrary. We could eliminate the difference between consumption time and free time, for example, by pointing out that the French consume beds and the Machiguenga consume mats during sleep. But we want to distinguish time spent at the movies or driving a car from time spent doing nothing — sitting idly by the door or casually visiting neighbors. This supports a main contention of our research: that little agreement now exists on exactly how to measure the differences between dissimilar societies.

For comparative purposes, we broke down our data into five categories of people, two for the Machiguenga and three for the French. For the relatively simple Machiguenga society, a division by gender was sufficient for studying patterns in time use. But for the more complex French society, a male-female breakdown was insufficient because such a division does not allow for working women. We divided the French data into three categories: men, working women, and housewives.

In production time French workers, both men and women, spend more time working outside the home than the Machiguenga do. French men work one and a half hours more per day away from home than do Machiguenga men;

employed French women work four hours more per day than do Machiguenga women. French housewives work less outside the home than Machiguenga women do, but they make up for this difference by exceeding their Machiguenga counterparts in work inside the home. French men spend more time working inside the home than do Machi-

guenga men. All told, French men spend more time engaged in production than do Machiguenga men, and French women (both working and housewives) spend more time in production activities than do Machiguenga women.

The French score equal to or higher than the Machiguenga on all measures of consumption. French men spend more

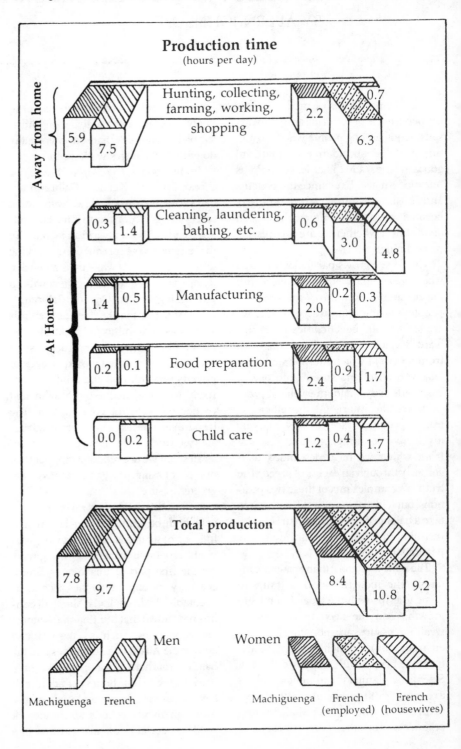

than three times as many hours in consumption as do Machiguenga men; French women consume goods at four or five times the rate of Machiguenga women, depending on whether they are employed or are housewives.

It is in the category of free time that the Machiguenga clearly surpass the French. Machiguenga men spend more than 14 hours per day engaged in free time, compared with nearly 10 hours for their French counterparts, and Machiguenga women have much more free time than French women do—whether or not the French women work.

The immediate question concerns differences in the overall pattern. It seems undeniable, as Sahlins has argued, that modern technological progress has not resulted in more free time for most people. The shrinking of the work week in the last century is probably nothing more than a short-term wrinkle in the historical trend toward longer work weeks. If our modern economy provides us with more goods, it is not simply because technical efficiency has increased. Indeed, the trend toward a shorter work week ended with World War II; since then, the length of the work week has remained about the same.

The increase of consumption time at the expense of free time is both a loss and a gain. Here we encounter a subtle, complex problem. Increased consumption may add excitement and pleasure to what would otherwise be considered boring time. On the other hand, this increase has the effect of crowding time with consumption activities so that people begin to feel that "time is short"—which may detract from the enjoyment of consumption.

Economist Staffan Burenstam Linder has looked at the effects of higher production and consumption of goods on our sense of time. To follow his argument we must move from the level of clock time to that of subjective time, as measured by our inner sense of the tempo of our lives. According to Linder, as a result of producing and consuming more, we are experiencing an increasing scarcity of time. This works in the following way. Increasing efficiency in production means that each individual

must produce more goods per hour; increased productivity means, though it is not often mentioned in this context, that to keep the system going we must consume more goods. Free time gets converted into consumption time because time spent neither producing nor consuming comes increasingly to be viewed as wasted. Linder's theory may account for the differences between the ways the Machiguenga and the French use their time.

The increase in the value of time (its increasing scarcity) is felt subjectively as an increase in tempo or pace. We are always in danger of being slow on the production line or late to work; and in our leisure we are always in danger of wasting time. I have been forcefully impressed with this aspect of time during several field visits to the Machiguenga. It happens each time I return to their communities that, after a period of two or three days, I sense a definite decrease in time pressure; this is a physiological as well as a psychological sensation.

This feeling of a leisurely pace of life reflects the fact that among the Machiguenga daily activities are never hurried or desperate. Each task is allotted its full measure of time, and free time is not felt to be boring or lost but is accepted as entirely natural. These feelings last throughout the field visit, but when I return home I am conscious of the pressure and sense of hurry building up to its former level. Something similar, though fleeting, happens on vacation trips—but here the pressure to consume, to see more sights while traveling, or to get one's money's worth in entertainment constantly asserts itself, and the tempo is usually kept up.

Linder sees a kind of evolutionary progression from "time surplus" societies through "time affluence" societies, ending with the "time famine" society of developed countries. The famine is expressed not only in a hectic pace, but also in a decline of activities in which goods are not consumed rapidly enough, such as spending time with the elderly and providing other social services. As Galbraith has pointed out, we neglect basic social needs because they are seen as economically unproductive.

Not only do we use our time for almost frantic consumption, but more of our time is also devoted to caring for the increasing number of goods we possess. The Machiguenga devote three to four times more of their production time at home to manufacturing (cloth and baskets, for example) than they do to maintenance activities, such as cleaning and doing the laundry; the French pattern is the reverse. This may help account for the failure of modern housewives to acquire more leisure time from their appliances, a situation that has prompted anthropologist Marvin Harris to refer to appliances as "labor-saving devices that don't save work."

On both objective and subjective grounds, then, it appears that economic growth has not given us more leisure time. If anything, the increasingly hectic pace of leisure activities detracts from our enjoyment of play, even when the increased stimulation they bring is taken into account. When we consider the abundance of goods, however, the situation is obviously different. The superiority of modern industrial technology in producing material goods is clear. The Machiguenga, and other people at a similar technological level, have no doubts on this score either. Despite their caution, which outsiders are apt to label "traditionalism," they really do undertake far-reaching changes in their ways of life in order to obtain even small quantities of industrial output.

One area in which the Machiguenga clearly need (and warmly welcome) Western goods is medicine. Despite hopeful speculations in popular writings that Amazon Indians have secret herbal remedies that are effective against infections, cancer, and other conditions, the curative powers of Machiguenga medicine are circumscribed. Antibiotics, even the lowly sulfa pill, are highly effective and much in demand for skin sores, eye infections, and other painful endemic health problems. Medicines to control such parasites as amoebae and intestinal worms bring immediate relief to a community, although people are eventually reinfected. In terms of human well-being, then, even the most romantic defender of the simple life must grant that modern medicines improve the lives of primitive people.

I am much less certain about what other Western goods to offer as evidence of the comparative lack of affluence among the Machiguenga. They have a great abundance of food, for example; they produce at least twice as many calories of food energy as they consume. (The excess production is not surplus so much as a security margin in case someone should fall ill or relatives unexpectedly come to stay for a time.) The Machiguenga diet is highly varied and at times very tasty. The people are attractive and healthy, with no apparent signs of malnutrition. Although they are somewhat underweight by modern standards, these standards may reflect average weights of modern populations that the Machiguenga would regard as overweight.

The highly productive food economy of the Machiguenga depends on metal tools obtained from Peruvian traders. Without an outside source of axes, the Machiguenga would have to give up their semisedentary existence and roam the forest as nomads. Should this happen, they could support fewer people in the same territory — but, if other hunter-collector groups can be used as evidence, nomadic life would result in even shorter workdays. Once again, in quantities of food as well as in quantities of time, the Machiguenga fit Sahlin's model of primitive affluence.

Our affluence exceeds Machiguenga affluence, but as in the case of time, there is the quality of life to take into account. My personal experiences in the field illustrate this aspect of the contrast. In preparing to leave for our first year-long visit to the Machiguenga, Orna and I decided to limit ourselves to the clothing and supplies that would fit into two trunks. This decision led to much agonizing over what to take and what to leave behind. Although we had both been in the field before, we had never gone anywhere quite so remote and we could not imagine how we would get along with so few goods.

The truth, however, was that we were absurdly oversupplied. As our field work progressed we used less and less of our store of goods. It even became a burden to us, since our possessions had to be dried in the sun periodically to prevent rot. As we grew close to the people we were living among, we began to be embarrassed by having so many things we did not really need.

Once, after a long rainy period, I laid my various footgear side by side in the sun to dry. There were a pair of hiking boots, a pair of canvas-topped jungle boots, and two pairs of sneakers. Some men came to visit and began inspecting the shoes, fingering the materials, commenting on the cleats, and trying them on for size. Then the discussion turned to how numerous my shoes were, and one man remarked that I had still another pair. There were protests of disbelief and I was asked if that was true. I said, "No, that's all I have." The man then said,

"Wait," and went inside the house, returning with an "extra pair" of sneakers that I had left forgotten and unused in a corner of the room for months. This was not the only occasion on which I could not keep track of my possessions, a deficiency unknown to the Machiguenga.

My feelings about this incident were compounded when I discovered that, no matter which pair of shoes I wore, I could never keep up with these men, whose bare feet seemed magically to grip the slipperiest rocks or to find toe holds in the muddy trails. At about this time I was reading Alfred Russel Wallace's narrative of his years in the Amazon, in which he relates that his boots soon wore out and he spent his remaining time there barefoot — an achievement that continues to fill me with awe. My origi-

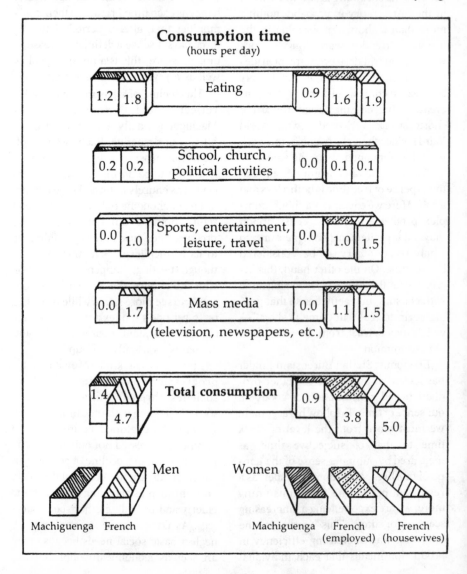

nal pride in being well shod was diminished to something closely resembling embarrassment.

This experience brings up the question of whether goods are needed in themselves or because demand for them has been created by the producers. Galbraith stresses that we cannot simply assume that goods are produced to meet people's real needs. The billions of dollars spent each year on advertising indicate that not all consumer wants arise from basic needs of the individual, but that some are created in consumers by the producers themselves. This turns things around. Instead of arguing, as economists usually do, that our economic system serves us well, we are forced to consider that it may be we who serve the system by somehow agreeing to want the things it seems bent on producing, like dozens of kinds of shoes.

To most economists there is no justification for criticizing the purchasing habits of modern consumers. Purchases simply reflect personal preference, and it smacks of arrogance and authoritarianism to judge the individual decisions of free men and women. Economist Kenneth Boulding has referred sarcastically to such attempts as "theonomics." Economists assume that if there were more satisfying pathways of consumption, people would choose them. But the role of advertising in creating wants leaves open the question of the relationship between the consumption of goods and the fulfillment of needs.

When the task is to consume more, there are three ways of complying. One is to increase the amount of time spent consuming; this is one way the French differ from the Machiguenga. Another way is to increase the total number of goods we possess and to devote less time to each one individually. In a sense, this is what I was doing with the five pairs of shoes. The third way is to increase the elaborateness (and hence the cost of production) of the items we consume. The following instance, which took place at a Machiguenga beer feast, demonstrates that even those manufactured items we consider most practical are both elaborate and costly.

At Machiguenga beer feasts, which last for two or three days until the beer is gone, men often make recreational items like drums and toys. At one beer feast that had been going on for a day and a half, I watched a drum being made. The monkey-skin drumheads were being readied, and I noticed that the man next to me was about to make holes in the edge of the skin for the gut that would be used to tighten the drumhead. I had in my pocket an elaborate knife of fine steel, which had among its dozen separate functions (scissors, file, tweezers, etc.) a leather punch. By the time I had pulled the knife out and opened the punch, my neighbor had already made a

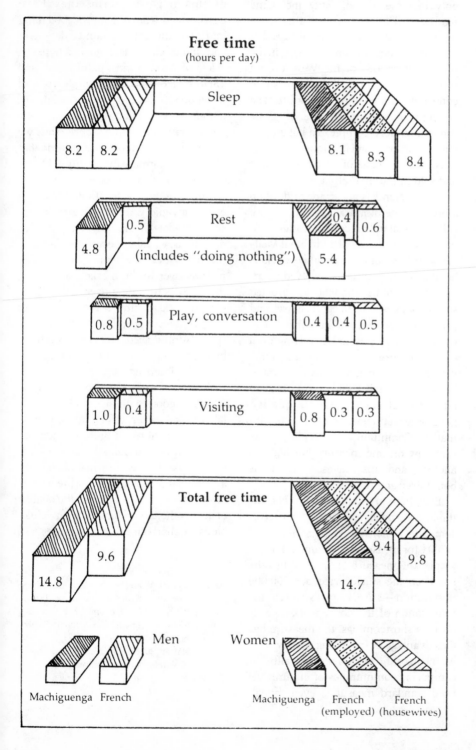

Free time
(hours per day)

Sleep   8.2 8.2   8.1 8.3 8.4

Rest (includes "doing nothing")   0.5 4.8   0.4 0.6 5.4

Play, conversation   0.8 0.5   0.4 0.4 0.5

Visiting   1.0 0.4   0.8 0.3 0.3

Total free time   14.8 9.6   9.4 9.8 14.7

Men   Women
Machiguenga French   Machiguenga French (employed) French (housewives)

perfect hole with a scrap of broken kitchen knife he had kept close at hand.

Then he noticed my knife and wanted to see it. He noted its fine workmanship and passed it around to others, who tested its sharpness and opened all its parts, asking me to explain each one. They wanted to know how much it cost and how they could obtain one.

I interpret this experience in two ways. First, the knife was overelaborate. The Machiguenga met all their own needs for clothing, shelter, and containers with much simpler tools. Second, the elaborateness of the knife was itself an attraction, and its remarkable design and quality of materials could not help but draw the men's attention. They wanted the knife—not craving it, but willing to make serious efforts to get it or something similar if the opportunity arose. It is characteristic of a developed culture's contact with small, isolated societies that the developed culture is not met as a whole, but rather in highly selective ways that emphasize manufactured goods and the aura of the great, mysterious power that made them.

Our examples do not prove that the Machiguenga enjoy a higher quality of life than people who live in an industrial society, but they are not intended to. They do show that the quantitative abundance of consumption goods does not automatically guarantee an advantage to the consumer. And although our experiences among the Machiguenga make it easy to argue for the high quality of their lives—as reflected in their warm family ties, peaceable manners, good humor, intimacy with nature, and impressive integrity—it is also true that we would have regarded a permanent life there as a great personal sacrifice. Orna and I came home partly because it is home, where our lives have meaning, and partly because we did not want to go without some creature comforts that we, for better or worse, regard as highly desirable.

It seems likely, however, that an increasing supply of creature comforts and stimulation will bring us into a dan-gerous relationship with our environment. Such a confrontation might lead us to think about the costs involved in producing and consuming less. In traditional terms this is almost unthinkable, because the relative affluence of communities has been restricted to quantitative measures such as per capita income or gross national product, which can only increase (good), stay the same (bad), or decline (worse). But these numerical measures, which always discover the highest standard of living in the developed nations of the West, do not necessarily touch on all the factors that contribute to a good quality of life. The concept of quality of life suggests something more complex: a balancing-out of diverse satisfactions and dissatisfactions, not all of which are bought and sold in the marketplace.

Social scientists are trying to develop a broad range of indexes, such as those called "social indicators," that attempt to measure the quality of individual well-being. It has not been the theoreticians but the planners directly involved in applying economic thought to directed social changes, like urban renewal and rural development, who have insisted on such measures. Instead of relying on a single measure, like per capita income, they have added unemployment rates, housing, mental health, cultural and educational resources, air quality, government efficiency, and social participation. Communities, or nations, may rank low on one measure but high on another, and this makes comparisons both fairer and more realistic.

Even here problems remain. For one thing, the social indicators themselves sometimes sacrifice understanding of quality for measures of quantity. For example, the measure of "mental health" has been the suicide rate per 100,000 population—surely a restricted interpretation of the concept. Despite its obvious shortcomings, the measure has the advantage of specifying exactly what we mean by the term "mental health." In comparing communities or cultures we need standard measures, even though quality and quantity are ultimately incompatible.

When we discuss non-Western societies, the existing social indicators do not work very well. Unemployment, housing, and mental health all become hard to define. Economists, for example, often label free time in other cultures as "hidden unemployment"; by clever use of this negative term, they have transformed what might be a good thing into something that sounds definitely bad. In our case, Machiguenga housing, made of palm fronds, palm wood, and various tropical hardwoods, would never qualify as good housing in terms of a housing code, but it is cool, well ventilated, comfortable, and secure. Thus we are still far from developing criteria that allow us to compare the quality of life, or affluence, in diverse societies.

The economy of the United States is changing rapidly. Yet when we try to construct models of the alternative futures open to us, we falter because we lack the means to evaluate them. To turn this process over to the marketplace is not the same as turning it over to the "people" in some absolute democratic sense. People's behavior in the marketplace is strongly influenced, often by subterfuge, by producers who try to convince them that their interests coincide.

To accept the influence of the producers of goods without criticism, while labeling all other efforts to influence consumer patterns as "interference" or "theonomics," amounts to simple bias. Certainly a degree of open-mindedness about what a good quality of life is, and more efforts at learning about the quality of life in other communities, are invaluable as we chart our uncertain future.

For further information:

Andrews, Frank M. and Stephen B. Withey. *Social Indicators of Well-Being: Americans' Perception of Life Quality.* Plenum, 1976.

Galbraith, John Kenneth. *The Affluent Society.* Houghton Mifflin, 1958.

Linder, Staffan Burenstam. *The Harried Leisure Class.* Columbia University Press, 1970.

Sahlins, Marshall. *Stone Age Economics.* Aldine-Atherton, 1972.

TOPIC ELEVEN

Cultural Ecology

· ·

Cultural ecology is rather a new subfield of anthropology, although it was anticipated by environmental determinism, which flourished around the turn of the century and later was discredited. Cultural ecologists study the ways in which cultural patterns act to adapt people to the stressful conditions imposed on them by their environment. They avoid a deterministic stance by acknowledging that there are many alternative patterns of behavior that can adapt a group to a given environment. Thus, when cultural ecologists explain a pattern of behavior in terms of its adaptive significance, they do not claim to be able to say *why* a particular pattern is adopted in preference to others. Instead, they contend that, given the facts of the environment, it is possible to make sense of a pattern of behavior that seems at first glance to be curious, or even "foolish" or damaging.

Marvin Harris, perhaps the best known exponent of cultural ecology, tackles the question of the taboo among Jews and Muslims against eating pork in "The Riddle of the Pig." He goes beneath the surface of religious prohibition and finds the logic of this proscription in the environment of the Middle East—and in the tastiness of pork. Similarly Michael Harner provides a new way of understanding "The Enigma of Aztec Sacrifice" by pointing to the severe protein shortage in Mexico and Mesoamerica at the time of the rise of their high civilizations. Harner's theory (and even his acceptance of the assumption of a protein shortage) has generated considerable debate among anthropologists. It is explained in greater detail in his more technical article,

"The Ecological Basis for Aztec Sacrifice" (*American Ethnologist*, February 1977).

Harner's critics question his data on the frequency of famine in Aztec Mexico and point out that the Spanish chronicles on which Harner relies were, at least to some degree, self-serving in justifying the Spanish conquest and, therefore, would be likely to embellish on Aztec atrocities. Several of his critics have further noted that many of the human sacrifices came at harvest time—precisely when the Aztecs did not need additional protein. Finally, Barbara Price argues that Harner's method of analysis is simplistic. She believes it is important to analyze cannibalism in Aztec society in terms of the interaction of all major Aztec social institutions, the political system in particular. In her view, human flesh was consumed mostly by the noble families and represented a perquisite of power in Aztec society, not a staple protein commodity.

John B. Calhoun's "Plight of the Ik and Kaiadilt Is Seen as a Chilling Possible End for Man" takes the horrifying testimony produced by the research of Colin Turnbull among the Ik of Uganda and Geoffrey Bianchi among the Kaiadilt in Australia, and shows that the decay of virtually all sustaining aspects of a society is predictable in certain contexts. Calhoun has investigated these contexts experimentally among populations of mice and sees alarming parallels there to the fate of the two peoples discussed in this essay. One cannot read this article without becoming deeply concerned over the directions taken by our own society.

Riddle of the Pig

BY MARVIN HARRIS

When the God of the ancient Hebrews told them not to eat pork, He must have realized that generations of scholars were going to try to figure out why. From my ecological perspective, I would like to offer an explanation that relates Jewish and Muslim attitudes toward the pig to the cultural and natural ecosystems of the Middle East.

Naturalistic explanations for the taboo on pork go back to Maimonides, who lived in the twelfth century. Maimonides said that God had intended the ban on pork as a public health measure since swine's flesh "had a bad and damaging effect upon the body." This explanation gained favor in the mid-nineteenth century when it was discovered that there was a parasite present in undercooked pork that caused trichinosis.

Impressed by this rational answer to the ancient riddle, American Jews who belonged to the reformed congregations proceeded forthwith to revoke the scriptural taboo on the grounds that if properly cooked, pork no longer menaced the community's health. But Maimonides's explanation has a big hole in it: the flesh of all undercooked domestic animals can serve as a vector for human diseases. Cattle, sheep, and goats, for example, transmit brucellosis and anthrax, both of which have fatality rates as high as that of trichinosis.

Although Maimonides's explanation must be rejected, I think he was closer to the truth than modern anthropologists, including Sir James Frazer, renowned author of *The Golden Bough*. Frazer declared that pigs, like "all so-called unclean animals were originally sacred; the reason for not eating them was that many were originally divine." This doesn't help us very much since the sheep, goat, and cow were also once worshiped in the Middle East, and yet their meat is much enjoyed by all ethnic and religious groups in the area.

Other scholars have suggested that pigs, along with the rest of the foods prohibited in the Bible, were the original totem animals of the Hebrew clans. But why interdict the consumption of a valuable food resource? After all, eagles, ravens, spiders, and other animals that are of only limited significance as a source of human food are also used as clan totems.

Maimonides at least tried to place the taboo in a natural context in which definite, intelligible forces were at work. His mistake was that he conceived of public health much too narrowly. What he lacked was an understanding of the threat that the pig posed to the integrity of the broad cultural and natural ecosystem of the ancient Hebrew habitat.

I think we have to take into account that the protohistoric Hebrews—the children of Abraham—were adapted to life in the rugged, sparsely inhabited arid lands between Mesopotamia and Egypt. Until their conquest of the Jordan Valley in Palestine, which began in the thirteenth century B.C., they were primarily nomadic pastoralists, living almost entirely on their sheep, goats, and cattle. But like all pastoral peoples they maintained close relationships with sedentary agriculturalists who held the oasis and fertile river valley.

From time to time certain Hebrew lineages adopted a more sedentary, agriculturally oriented mode of existence, as appears to have been the case with the Abrahamites in Mesopotamia, the Josephites in Egypt, and the Isaacites in the western Negev. But even during the climax of urban and village life under David and Solomon, the herding of sheep, goats, and cattle continued to play a vital, if not predominant, economic role everywhere except in the irrigated portions of the Jordan Valley.

Within the over-all pattern of this mixed farming and pastoral complex, the divine prohibition against pork constituted a sound ecological strategy. During periods of maximum nomadism, it was impossible for the Israelites to raise pigs, while during the semisedentary and even fully village farming phases, pigs were more of a threat than an asset. The basic reason for this is that the world zones of pastoral nomadism correspond to unforested plains and hills that are too arid for rainfall agriculture and that cannot easily be irrigated. The domestic animals best adapted to these zones are the ruminants—cattle, sheep, and goats. Because ruminants have sacks anterior to their stomachs, they are able to digest grass, leaves, and other foods consisting mainly of cellulose more efficiently than any other mammals.

The pig, however, is primarily a creature of forests and shaded river banks. Although it is omnivorous, its best weight gain is from food low in cellulose—nuts, fruits, tubers, and especially grains, making it a direct competitor of man. It cannot subsist on grass alone and nowhere in the world do fully nomadic pastoralists raise significant numbers of pigs. The pig has the further disadvantage of not being a practical source of milk and of being difficult to herd over long distances.

Above all, the pig is ill-adapted to the heat of the Negev, the Jordan Valley, and the other biblical lands. Compared to cattle, goats, and sheep, the pig is markedly incapable of maintaining a constant body temperature when the temperature rises.

In spite of the expression "to sweat like a pig," it has now become clear that pigs can't sweat through their relatively hairless skins. Human beings, the sweatiest of all mammals, cool themselves by evaporating as much as three ounces of body liquid per hour from each square foot of body surface. The best a pig can manage is one-tenth ounce per square foot, and none of this is sweat. Even sheep evaporate twice as much body liquid through their skins as pigs. And sheep have the advantage of thick white wool, which both reflects the sun's rays and provides insulation when the ambient temperature rises above body temperature. According to L. E. Mount of the Agricultural Research Council Institute of Animal Physiology in Cambridge, England, adult pigs will die if exposed to direct sunlight and air temperatures over 97 degrees F. In the Jordan Valley, air temperatures of 110 degrees occur almost every summer and there is intense sunshine throughout the year.

To compensate for its lack of protective hair and its inability to sweat, the pig must dampen its skin with external moisture. It usually does this by wallowing in fresh, clean mud, but if nothing else is available, it will cover its skin with its own urine and feces. Mount reports that below 84 degrees F. pigs kept in pens deposit their excreta away from their sleeping and feeding areas, while above 84 degrees they excrete throughout the pen.

Sheep and goats were the first animals to be domesticated in the Middle East, possibly as early as 9000 B.C. Pigs were domesticated in the same general region about 2,000 years later. Bone counts conducted by archeologists at early prehistoric village farming sites show that sheep and goats were in the majority while the domesticated pig was almost always a relatively minor part—about 5 percent—of the village fauna. This is what one would expect of a creature that ate the same food as man, couldn't be milked, and had to be provided with shade and mudholes. Domesticated pigs were from the beginning an economical and ecological luxury, especially since goats, sheep, and cattle provided milk, cheese, meat, hides, dung, fiber, and traction for plowing. But the pig, with its rich, fatty meat, was a delectable temptation—the kind, like incest and adultery, that mankind finds difficult to resist. And so God was heard to say that swine were unclean, not only as food, but to the touch as well. This message was repeated by Mohammed for the same reason: it was ecologically more adaptive for the people of the Middle East to cater to their goats, sheep, and cattle. Pigs tasted good but they ate you out of house and home and, if you gave them a chance, used up your water as well. Well, that's my answer to the riddle of why God told the Jews and the Muslims not to eat pork. Anyone have a better idea?

The Enigma of Aztec Sacrifice

BY MICHAEL HARNER

On the morning of November 8, 1519, a small band of bearded, dirty, exhausted Spanish adventurers stood at the edge of a great inland lake in central Mexico, staring in disbelief at the sight before them. Rising from the center of the lake was a magnificent island city, shining chalk white in the early sun. Stretching over the lake were long causeways teeming with travelers to and from the metropolis, Tenochtitlán, the capital of the Aztec empire, now known as Mexico City.

The Spaniards, under the command of Hernán Cortés, were fresh from the wars of the Mediterranean and the conquest of the Caribbean. Tough and ruthless men, numbering fewer than four hundred, they had fought their way up from the eastern tropical coast of Mexico. Many had been wounded or killed in battles with hostile Indians on the long march. Possibly all would have died but for their minuscule cavalry of fifteen horses—which terrified the Indians, who thought the animals were gods— and the aid of a small army of Indian allies, enemies of the Aztecs.

The panorama of the Aztec citadel across the water seemed to promise the Spaniards the riches that had eluded them all their lives. One of them, Bernal Díaz del Castillo, later wrote: "To many of us it appeared doubtful whether we were asleep or awake . . . never yet did man see, hear, or dream of anything equal to our eyes this day." For the Spaniards, it was a vision of heaven.

Slightly more than a year and half later, in the early summer of 1521, it was a glimpse of hell. Again the Spaniards found themselves on the lakeshore, looking toward the great capital. But this time they had just been driven back from the city by the Aztec army. Sixty-two of their companions had been captured, and Cortés and the other survivors helplessly watched a pageant being enacted a mile away across the water on one of the major temple-pyramids of the city. As Bernal Díaz later described it,

The dismal drum of Huichilobos sounded again, accompanied by conches, horns, and trumpetlike instruments. It was a terrifying sound, and when we looked at the tall *cue* [temple-pyramid] from which it came we saw our comrades who had been captured in Cortés' defeat being dragged up the steps to be sacrificed. When they had hauled them up to a small platform in front of the shrine where they kept their accursed idols we saw them put plumes on the heads of many of them; and then they made them dance with a sort of fan in front of Huichilobos. Then after they had danced the *papas* [Aztec priests] laid them down on their backs on some narrow stones of sacrifice and, cutting open their chests, drew out their palpitating hearts which they offered to the idols before them.

Cortés and his men were the only Europeans to see the human sacrifices of the Aztecs, for the practice ended shortly after the successful Spanish conquest of the Aztec empire. But the extremity of Aztec sacrifice has long persisted in puzzling scholars. No human society known to history

A temple-pyramid at the Maya site of Tikal, Guatemala. The steep steps of Mesoamerican pyramids may have facilitated tumbling down the bodies of victims after sacrifice.

52.

approached that of the Aztecs in the qualities of people offered as religious sacrifices: 20,000 a year is a common estimate.

A typical anthropological explanation is that the religion of the Aztecs required human sacrifices; that their gods demanded these extravagant, frequent offerings. This explanation fails to suggest why that particular form of religion should have evolved when and where it did. I suggest that the Aztec sacrifices, and the cultural patterns surrounding them, were a natural result of distinctive ecological circumstances.

Some of the Aztecs' ecological circumstances were common to ancient civilizations in general. Recent theoretical work in anthropology indicates that the rise of early civilizations was a consequence of the pressures that growing populations brought to bear on natural resources. As human populations slowly multiplied, even before the development of plant and animal domestication, they gradually reduced the wild flora and fauna available for food and disrupted the ecological equilibriums of their environments. The earliest strong evidence of humans causing environmental damage was the extinction of many big game species in Europe by about 10,000 B.C., and in America north of Mexico by about 9,000 B.C. Simultaneously, human populations in broad regions of the Old and New Worlds had to shift increasingly to marine food resources and small-game hunting. Finally, declining quantities of wild game and food plants made domestication of plants and animals essential in most regions of the planet.

Two sixteenth-century drawings from the Florentine Codex *of Bernardino de Sahagun. On the preceding page, the victim's heart is offered to the sun. At right, priests sacrifice a youth who had been chosen to personify the Aztec deity Tezcatlipoca for a year. Accompanied by a retinue, the future victim often strolled as a god on earth, playing one of his clay flutes. When he finally ascended to the temple-pyramid platform, he broke his flutes, one by one, on the steps. The vast majority of victims did not enjoy such presacrificial status.*

In the Old World, domestication of herbivorous mammals, such as cattle, sheep, and pigs, proceeded apace with that of food plants. By about 7,200 B.C. in the New World, however, ancient hunters had completely eliminated herbivores suitable for domestication from the area anthropologists call Mesoamerica, the region of the future high civilizations of Mexico and Guatemala. Only in the Andean region and southern South America did some camel-related species, especially the llama and the alpaca, manage to survive hunters' onslaughts, and thus could be domesticated later, along with another important local herbivore, the guinea pig. In Mesoamerica, the guinea pig was not available, and the Camelidae species became extinct several thousand years before domesticated food production had to be seriously undertaken. Dogs, such as the Mexican hairless, and wildfowl, such as the turkey, had to be bred for protein. The dog, however, was a far from satisfactory solution because, as a

carnivore, it competed with its breeders for animal protein.

The need for intensified domesticated food production was felt early, as anthropologist Robert Carneiro has pointed out, by growing populations in fertile localities circumscribed by terrain poorly suited to farming. In such cases, plants always became domesticated, climate and environment permitting, but herbivorous mammals apparently could not, unless appropriate species existed. In Mesoamerica, the Valley of Mexico, with its fertile and well-watered bottomlands surrounded by mountains, fits well Carneiro's environmental model. In this confined area, population was increasing up to the time of the Spanish conquest, and the supply of wild game was declining. Deer were nearly gone from the Valley by the Aztec period.

The Aztecs responded to their increasing problems of food supply by intensifying agricultural production with a variety of ingenious techniques, including the reclamation of

17.

soil from marsh and lake bottoms in the chinampa, or floating garden, method. Unfortunately, their ingenuity could not correct their lack of a suitable domesticable herbivore that could provide animal protein and fats. Hence, the ecological situation of the Aztecs and their Mesoamerican neighbors was unique among the world's major civilizations. I have recently proposed the theory that large-scale cannibalism, disguised as sacrifice, was the natural consequence of these ecological circumstances.

The contrast between Mesoamerica and the Andes, in terms of the existence of domesticated herbivores, was also reflected in the numbers of human victims sacrificed in the two areas. In the huge Andean Inca empire, the other major political entity in the New World at the time of the conquest, annual human sacrifices apparently amounted to a few hundred at most. Among the Aztecs, the numbers were incomparably greater. The commonly mentioned figure of 20,000, however, is unreliable. For example, one sixteenth-century account states that 20,000 were sacrificed yearly in the capital city alone, another reports this as 20,000 infants, and a third claims the same number as being slaughtered throughout the Aztec empire on a single particular day. The most famous specific sacrifice took place in 1487 at the dedication of the main pyramid in Tenochtitlán. Here, too, figures vary: one source states 20,000, another 72,344, and several give 80,400.

In 1946 Sherburne Cook, a demographer specializing in American Indian populations, estimated an overall annual mean of 15,000 victims in a central Mexican population reckoned at two million. Later, however, he and his colleague Woodrow Borah revised his estimate of the total central Mexican population upward to 25 million. Recently, Borah, possibly the leading authority on the demography of Mexico at the time of the conquest, has also revised the estimated number of persons sacrificed in central Mexico in the fifteenth century to 250,000 per year, equivalent to one percent of the total population. According to Borah, this figure is consistent with the sacrifice of an esti-

mated 1,000 to 3,000 persons yearly at the largest of the thousands of temples scattered throughout the Aztec Triple Alliance. The numbers, of course, were fewer at the lesser temples, and may have shaded down to zero at the smallest.

These enormous numbers call for consideration of what the Aztecs did with the bodies after the sacrifices. Evidence of Aztec cannibalism has been largely ignored or consciously or unconsciously covered up. For example, the major twentieth-century books on the Aztecs barely mention it; others bypass the subject completely. Probably some modern Mexicans and anthropologists have been embarrassed by the topic: the former partly for nationalistic reasons; the latter partly out of a desire to portray native peoples in the best possible light. Ironically, both these attitudes may represent European ethnocentrism regarding cannibalism—a viewpoint to be expected from a culture that has had relatively abundant livestock for meat and milk.

A search of the sixteenth-century literature, however, leaves no doubt as to the prevalence of cannibalism among the central Mexicans. The Spanish conquistadores wrote amply about it, as did several Spanish priests who engaged in ethnological research on Aztec culture shortly after the conquest. Among the latter, Bernardino de Sahagún is of particular interest because his informants were former Aztec nobles, who supplied dictated or written information in the Aztec language, Nahuatl.

According to these early accounts, some sacrificial victims were not eaten, such as children offered by drowning to the rain god, Tlaloc, or persons suffering skin diseases. But the overwhelming majority of the sacrificed captives apparently were consumed. A principal—and sometimes only—objective of Aztec war expeditions was to capture prisoners for sacrifice. While some might be sacrificed and eaten on the field of battle, most were taken to home communities or to the capital, where they were kept in wooden cages to be fattened until sacrificed by the priests at the temple-pyramids. Most of the sacrifices involved tearing out the

heart, offering it to the sun and, with some blood, also to the idols. The corpse was then tumbled down the steps of the pyramid and carried off to be butchered. The head went on the local skull rack, displayed in central plazas alongside the temple-pyramids. At least three of the limbs were the property of the captor if he had seized the prisoner without assistance in battle. Later, at a feast given at the captor's quarters, the central dish was a stew of tomatoes, peppers, and the limbs of his victim. The remaining torso, in Tenochtitlán at least, went to the royal zoo where it was used to feed carnivorous mammals, birds, and snakes.

Recent archeological research lends support to conquistadores' and informants' vivid and detailed accounts of Aztec cannibalism. Mexican archeologists excavating at an Aztec sacrificial site in the Tlatelolco section of Mexico City between 1960 and 1969 uncovered headless human rib cages completely lacking the limb bones. Associated with these remains were some razorlike obsidian blades, which the archeologists believe were used in the butchering. Nearby they also discovered piles of human skulls, which apparently had been broken open to obtain the brains, possibly a choice delicacy reserved for the priesthood, and to mount the skulls on a ceremonial rack.

Through cannibalism, the Aztecs appear to have been attempting to reduce very particular nutritional deficiencies. Under the conditions of high population pressure and class stratification that characterized the Aztec state, commoners or lower-class persons rarely had the opportunity to eat any game, even the domesticated turkey, except on great occasions. They often had to content themselves with such creatures as worms and snakes and an edible lake-surface scum called "stone dung," which may have been algae fostered by pollution from Tenochtitlán. Preliminary research seems to indicate that although fish and waterfowl were taken from the lakes, most of the Aztec poor did not have significant access to this protein source and were forced to be near-vegetarians, subsisting mainly on domesticated plant

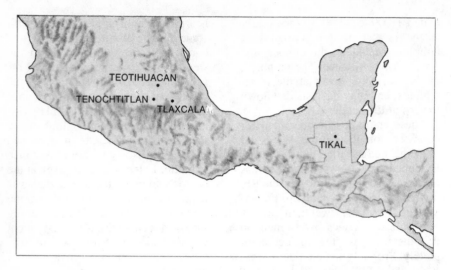

foods such as maize and beans.

The commoners theoretically could get the eight essential amino acids necessary for building body tissues from maize and beans. (A combination of the two foods complement each other in their essential amino acid components.) However, recent nutritional research indicates that in order to assure that their bodies would use the eight essential amino acids to rebuild body tissues, and not simply siphon off the dietary protein as energy, the Aztec commoners would have had to consume large quantities of maize and beans simultaneously or nearly simultaneously year-round. But crop failures and famines were common. According to Durán, a sixteenth-century chronicler, poor people often could not obtain maize and beans in the same season, and hence could not rely upon these plants as a source of the essential amino acids. How did the Aztecs know they needed the essential amino acids? Like other organisms perfected under natural selection, the human body is a homeostatic system that, under conditions of nutritional stress, tends to seek out the dietary elements in which it is deficient. Without this innate capacity, living organisms could not survive.

Another Aztec dietary problem was the paucity of fats, which were so scarce in central Mexico that the Spaniards resorted to boiling down the bodies of Indians killed in battle in order to obtain fat for dressing wounds and tallow for caulking boats. While the exact amount of fatty acids required by the human body remains a subject of uncertainty among nutritionists, they agree that fats, due to their slower rate of metabolism, provide a longer-lasting energy source than carbohydrates. Fatty meat, by providing not only fat, which the body will use as energy, but also essential proteins, assures the utilization of the essential amino acids for tissue building. Interestingly, prisoners confined by the Aztecs in wooden cages prior to sacrifice could be fed purely on carbohydrates to build up fat.

In contrast to the commoners, the Aztec elite normally had a diet enriched by wild game imported from the far reaches of the empire where species had not been so depleted. But even nobles could suffer from famines and sometimes had to sell their children into slavery in order to survive. Not surprisingly, the Aztec elite apparently reserved for themselves the right to eat human flesh, and conveniently, times of famine meant that the gods demanded appeasement through many human sacrifices.

At first glance, this prohibition against commoners eating human flesh casts doubt on cannibalism's potential to mobilize the masses of Aztec society to engage in wars for prisoners. Actually, the prohibition was, if anything, a goad to the lower class to participate in these wars since those who single-handedly took captives several times gained the right to eat human flesh. Successful warriors became members of the Aztec elite and their descendants shared their privileges. Through the reward of flesh-eating rights to the group most in need of them, the Aztec rulers assured themselves an aggressive war machine and were able to motivate the bulk of the population, the poor, to contribute to state and upper-class maintenance through active participation in offensive military operations. Underlying the war machine's victories, and the resultant sacrifices, were the ecological extremities of the Valley of Mexico.

With an understanding of the importance of cannibalism in Aztec culture, and of the ecological reasons for its existence, some of the Aztecs' more distinctive institutions begin to make anthropological sense. For example, the old question of whether the Aztecs' political structure was or was not an "empire" can be reexamined. One part of this problem is that the Aztecs frequently withdrew from conquered territory without establishing administrative centers or garrisons. This "failure" to consolidate conquest in the Old World fashion puzzled Cortés, who asked Moctezuma to explain why he allowed the surrounded Tlaxcalans to maintain their independence. Moctezuma reportedly replied that his people could thus obtain captives for sacrifice. Since the Aztecs did not normally eat people of their own polity, which would have been socially and politically disruptive, they needed nearby "enemy" populations on whom they could prey for captives. This behavior makes sense in terms of Aztec cannibalism: from the Aztec point of view, the Tlaxcalan state was preserved as a stockyard. The Aztecs were unique among the world's states in having a cannibal empire. Understandably, they did not conform to Old World concepts of empire, based on economies with domesticated herbivores providing meat or milk.

The ecological situation of the Aztecs was probably an extreme case of problems general to the high population pressure societies of Mesoamerica. Cannibalism encouraged the definition of the gods as eaters of human flesh and led almost inevitably to emphasis on fierce, ravenous, and carnivorous deities, such as the jaguar and the serpent, which are characteristic of Mesoamerican pantheons. Pre-Columbian populations could, in turn, rationalize the more grisly aspects of large-scale cannibalism as consequences of the gods' demands. Mesoamerican cannibalism, disguised as propitiation of the gods, bequeathed to the world some of its most distinctive art and architecture. The temple-pyramids of the Maya and the Toltecs, and of the pre-Aztec site at Teotihuacán in the valley of Mexico, resemble those of the Aztecs in appearance and probably had similar uses. Even small touches, such as the steepness of the steps on pyramids in Aztec and other Mesoamerican ruins, become understandable given the need for efficiently tumbling the bodies from the sacrificial altars to the multitudes below. Perhaps those prehistoric scenes were not too dissimilar from that which Bernal Díaz described when his companions were sacrificed before his eyes in Tenochtitlán:

Then they kicked the bodies down the steps, and the Indian butchers who were waiting below cut off their arms and legs and flayed their faces, which they afterwards prepared like glove leather, with their beards on, and kept for their drunken festivals. Then they ate their flesh with a sauce of peppers and tomatoes.

Gruesome as these practices may seem, an ecological perspective and population pressure theory render the Aztec emphasis on human sacrifice understandable as a natural and rational response to the material conditions of their existence. In *Tristes Tropiques,* the French anthropologist Claude Levi-Strauss described the Aztecs as suffering from "a maniacal obsession with blood and torture." A materialist ecological approach reveals the Aztecs to be neither irrational nor mentally ill, but merely human beings who, faced with unusual survival problems, responded with unusual behavior.

Plight of the Ik and Kaiadilt Is Seen as a Chilling Possible End for Man

BY JOHN B. CALHOUN

The Mountain—how pervasive in the history of man. A still small voice on Horeb, mount of God, guided Elijah. There, earlier, Moses standing before God received the Word. And Zion: "I am the Lord your God dwelling in Zion, my holy mountain."

Then there was Atum, mountain, God and first man, one and all together. The mountain rose out of a primordial sea of nothingness—Nun. Atum, the spirit of life, existed within Nun. In creating himself, Atum became the evolving ancestor of the human race. So goes the Egyptian mythology of creation, in which the Judaic Adam has his roots.

And there is a last Atum, united in his youth with another mountain of God, Mt. Morungole in northeasternmost Uganda. His people are the Ik, pronounced eek. They are the subject of an important new book, *The Mountain People,* by Colin M. Turnbull (Simon and Schuster, $6.95). They still speak Middle-Kingdom Egyptian, a language thought to be dead. But perhaps their persistence is not so strange. Egyptian mythology held that the waters of the life-giving Nile had their origin in Nun. Could this Nun have been the much more extensive Lake Victoria of 40 to 50 millennia ago when, near its borders, man groped upward to cloak his biological self with culture?

Well might the Ik have preserved the essence of this ancient tradition that affirms human beginnings. Isolated as they have been in their jagged mountain fastness, near the upper tributaries of the White Nile, the Ik have been protected from cultural evolution.

What a Shangri-la, this land of the Ik. In its center, the Kidepo valley, 35 miles across, home of abundant game; to the south, mist-topped Mt. Morungole; to the west the Niangea range; to the north, bordering the Sudan, the Didinga range; to the east on the Kenya border, a sheer drop of 2,000 feet into the Turkanaland of cattle herdsmen. Through ages of dawning history few people must have been interested in encroaching on this rugged land. Until 1964 anthropologists knew little of the Ik's existence. Their very name, much less their language, remained a mystery until, quite by chance, anthropologist Colin M. Turnbull found himself among them. What an opportunity to study pristine man! Here one should encounter the basic qualities of humanity unmarred by war, technology, pollution, over-population.

Turnbull rested in his bright red Land Rover at an 8,000-foot-high pass. A bit beyond this only "navigable" pass into the Kidepo Valley, lay Pirre, a police outpost watching over a cluster of Ik villages. There to welcome him came Atum of the warm, open smile and gentle voice. Gray-haired at 40, appearing 65, he was the senior elder of the Ik, senior in authority if not quite so in age. Nattily attired in shorts and woolen sweater—in contrast to his mostly naked colleagues—Atum bounced forward with his ebony walking stick, greeted Turnbull in Swahili, and from that moment on took command as best he could of Turnbull's life. At Atum's village a plaintive woman's voice called out. Atum remarked that that was his wife—sick, too weak to work in the fields. Turnbull offered to bring her food and medicine. Atum suggested he handle Turnbull's gifts. As the weeks wore on Atum picked up the parcels that Turnbull was supplying for Atum's wife.

One day Atum's brother-in-law, Lomongin, laughingly asked Turnbull if he didn't know that Atum's wife had been dead for weeks. She had received no food or medicine. Atum had sold it. So she just died. All of this was revealed with no embarrassment. Atum joined the laughter over the joke played on Turnbull.

Another time Atum and Lojieri were guiding Turnbull over the mountains, and at one point induced him to push ahead through high grass until he broke through into a clearing. The clearing was a sheer 1,500-foot drop. The two Iks rolled on the ground, nearly bursting with laughter because Turnbull just managed to catch himself. What a lovable cherub this Atum! His laughter never ended.

New meaning of laughter

Laughter, hallmark of mankind, not shared with any other animal, not even primates, was an outstanding trait of the Ik. A whole village rushed to the edge of a low cliff and joined in communal laughter at blind old Lo'ono who lay thrashing on her back, near death after stumbling over. One evening Iks around a fire watched a child as it crawled toward the flames, then writhed back screaming after it grasped a gleaming coal. Laughter erupted. Quiet came to the child as its mother cuddled it in a kind of respect for the merriment it had caused. Then there was the laughter of innocent childhood as boys and girls gathered around a grandfather, too weak to walk, and drummed upon his head with sticks or pelted him with stones until he cried. There was the laughter that binds families together: Kimat, shrieking for joy as she dashed off with the mug of tea she had snatched from her dying brother Lomeja's hand an instant after Turnbull had given it to him as a last token of their friendship.

Laughter there had always been. A few old people remembered times, 25 to 30 years ago, when laughter mirrored love and joy and fullness of life, times when beliefs and rituals and traditions kept a bond with the "millions of years" ago when time began for the Ik. That was when their god, Didigwari, let the Ik down from heaven on a vine, one at a time. He gave them the digging stick with the instruction that they could not kill one another. He let down other people. To the Dodos and Turkana he gave cattle and spears to kill with. But the Ik remained true to their instruction and did not kill one another or neighboring tribesmen.

For them the bow, the net and the pitfall were for capturing game. For them the greatest sin was to overhunt. Mobility and cooperation ever were part of them. Often the netting of game required the collaboration of a whole band of 100 or more, some to hold the net and some to drive game into it. Between the big hunts, bands broke up into smaller groups to spread over their domain, then to gather again. The several bands would each settle for the best part of the year along the edge of the Kidepo Valley in the foothills of Mt. Morungole. There they were once again fully one with the mountain. "The Ik, without their mountains, would no longer be the Ik and similarly, they say, the mountains without the Ik would no longer be the same mountains, if indeed they continued to exist at all."

In this unity of people and place, rituals, traditions, beliefs and values molded and preserved a continuity of life. All rites of passage were marked by ceremony. Of these, the rituals surrounding death gave greatest meaning to life. Folded in a fetal position, the body was buried with favorite possessions, facing the rising sun to mark celestial rebirth. All accompanying rituals of fasting and feasting, of libations of beer sprinkled over the grave, of seeds of favorite foods planted on the grave to draw life from the dust of the dead, showed that death is merely another form of life, and reminded the living of the good things of life and of the good way to live. In so honoring the dead by creating goodness the Ik helped speed the soul, content, on its journey.

Such were the Ik until wildlife conservation intruded into their homeland. Uganda decided to make a national park out of the Kidepo Valley, the main hunting ground of the Ik. What then happened stands as an indictment of the myopia that science can generate. No one looked to the Ik to note that their hunter-gatherer way of life marked the epitome of conservation, that the continuance of their way of life would have added to the success of the park. Instead they were forbidden to hunt any longer in the Kidepo Valley. They were herded to the periphery of the park and encouraged to become farmers on dry mountain slopes so steep as to test the poise of a goat. As an example to the more remote villages, a number of villages were brought together in a tight little cluster below the southwest pass into the valley. Here the police post, which formed this settlement of Pirre, could watch over the Ik to see that they didn't revert to hunting.

These events contained two of the three strikes that knocked out the spirit of the Ik. *Strike No. 1:* The shift from a mobile hunter-gatherer way of life to a sedentary farming way of life made irrelevant the Ik's entire repertoire of beliefs, habits and traditions. Their guidelines for life were inappropriate to farming. They seemed to adapt, but at heart they remained hunters and gatherers. Their cultural templates fitted them for that one way of life.

Strike No. 2: They were suddenly crowded together at a density, intimacy and frequency of contact far greater than they had ever before been required to experience. Throughout their long past each band of 100 or so individuals only temporarily coalesced into a whole. The intervening breaking up into smaller groups permitted realignment of relationships that tempered conflicts from earlier associations. But at the resettlement, more than 450 individuals were forced to form a permanent cluster of villages within shouting distance of each other. Suppose the seven million or so inhabitants of Los Angeles County were forced to move and join the more than one million inhabitants of the more arid San Diego County. Then after they arrived all water, land and air communication to the rest of the world was cut off abruptly and completely. These eight million people would then have to seek survival completely on local resources without any communication with others. It would be a test of the ability of human beings to remain human.

Such a test is what Dr. Turnbull's book on the Mountain People is all about. The Ik failed to remain human. I have put mice to the same test and they failed to remain mice. Those of you who have been following SMITHSONIAN may recall from the April 1970 and the January 1971 issues something about the projected demise of a mouse population experiencing the same two strikes against it as did the Ik.

Fate of a mouse population

Last summer I spoke in London behind the lectern where Charles Darwin and Alfred Wallace had presented their papers on evolution—which during the next century caused a complete revision of our insight into what life is all about and what man is and may become. In summing up that session of 1858 the president remarked that nothing of importance had been presented before the Linnean Society at that year's meeting! I spoke behind this same lectern to a session of the Royal Society of Medicine during its symposium on "Man in His Place." At the end of my paper, "Death Squared: The Explosive Growth and Demise of a Mouse Population," the chairman admonished me to stick to my mice; the insights I had presented could have no implication for man. Wonderful if the chairman could be correct—but now I have read about the Mountain People, and I have a hollow feeling that perhaps we, too, are close to losing our "mountain."

Turnbull lived for 18 months as a member of the Ik tribe. His identity transfer became so strong that he acquired the Ik laughter. He laughed at seeing Atum suffer as they were completing an extremely arduous journey on foot back across the mountains and the Kidepo Valley from the Sudan. He felt pleasure at seeing Lokwam, local "Lord of the Flies," cry in agony from the beating given him by his two beautiful sisters.

Well, for five years I have identified with my mice, as they lived in their own "Kidepo Valley"—their contrived Utopia where resources are always abundant and all mortality factors except aging eliminated. I watched their population grow rapidly from the first few colonizers. I watched them fill their metal "universe" with organized social groups. I watched them bring up a host of young with loving maternal care and paternal territorial protection—all of these young well educated for mouse society. But then there were too many of these young mice, ready to become in-

Unwanted by Ik society, an old man, who remembered times of human caring, lies among the rocks of the mountain, quietly awaiting a lonely death.

volved in all that mice can become, with nowhere to go, no physical escape from their closed environment, no opportunity to gain a niche where they could play a meaningful role. They tried, but being younger and less experienced they were nearly always rejected.

Rejecting so many of these probing youngsters overtaxed the territorial males. So defense then fell to lactating females. They became aggressive. They turned against their own young and ejected them before normal weaning and before adequate social bonds between mother and young had developed. During this time of social tension, rate of growth of the population was only one third of that during the earlier, more favorable phase.

Strike No. 1 against these mice: They lost the opportunity to express the capacities developed by older mice born during the rapid population growth. After a while they became so rejected that they were treated as so many sticks and stones by their still relatively well-adjusted elders. These rejected mice withdrew, physically and psychologically, to live packed tightly together in large pools. Amongst themselves they became vicious, lashing out and biting each other now and then with hardly any provocation.

Strike No. 2 against the mice: They reached great numbers despite reduced conceptions and increased deaths of newborn young resulting from the dissolution of maternal care. Many had early been rejected by their mothers and knew little about social bonds.

*Rains temporarily turned the Ik's mountain green just before
Turnbull returned for a visit.*

Often their later attempts at interaction were interrupted by some other mouse intervening unintentionally as it passed between two potential actors.

I came to call such mice the "Beautiful Ones." They never learned such effective social interactions as courtship, mating and aggressive defense of territory. Never copulating, never fighting, they were unstressed and essentially unaware of their associates. They spent their time grooming themselves, eating and sleeping, totally individualistic, totally isolated socially except for a peculiar acquired need for simple proximity to others. This produced what I have called the "behavioral sink," the continual accentuation of aggregations to the point that much available space was unused despite a population increase to nearly 15 times the optimum.

All true "mousity" was lost. Though physically they still appeared to be mice, they had no essential capacities for survival and continuation of mouse society.

Suddenly, population growth ceased. In what seemed an instant they passed over a threshold beyond which there was no likelihood of their ever recouping the capacity to become real mice again. No more young were born. From a peak population of 2,200 mice nearly three years ago, aging has gradually taken its toll until now there are only 46 sluggish near-cadavers comparable to people more than 100 years old.

It was just such a fading universe Colin Turnbull found in 1964. Just before he arrived, *Strike No. 3* had set in: starvation. Any such crisis could have added the coup de grace after the other two strikes. Normally the Ik could count on only making three crops every four years. At this time a two-year drought set in and destroyed almost all crops. Neighboring tribes survived with their cultures intact. Turkana herdsmen, facing starvation and death, kept their societies in contact with each other and continued to sing songs of praise to God for the goodness of life.

By the beginning of the long drought, "goodness" to the Ik simply meant to have food—to have food for one's self alone. Collaborative hunts were a thing of the past, long since stopped by the police and probably no longer possible as a social effort, anyway. Solitary hunting, now designated as poaching, became a necessity for sheer survival. But the solitary hunter took every precaution not to let others know of his success. He would gorge himself far off in the bush and bring the surplus back to sell to the police, who were not above profiting from this traffic. Withholding food from wife, children and aging parents became an accomplishment to brag and laugh about. It became a way of life, continuing after the government began providing famine relief. Those strong enough to go to the police station to get rations for themselves and their families would stop halfway home and gorge all the food, even though it caused them to vomit.

Village of mutual hatred

The village reflected this reversal of humanity. Instead of open courtyards around each group of huts within the large compound, there was a maze of walls and tunnels booby trapped with spears to ward off intrusion by neighbors.

In Atum's village a whole band of more than 100 individuals was crowded together in mutual hostility and aloneness. They would gather at their sitting place and sit for hours in a kind of suspended animation, not looking directly at each other, yet scanning slowly all others who might be engaged in some solitary task, watching for someone to make a mistake that would elicit the symbolic violence of laughter and derision. They resembled my pools of rejected withdrawn mice. Homemaking deteriorated, feces littered doorsteps and courtyard. Universal adultery and incest replaced the old taboo. The beaded virgins' aprons of eight-to-twelve-year-old girls became symbols that these were proficient whores accustomed to selling their wares to passing herdsmen.

One ray of humanity left in this cesspool was 12-year-old, retarded Adupa. Because she believed that food was for sharing and savoring, her playmates beat her. She still believed that parents were for loving and to be loved by. They cured her madness by locking her in her hut until she died and decayed.

The six other villages were smaller and their people could retain a few glimmers of the goodness and fullness of life. There was Kuaur, devoted to Turnbull, hiking four days to deliver mail, taunted for bringing food home to share with his wife and child. There was Losiké, the potter, regarded as a witch. She offered water to visitors and made pots for others. When the famine got so bad that there was no need for pots to cook in, her husband left her. She was no longer bringing in any income. And then there was old Nangoli, still capable of mourning when her husband died. She went with her family and village across Kidepo and into the Sudan where their village life turned for a while back to normality. But it was not normal enough to keep them. Back to Pirre, to death, they returned.

All goodness was gone from the Ik, leaving merely emptiness, valuelessness, nothingness, the chaos of Nun. They reentered the womb of beginning time from which there is no return. Urination beside the partial graves of the dead marked the death of God, the final fading of Mount Morungole.

My poor words give only a shadowy image of the cold coffin of Ik humanity that Turnbull describes. His two years with the Ik left him in a slough of despondency from which he only extricated himself with difficulty, never wanting to see them again. Time and distance brought him comfort. He did return for a brief visit some months later. Rain had come in abundance. Gardens had sprung up untended from hidden seeds in the earth. Each Ik gleaned only for his immediate needs. Granaries stood empty, not refilled for inevitable scarcities ahead. The future had ceased to exist. Individual and social decay continued on its downward spiral. Sadly Turnbull departed again from this land of lost hope and faith.

Last summer in London I knew nothing about the Ik when I was so publicly and thoroughly chastised for having the temerity to suspect that the behavioral and spiritual death my mice had exhibited might also befall man. But a psychiatrist in the audience arose in defense of my suspicion. Dr. Geoffrey N. Bianchi remarked that an isolated tribe of Australian Aborigines mirrored the changes and kinds of pathology I had seen among mice. I did not know that Dr. Bianchi was a member of the team that had studied these people, the Kaiadilt, and that a book about them was in preparation, Cruel, Poor and Brutal Nations by John Cawte (The University Press of Hawaii). In galley proof I have read about the Kaiadilt and find it so shattering to my faith in humanity that I now sometimes wish I had never heard of it. Yet there is some glimmer of hope that the Kaiadilt may recover—not what they were but possibly some new life.

A frail, tenacious people, the Kaiadilt never numbered more than 150 souls where they lived on Bentinck Island in the Gulf of Carpentaria. So isolated were they that not even their nearest Aboriginal neighbors, 20 miles away, had any knowledge of their existence until in this century; so isolated were the Kaiadilt from their nearest neighbors that they differ from them in such heredity markers as blood type and fingerprints. Not until the early years of this century did an occasional visitor from the Queensland Government even note their existence.

For all practical purposes the first real contact the Kaiadilt had with Western "culture" came in 1916 when a man by the name of McKenzie came to Bentinck with a group of male mainland Aborigines to try to establish a lime kiln. McKenzie's favorite sport was to ride about shooting Kaiadilt. His helpers' sport was to commandeer as many women as they could, and take them to their headquarters on a neighboring island. In 1948 a tidal wave poisoned most of the freshwater sources. Small groups of Kaiadilt were rounded up and transported to larger Mornington Island where they were placed under the supervision of a Presbyterian mission. They were crowded into a dense cluster settlement just as the Ik had been at Pirre.

Here they still existed when the psychiatric field team came into their midst 15 years later. They were much like the Ik: dissolution of family life, total valuelessness, apathy. I could find no mention of laughter, normal or pathological. Perhaps the Kaiadilt didn't laugh. They had essentially ceased the singing that had been so much a part of their traditional way.

The spiritual decay of the Kaiadilt was marked by withdrawal, depression, suicide and tendency to engage in such self-mutilation as ripping out one's testes or chopping off one's nose. In their passiveness some of the anxiety ridden children are accepting the new mold of life forced upon them by a benevolent culture they do not understand. Survival with a new mold totally obliterating all past seems their only hope.

So the lesson comes clear, and Colin Turnbull sums it up in the final paragraph of his book: "The Ik teach us that our much vaunted human values are not inherent in humanity at all, but are associated only with a particular form of survival called society, and that all, even society itself, are luxuries that can be dispensed with. That does not make them any the less wonderful or desirable, and if man has any greatness it is surely in his ability to maintain these values, clinging to them to an often very bitter end, even shortening an already pitifully short life rather than sacrifice his humanity. But that too involves choice, and the Ik teach us that man can lose the will to make it."

Personality and Sex Roles

· ·

In the first part of this century, social events (including the Russian revolution and the rise of socialism) and academic schools of thought (such as behaviorism in psychology) underlined the view that human beings are extraordinarily malleable and that social, historical, and cultural factors are preeminent over biological causes in shaping human behavior. Thus, the noted anthropologist Franz Boas and his students led the intellectual movement that, among other things, attacked the viability of the concept of "race" and took an activist stance in combatting racism.

In this context, the subject of differences between the human sexes became critical. One feature of the organization of social life that is present in all known societies is the cultural attribution of significance to differences between males and females. Notions of "maleness" and "femaleness" vary enormously across cultures, but the distinction between the sexes is made universally, and sex-role attributions and expectations are important organizers of social existence everywhere. Do innate biological differences between the sexes account for these distinctions?

In the early 1930s, Margaret Mead studied and lived with three societies in New Guinea. As she reported in her book *Sex and Temperament*, she found that in these societies the attribution of qualities of character to the two sexes differed remarkably—both among those societies and in contrast to ours. In her book, which quickly achieved notoriety, Mead argued for the point of view that human nature is "not rigid and unyielding" and that "cultural rhythms are stronger and more compelling than the physiological rhythms which they overlay and distort."

The public was more enthusiastic over *Sex and Temperament* than were anthropologists, who noted that her research was limited to a matter of months, that she relied on data provided by only one or two informants, that data and hypotheses were poorly separated, and that a subjective bias in the interpretation of the data was all too evident. Even Mead's hus-

band Reo Fortune, who had collaborated with her in this research, rejected her view that the Arapesh did not distinguish between male and female temperaments.

With the reemergence of feminism in America during the late 1960s and 1970s, *Sex and Temperament* was enshrined as a "classic," and its obvious shortcomings were overlooked, because its contents could be used to validate feminist critiques of contemporary social life. Mead herself participated in the feminist movement, but at the same time she expressed unease about the overinterpretation of her New Guinea materials by the writers of feminist tracts.

An early book by Mead also had become a bestseller (and remains a classic today). In *Coming of Age in Samoa* (1928), Mead described Ta'u village in 1925 as a paradise, untouched by competition, sexual inhibition, or guilt. She rejected heredity as accounting for the "storm and stress" commonly associated with adolescence and described Samoa as a place where the passage to adulthood involved only a minimum of stress and pain. In 1983, five years after Mead's death, Australian anthropologist Derek Freeman published *Margaret Mead and Samoa: The Making and Unmaking of An Anthropological Myth*, in which he attacked both Mead's research and her motives. Freeman sees Samoans as sexually inhibited, aggressive, highly competitive, prone to jealousy, and subject to psychological disorders. Not only is it *more* difficult to come of age in Samoa than in the United States, Freeman argues, but Samoans are prone to such pathological behavior as assault, murder, suicide, and rape. How could two, presumably unbiased, researchers come up with such diametrically opposite views of the same society? In "South Seas Squall," Lowell D. Holmes reviews Mead's research and Freeman's criticisms, explores some of the important underlying issues, and arrives at a resolution of the conflict.

In "Society and Sex Roles," Ernestine Friedl asks this question: Why do men have power over women in most societies? Her study of societies at differing levels of complexity shows a broad range to such dominance—from the extreme dominance of the Inuit (Eskimo) men to the relative social equality of the Hadza men and women of Tanzania. Friedl finds a positive correlation between the degree to which men control the production of food and the sexual stratification of social life. She ends her article with some extrapolations to sex-role changes we might expect in modern industrial society.

Finally, in "Life Behind the Veil," Cherry and Charles Lindholm explore the secret world of Moslem women. Though it may appear to Westerners that Moslem women are the personification of powerlessness, in fact, the Lindholms report, they are viewed in traditional Islamic society as powerful and dangerous beings.

35

South Seas Squall

BY LOWELL D. HOLMES

. . . .

NEW SAMOA BOOK Challenges Margaret Mead's Conclusions" ran the front-page headline in *The New York Times* last January. "Two months before its official publication date," the article reported, "a book maintaining that the late Margaret Mead seriously misrepresented the culture and character of Samoa has ignited heated discussion within the behavioral sciences."

The book that stirred this advance notice and notoriety was *Margaret Mead and Samoa: The Making and Unmaking of An Anthropological Myth,* by Derek Freeman, an emeritus professor of anthropology at the Australian National University, in Canberra. It attacks the conclusions of Mead's first research project, which she began when she was only twenty-three, and which she documented in *Coming of Age in Samoa.* "The entire academic establishment and all the encyclopedias and all the textbooks accepted the conclusions in her book, and these conclusions are fundamentally in error," Freeman told the *Times* reporter. "There isn't another example of such wholesale deception in the history of the behavioral sciences."

The *Times* article had special meaning for me, because, in 1954, I lived in Ta'u, where Mead had worked twenty-nine years earlier, talked to many of her informants, and analyzed every word she had written about life in that Samoan village. In that year I was conducting what is known as a methodological restudy. I retraced Mead's steps with the express purpose of testing the reliability and validity of her investigation and establishing the kinds of errors of interpretation that she might have made. Margaret Mead was a woman in a male-dominated society; she was young in a culture that venerates age; she was on her first field trip at a time when research methods were crude; and she was a student of the influential anthropologist Franz Boas, and so went armed with a particular theoretical frame of reference. Not only was I to analyze how my findings differed from hers (if they did), I was also to speculate how our differences in age, status, personality, and outlook might have accounted for differences in our collecting and interpreting of data.

As of 1954, a number of anthropologists favored restudies as a way of understanding the anthropologist's role in fieldwork. But Mead thought restudies a wasteful use of limited research funds, though she had written that "there is no such thing as an unbiased report on any social situation," and at one point had even suggested that, in order to control personal bias, a fieldworker ought to be psychoanalyzed before going into the field.

On the day the *Times* story appeared, my phone began to ring. News people who had been directed to me by anthropologists familiar with my 1954 restudy wanted comment on the controversy. While many of these reporters had received advance copies of Freeman's book in the form of bound page proofs, I had not been among the privileged. So, although I had some idea of Freeman's viewpoint from correspondence I had had with him in 1966 and 1967, I was not ready to comment. A phone call to Harvard University Press, Freeman's publisher, brought a copy of the page proofs, which I read with considerable interest. Now I am ready to respond.

IN HIS BOOK, Freeman argues that Mead perpetrated a hoax comparable in scope to that of the Piltdown Man when, in 1928, she described Samoa as a paradise relatively untouched by competition, sexual inhibition, or guilt. Refusing to believe that adolescents inevitably experience emotional crises because of biological changes associated with puberty (the psychological theory that then held sway), Mead had set out to discover a society where passage to adulthood involves only a minimum of stress and strain. She described such a society in *Coming of Age in Samoa.*

In relating this "negative instance," as Freeman calls it, Mead established that nurture is more critical than nature, or heredity, in accounting for adolescent behavior. Freeman, who rejects the idea that humans are shaped primarily by culture and environment, and who believes that Boas and Mead have totally ignored the influence of genes and heredity, maintains that Mead's Samoan research has led anthropology, psychology, and education down the primrose path. He is out to rescue these disciplines, armed with the real truth about Samoa and Samoans.

In Freeman's view, Samoans are sexually inhibited (even

puritanical), aggressive and highly competitive, prone to jealousy, and subject to psychological disturbances because of the rigid authority system under which they live. Not only is it more difficult to come of age in Samoa than in the United States, but Samoans also exhibit an unnatural range of pathological behavior; they assault, rape, and commit suicide and murder. Freeman claims that he could not publish these findings during Mead's lifetime because, until recently, he did not have access to government statistics that, he says, show rates of criminal behavior in Samoa many times higher than those found in the United States.

But Freeman's characterizations of Samoan personality and culture, and of Mead's work, do not jibe with what I saw. Freeman implies that, while I found much of Mead's research invalid, I was so awed by her reputation and so firmly under the thumb of Melville Herskovits, one of my professors at Northwestern, that I was afraid to reveal my true findings. The truth is that I would have loved to play the "giant killer," as Freeman now is trying to do. (What graduate student wouldn't?) But I couldn't. I had found the village and the behavior of its inhabitants to be much as Mead had described. *Coming of Age in Samoa* was like a map that represented the territory so well that I met with few surprises when I arrived. As for Herskovits's influence, all he demanded was that my criticisms of Mead's work be made with "icy objectivity," and that I deal with major issues and not trivial details.

After exhaustively reviewing Mead's writings on Samoa, I did find that the culture was not quite as simple as she had claimed, nor was Ta'u village quite the paradise that she would have us believe. For instance, Mead took some literary license in her chapter "A Day in Samoa"; she crowded typical activities into a "typical" day, and thus sketched a more bustling, vibrant scene than I ever encountered in any single twenty-four-hour period. I also could not agree with Mead on the degree of sexual freedom supposedly enjoyed by her informants, but then I am sure that she had greater rapport with teenagers than I (and probably Freeman). In fact, I found it extremely difficult to investigate anything of a sexual nature. There was considerable family and even village pressure for young people to maintain at least the outward appearance of chaste behavior. Yet the number of illegitimate children in the village, and the fact that grounds for divorce frequently involved adultery, gave the impression that more was going on than met the eye.

I also saw Samoan culture as considerably more competitive than Mead did, though I never saw it as inflexible or aggressive as Freeman does. I sensed a great preoccupation with status, power, and prestige, and on more than one occasion I observed fierce verbal duels between talking chiefs trying to enhance their own prestige or that of their village. The best fisherman, housebuilder, dancer, or orator was often pointed out to me. But I also learned that one was respected more for modesty than conceit, that it was better to have someone else laud your abilities than to do it yourself. And in matters of the heart, it

seemed that Samoans often played for higher stakes than Mead had indicated. I sensed that there was a concept of romantic love—in folklore and in contemporary life—and there were even cases of unrequited love ending unhappily in suicide. These were rare, but they did exist.

I communicated my criticisms concerning life in Ta'u village to Mead, and she discussed them, in a chapter titled "Conclusion 1969," in a reissue of *Social Organization of Manua,* published by the Bishop Museum. We differed on a number of matters. But despite her tender age, her inexperience, and the great possibilities for error in a seminal scientific study, I found Mead's Samoan research remarkably reliable. The differences between our findings that could not be attributed to change were relatively minor and, in most cases, involved not discrepancies in data but differences in interpretation. In short, I confirmed Mead's conclusion that in 1925 it was undoubtedly easier to come of age in Samoa than in the United States.

T HE LINE BETWEEN the child's world and the adult's world is effectively erased in Ta'u village, making for a more tranquil passage through adolescence. Since each household has a number of adults, any of whom may discipline children and respond to their needs, both authority and affection are diffused, easing the intensity of individual parent-child relationships. And if tensions do arise, flexible patterns of residence permit young people to flee to households of kinsmen. (While Freeman maintains that this does not happen in Samoa, I know of several such cases in Ta'u village; one informant revealed that when he was growing up he moved from house to house to avoid onerous work assignments.)

In Samoan homes, children are exposed to the facts of life—to sex, death, childbirth, and family leadership responsibilities—before they assume these responsibilities themselves. Coming of age is thus not a jolting experience; whenever the child is physically and mentally able, he simply assumes family chores and responsibilities. A child may begin caring for siblings as early as five or six years of age, and many adolescents take on plantation work, fishing chores, or household tasks long before such weighty responsibilities would be thrust upon an American child. While some observers have emphasized the oppressive work load forced upon teenagers, in this relatively bountiful environment no one puts in a forty-hour week or is required to work beyond his or her capacity.

Provided they stay out of serious trouble, teenage and young adult males are given a great deal of personal freedom. Members of *Aumaga* (a society of untitled men), some of whom are teenagers, often sleep together in the home of one of the village families, and frequently sit up until wee hours strumming guitars, joking, and playing cards. If these young people are repressed, they are also adept at hiding it. Young women are perhaps more restricted and given more household responsibility than men. But even they seem relaxed in family interactions.

By adolescence, Samoans have learned to regulate their

own personal conduct, and there is practically no testing of the limits of sanctioned behavior. While young children are punished for misbehaving—mostly for making noise or standing up in the house when chiefs are seated—no Samoan child was ever forced to finish dinner, go to bed at a particular time, or stop fighting with siblings. Nor have I ever seen an adolescent struck by a parent, or even severely lectured for misbehavior. And when limits are violated, punishment is expected, not resented.

Indeed, Samoans seemed to go to extremes to avoid conflict and to arrive at compromises. Village council decisions always had to be unanimous, and council meetings often dragged on for days while the assembled chiefs made minor concessions until everyone was satisfied with the collective decision. Breaches of acceptable conduct or the moral code often involved elaborate ceremonies of apology, called *ifoga,* during which persons, families, or even entire villages publicly humbled themselves, sitting cross-legged with mats over their bowed heads, until forgiven by the offended party. Even murder and manslaughter were handled this way if government authorities permitted it.

All in all, life in Samoa was simpler and encumbered by fewer decision-making dilemmas than in the United States. In 1954 (and certainly in 1925), there were fewer career choices, fewer alternative lifestyles, and fewer conflicting moral and ethical codes to choose from. In Mead's Samoa, young people grew up knowing that they would spend their lifetimes as farmers or farmers' wives; most men knew that if they worked hard for their family and their village they would someday acquire a chief's title and responsibility for a household unit. In Ta'u, there was but one sanctioned denomination—the London Missionary Society—and church membership and attendance were compulsory.

I observed all of these things in Ta'u village as late as 1954. Undoubtedly they were true during the years of Mead's investigation, for it was only in 1963 that television, increasing commercialization, and industrialization began to change the lives of young Samoans, exposing them to a much broader world. Then, rather abruptly, teenagers were faced with new choices: whether to farm family land or seek a salaried job in government or industry; whether to stay in Samoa or migrate to Hawaii or California, there to further an education and seek a fortune. But until that point in history, Samoan adolescents did indeed have an easier time coming of age than Americans did, just as Mead had reported.

MEAD'S WORK and my restudy may now be out of date, but Freeman's description of Samoan behavior does not run such a risk; he completely disregards time, change, and locality. In criticizing Mead's data gathered in Ta'u village in 1925 and 1926, he indiscriminately draws upon his own observations in Sa'anapu village, in Western Samoa, collected in the early 1940s, in 1966 and 1967, and in 1981, thus ignoring not only historical changes in this village, but also the fact that Sa'anapu was quite distinct from Ta'u. While in 1967 there were a handful of government jobs on the tiny island of Ta'u, there was almost nothing in the way of cash cropping. Since the island had no dock and was served by inter-island vessels that only appeared once a month, the people remained relatively isolated from outside influences. Sa'anapu, on the other hand, not only had a money economy, with income from copra, banana, and cocoa crops, but was also within a few hours' bus-ride of the town of Apia, with its movie theaters, department stores, nightclubs, bookstores, banks, public library, and government offices.

While Freeman is correct that Samoans share a common culture throughout the archipelago, they don't behave exactly the same everywhere, as he implies. There is a great deal more criminal and deviant behavior in urban centers, such as Apia or Pago Pago, than in the smaller, more isolated communities in remote parts of Savai'i or the Manu'a Islands. In metropolitan areas, family heads and village councils of chiefs no longer hold control, and young men who migrate from outer villages to these areas, seeking work or excitement, often become intoxicated with their new-found freedom and behave in very nontraditional ways. The court and police records that Freeman makes so much of are excellent evidence of the social disorganization now poisoning urban areas, though I fail to see how statistics relating to rape, assault, and murder have anything to do with the nature of normal Samoan culture. One would not study American national character or typical behavior in a state prison.

Freeman should have compared Ta'u with Ta'u. When I visited there in 1954, I found little of the deviant behavior he describes, and I can only assume that it was even rarer in 1925. William Green, the principal of the government school in American Samoa, in 1924, observed, "There has been no murder case in American Samoa since our flag was raised in 1900. Natives will suffer indignities for a long time before resorting to a fight."

Considering that Freeman is often described as a brilliant researcher, one might wonder at his methods for building a case. Not only does he ignore the differences between different places in Samoa, he also uses literature selectively to support his position—a technique that is quite distinct from the way most anthropologists were taught to do research. If the quote supports his viewpoint, it seems to make no difference who authored it. While he often uses my own critical statements about Mead's work, he either completely ignores or discounts my statements of corroboration. On one occasion Freeman even quotes Nicholas Von Hoffman, whose book *Tales from the Margaret Mead Taproom* is nothing but a spoof on anthropology, Mead, and Samoa, written almost entirely from information gathered in the bar of the Rainmaker Hotel, in Pago Pago. And while Freeman cites the reminiscences of missionaries and explorers who condemned the Samoans for their cruel and savage ways, he conveniently ignores those who characterized Samoans as friendly. He neglects to mention, for instance, that Dutch Commodore Jacob Roggeveen, who, in 1722, was the first white navigator to establish contact with the people of

Ta'u, reported that they paddled out to his ship in their outriggers and impressed him as a "harmless good sort of people, and very brisk and likely . . . with visible marks of civility."

Every culture projects ideal behavior in its ceremonies, and real behavior in its streets and homes. Freeman shifts back and forth between these, always to the advantage of his theory. When, for example, he is out to impress the reader with the restrictive nature of the Samoan sexual code, he points to the defloration ceremony (which was only performed on girls of high rank, such as *taupous* or paramount chiefs' daughters), or to the fact that the village councils (*fono*) fined family heads (*matai*) when teen-aged members of their households became pregnant out of wedlock. On the other hand, he ignores real behavior that indicates Samoans take a rather natural attitude toward sex before and outside of marriage. While young people in Samoa are not promiscuous, as Mead indicated, neither are they models of chastity, as Freeman would have us believe. I recall a pastor once remarking during a sermon in the Ta'u village church, in 1954, that some Man'-uan villages had reported record crops of breadfruit and bananas, but that, as usual, Ta'u had its record crop of *tama o le po* (literally, "children of the night"—illegitimate, in other words). This, of course, was an exaggeration, but it attests that sexual experience was far from nonexistent among young people.

While Freeman calls upon ideal behavior to document the sexual nature of Samoan culture, he draws from an observed case (though a deviant and atypical one) to show how aggressive and touchy Samoans really are. He reports that when a chief who had arrived late at a village council meeting demanded another kava ceremony that would include him, he and another chief ended up fighting furiously just outside the *fono* house. Such behavior would not be tolerated in the village of Ta'u; chiefs have far too much respect for the village council. While Freeman might have observed this behavior, such a grossly abnormal incident has no bearing on Samoan cultural norms or Samoan personality.

Clearly, Freeman and I disagree, much as Freeman and Mead would have. So it's a pity that he didn't have the courage to publish his restudy of Mead's work while she was still alive and able to defend herself. It would have been great sport and good for the science of anthropology. As a friend wrote in a recent letter, "Whatever else she was, Margaret was a feisty old gal and would have put up a spirited defense which would quickly have turned into a snotty offense." I would have put my money on the plump little lady with the no-nonsense attitude and the compulsion to "get on with it."

36

Society and Sex Roles

BY ERNESTINE FRIEDL

"Women must respond quickly to the demands of their husbands," says anthropologist Napoleon Chagnon describing the horticultural Yanomamo Indians of Venezuela. When a man returns from a hunting trip, "the woman, no matter what she is doing, hurries home and quietly but rapidly prepares a meal for her husband. Should the wife be slow in doing this, the husband is within his rights to beat her. Most reprimands ... take the form of blows with the hand or with a piece of firewood. .... Some of them chop their wives with the sharp edge of a machete or axe, or shoot them with a barbed arrow in some nonvital area, such as the buttocks or leg."

Among the Semai agriculturalists of central Malaya, when one person refuses the request of another, the offended party suffers *punan*, a mixture of emotional pain and frustration. "Enduring *punan* is commonest when a girl has refused the victim her sexual favors," reports Robert Dentan. "The jilted man's 'heart becomes sad.' He loses his energy and his appetite. Much of the time he sleeps, dreaming of his lost love. In this state he is in fact very likely to injure himself 'accidentally.' " The Semai are afraid of violence; a man would never strike a woman.

The social relationship between men and women has emerged as one of the principal disputes occupying the attention of scholars and the public in recent years. Although the discord is sharpest in the United States, the controversy has spread throughout the world. Numerous national and international conferences, including one in Mexico sponsored by the United Nations, have drawn together delegates from all walks of life to discuss such questions as the social and political rights of each sex, and even the basic nature of males and females.

Whatever their position, partisans often invoke examples from other cultures to support their ideas about the proper role of each sex. Because women are clearly subservient to men in many societies, like the Yanomamo, some experts conclude that the natural pattern is for men to dominate. But among the Semai no one has the right to command others, and in West Africa women are often chiefs. The place of women in these societies supports the argument of those who believe that sex roles are not fixed, that if there is a natural order, it allows for many different arrangements.

The argument will never be settled as long as the opposing sides toss examples from the world's cultures at each other like intellectual stones. But the effect of biological differences on male and female behavior can be clarified by looking at known examples of the earliest forms of human society and examining the relationship between technology, social organization, environment, and sex roles. The problem is to determine the conditions in which different degrees of male dominance are found, to try to discover the social and cultural arrangements that give rise to equality or inequality between the sexes, and to attempt to apply this knowledge to our understanding of the changes taking place in modern industrial society.

As Western history and the anthropological record have told us, equality between the sexes is rare; in most known societies females are subordinate. Male dominance is so widespread that it is virtually a human universal; societies in which women are consistently dominant do not exist and have never existed.

Evidence of a society in which women control all strategic resources like food and water, and in which women's activities are the most prestigious has never been found. The Iroquois of North America and the Lovedu of Africa came closest. Among the Iroquois, women raised food, controlled its distribution, and helped to choose male political leaders. Lovedu women ruled as queens, exchanged valuable cattle, led ceremonies, and controlled their own sex lives. But among both the Iroquois and the Lovedu, men owned the land and held other positions of power and prestige. Women were equal to men; they did not have ultimate authority over them. Neither culture was a true matriarchy.

Patriarchies are prevalent, and they appear to be strongest in societies in which men control significant goods that are exchanged with people outside the family. Regardless of who produces food, the person who gives it to others creates the obligations and alliances that are at the center of all political relations. The greater the male monopoly on the distribution of scarce items, the stronger their control of women seems to be. This is most obvious in relatively simple hunter-gatherer societies.

Hunter-gatherers, or foragers, subsist on wild plants, small land animals, and small river or sea creatures gathered by hand; large land animals and sea mammals hunted with spears, bows and arrows, and blow guns; and fish caught with hooks and nets. The 300,000 hunter-gatherers alive in the world today include the Eskimos, the Australian aborigines, and the Pygmies of Central Africa.

Foraging has endured for two million years and was replaced by farming and animal husbandry only 10,000 years ago; it covers more than 99 percent of human history. Our foraging ancestry is not far behind us and provides a clue to our understanding of the human condition.

Hunter-gatherers are people whose ways of life are technologically simple and socially and politically egalitarian. They live in small groups of 50 to 200 and have neither kings, nor priests, nor social classes. These conditions permit anthropologists to observe the essential bases for inequalities between the sexes without the distortions induced by the complexities of contemporary industrial society.

The source of male power among hunter-gatherers lies in their control of a scarce, hard to acquire, but necessary nutrient — animal protein. When men in a hunter-gatherer society return to camp with game, they divide the meat in some customary way. Among the !Kung San of Africa, certain parts of the animal are given to the owner of the arrow that killed the beast, to the first hunter to sight the game, to the one who threw the first spear, and to all men in the hunting party. After the meat has been divided, each hunter distributes his share to his blood relatives and his in-laws, who in turn share it with others. If an animal is large enough, every member of the band will receive some meat.

Vegetable foods, in contrast, are not distributed beyond the immediate household. Women give food to their children, to their husbands, to other members of the household, and rarely, to the occasional visitor. No one outside the family regularly eats any of the wild fruits and vegetables that are gathered by the women.

The meat distributed by the men is a public gift. Its source is widely known, and the donor expects a reciprocal gift when other men return from a successful hunt. He gains honor as a supplier of a scarce item and simultaneously obligates others to him.

These obligations constitute a form of power or control over others, both men and women. The opinions of hunters play an important part in decisions to move the village; good hunters attract the most desirable women; people in other groups join camps with good hunters; and hunters, because they already participate in an internal system of exchange, control exchange with other groups for flint, salt, and steel axes. The male monopoly on hunting unites men in a system of exchange and gives them power; gathering vegetable food does not give women equal power even among foragers who live in the tropics, where the food collected by women provides more than half the hunter-gatherer diet.

If dominance arises from a monopoly on big-game hunting, why has the male monopoly remained unchallenged? Some women are strong enough to participate in the hunt and their endurance is certainly equal to that of men. Dobe San women of the Kalahari Desert in Africa walk an average of 10 miles a day carrying from 15 to 33 pounds of food plus a baby.

Women do not hunt, I believe, because of four interrelated factors: variability in the supply of game; the different skills required for hunting and gathering; the incompatibility between carrying burdens and hunting; and the small size of seminomadic foraging populations.

Because the meat supply is unstable, foragers must make frequent expeditions to provide the band with gathered food. Environmental factors such as seasonal and annual variation in rainful often affect the size of the wildlife population. Hunters cannot always find game, and when they do encounter animals, they are not always successful in killing their prey. In northern latitudes, where meat is the primary food, periods of starvation are known in every generation. The irregularity of the game supply leads hunter-gatherers in areas where plant foods are available to depend on these predictable foods a good part of the time. Someone must gather the fruits, nuts, and roots and carry them back to camp to feed unsuccessful hunters, children, the elderly, and anyone who might not have gone foraging that day.

Foraging falls to the women because hunting and gathering cannot be combined on the same expedition. Although gatherers sometimes notice signs of game as they work, the skills required to track game are not the same as those required to find edible roots or plants. Hunters scan the horizon and the land for traces of large game; gatherers keep their eyes to the ground, studying the distribution of plants and the texture of the soil for hidden roots and animal holes. Even if a woman who was collecting plants came across the track of an antelope, she could not follow it; it is impossible to carry a load and hunt at the same time. Running with a heavy load is difficult, and should the animal be sighted, the hunter would be off balance and could neither shoot an arrow nor throw a spear accurately.

Pregnancy and child care would also present difficulties for a hunter. An unborn child affects a woman's body balance, as does a child in her arms, on her back, or slung at her side. Until they are two years old, many hunter-gatherer children are carried at all times, and until they are four, they are carried some of the time.

An observer might wonder why young women do not hunt until they become pregnant, or why mature women and men do not hunt and gather on alternate days, with some women staying in camp to act as wet nurses for the young. Apart from the effects hunting might have on a mother's milk production, there are two reasons. First, young girls begin to bear children as soon as they are physically mature and strong enough to hunt, and second, hunter-gatherer bands are so small that there are unlikely to be enough lactating women to serve as wet nurses. No hunter-gatherer group could afford to maintain a specialized female hunting force.

Because game is not always available, because hunting and gathering are specialized skills, because women carrying heavy loads cannot hunt, and because women in hunter-gatherer societies are usually either pregnant or caring for young children, for most of the last two million years of human history men have hunted and women have gathered.

If male dominance depends on controlling the supply of meat, then the degree of male dominance in a society should vary with the amount of meat available and the amount supplied by the men. Some regions, like the East African grasslands and the North American woodlands, abounded with species of large mammals; other zones, like tropical forests and semideserts, are thinly populated with prey. Many elements affect the supply of game, but theoretically, the less meat provided exclusively by the men, the more egalitarian the society.

All known hunter-gatherer societies fit into four basic types: those in which men and women work together in communal hunts and as teams gathering edible plants, as did the Washo Indians of North America; those in which men and women each collect their own plant foods although the men supply some meat to the group, as do the Hadza of Tanzania; those in which male hunters and female gatherers work apart but return to camp each evening to share their acquisitions, as do the Tiwi of North Australia; and those in which the men provide all the food by hunting large game, as do the Eskimo. In each case the extent of male dominance increases directly with the proportion of meat sup-

plied by individual men and small hunting parties.

Among the most egalitarian of hunter-gatherer societies are the Washo Indians, who inhabited the valleys of the Sierra Nevada in what is now southern California and Nevada. In the spring they moved north to Lake Tahoe for the large fish runs of sucker and native trout. Everyone—men, women, and children—participated in the fishing. Women spent the summer gathering edible berries and seeds while the men continued to fish. In the fall some men hunted deer but the most important source of animal protein was the jack rabbit, which was captured in communal hunts. Men and women together drove the rabbits into nets tied end to end. To provide food for the winter, husbands and wives worked as teams in the late fall to collect pine nuts.

Since everyone participated in most food-gathering activities, there were no individual distributors of food and relatively little difference in male and female rights. Men and women were not segregated from each other in daily activities; both were free to take lovers after marriage; both had the right to separate whenever they chose; menstruating women were not isolated from the rest of the group; and one of the two major Washo rituals celebrated hunting while the other celebrated gathering. Men were accorded more prestige if they had killed a deer, and men directed decisions about the seasonal movement of the group. But if no male leader stepped forward, women were permitted to lead. The distinctive feature of groups such as the Washo is the relative equality of the sexes.

The sexes are also relatively equal among the Hadza of Tanzania but this near-equality arises because men and women tend to work alone to feed themselves. They exchange little food. The Hadza lead a leisurely life in the seemingly barren environment of the East African Rift Gorge that is, in fact, rich in edible berries, roots, and small game. As a result of this abundance, from the time they are 10 years old,

Hadza men and women gather much of their own food. Women take their young children with them into the bush, eating as they forage, and collect only enough food for a light family meal in the evening. The men eat berries and roots as they hunt for small game, and should they bring down a rabbit or a hyrax, they eat the meat on the spot. Meat is carried back to the camp and shared with the rest of the group only on those rare occasions when a poisoned arrow brings down a large animal—an impala, a zebra, an eland, or a giraffe.

Because Hadza men distribute little meat, their status is only slightly higher than that of the women. People flock to the camp of a good hunter and the camp might take on his name because of his popularity, but he is in no sense a leader of the group. A Hadza man and a woman have an equal right to divorce and each can repudiate a marriage simply by living apart for a few weeks. Couples tend to live in the same camp as the wife's mother but they sometimes make long visits to the camp of the husband's mother. Although a man may take more than one wife, most Hadza males cannot afford to indulge in this luxury. In order to maintain a marriage, a man must supply both his wife and his mother-in-law with some meat and trade goods, such as beads and cloth, and the Hadza economy gives few men the wealth to provide for more than one wife and mother-in-law. Washo equality is based on cooperation; Hadza equality is based on independence.

In contrast to both these groups, among the Tiwi of Melville and Bathurst Islands off the northern coast of Australia, male hunters dominate female gatherers. The Tiwi are representative of the most common form of foraging society, in which the men supply large quantities of meat, although less than half the food consumed by the group. Each morning Tiwi women, most with babies on their backs, scatter in different directions in search of vegetables, grubs, worms, and small game such as bandicoots, lizards, and opossums. To track the game, they use hunting dogs. On most days women return to camp with some meat and with baskets full of *korka*, the nut of a native palm, which is soaked and mashed to make a porridge-like dish. The Tiwi men do not hunt small game and do not hunt every day, but when they do they often return with kangaroo, large lizards, fish, and game birds.

The porridge is cooked separately by each household and rarely shared outside the family, but the meat is prepared by a volunteer cook, who can be male or female. After the cook takes one of the parts of the animal traditionally reserved for him or her, the animal's "boss," the one who caught it, distributes the rest to all near kin and then to all others residing with the band. Although the small game supplied by the women is distributed in the same way as the big game supplied by the men, Tiwi men are dominant because the game they kill provides most of the meat.

The power of Tiwi men is clearest in their betrothal practices. Among the Tiwi, a woman must always be married. To ensure this, female infants are betrothed at birth and widows are remarried at the gravesides of their late husbands. Men form alliances by exchanging daughters, sisters, and mothers in marriage and some collect as many as 25 wives. Tiwi men value the quantity and quality of the food many wives can collect and the many children they can produce.

The dominance of the men is offset somewhat by the influence of adult women in selecting their next husbands. Many women are active strategists in the political careers of their male relatives, but to the exasperation of some sons attempting to promote their own futures, widowed mothers sometimes insist on selecting their own partners. Women also influence the marriages of their daughters and granddaughters, especially when the selected husband dies before the bestowed child moves to his camp.

Among the Eskimo, representative of the rarest type of forager society, inequality between the sexes is matched by inequality in supplying the group with food. Inland Eskimo men hunt caribou throughout the year to provision the entire society, and maritime Eskimo men depend on whaling, fishing, and some hunting to feed their extended families. The women process the carcasses, cut and sew skins to make clothing, cook, and care for the young; but they collect no food of their own and depend on the men to supply all the raw materials for their work. Since men provide all the meat, they also control the trade in hides, whale oil, seal oil, and other items that move between the maritime and inland Eskimos.

Eskimo women are treated almost exclusively as objects to be used, abused, and traded by men. After puberty all Eskimo girls are fair game for any interested male. A man shows his intentions by grabbing the belt of a woman and if she protests, he cuts off her trousers and forces himself upon her. These encounters are considered unimportant by the rest of the group. Men offer their wives' sexual services to establish alliances with trading partners and members of hunting and whaling parties.

Despite the consistent pattern of some degree of male dominance among foragers, most of these societies are egalitarian compared with agricultural and industrial societies. No forager has any significant opportunity for political leadership. Foragers, as a rule, do not like to give or take orders, and assume leadership only with reluctance. Shamans (those who are thought to be possessed by spirits) may be either male or female. Public rituals conducted by women in order to celebrate the first menstruation of girls are common, and the symbolism in these rituals is similar to that in the ceremonies that follow a boy's first kill.

In any society, status goes to those who control the distribution of valued goods and services outside the family. Equality arises when both sexes work side by side in food production, as do the Washo, and the products are simply distributed among the workers. In such circumstances, no person or sex has greater access to valued items than do others. But when women make no contribution to the food supply, as in the case of the Eskimo, they are completely subordinate.

When we attempt to apply these generalizations to contemporary industrial society, we can predict that as long as women spend their discretionary income from jobs on domestic needs, they will gain little social recognition and power. To be an effective source of power, money must be exchanged in ways that require returns and create obligations. In other words, it must be invested.

Jobs that do not give women control over valued resources will do little to advance their general status. Only as managers, executives, and professionals are women in a position to trade goods and services, to do others favors, and therefore to obligate others to them. Only as controllers of valued resources can women achieve prestige, power, and equality.

Within the household, women who bring in income from jobs are able to function on a more nearly equal basis with their husbands. Women who contribute services to their husbands and children without pay, as do some middle-class Western housewives, are especially vulnerable to dominance. Like Eskimo women, as long as their services are limited to domestic distribution they have little power relative to their husbands and none with respect to the outside world.

As for the limits imposed on women by their procreative functions in hunter-gatherer societies, childbearing and child care are organized around work as much as work is organized around reproduction. Some foraging groups space their children three to four years apart and have an average of only four to six children, far fewer than many women in other cultures. Hunter-gatherers nurse their infants for extended periods, sometimes for as long as four years. This custom suppresses ovulation and limits the size of their families. Sometimes, although rarely, they practice infanticide. By limiting reproduction, a woman who is gathering food has only one child to carry.

Different societies can and do adjust the frequency of birth and the care of children to accommodate whatever productive activities women customarily engage in. In horticultural societies, where women work long hours in gardens that may be far from home, infants get food to supplement their mothers' milk, older children take care of younger children, and pregnancies are widely spaced. Throughout the world, if a society requires a woman's labor, it finds ways to care for her children.

In the United States, as in some other industrial societies, the accelerated entry of women with preschool children into the labor force has resulted in the development of a variety of child-care arrangements. Individual women have called on friends, relatives, and neighbors. Public and private child-care centers are growing. We should realize that the declining birth rate, the increasing acceptance of childless or single-child families, and a de-emphasis on motherhood are adaptations to a sexual division of labor reminiscent of the system of production found in hunter-gatherer societies.

In many countries where women no longer devote most of their productive years to childbearing, they are beginning to demand a change in the social relationship of the sexes. As women gain access to positions that control the exchange of resources, male dominance may become archaic, and industrial societies may one day become as egalitarian as the Washo.

For further information:

Friedl, Ernestine. *Women and Men: An Anthropologist's View.* Holt, Rinehart and Winston, 1975.

Martin, M. Kay, and Barbara Voorhies, eds. *Female of the Species.* Columbia University Press, 1977.

Murphy, Yolanda, and Robert Murphy. *Women of the Forest.* Columbia University Press, 1974.

Reiter, Rayna, ed. *Toward an Anthropology of Women.* Monthly Review Press, 1975.

Rosaldo, M. Z., and Louise Lamphere, eds. *Women, Culture, and Society.* Stanford University Press, 1974.

Schlegel, Alice, ed. *Sexual Stratification: A Cross-Cultural View.* Columbia University Press, 1977.

Strathern, Marilyn. *Women In Between: Female Roles in a Male World.* Academic Press, 1972.

37

Life Behind the Veil

BY CHERRY LINDHOLM AND CHARLES LINDHOLM

The bazaar teems with activity. Pedestrians throng the narrow streets, wending past donkey carts, cyclists and overloaded vehicles. Vendors haggle in the dark doorways of their shops. Pitiful beggars shuffle among the crowds, while bearded religious mendicants wander about, their eyes fixed on a distant world.

Drifting among the mobs of men are, here and there, anonymous figures hidden beneath voluminous folds of material, who float along like ships in full sail, graceful, mysterious, faceless, instilling in the observer a sense both of awe and of curiosity. These are the Moslem women of the Middle East. Their dress is the customary *chador*, which they wear when obliged to leave the privacy of their homes. The *chador* is but one means by which women maintain their *purdah*, the institution of female seclusion, which requires that women should remain unseen by men who are not close relatives and strikes Westerners as so totally foreign and incomprehensible.

Sometimes the alien aspect is tempered with a touch of Western familiarity. A pair of plastic sunglasses may gleam from behind the lace that covers the eyes, or a platform shoe might peep forth from beneath the hem of the flowing *chador*. Nevertheless, the overall presence remains one of inscrutability and is perhaps the most striking image of Middle Eastern societies.

We spent nine months in one of the most strict of all the *purdah* societies, the Yusufzai Pakhtun of the Swat Valley in the North-West Frontier Province of Pakistan. ("Pakhtun" is the designation preferred by the tribesmen, who were generally called Pathans in the days of the British *raj*.)

We had come to the Swat Valley after a hair-raising ride on a rickety bus from Peshawar over the 10,280-foot Malakand Pass. Winston Churchill came this way as a young war correspondent attached to the Malakand Field Force in 1897. As we came into the valley, about half the size of Connecticut, we passed a sign that said WELCOME TO SWAT. We were fortunate to have entrée into the community through a Swati friend we had made eight years before. In Swat, women are secluded inside the domestic compound except for family rituals, such as marriage, circumcision and funerals, or visits to saints' tombs. A woman must always be in the protective company of other women and is never allowed out alone. It tells a great deal about the community that the word for husband in Pakhto, the language of the Pakhtun, is *khawund*, which also means God.

However, as everywhere, rules are sometimes broken or, more frequently, cleverly manipulated. Our Pakhtun host's stepmother, Bibi, an intelligent and forceful woman, was renowned for her tactics. Once, when all the females of the household had been forbidden to leave the compound to receive cholera inoculations at the temporary clinic next door, Bibi respectfully bowed her head and assured the men they could visit the mosque with easy minds. Once the men had gone, she promptly climbed the ladder to the flat roof and summoned the doctor to the door of her compound. One by one, the women extended their bare arms through the doorway and received their shots. Later, Bibi could honestly swear that no woman had set foot outside the compound walls.

Despite such circumventions, *purdah* is of paramount importance in Swat. As one Pakhtun proverb succinctly states: "The woman's place is in the home or the grave." Years ago in Swat, if a woman broke her *purdah*, her husband might kill her or cut off her nose as punishment and as a means of cleansing his honor. If a woman is caught alone with a unrelated man, it will always be assumed that the liaison is sexual, and public opinion will oblige her husband to shoot her, even if he does not desire her death; to go unavenged is to be known henceforth as *begherata*, or man without honor. As such, he would no longer have the right to call himself Pakhtun.

A shameless woman is a threat to the whole society. Our host remembered witnessing, 30 years ago when he was a child, the entire village stoning an adulteress. This punishment is prescribed by Islamic law, though the law requires there be four witnesses to the sexual act itself to establish guilt. Nowadays, punishments for wifely misdemeanors have become less harsh, though adulterous wives are still killed.

SEDUCTION

In the rural areas, poorer families generally cannot maintain *purdah* as rigorously as their wealthier neighbors, for often the wife must help her husband in the fields or become a servant. Nevertheless, she is required to keep her hair covered at all times and to interact with men to a minimum. Here again, the rules are sometimes flouted, and a poor woman might entice a man with her eyes or even, according to village men who claimed personal experiences, become more aggressive in her seductive attempts and actually seize a man in a deserted alleyway and lure him into her house. Often, the man is persuaded. Such a woman will accept money from her lover, who is usually a man from a wealthy family. Her husband is then a *begherata*, but some men acquiesce to the situation because of the money the wife is earning or because of fear of the wife's socially superior and more powerful lover. But most poor men,

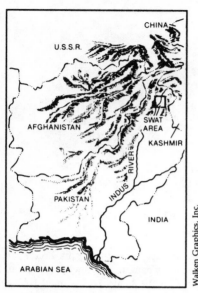

Swat is reached by a 10,280-foot deep pass in the mountains of the Hindu Kush.

and certainly all of the elite, keep their women under strict control.

In the Islamic Middle East, women are viewed as powerful and dangerous beings, highly sexual and lacking in personal discipline and discrimination. In Middle Eastern thought, sexual intercourse itself, though polluting, lacks the same negative connotations it has in the West. It has always been believed that women have sexual climaxes, and there is no notion of female frigidity. Male impotence, however, is well-documented, and some middle-aged and even young men admitted to us that they had lost their interest in women. Sometimes, though rarely, a young bridegroom will find himself incapable of consummating his marriage, either because he finds his bride unattractive or because he has been previously enchanted by a male lover and has become impotent in a heterosexual relationship. Homosexuality has never been seen as aberrant in the Middle East. As a famous Afghan saying humorously declares: "A woman is for bearing children, a boy is for pleasure, but ecstasy is a ripe watermelon!" However, with Western influence, homosexuality in the Middle East is now less overt. But even when it was common and open, the man was still expected to marry and produce children.

Men must marry, though women are regarded as a chaotic and anarchic force. They are believed to possess many times the sexual desire of men and constitute a potential threat to the family and the family's honor, which is based in large measure on the possession and control of women and their excessive and dangerous sexuality.

Among the Pakhtun of Swat, where the male-female relation is one of the most hostile in the Middle East, the man avoids showing affection to his wife, for fear she will become too self-confident and will begin to assert herself in ways that insult his position and honor. She may start by leaving the compound without his permission and, if unchecked, may end by bringing outside men into the house for sexual encounters, secure in the knowledge that her husband, weakened by his affection for her, will not take action. This course of events is considered inevitable by men and women alike and was illustrated by a few actual cases in the village where we lived.

Women are therefore much feared, despite the pronouncements of male supremacy. They must be controlled, in order to prevent their alarming basic natures from coming to the fore and causing dishonor to their own lineages. *Purdah* is generally described as a system that serves to protect the woman, but implicitly it protects the men and society in general from the potentially disruptive actions of the powerful female sex.

Changes are occurring, however, particularly in the modern urban centers. The educated urban woman often dispenses with the *chador,* replacing it with a simple length of veiling draped over the head or across the shoulders; she may even decide to adopt modest Western dress. The extent of this transformation will depend partly upon the attitude of the community in which she lives.

In the urban centers of the stricter *purdah* regions the public display of *purdah* is scrupulous, sometimes even more striking than that of the tribal village. Behind the scenes, though, the city-dwelling woman does have more freedom than she would have in the village. She will be able to visit not only relatives but friends without specific permission from her husband, who is out at work all day. She may, suitably veiled, go shopping in the bazaar, a chore her husband would have undertaken in the village. On the whole, the city woman will have a great deal more independence, and city men sometimes lament this weakening of traditional male domination.

The urbanized male may speak of the custom-bound tribesmen (such as the Swat Pakhtun, the Bedouin nomads of Saudi Arabia or the Qashqai herdsmen of Iran) as country bumpkins, yet he still considers their central values, their sense of personal pride, honor and autonomy, as cultural ideals and views the tribesmen, in a very real way, as exemplars of the proper mode of life. Elite families in the cities proudly emphasize their tribal heritage and sometimes send their sons to live for a year or so with distant tribal cousins, in order to expose them to the tribesman's integrity and moral code. The tribesman, on the other hand, views his urbanized relatives as weak and womanly, especially with reference to the slackening of *purdah* in the cities. Though the *purdah* female, both in the cities and in the tribal areas, rarely personifies the ideal virtues of silence, submission and obedience, the concept of *purdah* and male supremacy remains central to the male identity and to the ideology of the culture as a whole.

The dynamic beneath the notion of male supremacy, the institution of *purdah* and the ideology of women's sexual power becomes apparent when one takes an overall view of the social structure. The family in the Middle East, particularly in the tribal regions, is not an isolated element; kinship and marriage are the underlying principles that structure action and thought. Individuals interact not so much according to personal preference as according to kinship.

The Middle Eastern kinship system is known to anthropologists as a segmentary-lineage organization; the basic idea is that kinship is traced through one line only. In the Middle East, the system is patrilineal, which means that the male line is followed, and all the links through women are ignored. An individual can therefore trace his relationship to any other individual in the society and know the exact genealogical distance between them; i.e., the distance that must be traced to reach a common male ancestor. The system obliges men to defend their patrilineal relatives if they are attacked, but if there is no external force threatening the lineage, then men struggle against one another according to the principle of genealogical distance. This principle is nicely stated in a famous Middle Eastern proverb: "I against my brothers; my brothers and I against my cousins; my cousins, my brothers and I against the world." The cousins in question are of course patrilineal.

PROMISCUITY PHOBIA

Within this system, women appear to have no role, though they are the units of reproduction, the mothers of the sons who will carry on the patriline. Strange as it may seem, this is the core contradiction of the society: The "pure" patriline itself is actually descended from a woman. This helps explain the exaggerated fear of women's promiscuity and supposedly voracious sexuality. In order to protect the patriline, women must be isolated and guarded. Their sexuality, which threatens the integrity of the patriline, must be made the exclusive property of their husbands. Women, while being absolutely necessary for the perpetuation of the social order, are simultaneously the greatest threat to it.

The persistent denigration of women is explained by this core contradiction. Moslem society considers women naturally inferior in intelligence and ability—childlike, incapable of discernment, incompetent to testify in court, prey to whims and fancies. In tribal areas, women are prohibited from inheritance, despite a Koranic injunction, and in marriage they are purchased from their fathers like a commodity. Were women not feared, these denials of her personhood would be unnecessary.

Another unique element of Middle Eastern culture is the prevalence of marriage with the father's brother's daughter. In many areas, in fact, this marriage is so favored that a boy must give explicit permission to allow his patrilineal female cousin to marry elsewhere. This peculiar marriage form, which is found nowhere else in the world, also serves to negate the woman by merging her lineage with that of her husband, since both are members of the same patriline (indeed, are the offspring of brothers). No new blood enters, and the sanctity of the patriline is steadily maintained.

However, this ploy gives rise to other problems: Cousin marriage often divides the brothers rather than uniting them. Although the bride-price is usually reduced in such marriages, it is always demanded, thus turning the brothers into opponents in a business negotiation. Furthermore, giving a woman in Swat carries an implication of inferiority; historically, victors in war took women from the vanquished. Cousin marriage thus renders the brothers' equality questionable. Finally, the young couple's fights will further alienate the brothers, especially since such marriages are notoriously contentious. This is because patrilineal male cousins are rivals for the common grandfather's inheritance (in fact, the Swati term for father's brother's son is *tarbur,* which also means enemy), and a man who marries his patrilineal cousin is mar-

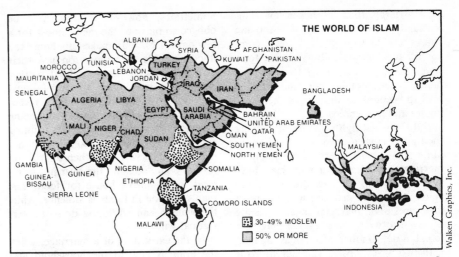

The world of Islam began when Mohammed preached in Saudi Arabia in the seventh century. It fanned out, carrying purdah with it, into Asia and into Africa south of the Sahara.

rying the sister of his lifelong opponent. Her loyalty is with her brother, and this is bound to cause frequent disputes.

Though the girl is treated like goods, she does not see herself as such. The fundamental premise of tribal life is the equality of the various landed families. There are very few hierarchies in these societies, and even the leaders are often no more than first among equals. Within this system, which has been described as a nearly perfect democracy, each *khan* (which means landowner and literally translates as king) family sees itself as superior to all others. The girls of the household feel the same pride in their lineage as their brothers and cannot help but regard their husbands' families through jaundiced eyes. The new bride is prepared to defend the honor of her family, even though they have partially repudiated her by negotiating the marriage. Her identity, like that of a man, rests on her lineage pride, which she will fight to uphold. The husband, meanwhile, is determined to demonstrate his domination and mastery, since control of women is the nexus of a man's sense of self-respect.

Hostility is thus built into marriage by the very structure of the society, which pits every lineage against every other in a never-ending contest to maintain an equilibrium of power within this markedly egalitarian culture. The hostility of the marriage bond is evident from its beginnings. The reluctant bride is torn from her cot in her family's house and ensconced on a palanquin that strongly resembles a bier. The war drums that announce the marriage procession indicate the nature of the tie, as does the stoning of the palanquin by the small boys of the

village as it is carried through the dusty streets. When the bride arrives at her new husband's house, his family triumphantly fires their rifles into the air. They have taken a woman! The young wife cowers in her veils as she is prodded and poked curiously by the females of the husband's house who try to persuade her to show her face. The groom himself is nowhere to be seen, having retreated to the men's house in shame. In three days, he will creep to her room and consummate the marriage. Taking the virginity of the bride is a highly charged symbolic act, and in some areas of the Middle East the display of the bloody nuptial sheet to the public is a vital part of the wedding rite. Breaking the hymen demonstrates the husband's possession of his wife's sexuality. She then becomes the most junior adult in the household, subordinate to everyone, but, most especially, under the heavy thumb of her mother-in-law.

The household the bride enters will be that of her husband's father, since the system, as well as being patrilineal, is also patrilocal. She will be surrounded by his relatives and will be alone with her husband only at night. During the day he will pay no attention to her, for it is considered shameful for a man to take note of his wife in front of others, particularly his father and mother. Within the compound walls, which shield the household from the rest of the world, she is at the mercy of her new family.

DOMESTIC BATTLES

Life within the compound is hardly peaceful. Wives squabble among themselves, and wives who have built a power base by having sons even quarrel with the old matriarch, their mother-in law. This is usually a prelude to a couple moving out of the house into their own compound, and husbands always blame their wives for the breakup of the extended family, even though they, too, will be glad to become the masters of their own homes and households.

But the worst fights among women are the fights between women married to the same man. Islam permits polygamous marriage, and legally a man may have four wives. Not all men are financially able to take more than one wife, but most men dream of marrying again, despite the Swati proverb that says, "I may be a fool, but not so much of a fool as the man with two wives." Men who can afford it often do take a second wife. The reason is not sexual desire, for wives do not mind if their husbands have liaisons with prostitutes or promiscuous poor women. Rather, the second wife is brought in to humiliate an overly assertive first wife. Bringing in a second wife is a terrible insult; it is an expression of contempt for the first wife and her entire lineage. The insult is especially cutting in Swat, where divorce is prohibited (though it is permitted in the Koran) and where a disliked wife must either endure her lot or retreat to her family's house and a life of celibacy. Small wonder then that households with two wives are pits of intrigue, vituperation and magical incantation, as each wife seeks to expel the other. The Koran says a man should only practice polygamy if he is sure he can treat each wife equally; the only man we met who was able to approximate this ideal was a man who never went home. He spent his time in the men's house, talking with his cronies and having his meals sent to him.

The men's house is the best-built structure in any village, along with the mosque, which is also prohibited to women. It is a meeting place for the clan, the center for hospitality and refuge and the arena for political manipulation. This is where the visitor will be received, surrounded by men who gossip, doze or clean their rifles. Here, the guest might well imagine that women do not even exist. Only the tea and food that is sent over from the compound nearby tell him of the women working behind the walls.

Formerly, in Swat, most men slept in the men's house, visiting their wives secretly late at night and returning before daybreak. But now only a few elders and some ne'er-do-well youths live permanently in the elegant, aging buildings.

Sometimes, however, a man may be obliged to move to the men's house for a few days if his wife makes his home too uncomfortable, for women too have their own weapons in the household battles. Arguments may flare up over almost anything: the husband buying a rotten piece of meat or forgetting to bring home a length of material, the wife ruining some curd or gossiping too much with a neighbor. The wife may then angrily refuse to cook, obliging the husband to retreat to the men's house for food. The man's weapon in fights is violence, while the woman can withdraw domestic services at will.

In the early days of a marriage, when the bride is new to the household and surrounded by her husband's people, she may be fairly meek. But when her status has improved as a result of producing sons, she will become more aggressive. Her lacerating tongue is renowned, and she will also begin to fight back physically as well as verbally. Finally, her exasperated husband may silence her with a blow from a heavy stick he keeps for that purpose. No shame is attached to beating one's wife, and men laugh about beatings they have administered. The women themselves, though they decry their men's brutality, proudly display their scars and bruises, characterizing a neighbor who is relatively gentle to his wife as "a man with no penis."

The older a woman gets, the more powerful and fearless she becomes. She is aided by her sons who, though respecting their father, regard him as an obstacle to their gaining rights in land. The old man, who gains his stature from his landholding, is always reluctant to allot shares to his grown sons. Furthermore, the sons' ties of affection are much stronger with the mother. The elderly father, who is generally 10 or 15 years older than his wife, is thus surrounded by animosity in his own house. The situation of the earlier years has reversed itself, and the wife, who began alone and friendless, gains allies in her old age, while the husband becomes isolated. Ghani Khan, a modern Pakhtun writer, has described the situation well: "The Pakhtun thinks he is as good as anyone else and his father rolled into one and is fool enough to try this even with his wife. She pays for it in her youth, and he in his old age."

But many women do not live to see their triumph. In northern Swat, for every 100 women over the age of 60 there are 149 men, compared to the more equal

100 to 108 ratio below 60. The women are worn out by continual childbearing, breast-feeding and a lack of protein. Though fertile in places, the Swat valley is heavily overpopulated with an estimated one million people, and survival is always difficult. The diet consists chiefly of bread, rice, seasonal vegetables and some dairy products. Meat is a rarity and goes to the men and boys as a matter of course. They perpetuate the patrilineal clan and must survive, while women can always be replaced. The lives of men are hard, but the lives of women are harder, as witnessed by their early deaths.

In this environment, people must learn to be tough, just as they must learn to fit the structure of the patrilineal system. Child-rearing serves both functions.

The birth of a boy in Swat is greeted by rejoicing, while the birth of a girl is an occasion for gloom. But the first few years for both sexes are virtually identical. Like most Middle Easterners, the Swatis practice swaddling, binding the baby tightly so that it is immobilized. Ostensibly, this is to help the baby sleep and prevent it from blinding itself with its flailing hands, but anthropologists have hypothesized that swaddling actually serves to develop a certain character type: a type which can withstand great restraint but which also tends to uncontrolled bursts of temper. This hypothesis fits Swat, where privation and the exigencies of the social structure demand stoicism, but where violent temper is also useful. We often saw Swati children of all ages lose themselves in tantrums to coerce their parents, and such coercion was usually successful. Grown men and women as well are prone to fits of temper, and this dangerous aspect makes their enemies leery of pressing them too hard.

Both sexes are indoctrinated in the virtues of their family and its lineage. In marital fights this training is obvious, as both partners heatedly assert, "Your ancestor was nothing, and mine was great!" At a man's death his sister, not his wife, is his chief mourner. And if a woman is killed it is her brother, not her husband, who avenges her.

Child training in Swat produces strong characters. When they give affection, they give it wholeheartedly, and when they hate, they hate bitterly. The conditions under which they live are cruel and cramped, and they respond with cruelty and rigidity in order to survive. But at the same time, the people are able to bear their hard lives with pride and dignity.

TOPIC THIRTEEN

Belief and Ritual

···

"As members of society, most of us see only what we expect to see, and what we expect to see is what we are conditioned to see when we have learned the definitions and classifications of our culture," anthropologist Victor Turner has observed. But the statement is incomplete; it omits any mention of *beliefs*—bodies of assumptions about the nature of things bolstered by selected facts—which are embedded in every culture and, along with the categories Turner mentions, powerfully organize our experiences of the world around us and our attempts to deal with the world thus conceived.

Belief systems deal with everything human beings can perceive and can imagine. Instrumental, or rational-technical, belief systems are concerned primarily with concrete phenomena and tasks. What kind of person makes a good spouse? Which stocks are likely to yield bushels of money to investors? What training methods and dietary regimens should Olympic swimmers undergo? Instrumental beliefs provide answers to these and countless other questions concerning day-to-day existence.

Other beliefs take us beyond daily concerns and address more profound questions, such as the purpose of human existence, the phenomenon of death, and the existence of entities that inherently cannot be verified by the human senses. Such transcendental beliefs always invoke the "larger picture" when they address concrete tasks or specific issues, as in the case of the Wape of New Guinea, described by William E. Mitchell in "A New Weapon Stirs Up Old Ghosts." The Wape center their religious beliefs around forest demons, who they believe cause illness, and the appeasement of the malevolent ghosts of their own ancestors. Mitchell describes how an item of western technology, a shotgun, was successfully integrated into the belief system of the Wape, creating a new shotgun cult.

Closer to home, Nathan L. Gerrard describes the beliefs of some fundamentalist Christian sects that have incorporated deadly snakes into their religious services in "The Serpent-Handling Religions of West Virginia." The adherents of these sects see each recovery from snakebite as a miracle wrought by God, whereas each death is evidence of how dangerous and difficult it is to obey the Lord's commandments.

Rituals are repeated and stereotyped activities, handed down from generation to generation, that express certain transcendental and instrumental beliefs. Often, rituals mark important social transitions, such as birth, puberty, marriage, and death. In "Cargo Cults," Peter M. Worsley narrates the emergence of a complex of beliefs and rituals in the South Pacific, as the indigenous cultures were subjected to severe stresses following contact with the industrial world. The cargo cults incorporated symbolic representations of industrial technology to bolster traditional belief systems, which were increasingly difficult to sustain in the context of invading armies during World War II. A paradox indeed—but rituals seem uniquely suited to the resolution, on an entirely different level, of those inevitable contradictions that people everywhere must cope with in their daily lives.

38

Cargo Cults

BY PETER M. WORSLEY

Patrols of the Australian Government venturing into the "uncontrolled" central highlands of New Guinea in 1946 found the primitive people there swept up in a wave of religious excitement. Prophecy was being fulfilled: The arrival of the Whites was the sign that the end of the world was at hand. The natives proceeded to butcher all of their pigs—animals that were not only a principal source of subsistence but also symbols of social status and ritual pre-eminence in their culture. They killed these valued animals in expression of the belief that after three days of darkness "Great Pigs" would appear from the sky. Food, firewood and other necessities had to be stock-piled to see the people through to the arrival of the Great Pigs. Mock wireless antennae of bamboo and rope had been erected to receive in advance the news of the millennium. Many believed that with the great event they would exchange their black skins for white ones.

This bizarre episode is by no means the single event of its kind in the murky history of the collision of European civilization with the indigenous cultures of the southwest Pacific. For more than 100 years traders and missionaries have been reporting similar disturbances among the peoples of Melanesia, the group of Negro-inhabited islands (including New Guinea, Fiji, the Solomons and the New Hebrides) lying between Australia and the open Pacific Ocean. Though their technologies were based largely upon stone and wood, these peoples had highly developed cultures, as measured by the standards of maritime and agricultural ingenuity, the complexity of their varied social organizations and the elaboration of religious belief and ritual. They were nonetheless ill prepared for

the shock of the encounter with the Whites, a people so radically different from themselves and so infinitely more powerful. The sudden transition from the society of the ceremonial stone ax to the society of sailing ships and now of airplanes has not been easy to make.

After four centuries of Western expansion, the densely populated central highlands of New Guinea remain one of the few regions where the people still carry on their primitive existence in complete independence of the world outside. Yet as the agents of the Australian Government penetrate into ever more remote mountain valleys, they find these backwaters of antiquity already deeply disturbed by contact with the ideas and artifacts of European civilization. For "cargo"—Pidgin English for trade goods—has long flowed along the indigenous channels of communication from the seacoast into the wilderness. With it has traveled the frightening knowledge of the white man's magical power. No small element in the white man's magic is the hopeful message sent abroad by his missionaries: the news that a Messiah will come and that the present order of Creation will end.

The people of the central highlands of New Guinea are only the latest to be gripped in the recurrent religious frenzy of the "cargo cults." However variously embellished with details from native myth and Christian belief, these cults all advance the same central theme: the world is about to end in a terrible cataclysm. Thereafter God, the ancestors or some local culture hero will appear and inaugurate a blissful paradise on earth. Death, old age, illness and evil will be unknown. The riches of the white man will accrue to the Melanesians.

Although the news of such a movement in one area has doubtless often inspired similar movements in other areas, the evidence indicates that these cults have arisen independently in many places as parallel responses to the same enormous social stress and strain. Among the movements best known to students of Melanesia are the "Taro Cult" of New Guinea, the "Vailala Madness" of Papua, the "Naked Cult" of Espiritu Santo, the "John Frum Movement" of the New Hebrides and the "Tuka Cult" of the Fiji Islands.

At times the cults have been so well organized and fanatically persistent that they have brought the work of government to a standstill. The outbreaks have often taken the authorities completely by surprise and have confronted them with mass opposition of an alarming kind. In the 1930s, for example, villagers in the vicinity of Wewak, New Guinea, were stirred by a succession of "Black King" movements. The prophets announced that the Europeans would soon leave the island, abandoning their property to the natives, and urged their followers to cease paying taxes, since the government station was about to disappear into the sea in a great earthquake. To the tiny community of Whites in charge of the region, such talk was dangerous. The authorities jailed four of the prophets and exiled three others. In yet another movement, that sprang up in declared opposition to the local Christian mission, the cult leader took Satan as his god.

Troops on both sides in World War II found their arrival in Melanesia heralded as a sign of the Apocalypse. The G.I.'s who landed in the New Hebrides, moving up for the bloody fighting on Guadalcanal, found the natives furiously at work preparing airfields, roads and docks for the magic ships and planes that they believed were coming from "Rusefel" (Roosevelt), the friendly king of America.

The Japanese also encountered millenarian visionaries during their southward march to Guadalcanal. Indeed, one of the strangest minor military actions of World War II occurred in Dutch New Guinea, when Japanese forces had to be turned against the local Papuan inhabitants of the Geelvink Bay region. The Japanese had at first been received with great joy, not because their "Greater East Asia Co-Prosperity Sphere" propaganda had made any great impact upon the Papuans, but because the natives regarded them as harbingers of the new world that was dawning, the flight of the Dutch having already given the first sign. Mansren, creator of the islands and their peoples, would now return, bringing with him the ancestral dead. All this had been known, the cult leaders declared, to the crafty Dutch, who had torn out the first page of the Bible where these truths were inscribed. When Mansren returned, the existing world order would be entirely overturned. White men would turn black like Papuans, Papuans would become Whites; root crops would grow in trees, and coconuts and fruits would grow like tubers. Some of the islanders now began to draw together into large "towns"; others took Biblical names such as "Jericho" and "Galilee" for their villages. Soon they adopted military uniforms and began drilling. The Japanese, by now highly unpopular, tried to disarm and disperse the Papuans; resistance inevitably developed. The climax of this tragedy came when several canoe-loads of fanatics sailed out to attack Japanese warships, believing themselves to be invulnerable by virtue of the holy water with which they had sprinkled themselves. But the bullets of the Japanese did not turn to water, and the attackers were mowed down by machine-gun fire.

Behind this incident lay a long history. As long ago as 1857 missionaries in the Geelvink Bay region had made note of the story of Mansren. It is typical of many Melanesian myths that became confounded with Christian doctrine to form the ideological basis of the movements. The legend tells how long ago there lived an old man named Manamakeri ("he who itches"), whose body was covered with sores. Manamakeri was extremely fond of palm wine, and used to climb a huge tree every day to tap the liquid from the flowers. He soon found that someone was getting there before him and removing the liquid. Eventually he trapped the thief, who turned out to be none other than the Morning Star. In return for his freedom, the Star gave the old man a wand that would produce as much fish as he liked, a magic tree and a magic staff. If he drew in the sand and stamped his foot, the drawing would become real. Manamakeri, aged as he was, now magically impregnated a young maiden; the child of this union was a miracle-child who spoke as soon as he was born. But the maiden's parents were horrified, and banished her, the child and the old man. The trio sailed off in a canoe created by Mansren ("The Lord"), as the old man now became known. On this journey Mansren rejuvenated himself by stepping into a fire and flaking off his scaly skin, which changed into valuables. He then sailed around Geelvink Bay, creating islands where he stopped, and peopling them with the ancestors of the present-day Papuans.

The Mansren myth is plainly a creation myth full of symbolic ideas relating to fertility and rebirth. Comparative evidence—especially the shedding of his scaly skin—confirms the suspicion that the old man is, in fact, the Snake in another guise. Psychoanalytic writers argue that the snake occupies such a prominent part in mythology the world over because it stands for the penis, another fertility symbol. This may be so, but its symbolic significance is surely more complex than this. It is the "rebirth" of the hero, whether Mansren or the Snake, that exercises such universal fascination over men's minds.

The 19th-century missionaries thought that the Mansren story would make the introduction of Christianity easier, since the concept of "resurrection," not to mention that of the "virgin birth" and the "second coming," was already there. By 1867, however, the first cult organized around the Mansren legend was reported.

Though such myths were widespread in Melanesia, and may have sparked occasional movements even in the pre-White era, they took on a new significance in the late 19th century, once the European powers had finished parceling out the Melanesian region among themselves. In many coastal areas the long history of "blackbirding"—the seizure of islanders for work on the plantations of Australia and Fiji—had built up a reservoir of hostility to Europeans. In other areas, however, the arrival of the Whites was accepted, even welcomed, for it meant access to bully beef and cigarettes, shirts and paraffin lamps, whisky and bicycles. It also meant access to the knowledge behind these material goods, for the Europeans brought missions and schools as well as cargo.

Practically the only teaching the natives received about European life came from the missions, which emphasized the central significance of religion in European society. The Melanesians already believed that man's activities—whether gardening, sailing canoes or bearing children—needed magical assistance. Ritual without human effort was not enough. But neither was human effort on its own. This outlook was reinforced by mission teaching.

The initial enthusiasm for European rule, however, was speedily dispelled. The rapid growth of the plantation economy removed the bulk of the able-bodied men from the villages, leaving women, children and old men to carry on as best they could. The splendid vision of the equality of all Christians began to seem a pious deception in face of the realities of the color bar, the multiplicity of rival Christian missions and the open irreligion of many Whites.

For a long time the natives accepted the European mission as the means by which the "cargo" would eventually be made available to them. But they found that acceptance of Christianity did not bring the cargo any nearer. They grew disillusioned. The story now began to be put about that it was not the Whites who made the cargo, but the dead ancestors. To people completely ignorant of factory production, this made good sense. White men did not work; they merely wrote secret signs on scraps of paper, for which they were given shiploads of goods. On the other hand, the Melanesians labored week after week for pitiful wages. Plainly the goods must be made for Melanesians somewhere, perhaps in the Land of the Dead. The Whites, who possessed the secret of the cargo, were intercepting it and keeping it from the hands of the islanders, to whom it was really consigned. In the Madang district of New Guinea, after some 40 years' experience of the missions, the natives went in a body one day with a petition demanding

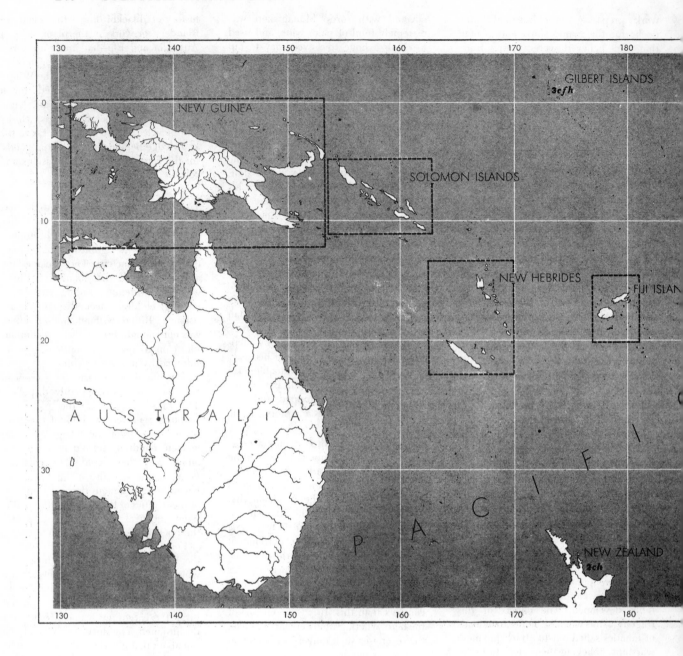

that the cargo secret should now be revealed to them, for they had been very patient.

So strong is this belief in the existence of a "secret" that the cargo cults generally contain some ritual in imitation of the mysterious European customs which are held to be the clue to the white man's extraordinary power over goods and men. The believers sit around tables with bottles of flowers in front of them, dressed in European clothes, waiting for the cargo ship or airplane to materialize; other cultists feature magic pieces of paper and cabalistic writing. Many of them deliberately turn their backs on the past by destroying secret ritual objects, or exposing them to the gaze of uninitiated youths and women, for whom formerly even a glimpse of the sacred objects would have meant the severest penalties, even death. The belief that they were the chosen people is further reinforced by their reading of the Bible, for the lives and customs of the people in the Old Testament resemble their own lives rather than those of the Europeans. In the New Testament they find the Apocalypse, with its prophecies of destruction and resurrection, particularly attractive.

Missions that stress the imminence of the Second Coming, like those of the Seventh Day Adventists, are often accused of stimulating millenarian cults among the islanders. In reality, however, the Melanesians themselves rework the doctrines the missionaries teach them, selecting from the Bible what they themselves find particularly congenial in it. Such movements have occurred in areas where missions of quite different types

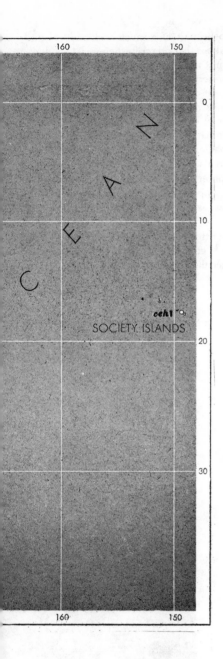

SOUTH PACIFIC, *scene of the religious disturbances known as cargo cults, is shown in this map. Most cargo cults have been in Melanesia, shown here as four regions enclosed in broken rectangles. Each of these regions is shown in a detailed map in the following pages. Also shown on this map are three outlying cargo cults, two of them Polynesian and the third Micronesian. Numbers on these maps indicate individual cults. Letters refer to typical features of cults (see number and letter keys accompanying each map).*

1 MAMAIA MOVEMENT TAHITI 1930-1944
2 HAU-HAU MOVEMENT NEW ZEALAND
1860-1871
3 ONOTOA TROUBLES GILBERT ISLANDS
1932

a MYTH OF THE RETURN OF THE DEAD
b REVIVAL OR MODIFICATION OF
PAGANISM
c INTRODUCTION OF CHRISTIAN
ELEMENTS
d CARGO MYTH
e BELIEF THAT NEGROES WILL
BECOME WHITE MEN AND
VICE VERSA
f BELIEF IN A COMING MESSIAH
g ATTEMPTS TO RESTORE NATIVE
POLITICAL AND ECONOMIC
CONTROL
h THREATS AND VIOLENCE AGAINST
WHITE MEN
i UNION OF TRADITIONALLY
SEPARATE AND UNFRIENDLY
GROUPS

ed overnight. Then came the Japanese, only to be ousted in turn largely by the previously unknown Americans. And among these Americans the Melanesians saw Negroes like themselves, living lives of luxury on equal terms with white G.I.'s. The sight of these Negroes seemed like a fulfillment of the old prophecies to many cargo cult leaders. Nor must we forget the sheer scale of this invasion. Around a million U. S. troops passed through the Admiralty Islands, completely swamping the inhabitants. It was a world of meaningless and chaotic changes, in which anything was possible. New ideas were imported and given local twists. Thus in the Loyalty Islands people expected the French Communist Party to bring the millennium. There is no real evidence, however, of any Communist influence in these movements, despite the rather hysterical belief among Solomon Island planters that the name of the local "Masinga Rule" movement was derived from the word "Marxian"! In reality the name comes from a Solomon Island tongue, and means "brotherhood."

Europeans who have witnessed outbreaks inspired by the cargo cults are usually at a loss to understand what they behold. The islanders throw away their money, break their most sacred taboos, abandon their gardens and destroy their precious livestock; they indulge in sexual license or, alternatively, rigidly separate men from women in huge communal establishments. Sometimes they spend days sitting gazing at the horizon for a glimpse of the long-awaited ship or airplane; sometimes they dance, pray and sing in mass congregations, becoming possessed and "speaking with tongues."

Observers have not hesitated to use such words as "madness," "mania," and "irrationality" to characterize the cults. But the cults reflect quite logical and rational attempts to make sense out of a social order that appears senseless and chaotic. Given the ignorance of the Melanesians about the wider European society, its economic organization and its highly developed technology, their reactions form a consistent and understandable pattern. They wrap up all their yearning and hope in an amalgam that combines the best counsel they can find in Christianity and their native belief. If the world is soon to end, gardening or fishing is unnecessary; everything will be provided. If the Melanesians are

have been dominant, from Roman Catholic to Seventh Day Adventist. The reasons for the emergence of these cults, of course, lie far deeper in the life-experience of the people.

The economy of most of the islands is very backward. Native agriculture produces little for the world market, and even the European plantations and mines export only a few primary products and raw materials: copra, rubber, gold. Melanesians are quite unable to understand why copra, for example,

fetches 30 pounds sterling per ton one month and but 5 pounds a few months later. With no notion of the workings of world-commodity markets, the natives see only the sudden closing of plantations, reduced wages and unemployment, and are inclined to attribute their insecurity to the whim or evil in the nature of individual planters.

Such shocks have not been confined to the economic order. Governments, too, have come and gone, especially during the two world wars: German, Dutch, British and French administrations melt-

NEW GUINEA has been a prolific breeder of cargo cults, resulting from the impact of Dutch, German, British and Japanese rule on its Stone Age cultures. At present the western portion is held by the Netherlands but claimed by Indonesia. The southeast (Papua) and northeast (U.N. Trust Territory of New Guinea) are governed by Australia.

a MYTH OF THE RETURN OF THE DEAD
b REVIVAL OR MODIFICATION OF PAGANISM
c INTRODUCTION OF CHRISTIAN ELEMENTS
d CARGO MYTH
e BELIEF THAT NEGROES WILL BECOME WHITE MEN AND VICE VERSA
f BELIEF IN A COMING MESSIAH
g ATTEMPTS TO RESTORE NATIVE POLITICAL AND ECONOMIC CONTROL
h THREATS AND VIOLENCE AGAINST WHITE MEN
i UNION OF TRADITIONALLY SEPARATE AND UNFRIENDLY GROUPS

4   KORERI MOVEMENT   NUMFOR, DUTCH NEW GUINEA   1911
5   KORERI MOVEMENT   BIAK, DUTCH NEW GUINEA   1939
6   KORERI MOVEMENT   BIAK, DUTCH NEW GUINEA   1886
7   KORERI MOVEMENT   BIAK, GEELVINK BAY, DUTCH NEW GUINEA   1942-1947
8   SIMSON INCIDENT   HOLLANDIA, DUTCH NEW GUINEA   1940- ?
9   PAMAI MOVEMENT   LAKE SENTANI, DUTCH NEW GUINEA   1928
10   NIMBORAN MOVEMENT   LAKE SENTANI, DUTCH NEW GUINEA   1945
11   NINIGO ISLANDS MOVEMENT   NINIGO ISLANDS, NEW GUINEA   1945- ?
12   BLACK KINGS MOVEMENT   AITAPE, WEWAK, NEW GUINEA   1930
13   GREAT PIGS   WEST-CENTRAL NEW GUINEA   1946
14   HINE MOVEMENT   WABAG, CENTRAL NEW GUINEA   1945
15   BLACK KINGS MOVEMENT   MOUNT HAGEN, NEW GUINEA   1940
16   NATIVE KING   KERAM RIVER, CENTRAL NEW GUINEA   1943-1945
17   GHOST WIND   KAINANTU, CENTRAL NEW GUINEA   1940-1947
18   TOMMY KABU COOPERATIVE MOVEMENT   PURARI DELTA, PAPUA   1945-1947
19   BATAWI INCIDENT   WESTERN PAPUA
20   GERMAN WISLIN   SAIBAI, TORRES STRAIT   1913-1915
21   VAILALA MADNESS   PAPUA   1919-1931
22   FILO INCIDENT   MEKEO, PAPUA   1940-1941
23   GOILALA AND GOGODARA CULT   PAPUA   1945
24   PIG KILLING   KAIRUKU, PAPUA   1937
25   THREE BLACK KINGS   WEWAK, NEW GUINEA   1948-1949
26   MAMBU MOVEMENT   MADANG, NEW GUINEA   1937-1940
27   TIFU INCIDENT   RAMU, MADANG, NEW GUINEA   1951
28   BLACK KING MOVEMENT   MADANG, NEW GUINEA   1935
29   KUKUAIK MOVEMENT   KARKAR ISLAND, NEW GUINEA   1940- ?
30   CARGO CULT   MADANG, NEW GUINEA   1940
31   CARGO CULT   MADANG, NEW GUINEA   1934
32   YALI INCIDENT   MADANG, NEW GUINEA   1945-1955
33   GARIA MOVEMENT   MADANG, NEW GUINEA   1940- ?
34   SECOND COMING OF CHRIST   RAI COAST, NEW GUINEA   1936
35   LETUB MOVEMENT   MADANG, NEW GUINEA   1939-1940
36   EEMASANG MOVEMENT   HUON PENINSULA, NEW GUINEA   1927- ?
37   COMING OF JESUS   EASTERN HIGHLANDS, CENTRAL NEW GUINEA   1943-1945
38   TIMO INCIDENT   HUON PENINSULA, NEW GUINEA   1922
39   THREE BLACK KINGS   FINSCHHAFEN, NEW GUINEA   1945- ?
40   LAZARUS MOVEMENT   HUON PENINSULA, NEW GUINEA   1933
41   SOSOM INCIDENT   MOUNT GOLDBERG, NEW GUINEA   1936
42   MOROBE MOVEMENT   MOROFE, NEW GUINEA   1933-1936
43   MARKHAM VALLEY MOVEMENT   MARKHAM VALLEY, NEW GUINEA   1932-1934
44   YERUMOT INCIDENT   TOEPFER RIVER, NEW GUINEA   1930- ?
45   SCHWAERMEREI   RAWLINSON RANGE, NEW GUINEA   1933
46   MARKHAM VALLEY MOVEMENT   MARKHAM VALLEY, NEW GUINEA   1932-1934
47   BAIGONA MOVEMENT   MASSIM, NEW GUINEA   1912-1919
48   TARO CULT   NORTHEAST NEW GUINEA   1914-1928
49   PIG KILLING   NORTH PAPUA   1930
50   PIG KILLING   NORTHEAST PAPUA   1930
51   ASSISI CULT   NORTHEAST PAPUA   1930-1944
52   MILNE BAY MOVEMENT   MASSIM, NEW GUINEA   1893- ?
53   PALIAU MOVEMENT   MANUS AND BALUAN, ADMIRALTY ISLANDS   1946-1954
54   THE NOISE   RAMBUDJON, ADMIRALTY ISLANDS   1946-1948 (?)
55   BATARI MOVEMENT   GALILO, NEW BRITAIN   1940-1946
56   BAINING TROUBLES   NEW BRITAIN   1955
57   BAINING MOVEMENT   NEW BRITAIN   1929-1930
58   KOKOPO MOVEMENT   NEW BRITAIN   1930 (?)
59   NAMATANAI MOVEMENT   NEW IRELAND   1939

to be part of a much wider order, the taboos that prescribe their social conduct must now be lifted or broken in a newly prescribed way.

Of course the cargo never comes. The cults nonetheless live on. If the millennium does not arrive on schedule, then perhaps there is some failure in the magic, some error in the ritual. New breakaway groups organize around "purer" faith and ritual. The cult rarely disappears, so long as the social situation which brings it into being persists.

At this point it should be observed that cults of this general kind are not peculiar to Melanesia. Men who feel

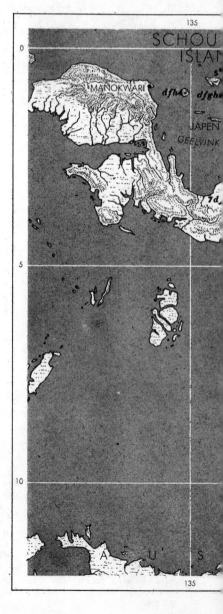

themselves oppressed and deceived have always been ready to pour their hopes and fears, their aspirations and frustrations, into dreams of a millennium to come or of a golden age to return. All parts of the world have had their counterparts of the cargo cults, from the American Indian ghost dance to the communist-millenarist "reign of the saints" in Münster during the Reformation, from medieval European apocalyptic cults to African "witch-finding" movements and Chinese Buddhist heresies. In some situations men have been content to wait and pray; in others they have sought to hasten the day by using their strong right arms to do the Lord's work. And always the cults serve to bring together scattered groups, notably the peasants and urban plebeians of agrarian societies and the peoples of "stateless" societies where the cult unites separate (and often hostile) villages, clans and tribes into a wider religio-political unity.

Once the people begin to develop secular political organizations, however, the sects tend to lose their importance as vehicles of protest. They begin to relegate the Second Coming to the distant future or to the next world. In Melanesia ordinary political bodies, trade unions and native councils are becoming the normal media through which the islanders express their aspirations. In recent years continued economic prosperity and political stability have taken some of the edge off their despair. It now seems unlikely that any major movement along cargo-cult lines will recur in areas where the transition to secular politics has been made, even if the insecurity of prewar times returned. I would predict that the embryonic nationalism represented by cargo cults is likely in future to take forms familiar in the history of other countries that have moved from subsistence agriculture to participation in the world economy.

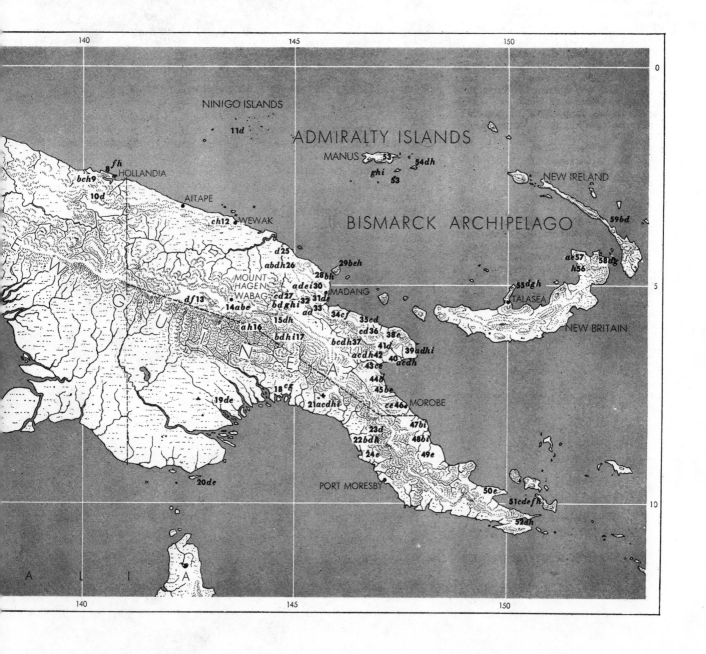

SOLOMON ISLANDS, administered by Australia and Great Britain, are another center of cargo cults, some caused by the cataclysmic impact of World War II. The data contained in these maps and tables, prepared by the author and Jean Guiart of the Ecole des Hautes Etudes in Paris, are not a complete list of cargo cults. Many dates are only approximate.

a MYTH OF THE RETURN OF THE DEAD
b REVIVAL OR MODIFICATION OF PAGANISM
c INTRODUCTION OF CHRISTIAN ELEMENTS
d CARGO MYTH
e BELIEF THAT NEGROES WILL BECOME WHITE MEN AND VICE VERSA
f BELIEF IN A COMING MESSIAH
g ATTEMPTS TO RESTORE NATIVE POLITICAL AND ECONOMIC CONTROL
h THREATS AND VIOLENCE AGAINST WHITE MEN
i UNION OF TRADITIONALLY SEPARATE AND UNFRIENDLY GROUPS

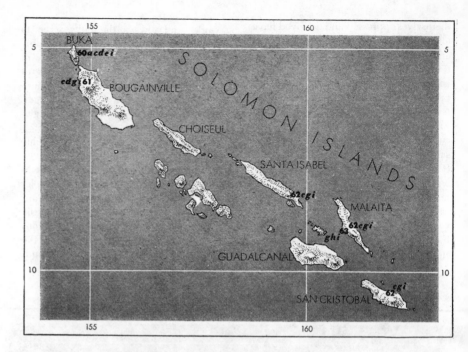

60 BUKA MOVEMENTS NORTHERN SOLOMON ISLANDS 1913-1935
61 BOUGAINVILLE MOVEMENT NORTHERN SOLOMON ISLANDS 1935-1939
62 MAASINA (MARCHING) RULE MALAITA, SOLOMON ISLANDS 1945-1958
63 CHAIR AND RULE CULT MALAITA, SOLOMON ISLANDS 1935

NEW HEBRIDES AND NEW CALEDONIA are, respectively, Anglo-French and French possessions. One New Caledonian cult placed Messianic hopes in the Communist Party.

FIJI ISLANDS are a British colony. Although generally Christianized, they have spawned several semi-Christian cargo cults.

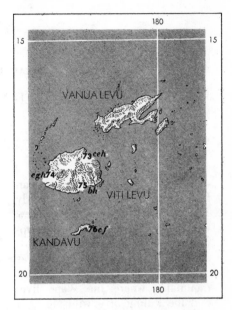

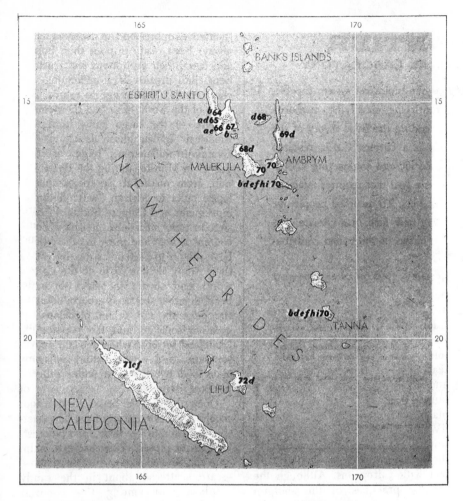

64 MAMARA MOVEMENT (NAKED CULT) WEST-CENTRAL ESPIRITU SANTO,
NEW HEBRIDES 1945-1951
65 ATORI INCIDENT SOUTH ESPIRITU SANTO, NEW HEBRIDES 1945
66 RONGOFURO AFFAIR SOUTH ESPIRITU SANTO, NEW HEBRIDES 1914-1923
67 AVA-AVU INCIDENT SOUTH-CENTRAL ESPIRITU SANTO, NEW HEBRIDES 1937
68 MALEKULA NATIVE COMPANY CENTRAL NEW HEBRIDES 1950
69 BULE INCIDENT MELSISI, PENTECOST, NEW HEBRIDES 1947
70 JOHN FRUM MOVEMENT TANNA, NEW HEBRIDES 1938-1958
71 PWAGAC INCIDENT NORTHERN NEW CALEDONIA 1941
72 "COMMUNIST PARTY" LIFU, NEW CALEDONIA 1947

a MYTH OF THE RETURN OF THE DEAD
b REVIVAL OR MODIFICATION OF
     PAGANISM
c INTRODUCTION OF CHRISTIAN
     ELEMENTS
d CARGO MYTH
e BELIEF THAT NEGROES WILL
     BECOME WHITE MEN AND
     VICE VERSA

f BELIEF IN A COMING MESSIAH
g ATTEMPTS TO RESTORE NATIVE
     POLITICAL AND ECONOMIC
     CONTROL
h THREATS AND VIOLENCE AGAINST
     WHITE MEN
i UNION OF TRADITIONALLY
     SEPARATE AND UNFRIENDLY
     GROUPS

73 TUKA MOVEMENT CENTRAL VITI LEVU,
FIJI 1873-1920
74 APOLOSI MOVEMENT WEST VITI LEVU,
FIJI 1914-1940
75 LUVE-NI-WAI CENTRAL VITI LEVU,
FIJI 1880- ?
76 KELEVI SECT KADAVU, FIJI 1945-1947

a MYTH OF THE RETURN OF THE DEAD
b REVIVAL OR MODIFICATION OF
     PAGANISM
c INTRODUCTION OF CHRISTIAN
     ELEMENTS
d CARGO MYTH
e BELIEF THAT NEGROES WILL
     BECOME WHITE MEN AND
     VICE VERSA
f BELIEF IN A COMING MESSIAH
g ATTEMPTS TO RESTORE NATIVE
     POLITICAL AND ECONOMIC
     CONTROL
h THREATS AND VIOLENCE AGAINST
     WHITE MEN
i UNION OF TRADITIONALLY
     SEPARATE AND UNFRIENDLY
     GROUPS

39

A New Weapon Stirs Up Old Ghosts

BY WILLIAM E. MITCHELL

When, in 1947, the Franciscan friars went to live among the nearly 10,000 Wape people of New Guinea, the principal native weapons were bone daggers and the bow and arrow. Even then, game was scarce in the heavily populated mountains where the Wape live, and the killing of a wild pig or a cassowary, New Guinea's major game animals, was an important village event. The Wape live in the western part of the Sepik River Basin. Their small villages lie along the narrow ridges of the Torricelli Mountains, above the sago palm swamps where women process palm pith, the Wape staff of life.

Today the Wape hunter's principal weapon is still the bow and arrow and game is even scarcer. This is partially the result of a new addition to the hunter's armory—the prosaic shotgun—which has had a profound moral impact on Wape village life.

The first guns were brought into this area in the late 1940s and early 1950s by missionaries, traders, and Australian government officials. Although natives were not permitted to own guns, they could use them if employed by a white man to shoot game for his table. This was a very prestigious job.

In 1960, government regulations were changed to permit natives to purchase single-shot shotguns. At first only a few Wape men, living in villages close to the government station and helpful to government officials, were granted gun permits. Eventually more permits were is-

sued, but today, in hopes of preserving the remaining game, one permit is issued for every 100 people.

Within ten years of the granting of the first gun permits, a belief and behavioral system had evolved around the shotgun. It was based on traditional Wape hunting lore but had distinctive elaborations stemming from native perceptions of the teachings of government officials and missionaries. For descriptive purposes I call this system of formalized beliefs and ritual the "Wape shotgun cult." It is one of several Wape ceremonial cults, but the only one originating after contact with Europeans. Although the specific practices of the shotgun cult vary from village to village, the underlying beliefs are the same.

In creating the shotgun cult the Wape faced the challenge of adapting an introduced implement to their culture. Unlike steel axes and knives, which replaced stone adzes and bamboo knives, the shotgun has never replaced the bow and arrow. The shotgun is a scarce and expensive machine. This, together with the European sanctions imposed upon its introduction, places it in a unique position, both symbolically and behaviorally, among the Wape.

The cult is a conservative institution. It breaks no new cognitive ground by challenging established Wape concepts. Instead it merges traditional hunting concepts with European moral teachings to create a coherent system. The cult upholds

traditional beliefs, accepts European authority, and most important, provides an explanation for unsuccessful hunting.

In 1970, my family and I arrived in Lumi, a small mountain settlement, which is the government's subdistrict headquarters in the middle of Wapeland. For the next year and a half, we lived in the village of Taute, near Lumi. There my wife and I studied Wape culture.

Taute, which has a population of 220, is reached by narrow foot trails, root strewn and muddy, passing through the dense, damp forest. The low houses—made of sago palm stems and roofed with sago thatch—are scattered about in the sandy plaza and among the coconut palms and breadfruit trees along the ridge. Towering poinsettias, red and pink hibiscus, and multicolored shrubs contrast with the encircling forest's greens and browns. A few small latrines perch on the steep slopes, concessions to Western concepts of hygiene. In the morning, flocks of screeching cockatoos glide below the ridge through the rising mists. When the breadfruit trees are bearing, giant fruit bats flop across the sky at dusk.

Since the mid-1950s the Franciscan friars have maintained, off and on, a religious school in Taute. There, Wape boys are instructed by a native catechist in Catholicism,

Mani, represented by a high conical mask, is a spirit who can insure good hunting. As he prances about the village, his joyful mien amuses the children.

simple arithmetic, and Melanesian Pidgin. A priest from Lumi visits the village several times a year, and the villagers, Catholic and heathen alike, are proud of their affiliation with the Franciscans and staunchly loyal to them. But their Catholicism is nominal and superficial—a scant and brittle frosting that does not mask their own religious beliefs, which dominate everyday life.

The ethos of Wape society is oriented around sacred curing rituals. Whereas some Sepik cultures aggressively center their ceremonial life around headhunting and the raising of sturdy and brave children, the Wape defensively center theirs in the ritual appeasement of malevolent ghosts and forest demons, who they believe cause sickness. Most men belong to one of the demon-curing cults where, once initiated as priests, they are responsible for producing the often elaborate curing ceremonies for exorcising the demon from the afflicted.

The little money that exists among the Wape is earned primarily by the men, who work as two-year contract laborers on the coastal and island copra plantations. Because of the lack of money to buy canned meats, the scarcity of game, and the paucity of fish in the mountain streams, the protein intake of the Wape is exceedingly low. The most common meal is sago dumplings and boiled leaves. Malnutrition is common among youngsters, and physical development is generally retarded. According to studies by Dr. Lyn Wark, a medical missionary who has worked widely among the Wape, the average birth weight of the Wape baby is the lowest recorded in the world. Correspondingly, secondary sex characteristics are delayed. For example, the mean age for the onset of menses is over eighteen years.

Before contact with Westerners, Wape men were naked and the women wore short string skirts. Today most men wear shorts and the women wear skirts purchased from Lumi's four small stores. To appear

in a semblance of European dress, however meager or worn, is a matter of pride and modesty to both sexes. "Savages" do not wear clothes, but white men and those who have been enlightened by white men do. In this sense, the Wape's Western-style dress represents an identification with the politically and materially powerful white man. The identification is with power; it is an ego-enhancing maneuver that permits the Wape to live with dignity, even though they are subservient to Western rule and influence. The tendency of the Wape to identify with, and incorporate, the alien when it serves to preserve their culture will help us to understand how they have woven diverse cultural strands into the creation of the shotgun cult.

From the first day I arrived in Taute, the men repeatedly made two urgent requests of me. One was to open a store in the village, saving them the difficult walk into Lumi; the other was to buy a shotgun to help them kill game. This was the

least, they seemed to indicate, a fair-minded and, in Wape terms, obviously rich neighbor should do. One of the hardest things the anthropologist in the field must learn is to say "no" to deserving people. To be stingy is almost to be un-American, but we had come halfway around the world to learn about the Wape way of life, not to introduce stores and shotguns that would alter the established trading and hunting patterns.

After several months the people of the major Taute hamlets, Kafiere, where we lived, and Mifu, a ten-minute walk away, each decided to buy a group-owned shotgun. The investment was a sizable forty-two Australian dollars; forty dollars for the gun and two dollars for the gun permit. Each hamlet made a volunteer collection from its members and I, as a fellow villager,

Left, men carry a wild pig into a hunting camp. There it will be ritually butchered and distributed to other villagers by the owner of the cartridge, which the gunman, below used to kill the animal.

contributed to both guns. A week later the villagers purchased the guns from one of the Lumi stores, and I began to learn about the shotgun's ritual and moral importance to the Wape. The villagers were already familiar with the significance of the shotgun for they had purchased one several years before. The cult ended, however, when the gun broke.

The shotgun, like Melanesian Pidgin, is associated by the Wape with Europeans and modernity. Not surprisingly, Pidgin is favored for shotgun parlance. The licensed gunman is not only called *sutboi* ("shootboy") but also *laman* ("law man"), the latter a term that connotes his official tie to European law and government as perceived by the villagers.

When a candidate for a gun permit appears before the government official in Lumi, he is examined orally on the use of firearms, then given an unloaded shotgun and tested on his handling knowledge. Under the direct and questioning gaze of the examining official, candidates sometimes become flustered. One inadvertently aimed the gun first toward the wife of the assistant district commissioner and then toward a group of observers. His examination ended ignominiously on the spot.

If the candidate passes the test and the examining official approves of his character, he is then lectured on the use of the gun: only the candidate can fire it, he must willingly shoot game for his fellow villagers, and the gun must be used exclusively for hunting. He is strongly warned that if any of these rules are broken or if there is trouble in the village, he will lose the gun and the permit and will be imprisoned.

The candidate's friends and the inevitable audience are present for the lecture. Here, as in many spheres of native life, the official's power is absolute, and the Wape know this from long experience. Guns have been confiscated or destroyed without reimbursement, and gunmen have been jailed.

The official's charge to the candidate is willingly accepted. Henceforth, he will never leave the village without carrying his gun. He is now a *laman*, and he has the gun and permit, printed entirely in English, to prove it.

The government official's strong sanctions against village quarrels are motivated by his fear that the gun might be used in a dispute among villagers. The sanctions are further upheld by the missionaries' and catechists' sermons against quarreling and wrongdoing as they attempt to teach the Christian doctrine of brotherly love. The message the villagers receive is this: To keep the white man's gun, they must follow the white man's rules. This the Wape do, not in servile submission, but with some pride because the presence of the gun and the public focus on morality mark the village as progressive and modern. The licensed gunman, therefore, is not only the guardian of the gun but of village morality as well.

Rain or shine, he is expected to go into the forest without compensation to hunt for his fellow villagers, who give him cartridges with some personal identifying mark upon them. After a gunman makes a kill, the owner of the cartridge receives the game and distributes it according to his economic obligations to others. But the gunman, like the bow and arrow hunter, is forbidden to eat from the kill; to do so would jeopardize further successful hunting.

In the hamlet of Kafiere, the clan that had contributed the most money toward the gun and on whose lands the most game was to be found appointed Auwe as gunman. But Auwe's wife, Naiasu, was initially against his selection. Her previous husband, Semer, now dead several years, had been Kafiere's first *sutboi* and she argued that the heavy hunting responsibilities of a *sutboi* took too much time, forcing him to neglect his own gardening and hunting obligations.

When Auwe first requested a gun permit he was turned away. The vil-

lagers believed that the ghost of Naiasu's dead husband, Semer, had followed Auwe to Lumi and influenced the examining official against him. Semer's ghost was acting to fulfill Naiasu's wish that her young son, now Auwe's stepson, would have a stepfather who was always available. This was the first of many stories I was to hear about the relationship between ghosts and the gun. When Auwe returned to Lumi for a second try, he passed the examination and was given the official permit.

The hamlet now had its own gun and hunting could begin in earnest. The first step was an annunciation feast called, in Pidgin, a *kapti* ("cup of tea"). Its purpose was to inform the villagers' dead ancestors about the new gun. This was important because ancestral ghosts roam the forest land of their lineage, protecting it from intruders and driving game to their hunting descendants. The hunter's most important hunting aide is his dead male relatives, to whom he prays for game upon entering his hunting lands. The dead remain active in the affairs of the living by protecting them from harm, providing them with meat, and punishing those who have wronged them.

The small sacrificial feast was held in front of Auwe's house. Placing the upright gun on a makeshift table in the midst of the food, Auwe rubbed it with sacred ginger. One of Auwe's elderly clansmen, standing and facing his land, called out to his ancestors by name and told them about the new gun. He implored them to send wild pigs and cassowaries to Auwe.

Several men spoke of the new morality that was to accompany hunting with a gun. The villagers should not argue or quarrel among themselves; problems must be settled quietly and without bitterness; malicious gossip and stealing were forbidden. If these rules were not obeyed, Auwe would not find game.

In traditional Wape culture there is no feast analogous to the *kapti*. Indeed, there are no general com-

munity-wide feasts. The *kapti* is apparently modeled on a European social gathering.

For the remainder of my stay in Taute, I followed closely the fortunes of the Taute guns and of guns in nearby villages as well. All seemed to be faced with the same two problems: game was rarely seen; and when seen, was rarely killed. Considering that a cartridge belongs to a villager, not the gunman, how was this economic loss handled? This presented a most intriguing and novel problem for there were no analogs to this type of predicament within the traditional culture. By Wape standards, the pecuniary implications of such a loss, although but a few Australian shillings, could not graciously be ignored by the loser. At the very least the loss had to be explained even if the money for the cartridges could not be retrieved.

Now I understood the concern about the ancestral ghosts. If the hunter shot and missed, the owner of the fired shells was being punished by being denied meat. Either he or a close family member had quarreled or wronged another person whose ghost-relative was securing revenge by causing the hunter to miss. This, then, was the functional meaning of the proscription against quarreling. By avoiding disputes, the villagers were trying to prevent the intervention of ancestral ghosts in human affairs. In a peaceful village without quarrels, the gunman could hunt undisturbed by vengeful ghosts chasing away game or misrouting costly shells.

Although a number of factors in European culture have influenced the shotgun cult, the cult's basic premise of a positive correlation between quarreling and bad hunting is derived directly from traditional Wape culture. In bow and arrow hunting, an individual who feels he was not given his fair share of a hunter's kill may punish the hunter by gossiping about him or quarreling openly with him. The aggrieved person's ancestral ghosts revenge the slight by chasing the game away from the offending hunter or misdirecting his arrows. But this is a private affair between the hunter and the angered person; their quarrel has no influence upon the hunting of others. And it is rare for an issue other than distribution of game to cause a ghost to hinder a bowman's success. The hunter's prowess is restored only when the angered person performs a brief supplication rite over the hunter.

This, then, is the conceptual basis for the tie between quarreling and bad hunting. Originally relevant only to bow and arrow hunting, it was then broadened to accommodate the government's pronouncements about the shotgun and keeping the village peace. And it applies perfectly to the special circumstances of shotgun hunting. Because the shotgun is community owned and many villagers buy cartridges for it, the villagers are identified with both the gun and the gunman. As a proxy hunter for the villagers, the gunman is potentially subject to the ghostly sanctions resulting from their collective wrongs. Thus gun hunting, unlike bow and arrow hunting, is a community affair and the community-wide taboo against quarrels and personal transgressions is the only effective way to prevent spiteful ghosts from wrecking the hunt.

No village, however, even if populated by people as disciplined and well behaved as the Wape, can constantly live in the state of pious peace considered necessary for continuous good gun hunting. When the hunting is poor, the gunman must discover the quarrels and wrongs within the village. After having identified the individuals whose ancestral ghosts are sabotaging the hunting, the gunman must also see to it that they implore the ghosts to stop. Embarrassed by the public disclosure, they will quickly comply.

The common method for detecting points of friction within the village is to bring the villagers together for a special meeting. The gunman will then document in detail his misfortunes and call on the villagers to find out what is ruining the hunting. If confessions of wrongdoing are not forthcoming, questioning accusations result. The meeting, beginning in Pidgin, moves into Wape as the discussion becomes more complex and voluble. It may last up to three hours; but even if there is no resolution, it always ends amiably—at least on the surface. For it is important to create no new antagonisms.

The other technique for locating the source of the hunting problem is to call in a professional clairvoyant. As the villagers must pay for his services, he is usually consulted only after a series of unsuccessful meetings. Clairvoyants have replaced the shamans, who were outlawed by the government and the mission because they practiced sorcery and ritual murders. The Wape do not consider a clairvoyant a sorcerer; he is a man with second sight who is experienced in discovering and treating the hidden causes of intractable problems. As such, shotguns are among his best patients.

Mewau, a clairvoyant from a neighboring village, held a "shotgun clinic" in Taute to examine the Mifu and Kafiere guns. For about an hour he examined the two guns and questioned the villagers. Then he declared the reasons for their misfortune.

Kapul, a dead Mifu shaman, was preventing the Mifu gun from killing game because a close relative of the gunman had allegedly stolen valuables from Kapul's daughter. Because of the family ties between the gunman and the thief, Kapul's ghost was punishing the gunman.

The Kafiere gun, Mewau declared, was not able to find game because a widow in the village felt that her dead husband's clan had not previously distributed game to her in a fair way. By interfering with the Kafiere gun, her husband's ghost was punishing his clan for the neglect of his family.

Once the source of trouble is named, there are several possible types of remedial ritual depending upon the seriousness of the situation. For example, the circumstances surrounding the naming of the husband's ghost were considered serious, and a *kapti* was held to placate him. Another, simpler ritual involves the preparation of taro soup, which the gunman consumes. But the simplest, commonest remedial rite is the supplication ritual without sacrificial food offerings, a ritual in which I became involved.

Mifu's gunman had shot a pig with one of his own cartridges but did not give me the small portion due me as a part owner of the gun. Partly as a test to see if my ancestors counted for anything in Taute and partly because I did not want to let this calculated slight go unchallenged, I, in typical Wape fashion, said nothing to the gunman but gossiped discreetly about his selfishness. The gunman continued to hunt but had no further success. When his bad luck persisted, a meeting was called to find out the reason. The gunman asked me if I was angry because I had not been given my portion of the pig. When I acknowledged my anger, he handed the shotgun to me and I dutifully spoke out to my ancestors to stop turning the game away from the gun.

But the gunman still had no success in the hunt, and the villagers decided there were other wrongs as well. The search for the offending ghosts continued. Eventually the villagers became so discouraged with the Mifu gun that they stopped giving cartridges to the gunman. The consensus was that a major undetected wrong existed in the hamlet, and until it was uncovered and the guilty ghost called off, hunting with the gun was senseless and extravagant. Thus the propriety of a remedial rite is established if there is success on the next hunt. The system is completely empirical; if no game is seen or if seen, is not killed, then the search for the wrong must continue.

Wape people are generally even tempered, and their villages, in contrast to many in New Guinea, strike the newcomer as almost serene. But the social impact of the guns at this time was pervasive, and life in Taute literally revolved around the guns and their hunting fortunes. Whereas the villagers previously had kept to their own affairs, they now became embroiled in meeting after meeting, seeking out transgressions, quarrels, and wrongdoing. As the gunman continued to have bad luck, his efforts to discover the cause became more zealous. A certain amount of polarization resulted: the gunman accused the villagers, the men accused the women, and the adults accused the young people of hiding their wrongs. And a few who had lost many cartridges wondered if the *sutboi* was keeping the game for himself. But no one ever suggested that he was an inexperienced shotgun hunter. The gunman was generally considered to be blameless; in fact, the more game he missed, the more self-righteous he became and the more miscreant the villagers.

Six months of poor hunting had gone by; the villagers felt that the only recourse left to them was to bring a bush demon named *mani* into the village from the jungle for a festival. The *mani*'s small stone heart is kept enshrined in a rustic altar in a corner of Kafiere's ceremonial house and after a kill the animal's blood is smeared upon it. The *mani* will reward the village with further kills only if he is fed with blood. *Mani* is the only spirit, other than ghosts, who can cause both good and bad hunting depending upon the way he is treated. Soon after the shotgun arrived in Taute, the gunman and some other men left their homes to sleep in the men's ceremonial house to keep *mani*'s stone heart warm. They thought *mani*, in appreciation, would send game to the gunman.

When little game was killed, the villagers decided on the hunting festival. In a special house outside of the village, men constructed the great conical mask that depicts *mani*. For several weeks they worked to cover the mask's frame with the spathes of sago palm fronds painted with designs traditional to *mani*. Finally, a priest of the *mani* cult, wearing a 20-foot-high mask festooned with feathers and leaves, pranced into the village to the thunderous beat of wooden drums.

For the next week and a half men from other villages who wished us well came and joined in the all-night singing of the *mani* song cycle. In the morning, if the weather was clear, *mani* led the bow and arrow hunters and the gunman to the edge of the village and sent them on their way to hunting success. But in spite of the careful attentions the villagers directed toward *mani*, he rewarded them with only one wild pig. The villagers became openly discouraged, then annoyed. Finally the hunters, disgusted and weary from numerous long futile hunts, and other men, their shoulders sore and bloody from constantly carrying the heavy mask around the plaza, decided that *mani* was simply taking advantage of them; all of their hard work was for nothing. Disgusted, they decided to send *mani* back to his home in the forest.

One late afternoon the *mani* appeared in the plaza but he did not prance. He walked slowly around the plaza, stopping at each house to throw ashes over himself with his single bark cloth arm. The villagers said he was in mourning because he had to leave by dusk and would miss the company of men. Silently the people watched the once gay and graceful *mani* lumber out of the village. The men and boys followed him into the forest. Then the gunman split open the mask, to insure the spirit's exit and eventual return to his forest home, and hurled it over the edge of the cliff into the bush below.

A few months after the *mani* hunting festival, the shotgun cult as I had known it in Taute ceased to function. All but one of the able young men of the hamlet of Kafiere went off to work on a coastal plantation for two years. With no young men, the ceremonial activities of the hunting and curing cults were suspended and the fault-finding meetings halted until their return. The drama and excitement of the previous months had vanished with the men.

40

The Serpent-Handling Religions of West Virginia

BY NATHAN L. GERRARD

. . . .

. . . And these signs shall follow them that believe; In my name shall they cast out devils; they shall speak with new tongues; They shall take up serpents; and if they drink any deadly thing, it shall not hurt them; they shall lay hands on the sick, and they shall recover.

Mark 16:17–18

In Southern Appalachia, two dozen or three dozen fundamentalist congregations take this passage literally and "take up serpents." They use copperheads, water moccasins, and rattlesnakes in their religious services.

The serpent-handling ritual was inaugurated between 1900 and 1910, probably by George Went Hensley. Hensley began evangelizing in rural Grasshopper Valley, Tenn., then traveled widely throughout the South, particularly in Kentucky, spreading his religion. He died in Florida at 70—of snakebite. To date, the press has reported about 20 such deaths among the serpent-handlers. One other death was recorded last year, in Kentucky.

For seven years, my wife and I have been studying a number of West Virginia serpent-handlers, primarily in order to discover what effect this unusual form of religious practice has on their lives. Although serpent-handling is outlawed by the state legislatures of Kentucky, Virginia, and Tennessee and by municipal ordinances in North Carolina, it is still legal in West Virginia. One center is the Scrabble Creek Church of All Nations in Fayette County, about 37 miles from Charleston. Another center is the Church of Jesus in Jolo, McDowell County, one of the most poverty-stricken areas of the state. Serpent-handling is also practiced sporadically elsewhere in West Virginia, where it is usually led by visitors from Scrabble Creek or Jolo.

The Jolo church attracts people from both Virginia and Kentucky, in addition to those from West Virginia.

Members of the Scrabble Creek church speak with awe of the Jolo services, where people pick up large handfuls of poisonous snakes, fling them to the ground, pick them up again, and thrust them under their shirts or blouses, dancing ecstatically. We attended one church service in Scrabble Creek where visitors from Jolo covered their heads with clusters of snakes and wore them as crowns.

Serpent-handling was introduced to Scrabble Creek in 1941 by a coal miner from Harlan, Ky. The practice really began to take hold in 1946, when the present leader of the Scrabble Creek church, then a member of the Church of God, first took up serpents. The four or five original serpent-handlers in Fayette County met at one another's homes until given the use of an abandoned one-room school house in Big Creek. In 1959, when their number had swelled several times over, they moved to a larger church in Scrabble Creek.

SNAKEBITES, SAINTS, AND SCOFFERS

During the course of our seven-year study, about a dozen members of the church received snakebites. (My wife and I were present on two of these occasions.) Although there were no deaths, each incident was widely and unfavorably publicized in the area. For their part, the serpent-handlers say the Lord causes a snake to strike in order to refute scoffers' claims that the snakes' fangs have been pulled. They see each recovery from snakebites as a miracle wrought by the Lord—and each death as a sign that the Lord "really had to show the scoffers how dangerous it is to obey His commandments." Since adherents believe that death brings one to the throne of God, some express an eagerness to die when He decides they are ready. Those who have been bitten and who have recovered seem to receive special deference from other members of the church.

The ritual of serpent-handling takes only 15 or 20 minutes in religious sessions that are seldom shorter than four hours. The rest of the service includes singing Christian hymns, ecstatic dancing, testifying, extemporaneous and impassioned sermons, faith-healing, "speaking in tongues," and foot-washing. These latter rituals are a part of the firmly-rooted Holiness movement, which encompasses thousands of churches in the Southern Appalachian region. The Holiness churches started in the 19th century as part of a perfectionist movement.

The social and psychological functions served by the Scrabble Creek church are probably very much the same as those served by the more conventional Holiness churches. Thus, the extreme danger of the Scrabble Creek rituals probably helps to validate the members' claims to holiness. After all, the claim that one is a living saint is pretentious even in a sacred society—and it is particularly difficult to maintain in a secular society. That the serpent-handler regularly risks his life for his religion is seen as evidence of his saintliness. As the serpent-handler stresses over and over, "I'm afraid of snakes like anybody else, but when God anoints me, I handle them with joy." The fact that he is usually not bitten, or if bitten usually recovers, is cited as further evidence of his claim to holiness.

After we had observed the Scrabble Creek serpent-handlers for some time, we decided to give them psychological tests. We enlisted the aid of Auke Tellegen, department of psychology, University of Minnesota, and three of his clinical associates: James Butcher, William Schofield, and Anne Wirt. They interpreted the Minnesota Multiphasic Personality Inventory that we administered to 50 serpent-handlers (46 were completed)—and also to 90 members of a conventional-denomination church 20 miles from Scrabble Creek. What we wanted to find out was how these two groups differed.

What we found were important personality differences not only between the serpent-handlers and the conventional church members, but also between the older and the younger generations within the conventional group. We believe that these differences are due, ultimately, to differences in social class: The serpent-handlers come from the nonmobile working class (average annual income: $3000), whereas members of the conventional church are upwardly mobile working-class people (average annual income: $5000) with their eyes on the future.

But first, let us consider the similarities between the two groups. Most of the people who live in the south central part of West Virginia, serpent-handlers or not, have similar backgrounds. The area is rural, nonfarm, with only about one-tenth of the population living in settlements of more than 2500. Until recently, the dominant industry was coal-mining, but in the last 15 years mining operations have been drastically curtailed. The result has been widespread unemployment. Scrabble Creek is in that part of Appalachia that has been officially declared a "depressed area"—which means that current unemployment rates there often equal those of the depression.

There are few foreign-born in this part of West Virginia. Most of the residents are of Scottish-Irish or Pennsylvania Dutch descent, and their ancestors came to the New World so long ago that there are no memories of an Old World past.

Generally, public schools in the area are below national standards. Few people over 50 have had more than six or seven years of elementary education.

Religion has always been important here. One or two generations ago, the immediate ancestors of both serpent-handlers and conventional-church members lived in the same mining communities and followed roughly the same religious practices. Today there is much "back-sliding," and the majority seldom attend church regularly. But there is still a great deal of talk about religion, and there are few professed atheists.

HYPOCHONDRIA AND THE HOLY SPIRIT

Though the people of both churches are native-born Protestants with fundamentalist religious beliefs, little education, and precarious employment, the two groups seem to handle their common problems in very different ways. One of the first differences we noticed was in the way the older members of both churches responded to illness and old age. Because the members of both churches had been impoverished and medically neglected during childhood and young adulthood, and because they had earned their livelihoods in hazardous and health-destroying ways, they were old before their time. They suffered from a wide variety of physical ailments. Yet while the older members of the conventional church seemed to dwell morbidly on their physical disabilities, the aged serpent-handlers seemed able to cheerfully ignore their ailments.

The serpent-handlers, in fact, went to the opposite extreme. Far from being pessimistic hypochondriacs like the conventional-church members, the serpent-handlers were so intent on placing their fate in God's benevolent hands that they usually failed to take even the normal precautions in caring for their health. Three old serpent-handlers we knew in Scrabble Creek were suffering from serious cardiac conditions. But when the Holy Spirit moved them, they danced ecstatically and violently. And they did this without any apparent harm.

No matter how ill the old serpent-handlers are, unless they are actually prostrate in their beds they manage to attend and enjoy church services lasting four to six hours, two or three times a week. Some have to travel long distances over the mountains to get to church. When the long sessions are over, they appear refreshed rather than weary.

One evening an elderly woman was carried into the serpent-handling church in a wheelchair. She had had a severe stroke and was almost completely paralyzed. Wheeled to the front of the church, she watched everything throughout the long services. During one particularly frenzied singing and dancing session, the fingers of her right hand tapped lightly against the arm of the chair. This was the only movement she was able to make, but obviously she was enjoying the service. When friends leaned over and offered to take her home, she made it clear she was not ready to go. She stayed until the end, and gave the impression of smiling when she was finally wheeled out. Others in the church apparently felt pleased rather than depressed by her presence.

Both old members of the conventional denomination and old serpent-handlers undoubtedly are frequently visited by the thought of death. Both rely on religion for solace, but the serpent-handlers evidently are more successful. The old serpent-handlers are not frightened by the prospect of death. This is true not only of those members who handle poisonous snakes in religious services, but also of the minority who do *not* handle serpents.

One 80-year-old member of the Scrabble Creek church—who did not handle serpents—testified in our presence: "I am not afraid to meet my Maker in Heaven. I am ready. If somebody was to wave a gun in my face, I would not turn away. I am in God's hands."

Another old church member, a serpent-handler, was dying from silicosis. When we visited him in the hospital he appeared serene, although he must have known that he would not live out the week.

The assertion of some modern theologians that whatever meaning and relevance God once may have had has been lost for modern man does not apply to the old serpent-handlers. To them, God is real. In fact, they often see Him during vivid hallucinations. He watches over the faithful. Misfortune and even death do not shake their faith, for misfortune is interpreted, in accordance with God's inscrutable will, as a hidden good.

Surprisingly, the contrast between the optimistic old serpent-handlers and the pessimistic elders of the conventional church all but disappeared when we

shifted to the younger members of the two groups. Both groups of young people, on the psychological tests, came out as remarkably well adjusted. They showed none of the neurotic and depressive tendencies of the older conventional-church members. And this cheerful attitude prevailed despite the fact that many of them, at least among the young serpent-handlers, had much to be depressed about.

The young members of the conventional church are much better off, socially and economically, than the young serpent-handlers. The parents of the young conventional-church members can usually provide the luxuries that most young Americans regard as necessities. Many conventional-church youths are active in extracurricular activities in high school or are attending college. The young serpent-handlers, in contrast, are shunned and stigmatized as "snakes." Most young members of the conventional denomination who are in high school intend to go on to college, and they will undoubtedly attain a higher socioeconomic status than their parents have attained. But most of the young serpent-handlers are not attending school. Many are unemployed. None attend or plan to attend college, and they often appear quite depressed about their economic prospects.

The young serpent-handlers spend a great deal of time wandering aimlessly up and down the roads of the hollows, and undoubtedly are bored when not attending church. Their conversation is sometimes marked by humor, with undertones of cynicism and bitterness. We are convinced that what prevents many of them from becoming delinquent or demoralized is their wholehearted participation in religious practices that provide an acceptable outlet for their excess energy, and strengthen their self-esteem by giving them the opportunity to achieve "holiness."

Now, how does all this relate to the class differences between the serpent-handlers and the conventional-church group? The answer is that what allows the serpent-handlers to cope so well with their problems— what allows the older members to rise above the worries of illness and approaching death, and the younger members to remain relatively well-adjusted despite their grim economic prospects—is a certain approach to life that is typical of them as members of the stationary working class. The key to this approach is hedonism.

HOPELESSNESS AND HEDONISM

The psychological tests shows that the young serpent-handlers, like their elders, were more impulsive and spontaneous than the members of the conventional church. This may account for the strong appeal of the

Holiness churches to those members of the stationary working class who prefer religious hedonism to reckless hedonism, with its high incidence of drunkenness and illegitimacy. Religious hedonism is compatible with a puritan morality—and it compensates for its constraints.

The feeling that one cannot plan for the future, expressed in religious terms as "being in God's hands," fosters the widespread conviction among members of the stationary working class that opportunities for pleasure must be exploited immediately. After all, they may never occur again. This attitude is markedly different from that of the upwardly mobile working class, whose members are willing to postpone immediate pleasures for the sake of long-term goals.

Hedonism in the stationary working class is fostered in childhood by parental practices that, while demanding obedience in the home, permit the child license outside the home. Later, during adulthood, this orientation toward enjoying the present and ignoring the future is reinforced by irregular employment and the other insecurities of stationary working-class life. In terms of middle-class values, hedonism is self-defeating. But from a psychiatric point of view, for those who actually have little control of their position in the social and economic structure of modern society, it may very well aid acceptance of the situation. This is particularly true when it takes a religious form of expression. Certainly, hedonism and the associated trait of spontaneity seen in the old serpent-handlers form a very appropriate attitude toward life among old people who can no longer plan for the future.

In addition to being more hedonistic than members of the conventional church, the serpent-handlers are also more exhibitionistic. This exhibitionism and the related need for self-revelation are, of course, directly related to the religious practices of the serpent-handling church. But frankness, both about others and themselves, is typical of stationary working-class people in general. To a large extent, this explains the appeal of the Holiness churches. Ordinarily, their members have little to lose from frankness, since their status pretensions are less than those of the upwardly mobile working class, who are continually trying to present favorable images of themselves.

Because the young members of the conventional denomination are upwardly mobile, they tend to regard their elders as "old-fashioned," "stick-in-the-muds," and "ignorant." Naturally, this lack of respect from their children and grandchildren further depresses the sagging morale of the older conventional-church members. They respond resentfully to the tendency of the young "to think they know more than their elders." The result is a vicious circle of increasing alienation and depression among the older members of the conventional denomination.

RESPECT FOR AGE

There appears to be much less psychological incompatibility between the old and the young serpent-handlers. This is partly because the old serpent-handlers manage to retain a youthful spontaneity in their approach to life. Then too, the young serpent-handlers do not take a superior attitude toward their elders. They admire their elders for their greater knowledge of the Bible, which both old and young accept as literally true. And they also admire their elders for their handling of serpents. The younger church members, who handle snakes much less often than the older members do, are much more likely to confess an ordinary, everyday fear of snakes—a fear that persists until overcome by strong religious emotion.

Furthermore, the young serpent-handlers do not expect to achieve higher socioeconomic status than their elders. In fact, several young men said they would be satisfied if they could accomplish as much. From the point of view of the stationary working class, many of the older serpent-handlers are quite well-off. They sometimes draw two pensions, one from Social Security and one from the United Mine Workers.

Religious serpent-handling, then—and all the other emotionalism of the Holiness churches that goes with it—serves a definite function in the lives of its adherents. It is a safety valve for many of the frustrations of life in present-day Appalachia. For the old, the serpent-handling religion helps soften the inevitability of poor health, illness, and death. For the young, with their poor educations and poor hopes of finding sound jobs, its promise of holiness is one of the few meaningful goals in a future dominated by the apparent inevitability of lifelong poverty and idleness.

TOPIC FOURTEEN

The Social Costs of Modernization

Modernization refers to the global transformation of society, a transformation that has its roots in the emergence of the industrial revolution. Although its particular manifestations vary widely due to local social, historical, cultural, political, and economic conditions (and also environmental riches and limitations), students of modernization have noted that certain elements characterize this phenomenon everywhere. As summarized by anthropologist Helen Henderson, these include the following:

1. Subsistence farming gives way to cultivation of agricultural products for the market, and new jobs are created in trade, manufacturing, and administration.

2. New sources of energy are exploited, and individual wage earners operate machines within the industrial system.

3. Specialized educational institutions are created to bring literacy to the masses and impart new skills and knowledge.

4. Urban areas develop rapidly as rural immigrants flow into cities in search of economic opportunities. Urbanites cut their ties with their extended kin, are freed from many traditional restraints, and step into new social roles.

5. The functions of the family change (and the form may as well). It is no longer a unit of production but specializes in the socialization of offspring and the organization of consumption.

6. Some scholars would add that modernization also introduces new forms of alienation into the lives of industrial workers, who lose control over the product of their labor and whose work tends to be repetitive and dull.

Modernization, therefore, means far more than a series of adjustments in indigenous economic systems. Rather, it refers to qualitative changes in the organization of society, in culture, and even in individual personalities.

Modernization is a European invention. It was exported from Europe (and America, its descendant) to the so-called Third World through the politics of colonialism and the sociopolitical economy of imperialism. Although its benefits to indigenous societies have been tabulated in terms of increased life spans, better health conditions, rising literacy, and broadened opportunities, the social costs of modernization have been high.

The imperialist nations systematically destroyed the indigenous societies' subsistence economies, converting them to specialized cash-crop (rubber, tobacco) or mineral (metal ores, diamonds) economies. Whereas before modernization the native populations easily could provide for their own subsistence needs, they suddenly were forced to participate in an economic system that was controlled from afar, that kept down the prices of what they had to offer, that made them dependent on imported goods priced high, and that kept their wages low. Thus modernization created poverty in many areas of the world whereas, before, the concept simply had no meaning.

In "Requiem for a Lost People," William W. Howells documents the horrifying story of the complete annihilation of the aboriginal population of Tasmania (an island south of Australia) by land-hungry European settlers in the nineteenth century. In "Societies on the Brink," David Maybury-Lewis lays out current rationales for the continuing destruction of small, semi-isolated societies and also presents anthropologically based arguments against this ongoing trend. He advocates social pluralism and suggests that the alternatives are grim.

Lauriston Sharp's classic article, "Steel Axes For Stone-Age Australians," illustrates Maybury-Lewis's point. She recounts how the introduction by missionaries of one small item of western technology—the steel axe—totally disrupted and destabilized the culture of an aboriginal people, the Yir Yoront.

Although it appears inevitable that small-scale societies will be transformed and absorbed as they come into contact with modern civilization, the final article strikes a somewhat hopeful, as well as pragmatic, note. Earlier in this book (article 19), Napoleon A. Chagnon described some of his fieldwork experiences among the Yąnomamö of Venezuela. Since the 1960s, he has returned several times to live among the Yąnomamö and to observe the changes that increasing contact with modern industrial society has wrought among "his" people. In "The Beginning of Western Acculturation," Chagnon argues that anthropologists have a special responsibility to see to it that the transformation and absorption of tribal societies occur in humane and enlightened ways. And he describes some of the measures he has taken to ease the Yąnomamö into the twentieth century.

41

Requiem for a Lost People

BY WILLIAM W. HOWELLS

No segment of humankind can have been rushed into oblivion as speedily as the aboriginals of Tasmania. Dark-skinned and woolly-haired, superficially they looked like Africans, though this is only skin-deep. Anthropologists regret their rapid passing; there is a great deal they would have liked to ask the Tasmanians, but in the early nineteenth century anthropology was a science unborn. There are other things to regret.

Tasmania is the shield-shaped island lying south of Australia's southeast corner. Its towns today give off a staid provincial air, and its countryside is rich in apples and flowers, but a hundred and fifty years ago the keynotes were kangaroos and violence. The island is a little like New England—north for south of course, since it lies in the other hemisphere. Its northern coast, nearest Australia, has the same latitude in the south as has New York in the north, and its southern end, with the city of Hobart, has about the latitude of Portland, Maine. But Tasmania lacks New England's antic weather. Deep snow may fall in the high interior, which is colder than the coast, and there are glaciers in the mountains. Still, while there was some risk from exposure if they were separated from companions and fire, the native Tasmanians essentially wore no clothes. On the shore, winters are mild and summers are cool. Over the year, the average temperature for the day changes only about eighteen degrees, from 46° to 64° Fahrenheit, compared with a swing of well over forty degrees in coastal New England. In fact, the thermometer may go up and down more during a single Tasmanian day than does the day's average during the whole year. Tell that in Boston.

During the late ice age it was colder, with larger glaciers in the center. Almost 25,000 years ago, while it was still a peninsula of Australia, aboriginal hunters are known to have entered Tasmania, to be marooned about twelve thousand years later, when the world's major ice sheets melted and the seas rose.

They were a culturally simple people, like their surviving cousins in Australia, and as time went on they became simpler still, their recent equipment being the most modest on record. When seen by Europeans, they lacked boomerangs, dogs, and hafted stone tools, all of which were invented or acquired in Australia after the original Tasmanians had left. And for some mysterious reason they gave up the catching of fish, although they continued to appreciate shellfish. Evidently the land was good

to them, with kangaroos and other marsupials to hunt, and the climate temperate enough so that an occasional cape of animal skin was all they ever wore. Two centuries ago about four thousand natives lived all over the island, except in the rugged mountains. Then, in thirty years, settlers from Australia and England wiped them out.

In the last crisis two men tried to stave off the extermination but only facilitated it, each in his own way. They were Governor George Arthur, with his printed proclamations and "picture boards," and G. A. Robinson, who went out to talk to the natives directly, in their own language. The Tasmanians themselves were neither ferocious nor hostile at first, as much testimony made clear too late. They were dangerous enough when provoked, and they fought to a limited extent among themselves over such things as trespass on hunting grounds or abduction of women, two offenses that the whites at once carried to intolerable excess. As for the "settlers," there could hardly have been a better team to carry out the annihilation. They were convicts, mostly hard cases from Australia. The first lot was accompanied by a handful of freemen given very small land grants to work with convict labor. Since a person might in those days be transported for what now pass as minor crimes (like stealing cars in Massachusetts?), some convicts were fairly decent men, but many, along with the soldiers sent to guard them, were capable of vicious brutality and in fact took pleasure in it. For a hundred years now, the fate of the Tasmanians has been a source of shame and lamentation, in today's high-minded Hobart as in the world at large. But in that time and place, it seems clear now, no other outcome was likely, as the repellent tragedy ran its course.

It started early, with the Risdon Massacre. The first arrivals from Sydney set up camp in 1803 along the mouth of the Derwent River in the vicinity of Hobart, founded a little later. They had already been officially enjoined to treat the natives with kindness, and threatened with punishment for violence to them. But there seems to have been little contact with Tasmanians as the first small farms were set up. Then, on a day in May 1804, about three hundred aboriginals—men, women, and children—appeared out of the woods forming a half-circle to surround kangaroos driven ahead of them. They had no spears, only clubs, and the fact that women and children joined in shows that they were not a war party. But a farmer a short distance away appears to have been frightened, and the semicircle seemed to be surrounding the camp. The officer in command of the soldiers (drunk, by accounts) was persuaded by the camp surgeon to fire on them with cannon loaded with grapeshot, killing a number. How many was not known, since the natives carried off some badly wounded members. The surgeon entertained the chaplain with a dissection of one corpse, and sent some pickled bones to Australia. Children were captured as well.

A few days later, the aboriginals retaliated with an attack on sailors gathering oysters, though no one was killed. In the next couple of years inexpert farming (the settlers were largely townspeople originally) and inept government supply led to a serious food shortage in the colony, which the governor met by setting a good price on kangaroo meat and encouraging hunting. Off into the bush went all who could be given a gun—not homesteaders, but their convict bond servants. Many of these saw at once how much better a free bush life was than harsh treatment and forced labor in the colony. Bushrangers increased in number as time went on, becoming dangerous men skilled in bushcraft, desperadoes of the worst sort who preyed on and murdered settlers, costing successive governors much effort in capturing and hanging them.

They also figured prominently in the long erosion of the native Tasmanians. But hostilities grew up gradually, and developed into the Black War only twenty years later. In spite of the Risdon Massacre, the local natives seemed not to be vindictive, only careful, and of course for some years aboriginals elsewhere in the large island knew little about the whites. Witnesses say they were friendly and helpful at the very start. Later, even when most settlers considered the Tasmanians enemies, other settlers could wander safely in the bush, and their young people joined aboriginal groups in hunting.

Nevertheless, new colonists were pressing up the whole fertile eastern side of the island, and from about 1818 people with more money and importance were taking out large grants of land. Beyond them roamed the bushrangers, capturing native women and often killing off a husband in the process—Tasmanian

The Conciliation, *oil painting by Benjamin Duterrau, 1840. George Augustus Robinson, protector of aboriginals, is shown with native Tasmanians on Bruny Island. The woman beside him is thought to be Truganini. Reproduced courtesy of the Tasmanian Museum and Art Gallery.*

men were very jealous of their wives. Wifeless settlers often did the same; Robinson, for example, was told of cases in which "stockkeepers had chained the females to their huts with bullock chains for the purpose of fornication." Partners in all this were seal hunters along the north coast, who had established themselves even before the colony in the south, and who remained effectively out of its control. They were American, British, New Zealander, or Polynesian, and as free of restraint or scruple as the bushrangers. Such a man usually supplied himself with two to five aboriginal women for sex and slavery, to help in sealing, hunting kangaroos, and skinning birds, and to be shot out of hand if they failed to get the work done or tried to escape. This glib description covers many specific accounts of atrocities, which we will do without. The point is that, whether or not a Tasmanian husband was actually dispatched for every woman taken, the women were removed as aboriginal mothers, with devastating effects on the next generation. When they gave birth to half-caste children, the women regarded them as despicable and usually killed them.

Bear in mind that the testimony, nauseating as it is, comes from our side, the European. If all the things Tasmanians saw and suffered could be known, the effect would be even more appalling. Settlers were outraged at

interference with their land-clearing, and the occasional spearing of cattle by natives: it did not occur to them that Tasmanians, not using the land for farming, might likewise have a sense of outrage—apart from their feelings at being shot up by any white man who took it into his mind. Of course, the Tasmanians were not passive, although reprisal on their part was long in becoming common. Their weapons were simple: carefully chosen stones, and long wooden javelins with fire-hardened points, both thrown with extraordinary marksmanship even at a distance. In later years they used ruses to draw a farmer away from his house, spearing the family in his absence. They were always skilled stalkers and ambushers. They developed the trick of walking while dragging a javelin, between the big toe and the next, through the grass where it could not be seen. Stark naked, such a man seemed to be unarmed—certainly with nothing up his sleeve—until he could approach a settler within easy spearing distance. (Tit for tat, one farmer taught himself to do the same thing with a shotgun.) Some such

Truganini, the last full-blooded Tasmanian aboriginal to live in Tasmania, died May 8, 1876, and was buried near Hobart. She reportedly had feared a fate similar to the last aboriginal male, William Lanne, who had died seven years before. On the eve of his funeral, a surgeon acting for a scientific society allegedly removed Lanne's skull and substituted another, and competitors made off with his hands and feet. The night after the burial, what remained of the corpse was removed from the grave and was never recovered.

Two years after Truganini's burial, she was exhumed and her skeleton put on display in the Tasmanian Museum and Art Gallery. There it remained for nearly a hundred years. Last April, in response to pressure from people of Tasmanian-aboriginal descent, Truganini's skeleton was cremated and the ashes scattered in Tasmania's D'Entrecasteaux Channel.

This photograph of Truganini was taken in 1866 by Charles A. Wooley and is reproduced courtesy of the Tasmanian Museum and Art Gallery.

things they invented on their own, and others they picked up from white bushrangers. They even made up bushranging groups themselves in a few instances. An Australian aboriginal convict named Mosquito was sent to Hobart to be a police scout. Bored, he ended by forming a gang of shantytown Tasmanians and taking to the bush, where he enjoyed a long outburst of crime before he was apprehended and suspended.

Back at the center, officialdom tried to control things, with ever smaller success, until at last its hand was forced against the natives willy-nilly, as a result of the cumulative acts of its own unruly subjects. Governor after governor tried in good conscience to carry out the early admonition not to harm the aboriginals, at least as far as words would serve. David Collins in 1810 ordered that violence against the natives be dealt with in the same manner as violence against a "civilized person." Thomas Davey in 1814 proclaimed that recent hostility of the natives was traceable to ill-treatment, especially the kidnapping of children. William Sorrell in 1817-1819 said the same, at great length, sternly forbidding such abductions. Governor Arthur arrived in 1824 and promptly issued a proclamation that he would punish ill-treatment of natives. And he did so, handing out 25 lashes to some colonists who had brutalized native women. (Such brutalities, which usually escaped punishment, were chaining a woman to a log, burning another with firebrands, and making another wear the head of her fresh-killed husband around her neck, and do not include outright murders by shooting, pushing onto a fire, and so on.)

In 1828, Arthur posted another proclamation, again admitting the depredations of the whites, but now trying to calm things by ordering the Tasmanians to stay out of the settled areas unless they procured official passports to gather shellfish on the coast. Of course the natives could not read this document even if they should see it; and the governor had no hot line to the interior—in fact one problem all along was that chiefs who one would expect could be negotiated with did not exist. So in early 1830, Arthur made one more try at proclaiming even-handed treatment for the natives, in a way they might grasp, with his famous picture boards.

They were the 1830 equivalent of propaganda leaflets dropped behind enemy lines. The message is clear enough, to us; its intentional simplicity read something like this: "Natives and whites can mingle in amity; natives should come meet Governor (recognize him by cocked hat); black spear white, black hang; white shoot black, white hang." Citizens who saw them thought them hilarious. But the idea was ingenious, and at least better than printed officialese in its promise of getting

across. (It seems to have been suggested by a colonist who had seen a charcoal drawing on a tree done by aboriginals, which showed a settler cart train they had been watching from hiding.) The boards were hung in trees where it was thought aboriginals would see them.

The picture boards had no effect. And the message was false, as earlier proclamations had been. Blacks had indeed been hanged in plenty, some for killing settlers and some who were falsely accused of murders committed by whites. But in the whole story no white was ever hanged for killing a black, in spite of cases of solid testimony to the killing. And little other punishment was handed out for all the murders, kidnappings, maimings, and other crimes against the blacks. This was not, however, squeamishness about using the gallows; on one occasion a single sitting of judges sentenced 37 whites to hang for offenses against whites.

The picture boards were a watershed—the last attempt at asserting native rights to justice. Actually, the wind had been blowing the other way ever more strongly, and the end came rather quickly. Although the governors wanted to protect the Tasmanians, or said they did, nobody else cared; and anyhow, a governor's constituency was the colonists, not the Tasmanians. Nor was a sense of moral responsibility the same as moral conviction. The government, whether local or back home in Britain, was nonplussed by the seemingly homeless, wandering naked savages, and compassion for these uncivilized folk did not extend to letting them interfere with the civilized spreading of farms and towns in a supposedly new and open land. As to spreading the gospel, for once the clergy sat on its hands and did nothing worth mentioning in behalf of the aboriginals. And the ordinary colonist's sense of humanity is epitomized by one of them. This jolly specimen amused a perfectly friendly black by holding an empty pistol to his own head and clicking the trigger. Then he suggested it was the native's turn at the same silly game, handed him a loaded pistol, and watched with satisfaction as the poor man blew his own brains out.

In any case, there was no road back. From about 1825 the Black War was on in earnest. After a generation of their special education by the whites, the

Tasmanians were waging total war, with their own cruelties and killings of personally innocent (not always, of course) settlers and their families. The Tasmanians were so successful, in spite of their primitive weapons and their dwindling numbers, that they were actually driving homesteaders back into the towns. The settlers demanded protection, and the government decided that the only solution to the aboriginal problem was extermination (certainly the settlers' choice) or holing them up somewhere out of the way. Governor Arthur's attempt to apply the second expedient was his most bizarre scheme of all, the Black Line.

This came in 1830, just after the picture boards, which were a last despairing cry and far too late. The Line was supposed to operate like a vast kangaroo surround, as used by the natives, starting at the perimeter of the whole settled southeastern third of the island and driving the Tasmanians before it into a cul-de-sac in the Tasman Peninsula at the island's corner. Such a drive had actually been used on the Australian mainland, with a degree of success. But the plains of Victoria were not the rugged and forested terrain of Tasmania. And the Black Line was not black, or thin red, but white, being composed partly of soldiers and partly of convicts but mostly of civilians, taking leave from whatever they were doing in farm or town to become instant woodsmen. It was a major effort for the still modest colony, although it was like executing the Schlieffen Plan with something over three thousand men having little or no training. The government doubtless had no idea how far aboriginal numbers had already ebbed, but there were still significant tribes in the area.

Governor Arthur organized the whole thing on paper in detail. D-day was October 7 and the Line, 120 miles long, started off with a man supposedly at every sixty yards. The story of the operation is a novel in itself. It would be superhuman, in that country, to maintain such a line in order. There were a few actual encounters with natives, and a few fancied ones. Some of these "Down Under Deerslayers" were wounded by their own comrades. One Tasmanian man was caught, as well as a boy about fifteen. Two more were shot dead. After seven weeks, the Line arrived at the neck of the Tasman Peninsula in great excitement and anticipation of the bag of aboriginals hemmed in there by the

human net. The peninsula was scoured; it was empty. Newspapers poured scorn on the campaign for having spent £30,000 of His Majesty's money to catch one black man. But the £30,000 had, after all, gone into colonial pockets, and the participants agreed they had had a very good time.

The operation was perhaps the least harmful thing that was ever visited on the Tasmanians, who must have been amazed as they slipped through the Line or watched it pass them by. More effective measures against them were already afoot. One was "roving parties."

With the Black War heating up and with settlers and natives shooting on sight, Governor Arthur in 1826 had proclaimed the need to capture certain natives who had become adept in directing attacks (by learning from the whites), and the next year he divided the country into military districts and then proclaimed martial law—all this, remember, before the picture boards and the Black Line. In 1829 Arthur authorized six parties, staffed by convicts but headed by relatively responsible men, to hunt for natives, and in 1830—but still before the ambitious Line—he offered rewards of £5 a head (£2 for a child) for natives taken alive. This is just the system that has brought the orang-utan to the verge of extinction because, as a newspaper predicted correctly at the time, several would be killed for one captured. The methods of such parties, official or informal, varied from attempts to capture with limited loss of life to outright search-and-destroy missions. In 1827 an informal posse to avenge the death of a settler reported killing or wounding about sixty Tasmanians; and in another case, a party of police that had come under a stone-throwing attack caught the attackers in a defile and killed seventy of them, dashing the brains of the children. The formal roving parties had by the end of 1832 captured 236 aboriginals, obviously at great cost to tribal life.

The other arm of the pincers was George Augustus Robinson, who earned the title of Conciliator. He was raised in the building trades in London, had come to Tasmania to improve himself, and would retire at last to England, living in affluence and mingling with the gentry in Bath, where he died. He was good-hearted though jealous of his prerogatives. He was a devout Wesleyan; he missionized and preached to the Tasmanians as opportunity afforded, but did not let it interfere with his main

object of communication. He had great fortitude, self-possession, and persistence. He became convinced by everything he heard, and by his own contacts, that the aboriginals were essentially mild and inoffensive, that their rights had been trampled on, and that they could be conciliated by decent treatment, if it were honest and official. His method was to go out among them everywhere; he had a few helpers, black and white, all unarmed, but he put himself at the head of his party and usually kept the other whites out of sight.

He had arrived in Tasmania in 1824, the same year as Governor Arthur. He soon formed his opinions but had no way of acting on them. Then in March 1829, the governor, in one of his deeds of good intention, published an advertisement in The Hobart Town Gazette seeking a man of good character who would try to effect friendly connections with the Tasmanians by taking charge of those on Bruny Island, across the bay from Hobart. The island was already partly settled by whites of the bad sort, and the surviving blacks needed protection and provisions, having little of either.

Robinson at once applied for and got the job, insisting on the salary being raised from £50 to £100 a year. He started his work in a week and carried it on for some months, but it does not seem to have been much of a success in helping the natives, who were a little too close to white civilization. However, it was an experience for Robinson. He observed a surprising mortality rate among the natives, from afflictions of unclear nature. In less than two months he had accumulated a vocabulary of 115 words of the local language and was also preaching in it to the aboriginals. With little formal education and no training he went on recording names and some words on his travels, noting where the languages were different; in spite of his crude renderings this has been an important source of information on these lost tongues. Finally, on Bruny he had met Truganini, an extraordinary girl of sixteen or seventeen, small of build, obviously intelligent, lively, resourceful, brave, and attractive. During his stay she was married (rather against her will) to Wooraddy, who had been mooning after her as the story opened. These two, and a few more Tasmanians from Bruny Island and elsewhere, were to accompany Robinson in all his travels, with Truganini as a constant source of intelligence he could not otherwise get, even when she did not know the language of an area.

At the beginning of 1830, Robinson started on his mission to conciliate outlying natives, a mission that would last some five years. He set out from Hobart westward along the coast, with his aboriginals and a few whites, including convicts. He was supported by a whaleboat and a schooner, but he himself went on foot—a trek sometimes extremely arduous—all around the shore, with inland excursions, until he reached Launceston in the northeast, just as the Black Line was kicking off to the south. He spent the next twelve months ranging through the northern interior and visiting the sealers, actually getting many of them to part with their Tasmanian women by threatening government action. The governor was impressed with the apparent success of Robinson in conciliating and bringing in natives, and promised him full support, giving him as his next objective the rounding up of the feared Big River tribe. On the last day of 1831, Robinson made friendly contact with two "sanguinary tribes," the Big River and Oyster Bay, and found that they came to a total of 26 persons: sixteen men, nine women, and one child, who put themselves under his protection. These figures alone reveal a people without a future.

Robinson made three more expeditions between 1832 and 1834, to remnant peoples in the still-wild west. In September 1832, a group of blacks he met in the northwest decided to spear him and his own natives, and he barely escaped by crossing a river on pieces of floating wood—he could not swim—pushed by Truganini. This was his closest call, as recorded in his long, immensely detailed journal. It is full of action, showing that his mission was no triumphal parade, but a long tussle of making contact in unmapped places through unknown languages, persuading aboriginals of his good intentions, and seeing many of those he persuaded change their minds and run off again. It contains his enumeration and naming of natives as he tried to learn facts; and it is larded with stories, some quite fresh, of horrors perpetrated by blacks and whites—though mostly by the latter and sometimes more sickening than any already mentioned. All this time he was bringing in parties of submitted aboriginals. The presumed last lot of Tasmanians was found at the

Tasmanian aboriginals at Oyster Cove. Taken in 1858 by Francis Russell (Bishop) Nixon, the photograph shows nearly all of the members of the race then living.

end of 1834 (by Robinson's sons after he had gone back to Hobart in August): it was made up of four women, one man, and three boys, who had wanted to turn themselves in but had been shot at by every white who saw them. One family or small group, however, is known to have remained at large until 1842.

The Conciliator had succeeded: he had rounded up Tasmania's aboriginals in a way everyone—official, humanitarian, or extirpationist—could approve. He was given public praise and reward, though he felt it was not prompt enough nor in a measure he was entitled to (he was recompensed for his captures at a kind of wholesale rate, less than the £5 a head previously offered). At his request he was made commandant of the new aboriginal settlement on Flinders Island, off the northeast corner of Tasmania, where all the natives were placed, after some smaller and less hospitable islands had been tried out.

In this windy place, now wearing clothing, which was probably often damp, the captives declined rapidly. There were not many, anyhow. Robinson's listing of natives he met is less than 300, showing how the population beyond the settlement zone had already shrunk, and he brought in less than 200—the roving parties rather more. Many Tasmanians never reached the settlement: of the tribe that had tried to kill him in September 1832, he and his people obtained the submission of eleven in July 1833; nine of these died inside three

weeks. When he took up residence on Flinders in 1835, there were only 106 on the island, not counting some he brought with him. Tuberculosis, influenza, and pneumonia continued the execution: in 1837 alone there were 29 deaths. There were a few births, but all infants died in a matter of weeks. Robinson left Tasmania in 1839, to become Protector of the Aborigines in Victoria, Australia. It is possible he took a few Tasmanians with him.

So aboriginal life was extinguished in Tasmania thirty years after the Risdon Massacre. Aboriginal bodies, it is true, went on breathing a while longer, like the mythical dead snake wriggling until sundown. Forty-four survivors (including some half-castes) were taken off Flinders in 1847 and brought down to Oyster Cove near Hobart. By 1854 sixteen were left. By 1870 there was one: hardy little Truganini herself.

She died in 1876, and so they ended. Actually, Robinson had been forced, some time earlier, to return a dozen or so aboriginal women to their sealer consorts on Cape Barren Island, and for all we know one or more of these may have outlived her. At any rate, from such unions there has grown up a present-day population of perhaps two thousand part-aboriginals. But with Truganini's death there went out the last known spark of native speech and ideas and memories. After twenty thousand years.

42

Societies on the Brink

BY DAVID MAYBURY-LEWIS

....

Small societies around the world are currently threatened with extinction. The threat, either implicit or explicit, that they must die so that we may live is something we normally conceal from ourselves under comfortable phrases like "the social costs of development," or "the price of progress." The assumptions behind this sort of thinking need to be examined.

We need first to try to develop some perspective on a problem that is often debated with considerable passion. If we consider the whole span of human history, then it is clear that the majority of the peoples of the world lived until quite recent times in relatively small and relatively isolated societies. The emergence of powerful tribes, nations, or empires threatened the physical existence and certainly the cultural continuity of smaller, weaker peoples. This is a process that is as old as humankind itself. What has rendered it more dramatic in recent centuries is the development of what we are pleased to call "Western technology." This placed the nations of Western Europe and, later, North America at an enormous advantage and hastened the process of physical and cultural extinction of weaker peoples. Even China, an ancient and powerful civilization which hardly qualifies as a small-scale society, was shaken to its very foundations by the impact of the West. It was able to recover because of its vast reserves, demographic and otherwise. Small societies cannot recover. Instead, they face destruction, either by physical extinction or by absorption into the larger ones that press in on them.

The process has long been recognized; scholars have tried to grapple with its implications since the earliest days of the European expansion. For a while it was a matter for serious debate whether humanoid creatures encountered in other lands were really humans at all. The people in the other lands were equally puzzled. A British party was at first kept in cages by the Singhalese, who tried to determine whether or not they were actually

human. We have similar reports from other parts of the world. In fact, even when the conventional attributes of humanity were granted to alien peoples, debate still raged as to whether they were fully human and therefore entitled to fully human treatment (whatever that might be by the standards of the time and place). Thus it became a matter of grave consequence whether they were or were not considered to be endowed with souls. Similarly, arguments raged as to whether peoples who apparently possessed the basic physical and mental equipment of human beings could nevertheless put themselves beyond the pale by practicing "inhuman" customs.

Cannibalism was usually regarded as one such practice. One can imagine with what *frisson* the Europeans of the sixteenth century read Hans Staden's *True History and Description of the Land of the Savage, Naked and Ugly Maneating Peoples of the New World of America* (1557). The Tupinamba Indians, who once held Staden captive, regularly and ritually killed and ate their prisoners. It was considered a heroic death. A captive warrior, who in some cases might have been living with his captors for years and might even have raised a family there, was led out and clubbed to death in a ceremonial duel, after which the entire community ate him to partake of his heroic essence. Staden also pointed out that the same Tupinamba were horrified by the cruelty of the Europeans with whom they came in contact. They considered the Europeans to be in some sense beyond the pale because of their inhuman customs, such as the routine use of torture in trials and punishments, and the practice of slavery.

The relativistic implications of the Tupinamba view were not, unfortunately, taken seriously by European scholars. The debates concerning the essential humanity of alien peoples and the rights to which they were entitled were conducted in strictly European terms. Even when the arguments were genuine—as in the case of the famous series of debates before the Spanish crown be-

264   Copyright © 1977 by Harvard Magazine, Inc. Reprinted by permission.

tween Las Casas and Sepúlveda—the results were self-serving. When the debate went against the Indians, the local authorities considered that they had learned opinion on their side. When it came out favorably to the Indians, the local authorities refused to abide by its outcome. In the last analysis, the principal argument was power. The stronger tended to find justifications for using the weaker, or at the very least for making the weaker over in the image of the conqueror.

I have referred to these centuries-old arguments because modern versions of them still persist in our own thinking, both in our conventional wisdom and in the assumptions made by our theorists. On the one hand we have what may be called the liberal, neo-Darwinian view that small, weak societies are fated for extinction and that there is not much that can be done about it. Perhaps indeed, according to this view, there is not much that should be done about it, for why expend energy and resources in trying to interfere with irreversible processes that are part of the order of things? On the other hand, there is an orthodox Marxist position that holds that such societies are backward and out of step historically. They must therefore be assisted in getting in phase with history as rapidly as possible or they will be crushed by the relentless and irreversible force of historical process. But the results in practical terms of these two views are monotonously similar. Small societies are extinguished, culturally, or physically, or both.

These arguments are unsatisfactory. There is no natural or historical law that militates against small societies. There are only political choices. In fact the rhetoric of both the United States and the Soviet Union, to take the two strongest powers in the world today, stresses cultural pluralism as a goal for their own

In the northern Kalahari of Botswana, a San boy squeezes water from a grass sponge into his sister's mouth. The scene reflects the traditional San hunting-and-gathering way of life; the water comes from a depression in the trunk of a monongo tree, whose protein-rich nuts are a vital food source. In the years since this picture was taken, however, cultural change among the San has increased dramatically as a neighboring cattle-keeping people, the Herero, have encroached on their territories.

societies and indeed for the world at large. The fact that this rhetoric is not often put into practice is not a matter of natural or historical necessity but of political convenience.

A small society is of course a relative concept. Many nations are small compared with the superpowers but overwhelmingly large compared with some peoples in remote jungle regions who have just come into contact with the outside world. It is the societies at the lower end of this continuum with which I am primarily concerned, although the fact that it is a continuum and that the problem transcends the fate of isolated, tribal populations has certain implications, which I shall also discuss.

Anthropologists have often come to the defense of these tiny, tribal peoples. When they do, these anthropologists are

normally attacked with a battery of arguments that need to be explicitly stated and examined.

First it is contended that anthropologists want tribal peoples left alone simply to preserve a traditional way of life. They therefore want to halt the push to explore and exploit the resources of the earth. They are sentimentalists who stand up for the right of a few to live their own lives in backwardness and ignorance as against the right of the many to use the resources available. Anthropologists are therefore the enemies of development.

This is a serious misrepresentation, which makes the defenders of the rights of small-scale societies seem like the nineteenth-century Luddites, who went around smashing machines in a futile effort to halt the Industrial Revolution. Whether isolated, tribal societies would be better off if the world left them alone is an academic matter. They are not going to be permitted to live in isolation. The people who speak up for them do not argue that they should be left alone or that all exploration and development should be halted. On the contrary, we assume that isolated societies will not be left alone and are therefore concerned with how to soften the impact of inevitable contact so that it will not destroy them in the name of progress. To return to the Luddite analogy for a moment, we do not try to stem the Industrial Revolution by breaking the machines. We accept its inevitability but question the necessity of chaining children to the machines (as was done in nineteenth-century England) as a means of capital formation.

A second argument is a malicious variation on the first one. According to that, it is claimed that anthropologists would like to keep tribal peoples isolated in what amount to human zoos for their own research purposes.

Again this is a misrepresentation. Anthropologists and others who take an interest in such small societies argue that these peoples' contacts with the outside world should be regulated if they are not to prove destructive. A small society must therefore have a guaranteed territory that it can call its own. This should not be a reservation in the sense that its inhabitants are confined to and imprisoned on it, but rather a home base, which the members of the society can use as a springboard in their efforts to come to terms with the outside world.

Another variation on these arguments stresses the immorality of preventing "backward" peoples from enjoying the benefits of civilization. Who, it is asked, has the right to insist that a relatively isolated society be left alone, to manage without modern medicine and modern consumer goods? Some ardent proponents of this theme wax so eloquent that they make the anxious anthropologist seem like a puritan who is determined to deny color TV to the natives. But the argument, once again, is a distortion of a position that gets little hearing.

Those people who are concerned about the effects of contact are merely urging caution, based on an understanding of the possible harmful effects of such contact. One would have thought that the grim historical record of death, disease, and despair that also accompany the arrival of civilization in remote areas would be sufficient grounds for advocating a cautious approach. We now know a good deal about the diseases that are introduced and we know too that they tend to be unremitting, while the provision of modern medicine is often fitful or inadequate. At a later stage in the process, we know too that the introduction of new industries in remote and not-so-remote areas can lead to cultural breakdown and personal despair within the local population *as well as* providing jobs, increasing income, and so on. This is a familiar dilemma even in advanced societies, which is why people are so anxious to have a say in what happens to their own communities. There is an uneasy suspicion that the arrival of, say, an oil refinery may on balance produce costs for the people of the community where it is located and benefits for people elsewhere. We understand this element of trade-off keenly enough in advanced societies and yet we often seek to impose oil refineries or their equivalents on societies much less able to cope with them. When the results are not cottages and TV sets but disruption and even death, we tend to shrug our shoulders and reassure ourselves that such costs are unavoidable. I am arguing here that this is not so, and that such costs can be minimized even if not avoided altogether.

But the most insidious argument used against those who speak up for small societies is insidious precisely because it seems so reasonable. Why, it is asked, should such societies be protected anyway? What are the advantages of protecting their way of life? There are in fact many that have been claimed. We can learn from their life styles, since we are clearly so desperately unhappy with our own. We can learn from their views of the world, particularly as concerns the general interrelatedness of things on earth. Many Americans are, for example, discovering a harmony in American Indian views of the world which they find conducive not only to inner peace but also to a more effective use of the environment. There are other arguments that are frequently advanced as reasons for protecting the life style of small societies in different parts of the world. We need to do so in order to further our understanding of human cultural variation. We know too little about how societies work and about how they can be made to work *for* people rather than against them. Besides, it is claimed, the members of the small society will be more useful citizens in the larger one if they come into it with something of their own heritage intact. Then again, there may be genetic advantages in seeing that such groups are not physically extinguished, and so on.

But these are the wrong questions. Supposing we decided that we had nothing more to learn from small societies; that there was no particular genetic advantage in seeing them survive physically and no particular social or philosophical advantage in seeing them survive culturally. Would that then give us the right to eliminate these cultures? Would we be willing to apply a similar reasoning to the sick, the weak, or the aged in our own culture? The question, put that way, is horrifying, which is precisely why I called the original question insidious. If we accept it as a legitimate question, then we find ourselves debating the question of whether it is *useful* to permit another culture to survive. But useful to whom? Presumably the usefulness of their physical and social existence is not in doubt for the members of that culture. What we are in fact debating is whether their existence is useful to *us*. Such thinking can lead to the gas chambers and has done so in our own time. That is why the original question is the wrong one. The fundamental reason why we must help other cultures to survive is because in all conscience we have no alternative. It is a moral imperative of the sort that insists that the strong ought not to trample on the rights of the weak.

Some writers have referred to the process by which a powerful society extinguishes a weaker culture as *ethnocide*, and have argued that this is (and should be recognized as) a crime analogous to genocide. I understand and sympathize with the passion that informs this view, but I find the formulation of it unhelpful. Homicide is hard enough to define and the arguments concerning the circumstances under which it may or may not be justified are complex. Genocide is even more difficult and its use as a term of opprobrium all too often depends on the point of view of the user. I find the concept of ethnocide more difficult still, and much too vague to be helpful. The moment of a culture's death, even more so than that of a person, is difficult to perceive. The manner of its passing, save in the most obvious cases, is hard to evaluate.

Take some hypothetical cases. A society may occupy the territory of another so that the members of the latter are deprived of their livelihood. Or it may send missionaries into a territory, who then seek to undermine the culture they find. Alternatively, a timber company may move into an area and pay the local people for cutting down the forests off which they have traditionally lived. Again, a new industry may move into an area and effect profound changes in its way of life. Now, all of these changes have some disruptive effect on the local culture. At the same time all of them, save presumably the first instance, bring some benefits. How is one to decide on the precise ratio of costs to benefits that constitutes ethnocide? Indeed, how does one deal with the paradox of a society that may collaborate in its own ethnocide, permitting its culture to be extinguished in exchange for the benefits obtained from another society? In my view, the concept of *ethnocide* is too much of an either/or, life-or-death concept, and does little to help us understand situations where often it is not clear how to knock the gun out of the murderer's hand, or even who the murderer is or which is the gun.

I would insist instead that we are dealing with processes of contact and rapidly induced change that have in the past been known to have serious and even fatal consequences. The problem then is how to soften the contact and how to regulate the change so that its consequences for the small societies are minimally harmful. We are seeking to minimize the costs and to maximize the benefits for the people contacted.

This is not easy to do, however, since the benefits usually accrue to the wider society while the costs are borne largely by the contacted culture. We are thus dealing with a problem as old as humankind itself, namely that of protecting the weak against the strong. It is a problem that is unlikely to disappear and for which there are no easy solutions. Yet there are some things that can be done.

In the first place it is important to insist, as I have done here, on the right of other societies to their own ways of life. Such an insistence is not banal. This right is neither generally accepted nor generally understood. That is why it must be established that small-scale societies are not condemned to disappear by the workings of some abstract historical process. On the contrary, small societies may be shattered and their members annihilated, but this happens as a result of political choices made by the societies that impinge upon them, and for which the powerful must take responsibility. It is not, in any case, inevitable. The smaller societies can be assisted to deal with the impact of the outside world at comparatively little cost to those who bear down upon them. We have now come to recognize the principle that it is reasonable to set aside some part of the profits from the extraction of resources from the earth to be used to offset the ecological damage that may have been done in the process of extracting them. A similar understanding of the human costs of development and a willingness to deal with them is all that is necessary.

Such understanding and willingness cannot be taken for granted. It has to be cultivated and the attempt to cultivate it will not always be successful. It is unlikely, for example, that anybody, however eloquent or theoretically brilliant, could have convinced Hitler of the right of German Jews to their own cultural integrity. In such cases there may be no redress other than warfare or revolution. In many instances, however, the ways of persuasion have hardly been tried, and it is largely out of ignorance that planners make decisions that have such fatal costs for the small societies caught up in their plans. It is therefore vital that anthropologists and others concerned about the problem make people aware of its dimensions and point out that the cost of assisting small societies to become successful ethnic minorities is a comparatively small one, which may well be offset in the long run by the benefits the wider society will reap as a result.

Of course, attempts to protect threatened small-scale societies will not always be successful. The politics of some situations indicate that the minorities are doomed, if not physically, then at least as distinct cultures or subcultures. Yet this is no reason to abandon the effort in despair, any more than we abandon the efforts to avoid war or to construct just societies because these efforts are so often frustrated. I consider the effort to protect the cultural integrity of small-scale societies an issue of equal importance. We are talking not merely about the fate of tiny enclaves of people, buried in the last jungle refuges of this earth. What we are really talking about is the ability of human beings to discover ways to live together in plural societies. It seems to me that this is the critical issue of our times. Our success or failure in this endeavor may well decide whether people anywhere will be able to live in societies based on a minimum of mutual tolerance and respect. The alternatives are unpleasant to contemplate.

43

Steel Axes for Stone-Age Australians

BY LAURISTON SHARP

I.

Like other Australian aboriginals, the Yir Yoront group which lives at the mouth of the Coleman River on the west coast of Cape York Peninsula originally had no knowledge of metals. Technologically their culture was of the old stone age or paleolithic type. They supported themselves by hunting and fishing, and obtained vegetables and other materials from the bush by simple gathering techniques. Their only domesticated animal was the dog; they had no cultivated plants of any kind. Unlike some other aboriginal groups, however, the Yir Yoront did have polished stone axes hafted in short handles which were most important in their economy.

Towards the end of the 19th century metal tools and other European artifacts began to filter into the Yir Yoront territory. The flow increased with the gradual expansion of the white frontier outward from southern and eastern Queensland. Of all the items of western technology thus made available, the hatchet, or short handled steel axe, was the most acceptable to and the most highly valued by all aboriginals.

In the mid 1930's an American anthropoligist lived alone in the bush among the Yir Yoront for 13 months without seeing another white man. The Yir Yoront were thus still relatively isolated and continued to live an essentially inde-

pendent economic existence, supporting themselves entirely by means of their old stone age techniques. Yet their polished stone axes were disappearing fast and being replaced by steel axes which came to them in considerable numbers, directly or indirectly, from various European sources to the south.

What changes in the life of the Yir Yoront still living under aboriginal conditions in the Australian bush could be expected as a result of their increasing possession and use of the steel axe?

II. THE COURSE OF EVENTS

Events leading up to the introduction of the steel axe among the Yir Yoront begin with the advent of the second known group of Europeans to reach the shores of the Australian continent. In 1623 a Dutch expedition landed on the coast where the Yir Yoront now live.[1] In 1935 the Yir Yoront were still using the few cultural items recorded in the Dutch log for the aboriginals they encountered. To this cultural inventory the Dutch added beads and pieces of iron which they offered in an effort to attract the frightened "Indians." Among these natives metal and beads have disappeared, together with any memory of this first encounter with whites.

The next recorded contact in this area was in 1864. Here there is more positive assurance that the natives

concerned were the immediate ancestors of the Yir Yoront community. These aboriginals had the temerity to attack a party of cattle men who were driving a small herd from southern Queensland through the length of the then unknown Cape York Peninsula to a newly established government station at the northern tip.[2] Known as the "Battle of the Mitchell River," this was one of the rare instances in which Australian aboriginals stood up to European gunfire for any length of time. A diary kept by the cattle men records that: " . . . 10 carbines poured volley after volley into them from all directions, killing and wounding with every shot with very little return, nearly all their spears having already been expended. . . . About 30 being killed, the leader thought it prudent to hold his hand, and let the rest escape. Many more must have been wounded and probably drowned, for 59 rounds were counted as discharged." The European party was in the Yir Yoront area for three days; they then disappeared over the horizon to the north and never returned. In the almost three-year long anthropological investigation conducted some 70 years later—in all the material of hundreds of free association interviews, in texts of hundreds of dreams and myths, in genealogies, and eventually in hundreds of answers to direct and indirect questioning on just this particular matter—there was nothing that could be interpreted as a reference to this shocking contact with Europeans.

The aboriginal accounts of their first remembered contact with whites begin in about 1900 with references to persons known to have had sporadic but lethal encounters with them. From that time on whites continued to remain on the southern periphery of Yir Yoront territory. With the establishment of cattle stations (ranches) to the south, cattle men made occasional excursions among the "wild back-fellows" in order to inspect the country and abduct natives to be trained as cattle boys and "house girls." At least one such expedition reached the Coleman River where a number of Yir Yoront men and women were shot for no apparent reason.

About this time the government was persuaded to sponsor the establishment of three mission stations along the 700-mile western coast of the Peninsula in an attempt to help regulate the treatment of natives. To further this purpose a strip of coastal territory was set aside as an aboriginal reserve and closed to further white settlement.

In 1915, an Anglican mission station was established near the mouth of the Mitchell River, about a three-day march from the heart of the Yir Yoront country. Some Yir Yoront refused to have anything to do with the mission, others visited it occasionally, while only a few eventually settled more or less permanently in one of the three "villages" established at the mission.

Thus the majority of the Yir Yoront continued to live their old self-supporting life in the bush, protected until 1942 by the government reserve and the intervening mission from the cruder realities of the encroaching new order from the south. To the east was poor, uninhabited country. To the north were other bush tribes extending on along the coast to the distant Archer River Presbyterian mission with which the Yir Yoront had no contact. Westward was the shallow Gulf of Carpentaria on which the natives saw only a mission lugger making its infrequent dry season trips to the Mitchell River. In this protected environment for over a generation the Yir Yoront were able to recuperate from shocks received at the hands of civilized society. During the 1930's their raiding and fighting, their trading and stealing of women, their evisceration and two- or three-year care of their dead, and their totemic ceremonies continued, apparently uninhibited by western influence. In 1931 they killed a European who wandered into their territory from the east, but the investigating police never approached the group whose members were responsible for the act.

As a direct result of the work of the Mitchell River mission, all Yir Yoront received a great many more western artifacts of all kinds than ever before. As part of their plan for raising native living standards, the missionaries made it possible for aboriginals living at the mission to earn some western goods, many of which were then given or traded to natives still living under bush conditions; they also handed out certain useful articles gratis to both mission and bush aboriginals. They prevented guns, liquor, and damaging narcotics, as well as decimating diseases, from reaching the tribes of this area, while encouraging the introduction of goods they considered "improving." As has been noted, no item of western technology available, with the possible exception of trade tobacco, was in greater demand among all groups of aboriginals than the short handled steel axe. The mission always kept a good supply of these axes in stock; at Christmas parties or other mission festivals they were given away to mission or visiting aboriginals indiscriminately and in considerable numbers. In addition, some steel axes as well as other European goods were still traded in to the Yir Yoront by natives in contact with cattle stations in the south. Indeed, steel axes had probably come to the Yir Yoront through established lines of aboriginal trade long before any regular contact with whites had occurred.

III. RELEVANT FACTORS

If we concentrate our attention on Yir Yoront behavior centering about the original stone axe (rather than on the axe—the object—itself) as a cultural trait or item of cultural equipment, we should get some conception of the role this implement played in aboriginal culture. This, in turn, should enable us to foresee with considerable accuracy some of the results stemming from the displacement of the stone axe by the steel axe.

The production of a stone axe required a number of simple technological skills. With the various details of the axe well in mind, adult men could set about producing it (a task not considered appropriate for women or children). First of all a man had to know the location and properties of several natural resources found in his immediate environment: pliable wood for a handle, which could be doubled or bent over the axe head and bound tightly; bark, which could be rolled into cord for the binding; and gum, to fix the stone head in the haft. These materials had to be correctly gathered, stored, prepared, cut to size and applied or manipulated. They were in plentiful supply, and could be taken from anyone's property without special permission. Postponing consideration of stone head, the axe could be made by any normal man who had a simple knowledge of nature and of the technological skills involved, together with fire (for heating the gum), and a few simple cutting tools—perhaps the sharp shells of plentiful bivalves.

The use of the stone axe as a piece of capital equipment used in producing other goods indicates its very great importance to the subsistence economy of the aboriginal. Anyone—man, woman, or child—could use the axe; indeed, it was used primarily by women, for their's was the task of obtaining sufficient wood to keep the family campfire burning all day, for cooking or other purposes, and all night against mosquitoes and cold (for in July, winter temperature might drop below 40 degrees). In a normal lifetime a woman would use the axe to cut or knock down literally tons of firewood. The axe was also used to make other tools or weapons, and a variety of material equipment required by the aboriginal in his daily life. The stone axe was essential in the construction of the wet season domed huts which keep out some rain and some insects; of platforms which provide dry storage; of shelters which give shade in the dry summer when days are bright and hot. In hunting and fishing and in gathering vegetable or animal food the axe was also a necessary tool, and in this tropical culture, where preservatives or other means of storage are lacking, the natives spend more time obtaining food than in any other occupation—except sleeping. In only two instances was the use of the stone axe strictly limited to adult men: for gathering wild honey, the most prized food known to the Yir Yoront; and for making the secret paraphernalia for ceremonies. From this brief listing of some of the activities involving the use of the axe, it is easy to understand why there was at least one stone axe in every camp, in every hunting or fighting party, and in every group out on a "walkabout" in the bush.

The stone axe was also promi-

nent in interpersonal relations. Yir Yoront men were dependent upon interpersonal relations for their stone axe heads, since the flat, geologically-recent alluvial country over which they range provides no suitable stone for this purpose. The stone they used came from quarries 400 miles to the south, reaching the Yir Yoront through long lines of male trading partners. Some of these chains terminated with the Yir Yoront men, others extended on farther north to other groups, using Yir Yoront men as links. Almost every older adult man had one or more regular trading partners, some to the north and some to the south. He provided his partner or partners in the south with surplus spears, particularly fighting spears tipped with the barbed spines of sting ray which snap into vicious fragments when they penetrate human flesh. For a dozen such spears, some of which he may have obtained from a partner to the north, he would receive one stone axe head. Studies have shown that the sting ray barb spears increased in value as they move south and farther from the sea. One hundred and fifty miles south of Yir Yoront one such spear may be exchanged for one stone axe head. Although actual investigations could not be made, it was presumed that farther south, nearer the quarries, one sting ray barb spear would bring several stone axe heads. Apparently people who acted as links in the middle of the chain and who made neither spears nor axe heads would receive a certain number of each as a middleman's profit.

Thus trading relations, which may extend the individual's personal relationships beyond that of his own group, were associated with spears and axes, two of the most important items in a man's equipment. Finally most of the exchanges took place during the dry season, at the time of the great aboriginal celebrations centering

about initiation rites or other totemic ceremonials which attracted hundreds and were the occasion for much exciting activity in addition to trading.

Returning to the Yir Yoront, we find that adult men kept their axes in camp with their other equipment, or carried them when travelling. Thus a woman or child who wanted to use an axe—as might frequently happen during the day—had to get one from a man, use it promptly, and return it in good condition. While a man might speak of "my axe," a woman or child could not.

This necessary and constant borrowing of axes from older men by women and children was in accordance with regular patterns of kinship behavior. A woman would expect to use her husband's axe unless he himself was using it; if unmarried, or if her husband was absent, a woman would go first to her older brother or to her father. Only in extraordinary circumstances would she seek a stone axe from other male kin. A girl, a boy, or a young man would look to a father or an older brother to provide an axe for their use. Older men, too, would follow similar rules if they had to borrow an axe.

It will be noted that all of these social relationships in which the stone axe had a place are pair relationships and that the use of the axe helped to define and maintain their character and the roles of the two individual participants. Every active relationship among the Yir Yoront involved a definite and accepted status of superordination or subordination. A person could have no dealings with another on exactly equal terms. The nearest approach to equality was between brothers, although the older was always superordinate to the younger. Since the exchange of goods in a trading relationship involved a mutual reciprocity, trading partners usually stood in a brotherly type of relationship, although one was always classified as older than the other and would have some advantage in case of dispute. It can be seen that repeated and widespread conduct centering around the use of the axe helped to generalize and standardize these sex, age, and kinship roles both in their normal benevolent and exceptional malevolent aspects.

The status of any individual Yir Yoront was determined not only by sex, age, and extended kin relationships, but also by membership in one of two dozen patrilineal totemic clans into which the entire community was divided.[3] Each clan had literally hundreds of totems, from one or two of which the clan derived its name, and the clan members their personal names. These totems included natural species or phenomena such as the sun, stars, and daybreak, as well as cultural "species": imagined ghosts, rainbow serpents, heroic ancestors; such external cultural verities as fires, spears, huts; and such human activities, conditions, or attributes as eating, vomiting, swimming, fighting, babies and corpses, milk and blood, lips and loins. While individual members of such totemic classes or species might disappear or be destroyed, the class itself was obviously ever-present and indestructable. The totems, therefore, lent a permanence and stability to the clans, to the groupings of human individuals who generation after generation were each associated with a set of totems which distinguished one clan from another.

The stone axe was one of the most important of the many totems of the Sunlit Cloud Iguana clan. The names of many members of this clan referred to the axe itself, to activities in which the axe played a vital part, or to the clan's mythical ancestors with whom the axe was prominently associated. When it was necessary to represent the stone axe in totemic ceremonies,

only men of this clan exhibited it or pantomimed its use. In secular life, the axe could be made by any man and used by all; but in the sacred realm of the totems it belonged exclusively to the Sunlit Cloud Iguana people.

Supporting those aspects of cultural behavior which we have called technology and conduct, is a third area of culture which includes ideas, sentiments, and values. These are most difficult to deal with, for they are latent and covert, and even unconscious, and must be deduced from overt actions and language or other communicating behavior. In this aspect of the culture lies the significance of the stone axe to the Yir Yoront and to their cultural way of life.

The stone axe was an important symbol of masculinity among the Yir Yoront (just as pants or pipes are to us). By a complicated set of ideas the axe was defined as "belonging" to males, and everyone in the society (except untrained infants) accepted these ideas. Similarly spears, spear throwers, and fire-making sticks were owned only by men and were also symbols of masculinity. But the masculine values represented by the stone axe were constantly being impressed on all members of society by the fact that females borrowed axes but not other masculine artifacts. Thus the axe stood for an important theme of Yir Yoront culture: the superiority and rightful dominance of the male, and the greater value of his concerns and of all things associated with him. As the axe also had to be borrowed by the younger people it represented the prestige of age, another important theme running through Yir Yoront behavior.

To understand the Yir Yoront culture it is necessary to be aware of a system of ideas which may be called their totemic ideology. A fundamental belief of the aboriginal divided time into two great epochs: (1) a distant and sacred period at the

beginning of the world when the earth was peopled by mildly marvelous ancestral beings or culture heroes who are in a special sense the forebears of the clans; and (2) a period when the old was succeded by a new order which includes the present. Originally there was no anticipation of another era supplanting the present. The future would simply be an eternal continuation and reproduction of the present which itself had remained unchanged since the epochal revolution of ancestral times.

The important thing to note is that the aboriginal believed that the present world, as a natural and cultural environment, was and should be simply a detailed reproduction of the world of the ancestors. He believed that the entire universe "is now as it was in the beginning" when it was established and left by the ancestors. The ordinary cultural life of the ancestors became the daily life of the Yir Yoront camps, and the extraordinary life of the ancestors remained extant in the recurring symbolic pantomimes and paraphernalia found only in the most sacred atmosphere of the totemic rites.

Such beliefs, accordingly, opened the way for ideas of what *should* be (because it supposedly *was*) to influence or help determine what actually is. A man called Dog-chases-iguana-up-a-tree-and-barks-at-him-all-night had that and other names because he believed his ancestral alter ego had also had them; he was a member of the Sunlit Cloud Iguana clan because his ancestor was; he was associated with particular countries and totems of this same ancestor; during an initiation he played the role of a dog and symbolically attacked and killed certain members of other clans because his ancestor (conveniently either anthropomorphic or kynomorphic) really did the same to the ancestral alter egos of these men; and he would avoid his mother-in-law, joke with a mother's distant brother, and make spears in a certain way because his and other people's ancestors did these things. His behavior in these specific ways was outlined, and to that extent determined for him, by a set of ideas concerning the past and the relation of the present to the past.

But when we are informed that Dog-chases-etc. had two wives from the Spear Black Duck clan and one from the Native Companion clan, one of them being blind, that he had four children with such and such names, that he had a broken wrist and was left handed, all because his ancestor had exactly these same attributes, then we know (though he apparently didn't) that the present has influenced the past, that the mythical world has been somewhat adjusted to meet the exigencies and accidents of the inescapably real present.

There was thus in Yir Yoront ideology a nice balance in which the mythical was adjusted in part to the real world, the real world in part to the ideal pre-existing mythical world, the adjustments occurring to maintain a fundamental tenet of native faith that the present must be a mirror of the past. Thus the stone axe in all its aspects, uses, and associations was integrated into the context of Yir Yoront technology and conduct because a myth, a set of ideas, had put it there.

IV. THE OUTCOME

The introduction of the steel axe indiscriminately and in large numbers into the Yir Yoront technology occurred simultaneously with many other changes. It is therefore impossible to separate all the results of this single innovation. Nevertheless, a number of specific effects of the change from stone to steel axes may be noted, and the steel axe may be used as an epitome of the increasing quantity of European goods and implements received by the aboriginals and of their general

influence on the native culture. The use of the steel axe to illustrate such influences would seem to be justified. It was one of the first European artifacts to be adopted for regular use by the Yir Yoront, and whether made of stone or steel, the axe was clearly one of the most important items of cultural equipment they possessed.

The shift from stone to steel axes provided no major technological difficulties. While the aboriginals themselves could not manufacture steel axe heads, a steady supply from outside continued; broken wooden handles could easily be replaced from bush timbers with aboriginal tools. Among the Yir Yoront the new axe was never used to the extent it was on mission or cattle stations (for carpentry work, pounding tent pegs, as a hammer, and so on); indeed, it had so few more uses than the stone axe that its practical effect on the native standard of living was negligible. It did some jobs better, and could be used longer without breakage. These factors were sufficient to make it of value to the native. The white man believed that a shift from steel to stone axe on his part would be a definite regression. He was convinced that his axe was much more efficient, that its use would save time, and that it therefore represented technical "progress" towards goals which he had set up for the native. But this assumption was hardly born out in aboriginal practice. Any leisure time the Yir Yoront might gain by using the steel axes or other western tools was not invested in "improving the conditions of life," nor, certainly, in developing aesthetic activities, but in sleep—an art they had mastered thoroughly.

Previously, a man in need of an axe would acquire a stone axe head through regular trading partners from whom he knew what to expect, and was then dependent solely upon a known and adequate

natural environment, and his own skills or easily acquired techniques. A man wanting a steel axe, however, was in no such self-reliant position. If he attended a mission festival when steel axes were handed out as gifts, he might receive one either by chance or by happening to impress upon the mission staff that he was one of the "better" bush aboriginals (the missionaries definition of "better" being quite different from that of his bush fellows). Or, again almost by pure chance, he might get some brief job in connection with the mission which would enable him to earn a steel axe. In either case, for older men a preference for the steel axe helped change the situation from one of self-reliance to one of dependence, and a shift in behavior from well-structured or defined situations in technology or conduct to ill-defined situations in conduct alone. Among the men, the older ones whose earlier experience or knowledge of the white man's harshness made them suspicious were particularly careful to avoid having relations with the mission, and thus excluded themselves from acquiring steel axes from that source.

In other aspects of conduct or social relations, the steel axe was even more significantly at the root of psychological stress among the Yir Yoront. This was the result of new factors which the missionary considered beneficial: the simple numerical increase in axes per capita as a result of mission distribution, and distribution directly to younger men, women, and even children. By winning the favor of the mission staff, a woman might be given a steel axe which was clearly intended to be hers, thus creating a situation quite different from the previous custom which necessitated her borrowing an axe from a male relative. As a result a woman would refer to the axe as "mine," a possessive form she was never able to use for the stone axe. In the same fashion, young men or even boys also obtained steel axes directly from the mission, with the result that older men no longer had a complete monopoly of all the axes in the bush community. All this led to a revolutionary confusion of sex, age, and kinship roles, with a major gain in independence and loss of subordination on the part of those who now owned steel axes when they had previously been unable to possess stone axes.

The trading partner relationship was also affected by the new situation. A Yir Yoront might have a trading partner in a tribe to the south whom he defined as a younger brother and over whom he would therefore have some authority. But if the partner were in contact with the mission or had other access to steel axes, his subordination obviously decreased. Among other things, this took some of the excitement away from the dry season fiesta-like tribal gatherings centering around initiations. These had traditionally been the climactic annual occasions for exchanges between trading partners, when a man might seek to acquire a whole year's supply of stone axe heads. Now he might find himself prostituting his wife to almost total strangers in return for steel axes or other white man's goods. With trading partnerships weakened, there was less reason to attend the ceremonies, and less fun for those who did.

Not only did an increase in steel axes and their distribution to women change the character of the relations between individuals (the paired relationships that have been noted), but a previously rare type of relationship was created in the Yir Yoront's conduct towards whites. In the aboriginal society there were few occasions outside of the immediate family when an individual would initiate action to several other people at once. In any average group, in accordance with the kin-

ship system, while a person might be superordinate to several people to whom he could suggest or command action, he was also subordinate to several others with whom such behavior would be tabu. There was thus no overall chieftanship or authoritarian leadership of any kind. Such complicated operations as grass-burning animal drives or totemic ceremonies could be carried out smoothly because each person was aware of his role.

On both mission and cattle stations, however, the whites imposed their conception of leadership roles upon the aboriginals, consisting of one person in a controlling relationship with a subordinate group. Aboriginals called together to receive gifts, including axes, at a mission Christmas party found themselves facing one or two whites who sought to control their behavior for the occasion who disregarded the age, sex, and kinship variables of which the aboriginals were so conscious, and who considered them all at one subordinate level. The white also sought to impose similar patterns on work parties. (However, if he placed an aboriginal in charge of a mixed group of post-hole diggers, for example, half of the group, those subordinate to the "boss," would work while the other half, who were superordinate to him, would sleep.) For the aboriginal, the steel axe and other European goods came to symbolize this new and uncomfortable form of social organization, the leader-group relationship.

The most disturbing effects of the steel axe, operating in conjunction with other elements also being introduced from the white man's several sub-cultures, developed in the realm of traditional ideas, sentiments, and values. These were undermined at a rapidly mounting rate, with no new conceptions being defined to replace them. The result was the erection of a mental and moral void which foreshad-

owed the collapse and destruction of all Yir Yoront culture, if not, indeed, the extinction of the biological group itself.

From what has been said it should be clear how changes in overt behavior, in technology and conduct, weakened the values inherent in a reliance on nature, in the prestige of masculinity and of age, and in the various kinship relations. A scene was set in which a wife, or a young son whose initiation may not yet have been completed, need no longer defer to the husband or father who, in turn, became confused and insecure as he was forced to borrow a steel axe from them. For the woman and boy the steel axe helped establish a new degree of freedom which they accepted readily as an escape from the unconscious stress of the old patterns—but they, too, were left confused and insecure. Ownership became less well defined with the result that stealing and trespassing were introduced into technology and conduct. Some of the excitement surrounding the great ceremonies evaporated and they lost their previous gaiety and interest. Indeed, life itself became less interesting, although this did not lead the Yir Yoront to discover suicide, a concept foreign to them.

The whole process may be most specifically illustrated in terms of totemic system, which also illustrates the significant role played by a system of ideas, in this case a totemic ideology, in the breakdown of a culture.

In the first place, under pre-European aboriginal conditions where the native culture has become adjusted to a relatively stable environment, few, if any, unheard of or catastrophic crises can occur. It is clear, therefore, that the totemic system serves very effectively in inhibiting radical cultural changes. The closed system of totemic ideas, explaining and categorizing a well-known universe as it was fixed at the beginning of time, presents a considerable obstacle to the adoption of new or the dropping of old culture traits. The obstacle is not insurmountable and the system allows for the minor variations which occur in the norms of daily life. But the inception of major changes cannot easily take place.

Among the bush Yir Yoront the only means of water transport is a light wood log to which they cling in their constant swimming of rivers, salt creeks, and tidal inlets. These natives know that tribes 45 miles further north have a bark canoe. They know these northern tribes can thus fish from midstream or out at sea, instead of clinging to the river banks and beaches, that they can cross coastal waters infested with crocodiles, sharks, sting rays, and Portuguese men-of-war without danger. They know the materials of which the canoe is made exist in their own environment. But they also know, as they say, that they do not have canoes because their own mythical ancestors did not have them. They assume that the canoe was part of the ancestral universe of the northern tribes. For them, then, the adoption of the canoe would not be simply a matter of learning a number of new behavioral skills for its manufacture and use. The adoption would require a much more difficult procedure; the acceptance by the entire society of a myth, either locally developed or borrowed, to explain the presence of the canoe, to associate it with some one or more of the several hundred mythical ancestors (and how to decide which?), and thus establish it as an accepted totem of one of the clans ready to be used by the whole community. The Yir Yoront have not made this adjustment, and in this case we can only say that for the time being at least, ideas have won out over very real pressures for technological change. In the elaborateness and explicitness of the totemic ideolo-

gies we seem to have one explanation for the notorious stability of Australian cultures under aborigininal conditions, an explanation which gives due weight to the importance of ideas in determining human behavior.

At a later stage of the contact situation, as has been indicated, phenomena unaccounted for by the totemic ideological system begin to appear with regularity and frequency and remain within the range of native experience. Accordingly, they cannot be ignored (as the "Battle of the Mitchell" was apparently ignored), and there is an attempt to assimilate them and account for them along the lines of principles inherent in the ideology. The bush Yir Yoront of the midthirties represent this stage of the acculturation process. Still trying to maintain their aboriginal definition of the situation, they accept European artifacts and behavior patterns, but fit them into their totemic system, assigning them to various clans on a par with original totems. There is an attempt to have the myth-making process keep up with these cultural changes so that the idea system can continue to support the rest of the culture. But analysis of overt behavior, of dreams, and of some of the new myths indicates that this arrangement is not entirely satisfactory, that the native clings to his totemic system with intellectual loyalty (lacking any substitute ideology), but that associated sentiments and values are weakened. His attitudes towards his own and towards European culture are found to be highly ambivalent.

All ghosts are totems of the Head-to-the-East Corpse clan, are thought of as white, and are of course closely associated with death. The white man, too, is closely associated with death, and he and all things pertaining to him are naturally assigned to the Corpse clan as totems. The steel axe, as a totem, was thus associated with the

Corpse clan. But as an "axe," clearly linked with the stone axe, it is a totem of the Sunlit Cloud Iguana clan. Moreover, the steel axe, like most European goods, has no distinctive origin myth, nor are mythical ancestors associated with it. Can anyone, sitting in the shade of a *ti* tree one afternoon, create a myth to resolve this confusion? No one has, and the horrid suspicion arises as to the authenticity of the origin myths, which failed to take into account this vast new universe of the white man. The steel axe, shifting hopelessly between one clan and the other, is not only replacing the stone axe physically, but is hacking at the supports of the entire cultural system.

The aboriginals to the south of the Yir Yoront have clearly passed beyond this stage. They are engulfed by European culture, either by the mission or cattle station subcultures or, for some natives, by a baffling, paradoxical combination of both incongruent varieties. The totemic ideology can no longer support the inrushing mass of foreign culture traits, and the myth-making process in its native form breaks down completely. Both intellectually and emotionally, a saturation point is reached so that the myriad new traits which can neither be ignored nor any longer assimilated simply force the aboriginal to abandon his totemic system. With the collapse of this system of ideas, which is so closely related to so many other aspects of the native culture, there follows an appallingly sudden and complete cultural disintegration, and a demoralization of the individual such as has seldom been recorded elsewhere. Without the support of a system of ideas well devised to provide cultural stablity in a stable environment, but admittedly too rigid for the new realities pressing in from outside, native sentiments and values are simply dead. Apathy reigns. The aboriginal has passed beyond the realm of any outsider who might wish to do him well or ill.

Returning from the broken natives huddled on cattle stations or on the fringes of frontier towns to the ambivalent but still lively aboriginals settled on the Mitchell River mission, we note one further devious result of the introduction of European artifacts. During a wet season stay at the mission, the anthropologist discovered that his supply of toothpaste was being depleted at an alarming rate. Investigation showed that it was being taken by old men for use in a new toothpaste cult. Old materials of magic having failed, new materials were being tried out in a malevolent magic directed towards the mission staff and some of the younger aboriginal men. Old males, largely ignored by the missionaries, were seeking to regain some of their lost power and prestige. This mild aggression proved hardly effective, but perhaps only because confidence in any kind of magic on the mission was by this time at a low ebb.

For the Yir Yoront still in the bush, a time could be predicted when personal deprivation and frustration in a confused culture would produce an overload of anxiety. The mythical past of the totemic ancestors would disappear as a guarantee of a present of which the future was supposed to be a stable continuation. Without the past, the present could be meaningless and the future unstructured and uncertain. Insecurities would be inevitable. Reaction to this stress might be some form of symbolic aggression, or withdrawal and apathy, or some more realistic approach. In such a situation the missionary with understanding of the processes going on about him would find his opportunity to introduce his forms of religion and to help create a new cultural universe.

Notes

[1] An account of this expedition from Amboina is given in R. Logan Jack, *Northmost Australia* (2 vols.), London, 1921, Vol. 1, pp. 18–57.

[2] Ibid, pp. 298–335.

[3] The best, although highly concentrated, summaries of totemism among the Yir Yoront and the other tribes of North Queensland will be found in R. Lauriston Sharp, "Tribes and Totemism in Northeast Australia," *Oceania*, Vol. 8, 1939, pp. 254–275 and 439–461 (especially pp. 268–275); also "Notes on Northeast Australian Totemism," in *Papers of the Peabody Museum of American Archaeology and Ethnology*, Vol. 20, *Studies in the Anthropology of Oceania and Asia*, Cambridge, 1943, pp. 66–71.

44

The Beginning of Western Acculturation

BY NAPOLEON A. CHAGNON

Those of us who live in industrialized societies look on change and progress as being "good" and "desirable." Our entire system of values and goals is constituted in such a way that we strive to make changes, improve and tinker with rules and technology, and reward those who are skillful at it. "Progress" for its own sake is beneficial by definition. The Yąnomamö are now entering a new and potentially hazardous time in their history, for our kind of culture is confronting them and urging, in the name of "progress," that they give up their way of life and adopt some rural form of ours. The agents of progress among the Yąnomamö are mostly missionaries—Salesian Catholics and several independent groups of Protestant Evangelists—whose presence among the Yąnomamö is permitted by Venezuelan and Brazilian law. Incorporation of the Yąnomamö into the national culture has been left almost entirely in the hands of the missionaries, who have been and continue to remain free to use whatever means or techniques they have to accomplish this objective. While the explicit goal of all the missionaries is the conversion of the Yąnomamö to Christianity and the salvation of their souls, a few far-sighted individuals in both groups have independently realized that they likewise have an obligation to prepare the Yąnomamö in other ways for their inevitable absorption into Western culture—teaching them to speak the Spanish or Portuguese language, reading, writing and counting, introducing domesticated animals that can later serve as predictable sources of protein, market principles, the use of money, scales of economic values, and so on. Other missionaries are more narrowly dedicated to saving souls at any cost, and are insensitive to the point of being inhumane in the techniques they use to bring salvation to the Yąnomamö.

It is inevitable that the Yąnomamö, and all tribal peoples, will be absorbed by the national cultures in whose territories they coincidentally reside. The process of acculturation is nearly as old as culture itself: all dominant cultures impinge on and transform their less-dominant neighbors. There are, however, enlightened and humane ways of accomplishing this . . . and there are insensitive and inhumane ways. Knowing that acculturation is inevitable, I must conclude that it is essential that a rational and sympathetic policy of acculturation be developed for the Yąnomamö, for the process of change has already begun at a number of mission villages, and it is off to a poor start. Such a policy will require the cooperation of missionaries, government officials, and field-experienced, informed anthropologists. It is yet to be developed.

This raises a dilemma for me. Anthropologists who have worked in "traditional" or "tribal" cultures are often frustrated and saddened by the vectors of change that transform the peoples they have grown to admire during their studies, especially when the changes diminish the freedom and dignity of those peoples. Many anthropologists are, in fact, alarmed by any change and would prefer to see native cultures persist indefinitely while the rest of the maddening world mires itself deeper and deeper into the technological, ecological, and political morass that is one certain artifact of cultural evolution and "progress." It is an open question whether particular anthropologists are attracted to primitive cultures because such cultures seemingly represent a more rational, more comprehensible means for coping with the external world . . . that is to say, a more human way. It is jokingly said that psychiatrists become what they are to better understand their own personal problems, and I suspect that some anthropologists, by analogy, are attracted to their craft for equally personal reasons. A few of my colleagues have even good-naturedly suggested to me that my own intensive involvement with the Yąnomamö is not without reason, for they suspect that I might fit as well in Yąnomamö culture as I do in my own!

But any similarity between an anthropologist and the people with whom he or she has spent a significant portion of his or her life is probably due more to association and learning than to initial equivalencies of personality. Anthropology as a science differs radically from, let us say, chemistry or genetics. Our subject matter is made essentially of the same kind of stuff as the observer—the "subject matter" itself has hopes, fears, desires, and emotions. It is easy to identify with people and become intimate with them; a chemist or geneticist cannot have much empathy for carbon or the genes that determine eye color.

My long association with the Yąnomamö, my intimate friendships among them, and my awareness of the values in their culture account for my sense of frustration and alarm when I reflect on the changes that are taking place in the mission posts and the means by which some of the changes have been effected. Some of them are wrong, in my estimation, perhaps even cruel. Others are ineffective and harmless. Still others are amusing and downright funny.

Acculturation is a subject that has all but become a major subdiscipline within anthropology. Perhaps the most appropriate way to end this case study would be to cast the process into academic terms and adopt a strictly formal, pedagogical stance as I discuss what is now happening to the Yąnomamö. I should like, however, to communicate something about the human dimension of the process, to relate a few incidents and anecdotes that reveal more than a neutral description can expose. What the Yąnomamö must now endure has happened to countless other tribesmen. Perhaps if more citizens of the twentieth century and industrialized culture knew, from the tribesman's point of view, what acculturation means, we might have more compassion and sympathy for the traumas they must endure as they are required to make, usually unwillingly, their transformation. Hopefully such knowledge will be used to a good end, and rational policies of directed change will be forged.

In addition, by looking at the means and methods of the changes that are being made in Yąnomamöland through their eyes we can gain insights into the nature of our own culture. Very often the things that we ourselves take to be normal, progressive, and desirable look very different when viewed through a tribal lens. Sometimes they appear to be merely humorous. At other times they appear to be hideous.

YĄNOMAMÖ GLIMPSES OF US

Rerebawä looked frail and dwarfed in my trousers and shirt as we sat in the blistering sun on the savannah of Esmeralda waiting for the Venezuelan Air Force cargo plane to appear out of the cloudy north. The *piums*—tiny, biting black gnats—were out in astronomical numbers; their annoying bites left miniscule blood clots, that itched for a day and then turned black. The *piums* liked the larger rivers and savanna areas, and I speculated about the distribution of the Yąnomamö villages—inland, on tiny streams, away from this annoying *plaga*. I pitied those groups that had started moving out to the Orinoco River to make contact with foreigners—to obtain the highly desirable steel tools that they brought with them. Life without clothing for them was unbearable in the dry season, and they would come to the mission stations to work for days at hard labor to earn a tattered garment that some charity had sent into the missions gratis. The Yąnomamö always looked so pathetic in European hand-me-downs, especially after wearing them for several months and not washing them. They would be crusted with filth and rancid, and their skins would begin to have boils and sores all over them.

I was in a gloomy mood, reflecting on the changes that I noticed were taking place among the Yąnomamö. Each year I returned to them there were more missionaries, new mission posts, and now alarming numbers of tourists were beginning to arrive. I did not like what I was seeing and it was no longer possible to ignore the problems that acculturation would bring the Yąnomamö. My personal relationships with the Yąnomamö had deepened and grown more intimate every year. As I observed what some mission activities and the tourists were doing to the Yąnomamö, my attitude hardened.

Rerebawä had indicated to me several times in the past few years that he would like to see Caracas and how the Caraca-teri lived, especially the Caracateri-yoma: "Perhaps I could abduct a few when nobody is looking and drag them back to Bisaasi-teri in the plane!" he would tease mischievously. "But they eat only cows and bread and sugar and would run away from you if you brought them only monkeys and *yei* fruits!" I teased back. "You have warts on your forehead!" he insulted me good-naturedly, and jabbed me in the ribs to make me laugh, for he knew I was ticklish. "You'd better be careful in Caraca-teri," I warned, "almost all the men run around with large guns like shotguns and they will ask you for your 'decorated leaves' they call 'papers' and if you don't have any, they will take you away . . . and me with you!" He puffed his chest out and said: "Huh! I'll just grab a large club and insult them and then we'll see who takes who away!" He adjusted the wad of chewing tobacco he always carried in his lip. "Will we bump into the upper layer when we fly to Caraca-teri?" he asked anxiously. I chuckled to myself. Rerebawä had spent many months with me during my annual returns to his people and he was quite cosmopolitan by Yąnomamö standards, but nevertheless a firm believer in the Yąnomamö notion of the cosmos—a series of rigid bowl-like layers, one over the other, separated by only a few hundred feet or yards. "No, the *Hedu kä misi* layer is too high for the plane to reach," I responded, choosing to confirm his beliefs about the cosmic layers rather than rouse his anxiety further by denying their existence. This would be his first plane ride and his first glimpse of the civilization that lay beyond Yąnomamöland, and I wanted him to enjoy his experience.

It was always difficult for me to impress the Yąnomamö with the size of the world beyond their villages and tropical forest, including Rerebawä. I recall being teased by my companions on one of my inland trips as we sat around the campfire before retiring to our hammocks for the evening. They were bantering me about how numerous the Yąnamamö were and how few foreigners there were by comparison. Rerebawä was among them, and just as vociferous. I stood up to underscore my argument, pointing dramatically to the north, northeast, east, reciting names of cities as they came indiscrimately to my mind: "Over there lie the New York-teri, the Boston-teri, the Washington-teri, the Miami-teri; and over there the London-teri, the Paris-teri, and Madrid-teri, and Berlin-teri . . ." and on, around the globe. They chuckled confidently, and one of them rose. "Over there lie the Shibariwä-teri, the Yabroba-teri, the Wabutawä-teri, the Yeisi-teri, the Auwei-teri and over there the Niyaiyoba-teri, the Maiyo-teri, the Boreta-teri, the Ihirubö-teri . . ." and on around the cardinal points of the compass. I protested, arguing that ". . . Caraca-teri is huge! There are many people there and you are just a few by comparison!" Their response would be, inevitably, "But have you seen the new Patanowä-teri *shabono* or Mishimishimaböwe-teri *shabono*? They stretch in a great arc, like this . . ." and an arm would slowly describe the vast arc while the others listened intently, clicking their tongues to exaggerate the size. Caracas, to them, was just another large *shabono*, with a large, thatched roof, and I knew that the only way to convince them otherwise was to bring one of them there to see it with his own eyes.

Perhaps if Rerebawä saw the scope and magnitude of the culture that was moving inexorably to assimilate his own he would be more prepared to understand and deal with it when it eventually came. Would the same thing happen to Yąnomamö culture that happened to so many North American Indian societies? Would the Yąnomamö be reduced biologically and culturally to a mere shadow of the proud and free people I had grown to know and admire during 12 years of research among them? My personal dilemma was that I hoped that the Yąnomamö would be permitted to remain sovereign and unchanged, but my sense of history and understanding of culture contact told me that change was inevitable.

Storm clouds were piling up over Duida, the massive, abrupt cliff that rose 10,000 feet up from the small savanna at Esmeralda, and I hoped the plane would arrive soon, for in an hour the clouds would obscure the landing strip and it might be weeks or months before another flight would be scheduled to Esmeralda. A free lift out to Caracas with Rerebawä today would be very convenient, for I could spend five days with him working in comfort on myth translations and return with my bush-pilot, who was coming in with my medical colleagues. There would be space for us in the plane.

"Avion! Avion!" shouted the Makiritare Indians who idly waited for the plane to arrive, for it always brought cargo for them. Rerebawä was on his feet in an instant, his hand over his brow, peering intently into the cloud-blackened northern sky. *"Kihamö kä a! A ösöwa he barohowä!"* he jabbered excitedly, and I agreed that indeed it was visible and very high. He raced over to his possessions, a small cluster of tightly bound cloth bags made from the remains of a shirt I had given him last year. "Hold on! It will not get here for a while yet. It has to circle the landing area and chase the Makiritare cows off the savanna." He sat down, clutching his bags and grinning. I hadn't noticed his bags until now, and asked him what he had in them. "Just some 'things,'" he responded nonchalantly. "What kind of 'things'?" I asked suspiciously. He untied the knot and opened the larger bag: it was full of grey wood ashes, about a quart of them. Before I could ask him why in the world he was bringing ashes to Caracas, he had opened the other bag: it was full of tightly bound cured tobacco leaves. I clicked my tongue approvingly and he wrapped them back up. The ashes were to mix with the chewing tobacco, and I recall that he had asked me earlier if the Caraca-teri made fires on the floor on their houses to cook by. He was way ahead of me.

The gigantic transport plane—a C-123 designed for paratroop drops and hauling heavy cargo—lumbered to a dusty stop and the Makiritare descended on it to unload the cargo. The crew was in a hurry, for they had caught the edge of the storm and wanted to be airborne as soon as possible. They were reluctant to fly over Amazonas, a vast jungle with no radio communications or emergency landing strips, in a tropical storm.

Within an hour the plane was unloaded and the crew motioning for any passengers who wanted a lift to get aboard. We stepped into the giant, empty belly of the plane and I strapped Rerebawä into his safety harness. He had grown very quiet and was now obviously worried . . . if we weren't going to crash into the upper layer, why is it necessary to tie ourselves into the seats? The plane lumbered to the end of the savanna, turned, and screeched to a halt. The pilot tested the motors, and the roar was deafening: Rerebawä's knuckles were white as he clutched the edge of his seat. The plane lurched forward and gathered speed, bouncing unpredictably over the irregularities of the unimproved dirt landing stirp. Then the nose tipped upward sharply and we were airborne.

It was one of the worst flights I ever had, for we hit the storm soon after we gained cruising altitude. The plane jerked and twisted violently, dipping first one wing and then, suddenly, the other. Gusts of wind bounced us around, and jarring losses of altitude would leave us breathless, pinning us against our safety harnesses and then, as the frail plane fought back upwards, forcing us into our canvas seats. We could hear the ominous beating of rain on the fuselage above the roar of the motors. In an hour we were over the llanos and the flight had become more calm, but the noise was still deafening as the two motors labored incessantly. I unsnapped my harness and walked around the plane, but I was unsuccessful in persuading Rerebawä to untie himself or look out one of the fogged-up portholes. He just sat there, staring blankly at the opposite side of the plane, his tobacco buried deeply between his lower lip and teeth, clutching his seat. He relaxed a bit when I told him that we were approaching our landing strip at Maracay, and whispered cautiously that he was very cold. I assured him that I, too, was cold but that it would be warm when we landed. He rolled his eyes back and nodded his understanding.

The tires squealed and gave off a puff of blue smoke as we touched the concrete runway, taxied in, and coasted to a stop in front of the gigantic hanger that Rerebawä immediately recognized as the "den" of the creature in which we were riding. The crew opened the tiny side doors of the plane, and a blast of hot, dry air burst in. Our ears continued to ring, even though the deafening engines had stopped. We climbed out and stood on the concrete pad that stretched as far as our eyes could see, disappearing in the shimmering heatwaves near the horizon. Rerebawä touched it carefully and asked me how we found so much flat stone to make such a huge trail. Before I could answer that question, a dozen more, equally startling, came from his dry lips. One of the crew asked me if I wanted a lift up to the headquarters, from which we could call a taxi to take us to Caracas, some 35 miles away. I accepted, and told Rerebawä that we were going to have a ride in a "car." "What is a 'car'?" he asked suspiciously, remembering his airplane trip. I pointed to the white Ford parked a short way off. "Why don't you get into it and wait for me there while I unload our things?" I suggested. He headed slowly for the car and I gathered our things from the plane. When I stepped out of the plane, he was standing by the car, examining it carefully, glancing periodically at me, then at the car. "Get into it!" I shouted, "I'll be right there!" I watched him walk slowly around the car, scratch his head, and look up at me with a puzzled expression. "Don't be afraid!" I shouted as I walked toward him. "Get in it!" He adjusted the tobacco in his mouth, took a half-step toward the car, and dived through the open window on the passenger's side, his feet and legs hanging curiously out the gaping hole in the side! I had forgotten to tell him about doors, and realized how much I had taken things for granted, and how incredibly bizarre much of our culture would be to the Yąnomamö.

The next week proved to be both sobering and outrageously funny at times as Rerebawä discovered what Caraca-teri and its customs and ways were like, and how much he would have to report to his co-villagers. The staggering size of the buildings reaching to the sky, built of stone laid upon stone, elevators, people staying up all night, the bright lights of the automobiles coming at an incredible speed at you during night travel, looking like the piercing eyes of the *bore* spirits, the ridiculous shoes that women wore with high heels and how they would cause you to trip if you tried to walk through the jungle in them, and the marvels of flush toilets and running water. He was astounded at how clean the floors were in the houses, was afraid to climb suspended stairs for fear they would collapse and could not drink enough orange soda pop, or get over the fact that a machine would dispense it when you put a coin in and pushed a button. "How could you invite these things to a feast?" he queried. "They certainly are generous and give their 'goods' away, but they expect to be reciprocated on the spot!"

He enjoyed himself in Caracas but was happy to return to his village, and spoke grandiloquently to his peers about the size of Caraca-teri. "Is it bigger than Patanowä-teri's *shabono*?" they asked him skeptically, and he looked at me, somewhat embarrassed, and knew that he could not explain it to them. We both knew that they would not be able to conceive of what Rerebawä had seen. His arm stretched out and he described a large arc, slowly, saying with the greatest of exaggeration his language permitted: "it stretches from here to . . . way over . . . there!" And they clicked their tongues, for it was bigger than they imagined.

In a few days Rerebawä had ceased discussing Caracas and his exciting trip there. He was busily and happily going about his normal Yąnomamö activities as if nothing extraordinary had happened. I marvelled at his resiliency and was relieved that the experience in Caracas had not diminished his enthusiastic view of his own culture as being inherently superior to and dominant over the ways of the *nabä*—the rest of the world that fell short of full humanness, the Non-Yąnomamö.

Glossary

....

Abbevillean (or Chellean) culture The earlier of two stages in the hand ax (bifacial core tool) tradition, lasting approximately 1,000,000 to 400,000 B.P.; found across southerly and medium latitudes of the Old World, radiating out from Africa to southwest Europe and as far east as India; associated with *Homo erectus*.

absolute dating Physical-chemical dating methods that tie archaeologically retrieved artifacts into clearly specified time ranges calculated in terms of an abstract standard, such as the calendar.

acclimatization The process by which an organism's sweat glands, metabolism, and associated mechanisms adjust to a new and different climate.

acculturation Those adaptive cultural changes that come about in a minority culture when its adherents come under the influence of a more dominant society and take up many of the dominant culture's traits.

Acheulian culture The second stage of the hand ax bifacial core tool tradition; associated primarily with *Homo erectus*; found in southern and middle latitudes all across the Old World from India to Africa and West Europe; lasting in toto from about 400,000 to 60,000 B.P.

adaptation The processes by which groups become fitted, physically and culturally, to particular environments over several generations. This comes about through natural selection on the biological level and the modification and selective passing on of cultural traits and practices on the cultural level.

adaptational approach A theoretical approach to cultural change with the underlying assumption that, in order to survive, human beings must organize themselves into social, economic, and political groups that somehow fit in with the resources and challenges of a particular environment.

adultery Sexual intercourse by a married person with a person other than the legal spouse.

Aegyptopithecus An especially important Oligocene ape form, dated to 28 million years ago, and found in the Fayum area of Egypt. It represents a probable evolutionary link between the prosimian primates of the Paleocene and Eocene, and the apes of the Miocene and Pliocene. *Aegyptopithecus* probably was ancestral to *Dryopithecus*, and thus possibly to modern apes and humans.

affinal kin A kin relationship involving one marriage link (for example, a husband is related by affinity to his wife and her consanguineals).

age grades Specialized hierarchical associations based on age that cut across entire societies.

agnatic kin Kin related to one through males.

agonistic interactions A term used mostly to refer to animal behavior that is aggressive or unfriendly, including the behavior of both the initiator and the recipient of aggression.

agriculture Domesticated food production involving minimally the cultivation of plants but usually also the raising of domesticated animals; more narrowly, plant domestication making use of the plow (versus horticulture).

alleles Alternative forms of a single gene.

alliance theory A theoretical approach to the study of descent that emphasizes reciprocal exchanges among descent groups as the basic mechanism of social integration.

allomorph In language, one of the different-sounding versions of the same morpheme (unit of meaning).

allophone In language, one of the different sounds (phones) that represent a single phoneme.

alveolar ridge Thickened portions of the upper and lower interior jaws in which the teeth are set.

ambilineal descent The reckoning of descent group membership by an individual through either the mother's or the father's line—at the individual's option. See also *cognatic descent*.

androgens The hormones, present in relatively large quantities in the testes, that are responsible for the development of the male secondary sex characteristics.

angular gyrus An area of the brain crucial to human linguistic ability that serves as a link between the parts of the brain that receive stimuli from the sense organs of sight, hearing, and touch.

animatism The attribution of life to inanimate objects.

animism The belief that objects (including people) in the concretely perceivable world have a nonconcrete, spiritual element. For human beings, this element is the soul.

anomie The state of normlessness, usually found in societies undergoing crises, that renders social control over individual behavior ineffective.

Anthropoidea Suborder of the order of Primates that includes monkeys, apes, and humans.

anthropology The systematic study of the nature of human beings and their works, past and present.

anthropometry A subdivision of physical anthropology concerned with measuring and statistically analyzing the dimensions of the human body.

anthropomorphism The ascription of human characteristics to objects not human—often deities or animals.

antigens Proteins with specific molecular properties located on the surface of red blood cells.

ape A large, tailless, semi-erect primate of the family *Pongidae*. Living species include the orangutan, gorilla, chimpanzee, gibbon, and siamang.

applied anthropology The use of anthropological concepts, methods, theories, and findings to achieve a desired social goal.

archaeological site See *site*.

archaeology The systematic retrieval, identification, and study of the physical and cultural remains that human beings and their ancestors have left behind them deposited in the earth.

aristocracy The privileged, usually land-owning, class of a society (for example, the ruling nobility of prerevolutionary France).

articulatory features Speech events described in terms of the speech organs employed in their utterance rather than from the nature of the sounds themselves.

artifact Any object manufactured, modified, or used by human beings to achieve a culturally defined goal.

ascribed status The social position a person comes to occupy on the basis of such uncontrollable characteristics as sex, age, or circumstances of birth.

assemblage The artifacts of one component of a site.

assimilation The disappearance of a minority group through the loss of particular identifying physical or sociocultural characteristics.

associated regions Broad regions surrounding the three geographical centers where agriculture was invented. Here different plants and animals were domesticated, and then spread individually throughout the whole area.

Aurignacian culture Upper Paleolithic culture that some scholars claim may represent a separate Middle Eastern migration into Europe; flourished in western Europe from 33,000 to 25,000 B.P. The Aurignacians began the European tradition of bone carving. The skeletal remains associated with this culture are the famous Cro-Magnon fossils.

australopithecine An extinct grade in hominid evolution found principally in early to mid-Pleistocene in eastern and southern Africa, usually accorded subfamily status (*Australopithecinae*, within *Hominidae*).

Australopithecus afarensis Early australopithecine form, dating to about 5.5 million years ago, found in the Afar region of Ethiopia and other parts of East Africa. Current debate centers on whether or not this form was directly ancestral to human beings.

Australopithecus africanus The original type specimen of australopithecines discovered in 1924 at Taung, South Africa, and dating from approximately 3.5 million years ago to approximately 1.6 million years ago. Belongs to the gracile line of the australopithecines.

Australopithecus boisei One of two species of robust australopithecines, appearing approximately 1.6 million years ago in sub-Saharan Africa.

Australopithecus habilis See *Homo habilis*.

Australopithecus robustus One of two species of robust australopithecines, found in both eastern and southern Africa, and dating from about 3.5 million years ago to about 1 million years ago.

avunculocal residence The practice by which a newlywed couple establishes residence with, or in the locale of, the groom's maternal uncle. A feature of some matrilineal societies that facilitates the men's maintaining their political power.

Aztec civilization Final Postclassic Mesoamerican civilization, dated from about A.D. 1300 to 1521, when Cortes conquered and destroyed the empire. The Aztec capital at Tenochtitlán (now Mexico City) housed some 300,000 people. Aztec society was highly stratified, dominated by a military elite.

balanced reciprocity The straightforward exchange of goods or services that both parties regard as equivalent at the time of the exchange.

baboon Large, terrestrial Old World monkey. Baboons have long, doglike muzzles, short tails, and are highly organized into troops.

band The simplest level of social organization; marked by very little political organization and consisting of small groups (50 to 300 persons) of families.

bartering The exchange of goods whose equivalent value is established by negotiation, usually in a market setting.

bifaces Stone artifacts that have been flaked on two opposite sides, most typically the hand axes produced by *Homo erectus*.

bifurcation Contrast among kin types based on the distinction between the mother's and father's kinfolk.

bilateral descent The reckoning of descent through both male and female lines. Typically found in Europe, the United States, and Southeast Asia.

bilateral kin A kin relationship in which an individual is linked equally to relatives of both sexes on both sides of the family.

bilocal residence The practice by which a newlywed couple has a choice of residence, but must establish residence with, or in the locale of, one or the other set of parents.

bipedalism The predominant use of the hind (two) legs for locomotion.

blade tool A long and narrow flake tool that has been knocked off a specially prepared core.

bound morpheme In language, a unit of meaning (represented by a sound sequence) that can only occur when linked to another morpheme (for example, suffixes and prefixes).

B.P. An abbreviation used in archaeology, meaning before the present.

brachiation A method of locomotion, characteristic of the pongids, in which the animal swings hand over hand through the trees, while its body is suspended by the arms.

breeding population In population genetics, all individuals in a given population who potentially, or actually, mate with one another.

brideprice A gift from the groom and his family to the bride and her family prior to their marriage. The custom legitimizes children born to the wife as members of her husband's descent group.

Broca's area An area of the brain located toward the front of the dominant side of the brain that activates, among other things, the muscles of the lips, jaw, tongue, and larynx. A crucial biological substratum of speech.

brow ridge A continuous ridge of bone in the skull, curving over the eyes and connected across the bridge of the nose.

burins Chisel-like Upper Paleolithic stone tools produced by knocking small chips off the end(s) of a blade, and used for carving wood, bone, and antlers to fashion spear and harpoon points. Unlike end scrapers, burins were used for fine engraving and delicate carving.

call systems Systems of communication of nonhuman primates, consisting of a limited number of specific sounds (calls) conveying specific meanings to members of the group, largely restricted to emotional or motivational states.

capitalism Economic system featuring private ownership of the means of production and distribution.

cargo cults Revitalization movements (also designated as revivalist, nativistic, or millenarian) that received their name from movements in Melanesia early in the twentieth century. Characterized by the belief that the millenium will be ushered in by the arrival of great ships or planes loaded with European trade goods (cargo).

carotene A yellowish pigment in the skin.

caste A hereditary, endogamous group of people bearing a common name and often having the same traditional occupation.

caste system A stratification system within which the social strata are hereditary and endogamous. The entire system is sanctioned by the mores, laws, and usually the religion of the society in question.

Catarrhini Old World anthropoids; one of two infraorders of the suborder of *Anthropoidea*, order of Primates. Includes Old World monkeys, apes, and humans.

catastrophism A school of thought, popular in the late eighteenth and early nineteenth centuries, proposing that old life forms became extinct through natural catastrophes, of which Noah's flood was the latest.

cephalic index A formula for computing long-headedness and narrow-headedness:

$$\frac{\text{head breadth}}{\text{head length}} \times 100$$

A low cephalic index indicates a narrow head.

Cercopithecoidea One of two superfamilies of the infraorder *Catarrhini*, consisting of the Old World monkeys.

cerebral cortex The "grey matter" of the brain, associated primarily with thinking and language use. The expansion of the cortex is the most recent evolutionary development of the brain.

ceremonial center Large permanent site that reveals no evidence of occupation on a day-to-day basis. Ceremonial centers are composed almost exclusively of structures used for religious purposes.

Chavin culture Highland Peruvian culture dating from about 1000 to 200 B.C. It was the dominant culture in the central Andes for some 700 years.

Chellean handax A bifacial core tool from which much (but not all) of the surface has been chipped away, characteristic of the Abbevillean (or Chellean) culture. Produced by *Homo erectus*.

chiefdom Estate, place, or dominion of a chief. Currently the term is used also to refer to a society at a level of social integration a stage above that of tribal society, characterized by a redistributive economy and centralized political authority.

chimpanzee (*Pan troglodytes*) Along with the gorilla and the orangutan, one of the great apes; found exclusively in Africa; one of *Homo sapiens'* closest relatives.

choppers Unifacial core tools, sometimes called pebble tools, found associated with *Homo habilis* in Olduvai sequence, and also with *Homo erectus* in East Asia.

chromosomal sex The sex identity of a person determined by the coded message in the sex chromosome contributed by each parent.

chromosome Helical strands of complex protein molecules found in the nuclei of all animal cells, along which the genes are located. Normal human somatic cells have forty-six chromosomes.

circumcision The removal of the foreskin of a male or the clitoral sheath of a female.

circumscription theory Theory of the origins of the state advanced by Robert Carneiro and others that emphasizes natural and social barriers to population expansion as major factors in producing the state.

civilization Consists of all those life-styles incorporating at least four of the following five elements: (1) agriculture; (2) urban living; (3) a high degree of occupational specialization and differentiation; (4) social stratification; and (5) literacy.

clan An exogamous unilineal kin group consisting of two or more lineages tracing descent from an unknown, perhaps legendary, founder.

class A stratum in a hierarchically organized social system; unlike a caste, endogamy is not a requirement (though it is often favored), and individuals do have the possibility (though not the probability) of moving to a neighboring stratum.

class consciousness An awareness by members of a social stratum of their common interests.

Classical archaeology A field within archaeology that concerns itself with the reconstruction of the classical civilizations, such as Greece, Rome, and Egypt.

Classic period Spectacular and sophisticated Mesoamerican cultural period dated from A.D. 300 to 900; marked by the rise of great civilizations and the building of huge religious complexes and cities. By A.D. 500, the Classical city of Teotihuacán housed some 120,000 people.

class system A stratification system in which the individual's position is usually determined by the economic status of the family head, but the individual may potentially rise or fall from one class to another through his or her own efforts or failings.

cognatic descent A form of descent by which the individual may choose to affiliate with either the mother's or father's kinship group. See also *ambilineal descent*.

cognatic kin Those relatives of all generations on both sides of the family, out to some culturally defined limit.

collateral kin Those nonlineal relatives in one's own generation on both sides of the family, out to some culturally defined limit.

colonialism The process by which a foreign power holds

political, economic, and social control over another people and establishes outposts of its own citizens among that people.

comparative linguistics (historical linguistics) A field of linguistics that attempts to describe formally the basic elements of languages and the rules by which they are ordered into intelligible speech.

communication The exchange of information between two or more organisms.

communist society A society marked by public or state ownership of the means of production and distribution.

composite family The situation in which multiple marriages are practiced or in which the residence rule requires a couple to reside with parents. See also *extended family; polygamy*.

consanguineal kin A kin relationship based on biological connections only.

continental drift Hypothesis introduced by Alfred Wegener, in the early twentieth century, of the breakup of a supercontinent, Pangaea, beginning around 225 million years ago and resulting in the present positions of the continents.

core tool A rough, unfinished stone tool shaped by knocking off flakes, used to crush the heads of small game, to skin them, and to dissect the carcasses.

couvade The custom, in many societies, for fathers to participate in the period of recuperation, after their wives give birth, by remaining inactive for a long period of time—often much longer than the women.

cranial index Anatomical measure computed on skeletal material, otherwise similar to the cephalic index.

cranium The skull, excluding the jaw.

creation myth A religiously validated tale, unique to each culture, in which ancestors become separated from the rest of the animal kingdom, accounting for the society's biological and social development.

Cro-Magnon A term broadly referring to the first modern humans, from 40,000 to 10,000 B.P. Specifically refers to humans living in southwestern France during the same period.

cross-cousins Cousins related through ascending generation linking kin (often parental siblings) of the opposite sex (for example, mother's brother's children or father's sister's children).

cultural anthropology The study of the cultural diversity of contemporary societies. It can be divided into two aspects: ethnography and ethnology.

cultural area A part of the world in which the inhabitants share many of the elements of culture, such as related languages, similar economic systems, social systems, and ideological systems; an outmoded concept that is seldom used.

cultural assemblage See *assemblage*.

cultural components (of a site) All the different divisions that can be found in a site.

cultural ecology (of a group) The ways in which a group copes with and exploits the potentials of its environment.

cultural evolution The process of invention, diffusion, and elaboration of the behavior that is learned and taught in groups and is transmitted from generation to generation; often used to refer to the development of social complexity.

cultural relativism A methodological orientation in anthropology, the basis of which is the idea that every culture is unique and therefore each cultural item must be understood in its own terms.

culture The patterned behavior and mental constructs that individuals learn, are taught, and share within the context of the groups to which they belong.

cuneiform Wedged-shaped writing developed by the Sumerian civilization.

cytoplasm The living matter in a cell, except the nucleus.

Darwinism The theoretical approach to biological evolution first presented by Charles Darwin and Alfred Russel Wallace in 1858. The central concept of the theory is natural selection, referring to the greater probability of survival and reproduction of those individuals of a species having adaptive characteristics for a given environment.

demographic study Population study, primarily concerned with such aspects of population as analyses of fertility, mortality, and migration.

dental formula The number of incisors, canines, premolars, and molars found in one upper and one lower quandrant of a jaw. The human formula, which we share with the apes and Old World monkeys, is shown below:

I	C	P	M
2	1	2	3
2	1	2	3

deoxyribonucleic acid (DNA) The hereditary material of the cell, capable of self-replication and of coding the production of proteins carrying on metabolic functions.

descent The practice of bestowing a specific social identity on a person as a consequence of his or her being born to a specific mother and/or father.

descent group A corporate entity whose membership is acquired automatically as a consequence of the genealogical connections between members and their offspring.

descent rule The principle used to trace lineal kin links from generation to generation. A child is filiated to both of its parents, but the descent rule stresses one parent's line and sex as links with others, over the other parent's line and sex.

descriptive kinship terminology The classification of kinspeople in ego's (the individual's) own generation, with a separate kin term for each kin type.

descriptive linguistics The careful recording, description of, and structural analysis of existing languages.

diachronics The comparative study of culture and society as they change through time in a specified geographical area.

differential fertility A major emphasis in the modern (or synthetic) theory of evolution, which stresses the importance of an organism actually reproducing and transmitting its genes to the next generation.

diffusion The spread of cultural traits from one people to another.

diffusionism The belief held by some European cultural anthropologists of the nineteenth and early twentieth century that all culture began in one or a few areas of the world and then spread outward.

diluvialism A school of thought, popular in the late eighteenth and early nineteenth centuries, claiming that Noah's flood accounted for the existence of extinct fossil forms.

diploid number The number of chromosomes normally found in the nucleus of somatic cells. In humans, the number is forty-six.

displacement The process by which sexual, aggressive, or other energies are diverted into other outlets. When these outlets are socially approved, the process is called sublimation.

divination The use of magic to predict the behavior of another person or persons, or even the course of natural events.

division of labor The universally practiced allotment of different work tasks to subgroupings of a society. Even the least complex societies allot different tasks to the two sexes and also distinguish different age groups for work purposes.

DNA See *deoxyribonucleic acid*.

domesticants Domesticated plants and/or animals.

dominance hierarchy The social ranking order supposed to be present in most or all primate species.

dominant allele The version of a gene that masks out other versions' ability to affect the phenotype of an organism when both alleles co-occur heterozygotically.

double descent A form of descent by which an individual belongs both to a patriline and a separate matriline, but usually exercises the rights of membership in each group separately and situationally.

dowry The wealth bestowed on a bride or a new couple by her parents.

Dryopithecus The most common Miocene ape genus, known from Africa, Europe, and Asia, and dated from 20 to 10 million years ago. A forest-dwelling ape with about six or seven species, *Dryopithecus* was most probably ancestral to modern apes and may have been ancestral to humans.

duality of patterning A feature of human language, it consists of sequences of sounds that are themselves meaningless (phonemes) and also of units of meaning (morphemes).

ecological niche Features of the environment(s) that an organism inhabits, that pose problems and create opportunities for the organism's survival.

ecology The science of the interrelationships between living organisms and their natural environments.

ecosystem A system containing both the physical environment and the organisms that inhabit it.

egalitarian society A society that makes all achieved statuses equally accessible to all its adult members.

emics The culturally organized cognitive constructs of a people being investigated (the "folk perspective"). See *etics*.

enculturation The lifelong process of learning one's culture and its values and learning how to act within the acceptable limits of behavior in culturally defined contexts.

endogamy The custom by which members of a group marry exclusively within the group.

environment All aspects of the surroundings in which an individual or group finds itself, from the geology, topography, and climate of the area to its vegetational cover and insect, bird, and animal life.

estrogens The hormones, produced in relatively large quantities by the ovaries, that are responsible for the development of female secondary sex characteristics.

estrous cycle The approximately four-week reproductive cycle of female mammals.

estrus The phase of the approximately four-week cycle in female mammals during which the female is receptive to males and encourages copulation.

ethnic group A group of people within a larger social and cultural unit who identify themselves as a culturally and historically distinct entity, separate from the rest of that society.

ethnicity The characteristic cultural, linguistic, and religious traditions that a given group of people use to establish their distinct social identity—usually within a larger social unit.

ethnocentrism The tendency of all human groups to consider their own way of life superior to all others and to judge the life-styles of other groups (usually negatively) in terms of their own value system.

enthnographic analogy A method of archaeological interpretation in which the behavior of the ancient inhabitants of an archaeological site is inferred from the similarity of their artifacts to those used by living peoples.

ethnography The intensive description of individual societies, usually small, isolated, and relatively homogeneous.

ethnology The systematic comparison and analysis of ethnographic materials, usually with the specification of evolutionary stages of development of legal, political, economic, technological, kinship, religious, and other systems.

etics The perspective of Western social science in general and anthropology in particular, as applied to the study of different cultures. See *emics*.

evolution The progress of life forms and social forms from the simple to the complex. In Herbert Spencer's terms, evolution is "change from an indefinite, incoherent homogeneity to a definite, coherent heterogeneity; through continuous differentiations and integrations." In narrow biological terms, evolution is the change in gene and allele frequencies within a breeding population over generations.

evolutionary progress The process by which a social or biological form can respond to the demands of the environment by becoming more adaptable and flexible. In order to achieve this, the form must develop to a new stage of organization that makes it more versatile in coping with problems of survival posed by the environment.

excessive fertility The notion that organisms tend to reproduce more offspring than actually survive; one of the principal points in Darwin's theory of organic evolution.

exchange marriage Usually describes the situation in which two men marry each other's sister. The term is sometimes used for more complicated patterns in which groups exchange women to provide wives for the men.

exogamy The custom by which members of a group regularly marry outside the group.

extended family A linking together of two or more nuclear families: horizontally, through a sibling link; or vertically, through the parent-child link.

family A married couple or other group of adult kinsfolk and their immature offspring, all or most of whom share a common dwelling and who cooperate economically.

family of orientation (family of origin) Nuclear or elementary family (consisting of husband, wife, and offspring) into which an individual is born and is reared and in which he or she is considered a child in relation to the parents.

family of procreation Nuclear or elementary family (consisting of husband, wife, and offspring) formed by the marriage of an individual, in which he or she is a parent.

feudalism The sociopolitical system characterizing medieval Europe, in which all land was owned by a ruling aristocracy that extracted money, goods, and labor (often forced) from the peasant class in return for letting the peasants till the soil.

fictive kin Extensions of the affect and social behavior usually shown toward genealogically related kin to particular persons with whom one has special relationships—godparents, blood brothers, and so on.

field study The principal methods by which anthropologists gather information, using either the participant-observation technique to investigate social behavior, excavation techniques to retrieve archaeological data, or recording techniques to study languages.

flake tool A tool made by preparing a flint core, then striking it to knock off a flake, which then can be worked further to produce the particular tool needed.

folklore Refers to a series of genres or types of culturally standardized stories transmitted from person to person (usually orally or by example).

folk taxonomy The cognitive categories and their hierarchical relations characteristic of a particular culture by which a specific group classifies all the objects of the universe it recognizes.

foraging society A society with an economy based solely on the collection of wild plant foods, the hunting of animals, and/or fishing.

Foramen magnum The "large opening" in the cranium of vertebrates through which the spinal cord passes.

formal negative sanction Deliberately organized, social response to individuals' behavior that usually takes the form of legal punishment.

formal positive sanction Deliberately organized, social response to individuals' behavior that takes the form of a ceremony sponsored by a central authority conveying social approval.

formal sanction Socially organized (positive or negative) response to individuals' behavior that is applied in a very visible, patterned manner under the direct or indirect leadership of authority figures.

fossils Remains of plant and animal forms that lived in the past and that have been preserved through a process by which they either leave impressions in stone or become stonelike themselves.

free morpheme In language, a unit of meaning (represented by a sound sequence) that can stand alone.

functionalism A mode of analysis, used particularly in the social sciences, that attempts to explain social and cultural phenomena in terms of the contributions they make to the maintenance of sociocultural systems.

functionalist anthropology A perspective of anthropology associated with Bronislaw Malinowski and A. R. Radcliffe-Brown. The former emphasized the meeting of biological and psychological "needs," the latter social "needs."

gametes The sex cells that, as sperm in males and eggs in females, combine to form a new human being as a fetus in a mother's womb.

gender identity The attachment of significance to a self-identification as a member of a sexually defined group and the adopting of behavior culturally appropriate to that group.

gender roles Socially learned behaviors that are typically manifested by persons of one sex and rarely by persons of the opposite sex in a particular culture.

gene The unit of biological heredity; a segment of DNA that codes for the synthesis of a single protein.

gene flow (admixture) The movement of genes from one population into another as a result of interbreeding in cases where previous intergroup contact had been impossible or avoided because of geographical, social, cultural, or political barriers.

gene frequency The relative presence of one allele in relation to another in a population's gene pool.

gene pool The sum total of all individuals' genotypes included within a given breeding population.

generalized exchange (reciprocity) The giving of gifts without expecting a direct return but in expectation of an "evening out" of gifts in the long run.

generative grammar (transformational grammar) A theory about a specific language that accounts in a formal manner for all the possible (permitted) strings of elements of that language and also for the structural relationships among the elements constituting such strings.

genetic drift The shift of gene frequencies as a consequence of genetic sampling errors that come from the migration of small subpopulations away from the parent group, or natural disasters that wipe out a large part of a population.

genetic load The number of deleterious or maladaptive genes that exist in the gene pool of a population or entire species.

genetic plasticity A characteristic of the human species that allows humans to develop a variety of limited physiological and anatomical responses or adjustments to a given environment.

genotype The genetic component that each individual inherits from his or her parents.

geographic center One of three regions in the world—the Middle East, East Asia, and the Americas—in which agriculture probably was invented independently.

gift exchange The giving of a gift from one group or individual to another with the expectation that the gift will be returned in similar form and quantity at the time or at a later date.

glottochronology A mathematical technique for dating language change.

gonadal sex Refers to the form, structure, and position of the hormone-producing gonads (ovaries, located within the pelvic cavity in females, and testes, located in the scrotum in males).

gorilla (*Gorilla gorilla*) The largest of the anthropoid (Great) apes and of the living primates; found exclusively in Africa.

government The administrative apparatus of the political organization in a society.

gracile australopithecines One of the two lines of australopithecine development, first appearing about 5.5 million years ago; usually refers to the fossil forms *Australopithecus africanus* and *Australopithecus afarensis*.

grammar According to Leonard Bloomfield, "the meaningful arrangements of forms in a language."

grid system A method of retrieving and recording the positions of remains from an archaeological dig.

Habilis. See *Homo habilis.*

habitation site A place where whole groups of people spent some time engaged in the generalized activities of day-to-day living.

hand ax An unspecialized flint bifacial core tool, primarily characteristic of the Lower and Middle Paleolithic, made by chipping flakes off a flint nodule and using the remaining core as the tool; produced by *Homo erectus*, later by *Homo sapiens neanderthalensis*.

hand ax tradition A technological tradition developed out of the pebble tool tradition, occuring from about 600,000 to about 60,000 years ago during the Lower and Middle Paleolithic; primarily associated with *Homo erectus*.

haploid number The number of chromosomes normally occurring in the nucleus of a gamete (sex cell). For humans, the number is twenty-three (one-half the diploid number).

Harappan civilization Civilization in the northwest corner of the Indian subcontinent (roughly, in present-day Pakistan), which reached its peak about 2000 B.C. Its major cities were Mohenjo-Daro and Harappa.

Hardy-Weinberg law The principle that in large breeding populations, under conditions of random mating and where natural selection is not operating, the frequencies of genes or alleles will remain constant from one generation to the next.

hemoglobin Complex protein molecule that carries oxygen through the bloodstream, giving blood its red color.

heredity (genetics) The innate capacity of an individual to develop characteristics possessed by its parents and other lineal ancestors.

heritability The proportion of the measurable variation in a given trait in a specified population estimated to result from hereditary rather than environmental factors.

heterozygote The new cell formed when the sperm and egg contain different alleles of the same gene.

heterozygous A condition in which two different alleles occur at a given locus (place) on a pair of homologous (matched pair of) chromosomes.

historical archaeology The investigation of all literate societies through archaeological means.

historical linguistics The study of the evolutionary tree of language. Historical linguistics reconstructs extinct "proto" forms by systematically comparing surviving language branches.

holism The viewing of the whole context of human behavior—a fundamental theme of anthropology.

Holocene The most recent geologic epoch; it began about 10,000 years ago.

homeostasis The process by which a system maintains its equilibrium using feedback mechanisms to accommodate inputs from its environment.

home range (of a primate group) An area through which a primate group habitually moves in the course of its daily activities.

hominid The common name for those primates referred to in the taxonomic family *Hominidae* (modern humans and their nearest evolutionary predecessors).

Hominidae Human beings, one of *Hominoidea*. See also *hominid*.

Hominoidea One of two superfamilies of *Catarrhini*, consisting of apes and human beings.

Homo erectus Middle Pleistocene hominid form that is the direct ancestor of *Homo sapiens*. It appeared about 1.9 million years ago, flourished until about 200,000 to 250,000 years ago. *H. erectus* was at least five feet tall, with a body and limbs that were within the range of variation of modern humans, and had a cranial capacity ranging from 900 to 1200 cubic centimeters.

Homo habilis ("handy man") A fossil form, dating from more than 2 million years ago, whose evolutionary status is disputed. Some physical anthropologists regard it as early *Homo*—the first members of our own genus. Others regard it as an advanced form of gracile australopithecine. This is the earliest hominid with which stone tools have been found in unambiguous relationship.

Homo sapiens neanderthalensis The first subspecies of *Homo sapiens*, appearing some 300,000 years ago and becoming extinct about 35,000 B.P. Commonly known as Neanderthal man.

Homo sapiens sapiens The second subspecies of *Homo sapiens*, including all contemporary humans, appearing about 60,000 years ago. The first human subspecies was the now extinct *Homo sapiens neanderthalensis*.

homologous A matched pair; usually refers to chromosomes, one from each parent, having the same genes in the same order.

homozygote The new cell formed when the sperm and egg contain the same allele of a particular gene.

homozygous A condition in which identical genes occur at a certain locus on homologous (matched pair) chromosomes.

horizontal extended family A household and cooperating unit of two siblings and their respective spouses and children.

hormonal sex The type of hormone mix (estrogens or androgens) produced by the gonads.

horticulture The preparation of land for planting and the tending of crops using only the hoe or digging stick; characterized especially by the absence of use of the plow.

hunting and gathering society A society that subsists on the collection of plants and animals existing in the natural environment. See *foraging society*.

hybrid vigor The phenomenon that occurs when a new generation, whose parent groups were from previously separated breeding populations, is generally healthier and larger than either of the parent populations.

hydraulic theory A theory of the origins of the state advanced by Karl Wittfogel that traces the rise of the state to the organization, construction, and maintenance of vast dam and irrigation projects.

hypothesis A tentative assumption, which must be tested, about the relationship(s) between specific events or phenomena.

ideology A belief system linked to and legitimating the political and economic interests of the group that subscribes to it.

imperialism The expansionist policy of nation-states by

which one state assumes political and economic control over another.

Inca Empire Empire of the Late Horizon period of Peruvian prehistory, dated about A.D. 1438 to 1540. The ninth and tenth Incas (kings) seized control of a 3,000-mile-long empire stretching from Quito to central Chile. The Incas had a highly sophisticated political organization.

incest Usually refers to sexual relations between father and daughter, mother and son, or brother and sister. In some societies the definition is extended to include larger numbers of consanguineal relatives, especially if the society is organized along the principle of lineages and clans.

incest taboo The nearly universal prohibition against sexual intercourse between family members, with the limits of incest varying from culture to culture on the basis of the society's kinship system and forms of social organization.

independent invention The process whereby two or more cultures develop similar elements without the benefit of cultural exchange or even contact.

independent assortment See *Law of Independent Assortment*.

Indus Valley civilization See *Harappan civilization*.

industrialism The form of production characterizing post-agricultural societies, in which goods are produced by mechanical means using machines and labor organized into narrowly defined task groups that engage in repetitive, physically simplified, and highly segmented work.

industrialization The process involving the growth of manufacturing industries in hitherto predominantly agrarian, pastoral, or foraging societies.

industrial society A society with a high degree of economic development that largely utilizes mechanization and highly segmented labor specialization for the production of its goods and services.

infanticide The killing of a baby soon after birth.

informal sanction A social response to an individual's behavior that is enacted individually by group members, with minimal organization by social authority.

informant A member of a society who establishes a working relationship with a fieldworker, providing him or her with information regarding that society.

instrumental belief system An organized set of ideas about phenomena necessary for survival and for performing day-to-day (functional) tasks.

integration, cultural The condition of harmonious pattern maintenance potentially characterizing cultural systems.

interglacial Refers to periods during which glaciers retreat and a general warming trend occurs in the climate.

internalized controls An individual's beliefs and values that mirror the beliefs and values of the group culture and that induce the individual to behave in ways appropriate to that culture.

invention The development of new ideas, techniques, resources, aptitudes, or applications that are adopted by a society and become part of its cultural repertoire.

involution Evolution through which a biological or social form adapts to its environment by becoming more and more specialized and efficient in exploiting the resources of that environment. Sometimes called specific evolution.

irrigation The artificial use of water for agriculture by means of human technology when naturally available water (rainfall or seasonal flooding) is insufficient or potentially too destructive to sustain desired crop production.

ischial callosities Bare, calloused areas of skin on the hindquarters, frequently found in terrestrial or semiterrestrial Old World monkeys.

kill site A place where prehistoric people killed and butchered animals.

kibbutz A collective settlement in Israel with strong emphasis on communal life and values; one of the forms of cooperative agricultural villages in Israel that is collective (to a greater or less degree) in the organization of work, ownership of all resources, child rearing, and living arrangements.

kin category A terminologically distinguished aggregate of persons with whom one might or might not have frequent interaction, but who are conceived to stand in a clearly understood genealogical relationship to the user of the term.

kindred The network of relatives linked genealogically to a person in a culturally specified manner. Each such network is different for each person, with the exception of siblings.

kinesics The study of body movement as a mode of communication.

kin group A terminologically distinguished aggregate of persons with whom one stands in specified genealogical relationships and with whom one interacts frequently in terms of these relationships.

kinship The social phenomenon whereby people establish connections with each other on the basis of genealogical linkages in culturally specified ways.

kinship terminology The set of contrasting terms that designate the culturally significant genealogical linkages between people and the social networks these perceived relationships generate.

knuckle walking The characteristic mode of terrestrial locomotion of orangutans, chimpanzees, and gorillas. These apes walk with a partially erect body posture, with the forward weight of the body supported by the arms and the hands touching the ground, fingers curled into the palm so that the back of the fingers bear the weight.

language The characteristic mode of communication practiced by all human beings, consisting of sounds (phonemes) that are strung together into a virtually limitless number of meaningful sequences.

Law of Independent Assortment Gregor Mendel's second principle. It refers to the fact that the particular assortment of alleles found in a given gamete is independently determined.

Law of Segregation Gregor Mendel's first principle. It states that, in reproduction, a set of paired alleles separate (segregate) in a process called meiosis into different sex cells (gametes); thus, either allele can be passed on to offspring.

legal sanction A formal, socially enacted negative response to an individual's or group's noncompliance with the law, or a legal decision meant to compel that compliance.

lemur A diurnal, semiterrestrial prosimian having stereoscopic vision. Lemurs are found only on the island of Madagascar.

levirate The practice by which a man is expected to marry the wife or wives of a deceased brother.

lineage A unilineal, consanguineal kin group tracing descent from a known ancestor and found in two forms: patrilineage, in which the relationship is traced through males; and matrilineage, in which the relationship is traced through females.

linguistic anthropology A subfield of anthropology entailing the study of language forms across space and time and their relation to culture and social behavior.

linguistics The study of language, consisting of two large subcategories: (1) historical linguistics, which is concerned with the evolution of languages and language groups through time, and with reconstructing extinct protolanguages from which historically known languages differentiate; and (2) descriptive linguistics, which focuses on recording, transcribing, and analyzing the structures of languages distributed across the world today.

little tradition The localized cultures of rural villagers living in the broader cultural and social contexts of mass industrial society, with its "great tradition." Currently the term is rarely used because it is very ethnocentric.

locus The position of a gene on a chromosome.

"Lucy" See *Australopithecus afarensis*.

Magdalenian culture The most advanced of the Upper Paleolithic cultures, dating from 17,000 to 10,000 B.P. Confined to France and northern Spain, the Magdalenian culture marks the climax of the Upper Paleolithic in Europe. The Magdalenians produced a highly diversified tool kit but are most famous for their spectacular cave art.

magic The usually ritualized behavior that is intended to control, or at least to influence significantly, the basic processes of the universe without recourse to perceptibly instrumental acts.

mana A diffuse force or energy-like entity that suffuses through various objects, places, and even people; recognized in various parts of the world but especially well known in Polynesia and Melanesia.

market economy A system in which goods and services are exchanged, and their relative values established, in marketplaces, generally via the use of money as a standard of value.

market exchange The process of distributing goods and services and establishing their relative value (frequently in terms of money) at centers of trade known as markets.

marriage A difficult term to define, given enormous cross-cultural variety. However, all societies recognize (publicly) connections between two or more persons that confer social legitimacy to their children—which is the basic minimum of marriage.

matriarchy A form of family organization characterized by the domination of domestic life or society as a whole by women.

matricentric family A family that is headed by a woman, often serially married to a number of men.

matrifocal family A family form in which the mother, sometimes assisted by other women of the household, is the most influential socializing agent and is central in terms of cultural values, family finances, patterns of decision-making, and affective ties.

matrilateral prescriptive cross-cousin marriage The rule by which a man must choose his spouse from among his mother's brother's daughters or their social equivalents.

matrilineage A kinship group made up of people all of whom trace relationships to one another through female links and are descended from a known female ancestor.

matrilineal descent The principle by which lineal kin links are traced exclusively through females—that is, a child is descended from his or her mother, mother's mother, and so on.

matrilocal residence The practice by which a newlywed couple moves into residence with, or in the locale of, the bride's mother's kin group.

Maya civilization The best-known Classic Mesoamerican civilization, located on the Yucatan peninsula and dated from before A.D. 300 to 900. Less intensely urban than Teotihuacán, it is marked by the building of huge ceremonial centers, such as Tikal in Guatemala.

melanin The brown, granular sustance found in the skin, hair, and some internal organs that gives a brownish tint or color to the areas in which it is found.

Mesolithic (Middle Stone Age) A term of convenience used by archaeologists to designate immediately preagricultural societies in the Old World, 13,000 to 6,000 B.C. A frequently used diagnostic characteristic is the presence of microliths, small blades often set into bone or wood handles to make sickles for the harvesting of wild grains. In Europe, this period also featured the invention of the bow and arrow as a response to the emergence of forests with the shift from Pleistocene to Holocene climate.

messianic movement A revitalization movement based on the belief that a person or god will arrive to cure the evils of the world.

metallurgy The techniques of separating metals from their ores and working them into finished products.

microlith A small stone tool made from bladettes, or fragments of blades, associated with the Mesolithic period, approximately 13,000 to 6,000 B.C.

migration A permanent or semipermanent change of residence by a group, usually involving movement over large distances.

millenarianism A revivalistic movement reacting to the perceived disparity between ideal and real social conditions, with the belief that this gap is about to close, usually with disastrous consequences for nonbelievers.

minority A group that is distinguished from the larger society of which it is a part by particular traits, such as language, national origin, religion, values, or customs. The term may also be used to refer to groups that, though a plurality in numbers, are nevertheless discriminated against socially, politically, and/or economically by the society's dominant patterns (for example, women in the United States).

modernization The process whereby traditional social units (such as tribes or villages) are integrated into larger, overarching units (such as nation-states), while at the same time being split into units of production (such as factories) and consumption (such as nuclear families) that are characteristic of industrial societies.

moiety The name used to refer to a group that is one of two units of a larger group (for example, each clan of a society composed of two clans is a moiety). Both groups are usually, but not always, based on unilineal descent and are exogamous.

money A medium of exchange characteristic of market economies that is easily replaceable and/or exchangeable for another of like kind, portable, divisible into combinable units, and accepted by all participants in the market system in which it is used.

monkey A small or medium-sized quadrupedal primate. There are two groups of monkeys: Old World and New World. Only New World monkeys have prehensile tails. Most monkeys are arboreal, have long tails, and are vegetarians.

monogamy The marriage rule that permits both the man and the woman only one spouse at a time.

monogenesis The theory that the human species had only one origin.

mores The important norms of a society. They have compelling social and emotional commitment and are rationalized by the society's belief system.

morpheme The smallest unit of meaning in a language.

morphological sex The physical appearance of a person's genitals and secondary sex characteristics.

multilinear evolution The study of cultural evolution recognizing regional variation and divergent evolutionary sequences.

mutation A rapid and permanent change in genetic material.

myths Sacred tales or narratives that usually deal with the issue of origins (of nature, society, humans) and/or transformations.

nasal index The ratio calculated from the width and height measurements of the nose; it was used by early physical anthropoligists to classify human "races."

national character Personality characteristics shared by the inhabitants of a nation—no longer a scientifically valued concept.

nativism A revitalization movement initiated by members of a society to eliminate foreign persons, customs, and objects in order to improve their own way of life.

natural selection The process through which certain environmentally adaptive biological features are perpetuated at the expense of less adaptive features.

Neanderthal man (*Homo sapiens neanderthalensis*) A subspecies of *Homo sapiens* living from approximately 300,000 years ago to about 35,000 years ago and thought to have been descended from *Homo erectus*. See also *Homo sapiens neanderthalensis*.

negative reciprocity A form of gift exchange in which the giver attempts to get the better of the exchange.

negative sanction A punitive social response to an individual's behavior that does not meet with group approval.

neoclassicism A new school of geneticists who propose that most of the molecular variations in natural populations are selectively neutral.

Neolithic (New Stone Age) A stage in cultural evolution marked by the appearance of ground stone tools and frequently by the domestication of plants and animals, starting some 10,000 years ago.

neolocal residence The practice by which a newlywed couple is expected to establish its own independent residence, living with neither the husband's nor the wife's parents or relatives.

neontology A division of physical anthropology that deals with the comparative study of living primates, with special emphasis on the biological features of human beings.

network study An analysis of interpersonal relations, usually focused on a particular individual (ego), that examines the character of interactions between ego and other individuals.

New Archaeology Primarily an American development, the New Archaeology attempts to develop archaeological theory by using rigorous, statistical analysis of archaeological data within a deductive, logical framework.

nomadism A characteristic trait associated with a number of ecologically adaptive systems, in which continuing residential mobility is necessary for the subsistence of the group, with a resulting lack of permanent abode.

nonverbal communication The transmission of communication between organisms without the use of speech. Modes of communication include gesturing (with voice and body) and manipulating space between the communicating organisms.

norm A standard shared by members of a social group to which members are expected to conform.

nuclear family A small social unit consisting of a husband and wife and their children, typical of a monogamous marriage with neolocal residence; also forms a functioning subunit of extended and otherwise composite families.

oasis hypothesis A theory of plant and animal domestication advanced by V. Gordon Childe, in which he suggests that in the arid Pleistocene environment, humans and animals congregated around water resources, where they developed patterns of mutual dependence.

Oldowan culture The oldest recognized Lower Paleolithic assemblage, whose type site is Olduvai Gorge (Tanzania), dating from about 2.2 to 1 million years ago and comprising unifacial core (pebble) tools and crude flakes

Olmec culture The first civilization in Mesoamerica and the base from which all subsequent Mesoamerican civilizations evolved. Located in the Yucatan peninsula, it is dated from 1500 to 400 B.C., Olmec art first appeared in 1250 B.C., and the civilization flourished at its height from 1150 to 900 B.C.

order A taxonomic rank. *Homo sapiens* belongs to the order of Primates.

orangutan (*Pongo pygmaeus*) A tree-dwelling great ape found only in Borneo and Sumatra. It has four prehensile limbs capable of seizing and grasping, and very long arms. The orangutan is almost completely arboreal.

ovaries The female gonads, located within the pelvic cavity.

Paleolithic (Old Stone Age) A stage in cultural evolution, dated from about 2.5 million to 10,000 years ago, during which chipped stone tools, but not ground stone tools, were made.

paleontology, human A subdivision of physical anthropology that deals with the study of human and hominid fossil remains.

paradigm, scientific A concept introduced by Thomas Kuhn (1962): the orthodox doctrine of a science, its training exercises, and a set of beliefs with which new scientists are enculturated.

paralinguistics The study of the nonphonemic phonetic overlays onto the phonological system used to convey special (connotative) meanings.

parallel cousins Cousins linked by ascending generation relatives (often parental siblings) of the same generation and sex (for example, mother's sister's or father's brother's children).

participant observation A major anthropological field research method formally conceptualized by Bronislaw Malinowski, in which the ethnographer is immersed in the day-to-day activities of the community being studied.

pastoralism A type of ecological adaptation found in geographically marginal areas of Europe, Asia, and Africa where natural resources cannot support agriculture, and hence the people are partially or entirely devoted to the care and herding of animals.

patriarchy A form of family organization in which power and authority are vested in the males and in which descent is usually in the male line, with the children being members of the father's lineage, clan, or tribe.

patrilateral parallel cousin marriage A marriage between brothers' children.

patrilineage An exogamous descent group based on genealogical links between males that are traceable back to a known male ancestor.

patrilineal descent The principle by which lineal kin links are traced through males (that is, a child is descended from his or her father, father's father, and so forth).

patrilocal residence A postmarital residence rule by which a newlywed couple takes up permanent residence with or near the groom's father's extended kin group.

peasants Rural, agricultural members of civilizations who maintain a very traditional life-style (often rejecting urban values) while tied into the wider economic system of the whole society through markets, where they sell their produce and purchase goods.

pebble tool The first manufactured stone tools consisting of somewhat larger than fist-sized pieces of flint that have had some six or seven flakes knocked off them; unifacial core tools; associated with *Homo habilis* in Africa and also *Homo erectus* in East Asia.

persistence hunting A unique hunting ability of humans in which prey is hunted over vast distances, often for days at a time.

pharynx The throat above the larynx.

phenotype The visible expression of a gene or pair of genes.

phoneme In language, the basic unit of recognized but meaningless sound.

phylogeny The tracing of the history of the evolutionary development of a life form.

phonetic laws Patterns of change in the sounds used by languages as they evolved, expressed as rules or principles of change.

phonological system The articulatory phonetics and the phonemic system of a language.

phonology The combined study of phonetics and phonemics.

phratry A unilineal descent group composed of at least two clans claiming to be related by kinship. When there are only two such clans, each is called a moiety.

physical anthropology The study of human beings as biological organisms across space and time. Physical anthropology is divided into two areas: (1) paleontology, which is the study of the fossil evidence of primate evolution, and (2)

neontology, which is the comparative biology of living primates.

pigmentation Skin color.

Piltdown man A human skull and ape jaw "discovered" in England in 1911 and thought by some to be a "missing link" in human evolution. It was exposed as a fraud in 1953.

Pithecanthropus erectus See *Homo erectus.*

plate tectonics The branch of geology that studies the movement of the continental plates over time; popularly known as "continental drift."

Platyrrhini One of two infraorders of the primate suborder *Anthropoidea*, consisting of all the New World monkeys; characterized by vertical nostrils and, often, prehensile tails.

plow An agricultural tool generally requiring animal power, used to loosen, aerate, and invert the soil so as to cover weeds, expose a large area of soil to weathering, and prepare a seed bed. Its presence differentiates agriculture from horticulture (limited to the use of digging sticks and hoes).

pluralism A characteristic of many complex societies, marked by the presence of several or numerous subgroups that coexist within a common political and economic system.

political anthropology The field of cultural anthropology that deals with that aspect of social behavior known as political organization and that concerns itself specifically with the organization and management of the public affairs of a society, especially pertaining to the sources and uses of power.

political economy The interpretation of the economy and the system of power and authority in a society, most frequently studied from a conflict theory perspective.

political organization That subsystem of social organization that specifically relates to the individuals or groups who are responsible for managing affairs of public policy or who control the appointment or action of those individuals or groups.

polyandrous family A family in which a woman has more than one husband at the same time.

polyandry A relatively rare form of multiple marriage in which a woman has more than one husband at the same time.

polygamy Any form of marriage in which more than two persons are married to one another.

polygenesis The theory that the human species had more than one origin.

polygynous family A family in which a man has more than one wife at the same time.

polygyny The most common form of multiple marriage, allowing a man to have more than one wife at the same time.

pongid A common term for the members of the *Pongidae* family, including the five modern apes: the orangutan, gorilla, chimpanzee, gibbon, and siamang.

positive sanctions A social response to an individual's behavior that takes the form of a reward.

positivism An approach to knowledge embodying empiricism and the scientific method, with its built-in tests for truth.

possession A trance state based on the culturally supported belief that curative or malevolent spirits may displace people's personalities and use their bodies as vehicles for temporary residence.

potassium-argon (KAr) dating An absolute dating technique that uses the rate of decay of radioactive potassium (K^{40}) into argon (Ar^{40}) as its basis. The half-life of K^{40} is 1.3 billion ± 40 million years.

potlatch Ceremonial feasting accompanied by the giving of gifts to guests according to rank; practiced by the Indians of the Northwest Coast of the United States and Canada; a form of economic redistribution.

power, political The ability of leaders to compel compliance with their orders.

prehistoric archaeology The use of archaeology to reconstruct prehistoric times.

Primates The order of mammals that includes humans, the apes, Old and New World monkeys, and prosimians.

primatologist One who studies primates.

profane All that which is ordinary, or not sacred.

prosimii (prosimian) The most primitive suborder of Primates, including lemurs, lorises, tarsiers, and similar creatures.

Protestant ethic A set of values, originally associated with the rise and spread of Protestantism in Europe, that celebrates the virtues of self-discipline, hard work, initiative, acquisitiveness, and thrift.

proxemics The study of the manipulation and meaning of space.

psychological sex The self-image that a person holds about his or her own sexual identity.

quadrupedalism Locomotion by the use of four feet.

quarry site In archaeology, a place where prehistoric people dug for flint, tin, copper, and other materials.

race A folk category of the English language that refers to discrete groups of human beings who are uniformly separated from one another on the basis of arbitrarily selected phenotypic traits.

racial minorities Groups that are categorically separated from the majority members of the larger society on the basis of arbitrarily selected phenotypic traits.

radiocarbon (C^{14}) dating An absolute physical-chemical dating technique that uses the rate of decay of radioactive carbon (C^{14}) which is present in all plants, to stable carbon (C^{12}) as its basis. The half-life of C^{14} is 5568 ± 30 years. The technique is useful for dating remains from 5000 to 50,000 years old, although a new technique may extend its range to about 100,000 years while reducing the margin of error.

Ramapithecus A late Miocene hominoid, found in India, Kenya, and Europe, who lived from 14 to 9 million years ago. Until recently, *Ramapithecus* was accepted by some scholars as the first true hominid, though recent discoveries have placed this form in the evolutionary lineage of the orang-utan.

random (genetic) drift A shift in gene and allele frequencies in a population due to sampling "error." When a small breeding population splits off from a larger one, its collection of genes may not adequately represent the allele frequencies of the larger population. These differences compound over succeeding generations, until the two populations are quite distinct. Along with mutation, gene flow, and natural selection, random drift is one of the mechanisms of organic evolution.

range (of a primate) See *home range*.

rank society A society in which there is equal access to land and other economic resources but unequal access to positions of prestige.

recessive allele A version of a gene that is not able to influence an organism's phenotype when it is homologous with another version of the gene. See also *dominant allele*.

reciprocity The giving and receiving of gifts, usually consisting of material items, favors, or specific forms of labor.

redistribution The enforced giving of surplus goods to a centralized authority, who then distributes them back to members of the society according to social conventions and his own predilections.

reference group The aggregate of people that an individual uses for comparison when assessing or evaluating his or her own and others' behavior.

reformulation The modification of a new cultural trait, or cluster of traits, by a group to fit its own traditions and circumstances; part of the process of culture trait diffusion.

relative dating In archaeology, the determination of the sequence of events; a relative date specifies that one thing is older or younger than another.

religious beliefs The sets of convictions held by members of a society with regard to the supernatural, transcendental, and fundamental issues, such as life's meaning.

revitalization movements Religious movements of a reformative nature that arise among exploited or disorganized groups (often after socioeconomic or political traumas) and that attempt to reinject culturally salient meaning into people's lives—often through a radical assault on existing conditions and/or institutions.

revivalistic movement A revitalization movement espousing the reintroduction of previous religious (or political) forms.

ribonucleic acid (RNA) Any of the nucleic acids containing ribose. One type—messenger RNA—carries the information encoded in the DNA to the site of protein synthesis located outside the nucleus.

rifting The sliding of the continental masses against one another's edges.

rites of passage Rituals marking changes in status or social position undergone as a person passes through the culturally recognized life phases of his or her society.

rites of solidarity Various rituals, usually but not necessarily religious, which in addition to their intended purposes also develop and maintain feelings of group cohesiveness among participants.

rituals Culturally prescribed, consistently repeated, patterned sequences of (group) behavior.

RNA See *Ribonucleic acid*.

robust australopithecines One of two lines of australopithecines, appearing some 3.5 million years ago and surviving until approximately 1 million years ago or even later; thought to have embodied two successive species, *Australopithecus robustus* and *Australopithecus boisei*.

role conflict The emotional stress experienced by a person whose socially expected behaviors are irreconcilable. This happens when a person occupies diverse social positions (statuses) yet in a given situation must act in terms of two or more of them (for instance, a U.S. senator who is also a stockholder asked to vote on legislation that would affect the corporation in which he or she owns shares).

roles The expected (normative) behaviors that every society associates with each of its statuses.

Rosetta stone A tablet containing three parallel texts written in Egyptian hieroglyphics, demotic script, and Greek. In 1822, Jean François Champollion used the stone to decode the hieroglyphics.

sacred A category of things, actions, and so on set apart as holy and entitled to reverence.

salvage archaeology The attempt to preserve archaeological remains from destruction by large-scale projects of industrial society (such as a dam or highway construction).

sanctions, social The responses a social group makes as a consequence of an individual's behavior.

savanna Tropical or subtropical grasslands.

scapulimancy The use of charred cracks in the burned scapula (shoulder bone) of an animal to divine the future.

scientific racism Research strategies based on the assumption that groups' biological features underlie significant social and cultural differences. Not surprisingly, this kind of research always manages to find "significant" differences between "races."

scraper An Upper Paleolithic stone tool made from blades with a retouched end; used for carving wood, bone, and antlers to make spear points.

secondary sex characteristics Physiological changes developing at and after puberty, such as body hair, breasts, and voice changes.

Segregation, Law of See *Law of Segregation*.

self-concept A person's perceptions and evaluative feelings about his or her continuity, boundaries, and qualities.

semantics The relationship between signs and what they represent; the study of semantics is essentially the study of meaning.

semiotic The study of signs and sign-using behavior in general.

serial marriage The process by which a man or woman marries and divorces a series of partners in succession.

seriation A technique of relative dating in which the relative dates of artifacts may be reconstructed by arranging them so that variations in form or style can be inferred to represent a developmental sequence and, hence, chronological order.

sexual dimorphism A difference between the males and females of a species that is not related directly to reproductive functions.

sexual identity The expectations about male and female behavior that affect the individual's learning ability, choice of work, and feelings about herself or himself.

shamanism The process by which certain gifted persons establish (usually with the aid of a trance or an ecstatic state of excitement) direct communication with the supernatural for the benefit of their social group.

sickle cell A red blood cell that has lost its normal circular shape and has collapsed into a half-moon shape.

sickle-cell anemia An often fatal disease caused by a chemical mutation that changes one of the amino acids in normal hemoglobin. The mutant sickle-cell gene occurs in unusually high frequency in parts of Africa and the Arabian peninsula. Individuals heterozygotic for the sickle-cell gene have a special resistance to malaria; homozygots suffer the severe anemia.

sign An object, gesture, or sound that represents something else.

silent trade A form of exchange with no face-to-face interaction between the parties involved, often practiced where potential for conflict between groups exists. Traded items are simply left at agreed-upon places by both parties.

site A concentration of the remains of (human) activities, or artifacts.

Sivapithecus A late Miocene hominoid found in India and Kenya, closely related to *Ramapithecus*, and thought by some scholars to be the first true hominid.

slash-and-burn agriculture A shifting form of cultivation with recurrent, alternate clearing and burning of vegetation and planting in the burnt fields; also called swidden (or shifting) cultivation.

slavery An extreme form of coerced work organization wherein the rights to people and their labor are owned by others, and in which both subordinate and superordinate positions are inherited.

social class A stratum in a social hierarchy based on differential group access to means of production and control over distribution; usually but not necessarily endogamous, with little—but some—openness.

social control Practices that induce members of a society to conform to the expected behavior patterns of their culture; also, mechanisms through which a society's rulers ensure the masses' conformity with the rules of the social order.

Social Darwinism The doctrine that makes use, or misuse, of Charles Darwin's biological evolutionary principles to explain or justify existing forms of social organization. The theory was actually formulated by Herbert Spencer.

social identity The socially recognized characteristics of a person that indicate his or her social position(s).

socialism A socioeconomic form characterized by public ownership of all strategic resources and major distribution mechanisms. It features centralized economic and social planning, and it is conceived by some Marxists to be a transitional stage to communism, in which centralized bureaucracies will "wither away."

social mobility The upward or downward movement of individuals or groups of individuals in a society consisting of social hierarchies and unequal distribution of such social resources as occupations, education, power, and wealth.

social organization The ordering of social relations within social groups whereby individuals' choices and decisions are visibly patterned.

social stratification An arrangement of statuses or groups within a society into a pattern of socially superior and inferior ranks (or groups) that are open to a greater or lesser degree.

social structure The total pattern of eco-centered relationships (such as kinship systems and friendship networks) that occur within a society.

societal structure The total aggregate of discrete, bounded subgroups that compose a society.

society A socially bounded, spacially contiguous aggregation of people who participate in a number of overarching institutions and share to some degree an identifiable culture, and that contains within its boundaries some means of production and units of consumption—with relative stability across generations.

sociobiology The systematic study of the biological basis of social behavior.

sociogram The full description, in the form of a catalog, of all the social behaviors of a species.

sociolinguistics The study of the societal correlates to variations in the patterning of linguistic behavior.

somatic cells The cells that make up all the bodily parts and that are constantly dying and being replaced; does not include central nervous system cells or sex cells.

sorcery A negatively connotative term to refer to magic—the use of supernatural agencies—to further the practitioner's goals.

sororal polygyny A marriage involving two or more sisters as wives of the same man at one time.

sororate The practice by which women are expected to marry the husband of a deceased sister.

spacing mechanisms The behaviors between neighboring groups of animals that help to maintain them at some distance from each other.

speciation The process of gradual separation of one interbreeding population into two or more separate, noninterbreeding populations.

species The largest naturally occurring population that interbreeds (or is capable of interbreeding) and produces fully fertile offspring.

speech community An aggregate of persons who share a set of conventions about how verbal communication is to take place.

state A set of institutions in a stratified society that operates to maintain the status quo by: (1) organizing the provision of needed services; (2) planning the production and use of needed resources; (3) quelling internal discontent by buying off or subduing rebellious minorities or subordinate classes; and (4) organizing, administering, and financing the protection of the society against hostile external forces.

statuses The interrelated positions in a society, with each position carrying certain expectations of behavior (roles) with respect to those persons occupying the same and/or interrelated positions.

stereoscopic vision Overlapping fields of vision resulting when the eyes are located toward the front of the skull, improving depth perception.

stereotype The attribution of certain presumed, invariable personality or behavioral characteristics to all members of a particular group, most notably those groups defined by religion, sex, nationality, or ethnicity.

stimulus diffusion The transfer of a basic idea from one culture to another, in which the idea is reinterpreted and modified to the extent that it becomes unique to the receiving group.

strategic resources The category of resources vital to a group's survival.

stratified society A society in which there is a structured inequality of access among groups not only to power and prestige, but also to the strategic resources that sustain life.

stratigraphy The arrangement of archaeological deposits in superimposed layers, or strata.

structural-functionalism An anthropological school of thought emphasizing the mutual interdependence of all parts and subgroups of a society, interpreting relationships between such groupings as contributing to the ongoing pattern maintenance of the society.

structuralism An analytical approach based on the assumption that observed phenomena are specific instances of the underlying, generalized principles of relationship or structure.

structural linguistics The study of the internal structures of the world's languages.

subculture The culture of a subgroup of a society that shares its fundamental values, but that also has its own distinctive folkways, mores, values, and world view.

subsistence strategies Technological skills, tools, and behaviors that a society uses to meet its subsistence needs.

substantivists A group of economic anthroplogists who deny that economic models derived from developed market economies can be applied universally to all economic systems.

supernatural Refers to all things that are believed to exist but are beyond verifiability through the human senses.

supernatural beliefs Organized systems of thoughts, ideas, and concerns regarding entities whose existence is not verifiable through the human senses.

superposition In archaeology, the perception that, under normal circumstances, a stratum found lying under another stratum is relatively older than the stratum under which it is lying.

supraorbital ridge The torus, or bony bar, surmounting orbital (eyeball) cavities; it is large and continuous in apes and quite small and divided in *Homo sapiens*.

swidden farming Shifting cultivation, with recurrent, alternate clearing and burning of vegetation and planting in the burnt fields. Fallow periods for each plot last many times longer than the periods of cultivation. See also *slash-and-burn agriculture.*

symbol A sign that represents some other (complex) thing with which it has no intrinsic connection.

synchronics The comparison of biological, linguistic, archaeological, and ethnographic data across a wide geographical area at one arbitrarily selected point in time.

syntax The relationships between signs. The study of syntax is the study of the rules of sequence and combination of signs.

synthetic theory (of evolution) A modern theory of evolution based on the Darwinian theory but emphasizing differential fertility (as opposed to differential mortality).

systematics The study of the kinds and diversity of objects and of the types of relationships existing among them.

taboo (tabu) The belief in negative supernatural consequences that attach to the performance of certain acts or the violation of certain objects or places.

tabula rasa The concept proposed by John Locke (1690) that people are born with blank minds and that they learn everything they come to know through their life experiences, socialization, and enculturation into groups.

taxonomy The science of constructing classifications of ganisms.

technology A society's use of knowledge, skills, implemen and sources of power in order (1) to exploit and partia control the natural environment and (2) to engage in p duction and reproduction of its goods and services.

tell A stratified mound created entirely through long peric of successive occupation by a series of groups.

tenancy A form of forced agricultural labor under which f mers plant their crops in the land owner's fields but o the land owner a certain proportion of the crops they h vest.

territoriality Defense by an animal of a geographically de-limited area.

testes The male gonads, suspended outside the body cavity in the scrotum.

test pit In archaeology, a pit that is dug at carefully selected positions in a site to reveal information about buried ar-tifacts and stratigraphy.

thalassemia Like sickle-cell anemia, a blood anemia carried by populations that are or have been in malaria-infested areas of the world—especially around the Mediterranean, Asia Minor, and southern Asia. Like sickle-cell anemia, it also represents an example of balanced polymorphism.

Third World Originally referred to non-Western peoples of the colonized societies of Asia, Africa, and Latin America. More recently, the term has also been associated with na-tional minorities within the United States and Canada, such as Chicanos, blacks, Native Americans, Puerto Ri-cans, and Asian-Americans.

Three-Age System The concept delineated by Christian Thomsen (1836) in which he identified three successive stages in cultural evolution: the Stone Age, the Bronze Age, and the Iron Age.

Toltec civilization Postclassic Mesoamerican civilization, dated from A.D. 900 to about 1300. The Toltecs perpetuated many of the themes of Classic culture. Their capital of Tula was sacked around 1160, and they were eventually re-placed by the Aztecs.

totemism The symbolic association of plants, animals, and objects with groups of people, especially the association of exogamous clans with animal species as their emblems and/or mythological ancestors.

trade The exchange of goods between people.

traditionalizm The organizing of behavior in terms of stan-dards derived from the past.

tradition (archaeological) The similarity in cultural elements and forms over a considerable span of time at a given site or group of sites in a geographically delimited area.

transcendental belief system A belief system providing people with organized ideas regarding states of existence inherently beyond the capacities of their senses to register and about things that are impossible for them to learn from their personal experience.

transhumance The seasonal migration of domesticated live-stock and their herders for the purpose of grazing different pastures at different times of the year; usually rotation between highlands and lowlands.

tribalism The orientation toward tribal membership—rather than toward citizenship in nation-states—as the criterion

of political allegiance and behavior.

tribe A relatively small group of people (small society) who share a culture, speak a common language or dialect, and share a perception of their common history and unique-ness. Often refers to unstratified social groups with a minimum of (or no) centralized political authority at all, organized around kinship lines.

type site In archaeology, a site used to represent the charac-teristic features of a culture.

typology A method of classifying objects according to hierar-chically arranged sets of diagnostic criteris.

underdevelopment The condition of state-level societies that have been exploited by the industrialization of the Euro-pean, American, and Japanese nations and that have themselves failed to benefit from industrialization.

underwater archaeology The retrieval and study of ships, dwellings, and other human remains that have been cov-ered over by waters in the course of time.

undifferentiated (social) system A social system in which the ascriptive qualities of sex, age, or kinship determine social relations in most domains of society.

Uniformitarianism The theory, developed by Charles Lyell, that the geological processes shaping the earth are uniform and continuous in character.

unilineal descent The reckoning of kinship connections through either exclusively female (matrilineal descent) or male (patrilineal descent) links.

unilineal evolution The theory that all human societies evolve through specific stages that are usually defined in terms of the occurrence of increasingly complex social and cultural elements.

unit of deposition All the contents of each stratum in an archaeological site that are conceived to have been depo-sited at the same point in time (as measured by ar-chaeologists).

unit of excavation Subdivision of an archaeological site made by an archaeologist to record the context in which each remain is found.

Upper Paleolithic culture The culture produced by modern *Homo sapiens sapiens*, beginning about 35,000 years ago. It is characterized by pervasive blade tool production, an "ex-plosion" of artistic endeavors (cave painting), highly or-ganized large-game hunting, and the efficient exploitation of previously uninhabited ecological niches—including the population of the New World, perhaps beginning as early as 40,000 years ago.

urban anthropology The application of anthropological re-search techniques and methods of analysis to the study of people living in cities.

urbanism An ill-defined term designating those qualities of life that presumably characterize all city life-styles.

urbanization The worldwide process of the growth of cities at the expense of rural populations.

uterine kin Kin related to one through female links.

uxorilocal residence The practice by which a newlywed couple takes up residence near the bride's mother's family but does not become a subordinate group contained within a larger extended family.

Valdivian culture A coastal Ecuadorian culture, dated from 3200 B.C., in which the earliest pottery found in the

Americas has been unearthed. Some archaeologists believe the pottery was introduced to the New World by Japanese visitors from the Jomon culture—a view hotly disputed by others.

values The ideals of a culture that are concerned with appropriate goals and behavior.

verbal communication The uniquely human use of language to communicate.

vertical extended family A family in which parents, their married children, and their grandchildren share a residence and constitute a functioning social unit.

virilocal residence The practice by which a newlywed couple moves near the residence of the groom's father but does not become a subordinate group contained within a larger extended family.

voluntary association A group of persons who join together for a common objective or on the basis of a mutual interest.

Wernicke's area The brain site where verbal comprehension takes place, located in the temporal lobe of the dominant hemisphere.

Westernization The transplanting of industrial European-American institutions to developing countries.

witchcraft The use of magic to control the behavior of another person or persons.

world view *(Weltanschauüng)* The corpus of beliefs about the world shared by members of a society, and represented in their myths, lore, ceremonies, social conduct, general values, and so on.

yeomanry In feudal societies, those who were granted special privileges in land and produce in exchange for military service in the militia of the lord.

Zinjanthropus A 1.75-million-year-old australopithecine fossil found in Kenya by Mary Leakey and thought to be a form of *Australopithecus robustus*.

DATE DUE

COL AUG - 2 1985			
	201-6503		Printed in USA

DATE DUE